WELLNESS
THE TOTAL PACKAGE

THIRD EDITION

University of Indianapolis

URGENT
HANDLE WITH CARE
because it's only your life
we're talking about here

mindy
hartman
mayol

Kendall Hunt
publishing company

D0088181

Cover image © Shutterstock.com

Kendall Hunt
publishing company

www.kendallhunt.com
Send all inquiries to:
4050 Westmark Drive
Dubuque, IA 52004-1840

Copyright © 2008, 2012, 2019 by Kendall Hunt Publishing Company

PAK ISBN: 978-1-5249-6151-0
Text Alone ISBN: 978-1-5249-6352-1

Published in the United States of America

Contents

Acknowledgements

To my boys, Alexander and Vincent, thank you for loving me no matter what.

To our students—You are embarking on a most special time in your life. Take care of yourself. Love yourself. Respect yourself. Learn from yourself. Take care of others. Love others. Respect others. Learn from others.

About the Author

Mindy Hartman Mayol, PhD, ACSM EP-C, is currently an Assistant Professor at the University of Indianapolis in the College of Health Sciences' Department of Kinesiology where she teaches a variety of courses in the Exercise Science program as well as coordinates the Wellness & Fitness courses for all undergraduate students.

She graduated with a PhD in Health and Rehabilitation Sciences with a minor in Public Health-Social and Behavioral Sciences from Indiana University in Indianapolis, IN, and also graduated from Indiana University in Bloomington, IN, with both a Bachelor of Science in Kinesiology with an emphasis in Exercise Science and a Master of Science in Kinesiology in Applied Sport Science.

Dr. Mayol has given over 50 presentations at local, state and national professional conferences and has published 10 articles and 14 published research abstracts in the exercise science and health and wellness field. Her current research interests include sport motivation and holistic wellness in collegiate athletes, multidimensional wellness in emerging adults, and health and lifestyle perceptions and behaviors in special populations.

Dr. Mayol is a member and Certified Exercise Physiologist through the American College of Sports Medicine (ACSM) as well sits on ACSM's Committee on Certification and Registry Board. Dr. Mayol also served as an Associate Editor for ACSM's Resources for the Personal Trainer, 5th Ed., (2017 © Wolters-Kluwer, Philadelphia, PA). She was awarded the 2014 UIndy Faculty Achievement Award and the IAHPERD Recreation Professional/Leisure Educator of the Year Award in 2010.

Previously, she worked for the National Institute for Fitness and Sport and St. Vincent Health in corporate fitness management and The Care Group Cardiology in marketing and health promotion—all based out of Indianapolis, Indiana. Mayol currently resides in Indianapolis, IN, and is the mother of two rambunctious boys, Alexander and Vincent.

Wellness

"*Live with intention. Walk to the edge. Listen hard. Practice wellness. Play with abandon. Laugh. Choose with no regret. Appreciate your friends. Continue to learn. Do what you love. Live as if this is all there is.*"

— Mary Anne Radmacher

The objectives in this introduction include the understanding of:

- Wellness and its many dimensions
- The balance of these dimensions
- Decisional balance and how energy drainers and energy fuelers play a role
- Identifying your overall goals for wellness
- The readiness to change
- Setting your goals and commitment of these goals
- How to get to your goals when faced with challenges and obstacles

Online Reminders

- Complete the poll question before the next class meeting.
- Complete the interactive activities for this chapter.
- Complete all of the online assignments for this chapter.
- Complete the Pre-Course Assessment: Multi-Dimensional Wellness Inventory.

Wellness—Isn't it just the same thing as health or exercise? Doesn't wellness mean that you eat right, you're active, and you try to prevent getting illnesses or diseases? Is there more to it than that?

These are questions you may be asking yourself, and they are appropriate questions to ask.

The term "wellness" has been traced back to the 1650s but was not often used in the media and within the medical and health profession until the 1950s. As a part of the 1948 World Health Organization's constitution, the promotion of healthy lifestyles began to materialize as: "Health is a state of complete physical, mental and social well-being and not merely the absence of disease or infirmity." In the late 1950s, Halbert L. Dunn, chief of the National Office of vital statistics, defined wellness as "an integrated

© Kendall Hunt Publishing Company

method of functioning, which is oriented toward maximizing the potential of which the individual is capable." Through the decades, "wellness" certainly has become trendy shorthand for physical fitness or health.

According to the Merriam-Webster dictionary, wellness is the quality or state of being in good health especially as an actively sought goal with synonyms fitness and health often used in its place. Health is (*a*) the condition of being sound in body, mind, or spirit; especially the freedom from physical disease or pain (*b*) the general condition of the body with wellness and fitness used synonymously. Fitness is the quality or state of being fit with—*you guessed it*—wellness and health used as synonyms.

Writer, Ben Zimmer, wrote "Wellness" an article that appeared in the New York Times discussing the popular gain of the word itself. Zimmer writes: "'Wellness,' intoned Dan Rather in November 1979, introducing a "60 Minutes" segment on a new health movement known by that name. "There's a word you don't hear every day."

Zimmer then talks of committed groups of early followers of the wellness movement, such as Drs. John W. Travis, Donald B. Ardell, Bill Hettler, Tom Dickey and Rodney Friedman, whose motivations and missions included "using self-directed approaches to well-being as an alternative to the traditional illness-oriented care of physicians" and "providing health promotion and wellness professionals unparalleled resources and services that fuel professional and personal growth." Zimmer summed up his article saying "But carping over wellness faded away in the '90s as the term gained a foothold in everyday use. A word that once sounded strange and unnecessary, even to its original boosters, has become tacitly accepted as part of our lexicon of health. Well, well, well."

Wellness isn't just one simple thing—it is multidimensional with each dimension as important as the next. One dimension of wellness does not work without the other. There is certainly crossover between each of the dimensions. There is a delicate but practical balance to each of these dimensions that make the state of your wellness secure.

Here it is folks:

If one of your wellness dimensions is negatively affected, it will certainly put more strain on the other supporting dimensions. That is why BALANCE is key to our everyday living, our everyday function, and in our everyday outlook. We must give ourselves a chance to cope with various afflictions and issues that come our way in life, because they will come and go.

The following ten chapters will introduce you to these dimensions of wellness, and the assignments within the chapters will help you in the discovery of your current wellness status and goals for BALANCE in your life! The approach of this book focuses on prevention as its sole purpose. However, most of us are managing certain dimensions of wellness or states that are past the "prevention" stage. If you find, when reading this book, that you are past the prevention stage of certain items, manage them to the best of your ability and keep making plans and goals to sustain your overall wellness state.

It is the hope that this book commences a journey to healthy, energetic, and productive planning for your current and future health. But, of course, your own continuous engagement in practicing healthy behaviors is a must-have not only as you read through this book but as your overall mindset.

We are always trying to improve our wellness status—we all strive for balance and for optimal health. Decisional balance is one of the major components of the model of behavior change, and it involves looking at the pros and cons of a given health behavior or choice. It is like a cost-benefit analysis designed to assist you in considering change, to help you understand what keeps you from changing (payoffs) and to provide incentive for change.

Online Assignment: Energy Drainers and Fuelers

Complete this assignment online. Go to:

www.grtep.com

Select >Chapter Content>Introduction>Enter your username and password

Now, refer to the various dimensions of wellness and your energy drainers to figure out what the changes or improvements you want to make to your life are. Again, the ultimate goal is BALANCE.

ASSIGNMENT: Complete the sections below to help you determine your three overall goals for change or improvement.

A. Identify three behaviors relating to wellness that you would like to change or improve.

1. _____
2. _____
3. _____

B. Now make each of the above behaviors into a question.

1. _____ ?
2. _____ ?
3. _____ ?

C. Read the statements below and choose a response to match 1, 2, and 3 listed above. You may have the same response for one or more of your behaviors.

1. _____
2. _____
3. _____

YES, I have been for MORE than 6 months.

YES, I have been, but for LESS than 6 months.

NO, but I intend to in the next 30 days.

NO, but I intend to in the next 6 months.

NO, and I do NOT intend to in the next 6 months.

D. So, what does all of this mean for each of your behaviors?

YES, I have been for MORE than 6 months = Maintenance Stage

YES, I have been, but for LESS than 6 months = Action Stage

NO, but I intend to in the next 30 days = Preparation Stage

NO, but I intend to in the next 6 months = Contemplation Stage

NO, and I do NOT intend to in the next 6 months = Pre-contemplation Stage

We all progress through a series of changes as we are looking to make a change in our current behavior. This is also called your readiness to change. These five series of changes are pre-contemplation, contemplation, preparation, action and maintenance.

Maintenance Stage = You are keeping up with your new goal and doing everything possible for goal sustainability.

Action Stage = You are starting to move toward a healthier behavior. You have your motivation, you understand that you are in control for being responsible for your changes, and you have your sights set on your goal.

Preparation Stage = You are monitoring your behavior, analyzing and identifying patterns in your activity, and setting a goal.

Contemplation Stage = You are aware that a problem exists and are seriously thinking about overcoming it but have not made a commitment to take action.

Pre-contemplation Stage = You are not ready to make a change in your life in the foreseeable future.

Just as people have their own personal goals in mind, they also may be at a different stage of change for each of the goals. Wellness, fitness, health—they are individualistic. One size does not fit all. Therefore, it is ultimately up to you to identify the change, to identify your readiness to change and to MAKE the change!

In order to make positive changes in your life, you must identify behaviors that need modification and behavior changes that would support your life change goals. When setting goals:

- Make achievable and measurable goals.

- Establish long-term goals, with weekly or monthly short-term goals that support the long-term goals.

- Identify behavior changes that will directly support your short term goals.

- Identify how you will measure your goals.

- Set target dates and reasonable rewards for goal achievement. A reward should be something that you enjoy but might not always get to do. It should be relatively inexpensive and accessible. It should not be anything that would reinforce the behavior you are trying to change.

Pick one number for each personal rulers that best corresponds to have ready, willing and able you feel about your goals. If you find yourself at a 6 or above, this indicates you are ready, willing and/or able to make efforts toward your goal. If you find yourself at a 5 or below, this indicates that you may want to spend more time exploring the value of this goal and possibly revise your goal.

PERSONAL RULERS

How **important** is it for you to make a change?

Not at All		Maybe		Some-what		Pretty Much		Very		Extremely
0	1	2	3	4	5	6	7	8	9	10

How **ready** are you to make a change?

Not at All		Maybe		Some-what		Pretty Much		Very		Extremely
0	1	2	3	4	5	6	7	8	9	10

How **able** are you to make a change?

Not at All		Maybe		Some-what		Pretty Much		Very		Extremely
0	1	2	3	4	5	6	7	8	9	10

ASSIGNMENT: Complete Your Personal Behavior Change Contract

A. Write down your three behaviors relating to wellness (completed in the previous assignment) that you've identified and would like to change. Consider these your long-term goals.

    1. _____

    2. _____

    3. _____

B. Write down pros for each of these goals.

    1. _____

    2. _____

    3. _____

C. Write down cons for each of these goals.

    1. _____

    2. _____

    3. _____

D. What will your short-term goals be that will support you reaching your long-term goals? Write down short-term goals for each long-term goal.

    1. _____

    2. _____

    3. _____

E. Specific behavior changes that will support my short-term goals are:

    1. _____

    2. _____

    3. _____

F. I will achieve my long-term goals by (enter a target date for each goal):

    1. _____

    2. _____

    3. _____

G. My rewards for reaching each long-term goal will be:

1. _____

2. _____

3. _____

I, _____, agree to what I have written above and will comply with the goals and target dates I have set for myself.

Signature: _____ Date: _____

Witness: _____ Date: _____

A note for the future: After achieving your goals, congratulate yourself and then make new goals. If you did not succeed with your goals, examine what behavior changes you were not able to do in order to support your short-term goals. Learn from your mistakes and try again. Perhaps you made your goals too challenging.

You Are a Work in Progress: Suggestions for Getting There!

When making any change, you will face self-doubts and remarks even from those with your "best interest" in mind. Here are some common reactions to expect:

External factors that may be hindering your choices or attempts to change	■ Family obligations, real or imagined ■ Stereotyping others hold about you (e.g., age, gender, ethnicity, personality) ■ Financial obligations or limitations ■ Regional limitations (partly due to unwillingness to leave family or friends)
Internal factors that may be limiting your possibilities for change	■ Lack of skills, education or credentials (e.g., degrees, licenses ■ Lack of willingness to ask for and accept help ■ Lack of knowledge of how to work with others (interpersonal skills) ■ Limiting your choices due to your own stereotypes of yourself (may include false beliefs about what a choice requires—how hard it will be, skills required) ■ Beliefs that your personality, motivation, temperament or past limit your choices ■ Lack of knowledge of available choices (e.g., what a major or career really is, how to find out about options or careers, where to get information, how to get started)

Some common fears that may be roadblocks for you

- Fear of change
- Fear of failure
- Fear of making a "wrong" choice
- Fear of not having enough confidence, motivation or skill to pursue a choice
- Fear of adverse impact on present relationships (e.g., loss due to move, time pressures, "growing apart"
- Fear of rejection, disapproval, or ridicule
- Fear that it really won't make life better or that it isn't better anywhere else
- Fear of making a fool of yourself or of embarrassment while learning a new path
- Fear of losing security, of abandoning a "safe," familiar behavior, situation, or person

How Do I Cope with These Real or Imagined Fears or Limitations?

Here are some ideas:

- Take one step at a time (break large steps into smaller steps).
- Visualize yourself coping successfully with the next step of your goal.
- Minimize risk by taking a "practice tour" of a choice you might make.
- Use positive self-talk, "psych" yourself up, be optimistic.
- Sometimes you think you need change when you're just bored. Examine your current life.
- Avoid self-limiting talk (too old . . . too young . . . too shy . . . too unlovable . . . too afraid . . . too inexperienced).
- Self-help groups can be very useful for major long-term changes.
- Realize you have many options and choices available.
- If you can, talk to someone who has already made the change you are planning.
- Allow time for change to become "natural."
- Realize that persistence is more useful than mere confidence when making changes.
- When making changes, be honest about the costs and rewards for a change.

References

Bounds, L. et al. *Health and Fitness: A Guide to a Healthy Lifestyle.* Behavior Change and Goal Setting. Kendall Hunt Publishing Company (2006): 117.

Geithner, C. et al. *American College of Sports Medicine's Health & Fitness Journal.* Personal Balance: Its Importance and How to Achieve It (2007): Vol. 11, Issue 1: 9–11.

Hettler, B. The National Wellness Institute. The Interdependent Model/The Six Dimensions of Wellness. *www.nationalwellness.org* accessed on 12.7.07

Thygerson, A. and Larson, K. *Lab Manual to Accompany Fit to Be Well.* Jones and Bartlett: 2006: 9–10

Prochaska, J. and Velicer, W. The Transtheoretical Model of Health Behavior Change. *American Journal of Health Promotion.* 1997: 12:38–48

Richardson, C. *Take Time for Your Life.* Broadway Books: (1998).

Schick, C. et al. *Surviving College: A "Real World" Experience.* "In Hot Pursuit of Happiness." Kendall Hunt Publishing Company (2001): 191–194

Zimmer, B. *The New York Times Reprints.* Wellness (2010): Apr. 12. nytimes.com/2010/04/18/magazine/18FOB-onlanguage-t.html accessed on April 26, 2010.

CHAPTER 1

Physical Wellness— Exercise

"Whatever it takes. No excuses.

No explanations."

— Coach Tony Dungy

The objectives in this chapter include the understanding of: ——

- ■ **The meaning of physical wellness in relation to exercise and its direct application to you**
- ■ **The three energy systems used during exercise and the principles of fitness training**
- ■ **Cardiovascular exercise**
- ■ **Strength training exercise**
- ■ **Flexibility exercise**
- ■ **Fitness and health tests**
- ■ **Pedometers and their use**
- ■ **Alternative exercise methods**
- ■ **Proper footwear when exercising**
- ■ **Obesity**
- ■ **Body image**

Online Reminders

- ■ Complete the poll question before the next class meeting.
- ■ Complete the interactive activities for this chapter.
- ■ Complete all of the online assignments for this chapter.

Physical Wellness—Physical wellness recognizes the need for regular physical activity, having healthy eating habits, and preventing heart disease, cancers, and other disease states. This chapter focuses on exercise and its components, which are: cardiovascular, strength training, and flexibility. In Chapter 2, the focus is on nutrition and how you'll understand and appreciate the relationship between how nutrition and exercise play a role in your overall health. In Chapter 10, the focus is on being responsible for your health (e.g., prevention of heart disease, how smoking plays a role in your health).

As The National Wellness Institute states, physical wellness follows these tenets:

1. It is better to consume foods and beverages that enhance good health than those that impair it.

2. It is better to be physically fit than not.

PRE-CLASS SURVEY: Take this physical wellness self-survey before your next class meeting Circle either Yes or No, total up each column, and check your score.

I believe that exercising holds many benefits for me.	YES	NO
I practice regular cardiovascular exercise on most days of the week.	YES	NO
I practice regular strengthening exercises at least twice a week.	YES	NO
I practice regular flexibility exercises on a weekly basis.	YES	NO
I think that being sedentary can contribute to obesity, heart disease, and many other disease states.	YES	NO
I ask questions frequently to fitness professionals if I don't know how to do something or don't know the answers to fitness questions.	YES	NO
I understand that I need to challenge myself and my cardiovascular and musculoskeletal systems when I exercise in order to gain the benefits and in order to see results.	YES	NO
I always exercise in a safe and conducive environment.	YES	NO
I have used a pedometer and understand why I should be taking 10,000 steps per day.	YES	NO
I understand the risks that obesity poses to me.	YES	NO
I feel I have a healthy body image of myself.	YES	NO
I complete my daily living and occupational activities and still have energy left to participate in recreational activities.	YES	NO
TOTAL		

WHAT YOUR TOTAL MEANS:

9 or more Yes answers	Excellent	Your habits are positively enhancing your health.
6–8 Yes answers	Average	You are obviously trying but there is room to improve.
5 or less Yes answers	Not So Good	There is a need for improvement in your daily habits.

SOURCE: "Wellness for Healthy Positive Living." *Physical Wellness Inventory.* www.for.gov.bc.ca/hrb/hw/index.htm

The Centers for Disease Control (CDC) states that over 50% of us (in the U.S. population) don't exercise—even though most of us know the importance and the benefits associated with physical activity. Why don't you think people exercise as often (or at all) as they should?

According to the CDC, heart disease is the #1 killer for both men and women with the #2 killer being all cancers combined. Following these top killers is unintentional injuies, chronic lower respiratory diseases, stroke, Alzheimer's disease, diabetes, influenza/pneumonia, kidney disease, and suicide. Do you think most of these are just genetically linked or are because of a person's lifestyle? Actually, it can be either or both. You should get to know your family's health history and be on the lookout for any unhealthy behaviors you can modify NOW. Do you know all of the risk factors associated with heart disease? If you don't, you should. The American Heart Association states that heart disease is the #1 killer of men AND women. These risk factors affect you more than you know. Approximately one in two people die from heart disease."

SOURCE: https://www.cdc.gov/nchs/products/databriefs/db293.htm

Do you think that not exercising is one of the risk factors that contribute to heart disease?

YES   or   **NO**

BENEFITS OF EXERCISE

Why exercise? Why not? Your body was designed to move, and it wants to move. When you don't exercise, you also put yourself at risk for heart disease, among other health problems, and, yes, your risk starts accumulating now. Exercise is medicine! Your physician will always prescribe some dose of exercise for you throughout your entire lifetime. The same benefits you gain from exercise now are the same benefits you will reap in your life downstream. According to the American College of Sports Medicine and the American Heart Association, these benefits include:

- helping manage your body weight/body composition or helping you lose weight/body fat percentage if that's your goal,
- raising energy levels and stamina
- aiding in alleviating daily stress and tension,
- helping you sleep more effectively,
- improving your self-image and self-confidence,
- countering anxiety and depression,
- increasing your outlook on life and helping you think clearly,
- increasing your muscular strength and your overall functional strength,
- improving posture,
- increased metabolic rate,
- decreasing your chances for injuries, especially low back injuries,
- increasing your range of motion,
- improving blood circulation throughout the body and blood cholesterol levels,
- reducing blood triglyceride levels and increasing HDL or good cholesterol levels,
- preventing high blood pressure,
- reducing risk for diabetes,

- helping to delay or prevent chronic illnesses and diseases associated with aging,

- maintaining quality of life and independence longer,

- preventing bone loss,

- and, oh yes, helping prevent heart disease among many other disease states!

The American College of Sports Medicine (ACSM) and the American Heart Association (AHA) jointly announced in 2011 physical activity guidelines relating to cardiovascular health that consisted of focus on individuals exercising using a moderate form of intensity for at least 30 minutes in duration for a frequency of five days a week (2011a). Garber, Blissmer, Deschenes, Franklin, Lamonte, Lee, Nieman, Swain and ACSM (2011a) gave these more specific recommendations for adults regarding all modes and levels of exercise:

- **Cardiovascular Exercise:** Adults are recommended to participate in a form of moderate (at least five days/week for 30 to 60 minutes) or vigorous (at least three days/week for 20 to 60 minutes) cardiovascular exercise via one continuous exercise bout per day or via multiple shorter exercise bouts per day of at least 10 minutes.

- **Strength Training:** Adults are recommended to participate in muscular strengthening exercises that use each major muscle group (at least two to three days/week) via a variety of modes and equipment (e.g., machines, free weights, body weight training). The spectrum for resistance training prescriptions vary for those that are novices to resistance exercise or those who have been sedentary, for older adults and for those will goals to increase muscular endurance, functional strength or for strength and power.

- **Flexibility Exercise:** Adults are recommended to participate in flexibility or stretching exercises (at least two or three days/week) to improve functionality of muscle and range of motion by stretching each muscle group (ten to 30 seconds static holds to the point of tightness or slight discomfort with an accumulation of 60 seconds/stretch).

- **Neuromotor Exercise:** Adults are recommended to participate in neuromotor exercise or functional fitness training (two or three days/week for 20 to 30 minutes per day) involving motor skills (balance, agility, coordination and gait), proprioceptive exercise training, and multi-faceted activities (yoga) to improve physical function and prevent falls in older adults.

SOURCE: Garber, C.E., Blissmer, B., Deschenes, M.R., Franklin, B.A., Lamonte, M.J., Lee, I.M., Nieman, D.C., Swain, D.P., & American College of Sports Medicine. (2011). American College of Sports Medicine position stand. Quantity and quality of exercise for developing and maintaining cardiorespiratory, musculoskeletal, and neuromotor fitness in apparently healthy adults: guidance for prescribing exercise. *Medicine & Science in Sports & Exercise, 43*(7), 1334–59. doi: 10.1249/MSS.0b013e318213fefb

Before beginning any exercise program, you should always check in with your doctor, especially if you have any pre-existing conditions (e.g., diabetes, orthopedic problems, previous injuries, etc). A PAR-Q questionnaire is a typical form completed by many adults that asks them questions about their health. Again, you should do this before working out in most fitness facilities. It provides a clearance for you, personally, as well as for the instructors or professionals that will be supervising your workouts. You also may complete a PAR-Q before undergoing various fitness tests. We will be discussing fitness tests later in this chapter.

ASSIGNMENT: Complete this PAR-Q and YOU form.

Safety of Exercise Participation: PAR-Q and You

(A Questionnaire for People Aged 15 to 69)

Regular physical activity is fun and healthy, and increasingly more people are starting to become more active every day. Being more active is very safe for most people. However, some people should check with their doctor before they start becoming much more physically active.

If you are planning to become much more physically active than you are now, start by answering the seven questions in the box below. If you are between the ages of 15 and 69, the PAR-Q will tell you if you should check with your doctor before you start. If you are over 69 years of age, and you are not used to being very active, check with your doctor.

Common sense is your best guide when you answer these questions. Please read the questions carefully and answer each one honestly: Check YES or NO.

YES	NO	
☐	☐	1. Has your doctor ever said that you have a heart condition *and* that you should only do physical activity recommended by a doctor?
☐	☐	2. Do you feel pain in your chest when you do physical activity?
☐	☐	3. In the past month, have you had chest pain when you were not doing physical activity?
☐	☐	4. Do you lose your balance because of dizziness, or do you ever lose consciousness?
☐	☐	5. Do you have a bone or joint problem that could be made worse by a change in your physical activity?
☐	☐	6. Is your doctor currently prescribing drugs (for example, water pills) for your blood pressure or heart condition?
☐	☐	7. Do you know of *any other reason* why you should not do physical activity?

If you answered

YES to one or more questions

Talk with your doctor by phone or in person BEFORE you start becoming much more physically active or BEFORE you have a fitness appraisal. Tell your doctor about the PAR-Q and which questions you answered YES.

- You may be able to do any activity you want—as long as you start slowly and build up gradually. Or, you may need to restrict your activities to those that are safe for you. Talk with your doctor about the kinds of activities you wish to participate in and follow his/her advice.
- Find out which community programs are safe and helpful for you.

NO to all questions

If you answered NO honestly to *all* PAR-Q questions, you can be reasonably sure that you can:
- start becoming much more physically active—begin slowly and build up gradually. This is the safest and easiest way to go.
- take part in a fitness appraisal—this is an excellent way to determine your basic fitness so that you can plan the best way for you to live actively.

DELAY BECOMING MUCH MORE ACTIVE:
- if you are not feeling well because of a temporary illness such as a cold or a fever—wait until you feel better, or
- if you are or may be pregnant—talk to your doctor before you start becoming more active.

Please note: If your health changes so that you then answer YES to any of the above questions, tell your fitness or health professional. Ask whether you should change your physical activity plan.

Informed Use of the PAR-Q: The Canadian Society for Exercise Physiology, Health Canada, and their agents assume no liability for persons who undertake physical activity, and if in doubt after completing this questionnaire, consult your doctor prior to physical activity.

You are encouraged to copy the PAR-Q but only if you use the entire form.

Note: If the PAR-Q is being given to a person before he or she participates in a physical activity program or a fitness appraisal, this section may be used for legal or administrative purposes.

I have read, understood and completed this questionnaire. Any questions I had were answered to my full satisfaction.

NAME _____

SIGNATURE _____   DATE _____

SIGNATURE OF PARENT _____   WITNESS_____

or GUARDIAN (for participants under the age of majority)
© Canadian Society for Exercise Physiology
Société canadienne de physiologie de l'exercice   Supported by: Health   Santé
                                                                             Canada   Canada

PAR-Q: Reprinted from the 1994 revised version of the Physical Activity Readiness Questionnaire (PAR-Q and YOU). The PAR-Q and YOU is a copyrighted, pre-exercise screen owned by the Canadian Society for Exercise Physiology.

SOURCE: *Physical Activity Readiness Questionnaire (PAR-Q)* © 2002. Used with permission from the Canadian Society for Exercise Physiology www.csep.ca.

ENERGY SYSTEMS AND PRINCIPLES OF FITNESS TRAINING

❝*And what is a man without energy? Nothing–nothing at all.*❞

— Mark Twain

Energy Systems

In order for you to move at all, your body must have a sufficient supply of energy. Basic economics of the body is all about supply (the food you eat) and demand (resting metabolism, daily functional activities, and exercise). When you're not active, your metabolism is low; when you are active, your metabolism increases. The food you eat is converted to adenosine tri-phosphate (ATP) through a series of chemical reactions. ATP provides energy to your body (e.g., contracting your muscles) as this high-energy compound breaks down. ATP is either used anaerobically (without the presence of oxygen) or aerobically (with the presence of oxygen). The three systems listed below are defined by the ways they produce and use ATP:

CHARACTERISTICS OF THE BODY'S ENERGY SYSTEMS

	IMMEDIATE	ENERGY SYSTEM* NONOXIDATIVE	OXIDATIVE
Duration of activity for which system predominates	0–10 seconds	10 seconds–2 minutes	>2 minutes
Intensity of activity for which system predominates	High	High	Low to moderately high
Rate of ATP production	Immediate, very rapid	Rapid	Slower but prolonged
Fuel	Adenosine triphosphate (ATP), creatine phosphate (CP)	Muscle stores of glycogen and glucose	Body stores of glycogen, glucose, fat, and protein
Oxygen used?	No	No	Yes
Sample activities	Weight lifting, picking up a bag of groceries	400-meter run, running up several flights of stairs	1,500-meter run, 30-minute walk, standing in line for a long time

*For most activities, all three systems contribute to energy production; the duration and intensity of the activity determine which system predominates.

Source: Adapted from Brooks, G. A., T. D. Fahey, and T. P. White. 1996. *Exercise Physiology: Human Bioenergetics and Its Applications,* 2d ed. Mountain View, Calif.: Mayfield.

All three systems use carbohydrates as an energy source, but the oxidative system also uses fat as an energy source. Proteins are reserved for making and repairing tissues and are not considered a preferred fuel source. However, the body can use proteins from body fat for energy if needed. The main factors of these energy systems are:

- As your exercise time increases, a shift occurs from your nonoxidative systems to your oxidative systems.

- As your exercise intensity increases, your body needs more energy to keep moving, which increases your need for more oxygen. Notice which system uses oxygen.

- People who are currently active use more energy; therefore, they use more body fat as an energy source, which helps sustain a longer workout. This also assists with keeping an ideal body composition or weight.

Principles of Fitness Training

There are principles of fitness training that you must apply to your exercise program in order to increase your chance of success with it:

Overload Principle	In order for a body system to become more efficient or stronger, it must be stressed beyond its normal working level. When overloading occurs, the system will respond by gradually adapting this new load and increasing its work efficiency until it reaches another plateau. When this occurs, additional overload must be applied for gain.
Specificity Principle	This refers to training specifically for an activity or isolating a specific muscle group and/or movement pattern one would like to improve.
Progression Principle	By gradually increasing the intensity, duration, and frequency, the body is able to gain improvement in strength and endurance.
Reversibility Principle	The old adage "if you don't use it, you lose it" applies with this principle.

Let's cut to the chase. It's easy to prescribe yourself effective cardiovascular, strength training, and flexibility workouts. These five key items will keep you on track: goals, mode, frequency, duration, and intensity.

CARDIOVASCULAR EXERCISE

> ❝We are under exercised as a nation. We look instead of play. We ride instead of walk. Our existence deprives us of the minimum of physical activity essential for healthy living.❞
>
> — President John F. Kennedy

According to the American College of Sports Medicine, cardiovascular fitness is the ability of the body's heart, lungs, blood vessels, and major muscle groups to persist in continuous rhythmic exercise. With regular cardiovascular exercise, your body is subjected to vigorous stress of the heart, lungs, and muscles. This improves the efficiency of how these systems function and allows the body to easily adjust to increased physical demands, ultimately improving everyday quality of life. A more efficient heart beats at a lower rate and pumps more blood per beat at rest. As a result, the body's capacity to use oxygen increases, giving you more energy to enjoy life. VO2Max is the measure of the maximum amount of oxygen that you can utilize per minute. As aerobic capacity increases, so does VO2Max. It's important to appraise your current level of health and fitness before anything else. You need to figure out what your base level of cardiovascular endurance is before setting up an effective plan for yourself.

The following are recommendations for cardiovascular exercise prescription plans for:

GOAL	INTENSITY	FREQUENCY	DURATION
Fitness aerobic benefits	Moderate to vigorous intensity: @ 60–80% HRR (examples: walking = 4.0 to 4.5 mph, jogging = 5 mph, biking = 10 mph)	3–5 day per week	20 to 60 minutes (20 to 30 minutes minimum)
Health benefits	Moderate intensity: @ 40–60% HRR (example: walking 3.5 mph)	Most days of the week	30 minutes
Weight loss or to prevent weight gain	Moderate intensity: @ 40–60% HRR (example: walking 3.5 mph)	Most days of the week	60 minutes
For weight loss maintenance (in previously overweight individuals	Moderate intensity: @ 40–60% HRR (example: walking 3.5 mph)	Most days of the week	60 to 90 minutes
Stretching: Make sure to stretch all muscle groups, but be sure to focus on the muscles primarily used in your workout. Always stretch your muscles after your warm-up and especially after your cool-down.			
Rest: You can exercise for consecutive days. However, if you have just begun exercising it would be wise to take a few days off in between workouts.			

Adapted from *A Wellness Way of Life's FITT Prescription* and from the American College of Sports Medicine's Guidelines for Exercise Testing & Prescription.

Warm-Up and Cool-Down

It is imperative that you perform and allow time for a warm-up and a cool-down. What exactly is a warm-up? A warm-up prepares your body and especially your cardiovascular system for more moderate to vigorous intensities to come. Warming-up increases body temperature, heart rate, and blood flow to the muscles you will work. This also helps prevent musculoskeletal injuries. You should gauge your warm-up by checking your heart rate. Your heart rate should be raised from a resting level to a rate near the lower end of your target heart rate zone. What exactly is a cool-down? Cooling-down helps you gradually lower your heart rate and allows your breathing and circulation to return to normal by slowly reducing the intensity of your workout. Cool-downs should last 5–10 minutes.

Your Cardiovascular Exercise Plan

ASSIGNMENT: Complete the items below for goals, modes, frequency, duration, and intensity.

Here's how to effectively plan your cardiovascular workout:

GOALS

What are your cardiovascular exercise goals?

1. _____
2. _____
3. _____

MODES

What kind of cardiovascular exercise do you like the most?

1. _____
2. _____
3. _____

NOTE: Keep in mind that you can change your modes around as you like. Some people like to stick with one or two of their preferred modes while others like to try out different modes. Your preference can help with adherence and with motivation factors. If you are trying out a different mode, make sure it will fit into your daily schedule or else you might find yourself more frustrated than anything else. Remember that modes can include using machines, taking group fitness classes, or simply walking, running, or cycling outdoors.

FREQUENCY

How many days per week do you have time for cardiovascular exercise (frequency)? _____

What days of the week work best for your weekly schedule? _____

DURATION

How much time per day can you set aside for cardiovascular exercise (duration)? _____

What time of the day works best for your daily schedule? _____

INTENSITY

How were you planning to measure your intensity levels while doing cardiovascular exercises? You will find you need a gauge for your intensity levels as sometimes your cardiovascular system is working harder than you perceive or sometimes the opposite. What is your goal for intensity each time you work out? Here's some help figuring it out:

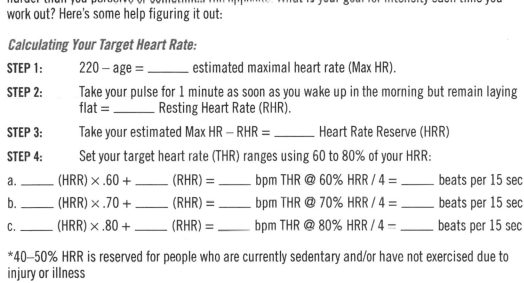

Calculating Your Target Heart Rate:

STEP 1: 220 – age = _____ estimated maximal heart rate (Max HR).

STEP 2: Take your pulse for 1 minute as soon as you wake up in the morning but remain laying flat = _____ Resting Heart Rate (RHR).

STEP 3: Take your estimated Max HR – RHR = _____ Heart Rate Reserve (HRR)

STEP 4: Set your target heart rate (THR) ranges using 60 to 80% of your HRR:

a. _____ (HRR) × .60 + _____ (RHR) = _____ bpm THR @ 60% HRR / 4 = _____ beats per 15 sec

b. _____ (HRR) × .70 + _____ (RHR) = _____ bpm THR @ 70% HRR / 4 = _____ beats per 15 sec

c. _____ (HRR) × .80 + _____ (RHR) = _____ bpm THR @ 80% HRR / 4 = _____ beats per 15 sec

*40–50% HRR is reserved for people who are currently sedentary and/or have not exercised due to injury or illness

d. _____ (HRR) × .50 + _____ (RHR) = _____ bpm THR @ 50% HRR / 4 = _____ beats per 15 sec

e. _____ (HRR) × .40 + _____ (RHR) = _____ bpm THR @ 40% HRR / 4 = _____ beats per 15 sec

Online Assignment: Cardiovascular Exercise Plan

Complete this assignment online. Go to:

www.grtep.com

Select >Chapter Content>Chapter 1>Enter your username and password

Other varieties of determining your intensity levels are also available. You may see a Rating of Perceived Exertion (RPE) Scale available at your fitness center (see Borg's RPE scale below) or perhaps you may conduct your own Talk Test. Some people choose these options to check their intensity levels; they will help you rate what you are perceiving as an easy or a hard workout.

The RPE scale helps you determine if you are working in your target heart rate zone by using the corresponding numbers below. The American College of Sports Medicine recommends training in the 12 to 16 range of the perceived exertion scale. The talk test simply assesses your intensity levels by seeing if you can carry a conversation while exercising. Various studies have shown that you are working in your target heart rate zone when your conversations are just at the point of becoming difficult. When it becomes harder to hold a conversation, you may be working at a level above your target heart rate zone.

THE BORG RPE SCALE

SCORE	DEGREE OF EXERTION
6	No exertion at all
7	Extremely light
8	
9	Very light
10	
11	Light
12	
13	Somewhat hard
14	
15	Hard (heavy)
16	
17	Very hard
18	Extremely hard
19	
20	Maximal exertion

Taking Your Heart Rate Manually

If you do not have a heart rate monitor to use, here are some simple steps to take your heart rate manually while exercising:

a. Find your heart rate with your index and middle fingers pressed gently on your wrist (on the inner edge of the wrist below the base of the thumb) or neck (below the ear along the jaw) and count for 15 seconds.

b. Multiply by 4 to get your beats per minute (bpm) value. It is recommended that you take your heart rate at the wrist. (Heart rate monitors will display your heart rate in beats per minute.)

c. Monitor your heart rate before, after three to five minutes of cardiovascular exercise, during cardiovascular exercise, and upon completion of your cardiovascular workout.

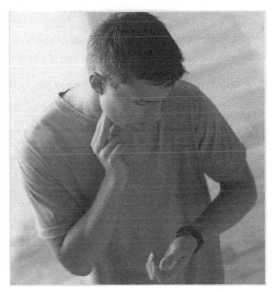

© PhotoDisc

d. Do not take your heart rate manually for a full minute as your slowing heart rate will give you inaccurate exercise heart rates.

Progression

Once you've got a plan, you also need to think about how you will improve and then maintain your cardiovascular fitness levels. According to the American College of Sports Medicine, the recommended rate of progression in an exercise program depends on your level of fitness, your medical and health status, your age, individual activity preferences and goals, and tolerance to the current level of training. The three stages of progression are: initial, improvement, and maintenance. In Appendix B, there are blank log sheets available for your use to log your activity each day.

TRAINING PROGRESSION FOR THE SEDENTARY LOW-RISK* PARTICIPANTS

PROGRAM STAGE	WEEK	EXERCISE FREQUENCY (SESSIONS • WK^{-1})	EXERCISE INTENSITY (% HRR)	EXERCISE DURATION (MIN)
Initial stage	1	3	40–50	15–20
	2	3–4	40–50	20–25
	3	3–4	50–60	20–25
	4	3–4	50–60	25–30
Improvement stage	5–7	3–4	60–70	25–30
	8–10	3–4	60–70	30–35
	11–13	3–4	65–75	30–35
	14–16	3–5	65–75	30–35
	17–20	3–5	70–85	35–40
	21–24	3–5	70–85	35–40
Maintenance stage[†]	24+	3–5	70–85	20–60

* Defined as the lowest risk categories.

[†] Depending on long-term goals of program, the intensity, frequency, and duration may vary

Abbreviations: HRR, heart rate reserve; it is recommended that low-risk cardiac patients train at the lower end of these ranges.

Heat and Humidity

When exercising in these conditions, be sure to stay plenty hydrated with cool water before, during, and after exercising. It is also important to wear clothes that can wick away moisture from your body as well as lightweight eyeglasses for eye protection against the sun's glare. Try your best to exercise in the coolest time of day or limit exposure time and check the heat index to make sure it is safe to exercise. If you feel nauseated, dizzy, or come down with an extreme headache, stop exercising!

HEAT AND HUMIDITY CHART

AIR TEMPERATURE °F	APPARENT TEMPERATURE (WHAT IT FEELS LIKE)									
	70°	75°	80°	85°	90°	95°	100°	105°	110°	115°
0%	64°	69°	73°	78°	83°	87°	91°	95°	99°	103°
10%	65°	70°	75°	80°	85°	90°	95°	100°	105°	111°
20%	66°	72°	77°	82°	87°	93°	99°	105°	112°	120°
30%	67°	73°	78°	84°	90°	96°	104°	113°	123°	135°
40%	68°	74°	79°	86°	93°	101°	110°	123°	137°	151°
50%	69°	75°	81°	88°	96°	107°	120°	135°	150°	
60%	70°	76°	82°	90°	100°	114°	132°	149°		
70%	70°	77°	85°	93°	106°	124°	144°			
80%	71°	78°	86°	97°	113°	136°				
90%	71°	79°	88°	102°	122°					
100%	72°	80°	91°	108°						

(RELATIVE HUMIDITY — left vertical scale)

Apparent temperature:	Heat stress risk with exertion:
90°–105°	Heat cramps and heat exhaustion possible.
105°–130°	Heat cramps or heat exhaustion likely; heat stroke possible.
130° and above	Heat stroke highly likely with continued exposure.

To determine the risk of exercising in the heat, locate the outside air temperature on the top horizontal scale and the relative humidity on the left vertical scale. Where these two values intersect is the *apparent temperature*. For example, on a 90°F day with 70 percent humidity, the apparent temperature is 106°F. Heat cramps or heat exhaustion are likely to occur, and heat stroke is possible during exercise under these conditions. (Adapted from U.S. Department of Commerce, National Oceanic and Atmospheric Administration, Heat index chart, in *Heat wave: A major summer killer.* Washington, D.C.: Government Printing Office, 1992.

STRENGTH TRAINING

"Lack of activity destroys the good condition of every human being, while movement and methodical physical exercise save it and preserve it."

— Plato

Strength training is a specialized method of conditioning that involves the progressive use of resistance to increase your ability to exert or resist force. Strength training is also known as resistance training, weight training, sculpting, and toning. It's important to appraise your current level of health and fitness before anything else. You need to figure out what your base level of muscular strength and endurance is before setting up an effective plan for yourself.

It's important that you know your muscle groups and their locations on your body.

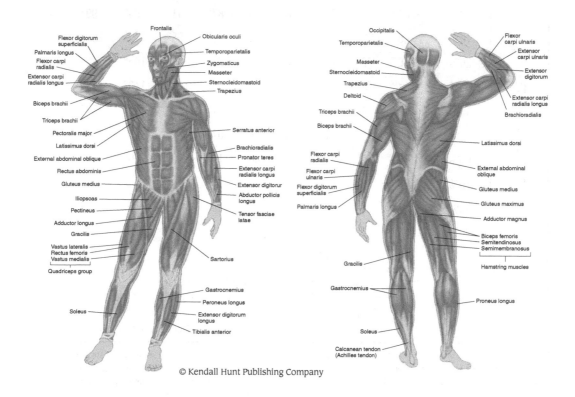

© Kendall Hunt Publishing Company

Strength training is very specific. The following are must-knows for strength training:

- A warm-up is imperative. Incorporate a 5–10 minute warm-up before starting.
- In order to gain the benefits of strength training whatever your goal may be, you must apply the overload principle (see under intensity).
- Increase your weight when you reach the top of your rep range, but by only 10% per week.
- Make sure to strengthen each muscle group. Do not leave a muscle group out of your plan.
- Include a strength training plan that incorporates working opposing muscle groups (for example, quadriceps and hamstrings).
- Work your larger muscle groups first and your smaller muscle groups second (for example, chest press then triceps extension).

- Perform multi-joint exercises first and single-joint exercises second (for example, leg squats and then leg curls).
- You should incorporate core stabilizers such as your lower back and abdominals at the end of your workout.
- Not only should your movements be slow and controlled (3 seconds concentric, 3 seconds eccentric), you should also maintain proper posture and good technique while performing the movement.
- Good posture includes not arching your back, bouncing weights against your body, twisting your body unnecessarily, or bending at the waist with straight legs while lifting.
- On the same note, fast, jerky movements that rely on momentum to make them happen are also contraindicative.
- If you are not able to keep your posture or perform your movements as stated above, decrease your weight.
- Do not hold your breath while strength training at any time.
- Always make sure the equipment or machines (set, leg, arm adjustments) are set up appropriately for you BEFORE you start doing any exercises.

If you are new to strength training or it has been a long time since you've done any strengthening exercises and you are trying to figure out where to begin, follow the muscular endurance plan above. Make a few adaptations to this plan by performing only 1–2 sets per workout and only 2 workouts per week for the first two weeks. This will ensure you a safe but also effective start to strength training. Once you've established a solid strength training base, then figure out what your goal is, choose a plan, and follow that plan. Remember, you will more than likely tweak any plan from above to meet your exercise needs while also working with your own personal schedule.

Your Strength Training Exercise Plan

ASSIGNMENT: Complete the items below for goals, modes, frequency, duration, and intensity.

Here's how to effectively plan your strength training workout:

GOALS

What are your strength training goals?

1. _____

2. _____

3. _____

GOAL	INTENSITY (using machines or free weights)	FREQUENCY	DURATION	REST BETWEEN SETS
Muscular Endurance	2–3 sets 12–15 reps Using a weight that cannot be lifted more than 15 times	3–5 workouts per week	Depends on efficiency of workout, rest between sets, and accessibility of equipment. You can decrease your overall time and rest between sets by working alternating body parts.	½– 1 minute
Health Benefits	1–2 sets 8–12 reps Using a weight that cannot be lifted more than 12 times	2–3 workouts per week		1–2 minutes
Bodybuilding	3–5 sets 5–10 reps Using a weight that cannot be lifted more than 10 times	4–10 workouts per week		1–3 minutes
Muscular Strength and Power	3–5 sets 2–8 reps Using a weight that cannot be lifted more than 8 times	2–3 workouts per week		2–4 minutes

Stretching: Make sure to stretch all muscle groups, but be sure to focus on the muscles primarily used in your workout. Always stretch your muscles after your warm-up and especially after your workout session.

Rest: You will need to rest your worked muscle groups for at least 48 hours before performing the same strength training exercises again. Your muscles need this time for repair and recovery as well as to minimize risk for injury.

Adapted from *A Wellness Way of Life: Guidelines for Resistance Training Programs*, American College of Sports Medicine's Guidelines for Exercise Testing & Guidelines and Fit to be Well: Exercise Guidelines.

MODES

What kinds of strength training exercises do you like the most?

1. _____
2. _____
3. _____

What kinds of strength training exercises do you think you need to be doing in order to meet your strength training goals?

1. _____
2. _____
3. _____

There are various ways to strength train your muscles. The types you will more than likely use:

a. **Isotonic:** This is the most typical mode used for strength training. It is a two-phase, dynamic contraction of your muscles that changes muscle lengths throughout the movement. This involves a concentric (shortening) of the muscle and eccentric (lengthening) of the muscle.

b. **Isometric:** This is a static muscle contraction in which the muscle does not change its length and does not net any muscle movement.

c. **Plyometrics:** This mode of strengthening involves doing explosive movements that help develop quick, powerful movements typically reserved for specialty training or athletic performance.

There are several modes you can choose for strength training:

a. **Weight machines:** You will find these machines at most fitness facilities. They assist you in isolating specific muscles, assist with posture and proper body positioning, and offer variable resistances to you. It is recommended that beginners use the machines; however, people who have a solid base for strength training also use them frequently.

b. **Free weights:** You will also find these in most fitness facilities, but they are used in the home as well. Free weights (e.g., dumbbells, barbells, weight plates and kettlebells) require a solid strength training base and experience performing the movements with good posture and proper body positioning. Free weights allow a greater range of motion and the ability to mimic daily functional tasks, thus increasing overall functional strength. They also allow for a wider variety of exercises and dynamic movements.

c. **Resistive bands:** You will find these in the home as well as at some fitness facilities, in particular in the group fitness areas. You may find some that are small and round and some that are longer, with or without handles, and of various colors and band thicknesses. The thicker the band, the more resistance you'll get. It is recommended that beginners use thinner bands. You should also use thin bands for upper body work. Use thicker bands for lower body work as they provide more resistance.

d. **Body weight/gravity exercises:** You can do body weight/gravity exercises at your home or at your fitness facility. These exercises simply do what they say. You are using your own body weight and gravity as the resistance. Examples of these include push-ups and curl-ups.

A comprehensive fitness facility should provide its users with each of the types of equipment mentioned above per each person's goals and abilities.

FREQUENCY

How many days per week do you have time for strength training (frequency)? _____
What days of the week work best for your weekly schedule? _____

DURATION

How much time per day can you set aside for strength training (duration)? _____
What time of the day works best for your daily schedule? _____

INTENSITY

How were you planning to measure your intensity levels while doing strength training? What is your goal for intensity each time you work out? You must apply the "Overload Principle" that we discussed earlier in order to gain strength. This will all depend on how you structure your sets, repetitions, and weight for each strengthening exercise based upon your overall goal. Keep in mind that you will need to structure upper body exercises differently than lower body exercises in order to meet the requirements for "overloading" the muscle groups. The same is true for larger muscle groups and smaller muscle groups. You may want to add more categories below or you may want to make a more general plan than what you see below.

Shoulders:	_____ weight	_____ reps	_____ sets
Chest:	_____ weight	_____ reps	_____ sets
Back:	_____ weight	_____ reps	_____ sets
Biceps:	_____ weight	_____ reps	_____ sets
Triceps:	_____ weight	_____ reps	_____ sets
Abdominals:	_____ weight	_____ reps	_____ sets
Low Back:	_____ weight	_____ reps	_____ sets
Hips/Gluteals:	_____ weight	_____ reps	_____ sets
Quadriceps:	_____ weight	_____ reps	_____ sets
Hamstrings:	_____ weight	_____ reps	_____ sets
Adductors:	_____ weight	_____ reps	_____ sets
Abductors:	_____ weight	_____ reps	_____ sets
Calves/Lower Leg:	_____ weight	_____ reps	_____ sets

Online Assignment: Strength Plan

Complete this assignment online. Go to:

www.grtep.com

Select >Chapter Content>Chapter 1>Enter your username and password

Various Modes for Strength Training Exercises

Upper Body Exercises

SHOULDERS

Military or Shoulder Press

Shoulder Rollouts

Shoulder Rollouts

Shoulder Shrugs

Shoulder Raise

Shoulder Raise

NOTE: You can also do raises to the front and pushes to the back to work all three parts of the shoulder

CHEST

Bench Press

Chest Press

Wall Pushups

Pushups

Floor Pushups

Ball Pushups

Back

Lat Pulldown

Lat Pull

Lat Row

Bent Over Row

Lat Row

BICEPS

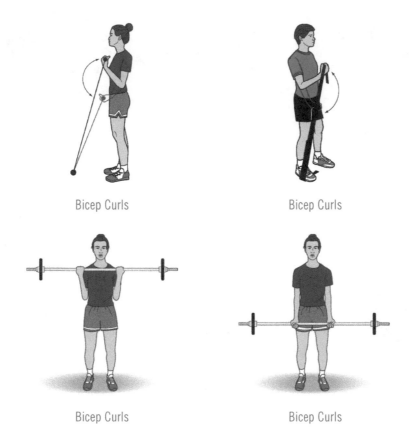

Bicep Curls   Bicep Curls

Bicep Curls   Bicep Curls

TRICEPS

Tricep Press   Tricep Press   Tricep Extension

Tricep Extension

Tricep Extension

Tricep Extension

Tricep Extension

Lower Body Exercises

2. PROGRESS TO DYNAMIC EXERCISES

| 2A | Two Handed Kettlebell Swing |

2B Kettlebell Squat

2C Kettlebell Lunge

© Kendall Hunt Publishing Company

1B Single Leg Deadlift

© Kendall Hunt Publishing Company

OVERALL LEG AND GLUTEAL EXERCISES

Squats

Squats

Back Wall Squat

Ball One Leg Squat

Leg Press

Lunge

Lunge

Quadriceps

Leg Extension

Leg Extension

Leg Extension

Leg Extension

Prone Knee Tucks

Prone Knee Tucks

Leg Extension

Leg Extension

HAMSTRINGS

Hamstring Curl

Hamstring Curl

Hamstring Tuck

Hamstring Tuck

HIPS AND GLUTEALS

Bridges

Bridges

Rear Leg Lift

Glute Squeeze

ABDUCTORS AND ADDUCTORS

Side Leg Lift

Side Leg Lift

Inner Leg Lift

Inner Leg Lift

Three Way Leg Pointer

Three Way Leg Pointer

CALVES AND LOWER LEGS

Calf Raises

Calf Raises

Calf Raises

Toe Press   Toe Press   Toe Press

Toe Lifts   Toe Lifts

CORE STABILIZERS (ABDOMINALS AND LOW BACK)

Abdominal Crunch   Long Arm Crunch   Abdominal Curl

Vertical Leg Crunch

Reverse Crunch

Abdominal Ball Transfer

Oblique Curls

Bicycle Exercise

Pelvic Tilt

Plank

Side Plank

Back Extension

Back Extensions   Opposite Arm Opposite Leg Lift   Opposite Arm Opposite Leg Lift

Back Extension

1. START WITH STABILIZATION EXERCISES

1A   **Turkish Get Up**

ASSIGNMENT: Complete your plan for repetitions, sets and weight for each muscle group.

SHOULDERS	Repetitions	Sets	Weight
1.			
2.			
3.			
4.			

CHEST	Repetitions	Sets	Weight
1.			
2.			
3.			
4.			

BACK	Repetitions	Sets	Weight
1.			
2.			
3.			
4.			

BICEPS	Repetitions	Sets	Weight
1.			
2.			
3.			
4.			

TRICEPS	Repetitions	Sets	Weight
1.			
2.			
3.			
4.			

ABDOMINALS	Repetitions	Sets	Weight
1.			
2.			
3.			
4.			

LOW BACK	Repetitions	Sets	Weight
1.			
2.			
3.			
4.			

HIPS/GLUTEALS	Repetitions	Sets	Weight
1.			
2.			
3.			
4.			

QUADRICEPS	Repetitions	Sets	Weight
1.			
2.			
3.			
4.			

HAMSTRINGS	Repetitions	Sets	Weight
1.			
2.			
3.			
4.			

ADDUCTORS	Repetitions	Sets	Weight
1.			
2.			
3.			
4.			

ABDUCTORS	Repetitions	Sets	Weight
1.			
2.			
3.			
4.			

CALVES/LOWER LEG	Repetitions	Sets	Weight
1.			
2.			
3.			
4.			

Progression

Once you've got a plan, you also need to think about how you will improve and then maintain your strength levels through a progression plan.

- Plan on changing the strengthening exercises for each muscle group every 1–2 months even if you keep the same sets and reps. This will work your muscles differently, help you become stronger, and help with boredom factors.

- Gradually increase the weight of each strengthening exercise as you find the movements becoming easier toward the end of your repetition range. For example, if you are doing 12–15 reps of a shoulder press, and after a few weeks the 10 lb. dumbbells you are using become too easy even at the 15th rep, you should increase your weight to keep applying that overload principle. Increase your weight by no more than 10% per week.

- In Appendix C, there are blank log sheets available for your use to log your activity each day.

FLEXIBILITY

> *"Like a beautiful flower that is colorful but has no fragrance,*
> *even well spoken words bear no fruit in one*
> *who does not put them into practice."*
>
> —The Buddha

Flexibility is the range of motion around a joint. Optimal function of your muscles, joints, and bones requires maintaining an adequate range of motion in all joints. It's important to appraise your current level of health and fitness before anything else. You need to figure out what your base level of flexibility is before setting up an effective plan for yourself.

Flexibility is achieved by stretching after each exercise session whether they are cardiovascular-based or strength training-based workouts. It is imperative to stretch those working muscles out after each workout to gain the benefits of flexibility, which includes the prevention of musculoskeletal injury. If you prefer to stretch both before and after a workout, you must make sure that you first warm up for 5 to 10 minutes, and then you can begin stretching. Warm muscles are most effectively and safely stretched.

The table on the following page lists recommendations for flexibility prescription plans.

GOAL	MODE	FREQUENCY	DURATION
General Health and Fitness	Static Stretching: Focus on muscle groups worked and those with a limited range of motion	After each exercise session, ideally 5–7 days/week	Depends on how many repetitions of stretching you do for each muscle group— *see* intensity.
	INTENSITY	**STRETCHING**	**REST**
	Hold each stretch for 15 to 30 seconds. Do 2 to 4 repetitions for each stretch.	Stretch to the end of the range of your range of motion to the point of tightness.	As long as you've warmed up your muscles, you can stretch daily.

Adapted from the American College of Sports Medicine's Guidelines for Exercise Testing & Guidelines.

Your Flexibility Plan

ASSIGNMENT: Complete the items below for goals, modes, frequency, duration, and intensity.

Here's how to effectively plan your flexibility exercise program:

GOALS

It's not okay to forget about including flexibility into your overall plan. What are your flexibility goals?

1. _____

2. _____

3. _____

MODES

What kinds of flexibility exercises do you think you need to do to meet your goals?

1. _____

2. _____

3. _____

What mode is highly recommended for flexibility? Static stretching is the correct answer. This involves slowly moving and stretching to the point of mild discomfort in the muscle and holding this stretch for 10–30 seconds.

NOTE: Ballistic stretching, which is not recommended, involves dynamic or bouncing movements. Plan to stay away from this mode of stretching unless you specifically use it for athletic performance. Proprioceptive Neuromuscular Facilitation (PNF) stretching is when you use a partner to provide resistance through isometric resistance. In this type of stretching, you resist against a partner using the muscle groups surrounding a particular joint, causing contraction, and then relaxing the muscle group. PNF stretching is highly specific and normally used in athletic performance workouts.

FREQUENCY

Flexibility exercises should be done after each exercise session. Are you planning on doing this? _____

DURATION

How much time per day can you set aside for flexibility exercises after your exercise sessions? _____

INTENSITY

How were you planning to measure your intensity levels while doing flexibility exercises? See the intensity guideline above for flexibility. Will you stretch to the end of your range of motion until you feel tightness or will you stretch until you feel discomfort or pain? _____

Progression

Once you've got a plan, you also need to think about how you will improve and then maintain your flexibility levels. Consistent flexibility exercises will lead to an increased range of motion at your various joints. So be on the lookout for improvement or ease of stretching for each flexibility exercise that you do. Once you feel that a stretch becomes easier, try to stretch just a bit further and hold. In Appendix D, there are blank log sheets available for your use to log your activity each day.

Online Assignment: Flexibility Plan

Complete this assignment online. Go to:
www.grtep.com
Select >Chapter Content>Chapter 1>Enter your username and password

The Dos and Don'ts of Flexibility Exercises

Flexibility Exercises

Half Head Roll

Deltoid Stretch

Tricep Stretch

Pectoral and Bicep Stretch

Spinal Twist

Lower Back Flex

Cat Stretch

Quadriceps Stretch

Calf and Lower Leg Stretch

Illiotibial Band Stretch

Hamstring Stretch

Flexibility Don'ts

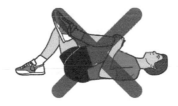

No Yoga Plow

No Single Knee

No Hurdler Stretch

No Standing Toe Touch

No Ballet Bar

No Head Roll

No Full Squat

PUTTING YOUR PLANS TOGETHER

> "*Physical fitness is not only one of the most important keys to a healthy body, it is the basis of dynamic and creative intellectual activity.*"
>
> — President John F. Kennedy, "The Soft American,"
> *Sports Illustrated*, December 26, 1960

Can you make it work? Do these plans all fit together in a weekly schedule that's realistic? Most of all, make sure your plans for exercising fit into your daily schedule. Plan it like an appointment you cannot miss. If what you've just planned out doesn't fit into your schedule then go back and change your plans. Otherwise, you're setting yourself up for failure.

WEEKLY PLAN FOR CARDIOVASCULAR, STRENGTH TRAINING AND FLEXIBILITY EXERCISES

	M	T	W	TH	F	SAT	SUN
Mode							
Frequency							
Duration							
Intensity							

FITNESS AND HEALTH TESTS

*"All parts of the body which have a function if used in moderation
and exercised in labors in which each is accustomed, become thereby
healthy, well developed and age more slowly, but if unused they
become liable to disease, defective in growth and age quickly."*

—Hippocrates

Do you know what your cardiovascular fitness, muscular strength and endurance, and flexibility levels are? Do you know what your body mass index (BMI) or body fat percentage is? Do you know what your numbers are for total cholesterol, LDL cholesterol, HDL cholesterol, triglycerides, and blood sugar, or if you are at risk? It's no secret that some people the same age as you don't know what their fitness levels are or if they are truly at risk for developing diseases.

If you think you are too young to worry about knowing any of these numbers, you are wrong. Most fitness and health professionals as well as physicians would argue that knowing your health and fitness levels is not only imperative but that the mindset of prevention HAS TO START NOW! Later in Chapter 10, you will complete an assignment comparing your numbers to the various risk factor tables provided for the various disease states.

Fitness and health testing is not only important for prevention reasons, it's also important for improvement and maintenance reasons. For example, if you don't know your current cardiovascular fitness level or your current total cholesterol level, how would you know what you need to improve or maintain? Your plan for health and for prevention has to begin somewhere, and this is usually where it begins.

ASSIGNMENT: Go to Appendix A to document and interpret your health and fitness appraisal outcomes.

USING WEARABLE TECHNOLOGY TO TRACK STEPS

*"Few people know how to take a walk. The qualifications are endurance,
plain clothes, old shoes, an eye for nature, good humor, vast curiosity,
good speech, good silence and nothing too much."*

— Ralph Waldo Emerson

Is there a relationship between physical activity and weight control? Absolutely! A goal of 10,000 steps per day is recommended in order for you to manage your weight, to increase fitness levels, and to assist in reducing health-related risks like heart disease, obesity, and diabetes. Taking 10,000 steps is equivalent to walking five miles with one mile being approximately 1,800 to 2,200 steps. Regardless of your cardiovascular fitness level or your weight, you can apply the recommendation of 10,000 steps a day to your overall plan. The box below shows you the average number of steps based on someone's current level:

Sedentary	2,000 to 4,000 steps per day
Somewhat active	5,000 to 7,000 steps per day
Active	At least 10,000 steps per day

By using wearable technology, you can simply and quickly check to see how many more steps you need to take to reach 10,000 steps that day. After a few days of using your wearable technology and checking your steps, you may find that it is tough to get in 10,000 steps in a day without incorporating some type of workout (i.e., jog, walk, using the elliptical machine, a game of basketball or racquetball, etc.). There are a multitude of fitness tracking apps on most smart phones that you can also use to track your steps and/or progress over time.

Another cool application aboutusing wearable technology is that it can measure various forms of physical activity (not just walking, jogging, and running). There are, however, some activities and reasons why wearable technology is not practical. Examples of these activities include: bicycling, swimming, skateboarding, in-line skating, and rowing.

If you don't see your activities listed below, you can go to *walking.about.com/od/measure/a/stepequivalents.htm* to convert your activities into steps. Below are examples of what you might find.

ACTIVITY	STEPS/MIN
Basketball (shooting baskets)	136
Basketball (game)	242
Bicycling	242
Circuit Training	242
In-line Skating	264
Martial Arts	303
Rowing Machine	212
Swimming	221
Weight Training (moderate effort)	121
Yoga or Stretching	76
Snow shoveling	150
Jumping rope	303

Working Your Way Up to 10,000 Steps per Day

The 10,000 step per day goal may be too much for some people at first. Follow these steps to safely reach your 10,000 steps per day goal:

1. Begin your first week off by using your wearable device for one full typical week and record how many steps you took each day. Then, figure out your daily average number of steps for one week, which will determine your baseline activity level and for setting your steps per day goal.

2. For the next two weeks, determine your steps per day goal by adding 10% more steps to your baseline activity level.

3. For the weeks after, you can increase or decrease your steps per day goal depending on how you feel about your progress from the past two weeks. Thereafter, you will need to make a plan to ultimately reach your 10,000 steps per day goal and how to maintain this.

4. Visit the conversion for steps Website mentioned above to estimate your steps if you enjoy doing activities that the pedometer may not accurately measure. These count toward your steps per day goal.

STEP CONVERSIONS	
1 step =	2.64 feet
1 mile =	2,000 steps
5 miles =	10,000 steps
10 miles =	20,000 steps
25 miles =	50,000 steps

In Appendix E, there are blank log sheets available for your use to track your steps each day.

YOGA, PILATES AND TAI CHI

> **"**It's good to have a goal of our journey,
> but it is the journey itself which influences the goal.**"**
>
> — Ursula LeGuinova

Yoga

Yoga is a mind and body practice with historical origins in ancient Indian philosophy. Like other meditative movement practices used for health purposes, various styles of yoga typically combine physical postures, breathing techniques, and meditation or relaxation. This fact sheet provides basic information about yoga, summarizes scientific research on effectiveness and safety, and suggests sources for additional information.

Key Facts

- Recent studies in people with chronic low-back pain suggest that a carefully adapted set of yoga poses may help reduce pain and improve function (the ability to walk and move). Studies also suggest that practicing yoga (as well as other forms of regular exercise) might have other health benefits such as reducing heart rate and blood pressure, and may also help relieve anxiety and depression. Other research suggests yoga is not helpful for asthma, and studies looking at yoga and arthritis have had mixed results.

- People with high blood pressure, glaucoma, or sciatica, and women who are pregnant should modify or avoid some yoga poses.

- Ask a trusted source (such as a health care provider or local hospital) to recommend a yoga practitioner. Contact professional organizations for the names of practitioners who have completed an acceptable training program.

- Tell all your health care providers about any complementary health approaches you use. Give them a full picture of what you do to manage your health. This will help ensure coordinated and safe care

About Yoga

- Yoga in its full form combines physical postures, breathing exercises, meditation, and a distinct philosophy. There are numerous styles of yoga. Hatha yoga, commonly practiced in the United States and Europe, emphasizes postures, breathing exercises, and meditation. Hatha yoga styles include Ananda, Anusara, Ashtanga, Bikram, Iyengar, Kripalu, Kundalini, Viniyoga, and others.

Side Effects and Risks

- Yoga is generally low-impact and safe for healthy people when practiced appropriately under the guidance of a well-trained instructor.

- Overall, those who practice yoga have a low rate of side effects, and the risk of serious injury from yoga is quite low. However, certain types of stroke as well as pain from nerve damage are among the rare possible side effects of practicing yoga.

- Women who are pregnant and people with certain medical conditions, such as high blood pressure, glaucoma (a condition in which fluid pressure within the eye slowly increases and may damage the eye's optic nerve), and sciatica (pain, weakness, numbing, or tingling that may extend from the lower back to the calf, foot, or even the toes), should modify or avoid some yoga poses.

Use of Yoga for Health in the United States

■ According to the 2007 National Health Interview Survey (NHIS), which included a comprehensive survey on the use of complementary health approaches by Americans, yoga is the sixth most commonly used complementary health practice among adults. More than 13 million adults practiced yoga in the previous year, and between the 2002 and 2007 NHIS, use of yoga among adults increased by 1 percent (or approximately 3 million people). The 2007 survey also found that more than 1.5 million children practiced yoga in the previous year.

■ Many people who practice yoga do so to maintain their health and well-being, improve physical fitness, relieve stress, and enhance quality of life. In addition, they may be addressing specific health conditions, such as back pain, neck pain, arthritis, and anxiety.

What the Science Says About Yoga

■ Current research suggests that a carefully adapted set of yoga poses may reduce low-back pain and improve function. Other studies also suggest that practicing yoga (as well as other forms of regular exercise) might improve quality of life; reduce stress; lower heart rate and blood pressure; help relieve anxiety, depression, and insomnia; and improve overall physical fitness, strength, and flexibility. But some research suggests yoga may not improve asthma, and studies looking at yoga and arthritis have had mixed results.

■ One NCCIH-funded study of 90 people with chronic low-back pain found that participants who practiced Iyengar yoga had significantly less disability, pain, and depression after 6 months.

■ In a 2011 study, also funded by NCCIH, researchers compared yoga with conventional stretching exercises or a self-care book in 228 adults with chronic low-back pain. The results showed that both yoga and stretching were more effective than a self-care book for improving function and reducing symptoms due to chronic low-back pain.

■ Conclusions from another 2011 study of 313 adults with chronic or recurring low-back pain suggested that 12 weekly yoga classes resulted in better function than usual medical care.

■ However, studies show that certain health conditions may not benefit from yoga.

■ A 2011 systematic review of clinical studies suggests that there is no sound evidence that yoga improves asthma.

■ A 2011 review of the literature reports that few published studies have looked at yoga and arthritis, and of those that have, results are inconclusive. The two main types of arthritis—osteoarthritis and rheumatoid arthritis—are different conditions, and the effects of yoga may not be the same for each. In addition, the reviewers suggested that even if a study showed that yoga helped osteoarthritic finger joints, it may not help osteoarthritic knee joints.

- Do not use yoga to replace conventional medical care or to postpone seeing a health care provider about pain or any other medical condition.

- If you have a medical condition, talk to your health care provider before starting yoga.

- Ask a trusted source (such as your health care provider or a nearby hospital) to recommend a yoga practitioner. Find out about the training and experience of any practitioner you are considering. To learn more, see Selecting a Complementary Medicine Practitioner.

- Everyone's body is different, and yoga postures should be modified based on individual abilities. Carefully selecting an instructor who is experienced with and attentive to your needs is an important step toward helping you practice yoga safely. Ask about the physical demands of the type of yoga in which you are interested and inform your yoga instructor about any medical issues you have.

- Carefully think about the type of yoga you are interested in. For example, hot yoga (such as Bikram yoga) may involve standing and moving in humid environments with temperatures as high as 105°F. Because such settings may be physically stressful, people who practice hot yoga should take certain precautions. These include drinking water before, during, and after a hot yoga practice and wearing suitable clothing. People with conditions that may be affected by excessive heat, such as heart disease, lung disease, and a prior history of heatstroke may want to avoid this form of yoga. Women who are pregnant may want to check with their health care providers before starting hot yoga.

- Tell all your health care providers about any complementary health approaches you use. Give them a full picture of what you do to manage your health. This will help ensure coordinated and safe care.

Source: nccih.gov

YOGA ESSENTIALS

11 Yoga Poses Everyone Should Know & Practice

Downward-Facing Dog

Garland Pose

Forward Bend

Plank Pose

Seated Spinal Twist

Warrior I

Camel Pose

Cat-Cow Pose

Crescent Lunge

Child's Pose

Corpse Pose

© Kendall Hunt Publishing Company

Pilates

How It Works

Pull out your gym mat and get ready to do a series of movements that will stabilize and strengthen your core.

The exercises are usually done in a specific order, one right after another. The movements have names, like "The 100," Criss-Cross," the "Elephant," and the "Swan."

The moves may look simple, but they take a lot of precision and control. It's not like doing a bunch of crunches; there's a strong emphasis on technique.

You can do Pilates on an exercise mat, either in a class or at home, using a DVD. Or you can go to a gym or studio that has special equipment, a class, or a trainer who can supervise you.

Pilates classes typically take 45 minutes to an hour, but you can do fewer moves in less time.

You'll get stronger, more sculpted muscles and gain flexibility. You may also have better posture and a better sense of well-being.

Plan on doing this workout a few days a week, in addition to cardio, since Pilates isn't aerobic.

INTENSITY LEVEL: MEDIUM

It's demanding, but it's not the kind of workout that always works up a sweat. It's all about concentration and breathing. But you'll definitely feel it in your muscles during each exercise.

AREAS IT TARGETS

Pilates' main focus is on core however, you can expect to see strength gains in your arms and legs. Positions and movements used to activate core rely on extremities to control &/or apply loads to the core and likewise will benefit from Pilates.

TYPE

- **Flexibility:** Yes. The exercises in a Pilates workout will boost your flexibility and joint mobility.

- **Aerobic:** No. This is not a cardio workout.

- **Strength:** Yes. This workout will make your muscles stronger. You'll use your own body weight instead of weights.

- **Sport:** No.

- **Low-Impact:** Yes. You'll engage your muscles in a strong but gentle way.

WHAT ELSE YOU SHOULD KNOW

- **Cost:** You can do it at home for the cost of a Pilates DVD (about $15). Or you can go to a Pilates class. Expect to pay $50 or more for a private session or $10–$30 for a group session.

- **Good for beginners?** Yes. You can start with basic exercises then try advanced moves as you get better. If you're starting out, opt for a class or private lessons so an instructor can keep an eye on your form to help prevent an injury.

- **Outdoors:** No. Expect to go to the gym or be in a room with a TV for this workout.

- **At home:** Yes. Pull out your mat and press play on your DVD player for a convenient at-home workout.

- **Equipment required?** Yes, you'll need a mat. Some gyms have special machines for Pilates, called a Reformer. You can get a modified version for your home, but you probably don't need it.

- **What Dr. Melinda Ratini Says:** If you are looking to strengthen your abdomen and pelvis as well as maintain good posture, then Pilates is for you. It also has a strong mind/body connection, so you may like it if you enjoy yoga but need a more intense core workout.

Pilates is great for strengthening and toning with a focus your core and for increasing your flexibility. Since it is not designed to be an aerobic activity, don't forget your cardio!

Pilates involves precise moves and specific breathing techniques. It's not for you if you prefer a less structured program. It also won't fit your needs if you are looking for an aerobic workout.

Pilates can be very demanding, so start slowly. Instructors do not have to be licensed, so it's best to get recommendations before selecting one.

Is It Good For Me If I Have a Health Condition?

You can tailor Pilates to your individual needs, so it can be a great addition to your aerobic workout, even if you have health issues like heart disease, high blood pressure, and cholesterol. Check with your doctor first.

If you have diabetes, you may need to make some adjustments in your diabetes treatment plan, since adding muscle mass helps your body make better use of glucose. Your doctor can tell you what changes you need to make. Tell your instructor that you have diabetes and particularly if you have any complications such as diabetic retinopathy. You may need to avoid certain Pilates moves.

If you have arthritis, a strength-training program such as Pilates is a very important part of your exercise program. Research shows that a combination of aerobic exercise and strength training can help curb symptoms, maintain balance, keep joints flexible, and help you get to and keep an ideal body weight.

If you have had a recent back or knee injury, put off Pilates until your doctor clears you. Pilates strengthens the thigh muscles (quadriceps), and this may help prevent arthritis and knee injuries. It may also help prevent greater disability if you have arthritis.

Ask your doctor if Pilates would be a good choice if you have chronic low back pain. It will help strengthen your weak core muscles that may be adding to your pain. For the best results, seek out a Pilates instructor who has at least several years of experience working with people with low back pain.

If you are pregnant check with your doctor. She will probably let you continue Pilates if you are already doing it, as long as your pregnancy is going well. There may be some changes needed as your belly grows. For example, after your first trimester you shouldn't exercise while lying flat on your back because this reduces blood flow to your baby. There are also special Pilates programs for pregnant women that you can try.

Source: WebMD

Tai Chi

Tai chi is a mind-body practice developed in China in approximately the 12th century A.D. It started as a martial art, or a practice for fighting or self-defense, usually without weapons. Over time, people began to use tai chi for health purposes as well. Many different styles of tai chi, and variations of each style, developed. The term "tai chi" has been translated in various ways, such as "internal martial art," "supreme ultimate boxing," "boundless fist," and "balance of the opposing forces of nature." While accounts of tai chi's history often differ, the most consistently important figure is a Taoist monk (and semi-legendary figure) in twelfth-century China named Chang San-Feng (or Zan Sanfeng). Chang is said to have observed five animals—the tiger, the dragon, the leopard, the snake, and the crane—and concluded that the snake and the crane, through their movements, were the ones most able to overcome strong, unyielding opponents. Chang developed an initial set of exercises that imitated the movements of animals. He also brought flexibility and suppleness in place of strength to the martial arts, as well as some key philosophical concepts.

A person practicing tai chi moves her body in a slow, relaxed, and graceful series of movements while breathing deeply and meditating. Tai chi is sometimes called "moving meditation." Many tai chi practitioners believe that tai chi helps the flow throughout the body of a proposed vital energy called "qi" (pronounced "chi"), which means air and power. In traditional Chinese medicine, qi is the vital energy or life force proposed to regulate a person's spiritual, emotional, mental, and physical health, influenced by the opposing forces of yin and yang. In the United States, tai chi for health purposes is part of complementary and alternative medicine (CAM).

The movements to tai chi make up what it calls forms (or routines). Some movements have the names of animals or birds, such as "White Crane Spreads Its Wings." The simplest style of tai chi uses 13 movements; more complex styles can have dozens. In tai chi, each movement flows into the next. The entire body is always in motion, with the movements performed gently and at uniform speed. It is considered important to keep the body upright, especially the upper body. Many tai chi practitioners use the image of a string that goes from the top of the head into the heavens and let the body's weight sink to the soles of the feet.

In addition to movement, two other important elements in tai chi are breathing and meditation. Tai chi considers it important to concentrate, to put aside distracting thoughts, and to breathe in a deep, relaxed, and focused manner. Practitioners believe that this breathing and meditation have many benefits, such as:

- Massaging the internal organs,
- Aiding the exchange of gases in the lungs,
- Helping the digestive system work better,
- Increasing calmness and awareness, and
- Improving balance.

Certain concepts from Chinese philosophy were important in tai chi's development (although not every person who practices tai chi for health purposes, especially in the West, learns or uses them). A few are as follows:

- A vital energy called qi underlies all living things,
- Qi flows in people through specific channels called meridians,
- Qi is important in health and disease, and
- Tai chi is a practice that supports, unblocks, and redirects the flow of qi.

Another concept in tai chi is that the forces of yin and yang should be in balance. Traditional Chinese medicine describes the concept of two opposing yet complementary forces. Yin represents cold, slow, or passive aspects of the person, while yang represents hot, excited, or active aspects. A major theory is that health becomes achieved through balancing yin and yang, and the cause of disease is an imbalance leading to a blockage in the flow of qi. In Chinese philosophy, yin and yang are two principles or elements that make up the universe and everything in it and that also oppose each other.

People practice tai chi for various health purposes, such as:

- For benefits from exercise: Tai chi is a low-impact form of exercise, but it is a weight-bearing exercise that can have certain health benefits and is an aerobic exercise to some.
- To improve physical condition, muscle strength, coordination and flexibility,
- To have better balance and a lower risk for falls, especially in elderly people,
- To ease pain and stiffness, for example, from arthritis,
- For health benefits that they may experience from meditation,
- To improve sleep, and
- For overall wellness.

Many people practice tai chi for health purposes. In the United States, a 2002 national survey on Americans' use of CAM found that 1.3% of the 31,000 survey participants had used tai chi for health reasons in the year before the survey. Tai chi is widely practiced in China (including in its hospitals and clinics) and in other countries with a substantial native-Chinese population. In Asia, many people consider tai chi the most beneficial exercise for older people, because it is gentle and easily modifiable if a person has health limitations.

In the United States, people do not have to be health professionals or licensed to practice or teach tai chi. State or federal governments do not regulate the practice. There is no standard training for tai chi teachers. If you are considering learning tai chi, ask about the teacher's training and experience. Learning tai chi from a teacher, compared with learning it from videos or books, allows a student to find out whether he is performing the movements correctly and safely.

National Institutes of Mental Health, U.S. Department of Health and Human Services.

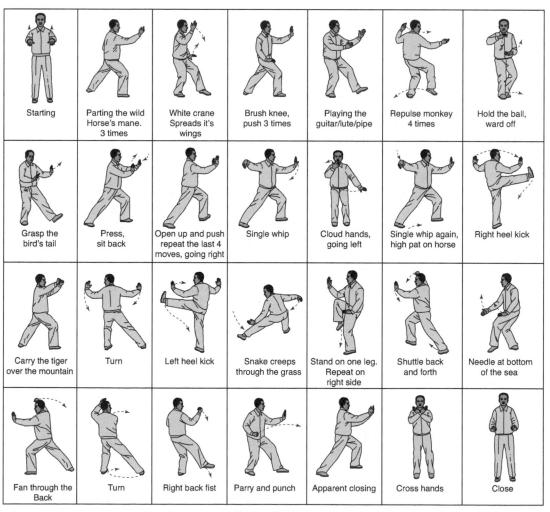

Starting	Parting the wild Horse's mane. 3 times	White crane Spreads it's wings	Brush knee, push 3 times	Playing the guitar/lute/pipe	Repulse monkey 4 times	Hold the ball, ward off
Grasp the bird's tail	Press, sit back	Open up and push repeat the last 4 moves, going right	Single whip	Cloud hands, going left	Single whip again, high pat on horse	Right heel kick
Carry the tiger over the mountain	Turn	Left heel kick	Snake creeps through the grass	Stand on one leg. Repeat on right side	Shuttle back and forth	Needle at bottom of the sea
Fan through the Back	Turn	Right back fist	Parry and punch	Apparent closing	Cross hands	Close

Proper Footwear

❝*Between saying and doing, many a pair of shoes is worn out.*❞

— Unknown

Believe it or not, footwear plays an important role with exercise. There are several sports-specific shoes to choose from, and it really depends on what types of exercise you'll be doing most of the time.

How to Buy Athletic Shoes

For many aerobic activities, good shoes are the most important purchase you'll make. Take the time to choose well. Here are some basic guidelines:

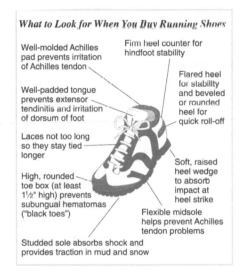

What to Look for When You Buy Running Shoes

Well-molded Achilles pad prevents irritation of Achilles tendon

Well-padded tongue prevents extensor tendinitis and irritation of dorsum of foot

Laces not too long so they stay tied longer

High, rounded toe box (at least 1½" high) prevents subungual hematomas ("black toes")

Studded sole absorbs shock and provides traction in mud and snow

Firm heel counter for hindfoot stability

Flared heel for stability and beveled or rounded heel for quick roll-off

Soft, raised heel wedge to absorb impact at heel strike

Flexible midsole helps prevent Achilles tendon problems

- Shop for shoes in the late afternoon, when your feet are most likely to be somewhat swollen—just as they will be after a workout.
- For walking shoes, look for a shoe that's lightweight, flexible, and roomy enough for your toes to wiggle, with a well-cushioned, curved sole; good support at the heel; and an upper made of a material that breathes (allows air in and out).
- For running shoes (see the figure), look for good cushioning, support, and stability. You should be able to wiggle your toes easily, but the front of your foot shouldn't slide from side to side, which could cause blisters. Your toes should not touch the end of the shoes because your feet will swell with activity. Allow about half an inch from the longest toe to the tip of the shoe.
- For racquetball shoes, look for reinforcement at the toe for protection during foot drag. The sole should allow minimal slippage. There should be some heel elevation to lessen strain on the back of the leg and Achilles tendon. The shoe should have a long throat to ensure greater control by the laces.
- For tennis shoes, look for reinforcement at the toe. The sole at the ball of the foot should be well padded because that's where most pressure is exerted. The sides of the shoe should be sturdy, for stability during continuous lateral movements. The toe box should allow ample room and some cushioning at the tips. A long throat ensures greater control by the laces.

Don't wear wet shoes for training. Let wet shoes air dry, because a heater will cause them to stiffen or shrink. Use powder in your shoes to absorb moisture, lessen friction, and prevent fungal infections. Break in new shoes for several days before wearing them for a long-distance run or during competition.

Source: Canadian Podiatric Sports Medicine Academy

OBESITY

On your body: **"***You may love it or hate it but it will be yours for the duration of your life on Earth. So take care of it.***"**

— Unknown

Worldwide, almost 2 billion adults were overweight with 600 million of these adults being clinically obese (World Health Organization, 2014). More specifically, obesity and overweight rates remain elevated within the United States with over 68% of adults being overweight and roughly 35% classified as clinically obese (Ogden, Carroll, Kit, & Flegal, 2013). It is a known fact that what is termed "preventable disease states" such heart disease, stroke, type 2 diabetes and certain types of cancers are often linked and attributed to obesity-related conditions (Centers for Disease Control and Prevention (CDC), 2015a). There is also a prevalence of higher obesity rates in middle-aged adults upwards of 30–40% for individuals ages 40 and above (CDC, 2015a). Medical expenses and costs associated with individuals with obesity are approximately $1400 higher per person than individuals who were not obese leading to an estimated annual medical cost of over $147 billion associated with obesity seen within the United States (CDC, 2015a).

SOURCES: World Health Organization. (2014). *Obesity and overweight.* Retrieved from who.int/mediacentre/factsheets/fs311/en/ Ogden, C.L., Carroll, M.D., Kit, B.K., Flegal, K.M. (2013). Prevalence of childhood and adult obesity in the United States, 2011–2012. *JAMA, 311*(8), 806–814.

Centers for Disease Control and Prevention. (2015a). *Obesity.* Retrieved from cdc.gov/obesity/data/adult.html

Remember: The criteria obesity is having a BMI of 30 or greater. Several health consequences are associated with obesity.

HEALTH CONSEQUENCES

- Coronary heart disease (the #1 killer of men and women)

- High blood pressure (twice as common in obese adults)

- Type 2 diabetes (more than 80% of diabetics are overweight)

(continues)

HEALTH CONSEQUENCES (CONTINUED)

- Back pain

- Asthma and shortness of breath

- High total cholesterol, high LDL cholesterol, decreased HDL, and high triglycerides

- Stroke

- Gallbladder disease (gallstones)

- Cancers: endometrial, breast, colon, prostate, kidney, gallbladder, and endometrial (women gaining more than 20 pounds from age 18 to midlife double their risk of postmenopausal breast cancer; 90,000 of yearly deaths due to cancer could be avoided if every U.S. adult could maintain a BMI under 25 throughout their lives)

- Osteoarthritis (degeneration of cartilage and its underlying bone within a joint)

- Bladder control problems (stress incontinence-urine leakage because of weak pelvic-floor muscles)

- Sleep apnea (on and off breathing while sleeping, which can decrease one's lifespan)

- Respiratory problems

- Menstrual irregularities and infertility

- Complications of pregnancy (obesity during pregnancy is associated with a increased risk of death in both mother and baby; a 10-fold increase of maternal high blood pressure; increased risk of neural tube defects like spina bifida; more likely to have gestational diabetes and problems with labor and delivery; infants born to obese women are more likely to have a high birth weight and low blood sugar, associated with brain damage and seizures)

- Premature death (people who are obese are at a 50%–100% increased risk of death from all causes).

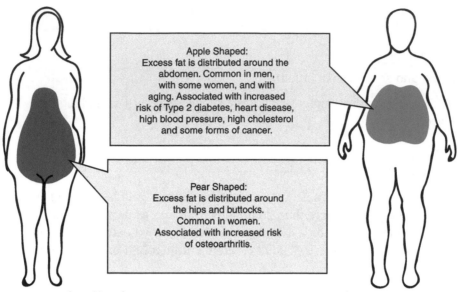

Apple Shaped:
Excess fat is distributed around the abdomen. Common in men, with some women, and with aging. Associated with increased risk of Type 2 diabetes, heart disease, high blood pressure, high cholesterol and some forms of cancer.

Pear Shaped:
Excess fat is distributed around the hips and buttocks. Common in women. Associated with increased risk of osteoarthritis.

Excess Fat Distribution

From *National Institute of Diabetes and Kidney Disease.*

Fat distribution is related to health risk. "Apples" describe male-fat patterned distribution with fat accumulating mostly around the torso. "Pears" describe female-fat patterned distribution with fat accumulating mostly on the hips and upper thighs (see figure). Apples have a higher health risk especially if they have visceral fat located around internal organs.

Supply and demand—the economics of the body.

Calories consumed > Calories Used = Weight Gain
Calories consumed < Calories Used = Weight Loss
Calories consumed = Calories Used = No Weight Gain

Body composition is the ratio of muscle mass (muscle, bone, organs, and other tissues and body fluids) to fat mass (total amount of essential and storage fat in the body). Exercise helps maintain body composition because:

- It uses calories (calories consumed either equal to the calories used or the calories used far exceed the calories consumed on a daily basis).

- It prevents the loss of lean muscle mass (lean muscle mass is associated with a higher metabolic rate because muscle cells are more metabolically active, and they burn more calories (at rest) than do fat cells).

- It decreases abdominal fat. (This fat is easier to mobilize through exercise than the fat in the hip/thigh area.)

- It is a natural appetite suppressor. (A decrease in appetite occurs for a time after exercising because the blood is now going to the skeletal muscles instead of to the digestive system.)

- It helps with weight management. (Regular exercise correlates with successful long-term weight management.)

- It improves self-esteem. (There is a decrease in anxiety and depression and an enhanced body image.)

Chapter 2 discusses more about weight loss and weight management as well as the reasons and factors for current weight gain.

BODY IMAGE

> **"***Nobody can make you feel inferior without your consent.***"**
>
> — Eleanor Roosevelt

Are you punishing yourself for being imperfect? Do you love your body? Are you saying, "Well, I like my arms, but my thighs are too big and I have this spare tire and . . ." Having a healthy body image means you feel good inside your own skin, despite any flaws you may have. Self-esteem influences body image more than how we actually look.

What Is Body Image?

- How you feel about how you look

- How you see yourself

- How you think others see you

- How you feel in your body

Are You Punishing Yourself?

Body image is defined as one's thoughts, perceptions, and attitudes about their physical appearance. How do you see yourself and feel about your body (e.g., height, shape, and weight) when you look in the mirror?

Positive body image is a clear, true perception of your shape; seeing the various parts of your body as they really are. Body positivity (or body satisfaction) involves feeling comfortable and confident in your body, accepting your natural body shape and size, and recognizing that physical appearance say very little about one's character and value as a person.

A negative body image, on the other hand, involves a distorted perception for one's shape. Negative body image (or body dissatisfaction) involves feelings of shame, anxiety, and self-consciousness. People who experience high levels of body dissatisfaction feel their bodies are flawed in comparison to others, and these folks are more likely to suffer from feelings of depression, isolation, low self-esteem, and eating disorders. While there is no single cause of eating disorders, research indicates that body dissatisfaction is the best-known contributor to the development of anorexia nervosa and bulimia nervosa (Stice, 2002). Learn more risk factors for eating disorders.

Body image concerns often begin at a young age and endure throughout life. By age 6, girls especially start to express concerns about their own weight or shape, and 40–60% of elementary school girls (ages 6–12) are concerned about their weight or about becoming too fat. (Smolak, 2011). Furthermore, over one-half of teenage girls and nearly one-third of teenage boys use unhealthy weight control behaviors such as skipping meals, fasting, smoking cigarettes, vomiting, and taking laxatives (Neumark-Sztainer, 2005). It is important to note that the age of onset differs depending on the individual, and these body image concerns may start younger, or never come up at all.

As with eating disorders, body image concerns can affect us all. While all ages, genders, and cultures are equally at risk for body image issues, there are traditionally different triggers and appearance-related pressures depending on one's gender. In our Western culture, girls often feel pressure to succumb to the societal appearance-ideal (sometimes referred to as the thin-, beauty-, or cultural-ideal), whereas boys are often faced with social pressures to be lean and muscular.

The body positive movement is making great strides to promote size diversity, body acceptance, and a healthier body image for all ages, genders, races, abilities, etc. It is important that we continue to embrace body diversity by recognizing all bodies as good bodies. While we all may have our days when we feel awkward or uncomfortable in our bodies, the key to developing positive body image is to recognize and respect our natural shape and learn to overpower those negative thoughts and feelings with positive, affirming, and accepting ones.

SOURCE: www.nationaleatingdisorders.org

Body image is how you see yourself when you look in the mirror or when you picture yourself in your mind. It encompasses:

- What you believe about your own appearance (including your memories, assumptions, and generalizations).

- How you feel about your body, including your height, shape, and weight.

- How you sense and control your body as you move. How you physically experience or feel in your body.

Many of us internalize messages starting at a young age that can lead to either positive or negative body image. Having a healthy body image is an important part of mental wellbeing and eating disorders prevention.

"Body image" is the way that someone perceives their body and assumes that others perceive them. This image is often affected by family, friends, social pressure and the media.

People who are unhappy with their bodies and don't seek healthy nutrition information may develop eating disorders. "Eating disorders" are unhealthy relationships with food that may include fasting, constant dieting, or binging and purging.

Body image is closely linked to self-esteem. Low self-esteem in adolescents can lead to eating disorders, early sexual activity, substance use and suicidal thoughts. You can post encouraging notes in your school bathrooms to brighten your classmates' day. Sign up for Mirror Messages.

Approximately 91% of women are unhappy with their bodies and resort to dieting to achieve their ideal body shape. Unfortunately, only 5% of women naturally possess the body type often portrayed by Americans in the media.

58% of college-aged girls feel pressured to be a certain weight.

Studies show that the more reality television a young girl watches, the more likely she is to find appearance important.

More than 1/3 of the people who admit to "normal dieting," will merge into pathological dieting. Roughly 1/4 of those will suffer from a partial or full-on eating disorder.

In a survey, more than 40% of women and about 20% of men agreed they would consider cosmetic surgery in the future. The statistics remain relatively constant across gender, age, marital status, and race.

Students, especially women, who consume more mainstream media, place a greater importance on sexiness and overall appearance than those who do not consume as much.

95% of people with eating disorders are between the ages of 12 and 25.

Only 10% of people suffering from an eating disorder will seek professional help.

SOURCE: www.dosomething.org

One list cannot automatically tell you how to turn negative body thoughts into positive body image, but it can introduce you to healthier ways of looking at yourself and your body. The more you practice these new thought patterns, the better you will feel about who you are and the body you naturally have.

Appreciate all that your body can do. Every day your body carries you closer to your dreams. Celebrate all of the amazing things your body does for you—running, dancing, breathing, laughing, dreaming, etc.

Keep a top-ten list of things you like about yourself—things that aren't related to how much you weigh or what you look like. Read your list often. Add to it as you become aware of more things to like about yourself.

Remind yourself that "true beauty" is not simply skin-deep. When you feel good about yourself and who you are, you carry yourself with a sense of confidence, self-acceptance, and openness that makes you beautiful. Beauty is a state of mind, not a state of your body.

Look at yourself as a whole person. When you see yourself in a mirror or in your mind, choose not to focus on specific body parts. See yourself as you want others to see you—as a whole person.

Surround yourself with positive people. It is easier to feel good about yourself and your body when you are around others who are supportive and who recognize the importance of liking yourself just as you naturally are.

Shut down those voices in your head that tell you your body is not "right" or that you are a "bad" person. You can overpower those negative thoughts with positive ones. The next time you start to tear yourself down, build yourself back up with a few quick affirmations that work for you.

Wear clothes that are comfortable and that make you feel good about your body. Work with your body, not against it.

Become a critical viewer of social and media messages. Pay attention to images, slogans, or attitudes that make you feel bad about yourself or your body. Protest these messages: write a letter to the advertiser or talk back to the image or message.

Do something nice for yourself—something that lets your body know you appreciate it. Take a bubble bath, make time for a nap, or find a peaceful place outside to relax.

Use the time and energy that you might have spent worrying about food, calories, and your weight to do something to help others. Sometimes reaching out to other people can help you feel better about yourself and can make a positive change in our world.

SOURCE: www.nationaleatingdisorders.org

Online Assignment: Take the "Real Age" Test

Complete this assignment online. Go to:

www.grtep.com

Select >Chapter Content>Chapter 1>Enter your username and password

TIPS TO BECOMING PHYSICALLY HEALTHY THROUGH EXERCISE

"Never, never, never quit!"
— Winston Churchill

- Make sure to set goals before figuring out mode, frequency, duration, and intensity.

- Always use a mode that you prefer or enjoy doing—this will help you stick to your program.

- If you are having troubles committing to an exercise program, find a workout partner or look into the details behind getting a personal trainer or taking a group fitness class.

- Make certain that any personal trainers or group fitness instructors have the proper education and experience before you begin a program or class with them.

- Be sure to keep an open mind and try out different modes or classes offered. You don't know if you're going to enjoy an activity or not unless you try it out.

- Ask a professional if you have questions about equipment, exercises, and even exercise myths.

- If you want to purchase a video or exercise equipment, do your homework first to make sure it fits your goal, suits your preference of mode, and before you spend your hard-earned money on it.

- Make it count! Apply the overload principle to each type of exercise you do.

- Wear breathable, comfortable clothing when exercising.

- Wear appropriate footwear when exercising.

- Stay plenty hydrated when exercising.

- Find ways to motivate and reward yourself for all of your time and hard work exercising!

Helpful Internet Sites

About.com. Identify Your Yoga Personality: yoga.about.com/od/typesofyoga/a/whatsyourtype.htm

American College of Sports Medicine: acsm.org

American Council on Exercise: acefitness.org

American Heart Association: americanheart.org or justmove.org

Balanced Body Pilates: pilates.com/BBAPP/V/home.html

Calories per Hour.com (Activity and Weight Loss Calculators): caloriesperhour.com

Conversion of Activities into Steps: walking.about.com/od/measure/a/stepequivalents.htm

Cooper Institute for Aerobics Research: cooperinst.org

Mayo Clinic: mayoclinic.com

RealAge Health Assessments: realage.com

Runner's World: runnersworld.com

Shape Up America! shapeup.org

U.S. Health & Human Services—Centers for Disease Control and Prevention: cdc.gov

U.S. National Institutes of Health—National Center for Complementary and Alternative Medicine: nccam.nih.gov

References

About.com. Improve Your Body Image.exercise.about.com/cs/exercisehealth/a/bodyimage_2.htm; *Yoga Style Guide:* yoga.about.com/od/typesofyoga/a/yogatypes.htm accessed on 4.4.08.

American Heart Association. *The Benefits of Daily Physical Activity.* americanheart.org accessed on 11.15.07.

Armstrong. L. et al. *ACSM's Guidelines for Exercise Testing and Prescription.* 7th Edition. Philadelphia: Lippincott Williams & Wilkins (2006). Exercise Prescription: Cardiovascular: 133–154; Strength: 154–158; Flexibility: 158–160.

Balanced Body Pilates. *Pilates—Its Benefits.* pilates.com/BBAPP/V/about/pilates-benefits.html accessed on 4.7.08.

Borg, G. *Perceived Exertion and Pain Scales.* Human Kinetics (1998).

Bounds, L. et al. *Health and Fitness: A Guide to a Healthy Lifestyle.* Kendall Hunt Publishing Company (2006): Warm-Up and Cool-Down: 34–35; Principles of Fitness Training: 35–36; Flexibility: 43–45; Par-Q and You: 55; Benefits of Aerobic Fitness Levels: 27; Energy for Exercise: 30–31; Heat and Humidity: 48; Excess Fat Distribution: 89.

Cooper, K. *The Aerobics Program for Total Well-Being.* 1.5 Mile Run Test. Bantam Books (1982).

Cooper Institute for Aerobics Research, Dallas, TX. *The Physical Fitness Specialist Manual.* Push-Up and Modified Push-Up Tests and Partial Curl-Up Test (2002).

Hettler, B. The National Wellness Institute. *The Six Dimensions of Wellness: Physical Wellness.* www.nationalwellness.org accessed on 12.7.07.

Karvonen, M., K. Kentala, and O. Mustala. The Effects of Training on Heart Rate: A Longitudinal Study. *Annals of Medicine and Experimental Biology* 35 (1957): 307–315.

Kravitz, L. *Anybody's Guide to Total Fitness.* 8th Edition. Kendall Hunt Publishing Company (2006). The Formula for Aerobic Fitness—Taking Your Heart Rate: 25.

Oz, M., M.D., and Roizen, M., M.D., realage.com accessed on 2.28.08.

Robbins, G. et al. *A Wellness Way of Life.* 7th Edition. McGraw-Hill (2008): FITT Prescription: 115; 10,000 Steps: A Daily Lifestyle Goal. 116–119.

The Rockport Company, Inc. *Rockport Fitness Walking Test.* (1993).

Shape Up America! *Everything You Want to Know about Body Fat: Healthy Body Fat Percentage Ranges.* shapeup.org/bodylab/basics/know3.php accessed on 4.8.08.

U.S. Department of Commerce. National Oceanic and Atmospheric Administration. *Heat Index Chart.* In *Heat Wave: A Major Summer Killer.* Government Printing Office (1992).

U.S. Department of Health and Human Services. Centers for Disease Control and Prevention. *National Health and Nutrition Examination Survey, 2009–2010.* NCHS Data Brief. No. 82. January 2012. cdc.gov/nchs/data/databriefs/db82.pdf accessed on June 18, 2012.

U.S. Department of Health and Human Services. Centers for Disease Control and Prevention. *National Center for Health Statistics, FastStats Leading Causes of Death, 2009–2010.* January 2012. cdc.gov/nchs/fastats/lcod.htm accessed on June 18, 2012.

U.S. Department of Health and Human Services. Centers for Disease Control and Prevention. Prevalence of Physical Activity, Including Lifestyle Activities Among Adults—United States, 2000–2001. *MMWR* August 15, 2003, 52(32):764–769. www.cdc.gov accessed on 11.5.07.

U.S. Department of Health and Human Services. Centers for Disease Control and Prevention. *National Health and Nutrition Examination Survey, 2009–2010.* NCHS Data Brief. No. 82. January 2012.

U.S. Centers for Disease Control and Prevention. *Obesity—Health Consequences.* cdc.gov/nccdphp/dnpa/obesity/consequences.htm accessed on 2.21.08.

U.S. National Institutes of Health. National Center for Complementary and Alternative Medicine. *Tai Chi for Health Purposes.* nccam.nih.gov/health/taichi/ accessed on 4.19.08.

YMCA Fitness Testing and Assessment Manual. 4th edition. *Percentiles by Age Groups and Gender for YMCA Sit-and-Reach Test* (2000).

Physical Wellness— Nutrition

"Food is an important part of a balanced diet."

— Fran Lebowitz

The objectives in this chapter include the understanding of:

- The meaning of physical wellness in relation to nutrition and its direct application to you
- The main nutrients and their functions such as carbohydrates, fats, proteins, vitamins, minerals, and water
- How to identify antioxidant-rich and phytochemical-rich foods
- Appropriate personal daily dietary and caloric recommendations
- The ChooseMyPlate.gov program
- Realistically identifying serving sizes
- Hunger/Fullness Cues and Scale
- How to read a food label and how to determine your personal daily grams/day intake
- How to determine healthier choices for meals and snacks
- The Mediterranean diet and the vegetarian diet
- Organic foods and healthier choices for fast foods and ethnic foods
- Obesity and its health consequences
- Weight loss, weight management, and weight gain

Online Reminders

- Complete the poll question before the next class meeting.
- Complete the interactive activities for this chapter.
- Complete all of the online assignments for this chapter.

Physical Wellness—Optimal physical wellness is achieved not only through exercise but rather the combination of BOTH regular exercise and healthy eating habits. Physical wellness, as it pertains to nutrition, involves learning about your daily diet and being aware of overall nutrition needs and necessities to make for a healthy lifestyle. Poor dietary habits, along with being sedentary, is one of the major factors that results in people becoming increasingly overweight or obese. Being overweight or obese is not only a major risk factor for heart disease (the #1 killer of men and women), but it also provides risks for other health problems that this chapter will discuss.

Because some nutrition information is hard to understand or appears overly complicated, people often either guess at what they are trying to interpret or just give up. That's not the way to maintain a healthy weight and body composition, to prevent heart disease and other disease states, and to live a healthy lifestyle. Knowledge is very powerful in this process of understanding nutrition. The United States Department of Agriculture (USDA) and the United States Department of Health and Human Services have teamed up in an effort to simplify and streamline nutritional information available to the general public. This effort is helping to decrease the amount of confusion with nutrition with easy to apply, user-friendly information.

Physical wellness follows these tenets, as stated by The National Wellness Institute:

1. It is better to consume foods and beverages that enhance good health than those that impair it.

2. It is better to be physically fit than not, as Chapter 1 discusses.

PRE-CLASS SURVEY: Take this physical wellness/nutrition self-survey before your next class meeting. Circle either Yes or No, total up each column, and check your score.

I eat fruits, vegetables, and whole grains every day.	YES	NO
I know how many calories I should consume (daily) without going over my limit.	YES	NO
I usually choose 100% whole-wheat bread or whole-grain bread.	YES	NO
I rarely eat fried or breaded meats, chicken, or fish.	YES	NO
I drink fat-free or low-fat milk.	YES	NO
I rarely eat a lot of high-fat foods and sweets.	YES	NO
I read food labels when making choices about the foods I buy.	YES	NO
I know what antioxidants and phytochemicals are and their benefits.	YES	NO
I consume 25 grams of fiber per day.	YES	NO
I am aware of which fats are bad and which fats are better for me.	YES	NO
I can identify healthy serving sizes.	YES	NO
I am familiar with the MyPyramid Food Guidance System.	YES	NO
	TOTAL	

WHAT YOUR TOTAL MEANS:

9 or more Yes answers	Excellent	Your habits are positively enhancing your health.
6–8 Yes answers	Average	You are obviously trying but there is room to improve.
5 or less Yes answers	Not So Good	There is a need for improvement in your daily habits.

NUTRIENTS

> **"***Thou shouldst eat to live; not live to eat.***"**
>
> — Socrates

Eating is a necessity for everyday function and for maintaining a healthy lifestyle. Making the effort to get the 40 essential nutrients through daily dietary consumption is something that most Americans aren't practicing day in and day out. The body makes some nutrients, but nutrients are found mainly in the foods you eat. Because no one food source contains all of these nutrients, eating a variety of foods is imperative to overall nutritional/physical wellness. To simplify things, let's classify these essential nutrients into macronutrients (needed by your body in large amounts) and micronutrients (needed by your body in small amounts). Together, these two categories of nutrients are responsible for growth, repair and maintenance of all tissues, regulation of body processes, and providing energy.

Macronutrients

Macronutrients provide energy to your body in the form of calories via carbohydrates, fats, and proteins.

Carbohydrates aka Carbs

This macronutrient is your body's main source of fuel. What happens is that your body breaks down the carbs you eat into a simple sugar called glucose (blood sugar)—the *most readily available* for fuel source for your body. Glucose can also be stored as glycogen in your muscles and liver and then converted to glucose when you need energy. Your body also uses carbohydrates as building blocks to make and repair cells.

Let's now classify carbs into two categories: simple and complex carbohydrates. Simple carbs are sugars that have little nutritive value beyond their energy content or what we call "empty calories." There are simple sugars found in milk, fruit, honey, and some vegetables, but they also exist in candy, jellies, cakes, sodas, and table sugar. Complex carbs consist of starch (digestible) and fiber (nondigestible), and you can find them in breads, grains, pastas, cereals, and potatoes. Complex carbohydrates should constitute most of your recommended daily carb intake since these are healthier for you.

What's the Deal with Fiber?

It is mainly present in leaves, roots, skins, and seeds and is the part of a plant not digested it the small intestine. Let's further categorize fiber into two categories:

insoluble and soluble. Insoluble fiber binds with water to help produce bowel movements. It allows food residues to pass through the intestinal tract more quickly, limiting the exposure and absorption time of toxic substances within the waste materials. Soluble fiber dissolves in water and helps the body excrete fats. Scientists have shown that it reduces levels of blood cholesterol and blood sugars. Soluble fiber travels through the digestive tract in gel-like form, pacing the absorption of cholesterol, which helps prevent dramatic shifts in blood sugar levels.

Evidence suggests that fiber in your diet may help by relieving and preventing constipation (wheat bran and oat bran), lowering the risk of diverticular disease (insoluble fiber), by lowering the risk of type 2 diabetes (high fiber consumption) and heart disease (high intake of fiber found in grains), and by promoting weight control by leaving you with a "full feeling."

FIBER-RICH FOODS YOU SHOULD INCORPORATE INTO YOUR DIET			
SOLUBLE FIBER		**INSOLUBLE FIBER**	
Oat bran	Cranberries	Brown Rice	Sprouts
Oatmeal	Grapefruit	Whole-wheat/	Apples
Legumes	Mango	grain breads	Bananas
Carrots	Oranges	Wheat-bran cereals	Berries
Broccoli	Apples	Legumes	Cherries
Brussels Sprouts	Pecans	Broccoli	Pears
Asparagus	Walnuts	Green peppers	Almonds
Peanuts		Red cabbage	Sesame seeds
		Spinach	Sunflower

Adapted from Shils et al., eds. *Modern Nutrition in Health and Disease,* 9th ed. Lippincott Williams and Wilkins, 1999.

Fats aka Lipids

This macronutrient is the body's major source of *stored* energy and provides energy during exercise. Fat has many other essential purposes—it insulates the body to preserve ideal body temperature, contributes to cellular structure, helps repair cells, assists in transporting fat soluble vitamins A, E, D, and K throughout your body, protects vital organs by cushioning, satisfies hunger because its digestion is slower, and adds flavor and texture to many foods. Fat is also necessary for normal growth and healthy skin and is essential in the making of key hormones (e.g., testosterone and estrogen). You see—dietary fat is very important to our health and to our diet. It's when people consume too much fat per day that they get into trouble with their health.

Let's again classify. Fats come in the following categories:

SATURATED FATS	TRANS FATS/ FATTY ACIDS	POLYUNSATURATED*	MONOUNSATURATED
"BAD FATS"	*"BAD FATS"*	*"GOOD FATS"*	*"GOOD FATS"*
Primarily found in animal products. All animal fats contain cholesterol.	Formed when liquid oils are made into solid fats by adding hydrogen atoms to the fats as a way to increase the shelf-life.	Primarily found in plants. Vegetable foods have no natural presence of cholesterol.	Also found in plants. Vegetable foods have no natural presence of cholesterol.
Elevates total cholesterol; elevates "bad" LDL cholesterol; increases the risk of heart disease and some cancers.	Elevates total cholesterol; elevates "bad" LDL cholesterol; lowers "good" HDL cholesterol; increases the risk of heart disease and some cancers.	Lowers total cholesterol; lowers "bad" cholesterol; may reduce the risk of heart disease.	Lowers total cholesterol; lowers "bad" cholesterol; may elevate "good" HDL cholesterol; may reduce the risk for heart disease and some cancers.
EXAMPLES: red meat, lard, cream, butter, cheese, whole milk, bacon, hot dogs, chocolates, coconut and palm oils	EXAMPLES: stick margarine, dips, shortenings, cookies, crackers, doughnuts, candy, pies, cakes, fried foods	EXAMPLES: corn, soybean, safflower and sunflower oils; tub margarines, pecans, mayonnaise, salad dressings	EXAMPLES: avocado, olives, cashews, almonds, peanuts and most nuts, peanut butter (without the hydrogenated oils), olive, peanut, and canola oils

* *Omega-3 fatty acid* is a specialized polyunsaturated fat ("good fat") found in cold-water fish such as salmon, tuna, halibut, mackerel, sardines, and herring. It also occurs in lesser amounts in walnuts, flaxseed, and flaxseed oil, green leafy vegetables, canola oil, wheat germ, and soybeans. Omega-3 fatty acids lower total cholesterol and the risk for heart disease and stroke by reducing the prevalence of atherosclerosis and inflammation in blood vessels, lowering blood pressure, and reducing blood clots. This fat can also reduce the occurrence of cancerous tumors. The American Heart Association recommends eating (the types of fish and foods already mentioned) at least twice a week.

Adapted from Robbins, G. et al. *A Wellness Way of Life.* 7th Edition. McGraw-Hill: 2008. Comparison of Fats.

What Exactly Is Cholesterol? HDL? LDL?

Cholesterol is a fat-like, waxy substance found in animal products. Your liver also makes it. The blood carries cholesterol by lipoproteins: high-density lipoproteins (HDL) and low-density lipoproteins (LDL). HDL ("good") carries cholesterol from the blood back to the liver, which prepares the cholesterol for elimination from the body. LDL ("bad") carries cholesterol from the liver to the rest of your body. When there is too much LDL in the blood, deposits of cholesterol can build up inside the arteries, which can narrow an artery enough to slow or block blood flow (atherosclerosis). Having higher LDL levels and lower HDL levels will put you at greater risk for heart disease. We will discuss this more in Chapter 10 as you learn about risk factors for cardiovascular disease.

Proteins

This macronutrient is essentially the "building block" of the body since proteins make up your cells. Proteins are necessary for the growth, maintenance, and repair of all body tissues (e.g., muscles, blood, bones, internal organs, skin, hair, and nails). Proteins also help maintain the normal balance of body fluids and are necessary to make enzymes, hormones, and antibodies that fight infection. At least 20 amino acids make up proteins, but there are *nine* the body cannot make (essential amino acids), which you must consume daily. Proteins occur in animal products (complete proteins) like meats, milk, fish, and eggs, AND they also occur in whole grains, beans, peas, pastas, rice, seeds, and nuts (incomplete proteins). Adults need approximately 4 grams of protein for every 10 pounds of ideal body weight. Athletes, pregnant, or lactating women and people over age 55 usually need a little extra protein.

You can use proteins as a fuel source for your body, but it is NOT the main source of energy like carbohydrates and fats are. Eating too much protein can also cause adverse health effects upon your bones because it requires lots of calcium, which can lead to your bones excreting too much of it. Excessive amounts of protein may also contribute to obesity, heart disease, and certain forms of cancer due to the saturated fats and cholesterol found in protein.

Micronutrients

Micronutrients regulate bodily functions such as metabolism, growth, and cellular development via vitamins, minerals, and water.

Vitamins

Your body does not consume these micronutrients, which you must obtain from food or a daily multiple vitamin. Vitamins do not provide energy for your body; rather, they allow the release of energy from carbs, fats, and proteins. They also help and grow tissue and maintain and support reproductive functions and immune system functions. Vitamins categorize into *either fat-soluble vitamins* or *water-soluble vitamins.* Fat-soluble vitamins are transported by the body's fat cells, are not excreted in the urine, and are stored in the body for long periods of time. Water-soluble vitamins are not stored in the body for a long time and are excreted through urine and sweat. Because of this, you must replace them daily.

Minerals

These micronutrients are inorganic substances acquired by eating foods every day, and they are critical to many functions in the body (as listed in the table below). Categories of minerals are either *macrominerals* (calcium, chloride, magnesium, phosphorus, potassium,

FACTS ABOUT VITAMINS

VITAMIN	FUNCTIONS	DEFICIENCY PROBLEMS	EFFECT OF EXCESS AMOUNTS	DIETARY SOURCES
Fat Soluble Vitamin A	Allows normal vision in the dark; promotes health and growth of cells and tissues; protects health of skin and tissues in the mouth, stomach, intestines, and respiratory and urogenital tract	Night blindness and other eye problems; dry, scaly skin; reproduction problems; poor growth	Birth defects, headaches; vomiting, double vision; hair loss; bone abnormalities; liver damage	Liver; fish oil; eggs; milk fortified with vitamin A; red, yellow, and orange fruits and vegetables; many dark green leafy vegetables
Vitamin D	Promotes absorption of calcium and phosphorus to develop and maintain bones and teeth	Osteoporosis and softening of the bones, rickets, defective bone growth	Kidney stones or damage, weak muscles and bones, excessive bleeding	Sunlight on the skin, cheese, eggs, some fish, fortified milk, breakfast cereals, and margarine
Vitamin E	Antioxidant and may protect against heart disease and some types of cancer	Nervous system problems	May interfere with vitamin K action and en hance the effect of some anticoagulant drugs	Vegetable oils and margarine, salad dressing and other foods made from vegetable oils, nuts, seeds, wheat germ, leafy green vegetables
Vitamin K	Helps blood clotting	Thin blood that does not clot	None observed	Green leafy vegetables, smaller amounts widespread in other foods

FACTS ABOUT VITAMINS *(CONTINUED)*

VITAMIN	FUNCTIONS	DEFICIENCY PROBLEMS	EFFECT OF EXCESS AMOUNTS	DIETARY SOURCES
Water Soluble				
Vitamin C	Helps produce collagen; maintenance and repair of red blood cells, bones, and other tissues; promotes healing; keeps immune system healthy	Scurvy, excessive bleeding, swollen gums, improper wound healing	Diarrhea, gastrointestinal discomfort	Citrus fruits, berries, melons, peppers, dark leafy green vegetables, tomatoes, potatoes
Thiamin	Conversion of carbohydrates into energy	Fatigue, weak muscles, and nerve damage	None reported	Whole-grain, enriched grain products, pork, liver, and other organ meats
Riboflavin	Energy metabolism, changes tryptophan into niacin	Eye disorders, dry and flaky skin, red tongue	None reported	Milk and other dairy products; enriched bread, cereal, and other grain products; eggs; meat; green leafy vegetables; nuts; liver; kidney; and heart
Niacin	Helps the body use sugars and fatty acids, produce energy, enzyme function	Diarrhea, mental disorientation, skin problems	Flushed skin, liver damage, stomach ulcers and high blood sugar	Poultry, fish, beef, peanut butter, and legumes

(continues)

FACTS ABOUT VITAMINS *(CONTINUED)*

VITAMIN	FUNCTIONS	DEFICIENCY PROBLEMS	EFFECT OF EXCESS AMOUNTS	DIETARY SOURCES
Vitamin B6	Converts tryptophan into niacin and serotonin, helps produce other body chemicals such as insulin, hemoglobin, and antibodies	Depression, nausea, mental convulsions in infants; greasy, flaky skin	Nerve damage	Chicken, fish, pork, liver, kidney, whole grains, nuts, and legumes
Folate	Produces DNA and RNA to make new body cells, works with vitamin B12 to form hemoglobin in red blood cells	Impaired cell division and growth, anemia	Medication interference, masking of vitamin B12 deficiencies	Leafy vegetables, orange juice and some fruits, legumes, liver, yeast breads, wheat germ, and some fortified cereals
Vitamin B12	Works with folate to make red blood cells, vital part of body chemicals	Anemia, fatigue, nerve damage, smooth tongue, very sensitive skin	None reported	Animal products and some fortified foods
Biotin	Metabolize fats, protein, and carbohydrates	Heart abnormalities, appetiteloss, fatigue, depressions, and dry skin	None reported	Eggs, liver, yeast breads, and cereal
Pantothenic Acid	Metabolize protein, fat, and carbohydrates	Rare	Diarrhea and water retention	Meat, poultry, fish, whole-grain cereals, and legumes; smaller amounts in milk, vegetables, and fruits

FACTS ABOUT SELECTED MINERALS

MINERAL	FUNCTIONS	DEFICIENCY PROBLEMS	EFFECT OF EXCESS AMOUNTS	DIETARY SOURCES
Calcium	Helps build strong bones and teeth, control of muscle contractions and nerve function, supports blood clotting	Stunted growth in children, bone mineral loss in adults	Muscle and abdominal pain, calcium kidney stones	Milk and milk products, tofu, green leafy vegetables, fortified orange juice, and bread
Fluoride	Formation and maintenance of bones and teeth	Higher occurrence of tooth decay	Increased bone density, mottling of teeth, impaired kidney function	Fluoridated drinking water, tea, seafood
Iron	Helps carry oxygen to body tissues	Anemia, weakness impaired immune function, cold hands and feet, gastrointestinal distress	Liver disease, arrhythmias, joint pain	Red meat, seafood, dried fruit, legumes, fortified cereals, green vegetables
Iodine	Component of thyroid hormones that help regulate growth, development, and metabolic rate	Enlarged thyroid, birth defect	Depression of thyroid activity, sometimes hyperthyroidism	Salt, seafood, bread, milk, cheese
Magnesium	Facilitates many cell processes	Neurological disorders, impaired immune function, kidney disorders nausea, weight loss	Nausea, vomiting, nervous system depression, coma, death in people with impaired kidney function	Widespread in foods

(continues)

FACTS ABOUT SELECTED MINERALS *(continued)*

MINERAL	FUNCTIONS	DEFICIENCY PROBLEMS	EFFECT OF EXCESS AMOUNTS	DIETARY SOURCES
Phosphorus	Works with calcium to build and maintain bones and teeth, helps convert food to energy	Bone loss, kidney disorders	Lowers blood calcium	Dairy products, egg yolks, meat, poultry, fish, legumes, soft drinks
Potassium	Vital for muscle contractions and nerve transmission, important for heart and kidney function, helps regulate fluid balance and blood pressure	Muscular weakness, nausea, drowsiness, paralysis, confusion, disruption of cardiac rhythm	Slower heart beat, kidney failure	Milk and yogurt, many fruits and vegetables (especially oranges, bananas, and potatoes)
Sodium	Maintains fluid and electrolyte balance, supports muscle contraction and nerve impulse transmissions	Muscle weakness, loss of appetite, nausea, vomiting	Edema, hypertension	Salt, soy sauce, bread, milk, meats
Zinc	Involved in production of genetic material and proteins, ability to taste, wound healing, sperm production, normal fetus development	Night blindness, loss of appetite, skin rash, impaired immune function, impaired taste, poor wound healing	Nausea and vomiting, abdominal pain	Seafood, meats, eggs, whole grains

sodium, and sulfur) or *microminerals* (chromium, cobalt, copper, fluoride, selenium, and zinc). Macronutrients are necessary in relatively large amounts (100 mg or more each day), and microminerals are necessary in smaller quantities (less than 100 mg per day).

What Are Antioxidants and Phytochemicals?

Antioxidants aid cells in your body facing ongoing battles with free radicals that can damage cell membranes and mutate genes (resulting from normal metabolism, environmental pollution, chemicals and pesticides, cigarette smoking, too much sunlight, additives in processed foods, and stress hormones). Studies show that antioxidants have the ability to suppress cell deterioration and may help "slow" the aging process. They also may reduce our risk for heart disease, cancer, stroke, high blood pressure, cataracts, and urinary tract infections. You can get your antioxidants by eating a wide variety of fruits and vegetables each day.

Phytochemicals are substances in plants that act as antioxidants. They have beneficial effects on the body, providing anticancer properties in particular. Generally fruits and vegetables that are bright colors—yellow, orange, red, green, blue, and purple—contain the most phytochemicals. This is why we derive the greatest health benefits from eating fruits and vegetables rather than taking supplements. Also, we are not able to duplicate all of the phytochemicals found in fruits and vegetables into pill or capsule form.

ANTIOXIDANTS AND THEIR PRIMARY FOOD SOURCES

Vitamin A	Fortified milk; egg yolk; cheese; liver; butter; fish oil; dark green, yellow, and orange vegetables and fruits
Vitamin C	Papaya, cantaloupe, melons, citrus fruits, grapefruit, strawberries, raspberries, kiwi, cauliflower, tomatoes, dark green vegetables, green and red peppers, asparagus, broccoli, cabbage, collard greens, orange juice, and tomato juice
Vitamin E	Vegetable oils, nuts and seeds, dried beans, egg yolk, green leafy vegetables, sweet potatoes, wheat germ, 100 percent whole wheat bread, 100 percent whole grain cereal, oatmeal, mayonnaise
Carotenoids	Sweet potatoes, carrots, squash, tomatoes, asparagus, broccoli, spinach, romaine lettuce, mango, cantaloupe, pumpkin, apricots, peaches, papaya
Flavenoids	Purple grapes, wine, apples, berries, peas, beets, onions, garlic, green tea
Selenium	Lean meat, seafood, kidney, liver, dairy products, 100 percent whole grain cereal, 100 percent whole wheat bread

EXAMPLES OF FUNCTIONAL COMPONENTS*

CLASS/COMPONENTS	SOURCE*	POTENTIAL BENEFIT
Carotenoids		
Beta-carotene	Carrots, pumpkin, sweet potato, cantaloupe	Neutralizes free radicals, which may damage cells; bolsters cellular antioxidant defenses; can be made into vitamin A in the body
Lutein, zeaxanthin	Kale, collards, spinach, corn, eggs, citrus	May contribute to maintenance of healthy vision
Lycopene	Tomatoes and processed tomato products, watermelon, red/pink grapefruit	May contribute to maintenance of prostate health
Dietary (functional and total) Fiber		
Insoluble fiber	Wheat bran, corn bran, fruit skins	May contribute to maintenance of a healthy digestive tract; may reduce the risk of some types of cancer
Beta glucan**	Oat bran, oatmeal, oat flour, barley, rye	May reduce risk of coronary heart disease (CHD)
Soluble fiber**	Psyllium seed husk, peas, beans, apples, citrus fruits	May reduce risk of CHD and some types of cance
Whole grains**	Cereal grains, whole wheat bread, oatmeal, brown rice	May reduce risk of CHD and some types of cancer; may contribute to maintenance of healthy blood glucose levels
Fatty Acids		
Monounsaturated fatty acids (MUFAs)**	Tree nuts, olive oil, canola oil	May reduce risk of CHD
Polyunsaturated fatty acids (PUFAs)—omega-3 fatty acids—ALA	Walnuts, flax	May contribute to maintenance of heart health; may contribute to maintenance of mental and visual function
PUFAs—omega-3 fatty acids—DHA/EPA**	Salmon, tuna, marine, and other fish oils	May reduce risk of CHD; may contribute to maintenance of mental and visual function
Conjugated linoleic acid (CLA)	Beef and lamb; some cheese	May contribute to maintenance of desirable body composition and healthy immune function

(continues)

EXAMPLES OF FUNCTIONAL COMPONENTS* *(continued)*

CLASS/COMPONENTS	SOURCE*	POTENTIAL BENEFIT
Flavonoids		
Anthocyanins—cyanidin, delphinidin, malvidin	Berries, cherries, red grapes	Bolsters, cellular antioxidant defenses; may contribute to maintenance of brain function
Flavanols—catechins, epicatechins, epigallocatechin, procyanidins	Tea, cocoa, chocolate, apples, grapes	May contribute to maintenance of heart health
Flavanones—hesperetin, naringenin	Citrus foods	Neutralize free radicals, which may damage cells; bolster cellular antioxidant defenses
Flavonols—quercetin, kaempferol, isorhamnetin, myricetin	Onions, apples, tea, broccoli	Neutralize free radicals, which may damage cells; bolster cellular antioxidant defenses
Proanthocyanidins	Cranberries, cocoa, apples, strawberries, grapes, wine, peanuts, cinnamon	May contribute to maintenance of urinary tract health and heart health
Isothiocyanates		
Sulforaphane	Cauliflower, broccoli, broccoli sprouts, cabbage, kale, horseradish	May enhance detoxification of undesirable compounds; bolsters cellular antioxidant defenses
Minerals		
Calcium**	Sardines, spinach, yogurt, low-fat dairy products, fortified foods and beverages	May reduce the risk of osteoporosis
Magnesium	Spinach, pumpkin seeds, whole-grain breads and cereals, halibut, brazil nuts	May contribute to maintenance of normal muscle and nerve function, healthy immune function, and bone health
Potassium**	Potatoes, low-fat dairy products, whole-grain breads and cereals, citrus juices, beans, bananas	May reduce the risk of high blood pressure and stroke, in combination with a low-sodium diet
Selenium	Fish, red meat, grains, garlic, liver, eggs	Neutralizes free radicals, which may damage cells; may contribute to healthy immune function

(continues)

EXAMPLES OF FUNCTIONAL COMPONENTS* *(continued)*

CLASS/COMPONENTS	SOURCE*	POTENTIAL BENEFIT
Phenolic Acids Caffeic acid, ferulic acid	Apples, pears, citrus fruits, some vegetables, coffee	May bolster cellular antioxidant defenses; may contribute to maintenance of healthy vision and heart health
Plant Stanols/Sterols Free stanols/sterols**	Corn, soy, wheat, wood oils, fortified foods and beverages	May reduce risk of CHD
Stanol/sterol esters**	Fortified table spreads, stanol ester dietary supplements	May reduce risk of CHD
Polyols Sugar alcohols**—xylitol, sorbitol, mannitol, lactitol	Some chewing gums and other food	Applications may reduce risk of dental caries
Prebiotics Inulin, fructo-oligosaccharides (FOS), polydextrose	Whole grains, onions, some fruits, garlic, honey, leeks, fortified foods and beverages	May improve gastrointestinal health; may improve calcium absorption
Probiotics Yeast, *Lactobacilli*, *Bifidobacteria* and other specific strains of beneficial bacteria	Certain yogurts and other cultured dairy and non-dairy applications	May improve gastrointestinal health and systemic immunity; benefits are strain-specific
Phytoestrogens Isoflavones—daidzein, genistein	Soybeans and soy-based foods	May contribute to maintenance of bone health, healthy brain and immune function; for women, may contribute to maintenance of menopausal health
Lignans	Flax, rye, some vegetables	May contribute to maintenance of heart health and healthy immune function
Soy Protein Soy protein**	Soybeans and soy-based foods	May reduce risk of CHD

(continues)

EXAMPLES OF FUNCTIONAL COMPONENTS* *(continued)*

CLASS/COMPONENTS	SOURCE*	POTENTIAL BENEFIT
Sulfides/Thiols		
Diallyl sulfide, allyl methyl trisulfide	Garlic, onions, leeks, scallions	May enhance detoxification of undesirable compounds; may contribute to maintenance of heart health and healthy immune function
Dithiolthiones	Cruciferous vegetables	May enhance detoxification of undesirable compounds; may contribute to maintenance of healthy immune function
Vitamins		
A***	Organ meats, milk, eggs, carrots, sweet potato, spinach	May contribute to maintenance of healthy vision, immune function, and bone health; may contribute to cell integrity
B1 (Thiamin)	Lentils, peas, long-grain brown rice, brazil nuts	May contribute to maintenance of mental function; helps regulate metabolism
B2 (Riboflavin)	Lean meats, eggs, green leafy vegetables	Helps support cell growth; helps regulate metabolism
B3 (Niacin)	Dairy products, poultry, fish, nuts, eggs	Helps support cell growth; helps regulate metabolism
B5 (Pantothenic acid)	Organ meats, lobster, soybeans, lentils helps regulate metabolism and hormone synthesis	Helps regulate metabolism and hormone synthesis
B6 (Pyridoxine)	Beans, nuts, legumes, fish, meat, whole grains	May contribute to maintenance of healthy immune function; helps regulate metabolism
B9 (Folate)**	Beans, legumes, citrus foods, green leafy vegetables, fortified breads and cereals	May reduce a woman's risk of having a child with a brain or spinal cord defect
B12 (Cobalamin)	Eggs, meat, poultry, milk	May contribute to maintenance of mental function; helps regulate metabolism and supports blood cell formation
Biotin	Liver, salmon, dairy, eggs, oysters	Helps regulate metabolism and hormone synthesis

(continues)

EXAMPLES OF FUNCTIONAL COMPONENTS* *(continued)*

CLASS/COMPONENTS	SOURCE*	POTENTIAL BENEFIT
C	Guava, sweet red/green pepper, kiwi, citrus fruit, strawberries	Neutralizes free radicals, which may damage cells; may contribute to maintenance of bone health and immune function
D	Sunlight, fish, fortified milk and cereals	Helps regulate calcium and phosphorus; helps contribute to bone health; may contribute to healthy immune function; helps support cell growth
E	Sunflower seeds, almonds, hazelnuts, turnip greens	Neutralizes free radicals, which may damage cells; may contribute to healthy immune function and maintenance of heart health

*Examples are not an all-inclusive list.

**FDA approved health claim established for component.

***Preformed vitamin A is found in foods that come from animals. Provitamin A carotenoids are found in many darkly colored fruits and vegetables and are a major source of vitamin A for vegetarians.

SOURCE: Reprinted from International Food Information Council Foundation, 2007–2009. Originally printed in the 2007–2009 Foundation Media Guide on Food Safety and Nutrition.

Is Chocolate an Antioxidant?

Yes! As stated by the American Dietetic Association, cocoa beans (which are actually not beans but seeds from the fruit of the cocoa tree) are rich in a specific type of antioxidant called flavonols. Chocolate is made from cocoa beans. Recent research suggests that cocoa and chocolate have the following benefits on vascular health: They help limit the buildup of plaque in arteries by lowering LDL cholesterol; they help raise HDL cholesterol; they help blood platelets to be less "sticky," which promotes healthy blood flow; they reduce blood pressure in people with high blood pressure; and they help maintain healthy blood sugar levels, thus increasing blood flow in the brain and keeping skin healthy. Look for non-alkalized or lightly alkalized cocoas (also called a "dutched" cocoa) but not "natural cocoa," which is not alkalized. Also look for darker chocolates made with at least 40% cocoa bean content or "cacao." Keep in mind that chocolate contains fat and added sugar that provides additional calories—eat chocolate in moderation.

Is Red Wine an Antioxidant, Too?

Yes! The National Cancer Institute states that red wine is a rich source of phytochemicals, in particular in compounds called polyphenols found in red wine (such as catechins and resveratrol). These are thought to have antioxidant or anticancer properties. Recent evidence from animal studies suggests this anti-inflammatory compound may be an effective chemopreventive agent in three stages of the cancer process: initiation, promotion, and progression. Research studies published in the International Journal of Cancer show that drinking one glass of red wine a day may cut a man's risk of prostate cancer in half and that the protective effect appears to be strongest against the most aggressive forms of the disease. It also reported that men who consumed four or more 4-ounce glasses of red wine per week have a 60% lower incidence of the more aggressive types of prostate cancer. However, studies of the association between red wine consumption and cancer in humans are in their initial stages. Although consumption of large amounts of alcoholic beverages may increase the risk of some cancers, there is growing evidence that the health benefits of red wine are related to its *nonalcoholic* components.

What about Red Wine and Heart Disease?

According to the American Heart Association and a series of scientific studies, the polyphenolic compounds in red wine, such as flavonoids and resveratrol, may contribute to limiting the start and progression of atherosclerosis (when blood vessels begin to lose their natural ability to relax, or vasodilate, due to risk factors such as smoking, high blood pressure, high cholesterol, and diabetes). Both the alcohol and polyphenolic compounds found in red wine appear to favorably maintain healthy blood vessels (vasculature) by promoting the formation of nitric oxide. This is the key chemical relaxing factor that plays a pivotal role in the regulation of vascular tone. Nitric oxide protects against vascular injury, inhibits the adhesion of inflammatory cells to the vessel wall, and limits the activation of platelets, the cell particles responsible for blood clotting.

Water

Although water is not an energy source for the body, it is essential to daily life functions. Water lubricates joints, absorbs shock, regulates body temperature, maintains blood volume, and transports fluids throughout the body. About 60% of your total body weight is water. If you lose even 4% of your body weight through sweat, you will lose the ability to make decisions, concentrate, or do physical work. If you lose as much as 20%, you will die.

PROGRESSIVE EFFECTS OF DEHYDRATION

% LOSS OF BODY WATER	EFFECTS OF DEHYDRATION
0–1%	Thirst
2–5%	Dry mouth, flushed skin, fatigue, headache, impaired physical performance
6%	Increased body temperature, breathing rate and heart rate, dizziness, increased weakness
8%	Dizziness, increased weakness, labored breathing with exercise
10%	Muscle spasms, swollen tongue, delirium
11%	Poor blood circulation, failing kidney function

Adapted from *The American Dietetic Association's Complete Food and Nutrition Guide.* Chronimed Publishing (1996): 168.

We lose water from breathing, sweating, and in urine and stool. We take water from eating foods (fruits, vegetables, soups, meats, grains), from drinking water in beverages (water itself, fruit juices, milk, and sports drinks), and from the metabolism process or chemical breakdown of foods. If you lose more water than you take in, you become dehydrated. Dehydration can happen if you are not drinking enough fluids daily, working or exercising in a hot or cold environment, living at high altitude, and drinking too much alcohol. Clear urine is a sign that you are well hydrated. The more dehydrated you are, the darker (and smellier) you urine will be although medications, vitamins, and diet can affect color.

DIETARY GUIDELINES 2015–2020

> *College students don't get a lot of great nutrition, mostly because they are in a hurry, so we give them counsel on healthy things to eat.*
>
> — Chris Linde

Executive Summary

Over the past century, deficiencies of essential nutrients have dramatically decreased, many infectious diseases have been conquered, and the majority of the U.S. population can now anticipate a long and productive life. At the same time, rates of chronic diseases—many of which are related to poor quality diet and physical inactivity—have increased. About half of all American adults have one or more preventable, diet-related chronic diseases, including cardiovascular disease, type 2 diabetes, and overweight and obesity.

However, a large body of evidence now shows that healthy eating patterns and regular physical activity can help people achieve and maintain good health and reduce the risk of chronic disease throughout all stages of the lifespan. The *2015–2020 Dietary Guidelines for Americans* reflects this evidence through its recommendations.

The *Dietary Guidelines* is required under the 1990 National Nutrition Monitoring and Related Research Act, which states that every 5 years, the U.S. Departments of Health and Human Services (HHS) and of Agriculture (USDA) must jointly publish a report containing nutritional and dietary information and guidelines for the general public. The statute (Public Law 101-445, 7 U.S.C. 5341 et seq.) requires that the *Dietary Guidelines* be based on the preponderance of current scientific and medical knowledge. The 2015–2020 edition of the *Dietary Guidelines* builds from the 2010 edition with revisions based on the *Scientific Report of the 2015 Dietary Guidelines Advisory Committee* and consideration of Federal agency and public comments.

Previous editions of the *Dietary Guidelines* focused primarily on individual dietary components such as food groups and nutrients. However, people do not eat food groups and nutrients in isolation but rather in combination, and the totality of the diet forms an overall eating pattern. As a result, eating patterns and their food and nutrient characteristics are a focus of the recommendations in the *2015–2020 Dietary Guidelines*.

The *2015–2020 Dietary Guidelines* provides five overarching Guidelines that encourage healthy eating patterns, recognize that individuals will need to make shifts in their food and beverage choices to achieve a healthy pattern, and acknowledge that all segments of our society have a role to play in supporting healthy choices.

The Guidelines

1. **Follow a healthy eating pattern across the lifespan.** All food and beverage choices matter. Choose a healthy eating pattern at an appropriate calorie level to help achieve and maintain a healthy body weight, support nutrient adequacy, and reduce the risk of chronic disease.

2. **Focus on variety, nutrient density, and amount.** To meet nutrient needs within calorie limits, choose a variety of nutrient-dense foods across and within all food groups in recommended amounts.

3. **Limit calories from added sugars and saturated fats and reduce sodium intake.** Consume an eating pattern low in added sugars, saturated fats, and sodium. Cut back on foods and beverages higher in these components to amounts that fit within healthy eating patterns.

4. **Shift to healthier food and beverage choices.** Choose nutrient-dense foods and beverages across and within all food groups in place of less healthy choices. Consider cultural and personal preferences to make these shifts easier to accomplish and maintain.

5. **Support healthy eating patterns for all.** Everyone has a role in helping to create and support healthy eating patterns in multiple settings nationwide, from home to school to work to communities.

Key Recommendations provide further guidance on how individuals can follow the five Guidelines:

Consume a healthy eating pattern that accounts for all foods and beverages within an appropriate calorie level.

A healthy eating pattern includes:

- A variety of vegetables from all of the subgroups—dark green, red and orange, legumes (beans and peas), starchy, and other

- Fruits, especially whole fruits

- Grains, at least half of which are whole grains

- Fat-free or low-fat dairy, including milk, yogurt, cheese, and/or fortified soy beverages

- A variety of protein foods, including seafood, lean meats and poultry, eggs, legumes (beans and peas), and nuts, seeds, and soy products

- Oils

A healthy eating pattern limits:

- Saturated fats and *trans* fats, added sugars, and sodium

- Consume less than 10 percent of calories per day from added sugars

- Consume less than 10 percent of calories per day from saturated fats

- Consume less than 2,300 milligrams (mg) per day of sodium

- If alcohol is consumed, it should be consumed in moderation—up to one drink per day for women and up to two drinks per day for men—and only by adults of legal drinking age.

ESTIMATED CALORIE NEEDS PER DAY, BY AGE, SEX, AND PHYSICAL ACTIVITY LEVEL

MALES

AGE	SEDENTARY	MODERATELY ACTIVE	ACTIVE
2	1,000	1,000	1,000
3	1,000	1,400	1,400
4	1,200	1,400	1,600
5	1,200	1,400	1,600
6	1,400	1,600	1,800
7	1,400	1,600	1,800
8	1,400	1,600	2,000
9	1,600	1,800	2,000
10	1,600	1,800	2,200
11	1,800	2,000	2,200
12	1,800	2,200	2,400
13	2,000	2,200	2,600
14	2,000	2,400	2,800
15	2,200	2,600	3,000
16	2,400	2,800	3,200
17	2,400	2,800	3,200
18	2,400	2,800	3,200
19–20	2,600	2,800	3,000
21–25	2,400	2,800	3,000
26–30	2,400	2,600	3,000
31–35	2,400	2,600	3,000
36–40	2,400	2,600	2,800
41–45	2,200	2,600	2,800
46–50	2,200	2,400	2,800
51–55	2,200	2,400	2,800
56–60	2,200	2,400	2,600

(continues)

ESTIMATED CALORIE NEEDS PER DAY, BY AGE, SEX, AND PHYSICAL ACTIVITY LEVEL
(CONTINUED)

MALES

AGE	SEDENTARY	MODERATELY ACTIVE	ACTIVE
61–65	2,000	2,400	2,600
66–70	2,000	2,200	2,600
71–75	2,000	2,200	2,600
76 and up	2,000	2,200	2,400

FEMALES

AGE	SEDENTARY	MODERATELY ACTIVE	ACTIVE
2	1,000	1,000	1,000
3	1,000	1,200	1,400
4	1,200	1,400	1,400
5	1,200	1,400	1,600
6	1,200	1,400	1,600
7	1,200	1,600	1,800
8	1,400	1,600	1,800
9	1,400	1,600	1,800
10	1,400	1,800	2,000
11	1,600	1,800	2,000
12	1,600	2,000	2,200
13	1,600	2,000	2,200
14	1,800	2,000	2,400
15	1,800	2,000	2,400
16	1,800	2,000	2,400
17	1,800	2,000	2,400
18	1,800	2,000	2,400
19–20	2,000	2,200	2,400
21–25	2,000	2,200	2,400

(continues)

ESTIMATED CALORIE NEEDS PER DAY, BY AGE, SEX, AND PHYSICAL ACTIVITY LEVEL
(CONTINUED)

FEMALES

AGE	SEDENTARY	MODERATELY ACTIVE	ACTIVE
26–30	1,800	2,000	2,400
31–35	1,800	2,000	2,200
36–40	1,800	2,000	2,200
41–45	1,800	2,000	2,200
46–50	1,800	2,000	2,200
51–55	1,600	1,800	2,200
56–60	1,600	1,800	2,200
61–65	1,600	1,800	2,000
66–70	1,600	1,800	2,000
71–75	1,600	1,800	2,000
76 and up	1,600	1,800	2,000

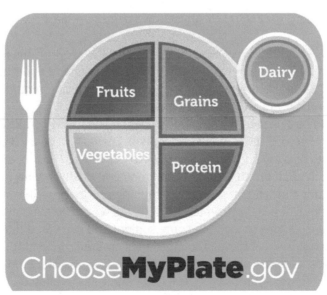

(Source: https://www.choosemyplate.gov/MyPlate)

The USDA's My Plate, was introduced in 2011 and is divided into four sections—fruits, vegetables, grains and protein. MyPlate is a reminder to find your healthy eating style and build it throughout your lifetime. Everything you eat and drink matters. The right mix can help you be healthier now and in the future. This means:

- Focus on variety, amount, and nutrition.
- Choose foods and beverages with less saturated fat, sodium, and added sugars.
- Start with small changes to build healthier eating styles.
- Support healthy eating for everyone.

Eating healthy is a journey shaped by many factors, including our stage of life, situations, preferences, access to food, culture, traditions, and the personal decisions we make over time. All your food and beverage choices count. MyPlate offers ideas and tips to help you create a healthier eating style that meets your individual needs and improves your health.

Online Assignment: ChooseMyPlate.gov/ Serving Sizes and Plan for Daily Diet

Complete this assignment online. Go to:
www.grtep.com
Select >Chapter Content>Chapter 2>Enter your username and password

Appendix 3. USDA Food Patterns: Healthy U.S.-Style Eating Pattern

The Healthy U.S.-Style Pattern is based on the types and proportions of foods Americans typically consume, but in nutrient-dense forms and appropriate amounts. It is designed to meet nutrient needs while not exceeding calorie requirements and while staying within limits for overconsumed dietary components.

The methodology used to develop and update this Pattern continues to be grounded in that of the food guides USDA has developed for the last 30 years. This methodology includes using current food consumption data to determine the mix and proportions of foods to include in each group, using current food composition data to select a nutrient-dense representative for each food, and calculating nutrient profiles for each food group using these nutrient-dense representative foods. As would be expected, most foods in their nutrient-dense forms do contain some sodium and saturated fatty acids. In a few cases, such as whole-wheat bread, the most appropriate representative in current Federal databases contains a small amount of added sugars. Detailed information about the representative foods, nutrient profiles, and Patterns is available on the USDA Center for Nutrition Policy and Promotion website.[1]

[1] For additional information and technical tables, see: U.S. Department of Agriculture. Center for Nutrition Policy and Promotion. USDA Food Patterns. Available at: http://www.cnpp.usda.gov/USDAFoodPatterns (http://www.cnpp.usda.gov/USDAFoodPatterns).

Amounts of each food group and subgroup are adjusted as needed, within the limits of the range of typical consumption when possible, to meet nutrient and *Dietary Guidelines* standards while staying within the limits for calories and overconsumed dietary components. Standards for nutrient adequacy aim to meet the Recommended Dietary Allowances (RDA), which are designed to cover the needs of 97 percent of the population, and Adequate Intakes (AI), which are used when an average nutrient requirement cannot be determined. The Patterns meet these standards for almost all nutrients. For a few nutrients (vitamin D, vitamin E, potassium, choline), amounts in the Patterns are marginal or below the RDA or AI standard for many or all age-sex groups. In most cases, an intake of these nutrients below the RDA or AI is not considered to be of public health concern. For more information on potassium and vitamin D, see Chapter 2, Underconsumed Nutrients and Nutrients of Public Health Concern (/dietaryguidelines/2015/guidelines/chapter-2/a-closer-look-at-current-intakes-and-recommended-shifts/#underconsumed-nutrients).

The Healthy U.S.-Style Pattern is the base USDA Food Pattern. While the Healthy U.S.-Style Pattern is substantially unchanged from the base USDA Food Pattern of the 2010 edition of the *Dietary Guidelines*, small changes in the recommended amounts reflect updating the Patterns based on current food consumption and composition data. The Healthy U.S.-Style Pattern includes 12 calorie levels to meet the needs of individuals across the lifespan. To follow this Pattern, identify the appropriate calorie level, choose a variety of foods in each group and subgroup over time in recommended amounts, and limit choices that are not in nutrient-dense forms so that the overall calorie limit is not exceeded.

HEALTHY U.S.-STYLE EATING PATTERN: RECOMMENDED AMOUNTS OF FOOD FROM EACH FOOD GROUP AT 12 CALORIE LEVELS

CALORIE LEVEL OF PATTERN[a]	1,000	1,200	1,400	1,600	1,800	2,000
Food Group[b]	**Daily Amount[c]** of Food From Each Group (vegetable and protein foods subgroup amounts are per week)					
Vegetables	1 c-eq	1½ c-eq	1½ c-eq	2 c-eq	2½ c-eq	2½ c-eq
Dark-green vegetables (c-eq/ wk)	½	1	1	1½	1½	1½
Red and orange vegetables (c-eq/wk)	2½	3	3	4	5½	5½
Legumes (beans and peas) (c-eq/wk)	½	½	½	1	1½	1½
Starchy vegetables (c-eq/wk)	2	3½	3½	4	5	5

(continues)

HEALTHY U.S.-STYLE EATING PATTERN: RECOMMENDED AMOUNTS OF FOOD FROM EACH FOOD GROUP AT 12 CALORIE LEVELS *(CONTINUED)*

CALORIE LEVEL OF PATTERN[a]	1,000	1,200	1,400	1,600	1,800	2,000
Other vegetables (c-eq/wk)	1½	2½	2½	3½	4	4
Fruits	**1 c-eq**	**1 c-eq**	**1½ c-eq**	**1½ c-eq**	**1½ c-eq**	**2 c-eq**
Grains	**3 oz-eq**	**4 oz-eq**	**5 oz-eq**	**5 oz-eq**	**6 oz-eq**	**6 oz-eq**
Whole grains[d] (oz-eq/day)	1½	2	2½	3	3	3
Refined grains (oz-eq/day)	1½	2	2½	2	3	3
Dairy	**2 c-eq**	**2½ c-eq**	**2½ c-eq**	**3 c-eq**	**3 c-eq**	**3 c-eq**
Protein Foods	**2 oz-eq**	**3 oz-eq**	**4 oz-eq**	**5 oz-eq**	**5 oz-eq**	**5½ oz-eq**
Seafood (oz-eq/wk)	3	4	6	8	8	8
Meats, poultry, eggs (oz-eq/wk)	10	14	19	23	23	26
Nuts seeds, soy products (oz-eq/wk)	2	2	3	4	4	5
Oils	**15 g**	**17 g**	**17 g**	**22 g**	**24 g**	**27 g**
Limit on Calories for Other Uses, calories (% of calories)[e,f]	150 (15%)	100 (8%)	110 (8%)	130 (8%)	170 (9%)	270 (14%)

[a] Food intake patterns at 1,000, 1,200, and 1,400 calories are designed to meet the nutritional needs of 2- to 8-year-old children. Patterns from 1,600 to 3,200 calories are designed to meet the nutritional needs of children 9 years and older and adults. If a child 4 to 8 years of age needs more calories and, therefore, is following a pattern at 1,600 calories or more, his/her recommended amount from the dairy group should be 2.5 cups per day. Children 9 years and older and adults should not use the 1,000-, 1,200-, or 1,400-calorie patterns.

[b] Foods in each group and subgroup are:

- Vegetables
  - Dark-green vegetables: All fresh, frozen, and canned dark-green leafy vegetables and broccoli, cooked or raw: for example, broccoli; spinach; romaine; kale; collard, turnip, and mustard greens.
  - Red and orange vegetables: All fresh, frozen, and canned red and orange vegetables or juice, cooked or raw: for example, tomatoes, tomato juice, red peppers, carrots, sweet potatoes, winter squash, and pumpkin.
  - Legumes (beans and peas): All cooked from dry or canned beans and peas: for example, kidney beans, white beans, black beans, lentils, chickpeas, pinto beans, split peas, and edamame (green soybeans). Does not include green beans or green peas.
  - Starchy vegetables: All fresh, frozen, and canned starchy vegetables: for example, white potatoes, corn, green peas, green lima beans, plantains, and cassava.
  - Other vegetables: All other fresh, frozen, and canned vegetables, cooked or raw: for example, iceberg lettuce, green beans, onions, cucumbers, cabbage, celery, zucchini, mushrooms, and green peppers.

- **Fruits**
  - All fresh, frozen, canned, and dried fruits and fruit juices: for example, oranges and orange juice, apples and apple juice, bananas, grapes, melons, berries, and raisins.
- **Grains**
  - Whole grains: All whole-grain products and whole grains used as ingredients: for example, whole-wheat bread, whole-grain cereals and crackers, oatmeal, quinoa, popcorn, and brown rice.
  - Refined grains: All refined-grain products and refined grains used as ingredients: for example, white breads, refined grain cereals and crackers, pasta, and white rice. Refined grain choices should be enriched.
- **Dairy**
  - All milk, including lactose-free and lactose-reduced products and fortified soy beverages (soymilk), yogurt, frozen yogurt, dairy desserts, and cheeses. Most choices should be fat-free or low-fat. Cream, sour cream, and cream cheese are not included due to their low calcium content.
- **Protein Foods**
  - All seafood, meats, poultry, eggs, soy products, nuts, and seeds. Meats and poultry should be lean or low-fat and nuts should be unsalted. Legumes (beans and peas) can be considered part of this group as well as the vegetable group, but should be counted in one group only.

^c Food group amounts shown in cup-(c) or ounce-equivalents (oz-eq). Oils are shown in grams (g). Quantity equivalents for each food group are:

- Vegetables and fruits, 1 cup-equivalent is: 1 cup raw or cooked vegetable or fruit; 1 cup vegetable or fruit juice, 2 cups leafy salad greens, ½ cup dried fruit or vegetable.
- Grains, 1 ounce-equivalent is: ½ cup cooked rice, pasta, or cereal; 1 ounce dry pasta or rice; 1 medium (1 ounce) slice bread; 1 ounce of ready-to-eat cereal (about 1 cup of flaked cereal).
- Dairy, 1 cup-equivalent is: 1 cup milk, yogurt, or fortified soymilk; 1½ ounces natural cheese such as cheddar cheese or 2 ounces of processed cheese.
- Protein Foods, 1 ounce-equivalent is: 1 ounce lean meat, poultry, or seafood; 1 egg; ¼ cup cooked beans or tofu; 1 Tbsp peanut butter; ½ ounce nuts or seeds.

^d Amounts of whole grains in the Patterns for children are less than the minimum of 3 oz-eq in all Patterns recommended for adults.

^e All foods are assumed to be in nutrient-dense forms, lean or low-fat and prepared without added fats, sugars, refined starches, or salt. If all food choices to meet food group recommendations are in nutrient-dense forms, a small number of calories remain within the overall calorie limit of the Pattern (i.e., limit on calories for other uses). The number of these calories depends on the overall calorie limit in the Pattern and the amounts of food from each food group required to meet nutritional goals. Nutritional goals are higher for the 1,200- to 1,600-calorie Patterns than for the 1,000-calorie Pattern, so the limit on calories for other uses is lower in the 1,200- to 1,600-calorie Patterns. Calories up to the specified limit can be used for added sugars, added refined starches, solid fats, alcohol, or to eat more than the recommended amount of food in a food group. The overall eating Pattern also should not exceed the limits of less than 10 percent of calories from added sugars and less than 10 percent of calories from saturated fats. At most calorie levels, amounts that can be accommodated are less than these limits. For adults of legal drinking age who choose to drink alcohol, a limit of up to 1 drink per day for women and up to 2 drinks per day for men within limits on calories for other uses applies (see Appendix 9. Alcohol (/dietaryguidelines/2015/guidelines/appendix-9/) for additional guidance); and calories from protein, carbohydrate, and total fats should be within the Acceptable Macronutrient Distribution Ranges (AMDRs).

^f Values are rounded.

Source: https://health.gov/dietaryguidelines/2015/guidelines/appendix-3/

Serving Sizes

Now you have determined what you should be eating and how much. The "how much" question is always the hardest to figure out for most of us. Healthy eating not only includes making healthful food choices but also understanding serving sizes. Once you get a good sense of serving sizes, you can compare them to the amount you eat and make any necessary changes. Serving sizes are units of measure used to describe the amount of food *recommended* from each food group. Portions are amounts of specific foods you *choose* to eat, which can be bigger or smaller than the recommended food servings. Here are some everyday comparisons to help you figure out your serving sizes based on your ChooseMyPlate suggestions:

Measurement	Size	Food item portion
1 cup	Fist	Medium fruit, Green salad, Frozen yogurt, Pasta, Rice, Pretzels, Snack food, Ice cream
1/2 cup (4 ounces)	Rounded handful	Cooked vegetables, Cup of fruit, Pasta, Rice, Snack food, Pretzels, Nuts, Small candy
3 ounces	Deck of cards	Fish, Meat, Poultry
1/4 cup	Golf ball	Dried fruit, such as Raisins, Apricots
1 1/2 ounces	6 dice	Cheese
1 teaspoon (tsp.)	Tip of thumb	Pat of butter

Online Assignment: ChooseMyPlate.gov/ Serving Sizes and Plan for Daily Diet

Complete this assignment online. Go to:

www.grtep.com

Select >Chapter Content>Chapter 2>Enter your username and password

Hunger/Fullness Cues and Scale

Your body has all of the things it needs to maintain a natural and healthy weight. But, you need to pay attention to the signals that your body gives you and eat (and stop eating) according to them. To pay closer attention to your body, use a Hunger and Fullness Scale. This type of scale can help you gauge whether or not you need to eat and can help you to determine when to stop eating as well. There are many hunger/fullness scales on the internet so do a quick search to find one that you like the best. Then make a copy of it and use it each time you feel that you want to eat or finish a meal. I have included a sample Hunger and Fullness scale below. This particular scale was developed by Barbara Craighead, PhD and uses a 1 through 7 rating. To use the scale, ask yourself "Am I really hungry?" before you start eating. Tune in to the physical sensations you're experiencing and then rate your hunger on the Hunger/Fullness Scale using the descriptions below. For this particular scale, it's recommended that you try to stay between a 2.5 and a 5.5. Avoid letting yourself get down to a 1 on the scale, which is "very hungry," by keeping planned snacks on hand that you can eat if you fall below a 2.5. As you eat, continually think about where you fall on the scale. Stop eating once you feel that you are at a 5.5. Using a Hunger and Fullness Scale can be difficult, but with focus and practice, you will eventually become more in tune with your internal signals of hunger and fullness and you will be able to realize when you are eating in response to emotions or stress as opposed to hunger. The next step would be finding alternatives to emotional eating.

VERY HUNGRY	MODERATELY HUNGRY	MILDLY HUNGRY	NO FEELING; NEUTRAL	MILDLY FULL	VERY FULL	MUCH TOO FULL
1	2	3	4	5	6	7
	2.5		— Desirable Zone —		5.5	

(1= Very hungry; starving, 2= Moderately hungry; ready to eat, 3= Mildly hungry; beginning hunger, 4= Neutral. You feel no sensations of hunger or fullness, 5: Mildly full. You feel satisfied, 6=Very full. Your stomach is beginning to feel a bit distended, 7= Much too full. Your stomach feels stuffed)

What's On The Nutrition Facts Label

The Nutrition Facts Label found on packaged foods and beverages is your daily tool for making informed food choices that contribute to healthy lifelong eating habits. Explore it today and discover the wealth of information it contains!

Serving Size

Serving Size is based on the **amount of food that is customarily eaten** at one time. All of the nutrition information listed on the Nutrition Facts Label is based on **one serving** of the food.

The serving size is shown as a common household measure that is appropriate to the food (such as cup, tablespoon, piece, slice, or jar), followed by the metric amount in grams (g).

When comparing calories and nutrients in different foods, check the serving size in order to make an accurate comparison.

Servings Per Container

Servings Per Container shows the **total number of servings** in the entire food package or container. It is common for one package of food to contain more than one serving.

The information listed on the Nutrition Facts Label is based on **one serving**. So, if a package contains *two servings* and you eat the entire package, you have consumed *twice the amount of calories and nutrients* listed on the label.

Calories

Calories refers to the **total number of calories**, or "energy," supplied from all sources (fat, carbohydrate, protein, and alcohol) in one serving of the food.

To achieve or maintain a healthy body weight, balance the number of calories you eat and drink with the number of calories you burn during physical activity and through your body's metabolic processes.

> As a general rule:
> **100 calories** per serving is **moderate**
> **400 calories** per serving is **high**

Nutrition Facts

Serving Size 1 package (272g)
Servings Per Container 1

Amount Per Serving

Calories 300   Calories from Fat 45

	% Daily Value*
Total Fat 5g	**8%**
Saturated Fat 1.5g	**8%**
Trans Fat 0g	
Cholesterol 30mg	**10%**
Sodium 430mg	**18%**
Total Carbohydrate 55g	**18%**
Dietary Fiber 6g	**24%**
Sugars 23g	
Protein 14g	
Vitamin A	80%
Vitamin C	35%
Calcium	6%
Iron	15%

* Percent Daily Values are based on a 2,000 calorie diet. Your Daily Values may be higher or lower depending on your calorie needs:

		Calories:	2,000	2,500
Total Fat	Less than		65g	80g
Saturated Fat	Less than		20g	25g
Cholesterol	Less than		300mg	300mg
Sodium	Less than		2,400mg	2,400mg
Total Carbohydrate			300g	375g
Dietary Fiber			25g	30g

> **Tip:** "Fat-free" doesn't mean "calorie-free." Some lower fat food items may have as many calories as the full-fat version. Always check the Nutrition Facts Label and compare the calories and nutrients in the fat-free version to the regular version.

Calories from Fat

Calories from Fat are *not* additional calories, but are **fat's contribution to the total number of calories** in one serving of the food. The Nutrition Facts Label lists the calories from fat because fat has more than *twice* the number of calories per gram than carbohydrate or protein.

For example, if the Nutrition Facts Label says one serving of food contains 150 calories and 100 calories from fat, the remaining 50 calories comes from carbohydrate, protein, and/or alcohol.

 http://www.fda.gov/nutritioneducation   **What's On The Nutrition Facts Label 1**

Percent Daily Value (%DV)

Percent Daily Value (%DV) shows **how much of a nutrient is in one serving** of the food. The %DVs are based on the Daily Values for key nutrients, which are the amounts (in grams, milligrams, or micrograms) of nutrients recommended per day for Americans 4 years of age and older. The %DV column doesn't add up vertically to 100%. Instead, the %DV is the percentage of the Daily Value for each nutrient in one serving of the food.

For example, the Daily Value for saturated fat is 20 grams (g), which equals 100% DV. If the Nutrition Facts Label says one serving of a food contains 1.5 g of saturated fat, then the %DV for saturated fat for this specific food is 8%. That means the food contains 8% of the maximum amount of saturated fat that an average person should eat in an entire day.

Using the %DV

Compare Foods: Use the %DV to compare food products (remember to make sure the serving size is the same) and to choose products that are higher in nutrients you want to get more of and lower in nutrients you want to get less of.

> As a general rule:
> **5% DV** or less of a nutrient per serving is **low**
> **20% DV** or more of a nutrient per serving is **high**

Understand Nutrient Content Claims: Use the %DV to help distinguish one claim from another, such as "light," "low," and "reduced." Simply compare the %DVs in each food product to see which one is higher or lower in a particular nutrient; there is no need to memorize definitions.

Manage "Dietary Trade-Offs": Use the %DV to make dietary trade-offs with other foods throughout the day. You don't have to give up a favorite food to eat a healthy diet. When a food you like is high in a nutrient you want to get less of – or low in a nutrient you want to get more of – balance it with foods that are low (or high) in that nutrient at other times of the day.

Nutrition Facts

Serving Size 1 package (272g)
Servings Per Container 1

Amount Per Serving

Calories 300   Calories from Fat 45

	% Daily Value*
Total Fat 5g	**8%**
Saturated Fat 1.5g	**8%**
Trans Fat 0g	
Cholesterol 30mg	**10%**
Sodium 430mg	**18%**
Total Carbohydrate 55g	**18%**
Dietary Fiber 6g	**24%**
Sugars 23g	
Protein 14g	
Vitamin A	80%
Vitamin C	35%
Calcium	6%
Iron	15%

* Percent Daily Values are based on a 2,000 calorie diet. Your Daily Values may be higher or lower depending on your calorie needs:

	Calories:	2,000	2,500
Total Fat	Less than	65g	80g
Saturated Fat	Less than	20g	25g
Cholesterol	Less than	300mg	300mg
Sodium	Less than	2,400mg	2,400mg
Total Carbohydrate		300g	375g
Dietary Fiber		25g	30g

Footnote

The Asterisk

The asterisk (*) following the heading "% Daily Value" on the Nutrition Facts Label refers to the standard footnote at the bottom of all labels, which specifies that some of the %DVs are based on a **2,000 calorie daily diet**. A 2,000 calorie daily diet is often used as the basis for general nutrition advice; however, your Daily Values may be higher or lower depending on your calorie needs. Calorie needs vary according to age, gender, height, weight, and physical activity level. Check your calorie needs at http://www.choosemyplate.gov.

Daily Value Recommendations

If there is enough space available on the food package, the footnote on the Nutrition Facts Label will also list the **Daily Values** for some key nutrients. These are given for both a 2,000 and 2,500 calorie daily diet. This section also includes **goals** regarding how much or how little of a nutrient to aim for in your daily diet. The Daily Values for some nutrients are different for a 2,000 or 2,500 calorie diet, while others (cholesterol and sodium) remain the same for both calorie amounts.

What's On The Nutrition Facts Label 2

Nutrients

The Nutrition Facts Label can help you learn about the **nutrient content** of many foods in your diet. It also enables you to compare foods to make healthy choices.

The Nutrition Facts Label must list: total fat, saturated fat, *trans* fat, cholesterol, sodium, total carbohydrate, dietary fiber, sugars, protein, vitamin A, vitamin C, calcium, and iron.

The Nutrition Facts Label may also list: monounsaturated fat, polyunsaturated fat, soluble fiber, insoluble fiber, sugar alcohol, other carbohydrate, vitamins (such as biotin, folate, niacin, riboflavin, pantothenic acid, thiamin, vitamin B_6, vitamin B_{12}, vitamin D, vitamin E, and vitamin K) and minerals (such as chromium, copper, iodine, magnesium, manganese, molybdenum, phosphorus, potassium, selenium, and zinc).

Nutrients to get less of – get less than 100% DV of these each day: saturated fat, *trans* fat, cholesterol, and sodium. (Note: *trans* fat has no %DV, so use the amount of grams as a guide)

Nutrients to get more of – get 100% DV of these on most days: dietary fiber, vitamin A, vitamin C, calcium, and iron.

Nutrition Facts

Serving Size 1 package (272g)
Servings Per Container 1

Amount Per Serving

Calories 300	Calories from Fat 45

	% Daily Value*
Total Fat 5g	**8%**
Saturated Fat 1.5g	**8%**
Trans Fat 0g	
Cholesterol 30mg	**10%**
Sodium 430mg	**18%**
Total Carbohydrate 55g	**18%**
Dietary Fiber 6g	**24%**
Sugars 23g	
Protein 14g	
Vitamin A	80%
Vitamin C	35%
Calcium	6%
Iron	15%

* Percent Daily Values are based on a 2,000 calorie diet. Your Daily Values may be higher or lower depending on your calorie needs:

	Calories:	2,000	2,500
Total Fat	Less than	65g	80g
Saturated Fat	Less than	20g	25g
Cholesterol	Less than	300mg	300mg
Sodium	Less than	2,400mg	2,400mg
Total Carbohydrate		300g	375g
Dietary Fiber		25g	30g

Ingredient List

The Ingredient List shows each ingredient in a food by its **common or usual name in descending order** by weight. So, the ingredient with the greatest contribution to the product weight is listed first, and the ingredient contributing the least by weight is listed last. The ingredient list is usually located near the name of the food's manufacturer and often below the Nutrition Facts Label.

Use this list to find out whether a food or beverage contains ingredients that are sources of nutrients you want to get less of, such as saturated fat (like shortening), *trans* fat (like partially hydrogenated oils), and added sugars (like syrups) – and sources of nutrients you want to get more of, such as whole grains (like whole oats).

INGREDIENTS: WHOLE WHEAT PASTA (WATER, WHOLE WHEAT FLOUR), COOKED WHITE MEAT CHICKEN (WHITE MEAT CHICKEN, WATER, MODIFIED TAPIOCA STARCH, CHICKEN FLAVOR [DRIED CHICKEN BROTH, CHICKEN POWDER, NATURAL FLAVOR], CARRAGEENAN, WHEY PROTEIN CONCENTRATE, SOYBEAN OIL, CORN SYRUP SOLIDS, SODIUM PHOSPHATE, SALT), WATER, CARROTS, GREEN BEANS, APPLE JUICE CONCENTRATE, DRIED CRANBERRIES (CRANBERRIES, SUGAR, SUNFLOWER OIL), APPLES (APPLES, CITRIC ACID, SALT, WATER), CONTAINS 2% OR LESS OF: BUTTER (CREAM, SALT), MODIFIED CORNSTARCH, CHICKEN BROTH, ORANGE JUICE CONCENTRATE, APPLE CIDER VINEGAR, SUGAR, SOYBEAN OIL, SEA SALT, GINGER PUREE (GINGER, WATER, CITRIC ACID), YEAST EXTRACT, SPICES, LEMON JUICE CONCENTRATE, CITRIC ACID.

Reading a Food Label

Knowing how to read a food label can help you put your serving sizes into action and to understand how various foods fit into your daily allowance. Food labels list ingredients by percentage of total weight, in order from heaviest or highest to lowest. By reading the listing of ingredients, you can figure out whether a food is relatively high in fat, sugar, salt, etc. Food labels are legally required to include the number of servings per container, the serving size, and the number of calories per serving. They must also list the percentage of the daily value of total fat, saturated fat, trans fat, cholesterol, sodium, total carbohydrates, (including dietary fiber and sugars), proteins, vitamins, and minerals. The bottom part of a food label on larger packages contains information on Daily Values (DVs) for 2000 and 2,500 caloric/day diets which is a *general* way to remind you of the USDA's recommendations.

ASSIGNMENT: Evaluate your knowledge of a "real life" food label.

1. Cut out a food label from something you've eaten in the past few days and staple it to this page.

   a. What constitutes one serving? _____

   b. What is total number of calories? _____ cal   Total number of fat calories? _____ cal

   c. How many grams of carbohydrates are in each serving? _____ grams

   d. How many grams of fats are in each serving? _____ grams

   e. How many grams of proteins are in each serving? _____ grams

   f. How many calories of carbohydrates is this? _____ carb calories (4 cal/gram = carbs)

   g. How many calories of fat is this? _____ fat calories (9 cal/gram = fat)

   h. How many calories of protein is this? _____ protein calories (4 cal/gram = proteins)

2. Now determine what you actually consumed.

   a. How many servings did you actually have? _____

   b. What then was the total number of calories you ate? _____ cal
   and the total number of fat calories? _____ cal

   c. How many grams of carbohydrates were in the number of servings you ate? _____ grams

   d. How many grams of fats were in the number of servings you ate? _____ grams

   e. How many grams of proteins were in the number of servings you ate? _____ grams

   f. How many calories of carbohydrates was this? _____ carb calories (4 cal/gram = carbs)

   g. How many calories of fat was this? _____ fat calories (9 cal/gram = fat)

   h. How many calories of protein was this? _____ protein calories (4 cal/gram = proteins)

United States Department of Agriculture

10 tips
Nutrition
Education Series

MyPlate
MyWins

Based on the
Dietary Guidelines for Americans

Build a healthy meal

Each meal is a building block in your healthy eating style. Make sure to include all the food groups throughout the day. Make fruits, vegetables, grains, dairy, and protein foods part of your daily meals and snacks. Also, limit added sugars, saturated fat, and sodium. Use the MyPlate Daily Checklist and the tips below to meet your needs throughout the day.

1 Make half your plate veggies and fruits

Vegetables and fruits are full of nutrients that support good health. Choose fruits and red, orange, and dark-green vegetables such as tomatoes, sweet potatoes, and broccoli.

2 Include whole grains
Aim to make at least half your grains whole grains. Look for the words "100% whole grain" or "100% whole wheat" on the food label. Whole grains provide more nutrients, like fiber, than refined grains.

3 Don't forget the dairy
Complete your meal with a cup of fat-free or low-fat milk. You will get the same amount of calcium and other essential nutrients as whole milk but fewer calories. Don't drink milk? Try a soy beverage (soymilk) as your drink or include low-fat yogurt in your meal or snack.

4 Add lean protein
Choose protein foods such as lean beef, pork, chicken, or turkey, and eggs, nuts, beans, or tofu. Twice a week, make seafood the protein on your plate.

5 Avoid extra fat
Using heavy gravies or sauces will add fat and calories to otherwise healthy choices. Try steamed broccoli with a sprinkling of low-fat parmesan cheese or a squeeze of lemon.

6 Get creative in the kitchen
Whether you are making a sandwich, a stir-fry, or a casserole, find ways to make them healthier. Try using less meat and cheese, which can be higher in saturated fat and sodium, and adding in more veggies that add new flavors and textures to your meals.

7 Take control of your food

Eat at home more often so you know exactly what you are eating. If you eat out, check and compare the nutrition information. Choose options that are lower in calories, saturated fat, and sodium.

8 Try new foods
Keep it interesting by picking out new foods you've never tried before, like mango, lentils, quinoa, kale, or sardines. You may find a new favorite! Trade fun and tasty recipes with friends or find them online.

9 Satisfy your sweet tooth in a healthy way
Indulge in a naturally sweet dessert dish—fruit! Serve a fresh fruit salad or a fruit parfait made with yogurt. For a hot dessert, bake apples and top with cinnamon.

10 Everything you eat and drink matters
The right mix of foods in your meals and snacks can help you be healthier now and into the future. Turn small changes in how you eat into your MyPlate, MyWins.

Center for Nutrition Policy and Promotion
USDA is an equal opportunity provider, employer, and lender.

Go to Choose**MyPlate**.gov
for more information.

DG TipSheet No. 7
June 2011
Revised October 2016

HEALTHY SNACKS FROM CHOOSEMYPLATE'S FOOD GROUPS

GRAINS

- Ready-to-eat cereals
- Low fat muffins
- English muffins
- Whole grain breads
- Bagels
- Tortillas
- Low sodium pretzels
- Low fat or reduced fat crackers
- Animal crackers
- Low fat granola bars
- Air popped popcorn

VEGETABLES

- Fresh vegetables cut into chunks
- Low sodium vegetable juices
- Low sodium V-8 juice

FRUITS

- Fresh fruit, in season
- Canned fruit, in its own juice or water packed
- Fruit juice (100% juice)—individual cans are very convenient
- Dried fruit: raisins, apricots, cranberries, and apples

DAIRY

- Skim or 1% milk, any flavor
- String cheese
- Low fat or reduced fat cheese (slices or chunks of cheese)
- Low fat yogurt with or without fruit
- Alba
- Carnation Instant Breakfast, variety of flavors
- Hot cocoa

PROTEIN FOODS

- Low fat or fat free sliced deli meats
- Canned tuna, salmon or chicken chunks, water packed
- Hummus
- Dry roasted nuts or seeds
- Peanut butter or other nut butters

Points to consider: Use leftover soups or grain mixtures for a snack. Mix and match your favorite grains, fruits, and vegetables for snacks. Plan for snacks and purchase individual-size portions when shopping. Use ChooseMyPlate.gov as your guide for healthy snacks as well as for menu choices. Remember to check serving sizes!

ASSIGNMENT: Determine what healthy snacks you will incorporate into your daily diet.

List which snacks you eat currently in between classes, meals, at night, etc. Then, to the right of your current snack, list which healthy snacks you will begin trying today or in the next few days.

CURRENT SNACKS
1.
2.
3.
4.
5.

HEALTHIER ALTERNATIVES FOR SNACKS
1.
2.
3.
4.
5.

Organic Foods

The USDA has put in place a set of national standards that food labeled "organic" must meet, whether grown in the U.S. or imported from other countries. Farmers who produce organic food emphasize the use of renewable resources and the conservation of soil and water to enhance environmental quality for future generations. Organic meat, poultry, eggs, and dairy products come from animals that receive no antibiotics or growth hormones. Organic food production occurs without using most conventional pesticides, fertilizers made with synthetic ingredients or sewage sludge, bioengineering, or ionizing radiation. Before a product can be labeled "organic," a government-approved certifier inspects the farm where the food is grown to make sure the farmer is following all the rules necessary to meet USDA organic standards. Companies that handle or process organic food before it gets to your local supermarket or restaurant must become certified, too.

Is Organic Food Better for Me?

The USDA makes no claims that organically produced food is safer or more nutritious than conventionally produced food. Organic food is grown, handled, and processed differently from conventionally produced food.

When I Go to the Supermarket, How Can I Tell Organically Produced Food from Conventionally Produced Food?

You must look at package labels and watch for signs in the supermarket. Along with the national organic standards, the USDA developed strict labeling rules to help consumers know the exact organic content of the food they buy. The *USDA Organic* seal also tells you that a product is at least 95% organic.

Single-Ingredient Foods

Look for the word "organic" and a small sticker version of the *USDA Organic* seal on vegetables or pieces of fruit. Or they may appear on the sign above the organic produce display. The word "organic" and the seal may also appear on packages of meat and on cartons of milk or eggs, cheese, and other single-ingredient foods.

Foods with More Than One Ingredient

Products with less than 70% organic ingredients may list specific organically-produced ingredients on the side panel of the package, but they may not make any organic claims on the front of the package. Look for the name and address of the government-approved certifier on all packaged products that contain at least 70% organic ingredients.

Will I Find the USDA Organic Seal on All 100% Organic Products, or Products with at Least 95% Organic Ingredients?

No. The use of the seal is voluntary.

How Is Use of the USDA Organic Seal Protected?

People who sell or label a product "organic" when they know it does not meet USDA standards can receive fines up to $11,000 for each violation.

Does Natural Mean Organic?

No. Natural and organic are not interchangeable. Other truthful claims, such as free-range, hormone-free, and natural, can still appear on food labels. However, don't confuse these terms with "organic." Only food labeled "organic" has certification meeting USDA organic standards.

SOURCE: USDA.gov

Appendix 4. USDA Food Patterns: Healthy Mediterranean-Style Eating Pattern

The Healthy Mediterranean-Style Pattern is adapted from the Healthy U.S.-Style Pattern, modifying amounts recommended from some food groups to more closely reflect eating patterns that have been associated with positive health outcomes in studies of Mediterranean-Style diets. Food group intakes from the studies that provided quantified data were compared to amounts in the Healthy U.S.-Style Pattern and adjustments were made to better reflect intakes of groups with Mediterranean-Style diets. The healthfulness of the Pattern was evaluated based on its similarity to food group intakes reported for groups with positive health outcomes in these studies rather than on meeting specified nutrient standards.

The Healthy Mediterranean-Style Pattern contains more fruits and seafood and less dairy than does the Healthy U.S.-Style Pattern. The changes in these amounts were limited to calorie levels appropriate for adults, because children were not part of the studies used in modifying the Pattern. The amounts of oils in the Pattern were not adjusted because the Healthy U.S.-Style Pattern already contains amounts of oils that are similar to amounts associated with positive health outcomes in the studies, and higher than typical intakes in the United States. Similarly, amounts of meat and poultry in the Healthy U.S.-Style Pattern are less than typical intakes in the United States and also similar to amounts associated with positive health outcomes in the studies. While not evaluated on nutrient-adequacy standards, nutrient levels in the Pattern were assessed. The Pattern is similar to the Healthy U.S.-Style Pattern in nutrient content, with the exception of calcium and vitamin D. Levels of calcium and vitamin D in the Pattern are lower because less dairy is included for adults. See table footnotes for amounts of dairy recommended for children and adolescents.

To follow this Pattern, identify the appropriate calorie level, choose a variety of foods in each group and subgroup over time in recommended amounts, and limit choices that are not in nutrient-dense forms so that the overall calorie limit is not exceeded.

HEALTHY MEDITERRANEAN-STYLE EATING PATTERN: RECOMMENDED AMOUNTS OF FOOD FROM EACH FOOD GROUP AT 12 CALORIE LEVELS

CALORIE LEVEL OF PATTERN[a]	1,000	1,200	1,400	1,600	1,800	2,000	2,200
Food Group[b]	**Daily Amount**[c] of Food From Each Group (vegetable and protein foods subgroup amounts are per week)						
Vegetables	1 c-eq	1½ c-eq	1½ c-eq	2 c-eq	2½ c-eq	2½ c-eq	3 c-eq
Dark-green vegetables (c-eq/wk)	½	1	1	1½	1½	1½	2
Red and orange vegetables (c-eq/wk)	2½	3	3	4	5½	5½	6

(continues)

HEALTHY MEDITERRANEAN-STYLE EATING PATTERN: RECOMMENDED AMOUNTS OF FOOD FROM EACH FOOD GROUP AT 12 CALORIE LEVELS *(CONTINUED)*

CALORIE LEVEL OF PATTERN[a]	1,000	1,200	1,400	1,600	1,800	2,000	2,200
Legumes (beans and peas) (c-eq/wk)	½	½	½	1	1½	1½	2
Starchy vegetables (c-eq/wk)	2	3½	3½	4	5	5	6
Other vegetables (c-eq/wk)	1½	2½	2½	3½	4	4	5
Fruits	1 c-eq	1 c-eq	1½ c-eq	2 c-eq	2 c-eq	2½ c-eq	2½ c-eq
Grains	3 oz-eq	4 oz-eq	5 oz-eq	5 oz-eq	6 oz-eq	6 oz-eq	7 oz-eq
Whole grains[d] (oz-eq/day)	1½	2	2½	3	3	3	3½
Refined grains (oz-eq/day)	1½	2	2½	2	3	3	3½
Dairy[e]	2 c-eq	2½ c-eq	2½ c-eq	2 c-eq	2 c-eq	2 c-eq	2 c-eq
Protein Foods	2 oz-eq	3 oz-eq	4 oz-eq	5½ oz-eq	6 oz-eq	6½ oz-eq	7 oz-eq
Seafood (oz-eq/wk)[f]	3	4	6	11	15	15	16
Meats, poultry, eggs (oz-eq/wk)	10	14	19	23	23	26	28
Nuts, seeds, soy products (ozeq/wk)	2	2	3	4	4	5	5
Oils	15 g	17 g	17 g	22 g	24 g	27 g	29 g
Limit on Calories for Other Uses, calories (% of calories)[g,h]	150 (15%)	100 (8%)	110 (8%)	140 (9%)	160 (9%)	260 (13%)	270 (12%)

[a,b,c,d]See Appendix 3. USDA Food Patterns: Healthy U.S.-Style Eating Pattern(/dietaryguidelines/2015/guidelines/appendix-3/#table-a3-note-a), notes a through d.

[e]Amounts of dairy recommended for children and adolescents are as follows, regardless of the caloric level of the Pattern: For 2 year-olds, 2 cup-eq per day; for 3 to 8 year-olds, 2 ½ cup-eq per day; for 9 to 18 year-olds, 3 cup-eq per day.

[f]The U.S. Food and Drug Administration (FDA) and the U.S. Environmental Protection Agency (EPA) provide joint guidance regarding seafood consumption for women who are pregnant or breastfeeding and young children. For more information, see the FDA or EPA websites www.FDA.gov/fishadvice (http://www.FDA.gov/fishadvice); www.EPA.gov/fishadvice (http://www.EPA.gov/fishadvice).

[g,h]See Appendix 3 (/dietaryguidelines/2015/guidelines/appendix-3/#table-a3-note-e), notes e through f.

SOURCE: https://health.gov/dietaryguidelines/2015/guidelines/appendix-4/

Appendix 5. USDA Food Patterns: Healthy Vegetarian Eating Pattern

The Healthy Vegetarian Pattern is adapted from the Healthy U.S.-Style Pattern, modifying amounts recommended from some food groups to more closely reflect eating patterns reported by self-identified vegetarians in the National Health and Nutrition Examination Survey (NHANES). This analysis allowed development of a Pattern that is based on evidence of the foods and amounts consumed by vegetarians, in addition to meeting the same nutrient and Dietary Guidelines standards as the Healthy U.S.-Style Pattern. Based on a comparison of the food choices of these vegetarians to nonvegetarians in NHANES, amounts of soy products (particularly tofu and other processed soy products), legumes, nuts and seeds, and whole grains were increased, and meat, poultry, and seafood were eliminated. Dairy and eggs were included because they were consumed by the majority of these vegetarians. This Pattern can be vegan if all dairy choices are comprised of fortified soy beverages (soymilk) or other plant-based dairy substitutes. Note that vegetarian adaptations of the USDA Food Patterns were included in the 2010 *Dietary Guidelines*. However, those adaptations did not modify the underlying structure of the Patterns, but substituted the same amounts of plant foods for animal foods in each food group. In contrast, the current Healthy Vegetarian Pattern includes changes in food group composition and amounts, based on assessing the food choices of vegetarians. The Pattern is similar in meeting nutrient standards to the Healthy U.S.-Style Pattern, but somewhat higher in calcium and fiber and lower in vitamin D due to differences in the foods included.

To follow this Pattern, identify the appropriate calorie level, choose a variety of foods in each group and subgroup over time in recommended amounts, and limit choices that are not in nutrient-dense forms so that the overall calorie limit is not exceeded.

HEALTHY VEGETARIAN EATING PATTERN: RECOMMENDED AMOUNTS OF FOOD FROM EACH FOOD GROUP AT 12 CALORIE LEVELS

CALORIE LEVEL OF PATTERN[a]	1,000	1,200	1,400	1,600	1,800	2,000
Food Group[b]	Daily Amount[c] of Food From Each Group (vegetable and protein foods subgroup amounts are per week)					
Vegetables	1 c-eq	1½ c-eq	1½ c-eq	2 c-eq	2½ c-eq	2½ c-eq
Dark-green vegetables (c-eq/wk)	½	1	1	1½	1½	1½
Red and orange vegetables (c-eq/wk)	2½	3	3	4	5½	5½

(continues)

HEALTHY VEGETARIAN EATING PATTERN: RECOMMENDED AMOUNTS OF FOOD FROM EACH FOOD GROUP AT 12 CALORIE LEVELS

CALORIE LEVEL OF PATTERN[a]	1,000	1,200	1,400	1,600	1,800	2,000
Legumes (beans and peas) (c-eq/wk)[d]	½	½	½	1	1½	1½
Starchy vegetables (c-eq/wk)	2	3½	3½	4	5	5
Other vegetables (c-eq/wk)	1½	2½	2½	3½	4	4
Fruits	1 c-eq	1 c-eq	1½ c-eq	1½ c-eq	1½ c-eq	2 c-eq
Grains	3 oz-eq	4 oz-eq	5 oz-eq	5½ oz-eq	6½ oz-eq	6½ oz-eq
Whole grains[e] (oz-eq/day)	1½	2	2½	3	3½	3½
Refined grains (oz-eq/day)	1½	2	2½	2½	3	3
Dairy	2 c-eq	2.5 c-eq	2.5 c-eq	3 c-eq	3 c-eq	3 c-eq
Protein Foods	1 oz-eq	1½ oz-eq	2 oz-eq	2½ oz-eq	3 oz-eq	3½ oz-eq
Eggs (oz-eq/wk)	2	3	3	3	3	3
Legumes (beans and peas) (oz-eq/wk)[d]	1	2	4	4	6	6
Soy products (oz-eq/wk)	2	3	4	6	6	8
Nuts and seeds (oz-eq/wk)	2	2	3	5	6	7
Oils	15 g	17 g	17 g	22 g	24 g	27 g
Limit on Calories for Other Uses, calories (% of calories)[f,g]	190 (19%)	170 (14%)	190 (14%)	180 (11%)	190 (11%)	290 (15%)
Total Legumes (beans and peas) (c-eq/wk)	1	1	1½	2	3	3 3½ 4

[a,b,c]See Appendix 3. USDA Food Patterns: Healthy U.S.-Style Eating Pattern, notes a through c (/dietaryguidelines/2015/guidelines/appendix-3/#table-a3-note-a).

[d]About half of total legumes are shown as vegetables, in cup-eq, and half as protein foods, in oz-eq. Total legumes in the Patterns, in cup-eq, is the amount in the vegetable group plus the amount in protein foods group (in oz-eq) divided by 4:

[e,f,g]See Appendix 3, notes d through f (/dietaryguidelines/2015/guidelines/appendix-3/#table-a3-note-d).

Source: https://health.gov/dietaryguidelines/2015/guidelines/appendix-5/

FAST FOOD AND ETHNIC FOODS

> **"***As a culture, we say we value physical activity and healthy eating,
> but in reality we're all about convenience and convenience foods
> because we have such busy schedules.***"**
>
> — Karen Olson

Fast foods . . . We've all probably have had some version of fast foods this week alone. Why not? They're quick, cheap, and "hit the spot." BUT what you might be forgetting is that fast foods are typically high in calories, fat, sugar, and sodium. This combination is not going to be your healthiest of choices, as you may already know. Eating any foods, whether fast foods or not, that have this combination can lead to overweight or obesity and then on to other disease states. The good news: Fast food restaurants and restaurants in general are now offering healthier menu options to help combat the high calories, fat, sugar, and sodium issues. Here are some tips for fast food dining:

- *Salads* are wise choices, but go easy on salad dressings, bacon bits, and cheeses. Make sure to choose a variety of vegetables along with your lettuce. Choose a lower-fat or fat-free salad dressing and ask for your salad dressing on the side.

- *Hamburgers:* A smart choice is a hamburger without cheese and sauces. Order your burger with extra tomatoes, lettuce, and onions instead. Try to order the small burger instead of the larger alternative or try a veggie burger.

- *Pizza* is a good choice if you top it with onions, mushrooms, green peppers, tomatoes, and other vegetables. Ask for less cheese and for meats such as pepperoni, sausage, and bacon. If you really want to eat a pizza loaded with cheese and meats, then eat fewer slices than normal.

- *Sandwiches* are great choices, especially if you choose lean turkey, beef, chicken breast, or ham, and if you avoid tuna salad, bacon, oils, regular mayonnaise, and high-fat cheeses. Choose more vegetables on your sandwich like tomatoes, lettuce, onions, and peppers and get whole grain breads instead of croissants or biscuits, which contain added fat.

- *Potatoes:* Go easy on cheese, butter-type sauces, bacon, or sour cream.

- *Meat, chicken and fish:* Select baked, grilled, roasted, or broiled items and not breaded or fried.

- *Drinks:* Choose skim milk or juices instead of a shake or a soda.

- *Breakfast:* Avoid croissants, biscuits, sausage, bacon, butter and Danishes. Smarter choices are pancakes, English muffins, bagels, bran muffins, and whole grain cereals.

ETHNIC DIET RECOMMENDATIONS

GOOD	NOT AS GOOD
Chinese Steamed, poached, boiled, roasted, barbecued, or lightly stir-fried fresh fish and seafood, skinless chicken, or tofu; with mixed vegetables, Chinese greens, steamed rice, steamed spring rolls, or soft noodles; with hoisin sauce, oyster sauce, wine sauce, plum sauce, velvet sauce, or hot mustard	Crab Rangoon, crispy duck or chicken, or anything breaded or deep-fried, including fried rice, fried wontons, egg rolls, and fried or crispy noodles
Thai Dishes barbecued, sauteed, broiled, boiled, steamed, braised, or marinated; skewered and grilled meats; with fish sauce, basil sauce, or hot sauces; bean thread noodles; Thai salad	Coconut milk soup; peanut sauce or dishes topped with nuts; crispy noodles; red, green, and yellow curries containing coconut milk
Japanese Dishes boiled or made in boiling broth, steamed, simmered, broiled, or grilled; with mixed rice, steamed rice, or buckwheat, wheat, or rice noodles	Dishes battered and fried or deep-fried; fried pork cutlet, fried tofu
Mexican Fish marinated in lime juice; soft corn or wheat tortillas, burritos, fajitas, enchiladas, soft tacos, tamales filled with beans, vegetables, or lean meats; with refried beans, nonfat or low-fat rice and beans; with salsa, enchilada sauce, or picante sauce; gazpacho, menudo, or black bean soup; fruit or flan	Crispy fried tortillas; fried dishes such as chile rellenos, chimichangas, flautas, or tostadas; nachos and cheese, chili con queso, and other dishes made with cheese or cheese sauce; guacamole, sour cream; refried beans made with lard; fried ice cream

(continues)

ETHNIC DIET RECOMMENDATIONS *(continued)*

GOOD	NOT AS GOOD
Italian Pasta primavera or pasta, polenta, risotto, or gnocchi; with marinara, red or white wine sauce, red or white clam sauce, light mushroom sauce; dishes grilled or made with tomato-based sauce, broth and wine sauce, or lemon sauce; seafood stew; vegetable, minestrone, or bean soups	Cheese or smoked meats; dishes prepared alfredo, carbonara, fried, creamed, or with cream; veal scallopini; chicken, veal, or eggplant parmigiana; Italian sausage, salami, or prosciutto; buttered garlic bread; cannoli
French Fresh fish, shrimp, scallops, mussels, or skinless chicken, steamed, skewered, and broiled or grilled; without sauces; clear soups	Dishes prepared in cream sauce, baked with cream and cheese, or in a pastry crust; drawn butter, hollandaise sauce, or mayonnaise-based sauce
Indian Dishes prepared with curry and roasted in a clay oven or pan-roasted; kabobs; yogurt and cucumber salad, and other yogurt-based dishes and sauces; lentils and basmati rice; baked bread	Any fried or coconut-milk–based dishes; meat in cream sauce; clarified butter; fried breads

Thygerson, A.and Larson, K. *Fit to be Well.* "Ethnic Diet Recommendations." Jones and Bartlett (2006): 108.

Online Assignment: Evaluate Your Favorite Fast Foods

Complete this assignment online. Go to:

www.grtep.com

Select >Chapter Content>Chapter 1>Enter your username and password

10 tips
Nutrition Education Series

eating better on a budget

ChooseMyPlate.gov

10 tips to help you stretch your food dollars

Get the most for your food budget! There are many ways to save money on the foods that you eat. The three main steps are planning before you shop, purchasing the items at the best price, and preparing meals that stretch your food dollars.

1 plan, plan, plan!
Before you head to the grocery store, plan your meals for the week. Include meals like stews, casseroles, or stir-fries, which "stretch" expensive items into more portions. Check to see what foods you already have and make a list for what you need to buy.

2 get the best price
Check the local newspaper, online, and at the store for sales and coupons. Ask about a loyalty card for extra savings at stores where you shop. Look for specials or sales on meat and seafood—often the most expensive items on your list.

3 compare and contrast
Locate the "Unit Price" on the shelf directly below the product. Use it to compare different brands and different sizes of the same brand to determine which is more economical.

4 buy in bulk
It is almost always cheaper to buy foods in bulk. Smart choices are family packs of chicken, steak, or fish and larger bags of potatoes and frozen vegetables. Before you shop, remember to check if you have enough freezer space.

5 buy in season
Buying fruits and vegetables in season can lower the cost and add to the freshness! If you are not going to use them all right away, buy some that still need time to ripen.

6 convenience costs... go back to the basics
Convenience foods like frozen dinners, pre-cut vegetables, and instant rice, oatmeal, or grits will cost you more than if you were to make them from scratch. Take the time to prepare your own—and save!

7 easy on your wallet
Certain foods are typically low-cost options all year round. Try beans for a less expensive protein food. For vegetables, buy carrots, greens, or potatoes. As for fruits, apples and bananas are good choices.

8 cook once...eat all week!
Prepare a large batch of favorite recipes on your day off (double or triple the recipe). Freeze in individual containers. Use them throughout the week and you won't have to spend money on take-out meals.

9 get your creative juices flowing
Spice up your leftovers—use them in new ways. For example, try leftover chicken in a stir-fry or over a garden salad, or to make chicken chili. Remember, throwing away food is throwing away your money!

10 eating out
Restaurants can be expensive. Save money by getting the early bird special, going out for lunch instead of dinner, or looking for "2 for 1" deals. Stick to water instead of ordering other beverages, which add to the bill.

United States
Department of Agriculture
Center for Nutrition
Policy and Promotion

Go to www.ChooseMyPlate.gov for more information.

DG TipSheet No. 16
December 2011
USDA is an equal opportunity provider and employer.

FAD DIETS AND DIET SUPPLEMENTS

"I've been on a diet for two weeks and all I've lost is two weeks."

—Totie Fields

Fad diets have been around for a long time, but now there are even more fad diets available for people to choose from. This may be due to the rising obesity epidemic with so many people looking to lose weight as well as the industry's competition for all of these people to use their products or services. Unfortunately, most of these plans actually fail to teach these people how to eat correctly. Thus, the problem of gaining the weight back after stopping the diet plan. In general, fad diets are flawed in the following ways:

- Most of these diet components place people at risk for coronary heart disease.

- Most of these diets describe some specific food or combination of foods as "fat-burning" foods. No scientific evidence exists to support this claim.

- Most fad diets require significant restrictions on the consumption of fats, carbs, and proteins, which tend to trigger strong cravings.

- Some people take on their own varieties of these diets plans, which can then become highly imbalanced. This can lead to ketosis (a state where the body believes it is starving and begins to metabolize muscle mass instead of fat).

- Most of the fad diets rarely discuss the importance of physical activity in weight loss and weight management.

Ask yourself the following questions for evaluating weight-loss programs:

1. Can I live with this program the rest of my life?

2. Does it allow for basic energy needs (never under 1,200 calories) and for safe weight loss (1–2 lbs per week)?

3. Does it encourage regular physical activity as a part of the program?

4. Does it allow for "favorite" foods in moderation?

5. Does it use real foods found in a supermarket?

According to the National Center for Complementary and Alternative Medicine, dietary supplements are vitamins, minerals, herbs and other substances *meant to improve* your diet usually in the form of pills, capsules, powders and liquids. In 2016,

CHARACTERISTICS OF DIET PLANS	KNOWN PLANS HAVING THESE PROPERTIES	DIET'S CLAIM TO FAME
Calorie controlled, low fat, high carbohydrates	Weight Watchers, Volumetrics, Ornish, Pritikin	Balanced plan; ease into maintenance
High protein, high fat, low carbohydrates	Atkins, Scarsdale, Carb Addicts, Sugar Busters, Protein Power, South Beach (initial stage)	Quick weight loss; no measuring/no hunger
High protein, moderate fat, moderate carbohydrates variety	Zone, South Beach (later stages) (emphasize glycemic index of foods)	Use fat for energy; no hunger
Meal replacement	Jenny Craig, Nutrasystems	Portion controlled; no meal preparation
Liquid protein shakes/bars (typically hp/lf)	Optifast, Medifast, Health Maintenance, Resources, Cambridge, Slimfast	Dealing with food minimally; quick initial weight loss
Others have very specific recommendations to make them unique, yet the diet composition is similar to others (low fat or low carb and low calorie)	Fit for Life, Food Combining, Fat Flush, Eat for Your Blood Type, Suzanne Sommers	Quick initial weight loss; structured plan

From the *American College of Sports Medicine's Certified News*. "What's New in the Realm of Weight Management?" (2008): Vol. 18, Issue 1: 7.

70 percent of 18–34 year-olds reported taking dietary supplements which is over two-thirds of the adults U.S. population. Safety is of the biggest concerns when considering taking diet supplements. These safety measures include working with your physician when initially deciding on whether or not taking a supplement would benefit you, making sure to take the correct doses as listed on the label or prescribed by your doctor and cease taking the supplement if side effects appear.

Truths and Considerations before Using Diet Supplements

- Dietary supplements are not tested by the FDA as drugs are. The manufacturers of the supplements are responsible for the safety of the products not the FDA (Dietary Supplement Health and Education Act, 1994).

■ The FDA does require, as of 2007, that manufacturers provide labels to make sure the supplement is labeled for its specific use, that it does not contain too little or too much of the ingredient and that it is not contaminated. Keep in mind the detail on the actual label is not required like it is for packaged foods we buy at the grocery store.

■ Labels on dietary supplements cannot make unsupported claims of disease prevention, treatment or diagnosis. Any such claims would be considered an unapproved or illegal drug according to the FDA.

■ There is no license needed for sellers of dietary supplements to sell them to consumers. Under current law, neither the manufacturers nor the diet supplements themselves have to be registered with the FDA to sell their products.

■ There are no special training and education requirements for those who sell dietary supplements to consumers. Always talk with your doctor before choosing or purchasing any supplements.

■ Side effects and interactions with other medicines/supplements can occur when taking dietary supplements no matter what the salesperson might tell you.

■ Even though there is recommended doses for some supplements, most supplements do not have a recommended dose because of a lack of scientific evidence.

Online Assignment: Diet Supplements Quiz

Complete this assignment online. Go to:
www.grtep.com
Select >Chapter Content>Chapter 1>Enter your username and password

WEIGHT LOSS, WEIGHT MANAGEMENT AND WEIGHT GAIN

"I eat like a vulture. Unfortunately the resemblance doesn't end there."

— Groucho Marx

Here are the simple facts again:

Calories consumed > Calories Used = Weight Gain
Calories consumed < Calories Used = Weight Loss
Calories consumed = Calories Used = No Weight Gain

As Chapter 1 discussed, it is usually the case of an imbalance of the body's economics of supply and demand—meaning that the body has more supply than demand placed on it per day. However, sometimes other involvements can exist.

Current Weight Gain Theories and Factors

Calories

Consumed portion size and the number of people who eat readily accessible foods (prepackaged foods, fast foods, and soft drinks) have increased. Readily accessible foods can be high in calories and also high in fat and sugar. However, some foods may be listed as healthy, low fat, or fat free but still contain a high amount of calories. When calories consumed exceed what the body really needs for energy for breathing, digestion, and daily activities, weight gain will occur.

Calories Used

Current lifestyles are showing a reduction in daily physical activity among many countries. This reduction of physical activity in one's day puts the "brakes on" when it comes to expending an excess energy to keep one in a "no weight gain" situation.

Environment

At home, people spend too much time watching television, on the Internet, or playing video games where physical activity isn't being built into the day. At school or work, sometimes they are unsure what healthier menu options or snacks are, or they don't plan or adjust for their day and may eat the readily accessible foods discussed previously for the majority of the day. Getting enough physical activity is another determinant.

Genetics

Some people are genetically (and sometimes culturally) predisposed to gaining weight and storing fat around the abdomen and chest more easily than others. Recently, several independent population-based studies reported that a gene of unknown function (FTO, fat mass and obesity-associated gene) might be responsible for up to 22% of all cases of common obesity in the general population. Interestingly, this gene also shows a strong association with diabetes. The mechanism by which this gene operates is currently under intense scientific investigation.

Diseases and Medications

Illnesses such as Cushing's disease or polycystic ovary syndrome (PCOS) may lead to weight gain. An endocrinologist diagnoses and treats these illnesses. Weight gain may also come through some medications (steroids and anti-depressants). A physician or pharmacist would be the most appropriate professionals to answer questions about medications causing weight gain.

Socioeconomics, Age and Gender

Age: Fatness increases during adulthood and declines in the elderly.

Gender: Obesity is more prevalent in women than men.

Culture: People in developed countries have more body fat than those in developing societies.

Race/ethnicity: Obesity is more prevalent is African Americans, Hispanics, Native Americans, and Pacific Islanders.

Income: Obesity is more prevalent in lower-income women.

Education: Less-educated women have a higher incidence of obesity.

Employment: Unemployed women have a higher incidence of obesity.

Residence: Rural women have a higher incidence of obesity.

Region: People living in the southern U.S. have a higher incidence of obesity.

Psychological

Some people try to reduce food intake by restraining from eating foods as long as possible (skipping meals or delaying eating), but they may overeat when emotionally stressed without realizing it. Others "yo-yo" diet (seen when a pattern of losing and gaining weight occurs over and over) while some people binge eat (compulsive overeating sometimes for days). The latter is common among people in weight loss programs.

Weight Loss

If weight loss is your goal, then read the following. If weight loss is not your goal, then refer to either the "Weight Management" or "Weight Gain" section. Losing weight is difficult—over 95% of people trying to lose weight permanently regain their lost weight and go on to add more weight. However, reducing calorie intake and increasing physical activity each day has helped the most successful dieters, BUT both must be incorporated in order to be successful. It took *time* to add the weight, so be patient as it will take some *time* to lose the weight.

- *Let's break it down per day*—you must decrease your caloric intake by 500 calories per day and maintain the same amount of activity or increase it so that your body uses 500 calories each day.

- *Now per week*—you must decrease your caloric intake by 3,500 calories (500 calories per day ? 7 days per week) and maintain the same amount of activity or increase physical activity so that your body uses 3,500 calories per week (3,500 calories = 1 pound).

- A safe and realistic weight loss goal is 1–2 pounds per week and no more. Some people may see more weight loss and some less per week due to calories consumed and calories used. With obese people, sometimes more weight loss occurs per week (initially).

- *What do I need to know about how to appropriately exercise for weight loss?* In Chapter 1, we looked at the recommendations for cardiovascular exercise prescription plans. Let's focus in now on exercise and weight loss:

Weight loss or to prevent weight gain	Moderate intensity: @ 40–60% HRR (example: walking 3.5 mph)	Most days of the week	60 minutes

Recent research indicates that you will need to burn the 500 calories per day, which equal the 60 minutes seen above, or walk approximately 4 to 5 miles. You can also use your 10,000 steps a day goal (discussed in Chapter 1), which equals approximately 5 miles. If you are exercising more vigorously than the 40–60% HRR, then 40 minutes per day is recommended.

- It is also important to note that adding strength training (in addition to the cardiovascular recommendations) also has proven a part of the success in weight loss and weight management.

- It is important to ease into an exercise program if you currently haven't been active. Increase your duration and frequency first before increasing your intensity levels.

- You should NOT attempt to lose weight when among the following groups: most pregnant and breastfeeding women, people with serious or uncontrolled mental illness, those actively engaged in a substance abuse program, those with a history of anorexia or bulimia, and those whose health caloric restriction would compromise.

Weight Management

Review the following helpful tips for managing your weight:

- Know how much you're eating on a daily basis. Keep a food journal to maximize awareness.

- When eating a snack, evaluate if you are truly hungry or if you are eating due to stress, boredom, habit, etc.

- Use smaller plates and do not place serving dishes on the table.

- Know how much you're exercising on a daily basis. Keep an activity journal to maximize awareness.

- When eating out, plan to share large portions with someone or take extras home for another meal.

- Eat in one room only. Sit at a table—don't stand.

- Keep healthy food accessible and visible.

- Plan strategies in advance for eating out and for special occasions like the holidays.

- Substitute other activities for eating like running errands, exercising, paying bills, etc.

- Don't use the kitchen for non-food-related activities, and close the kitchen down after a meal.

- Eat your "favorite" foods—in moderation.

- Eat and snack from a plate not a package so you don't eat more than you should.

- Keep away negative environmental triggers that could lead to overeating.

- Leave the table and clear the dishes once you're done with your meal. Chew gum or brush your teeth right after you've done this.

Weight Gain

Some people are underweight due to a number of reasons (genetics, stress, addiction, dieting, eating disorders, over exercising, or underlying diseases). If the cause is not due to genetics, one could become deficient in protein and other energy-producing nutrients, which can cause fatigue, reproductive issues, and susceptibility to disease. This would be a scenario where a physician and a psychological health professional would come into play. Those people who are genetically underweight and have a goal to gain weight should read the following:

- Understand that gaining weight will take time.

- *Let's break it down per day*—you must increase your caloric intake by 500 calories per day and maintain the same amount of activity each day.

- *Now per week*—you must increase your caloric intake by 3,500 calories (500 calories per day × 7 days per week) and maintain the same amount of activity per week so that your body nets that 3,500 calories per week (3,500 calories = 1 pound).

- Eat small and frequent meals. Eat snacks between meals.

- Eat high-calorie foods and drinks (but watch total fat, saturated fat/trans fat, and cholesterol content so you are not unsafe).

- Eat extra servings of nutritious carbohydrates.

- Incorporate strength training to increase your muscle mass.

- Ask a registered dietitian or physician about taking vitamin/mineral supplements to make sure you are not deficient in these essential micronutrients.

TIPS TO BECOMING PHYSICALLY HEALTHY THROUGH NUTRITION

"Good nutrition helps students be healthier and do better."

— Andrea Johnson

- Focus on a healthy eating plan, not a specialized diet.

- Don't skip meals, especially breakfast! This can lead to cravings, binging, lowering blood sugar and eventually metabolism.

- Make sure to consult your physician or a registered dietitian about diet supplements and fad diets before using these products or concepts for weight loss.

- Drink plenty of water throughout the day.

- Make it a point to become familiar with serving sizes from now on instead of guessing what they might be. Portion control is a required knowledge for managing weight or losing weight.

- Be "mindful" when you are eating a meal or snacking. Eating with a lot of distractions can lead to eating too much and too fast.

- Stick with baked, grilled, roasted, or broiled meats.

- Eat non-fried or breaded fish TWICE A WEEK (salmon, tuna, halibut, mackerel, sardines, and herring).

- Have your salad dressing in a separate cup or dish next to your salad. Dip your fork in it first and then into the salad.

- Grocery shop with a list and NOT on an empty stomach.

- Prepackage healthy snacks or meals yourself and take them with you.

- Allow yourself to have your "favorite" foods but in moderation.

- Use fresh, unprocessed foods whenever possible.

- Include fiber in your diet.

- Make sure to eat a little protein with each meal.

- Set realistic and attainable goals with weight loss, weight management, or weight gain. Doing so will lessen the chances you get frustrated and back out of your goals. Remember, small changes can bring you big results.

Glossary

Eating pattern—The combination of foods and beverages that constitute an individual's complete dietary intake over time. Often referred to as a "dietary pattern," an eating pattern may describe a customary way of eating or a combination of foods recommended for consumption. Specific examples include USDA Food Patterns and the Dietary Approaches to Stop Hypertension (DASH) Eating Plan.

Nutrient dense—A characteristic of foods and beverages that provide vitamins, minerals, and other substances that contribute to adequate nutrient intakes or may have positive health effects, with little or no solid fats and added sugars, refined starches, and sodium. Ideally, these foods and beverages also are in forms that retain naturally occurring components, such as dietary fiber. All vegetables, fruits, whole grains, seafood, eggs, beans and peas, unsalted nuts and seeds, fat-free and low-fat dairy products, and lean meats and poultry—when prepared with little or no added solid fats, sugars, refined starches, and sodium—are nutrient-dense foods. These foods contribute to meeting food group recommendations within calorie and sodium limits. The term "nutrient dense" indicates the nutrients and other beneficial substances in a food have not been "diluted" by the addition of calories from added solid fats, sugars, or refined starches, or by the solid fats naturally present in the food.

Variety—A diverse assortment of foods and beverages across and within all food groups and subgroups selected to fulfill the recommended amounts without exceeding the limits for calories and other dietary components. For example, in the vegetables food group, selecting a variety of foods could be accomplished over the course of a week by choosing from all subgroups, including dark green, red and orange, legumes (beans and peas), starchy, and other vegetables.

Helpful Internet Sites

American Heart Association: aha.org
American Heart Association—Delicious Decisions: deliciousdecisions.org
American Dietetic Association: eatright.org
Ask the Dietitian: dietitian.com
Ask Dr. Weil: drweil.com

The Calorie Control Council: caloriecontrol.org
Calorie King For Food Awareness: calorieking.com
Calories Per Hour.com (Activity and Weight Loss Calculators): caloriesperhour.com
Center for Science in the Public Interest: cspinet.org
ChooseMyPlate.gov
Diet Facts: dietfacts.com
Fast Food Facts: foodfacts.info
Food Safety: fightbac.org
International Food Information Council Foundation: ific.org
Lactose Intolerance: lactaid.com
National Dairy Council: nationaldairycouncil.org
National Osteoporosis Foundation: nof.org
National Institutes of Health—Office of Dietary Supplements: dietarysupplements.info.nih.gov
Nutrition Data: nutritiondata.com
U.S. Centers for Disease Control and Prevention: cdc.gov
USDA: nutrition.gov
USDA's Center for Policy and Nutrition: cnpp.usda.gov
USDA's Food and Nutrition Information Center: nal.usda.gov/fnic
U.S. Food and Drug Administration: fda.gov
The Vegetarian Resource Group: vrg.org
WebMD: assessyourdiet.webmd.com
3-a-Day of Dairy: 3aday.org
5 to 9 a day: 5aday.gov

Note: Several fast food and chain restaurants have nutritional information on their foods via the Internet.

References

American Dietetic Association's Complete Food and Nutrition Guide. *Progressive Effects of Dehydration.* Chronimed Publishing (1996): 168.

American Dietetic Association's Nutrition Fact Sheet sponsored by Hershey Center for Health & Nutrition. *Cocoa and Chocolate: Sweet News!* (2007): eatright.org accessed on 2.16.08.

American Heart Association. *Red Wine and Your Heart Circulation.* (2005): 111–119. circ.ahajournals.org/cgi/content/full/111/2/e10 accessed on 2.18.08.

Bounds, L. et al. *Health and Fitness: A Guide to a Healthy Lifestyle.* Nutrition. Kendall Hunt Publishing Company (2006): 125–136; 145.

The Care Group Cardiology. *Sources of Antioxidants and Phytochemicals and The Mediterranean Diet.* Behavior Modification for a Healthier Lifestyle CD. thecaregroup.com

Corbin, C. *American College of Sports Medicine's Health & Fitness Journal.* Dietary Supplements (2007): Vol. 11, Issue 5: 22–23.

Edlin, G. and Golanty, E. *Health & Wellness,* 8th Edition. "Phytochemicals in Fruits and Vegetables and Their Possible Benefits." Jones and Bartlett (2004): 99.

Hettler, B. The National Wellness Institute. "The Six Dimensions of Wellness: Physical Wellness." nationalwellness.org accessed on 2.10.08.

Insel, P. et al. *Discovering Nutrition.* Jones & Bartlett (2003): 268–270.

Kraus, S. *American College of Sports Medicine's Certified News.* "What's New in the Realm of Weight Management?" (2008): Vol. 18, Issue 1: 7.

National Academy of Sciences, Institute of Medicine. *Dietary Reference Intakes for Energy: Carbohydrates, Fiber, Fat, Fatty Acids, Cholesterol, Protein and Amino Acids.* (Sept. 5, 2002).

National Heart Lung Blood Institute. National Institutes of Health. *Serving Sizes Card.* Hin.nhlbi.nih. gov/portion/servingcard7.pdf accessed on 2.17.08.

The National Organic Council. Organic Foods Standards and Labels: The Facts. ams.usda.gov/nop/ Consumers/brochure.html accessed on 2.20.08.

The Princeton Longevity Center Medical News. 3 "Internal" Tools for Weight Control. http://www.the plc.net/Weight_Control_Tools.html accessed on January 11, 2012.

Robbins, G. et al. *A Wellness Way of Life.* 7th Edition. Comparison of Fats. McGraw-Hill (2008): 371; Factors that Affect Basal Metabolic Rate Table 12-4: 418; Behavior Modification Techniques Table 12-6: 423 and Fast Food Tips: 386.

Shils M. et al. *Modern Nutrition in Health and Disease,* 9th Edition. Foods Rich in Soluble and Insoluble Dietary Fiber. Lippincott Williams and Wilkins: (1999).

Thygerson, A.and Larson, K. *Fit to be Well.* "Water." Jones and Bartlett (2006): 99; "Ethnic Diet Recommendations:" 108; "Fad Diets:" 123; "Theories of Weight Gain:" 126–129; "How to Gain Weight:" 144 and "Fast Food Recommendations:" 106.

Thygerson, A.and Larson, K. *Lab Manual to Accompany Fit to be Well.* "Assess Your Total Daily Energy Needs." Jones and Bartlett (2006): 85–86.

U.S. Department of Agriculture. ChooseMyPlate.gov. http://www.choosemyplate.gov/ accessed June 18, 2011.

U.S. Department of Agriculture. Build A Healthy Meal. http://www.choosemyplate.gov/food-groups/downloads/TenTips/DGTipsheet7BuildAHealthyMeal.pdf accessed June 18, 2011.

U.S. Department of Agriculture. Eating Better on a Budget. http://www.choosemyplate.gov/food-groups/downloads/TenTips/DGTipsheet16EatingBetterOnABudget.pdf accessed on January 11, 2012.

U.S. Centers for Disease Control and Prevention. *Contributing Factors.* cdc.gov/nccdphp/dnpa/ obesity/contributing_factors.htm accessed on 2.21.08.

U.S. Centers for Disease Control and Prevention. The National Office of Public Genomics. *Obesity & Genetics.* cdc.gov/genomics/training/perspectives/files/obesedit.htm accessed on 2.21.08.

U.S. Centers for Disease Control and Prevention. The National Center for Health Statistics. *Obesity Among Adults in the U.S.—No Statistically Significant Change Since 2003–2004.* cdc.gov/nchs/ data/databriefs/db01.pdf accessed on 2.21.08.

U.S. Department of Agriculture. "Dietary Recommendations." nutrition.gov accessed on 2.10.08.

U.S. Department of Agriculture. "ChooseMyPlate." www.choosemyplate.gov accessed on 6.2.11.

U.S. Institutes of Health- National Cancer Institute. *Red Wine and Cancer Prevention Fact Sheet.* cancer.gov/cancertopics/factsheet/red-wine-and-cancer-prevention accessed on 2.18.08.

The Vegetarian Resource Group. *Vegetarianism in a Nutshell.* Vrg.org accessed on 2.20.08.

CHAPTER 3

Mental Wellness

"In the end, it's not the years in your life that count, it's the life in your years."

— Abraham Lincoln

The objectives in this chapter include the understanding of:

- The meaning of mental wellness and its direct application to you
- What stress is, what emotions are and how stress affects you and your health
- Stress management techniques and how you can use them to your benefit
- Resilience
- Time management and ways to get your time under control
- Learned Helplessness
- What grief is, coping strategies and how you can best help another who is grieving
- Mental disorders and their signs and symptoms

Online Reminders

- Complete the poll question before the next class meeting.
- Complete the interactive activities for this chapter.
- Complete all of the online assignments for this chapter.

Mental Wellness—Mental (also known as emotional) wellness is defined as the successful performance of mental function, resulting in productive activities, fulfilling relationships with other people, and the ability to adapt to change and to cope with adversity. From early childhood until late life, mental health is the springboard of thinking and communication skills, learning, emotional growth, resilience, and self-esteem. Having sound mental health is the ability to enjoy life despite unexpected challenges and problems. Effectively coping with life's difficulties and unexpected events is essential to maintaining good health. Equally important to good physical wellness is the ability to understand your feelings and to express those feelings or emotions outwardly in a positive and constructive manner. "Bottled up" negative emotions can affect the immune system and result in chronic stress. This in turn can lead to serious illnesses, such as high blood pressure, and can potentially lead to a premature death.

According to the National Wellness Institute, mental wellness includes the degree to which one feels positive and enthusiastic about oneself and life and has the ability to live and work independently while realizing the importance of seeking and appreciating the support and assistance of others. It also includes the ability to form interdependent relationships with others based upon a foundation of mutual commitment, trust, and respect and to take on challenges, take risks, and recognize conflict as being potentially healthy. Managing your life in personally rewarding ways, and taking responsibility for your actions, will help you see life as an exciting, hopeful adventure. Mental wellness follows these tenets:

1. It is better to be aware of and to accept our feelings than to deny them.

2. It is better to be optimistic in our approach to life than pessimistic.

PRE-CLASS SURVEY: Take your mental wellness survey before your next class meeting and identify your level of mental wellness. Circle either Yes or No, total up each column, and check your score.

I generally face up to problems and cope with change effectively.	YES	NO
I choose to feel confident and optimistic.	YES	NO
I focus on the positive aspects in difficult situations.	YES	NO
I seek help and support when I need it.	YES	NO
I seldom experience periods of depression.	YES	NO
I reflect on how it feels to have given up the burden of a grudge, and I recognize emotional relief.	YES	NO
I stick up for myself when necessary.	YES	NO
I have a positive self-image.	YES	NO
I ask for and accept feedback from others.	YES	NO
I am aware that my feelings provide me with information about myself and use them accordingly.	YES	NO
I have close relationships with my family and/or friends.	YES	NO
I have a sense of fun and laughter.	YES	NO
TOTAL		

WHAT YOUR TOTAL MEANS:

9 or more Yes answers	Excellent	Your habits are positively enhancing your health.
6–8 Yes answers	Average	You are obviously trying but there is room to improve.
5 or less Yes answers	Not So Good	There is a need for improvement in your daily habits.

Source: "Wellness for Healthy Positive Living." *Mental Wellness Inventory.* www.for.gov.bc.ca/hrb/hw/index.htm

STRESS

❝*If you ask what is the single most important key to longevity,
I would have to say it is avoiding worry, stress and tension.
And if you didn't ask me, I'd still have to say it.*❞

— George Burns

You probably didn't expect college to be easy, but many students are unprepared for how stressful going to college can be. As a college student, you are likely to have more roles than the average person. If you're just starting to live on your own, you have the pressure of paying bills, grocery shopping, and doing laundry—things that your parents used to do for you. If you live at home, you probably have additional responsibilities. If you are married and/or a parent, you are aware of the time and energy involved in building strong relationships and running a household. Some of you may work part-time and some full-time.

Many of you are also involved in activities either on campus or in the community. Now you've added the hours of homework and studying that it takes to maintain good grades. In addition, if you were not a strong student in high school, or if it has been a few years since you were in school, you might be feeling anxious about taking tests, working with math problems, or writing papers. College courses move very quickly, and the pace frequently accelerates after midterm. In addition to college stressors, many people are trying to deal with unreasonable feelings of anger.

If you're feeling a little stressed out these days, do know that it's normal because of all the change in your life, and know that you're not the only one! However, recognizing what may have triggered your stress or what may be triggering your stress lately is the key to managing it. (Aguilar)

What Is Stress Exactly?

Stress has been defined as any action or situation (stressor) that places special physical or psychological demands on a person—in other words, anything that unbalances one's equilibrium. Dr. Hans Selye, one of the greatest pioneers of medicine and the originator of the concept of stress, wrote in his famous 1956 classic, *The Stress of Life*, "In its medical sense, stress is essentially the rate of wear and tear in the body . . . the nonspecific response of the body to any demand."

In Dr. Selye's view, there are both good and bad stressors producing stress reactions in the body. A divorce is stressful—but so is getting married. Both upset the person's equilibrium and require adjustment and adaptation. But it is not the stressor itself that creates the response. Instead, it is the person's REACTION to the stressor. People will respond in varying ways to the same stressor based on their individual ways of reacting.

*Medical research on stress dates back to the 1920s, when Walter Cannon began experimenting with the physiological effect on stress on cats and dogs. Studying the animals' reactions to danger, the Harvard physiologist noted a regular and common pattern now known as the fight-or-flight response.

As you can see in the fight-or-flight response:

- The muscles tense and tighten.

- Breathing becomes deeper and faster.

- The heart rate rises and blood vessels constrict, raising blood pressure.
- The stomach and intestines temporarily halt digestion.
- Perspiration increases.
- The thyroid gland is stimulated while secretion of saliva and mucus slows.
- Sensory perception becomes sharpened.
- The body releases various stress hormones—in particular epinephrine and cortisol—which depress immune function and adversely affect bodily functions in many other ways.

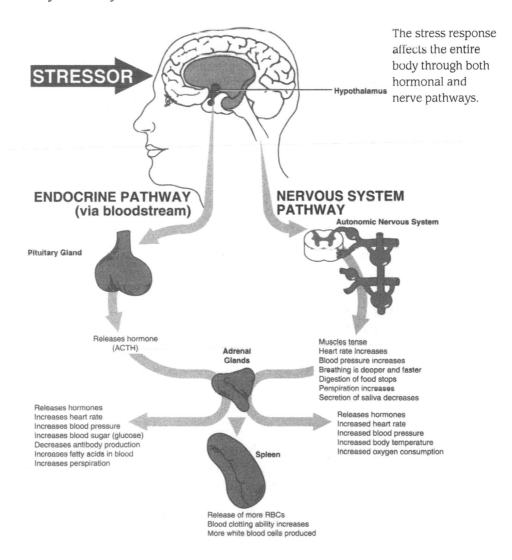

The stress response affects the entire body through both hormonal and nerve pathways.

STRESSOR

Hypothalamus

**ENDOCRINE PATHWAY
(via bloodstream)**

**NERVOUS SYSTEM
PATHWAY**

Autonomic Nervous System

Pituitary Gland

Releases hormone
(ACTH)

Adrenal
Glands

Muscles tense
Heart rate increases
Blood pressure increases
Breathing is deeper and faster
Digestion of food stops
Perspiration increases
Secretion of saliva decreases

Releases hormones
Increases heart rate
Increases blood pressure
Increases blood sugar (glucose)
Decreases antibody production
Increases fatty acids in blood
Increases perspiration

Spleen

Releases hormones
Increased heart rate
Increased blood pressure
Increased body temperature
Increased oxygen consumption

Release of more RBCs
Blood clotting ability increases
More white blood cells produced

In the 1940s and 1950s, Dr. Selye extended Cannon's work and laid the foundation for much of today's work on stress. In his experiments, he used various stressors and found a regular pattern of responses, which he described as the General Adaptation Syndrome (alarm, resistance, exhaustion). He discovered that if the stressor were maintained for a prolonged period of time, the body would first go through an alarm reaction (fight-or-flight response), followed by a stage of resistance where functions would return close to normal as the body strived to resist the stress. Finally, there would be a stage of exhaustion where the symptoms of the alarm reaction returned. (Nieman)

What Is Emotion?

In its most literal sense, the *Oxford English Dictionary* defines *emotion* as "any agitation or disturbance of mind, feeling, passion; any vehement or excited mental state."

Some theorists propose basic families, though not all agree on them. The main candidates and some of the members of their families:

- *Anger:* fury, outrage, resentment, wrath, exasperation, indignation, vexation, acrimony, animosity, annoyance, irritability, hostility, and, perhaps at the extreme, pathological hatred and violence.
- *Sadness:* grief, sorrow, cheerlessness, gloom, melancholy, self-pity, loneliness, dejection, despair, and, when pathological, severe depression.
- *Fear:* anxiety, apprehension, nervousness, concern, consternation, misgiving, wariness, qualm, edginess, dread, fright, terror; as a psychopathology, phobia and panic.
- *Enjoyment:* happiness, joy, relief, contentment, bliss, delight, amusement, pride, sensual pleasure, thrill, rapture, gratification, satisfaction, euphoria, whimsy, ecstasy, and at the far edge, mania.
- *Love:* acceptance, friendliness, trust, kindness, affinity, devotion, adoration, infatuation, agape.
- *Surprise:* shock, astonishment, amazement, wonder.
- *Disgust:* contempt, disdain, scorn, abhorrence, aversion, distaste, revulsion.
- *Shame:* guilt, embarrassment, chagrin, remorse, humiliation, regret, mortification, and contrition.

All emotions are, in essence, impulses to act, the instant plans for handling life that evolution has instilled in us. That emotions lead to actions is most obvious in watching animals or children; it is only in "civilized" adults we so often find the great anomaly in the animal kingdom, emotions—root impulses to act—divorced from obvious reaction.*

*Only in adults: An observation by Paul Ekman, University of California at San Francisco.

"What Are Emotions For?," and "What is Emotion?" from *Emotional Intelligence: Why It Can Matter More Than IQ* by Daniel Goleman, copyright © 1995 by Daniel Goleman. Used by permission of Bantam Books, an imprint of Random House, a division of Penguin Random House LLC. All rights reserved.

In our emotional repertoire each emotion plays a unique role, as revealed by their distinctive biological signatures. With new methods to peer into the body and brain, researchers are discovering more physiological details of how each emotion prepares the body for a very different kind of response:**

- With anger blood flows to the hands, making it easier to grasp a weapon or strike at a foe; heart rate increases, and a rush of hormones such as adrenaline generates a pulse of energy strong enough for vigorous action.

- With fear blood goes to the large skeletal muscles, such as in the legs, making it easier to flee-and making the face blanch as blood is shunted away from it (creating the feeling that the blood "runs cold"). At the same time, the body freezes, if only for a moment, perhaps allowing time to gauge whether hiding might be a better reaction. Circuits in the brain's emotional centers trigger a flood of hormones that put the body on general alert, making it edgy and ready for action, and attention fixates on the threat at hand, the better to evaluate what response to make.

- Among the main biological changes in happiness is an increased activity in a brain center that inhibits negative feelings and fosters an increase in available energy, and a quieting of those that generate worrisome thought. But there is no particular shift in physiology save a quiescence, which makes the body recover more quickly from the biological arousal of upsetting emotions. This configuration offers the body a general rest, as well as readiness and enthusiasm for whatever task is at hand and for striving toward a great variety of goals.

- Love, tender feelings, and sexual satisfaction entail parasympathetic arousal—the physiological opposite of the "fight-or-flight" mobilization shared by fear and anger. The parasympathetic pattern, dubbed the "relaxation response," is a bodywide set of reactions that generates a general state of calm and contentment, facilitating cooperation.

- The lifting of the eyebrows in surprise allows the taking in of a larger visual sweep and also permits more light to strike the retina. This offers more information about the unexpected event, making it easier to figure out exactly what is going on and concoct the best plan for action.

**Body changes in emotions and their evolutionary reasons: Some of the changes are documented in Robert W. Levenson, Paul Ekman and Wallace V. Friesen, "Voluntary Facial Action Generates Emotion-Specific Autonomous Nervous System Activity," *Psychophysiology*, 27, 1990. This list is culled from there and other sources. At this point such a list remains speculative to a degree; there is scientific debate over the precise biological signature of each emotion, with some researchers taking the position that there is far more overlap than difference among emotions, or that our present ability to measure the biological correlates of emotion is too immature to distinguish among them reliably. For this debate, see: Paul Ekman and Richard Davidson, eds., Fundamental Questions About Emotions (New York: Oxford university Press, 1994).

■ Around the world an expression of disgust looks the same, and sends the identical message: something is offensive in taste or smell, or metaphorically so. The facial expression of disgust—the upper lip curled to the side as the nose wrinkles slightly—suggests a primordial attempt, as Darwin observed, to close the nostrils against a noxious odor or to spit out a poisonous food.

■ A main function for sadness is to help adjust to a significant loss, such as the death of someone close or a major disappointment. Sadness brings a drop in energy and enthusiasm for life's activities, particularly diversions and pleasures, and, as it deepens and approaches depression, slows the body's metabolism. This introspective withdrawal creates the opportunity to mourn a loss or frustrated hope, grasp its consequences for one's life, and, as energy returns, plan new beginnings. This loss of energy may well have kept saddened—and vulnerable— early humans close to home, where they were safer.

ASSIGNMENT: Evaluate your stress levels. Check the appropriate boxes of events that have happened during the past six months or are likely to occur within the next six months. Total up your points and score yourself on the following page.

This has been modified from the Holmes and Rahe's Life Events Scale to gauge the stress level and corresponding health consequences for college-age adults. In the Student Stress Scale, each event, such as beginning or ending school, has a score that represents the amount of readjustment a person has to make in life as a result of the change. Change of any kind can produce stress.

1. Death of a close family member	❏	100
2. Death of a close friend	❏	73
3. Divorce between parents	❏	65
4. Jail term	❏	63
5. Major personal injury or illness	❏	63
6. Marriage	❏	58
7. Fired from job	❏	50
8. Failed important course	❏	47
9. Change in health of a family member	❏	45
10. Pregnancy	❏	45
11. Sexual problems	❏	44
12. Serious argument with close friend	❏	40
13. Change in financial status	❏	39
14. Change of major	❏	39
15. Trouble with parents	❏	39
16. New girl- or boyfriend	❏	38
17. Increased workload at school	❏	37

18. Outstanding personal achievement	❏	36
19. First quarter/semester in college	❏	35
20. Change in living conditions	❏	31
21. Serious argument with instructor	❏	30
22. Lower grades than expected	❏	29
23. Change in sleeping habits	❏	29
24. Change in social activities	❏	29
25. Change in eating habits	❏	26
26. Chronic car trouble	❏	26
27. Change in number of family get togethers	❏	26
28. Too many missed classes	❏	25
29. Change of college	❏	24
30. Dropped more than one class	❏	23
31. Minor traffic violations	❏	20

SOURCE: Adapted from T. H. Holmes and R. H. Rahe, 1967, *Journal of Psychosomatic Research* 11:213.

HOW TO DETERMINE YOUR SCORE:

300 points or higher = have a very high risk of developing a serious health condition

150–300 points = 50/50 chance of developing a serious health condition within the next two years

150 or less = 1 in 3 chance of developing a serious health condition

What was your result? _____

The Ill Effects of High Stress

Medical research on stress dates back to the 1920s, when Walter Cannon began experimenting with the physiological effect of stress on cats and dogs. Studying the animals' reactions to danger, the Harvard physiologist noted a regular and common pattern, now known as the fight-or-flight response.

In this response, the muscles tense and tighten, breathing becomes deeper and faster, the heart rate rises and blood vessels constrict (raising the blood pressure), the stomach and intestines temporarily halt digestion, perspiration increases, the thyroid gland is stimulated, while the secretion of saliva and mucus slows, and sensory perception becomes sharper. Various stress hormones are released in the body, in particular epinephrine and cortisol, depressing immune function, and adversely affecting bodily functions in many other ways (see figure).

In the 1940s and 1950s, Dr. Selye extended Cannon's work and laid the foundation for much of today's work on stress. Experimenting with rats, he used various stressors, and found a regular pattern of responses, which he described as the General Adaptation Syndrome (alarm, resistance, exhaustion).

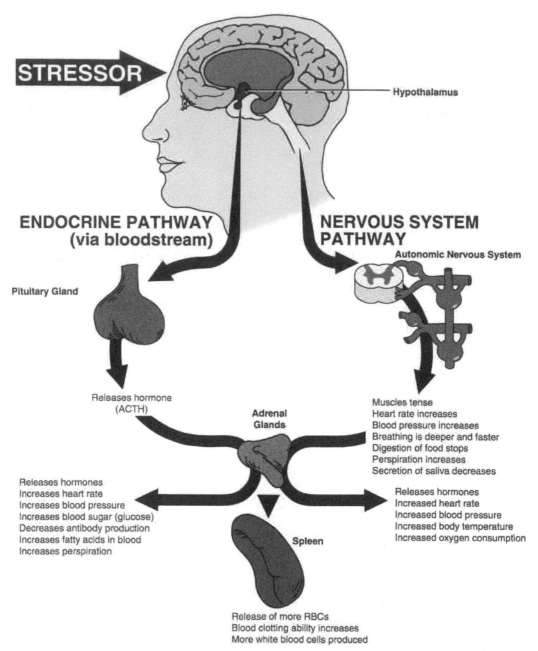

STRESSOR

Hypothalamus

**ENDOCRINE PATHWAY
(via bloodstream)**

**NERVOUS SYSTEM
PATHWAY**

Autonomic Nervous System

Pituitary Gland

Releases hormone
(ACTH)

Adrenal
Glands

Muscles tense
Heart rate increases
Blood pressure increases
Breathing is deeper and faster
Digestion of food stops
Perspiration increases
Secretion of saliva decreases

Releases hormones
Increases heart rate
Increases blood pressure
Increases blood sugar (glucose)
Decreases antibody production
Increases fatty acids in blood
Increases perspiration

Spleen

Releases hormones
Increased heart rate
Increased blood pressure
Increased body temperature
Increased oxygen consumption

Release of more RBCs
Blood clotting ability increases
More white blood cells produced

**The stress response affects the entire body through both hormonal
and nerve pathways.**

He discovered that if the stressor were maintained for a prolonged period of time, the body would first go through an alarm reaction (fight-or-flight response), followed by a stage of resistance where functions would return close to normal as the body strove to resist the stress. Finally, there would be a stage of exhaustion where the symptoms of the alarm reaction returned. In animal experiments, the animals would die.

Stress can have a profound effect on one's physical health. If you are chronically anxious, depressed, or emotionally distressed, your health can suffer.

For example, in one study of 1,300 graduates of the Johns Hopkins Medical School, depression was found to be an important predictor of heart disease. In England, people who experienced chronic mild anxiety and depression were more likely to develop heart disease than those who did not. In a study of 10,000 Israeli men, anxiety over problems and conflicts about finance, family, and relationships with co-workers was associated with 2 to 3 times the risk of developing heart disease.

In a 17-year study of 2,000 middle-aged men, depression has been associated with twice the risk of death from cancer. A one-year study of 100 people found that flus and colds were four times as prevalent following stressful life events. An Australian study found that stressed people had twice as many days when they had flu and cold symptoms.

Dr. Donald Girard from the Oregon Health Sciences University has reviewed the literature on this subject and concluded that repressed feelings of loss, denial, depression, inflexibility, conformity, lack of social ties, high levels of anxiety and dissatisfaction, and an over-abundance of life-change events are associated with increased cancers, heart disease, and infection. Writes Dr. Guard, "It seems that the best advice the physician can offer patients is that good mental health is important for maintaining physical well-being."

National surveys suggest that marital happiness contributes far more to happiness in societies throughout the world than any other variable, including satisfaction with work and friendships. Divorced and separated people have poorer mental and physical health than those who remain married, or are widowed or single. Marital disruption has been found to be the single most powerful predictor of stress-related physical illness; separated partners have about 30 percent more acute illnesses and physician visits than those who remain married. It has been concluded that depression of immune function is associated with marital discord.

A number of other studies have found bereavement and a lack of social and community ties to be associated with an overall increase in mortality. A study of 95,647 widows found more than double the normal mortality rate during the first week following widowhood, primarily from cardiovascular disease, violent causes, and suicides. Dr. Ruberman of New York has reported that highly stressed and socially isolated heart disease patients (few contacts with friends, relatives, church or club groups) had more than four times the risk of dying from heart disease of men with tow levels of isolation and stress.

A statement made by William Harvey in 1628 applies today: "Every affection of the mind that is attended with either pain or pleasure, hope or fear, is the cause of an agitation whose influence extends to the heart."

Dr. George Vaillant of Harvard University tracked 204 men over 40 years and found that poor mental health was associated with increased disease and death, after allowance had been made for the effects of drug abuse, obesity, and family history of long life. Concluded Vaillant: "Good mental health facilitates our survival."

Stress Management Principles

Much has been written about controlling stress. It can all be summarized under five basic stress management principles.

1. Control Stressors

Stressors are everywhere. They can't all be avoided, but you can do a great deal in the way of reducing, modifying, or avoiding many of them in a way that will allow you to accomplish your goals. For example, if you are going to climb a tall mountain, you can make the trip miserable by hiking too fast with a heavy backpack, or satisfying and pleasurable by walking at a moderate pace with a lighter load. Same goal, same path, but a completely different experience.

Let's say that a college student is taking a heavy academic load in a subject area (e.g., biochemistry) that is too difficult for him at present, working 15 hours a week to help pay for expenses, living in a crowded and noisy apartment with an unbearable roommate, experiencing constant transportation problems because of a car that keeps breaking down, and dealing with crushing family problems due to the divorce of his parents. The first step would be for the student to sit down, make a list of all his major goals, in order of importance, and then catalog each of the stressors, along with plans to either eliminate or modify them (see sample form, figure).

For example, finishing biochemistry has a high priority because he must do so to have a chance to achieve his major life goal of becoming a physician. He should give it his first attention (he could increase his study time by quitting work and taking out a loan). He could move closer to campus, find more desirable living accommodations, and walk or bicycle for transportation until finances improve.

Just as in climbing a mountain, the stressors of life often can be managed by controlling the pace of life and the load carried, A key is to avoid crowding too much into the schedule, and learning to control circumstances to allow the pace of life to flow with one's psychological makeup. The important objective is to control your circumstances—don't let them control you.

2. Let the Mind Choose the Reaction

This strategy is also called "stress reaction management." As we've seen, a stress reaction (the fight-or-flight response) stimulates production of various stress hormones, depressing immune function, increasing blood pressure, and so on. In all, the response has negative health effects, so the goal is to head off the stress reaction before it can take place.

To understand how to do this, one needs to remember that events only cause stress when they are seen, heard, felt, or sensed by the brain. The mind interprets the event, and the type of interpretation governs the reaction. The good news is that when a stressor presents itself, you can decide what kind of reaction you will have. The bad news is that usually we have "knee-jerk" reactions to potentially stressful events, without taking the opportunity to calmly reason them out. In other words, we are largely responsible for creating our emotional reactions and we miss our opportunities to control them.

Once again, the principle is not new. Marcus Aurelius said long ago: "If you are distressed by anything external, the pain is not due to the thing itself but to your estimate of it. This you have the power to revoke at any time."

So when an event takes place (e.g., a flat tire on your way to work or school), you can choose how you will react. You can either react with the stress response of anger (as you kick the tire and blame the tire manufacturer), or you can choose a calm response by considering your practical options (I'll call at the first opportunity and work it out with the boss or professor).

3. Seek the Social Support of Others

A survey has shown that as many as one fourth of the American population feel extremely lonely at some time during any given month—especially divorced parents, single mothers, people who have never married, and housewives.

It is now clear that when people are socially isolated (few social contacts with family and friends, neighbors or the "society at large"), they are more vulnerable to sickness, mental stress, and even early death. One nine-year study (of 7,000 residents of Alameda County, California) found that people with few ties to other people had death rates from various diseases two to five times higher than those with more ties. The researchers measured social ties by looking at whether or not people were married, the number of close friends and relatives they had and how often they were in contact with them, church attendance, and involvement in informal and formal group associations.

Step One	List top 5 major life goals, in order of importance.
Step Two	List stressors associated with each goal.
Step Three	Summarize plans to modify or eliminate stressors so that goals can be achieved.

STEP ONE Top 5 Goals	STEP TWO Major stressors associated with each goal
Goal 1	
Goal 2	
Goal 3	
Goal 4	
Goal 5	

STEP THREE Summarize plans to modify or eliminate stressors so that goals can be achieved.

1. _____

2. _____

3. _____

4. _____

5. _____

6. _____

7. _____

8. _____

9. _____

10. _____

Sample form for evaluating goals and stressor.

Social support means reaching out to other people, sharing emotional, social, physical, financial, and other types of comfort and assistance. The principle was summarized by the Government's Institute of Medicine (Division of Health Promotion and Disease Prevention) " . . . a lack of family and community supports plays an important role in the development of disease. An absence of social support weakens the body's defenses through psychological stress. Isolated individuals must be identified, and strategies for increasing social contact and diminishing feelings of loneliness must be developed. Clinicians, family, friends, and social institutions bear a responsibility for diminishing social isolation."

4. Find Satisfaction in Work and Service

Dr. Albert Schweitzer once wrote, "I don't know what your destiny will be. But I do know that the only ones among you who will find true happiness are those who find a place to serve." Dr. Selye echoed this thought in his book, *Stress Without Distress* (New York: New American Library, 1974): "My own code is based on the view that to achieve peace of mind and fulfillment through self-expression, most men need a commitment to work in the service of some cause that they can respect."

5. Keep Healthy

It is far easier to handle stressors when the body is healthy from adequate exercise, sleep, good food and water, clean air and sunshine, and relaxation.

Problems with sleep have become a modern epidemic that is taking an enormous toll on our bodies and minds. Desperately trying to fit more into the hours of the day, many people are stealing extra hours from the night. The result, say sleep researchers, is a sleep deficit that undermines health, sabotages productivity, blackens mood, clouds judgment, and increases the risk of accidents. See the Health and Fitness Insight at the end of this chapter for more information on sleep.*

Stress Management—Effects of Stress

Stress can affect you both immediately (acute stress) and over time (chronic stress).

Tension is often the first signal of acute stress. Tense muscles are tight and feel "hard" to the touch. A tense mind makes you feel jumpy, irritable, and unable to

* From *Fitness & Your Health*, 7th Edition by David Nieman. Copyright © 2015 by Kendall Hunt Publishing Company. Reprinted by permission.

concentrate. This could be your signal to do something about stress, both for your immediate comfort and to prevent the long-term effects of stress.

Symptoms of Stress

Common symptoms of stress include:

- Rapid heartbeat
- Headache
- Stiff neck and/or tight shoulders
- Backache
- Rapid breathing
- Sweating and sweaty palms
- Upset stomach, nausea, or diarrhea

You also may notice signs of stress in your thinking, behavior, or mood. You may:

- Become irritable and intolerant of even minor disturbances.
- Feel irritated or frustrated, lose your temper more often, and yell at others for no reason.
- Feel jumpy or exhausted all the time.
- Find it hard to concentrate or focus on tasks.
- Worry too much about insignificant things.
- Doubt your ability to do things.
- Imagine negative, worrisome, or terrifying scenes.
- Feel you are missing opportunities because you cannot act quickly.

Acute Stress Problems

Acute (short-term) stress is the body's immediate reaction to any situation that seems demanding or dangerous. Your stress level depends on how intense the stress is, how long it lasts, and how you cope with the situation. The body usually recovers quickly from acute stress, but it can cause problems if it happens too often or your body doesn't have a chance to return to normal. In people who have heart problems, acute stress can trigger an abnormal heartbeat (arrhythmia) and even a heart attack.

Life-threatening or traumatic events, such as sexual abuse or war experiences, can cause acute stress disorder or post-traumatic stress disorder (PTSD).

Chronic Stress Problems

Chronic stress can be the result of a host of irritating hassles or a long-term life condition, such as a difficult job situation or living with a chronic disease. In people who have higher levels of chronic stress, the stress response lasts longer. Over time, chronic stress can have an effect on:

The immune system. Under stress, the body becomes more vulnerable to illnesses, from colds and minor infections to major diseases. If you have a chronic illness such as AIDS, stress can make the symptoms worse.

Cardiovascular disease. Stress is linked to high blood pressure, abnormal heartbeat (arrhythmia), problems with blood clotting, and hardening of the arteries (atherosclerosis). It is also linked to coronary artery disease, heart attack, and heart failure.

Muscle pain. People who are stressed often have neck, shoulder, and low back pain. This may be caused by constant tension in the muscle because of stress. Stress also affects rheumatoid arthritis.

Stomach and intestinal problems. Stress may be a factor in gastroesophageal reflux disease (GERD), peptic ulcer disease, and irritable bowel syndrome.

Reproductive organs. Stress is linked to painful menstrual periods, decreased fertility, and erection problems.

The lungs. Stress can make symptoms of asthma and chronic obstructive pulmonary disease (COPD) worse.

Skin problems. Stress can make disorders such as acne or psoriasis worse.

Individual Differences

Stress can also cause migraine or tension headaches, insomnia, or other sleep problems and can lead to addictions such as to alcohol and drugs (misuse of over-the-counter or prescription drugs or using recreational drugs).

What about Stress-Induced Obesity?

Chronic stress can contribute to several harmful physiological events. When body tissues are exposed to high levels of cortisol for extended periods of time, some cellular and tissue alterations occur. Cortisol is a necessary hormone that is responsible for fuel regulation of carbohydrates, fats, and proteins, also released while exercising, eating, and awakening. Cortisol is released into the body as a part of the stress response. The problems start when there is too much stress that makes too much cortisol. Cortisol is associated with overeating and craving high caloric fatty and sugary foods. High levels of cortisol cause fat stores and excess circulating fat to relocate and deposit deep in the abdomen, which left unchecked can develop into or enhance obesity. In addition, there are links between elevated cortisol levels and high blood pressure, elevated cholesterol, and elevated blood sugar. Individuals with a high waist-to-hip ratio are at greater risk for developing cardiovascular disease, type 2 diabetes, and cerebrovascular disease (clogging of the arteries leading to and/or in the brain).

American College of Sports Medicine's *Health & Fitness Journal.* "Cortisol Connection: Tips on Managing Stress and Weight" (2005). Volume 9, Issue 5: 21–22.

Stress and Self-Esteem

A healthy regard for yourself is necessary if you are going to do your best in anything you do in life (e.g., school, work, relationships). Low self-esteem is a major mental health problem in this nation. Many psychologists and mental health professionals believe that it is at the core of many types of mental health problems: substance abuse, depression, eating disorders, etc. The amount of control you take over what happens in your life is generally influenced by self-esteem. The lower the self-esteem, the more likely you are to react negatively in situations that should not cause you to feel stressed. The higher the self-esteem, the more likely you are to do what is needed in the situation and feel that you are in control.

Anxiety is an unpleasant apprehension directed at future events and self-doubt at the ability to cope with those events. Anxiety may become higher if your self-esteem is low. Anxiety, tension, and worry are the wrong responses to stress and will have negative effects on your performance. Low self-esteem is something to watch and to keep in check if you are going to learn to cope with stress in a positive way. Focus on the things you do well. React to situations and events in a more positive way. Keep tension, worry, and anxiety to a minimum.

ASSIGNMENT: Evaluate possible signs of stress you have felt lately. Stress affects many dimensions of your life.

COMMON SIGNS OF STRESS

Check the signs of stress that you have experienced lately. Stress affects many dimensions of your life.

PHYSICAL

_____ Headaches

_____ Asthma attack

_____ Gastrointestinal (constipation and/or diarrhea, indigestion, stomach cramping or bloating, nausea or vomiting)

_____ Acne flare-up

_____ Excessive dryness of hair or skin

_____ Frequent colds, flu, low-grade infections/herpes flare-ups

_____ Chest pain

_____ Neck, back, or shoulder pain

_____ Increased perspiration (excess sweating cold sweaty hands)

_____ Allergy flare-up, rashes, hives

_____ Muscle twitches or eye twitches

_____ Heart pounding, racing, or beating erratically

_____ Restlessness

_____ Fatigue

_____ Stiff or tense muscles

_____ Difficulty sleeping (insomnia, sleeping too much, sleeping too little)

_____ Trembling hands

_____ Weight gain or loss

_____ Teeth grinding

EMOTIONAL/SOCIAL/BEHAVIORAL

_____ Depression

_____ Sadness

_____ Restlessness

_____ Feeling burned out

_____ Inability to relax

_____ Difficulty in completing work or school assignments

_____ Questioning your personal worth

_____ Feeling sensitive to criticism

_____ Often feeling suspicious

_____ Crying spells

_____ Being accident-prone

_____ Increased use of alcohol/drugs/smoking

_____ Loss of appetite or excessive eating

_____ Mood swings

_____ Fidgeting

_____ Paying less attention to appearance

_____ Resentment

_____ Impulsive actions

_____ Loneliness

_____ Bouts of anger/hostility

_____ Social withdrawal or need to be with people most or all of the time

_____ Trouble getting along with others

_____ Diminished sex drive

MENTAL

_____ Disorganization (losing things, making dumb mistakes)

_____ Irritability

_____ Difficulty making small decisions

_____ Restlessness, poor concentration, boredom

_____ Worrying, anxiety, phobias

_____ Forgetfulness (memory problems)

_____ Negative attitude and/or negative self-talk

_____ Confusion

_____ Lethargy

_____ Decreased productivity

_____ Depression

_____ Loss of sense of humor

SPIRITUAL	
_____ Emptiness	_____ Sadness
_____ Loss of meaning	_____ Intolerance
_____ Doubt	_____ Loss of direction
_____ Being unforgiving	_____ Cynicism
_____ Martyrdom	_____ Apathy
_____ Lack of intimacy	

From Robbins, G. et al. *A Wellness Way of Life.* 7th Edition. "Common Signs of Stress." McGraw-Hill (2008): 323.

STRESS MANAGEMENT

"In times of great stress or adversity, it's always best to keep busy, to plow your anger and your energy into something positive."

— Lee Iacocca

Despite this relatively high prevalence of stress as discussed in the section above, however, few adults seek help for personal or emotional problems. Most people suffering from depression do not receive treatment. Americans report taking steps to control or reduce stress, but most do so unsuccessfully. Obviously, a large percentage of the population could benefit by using various stress management techniques. (Nieman, 314)

Resilience

Resilience refers to the ability of an individual, family, organization, or community to cope with adversity and adapt to challenges or change. It is an ongoing process that requires time and effort and engages people in taking a number of steps to enhance their response to adverse circumstances. Resilience implies that after an event, a person or community may not only be able to cope and recover, but also change to reflect different priorities arising from the experience and prepare for the next stressful situation.

- Resilience is the most important defense people have against stress.

- It is important to build and foster resilience to be ready for future challenges.

- Resilience will enable the development of a reservoir of internal resources to draw upon during stressful situations.

RESILIENCE IS THE ABILITY TO:

- Bounce back

- Take on difficult challenges and still find meaning in life

- Respond positively to difficult situations

- Rise above adversity

- Cope when things look bleak

- Tap into hope

- Transform unfavorable situations into wisdom, insight, and compassion

- Endure

Research (Aguirre, 2007; American Psychological Association, 2006; Bonanno, 2004) has shown that resilience is ordinary, not extraordinary, and that people regularly demonstrate being resilient.

- Resilience is not a trait that people either have or do not have.

- Resilience involves behaviors, thoughts, and actions that can be learned and developed in anyone.

- Resilience is tremendously influenced by a person's environment.

Resilience changes over time. It fluctuates depending on how much a person nurtures internal resources or coping strategies. Some people are more resilient in work life, while others exhibit more resilience in their personal relationships. People can build resilience and promote the foundations of resilience in any aspect of life they choose.

What Is Individual or Personal Resilience?

Individual resilience is a person's ability to positively cope after failures, setbacks, and losses. Developing resilience is a personal journey. Individuals do not react the same way to traumatic or stressful life events. An approach to building resilience that works for one person might not work for another. People use varying strategies to build their resilience. Because resilience can be learned, it can be strengthened. Personal resilience is related to many factors including individual health and well-being, individual aspects, life history and experience, and social support.

INDIVIDUAL HEALTH AND WELL-BEING	INDIVIDUAL ASPECTS	LIFE HISTORY AND EXPERIENCE	SOCIAL SUPPORT
These are factors with which a person is born. ■ Personality ■ Ethnicity ■ Cultural background ■ Economic background	These are past events and relationships that influence how people approach current stressors. ■ Family history ■ Previous physical health ■ Previous mental health ■ Trauma history ■ Past social experiences ■ Past cultural experiences	These are support systems provided by family, friends, and members of the community, work, or school environments. ■ Feeling connected to others ■ A sense of security ■ Feeling connected to resources	

(Adapted from Simon, Murphy, & Smith, 2008)

Along with the factors listed above, there are several attributes that have been correlated with building and promoting resilience.

THE AMERICAN PSYCHOLOGICAL ASSOCIATION REPORTS THE FOLLOWING ATTRIBUTES REGARDING RESILIENCE:

■ The capacity to make and carry out realistic plans

■ Communication and problem-solving skills

■ A positive or optimistic view of life

■ Confidence in personal strengths and abilities

■ The capacity to manage strong feelings, emotions, and impulses

---

What Factors Promote Resilience?

Resilience involves the modification of a person's response to a potentially risky situation. People who are resilient are able to maintain high self-esteem and self-efficacy in spite of the challenges they face. By fostering resilience, people are building psychological defenses against stress. The more resources and defenses available during a time of struggle, the better able to cope and bounce back from adverse circumstances people will be. A person's ability to regain a sense of normalcy or define a new normalcy after adverse circumstances will be partially based on the resources available to him/her. Resilience building can begin at any time. Following is information regarding applicable ways to implement resilience practices, as well as situations that could inhibit resilience, situations that enhance resilience, and people who help facilitate the growth of resilience.

	DEMONSTRATING RESILIENCE	VULNERABILITY FACTORS INHIBITING RESILIENCE	PROTECTIVE FACTORS ENHANCING RESILIENCE	FACILITATORS OF RESILIENCE
Individual Resilience The ability for an individual to cope with adversity and change	▪ Optimism ▪ Flexibility ▪ Self-confidence ▪ Competence ▪ Insightfulness ▪ Perseverance ▪ Perspective ▪ Self-control ▪ Sociability	▪ Poor social skills ▪ Poor problem solving ▪ Lack of empathy ▪ Family violence ▪ Abuse or neglect ▪ Divorce or partner breakup ▪ Death or loss ▪ Lack of social support	▪ Social competence ▪ Problem-solving skills ▪ Good coping skills ▪ Empathy ▪ Secure or stable family ▪ Supportive relationships ▪ Intellectual abilities ▪ Self-efficacy ▪ Communication skills	▪ Individuals ▪ Parents ▪ Grandparents ▪ Caregivers ▪ Children ▪ Adolescents ▪ Friends ▪ Partners ▪ Spouses ▪ Teachers ▪ Faith Community

How Is Personal Resilience Built?

Developing resilience is a personal journey. People do not react the same way to traumatic events. Some ways to build resilience include the following actions:

- Making connections with others

- Looking for opportunities for self-discovery

- Nurturing a positive view of self

- Accepting that change is a part of living

- Taking decisive actions

- Learning from the past

The ability to be flexible is a great skill to obtain and facilitates resilience growth. Getting help when it is needed is crucial to building resilience. It is important to try to obtain information on resilience from books or other publications, self-help or support groups, and online resources like the ones found in this resource collection.

Online Assignment: Resiliency

Complete this assignment online. Go to:

www.grtep.com

Select >Chapter Content>Chapter 3>Enter your username and password

Before discussing positive ways to deal with stress management, let's look at some defense mechanisms. These are a way of coping and dealing with stress—some positive and some negative. Being able to identify possible defense mechanisms you may use will help increase your awareness of how you truly deal with stress and if you need to think about other ways to deal with stress.

https://www.authentichappiness.sas.upenn.edu/learn/grit

DEFENSE MECHANISMS

DEFENSE MECHANISM	POSITIVE OR NEGATIVE?	DEFINITION	SIMPLE EXAMPLE
Affiliation	Positive	Sharing your feelings of stress, without trying to make others take responsibility for it.	Talking with a close friend about the difficulties you are having with speaking in front of class.
Humor	Positive	Finding the humor or irony of a situation. Differs from sarcasm, which is an anger response.	At the end of a day filled with conflict, finding humor in the ridiculous odds that "all those things" could happen in the same day.
Denial	Negative	Pretending a stressor is minor or does not exist.	Failing to recognize the possibility one has an alcohol problem after receiving a third DUI citation.
Rationalization	Negative	Defending or justifying personal actions and feelings others find unacceptable.	"I only smoke when I drink, so I'm not really a smoker."
Splitting	Negative	Categorization of others in one's life; idolizing one group and disenfranchising the other.	After a major argument with all four roommates, ignoring and shutting out those who disagreed with you, while spending all your time with those who did agree.
Repression	Negative	Blocking disturbing thoughts or experiences from the conscious mind.	Often used by those having experienced physical, emotional, or sexual abuse as children so the upsetting thoughts are not always present.

SOURCE: Adapted from Levo L. M. Understanding defense mechanisms. *Lukenotes* 2003; 7.

https://positivepsychologyprogram.com/broaden-build-theory/

Much has been written about controlling stress. Five basic stress management principles can summarize it all:

1. *Control stressors.* They are everywhere and can't all be avoided. But you can do a great deal in the way of reducing, modifying, or avoiding many of them in a way that will allow you to accomplish your goals. Let's say you're taking a heavy academic load in a subject area (e.g., biochemistry). It is too difficult for you at present, as you are working 15 hours a week to help pay for expenses, living in a crowded and noisy apartment with an unbearable roommate, experiencing constant transportation problems because of a car that keeps breaking down, and dealing with crushing family problems due to the divorce of your parents. The first step would be for you to sit down and make a list of all your major goals, in order of importance, and then to catalog each of the stressors along with plans to either eliminate or modify them.

   A key is to avoid crowding too much into your schedule and to learn to control circumstances to allow the pace of life to flow with one's psychological make-up. The important objective is to control your circumstances—don't let them control you.

2. *Let the mind choose the reaction.* This is also called "stress reaction management." You've read about the stress reaction or "fight-or-flight response" and how it stimulates the production of various hormones, depresses the immune function, and so on. In all, the response has negative health effects, so the goal is to head off the stress reaction before it can take place.

   To understand how to do this, you need to remember that events only cause stress when the brain sees, hears, feels, or senses them. The mind interprets the event, and the type of interpretation governs the reaction. The good news is that when a stressor presents itself, you can decide what kind of reaction you will have. The bad news is that usually we have "knee-jerk" reactions to potentially stressful events, without taking the opportunity to calmly reason them out. In other words, we are largely responsible for creating our emotional reactions, and we miss our opportunities to control them. So when an event takes place, you can choose how you will react. You can either react with the stress response of anger or you can choose a calm response by considering your practical options.

3. *Seek the social support of others.* A survey has shown that as many as one-fourth of the American population feels extremely lonely at some time during any given month—especially divorced parents, single mothers, people who have never married, and housewives. It is now clear that when people are

socially isolated (few social contacts with family and friends, neighbors or the "society at large"), they are more vulnerable to sickness, mental stress, and even early death. One nine-year study (of 7,000 residents in California) found that people with few ties to other people had death rates from various diseases two to five times higher than those with more ties. The researchers measured social ties by looking at whether or not people were married, the number of close friends and relatives they had, and how often they were in contact with them, as well as whether they attended church and had involvement in informal and formal group associations. Social support means reaching out to other people and sharing emotional, social, physical, financial, and other types comfort and assistance.

4. ***Find satisfaction in work and service.*** Dr. Albert Schweitzer once wrote, "I don't know what your destiny will be. But I do know that the only ones among you who will find true happiness are those who find a place to serve." Dr. Selye echoed this thought in his book, *Stress Without Distress*, "My own code is based on the view that to achieve peace of mind and fulfillment through self-expression, most people need a commitment to work in the service of some cause that they can respect."

5. ***Keep healthy.*** It is far easier to handle stressors when the body is healthy from adequate sleep, exercise, good food and water, clean air and sunshine, and relaxation. Problems with sleep have become a modern epidemic that is taking an enormous toll on our bodies and minds. Desperately trying to fit more into the hours of the day, many people are stealing extra hours from the night. The results say sleep researchers is a sleep deficit that undermines health, sabotages productivity, blackens mood, clouds judgment, and increases the risk of accidents.

    One of the most important habits you can acquire to improve mood state and manage stress is the habit of regular exercise. The part of the brain that enables us to exercise (the motor cortex) lies only a few millimeters away from the part of the brain that deals with thought and feeling. Might this proximity mean that when exercise stimulates the motor cortex, it has a parallel effect on cognition and emotion? The highly acclaimed "Perrier Survey of Fitness in America," conducted by Louis Harris and Associates, showed that modern-day men and women strongly believe in the Greek concept of a "strong mind in a strong body." The survey found that those who have a deep commitment to exercise report feeling more relaxed, less tired, more disciplined, more attractive, more self-confident, more productive in work, and, in general, more at one with themselves. (Nieman, 317–320)

ASSIGNMENT: Evaluate your goals and stressors.

Step One   List top 5 major life goals, in order of importance.
Step Two   List stressors associated with each goal.
Step Three   Summarize plans to modify or eliminate stressors so that goals can be achieved.

STEP ONE Top 5 Goals	STEP TWO Major stressors associated with each goal
Goal 1	
Goal 2	
Goal 3	
Goal 4	
Goal 5	

STEP THREE   Summarize plans to modify or eliminate stressors so that goals can be achieved

1. _____

2. _____

3. _____

4. _____

5. _____

6. _____

7. _____

8. _____

9. _____

10. _____

Relaxation and Anger Management Techniques

It is difficult to eliminate all the stress in your life, but you can learn to reduce your anger and to control your frustrations or anxiety by practicing relaxation exercises. Some are more involved, but others are simple enough to do anywhere—even in the classroom. Try one or more of the following exercises whenever you feel yourself becoming angry, tense, or overly tired, or if you feel that others may be taking advantage of you.

Deep Breathing

- Anger and stress result in shallow, rapid breathing. Deep, slow breathing can reduce stress and help you relax. Oxygen is the body's natural stress-reducer, and increasing your body's oxygen intake helps relieve tension.
- *Begin by closing your eyes. Exhale slowly and clear the air from your lungs. The inhale deeply through your nose and hold your breath for a count of five. When taking a deep breath, your stomach (actually your diaphragm) should be expanded. Slowly exhale using your lips to control the rate of air that you move out of your lungs. Begin the cycle again. Repeat several times until you feel calmer.*

Deep Muscle Relaxation

- One of the most common reactions to anger and stress is muscle tension. Think of a time when you've been angry or frustrated and remember the tenseness in your jaw, neck, shoulders, arms, and hands. Deep and progressive muscle relaxation will help you relax your entire body from head to toe by first tensing and then relaxing various muscle groups. This type of relaxation may also help you sleep better.
- *Find a comfortable position either sitting or lying down. Close your eyes. Begin with your head and facial muscles—scalp, brow, eyes, lips, jaw, etc. Tighten your muscles and hold them tense for ten seconds; then relax. Continue contracting and relaxing your muscles by moving through your neck, shoulder, back, and chest areas. Keep doing this through every major muscle group. Concentrate on your breathing (slow, deep breaths) while you work your way down to your hips, legs, and feet.*

Meditation

- An ancient relaxation technique—meditation—can help you clear stressful thoughts from your mind, but it may take time to learn how to do it effectively.
- *Find a location where you are comfortable and won't be disturbed. Close your eyes and focus on a peaceful word or image. Your goal is to find a quiet, peaceful state of mind. Concentrate on something calming and do not let any other thoughts enter your mind. Learning to abandon all other thoughts is the hard part. Return to the one image or word you have selected, clearing your mind of any stress and worry. Breathe deeply. At the end of your meditation session, you will feel calm and relaxed.*

- Imagery is another type of mental exercise. It is like taking a mini-mental vacation or day-dreaming with a purpose. You can achieve the same feeling of tranquility that you do with meditation but the technique is different. Rather than concentrating on a single thought, you can create an entirely relaxing place of your own to which you can escape.

- *Once again, close your eyes and visualize the perfect place to relax. It might be in the woods by a brook, on a warm, sandy beach, in the mountains, floating on a cloud—wherever seems right to you. See yourself there, calm and satisfied with life. You can go to this special place in your mind whenever you need a few seconds of escape-time. You can also use this technique to build confidence. While your place is perfect, visualize yourself accomplishing one of your goals.*

- There are a variety of products currently on the market to help you relax. You can use everything from bubble bath to scented candles to create a soothing environment. Relaxing music, pleasant aromas, multimedia that captures the sights and sounds of ocean waves, raindrops, a crackling fire, or any number of other auditory and visual images can produce a tranquil state of mind.

- Massage therapy is now readily available in a variety of forms—chair massages for the neck and shoulders, pulse or wave massages, and full-body massages.

Especially for You, the College Student

Almost everyone feels some apprehension, fear, uneasiness, or worry about taking a test. A little pressure can be beneficial if it is moderate and controlled, and some students view an exam as an opportunity to show what they can do. Their attitude is similar to that of an athlete who enjoys competition because it enhances his or her own performance. If moderate anxiety keeps you alert and provides you with a burst of energy, it can help you do your best. Test anxiety may result in noticeable physical symptoms such as headaches, nausea, sweating, or dizziness. It can reduce your ability to concentrate and make you feel overwhelmed and unable to perform. The anxiety is self-induced, but contributing factors may come from outside pressures to maintain good grades. If you suffer from anxiety because you think you have to be perfect, you need to let go of some of your unrealistic expectations.

Test Anxiety Reduction

- *Attitude Adjustment*—Be realistic about the importance of any single test or exam. Recognize that your value as a person is not dependent on what you do on any one test or in any one course.

- *Effective Study Techniques*—Faithfully practicing note-taking, time management and test-taking strategies will give you the confidence you need to go into the test with a winning attitude. Be sure to use tutoring and other academic support services as needed.

- *Positive Self-Talk*—Negative thinking increases your anxiety level. Recognize any self-defeating thoughts you might have and replace them with positive thoughts designed to increase your confidence levels. Believe that you have the ability to control what happens and visualize yourself doing your absolute best. Practice positive statements to boost your confidence and self-esteem

(Aguilar, 205–207)

Humor and Stress Management

Laughter activates the chemistry of the will to live and increases our capacity to fight disease. Laughing relaxes the body and reduces problems associated with high blood pressure, strokes, arthritis, and ulcers. Some research suggests that laughter may also reduce the risk of heart disease. Historically, research has shown that distressing emotions (depression, anger, anxiety, and stress) are all related to heart disease. A study done at the University of Maryland Medical Center suggests that a good sense of humor and the ability to laugh at stressful situations help mitigate the damaging physical effects of distressing emotions.

Laughter's Effects on the Body

Laughter lowers blood pressure

People who laugh heartily on a regular basis have lower standing blood pressure than the average person. When people have a good laugh, initially the blood pressure increases, but then it decreases to levels below normal. Breathing then becomes deeper, which sends oxygen enriched blood and nutrients throughout the body.

Humor changes our biochemical state

Laughter decreases stress hormones and increases infection fighting antibodies. It increases our attentiveness, heart rate, and pulse.

Laughter protects the heart	Laughter, along with an active sense of humor, may help protect you against a heart attack, according to the study at the University of Maryland Medical Center (cited above). The study, which is the first to indicate that laughter may help prevent heart disease, found that people with heart disease were 40% less likely to laugh in a variety of situations compared to people of the same age without heart disease. Laughter gives our bodies a good workout.
Laughter gives our bodies a good workout	Laughter can be a great workout for your diaphragm, abdominal, respiratory, facial, leg, and back muscles. It massages abdominal organs, tones intestinal functioning, and strengthens the muscles that hold the abdominal organs in place. Not only does laughter give your midsection a workout, it can benefit digestion and absorption functioning as well. It is estimated that hearty laughter can burn calories equivalent to several minutes on the rowing machine or the exercise bike. Humor improves brain function and relieves stress.
Humor improves brain function and relieves stress	Laughter stimulates both sides of the brain to enhance learning. It eases muscle tension and psychological stress, which keeps the brain alert and allows people to retain more information.

A healthy sense of humor relates to the ability to laugh at oneself and at one's life. Laughing at oneself can be a way of accepting and respecting oneself. Lack of a sense of humor directly relates to lower self esteem. (Note that laughing at oneself can also be unhealthy if one laughs as a way of self degradation.)

Mental Health Benefits of Laughter

- Humor enhances our ability to affiliate or connect with others.

- Humor helps us replace distressing emotions with pleasurable feelings. You cannot feel angry, depressed, anxious, guilty, or resentful and experience humor at the same time.

- Lacking humor will cause one's thought processes to stagnate, leading to increased distress.

- Humor changes behavior—when we experience humor we talk more, make more eye contact with others, touch others more, etc.

- Humor increases energy, and with increased energy we may perform activities that we might otherwise avoid.

- Finally, humor is good for mental health because it makes us feel good!

Social Benefits of Humor and Laughter

Our work, marriage, and family all need humor, celebrations, play, and ritual as much as recordkeeping and problem-solving. We should ask the questions "Do we laugh together?" as well as "Can we get through this hardship together?" Humor binds us together, lightens our burdens, and helps us keep things in perspective. Some of the things that sap our energy are the time, focus, and effort we put into coping with life's problems, including each other's limitations. Our families, our friends, and our neighbors are not perfect, and neither are our marriages, our kids, or our inlaws. When we laugh together, it can bind us closer instead of pulling us apart.

Remember that even in the most difficult of times, a laugh, or even simply a smile, can go a long way in helping us feel better:

- Laughter is the shortest distance between two people.

- Humor unites us, especially when we laugh together.

- Laughter heals.

- We enjoy laughs and smiles best when we share them with others.

- To laugh or not to laugh is your choice.

Humor: How to Use Laughter

Improve your sense of humor

Humor CAN be learned. In fact, developing or refining your sense of humor may be easier than you think.

- **Put humor on your horizon.** Find a few photos, memes, movies, or videos that make you chuckle. Hang them up at home or at work. Look online at joke websites. Go to a comedy club.

- **Laugh and the world laughs with you.** Find a way to laugh about your own situations and watch your stress begin to fade away. Even if it feels forced at first, practice laughing. It does your body good.

- **Consider trying laughter yoga.** In laughter yoga, people practice laughter as a group. Laughter is forced at first, but it can soon turn into spontaneous laughter.

- **Share a laugh.** Make it a habit to spend time with friends who make you laugh. Return the favor by sharing funny stories or jokes with those around you.

Improve your sense of humor (continued)	■ **Knock, knock.** Browse through your local bookstore or library's selection of joke books and get a few rib ticklers in your repertoire that you can share with friends. ■ **Know what isn't funny.** Some forms of humor aren't appropriate or healthy. Use your best judgment to discern a good joke from a hurtful one. Laughter is good medicine. Once you've laughed, take stock of how you're feeling. Are your muscles a little less tense? Do you feel more relaxed or buoyant? That's the natural wonder of laughing at work.
Laughter is the best medicine	Go ahead and give it a try. Turn the corners of your mouth up into a smile and then give a laugh, even if it feels a little forced. Once you've had your chuckle, take stock of how you're feeling. Are your muscles a little less tense? Do you feel more relaxed or buoyant? That's the natural wonder of laughing at work.

What NOT to Do . . . Eating When You're Stressed

Medical New Today stated that research shows that 20% of Americans are worried that stress will affect their health, yet 36% say they deal with stress by eating or drinking alcohol. According to Kathleen M. Zelman, LD, MPH, RD, WebMD Weight Loss Clinic Expert, 75% of us are emotional eaters.

Why Is Food Used as a Coping Mechanism for Stress?

People use food as an escape or as a way to cope with stress for a variety of reasons. These include unhappiness, loneliness, low self-esteem, a distraction to mask nervousness in social situations, boredom, relationship break-ups, anxiety, spending the holidays with family, depression, etc.

Zelman states, "People who use food to heal emotions usually do so when they're not feeling good about themselves, and the result is usually unwanted weight gain. The excess weight leads to more negative feelings, triggering the cycle over and over again."

If you are an emotional eater, it's imperative that you start figuring out what triggers your emotional overeating so that you can begin to take steps to stop the cycle now. This is the first step. Once you've established what these triggers are, then the next step is to replace the old, unhealthy behaviors of emotional overeating with new behaviors and things to help you manage your feelings and emotions better. Here are some examples:

- Exercise.

- Meditate.

- Regimen your meals and snacks so you are on a routine.

- Listen to your favorite music or watch a movie.

- Call or visit a friend or family member.

- Start journaling your experiences and feelings.

- Take a drive.

- If these methods and others you try do not seem to help, look into talking with a healthcare professional about other alternatives.

ASSIGNMENT: Evaluate which stress management techniques you prefer.

Which stress management techniques will you try out today or in the next few days?

1. _____

_____

2. _____

_____

3. _____

_____

4. _____

_____

5. _____

_____

6. _____

_____

What made you choose the above techniques?

1. _____

   _____

2. _____

   _____

3. _____

   _____

4. _____

   _____

5. _____

   _____

6. _____

   _____

EXERCISE EFFECTS ON STRESS

"I'm really into my running workout.
Running really helps me clear my head and
makes me feel good, especially when I'm stressed."

— Katie Holmes

Several national surveys in the U.S. and Canada have studied the relationship between physical activity and feelings of mental well-being. One of the questionnaires used in Canadian studies was the "general well-being scale" (GWBS). The GWBS is highly regarded as one of the best measures of stress and mental health that the general public can use. The National Center for Health Statistics designed it with 18 questions covering such areas as energy level, satisfaction, freedom from worry, and self-control. A high score on the GWBS reflects an absence of bad feelings, an expression of positive mood state, and low stress.

Results from national surveys show that higher scores for the GWBS are significantly associated with increased amounts of physical activity for all age groups and for both men and women.

Cardiovascular Reactivity to Mental Stress

A considerable amount of recent research has indicated that aerobically unfit people show greater cardiovascular responses (in terms of elevated heart rates and blood pressure) to psychological stressors. When involved in stressful mental tasks, the less fit had heart rates nearly 30 beats per minute higher than the highly fit. And when originally unfit people participated in aerobic training programs, their heart rates were lower when they were subjected to psychological stressors.

One study randomly divided subjects into a meditation group, a music appreciation class (the control groups), and an exercise group involving 30 minutes of calisthenics and jogging four days per week for 10 weeks. At the end of 10 weeks, the exercise group demonstrated a faster recovery of the heart rate and autonomic system (skin electrical response) than the control groups in response to a battery of very stressful mental tasks. *The study concluded that this faster recovery is very important in coping with stress.* Since both exercise and mental stress increase the heart rate, blood pressure, adrenaline, and other biochemical measures, strengthening the body to adapt to exercise stress apparently strengthens it to handle mental stress.

Stressful Life Events and Somatic Illness

During the past 25 years, a large number of studies have shown that life events of all types (marriage, divorce, buying a house, losing one's job, moving to a new location, surgery, etc.) are significant stressors that lead to predictable physical and psychological health problems. Several recent studies have shown, however, that such life stress has less impact on the health of physically active people.

A study of 112 students showed that the less physically fit were more susceptible to stress-related health problems. In a second study of college students who had reported a high number of negative life events over the preceding year, aerobic exercise and relaxation training were both found effective for reducing depression.

Psychological Mood State

Depression and fatigue are very common complaints of Americans. Adults who are physically inactive are at much higher risk for fatigue and depression than those who are physically active. Depression, anxiety, and mood state in general appear to be favorably affected by regular aerobic exercise.

A team of researchers at Duke University studied 32 middle-aged men and women. They placed 16 in a 10-week program of walking and jogging for 45 minutes three times per week. Compared to the 16 who did not exercise, the exercising group showed less anxiety and depression, less fatigue and confusion, and elevated vigor. A similar 12-week study of 36 policemen and firemen reported comparable results.

Other types of aerobic exercise besides jogging or running have also proven mentally beneficial. Other studies have found that mixed aerobic programs of swimming, soccer, running, and aquatic and land calisthenics that are more moderate in intensity and more fun are helpful in reducing anxiety.

Self-Esteem

Exercise does more than reduce anxiety and depression and elevate mood. Self-esteem also improves, and many studies have strongly correlated it with exercise. A study of three groups of 40 college students divided the students into a 10-week exercise group, a 10-week exercise group with supportive counseling, and a control group receiving no exercise or counseling. The combination of running and supportive counseling helped those with low self-esteem gain more positive views of themselves.

Mental Cognition and Reaction Time

Results from some studies have suggested that short-term memory and intellectual function may improve during or shortly after an exercise session, but this area needs much more study. Several recent studies with elderly people have consistently shown that those who become physically active improve their ability to think and react mentally.

(Nieman, 320–324; 331)

Online Assignment: The General Well-Being Scale

Complete this assignment online. Go to:

www.grtep.com

Select >Chapter Content>Chapter 3>Enter your username and password

LEARNED HELPLESSNESS

❝ *We cannot change the cards we are dealt, just how we play the hand.* ❞

— Randy Pausch

Have you caught yourself ever saying, "What I think or what I do isn't going to change the situation anyway?" or "Why bother doing or saying anything at all?" Most people would answer yes.

But have you ever caught yourself saying these things to yourself often? Has it resulted in an overall feeling of loss of empowerment or helplessness?

The concept of learned helplessness is very real and is detrimental to one's mental wellness. It has been associated with various mental compromises such as depression, anxiety, loneliness and phobias. In 1967, psychologists, Martin Seligman and Steven F. Maier, accidentally discovered learned helplessness when conducting classical conditioning experiments with dogs. This study illustrated that "when an animal is repeatedly subjected to an aversive stimulus that it cannot escape, the animal will stop trying to avoid the stimulus and behave as if it is helpless to change the situation." Drs. Seligman and Maier then observed that despite given an opportunity to escape, the concept of learned helplessness in these dogs was preventing any further action to escape.

Learned helplessness is not just demonstrated in animals, it can also be seen in people. According to the learned helplessness theory, people's experiences with uncontrollable events may lead to the expectation that future events will render any action pointless or without control, resulting in people showing emotional defeat or "giving up" and less than desirable situations in future learning and motivation.

Dr. Seligman and his colleagues then further investigated into learned helplessness and pessimism and attribution style. Attribution style is one's understanding of the processes of how to explain the causes of behaviors and events. Their results show that "people who exhibit a style of attributing negative outcomes to global causes show greater generalization of learned helplessness to new situations than do people who do not exhibit the global attributional style for negative outcomes." Basically, Dr. Seligman introduces the concept of "explanatory style" and found that how we talk to ourselves about negative occurrences is the largest factor in determining optimism versus pessimism in an individual. For people who are more negatively oriented are more vulnerable to debilitating behavioral and emotional responses to less than desirable situations.

His research on helplessness and pessimism had significant findings with the prevention and treatment of depression. His evidence shows that most cases of depression are not biochemical or rooted in psychoanalytic causes but are due to continuous patterns of thinking that stem from the explanatory styles discussed above that lead to learned helplessness.

Online Reminders: Optimism Quiz
■ Complete the poll question before the next class meeting.
■ Complete the interactive activities for this chapter.
■ Complete all of the online assignments for this chapter.

GRIEF AND GRIEF MANAGEMENT

❝*Grief itself is a medicine.***❞**

— William Cowper

Grief is the normal response of sorrow, emotion, and confusion that comes from losing someone or something important to you. It is a natural part of life. Grief is a typical reaction to death, divorce, job loss, a move away from friends and family, or loss of good health due to illness.

How Does Grief Feel?

Just after a death or loss, you may feel empty and numb, as if you are in shock. You may notice physical changes such as trembling, nausea, trouble breathing, muscle weakness, dry mouth, or trouble sleeping and eating. You may become angry—at a situation, a particular person, or just angry in general. Almost everyone in grief also experiences guilt. Guilt is often expressed as "I could have, I should have, and I wish I would have" statements. People in grief may have strange dreams or nightmares, be absent-minded, withdraw socially, or lack the desire to return to work. While these feelings and behaviors are normal during grief, they will pass.

How Long Does Grief Last?

Grief lasts as long as it takes you to accept and learn to live with your loss. For some people, grief lasts a few months. For others, grieving may take years. The length of time spent grieving is different for each person. There are many reasons for the differences, including personality, health, coping style, culture, family background, and life experiences. The time spent grieving also depends on your relationship with the person lost and how prepared you were for the loss.

How Will I Know When I'm Done Grieving?

Every person who experiences a death or other loss must complete a four-step grieving process:

1. Accept the loss;
2. Work through and feel the physical and emotional pain of grief;
3. Adjust to living in a world without the person or item lost; and
4. Move on with life.

The grieving process is over only when a person completes the four steps.

How Does Grief Differ from Depression?

Depression is more than a feeling of grief after losing someone or something you love. Clinical depression is a whole body disorder. It can take over the way you think and feel. This chapter includes symptoms of depression later under "Mental Disorders." If you recently experienced a death or other loss, these feelings may be part of a normal grief reaction. But if these feelings persist with no lifting mood, ask for help.

HOW YOU CAN HELP SOMEONE WHO IS GRIEVING

- Listening is key in your efforts to support the person grieving. The mere presence of your attention, affection and willingness to listen can go a long way.

- Just as we are all unique beings, we will grieve in our own way. Be prepared for tears, outbursts, anger and even silence. Be open to the fact that all people cope differently and be that support to them.

- Ask the grieving person if they would like for you to go with them to the funeral home for the planning appointment and/or for any other funeral arrangements.

- Ask the bereaved person if you can assist them with making arrangements for transportation and hotel or housing arrangements for out-of-town family members or friends.

- As time moves on, make sure to visit with or call the bereaved person frequently. The calls and visits usually slow down after a few months of the funeral, etc. They will appreciate your support and consideration.

- Sometimes people who are grieving need quiet time, down time or the need to be alone. Keep an eye on them, however, if it seems to be shifting into a depression or a like thereof.

- Do not tell the bereaved to "get back to normal" since grief does not have a timetable and everyone copes differently and at different rates.

- Don't feel strange by speaking of the deceased person by his/her name especially when talking with the person grieving.

- Saying things like "They are now out of pain" or "It was God's will" may not always sit well with the bereaved person. Stay away from cliches. If you're not sure what to say, just provide your hand to hold or a hug to the person.

- Tell children the truth about the loved one that died. For example, say "She died" rather than "She is sleeping."

- Be open-minded and non-judgmental about the bereaved person's feelings of grief no matter the circumstance (for example if the deceased was very old or very sick).

- Let the bereaved person tell their story to you even if they have repeated it to you over and over again.

- Share a picture or a story of your own about the deceased to the person grieving. This may bring comfort to some but for others it can be a painful reminder of the death.

- There are no "should's" and "should not's" with grief.

MENTAL DISORDERS

> **❝***The statistics are that one out of every four Americans is suffering from some form of mental illness. Think of your three best friends. If they're okay, then it's you.***❞**
>
> — Rita Mae Brown

You may be thinking, "I don't have a mental disorder" or "Do I have a mental disorder?" Even though this book's purpose is all about prevention, how can you best practice prevention without being educated on what you're working on preventing in the first place? Do keep an open mind when reading this section. Mental disorders may affect you directly or indirectly—you'll see why when you read below.

According to the National Institute of Mental Health, mental illness refers collectively to all mental disorders, which are defined as "health conditions that are characterized by alterations in thinking, mood or behavior (or some combination thereof) associated with distress and/or impaired functioning." One in four or a little over 57 million Americans (26% adults) suffer from a diagnosable mental disorder in a given year.

Two of the most commonly talked about mental disorders are anxiety and depression. Anxiety is a condition characterized by apprehension, tension, or uneasiness, and it stems from the anticipation of real or imagined danger. If the anxiety becomes excessive and unrealistic, it can interfere with normal functioning.

Depression is a disparaging illness linked with episodes of long duration, relapse, and social and physical impairment. Most people with major depression are misdiagnosed, receive inappropriate or inadequate treatment, or receive no treatment at all. A depressive disorder is an illness that involves the body, mood, and thoughts. It affects the way a person eats and sleeps, the way one feels about oneself, and the way one thinks about things. Depression may range in severity from mild symptoms to more severe forms.

Mental Disorders in America

Even though mental disorders are widespread in the population, the main burden of illness is concentrated in a much smaller proportion—about 6% or 1 in 17—who suffer from a serious mental illness. In addition, MENTAL DISORDERS ARE THE LEADING CAUSE OF DISABILITY IN THE U.S. AND CANADA FOR AGES 15–44. Many people suffer from more than one mental disorder at a given time. Nearly half of those with any mental disorder (45% of people) meet criteria for two or more disorders. In the U.S., the *Diagnostic and Statistical Manual of Mental Disorders, fourth edition (DSM-IV)* is the basis for diagnosing mental disorders.

MOOD DISORDERS INCLUDE:	■ Approximately 20.9 million American adults, or about 9.5 percent of the U.S. population age 18 and older in a given year, have a mood disorder. ■ The median age of onset for mood disorders is 30 years. ■ Depressive disorders often co-occur with anxiety disorders and substance abuse.
Major Depressive Disorder	■ Depression is a serious medical illness; it's not something that you have made up in your head. It's more than just feeling "down in the dumps" or "blue" for a few days. It's feeling "down" and "low" and "hopeless" for weeks at a time. ■ Signs and symptoms include persistent sad, anxious, or "empty" mood, feelings of hopelessness, pessimism, feelings of guilt, worthlessness, helplessness, and loss of interest or pleasure in hobbies and activities once enjoyed. ■ Major Depressive Disorder is the leading cause of disability in the U.S. for ages 15–44. ■ Major depressive disorder affects approximately 14.8 million American adults, or about 6.7 percent of the U.S. population age 18 and older in a given year. ■ While major depressive disorder can develop at any age, the median age at onset is 32. ■ Major depressive disorder is more prevalent in women than in men. ■ The lifetime estimate for major depression is 17% and is most common among females, the elderly, young adults, and people with less than a college education.
Dysthymic Disorder	■ Dysthymic disorder symptoms (chronic, mild depression) must persist for at least two years in adults (one year in children) to meet criteria for the diagnosis. ■ Dysthymic disorder affects approximately 1.5 percent of the U.S. population age 18 and older in a given year. This figure translates to about 3.3 million American adults. ■ The median age of onset of dysthymic disorder is 31.

Bipolar Disorder

- Bipolar Disorder, also known as manic-depressive illness, is a serious medical illness that causes shifts in a person's mood, energy, and ability to function. The symptoms of bipolar disorder are severe and different from the normal ups and downs that everyone goes through.

- Bipolar disorder causes dramatic mood swings from overly "high" or irritable to sad and hopeless, and then back again, often with periods of normal mood in between. Severe changes in energy and behavior go along with these changes in mood. The periods of highs and lows are called episodes of mania and depression.

- Bipolar disorder affects approximately 5.7 million American adults, or about 2.6 percent of the U.S. population age 18 and older in a given year.

- The median age of onset for bipolar disorders is 25 years.

Borderline Personality Disorder (BPD)

- BPD is a serious mental illness characterized by pervasive instability in moods, interpersonal relationships, self-image, and behavior. This instability often disrupts family and work life, long-term planning, and the individual's sense of self-identity. Originally thought to be at the "borderline" of psychosis, people with BPD suffer from a disorder of emotion regulation.

- While less well known than schizophrenia or bipolar disorder (manic-depressive illness), BPD is more common, affecting 2 percent of adults, mostly young women. There is a high rate of self-injury without suicide intent, as well as a significant rate of suicide attempts and completed suicide in severe cases. Patients often need extensive mental health services and account for 20% of psychiatric hospitalizations. Yet, with help, many improve over time and are eventually able to lead productive lives.

- While a person with depression or bipolar disorder typically endures the same mood for weeks, a person with BPD may experience intense bouts of anger, depression, and anxiety that may last only hours, or at most a day. These may be associated with episodes of impulsive aggression, self-injury, and drug or alcohol abuse. Distortions in cognition and sense of self can lead to frequent changes in long-term goals, career plans, jobs, friendships, gender identity, and values. Sometimes people with BPD view themselves as fundamentally bad, or unworthy. They may feel unfairly misunderstood or mistreated, bored, empty, and have little idea who they are. Such symptoms are most acute when people with BPD feel isolated and lacking in social support, and they may result in frantic efforts to avoid being alone.

Borderline Personality Disorder (BPD) (continued)

- People with BPD often have highly unstable patterns of social relationships. While they can develop intense but stormy attachments, their attitudes towards family, friends, and loved ones may suddenly shift from idealization (great admiration and love) to devaluation (intense anger and dislike). Thus, they may form an immediate attachment and idealize the other person, but when a slight separation or conflict occurs, they switch unexpectedly to the other extreme and angrily accuse the other person of not caring for them at all. Even with family members, individuals with BPD are highly sensitive to rejection, reacting with anger and distress to such mild separations as a vacation, a business trip, or a sudden change in plans. These fears of abandonment seem related to difficulties feeling emotionally connected to important persons when they are physically absent, leaving the individual with BPD feeling lost and perhaps worthless. Suicide threats and attempts may occur along with anger at perceived abandonment and disappointments.

- People with BPD exhibit other impulsive behaviors, such as excessive spending, binge eating, and risky sex. BPD often occurs together with other psychiatric problems, particularly bipolar disorder, depression, anxiety disorders, substance abuse, and other personality disorders.

Suicide

- In 2004, 32,439 (approximately 11 per 100,000) people died by suicide in the U.S.

- More than 90% of people who kill themselves have a diagnosable mental disorder, most commonly a depressive disorder or a substance abuse disorder.

- Suicide is the third leading cause of death for people age 15–24.

- Most people know someone who has committed suicide.

- Four times as many men as women die by suicide; however, women attempt suicide two to three times as often as men.

SCHIZOPHRENIA

- Schizophrenia is a chronic, severe, and disabling brain disorder that affects about 1.1 percent of the U.S. population age 18 and older in a given year. People with schizophrenia sometimes hear voices others don't hear, believe that others are broadcasting their thoughts to the world, or become convinced that others are plotting to harm them. These experiences can make them fearful and withdrawn and cause difficulties when they try to have relationships with others.

- Symptoms usually develop in men in their late teens or early twenties and women in the twenties and thirties, but in rare cases they can appear in childhood. They can include hallucinations, delusions, disordered thinking, movement disorders, flat affect, social withdrawal, and cognitive deficits.

SCHIZOPHRENIA (continued)

- Approximately 2.4 million American adults have schizophrenia, or about 1.1% of the population age 18 and older in a given year.
- Schizophrenia affects men and women with equal frequency.
- Schizophrenia often first appears in men in their late teens or early twenties. In contrast, women are generally affected in their twenties or early thirties.

ANXIETY DISORDERS INCLUDE:

- Approximately 40 million American adults ages 18 and older have an anxiety disorder or about 18.1% of people in this age group in a given year.
- Anxiety disorders frequently co-occur with depressive disorders, eating disorders, or substance abuse.
- Most people with one anxiety disorder also have another anxiety disorder. Nearly three-quarters of those with an anxiety disorder will have their first episode by age 21.5.
- Anxiety disorders are two times as prevalent in females as in males.

Panic Disorder

- People with panic disorder have feelings of terror that strike suddenly and repeatedly with no warning.
- Unexpected and repeated episodes of intense fear characterize it, accompanied by physical symptoms that may include chest pain or smothering sensations, heart palpitations, shortness of breath, dizziness, abdominal distress, a sense of unreality or fear of impending doom or loss of control.
- Approximately 6 million American adults ages 18 and older, or about 2.7% of people in this age group in a given year, have panic disorder.
- Panic disorder typically develops in early adulthood (median age of onset is 24), but the age of onset extends throughout adulthood.
- About one in three people with panic disorder develops *agoraphobia,* a condition in which the individual becomes afraid of being in any place or situation where escape might be difficult or help unavailable in the event of a panic attack.

Obsessive-Compulsive Disorder (OCD)

- Persistent, unwelcome thoughts or images may plague people with OCD, or the urgent need to engage in certain rituals.
- Recurrent, unwanted thoughts (obsessions) and/or repetitive behaviors (compulsions) characterize it. Repetitive behaviors such as hand washing, counting, checking, or cleaning are often performed with the hope of preventing obsessive thoughts or making them go away. Performing these so-called "rituals," however, provides only temporary relief, and not performing them markedly increases anxiety.

Obsessive-Compulsive Disorder (con't.)

- Approximately 2.2 million American adults age 18 and older have OCD or about 1.0% of people in this age group in a given year.
- The first symptoms of OCD often begin during childhood or adolescence; however, the median age of onset is 19.

Post-Traumatic Stress Disorder (PTSD)

- People with PTSD have persistent frightening thoughts and memories of their ordeal and feel emotionally numb, especially with people they were once close to. They may experience sleep problems, feel detached or numb, or be easily startled.
- This disorder can develop after exposure to a terrifying event or ordeal in which grave physical harm occurred or was threatened. Traumatic events that may trigger PTSD include violent personal assaults, natural or human-caused disasters, accidents, or military combat.
- Approximately 7.7 million American adults age 18 and older have PTSD or about 3.5% of people in this age group in a given year.
- PTSD can develop at any age, including childhood, but research shows that the median age of onset is 23 years.
- About 19 percent of Vietnam veterans experienced PTSD at some point after the war. The disorder also frequently occurs after violent personal assaults such as rape, mugging, or domestic violence; terrorism; natural or human-caused disasters; and accidents.

Generalized Anxiety Disorder (GAD)

- People with GAD can't seem to shake their concerns. Their worries are accompanied by physical symptoms, especially fatigue, headaches, muscle tension, muscle aches, difficulty swallowing, trembling, twitching, irritability, sweating, and hot flashes.
- Chronic anxiety, exaggerated worry, and tension characterize it, even when there is little or nothing to provoke it.
- Approximately 6.8 million American adults have GAD in a given year or about 3.1% of people age 18 and over.
- GAD can begin across the life cycle, though the median age of onset is 31 years old.
- GAD is defined as constant, exaggerated worrisome thoughts and tension about everyday routine life events and activities, lasting at least six months and accompanied by physical symptoms, such as fatigue, trembling, muscle tension, headache, or nausea. The person almost always anticipates the worst even though there is little reason to expect it.

Social Phobia

- People with social phobia have a persistent, intense, and chronic fear of being watched and judged by others and being embarrassed or humiliated by their own actions. Their fear may become so severe that it interferes with work, school, and other ordinary activities. Physical symptoms often accompany the intense anxiety of social phobia and include blushing, profuse sweating, trembling, nausea, and difficulty talking.

- Overwhelming anxiety and excessive self-consciousness in everyday social situations are characteristics. Social phobia can be limited to only one type of situation—such as a fear of speaking in formal or informal situations, or eating or drinking in front of others—or, in its most severe form, it may become so broad that a person experiences symptoms almost anytime he or she is around other people.

- Approximately 15 million American adults age 18 and over have social phobia or about 6.8% of people in this age group in a given year.

- Social phobia begins in childhood or adolescence, typically around 13 years of age.

Agoraphobia

- *Agoraphobia* involves intense fear and anxiety of any place or situation where escape might be difficult, leading to avoidance of such situations as being alone outside of the home, traveling in a car, bus, or airplane, or being in a crowded area.

- Approximately 1.8 million American adults age 18 and over have agoraphobia without a history of panic disorder or about 0.8% of people in this age group in a given year.

- The median age of onset of agoraphobia is 20 years of age.

Specific Phobia

- *Specific phobia* involves marked and persistent fear and avoidance of a specific object or situation.

- Approximately 19.2 million American adults age 18 and over have some type of specific phobia or about 8.7% of people in this age group in a given year.

- Specific phobia typically begins in childhood; the median age of onset is seven years.

EATING DISORDERS

- Extremes mark an eating disorder. It is present when a person experiences severe disturbances in eating behavior, such as extreme reduction of food intake or extreme overeating, or feelings of extreme distress or concern about body weight or shape.

- The three main types of eating disorders are anorexia nervosa, bulimia nervosa, and binge-eating disorder.

- Characteristics of *anorexia nervosa* are emaciation, a relentless pursuit of thinness and unwillingness to maintain a normal or healthy weight, a distortion of body image and intense fear of gaining weight, a lack of menstruation among girls and women, and extremely disturbed eating behavior. Some people with anorexia lose weight by dieting and exercising excessively; others lose weight by self-induced vomiting or misusing laxatives, diuretics, or enemas.

- Characteristics of *bulimia nervosa* are recurrent and frequent episodes of eating unusually large amounts of food (e.g., binge-eating) and feeling a lack of control over the eating. A type of behavior that compensates for the binge follows this binge-eating, such as purging (e.g., vomiting, excessive use of laxatives or diuretics), fasting, or excessive exercise.

- Characteristics of *binge-eating disorder* are recurrent binge-eating episodes during which a person feels a loss of control over his or her eating. Unlike bulimia, purging, excessive exercise, or fasting do not follow binge-eating disorders. As a result, people with binge-eating disorder often are overweight or obese. They also experience guilt, shame, or distress about the binge-eating, which can lead to more binge-eating.

- Females are much more likely than males to develop an eating disorder. Only an estimated 5 to 15% of people with anorexia or bulimia and an estimated 35 percent of those with binge-eating disorder are male.

- In their lifetime, an estimated 0.5% to 3.7% of females suffer from anorexia, and an estimated 1.1% to 4.2% suffer from bulimia.

- Community surveys have estimated that between 2% and 5% of Americans experience binge-eating disorder in a six-month period.

- The mortality rate among people with anorexia has been estimated at 0.56% per year, or approximately 5.6% per decade, which is about 12 times higher than the annual death rate due to all causes of death among females ages 15–24 in the general population.

- Researchers are unsure of the underlying causes and nature of eating disorders. Unlike a neurological disorder, which generally points to a specific lesion on the brain, an eating disorder likely involves abnormal activity distributed across brain systems. With increased recognition that mental disorders are brain disorders, more researchers are using tools from both modern neuroscience and modern psychology to better understand eating disorders.

ATTENTION DEFICIT HYPERACTIVITY DISORDER (ADHD)

- ADHD is one of the most common mental disorders that develop in children. Children with ADHD have impaired functioning in multiple settings, including home, school, and in relationships with peers. If untreated, the disorder can have long-term adverse effects into adolescence and adulthood.

- Symptoms of ADHD will appear over the course of many months, and include impulsiveness (a child who acts quickly without thinking first), hyperactivity (a child who can't sit still and who walks, runs, or climbs around when others are seated and talks when others are talking), and inattention (a child who daydreams or seems in another world and gets sidetracked by what is going on around him or her).

- ADHD, one of the most common mental disorders in children and adolescents, also affects an estimated 4.1% of adults, ages 18–44, in a given year.

- ADHD usually becomes evident in preschool or early elementary years. The median age of onset of ADHD is seven years, although the disorder can persist into adolescence and occasionally into adulthood.

AUTISM

- Autism Spectrum Disorders (ASD), also known as Pervasive Developmental Disorders (PDDs), cause severe and pervasive impairment in thinking, feeling, language, and the ability to relate to others. These disorders are usually first diagnosed in early childhood and range from a severe form, called autistic disorder, through pervasive development disorder not otherwise specified (PDD-NOS), to a much milder form, Asperger syndrome. They also include two rare disorders, Rett syndrome and childhood disintegrative disorder.

- Parents are usually the first to notice unusual behaviors in their child. In some cases, the baby seemed "different" from birth, unresponsive to people or focusing intently on one item for long periods of time. The first signs of an autism spectrum disorder can also appear in children who had been developing normally. When an affectionate, babbling toddler suddenly becomes silent, withdrawn, self-abusive, or indifferent to social overtures, something is wrong.

- Autism is part of a group of disorders called autism spectrum disorders (ASDs), also known as pervasive developmental disorders. ASDs range in severity, with autism being the most debilitating form, while other disorders, such as Asperger syndrome, produce milder symptoms.

- Estimating the prevalence of autism is difficult and controversial due to differences in identifying and defining cases, as well as differences in study methods, and changes in diagnostic criteria. A recent study reported the prevalence of autism in 3–10 year-olds to be about 3.4 cases per 1,000 children.

AUTISM (continued)

- Autism and other ASDs develop in childhood and generally become diagnosed by age three.

- Autism is about four times more common in boys than girls. Girls with the disorder, however, tend to have more severe symptoms and greater cognitive impairment.

ALZHEIMER'S DISEASE (AD)

- Dementia is a brain disorder that seriously affects a person's ability to carry out daily activities. The most common form of dementia among older people is Alzheimer's disease (AD), which initially involves the parts of the brain that control thought, memory, and language. Although scientists are learning more every day, right now they still do not know what causes AD, and there is no cure.

- AD is named after Dr. Alois Alzheimer, a German doctor. In 1906, Dr. Alzheimer noticed changes in the brain tissue of a woman who had died of an unusual mental illness. He found abnormal clumps (now called amyloid plaques) and tangled bundles of fibers (now called neurofibrillary tangles). Today, scientists consider these plaques and tangles in the brain signs of AD.

- Scientists also have found other brain changes in people with AD. Nerve cells die in areas of the brain that are vital to memory and other mental abilities, and connections between nerve cells are disrupted. There also are lower levels of some of the chemicals in the brain that carry messages back and forth between nerve cells. AD may impair thinking and memory by disrupting these messages.

- AD affects an estimated 4.5 million Americans. The number of Americans with AD has more than doubled since 1980.

- AD is the most common cause of dementia among people age 65 and older.

- Increasing age is the greatest risk factor for Alzheimer's. In most people with AD, symptoms first appear after age 65. One in 10 individuals over 65 and nearly half of those over 85 are affected. Rare, inherited forms of Alzheimer's disease can strike individuals as early as their 30s and 40s.

- From the time of diagnosis, people with AD survive about half as long as those of similar age without dementia. From the National Institute of Mental Health.

From the National Institute of Mental Health.

Online Assignment: Risks for Eating Disorders

Complete this assignment online. Go to:

www.grtep.com

Select >Chapter Content>Chapter 3>Enter your username and password

TIPS TO BECOMING MENTALLY HEALTHY

"The ability to be in the present moment is a major component of mental wellness."

— Abraham Maslow

- Take a break and "play." Give yourself a brief break from thinking about stress or all the work that you do.
- Plan your time wisely to help reduce stress levels.
- Spend time with others. Connecting with others on a regular basis is important to emotional well-being.
- Laugh every day. Laughing has positive effects on both mental and physical health.
- Find time to relax or to do something fun.
- Call or text a friend to share a funny story.
- Keep expectations of yourself and others realistic.
- Don't give up when you still have something to give.
- Limit daily caffeine, sugar, alcohol, and sodium intake as well as the use of stimulating drugs, which can cause added agitation.
- Watch a funny or uplifting movie.
- Choose to be good to yourself.
- Spend time alone. It is important to have some time by yourself to quietly reflect on the day's events, to plan for the future, and to count your blessings.
- Get plenty of sleep—and restful sleep at that.
- Try to find the answers within yourself. Identify what you need by listening to your own mind, body, and spirit.
- Find the best way for you to cope with stress, and make an honest attempt to try it.
- Seek the support and help of others or of professionals to protect your mental stability during stressful times.

Helpful Internet Sites

About.com Stress Management: stress.about.com
American Association for Suicide Prevention: afsp.org
American College of Sports Medicine: acsm.org
American Institute of Stress: stress.org
American Psychological Association: apa.org
Ask Dr. Weil: drweil.com
Center for Anxiety and Stress Treatment: stressrelease.com
Compassionate Friends (Grief): compassionatefriends.org
GriefNet: griefnet.org
Healthfinder: healthfinder.gov
HolisticOnline.com
How to Meditate: how-to-meditate.org
The Humor Project: humorproject.com
Mayo Clinic: mayoclinic.com
Meditation Center: meditationcenter.com
The Meditation Society of America: meditationsociety.com
Mind/Body Medical Institute: mbmi.org
National Institute of Mental Health: nimh.nih.gov
PsychWatch: psychwatch.com
Darrin Zeer/Relax Yoga: relaxyoga.com
RENEW- Center for Personal Recovery: renew.net
Stress. Depression, Anxiety, Sleep Problems and Drug Use: teachhealth.com
Substance Abuse & Mental Health Services Administration: mentalhealth.samhsa.gov
WebMD: webmd.com

References

About.com. What Is Learned Helplessness? psychology.about.com/od/lindex/f/earned-helplessness.htm accessed on May 24, 2012.

Aguilar, L. *The Community College: A New Beginning.* Fourth Edition. Managing the Stresses of Life as a College Student. Kendall Hunt Publishing Company (2005): 201; 205–207.

Berk, L. and Tan, S. Therapeutic Benefits of Laughter. *Humor and Health Journal* September/October: 1996.

Bounds, L. *Health and Fitness: A Guide to a Healthy Lifestyle.* Definition of Emotional Health. Kendall Hunt Publishing Company (2006): 2–3; Student Stress Scale: 7.

Cooper, C. *Keys to Excellence.* Seventh Edition. Time Management. Kendall Hunt Publishing Company (2004): 85–92; 83; 93–108.

Funk, G. et al. *Practical Approaches for Building Study Skills and Vocabulary.* Second Edition. Stressing the Point. Kendall Hunt Publishing Company (1996): Self-Esteem: 651–652.

Hettler, B. The National Wellness Institute. *The Six Dimensions of Wellness: Emotional Wellness.* www.nationalwellness.org accessed on 12.7.07.

HolisticOnline.com. *Therapeutic Benefits of Humor.* holisticonline.com/Humor_Therapy/humor_therapy_benefits.htm accessed on 2.10.08.

Holmes, T. and Rahe, R. Life's Event Scale. *Journal of Psychosomatic Research* 11 1967: 213.

Maglione, C. et al. *American College of Sports Medicine's Health & Fitness Journal.* Cortisol Connection: Tips on Managing Stress and Weight (2005): Volume 9, Issue 5: 21–22.

National Catholic Ministry to the Bereaved. *Fifty Ways to Help a Grieving Friend.* (2001): griefwork.org.

National Institute of Mental Health. The Numbers Count in America. nimh.nih.gov/health/publications/the-numbers-count-mental-disorders-in-america.shtml accessed on 2.1.08; Mental Health Topics. nimh.nih.gov/health/topics/index.shtml accessed on 2.4.08.

Nieman, D. *Fitness & Your Health.* Third Edition. Stress Management and Mental Health. Kendall Hunt Publishing Company (2007): 313–314; 314–320; 320–324; 324–334.

Robbins, G. et al. *A Wellness Way of Life.* 7th Edition. Common Signs of Stress. McGraw-Hill (2008): 323 and Are You at Risk for An Eating Disorder: 447.

Scott, E. *The Stress Management and Health Benefits of Laughter: The Laughing Cure.* (About.com Health's Disease and Condition content reviewed by S. Gans, MD) stress.about.com/od/stresshealth/a/laughter.htm accessed on 2.10.08.

Seligman, M. *Learned Optimism.* Learning to be Helpless. Pocket Books, division of Simon & Schuster, Inc. (1998): 17–30.

Selye, H. *Stress without Distress.* New American Library (1974).

Selye, H. *The Stress of Life.* (1956).

Stephens, T. Physical Activity and Mental Health in the United States and Canada: Evidence from Four Population Surveys. *Prev Med* 17 1988: 35–47.

U.S. Department of Health and Human Services. Substance Abuse and Mental Health Services Administration. *Resilience and Stress Management: Resilience.* http://www.samsha.gov/dtac.dhhis/dbhis_stress/resilience.htm accessed on 1.11.12.

U.S. Department of Health and Human Services. Substance Abuse and Mental Health Services Administration. *How to Deal with Grief.* mentalhealth.samhsa.gov/publications/allpubs/KEN-01-0104/default.asp accessed on 2.18.08.

WebMD.com. Stress Management Health Center. webmd.com/balance/stress-management/stress-management-effects-of-stress accessed on 2.1.08.

WebMd.com Health & Diet. *Getting Over Overeating: 5 Ways to Break the Emotional Cycle.* webmd.com/diet/features/getting-over-overeating accessed on 2.27.08.

Wellness for Healthy Positive Living. Emotional Wellness Inventory and Emotional Wellness Facts & Tips. for.gov.bc.ca/hrb/hw/index.htm accessed on 2.4.08.

CHAPTER 4

Social
Wellness

"When an experience is viewed in a certain way, it presents nothing but doorways into the domain of the soul."

— Jon Kabat-Zinn

The objectives in this chapter include the understanding of:

- The meaning of social wellness and its direct application to you
- Attitude
- Personality and learning to work with other personalities
- The communication process and the communication styles
- Civility
- Multiculturalism/diversity in your life
- Friendships and relationships and how they affect your life

Online Reminders

- Complete the poll question before the next class meeting.
- Complete the interactive activities for this chapter.
- Complete all of the online assignments in this chapter.

Social wellness—are we talking about how to generate a conversation with someone? How many friends you have? How many parties you go to every weekend? Your rating for giving a presentation in a class? How healthy your relationship is with your parents, boyfriends, or girlfriends? Well, yes. You can include all of these your definition of social wellness but—hey, it's the theme—there's always more to it!

Social wellness is the contribution you make to your surroundings and community by becoming more aware of your importance in society and the impact you have on multiple environments. It is the discovery of your own power to make healthier choices when building friendships and relationships as well as your creation of better living and community spaces and more effective ways to communicate with others. The National Institute of Wellness states that social wellness follows these tenets (Hettler):

1. It is better to contribute to the common welfare of our community than to think only of ourselves.

2. It is better to live in harmony with others and our environment than to live in conflict with them.

PRE-CLASS SURVEY: Take your social wellness survey before your next class meeting and identify your level of social wellness. Circle either Yes or No, total up each column, and check your score.

I am striving to maintain a network of supportive friends, family, and social contacts.	YES	NO
I am accepting of the diversity in myself and others.	YES	NO
I know the qualities I am looking for in a significant relationship.	YES	NO
I am aware of and able to set and respect my own and others' boundaries.	YES	NO
I volunteer for activities or organizations at school, and I am an active member of my community at home.	YES	NO
I am told I have good communication skills and that I am a good listener.	YES	NO
I am aware of how my attitude and personality impacts my reactions and responses to others.	YES	NO
I know the qualities I am looking for in a meaningful friendship.	YES	NO
I engage in activities that are unfamiliar or different (e.g., talking with people from cultures different from my own and engaging in diverse cultural experiences).	YES	NO
I am aware of my professor's personality and how it may be similar or different than my own.	YES	NO
I am told that I am setting a good example to others or to those who look up to me.	YES	NO
I focus on talking to myself in a positive and not negative way.	YES	NO
TOTAL		

WHAT YOUR TOTAL MEANS:

9 or more Yes answers	Excellent	Your habits are positively enhancing your health.
6–8 Yes answers	Average	You are obviously trying but there is room to improve.
5 or less Yes answers	Not So Good	There is a need for improvement in your daily habits.

SOURCE: "Wellness for Healthy Positive Living." *Social Wellness/Inventory* for.gov.bc.ca/hrb/hw/index.htm

ATTITUDE

❝*The longer I live, the more I realize the impact of attitude on my life. This is so because the remarkable thing is we have a choice everyday regarding the attitude we will embrace for that day. I am convinced that life is 10% what happens to me and 90% how I react to it. And so it is with you, we are in charge of our attitudes.*❞

— Charles Swindoll

What's in an attitude? Your attitude is something that's developed over time. Yes, you were born with certain personality characteristics, but you also were exposed to various factors in your daily surroundings growing up that helped you develop your attitude. According to John C. Maxwell, while these factors continually impact people, they make the greatest impression during the following times of life:

STAGES	FACTORS	WHAT IT MEANS
Pre-birth	Inherent personality/temperament	Who I am
Birth	Environment	What's around me
Ages 1–6	Word expression, adult acceptance/affirmation	What I hear and what I feel
Ages 6–10	Self-image, exposure to new experiences	How I see myself and opportunities for growth
Ages 11–21	Peers, physical appearance	Who influences me and how I look to others
Ages 21–61	Marriage, family, job, success, adjustments, assessment of life	My security and status

Maxwell, John C. *Attitude 101.* Thomas Nelson, Inc. 2003: 29.

Attitude shapes who you are, your outlook on life, and your potential for success. It can influence your personal wellness and how those dimensions are working in your life. It also can influence how you choose to respond to situations in your life. Your attitude influences your relationships with people. In life, you form relationships with people and through those you build personal and professional friendships and working relationships. To be fulfilled and successful, you will need to figure out a way to form a healthy attitude and, therefore, healthy relationships.

Consider your proposed professional path for a moment. "The Stanford Research Institute states that the money you make in any endeavor is determined 12.5% by knowledge and 87.5% by your ability to deal with people." (Maxwell) Hmmm. . . . intriguing.

ASSIGNMENT: Evaluate your present attitude.

1. What attitudes make you feel the most negative about yourself?

_____

_____

2. What attitudes cause you the most problems when dealing with other people?

_____

3. What thoughts consistently control your mind?

_____

_____

4. What do your feelings tell you about how your attitude should be?

_____

_____

5. What must I do to change the negative thoughts or attitudes in my life?

_____

_____

6. Can I make an honest attempt to change some of the thoughts and attitudes listed above for the better?

_____

_____

ELIMINATE THESE WORDS COMPLETELY	MAKE THESE WORDS A PART OF YOUR VOCABULARY
I can't	I can
If	I will
Doubt	Expect the best
I don't think	I know
I don't have the time	I will make the time
Maybe	Positively
I'm afraid of	I am confident
I don't believe	I do believe
(minimize) I	(promote) You
It's impossible	All things are possible

Maxwell, J. *Attitude 101*. The Impact of an Attitude and The Formation of an Attitude. Thomas Nelson, Inc: (2003): 45; 48–49.

PERSONALITY

> **"** *Always be a first-rate version of yourself instead*
> *of a second-rate version of somebody else.* **"**
>
> — Judy Garland

According to the work of Carl Jung, Katharine Briggs, and Isabel Myers, personality has four dimensions:

1. Extroversion or Introversion
2. Sensing or Intuitive
3. Thinking or Feeling
4. Judging or Perceptive

Online Assignment: Personality Quiz

Complete this assignment online. Go to:
www.grtep.com
Select >Chapter Content>Chapter 4>Enter your username and password

Each personality type has a natural preference for how to learn. You will dive deeper into your personality types and how this applies to your learning style when reading about Intellectual Wellness in Chapter 6. (Fralick, 240)

Understanding Your Professor's Personality

Making the effort to understand how your professor operates is key to your success in college. Different personality types have different expectations of their teachers. Extraverts want faculty who encourage class discussion. Introverts want faculty who give clear lectures. Sensing types want faculty who give clear assignments. Intuitive types want faculty who encourage independent thinking. Thinking types want faculty who make logical presentations. Feeling types want faculty who establish personal rapport with students. Judging types want faculty to be organized. Perceptive types want faculty to be entertaining and inspiring.

What can you do if your personality and your professor's personality are different? This is often the case by the way. First, try to understand the professor's personality type on the first day of class by examining class materials and observing his or her manner of presentation. If you understand the professor's personality type, you will know what to expect. Next, try to appreciate what the professor has to offer. You may need to adapt your style to fit. If you are a perceptive type, be careful to meet the due dates or your assignments. Experiment with different study techniques so that you can learn the material presented.

You could call college a "dress rehearsal" for life after you graduate. Most students will agree that their objectives in college are to decide on a major, to try hard and learn as much as possible, to make friendships and new relationships, to get involved in extracurricular activities, and to graduate. No surprise there, but what you do now, and how, during college, will help lay a solid foundation for you to build on for the rest of your life. Make it count now, and continue to make it count later! Various social situations in college, from getting along with your professors to getting along with your roommates, will help you be better prepared for the working world when you face being on a team with co-workers or dealing with a demanding boss. The more you dive in to figure things out now, the better off you will be when you graduate.

(Adapted from Fralick)

COMMUNICATION

❝The single biggest problem in communication
is the illusion that it has taken place.❞

— George Bernard Shaw

As human beings, our lives revolve around our interpersonal relationships with others in our environment—family members, friends, significant others, co-workers, teachers, classmates, service personnel, supervisors, and many others with whom we interact on a daily basis. We solve problems, socialize, shop, and work with others by using communication skills. Communication is a two-way process involving both a sender and receiver.

> Sender = expresses feelings, ideas, or needs and sends a message
> Receiver/Listener = expected to respond in some way and gives feedback

The communication process is interactive—we act as both the sender and the receiver/listener during the course of any conversation. The message is carried and the feedback is sent both verbally and nonverbally.

Effective communication is the key to happiness and success—personally and professionally. The communication process begins at birth when a newborn's cry communicates a need for attention and results in his or her being fed, diapered, or held. As a child grows and matures, the level of communication becomes more advanced as his or her language abilities develop. As adults, we are capable of developing deep, personal relationships based primarily upon our ability to communicate with one another.

We also use our interpersonal skills to handle problems and conflicts in our daily lives that require the use of effective communication skills to solve problems. Unfortunately, many people never develop strong interpersonal skills and are unable to communicate effectively with others. However, developing effective communication skills can improve our relationships with others—at home, in school, at the workplace, in social or business situations, and in everyday interactions with the general public. To do so, we must develop specific skills in both parts of the communication process as the sender and receiver. (Aguilar, 183)

Strategies for becoming an effective listener

- Listen—don't talk. Allow the sender to communicate the message without interruption. Concentrate on the message rather than on trying to plan your responses to the message.
- Beware of non-verbal messages you send while listening.
- Consider your response before beginning to speak.
- Do not interrupt.
- Provide feedback by first summarizing what you heard like, "If I understand you correctly . . ." This allows you to clarify your understanding and to keep communication going.
- Respond in a non-judgmental manner.
- Respond to the sender's feelings as well as to his or her words.
- Be willing to acknowledge the speaker's views and his or her right to have them, even though they may differ from your own.

Strategies for becoming an effective sender

- Take responsibility for your ideas/feelings.
- Use "I" messages to get your point across without blaming, criticizing, or making personal attacks upon your listener. "You" messages make the receiver/listener defensive.
- Be aware of your nonverbal messages whether they are the tone of your voice, your body language, or avoiding eye contact.
- Clarify what you want to say in your own mind before beginning to speak.
- Be sensitive to issue appropriateness and timing. You don't want to show lack of care or concern.
- Avoid making demands using statements such as "you should" or "you have to."

Nonverbal Communication

Body language often nonverbally and silently communicates whether or not we're truly listening. It has been said that 90% of communication is nonverbal because human body language often communicates stronger and truer messages than spoken language. In the case of listening, our body language may be the best way to communicate interest in the speaker's words and interest in the person speaking. Similarly, if we're speaking, awareness of our listener's body language can also send us important clues about whether we are holding or losing interest. A good mnemonic device (memory-improvement method) for remembering the nonverbal signals we should send others while listening is the acronym, SOFTEN. This stands for:

S = **Smile**—periodically, but not continually as if your smile is permanently (and artificially) painted on your face.

O = **Open posture**—not a closed posture with arms crossed or hands folded together.

F = **Forward leaning**—as opposed to leaning back as if you're psychoanalyzing or evaluating.

T = **Touch** a light touch on the arm or hand can be a good way to communicate warmth

E = **Eye contact**—periodically, rather than little or no eye contact because this suggests you'd like the conversation to end; but don't make continuous or excessive eye contact because someone could interpret this as staring or glaring.

N = **Nod your head** slowly and every once in a while, not repeatedly and rapidly, because this sends the message that you want the speaker to hurry up and finish so you can start talking.

(Cuseo, 357–358)

BARRIERS TO COMMUNICATION

> **"**We were given mouths that close and ears that don't.
> That should tell us something.**"**
>
> — Unknown

Even when people want to communicate, barriers may exist that can cause a breakdown in the communication process. These barriers are usually internal blockers that can prevent us from either sending or receiving a clean, undistorted message. Common blockers are:

1. **Preoccupation/distractedness.** If you have something on your mind, you will not be able to listen effectively. Reading or doing something else while trying to listen, thinking about what else you need to do today, or worrying about a financial problem are just a few examples of ways that can lower your concentration. Being unable to give the speaker your full attention can cause misunderstandings or a total breakdown in the communication attempt.

2. **Stereotyping.** Stereotypes are fixed ideas about people as part of a group rather than considering each person as an individual. Ethnic and gender differences account for many stereotypes, but other differences such as political, sexual, or religious preferences may also result in stereotyping. Persons with disabilities, people whose body sizes fall outside the socially accepted norms, and others who exhibit some difference are all targets for stereotypes. Making false assumptions always interferes with clear, accurate communication. Stereotypes are also a form of discrimination and, as such, inhibit the communication process.

3. **Emotional blocks—anger/defensiveness/grief.** When either the sender or the receiver is attempting to communicate while angry or defensive, the communication attempt will most likely not be successful. An angry sender often communicates that anger through facial expressions and body language or through tone of voice, even though the words are not necessarily argumentative. Angry senders frequently use exaggerations like "always" and "never" to justify their attacks, often eliminating all possibilities of cooperation. An angry or defensive listener is likely to "tune out" much of the speaker's words or react in a hostile manner during the communication attempt. Grief, whether suffered by the sender or receiver, is also likely to cause a breakdown in the communication process.

4. **Past experience.** All of our past experiences also play a part in "filtering" our communication efforts with others. Students with previous negative experiences speaking in front of groups may resist their advisor's attempt to register them for speech class even though they require it. Boyfriends, girlfriends, or spouses may remember and bring up past difficulties or problems in the relationships whenever new disagreement arises.

These kinds of barriers can make effective communication extremely hard and sometimes impossible. Try to eliminate barriers you may bring to the process. Again, communication is one of the keys to your success in life whether in school work, personal friendships, relationships, family interaction, or the business world. Don't destroy your friendship with someone you care about just to win an argument. Be aware! Bad communication can damage relationships just as good communication can enhance them. (Aguilar, 185-186)

Negative Self-talk

Self-talk is what you say to yourself. It is the stream of consciousness or the little voice in your head. This self-talk affects how you communicate with others. If your self-talk is negative, you will have lower self-esteem and find it more difficult to communicate with others. There are some common irrational beliefs that lead to negative self-talk. Becoming aware of these beliefs can help you avoid them.

I have to be perfect.

If you believe this, you will think you have to be a perfect communicator and deliver flawless speeches. Since this goal is unattainable, it causes undue stress and anxiety and takes up much energy.

REDIRECTION: *Everyone makes mistakes! When you stop trying to be perfect and accept yourself as you are, you can begin to relax and work on the areas needing improvement.*

I need the approval of everyone.

If you believe this, you will find it necessary to have the approval of almost everyone and spend much energy gaining approval from others. If you do not obtain approval, you may feel nervous, embarrassed, or apologetic.

REDIRECTION: *It is not possible to win the approval of everyone because each person is unique. If you constantly seek approval, you will sacrifice your own values and what you think is right just to please others.*

That's always the way it is.

If you believe this, you are making generalizations of previous events and are using them to predict the future or exaggerate shortcomings.

REDIRECTION: *Remember that with a positive attitude, things can change in the future. Just because it was once that way doesn't mean it has to be the same way in the future. Be aware of "always" and "never" statements.*

You made me feel that way.

Your own self-talk, rather than the actions of others, is what causes emotions.

REDIRECTION: *No one can make you feel a certain way—YOU feel a certain way based on what you say to yourself about an event or a comment. You are always in control of how you CHOOSE to react.*

I'm helpless.

If you believe this, you think things are beyond your control and will be unlikely to do something to make the situation better.

REDIRECTION: *Believe that there is a way to change and you can make your life better by doing so.*

If something bad can happen, it will happen.

If you expect the worst, you may take actions that make it happen.

REDIRECTION: *There will be times when you make a poor speech, get turned down for a job, or have a relationship fail. Learn from these situations and make the change within yourself to do better next time.*

(Fralick, 353–354)

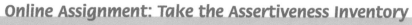

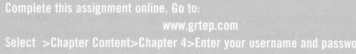

Online Assignment: Take the Assertiveness Inventory

Complete this assignment online. Go to:
www.grtep.com
Select >Chapter Content>Chapter 4>Enter your username and password

COMMUNICATION STYLES

❝*Art to me is about developing your own style of communication. And technology is about communication. So to integrate the two just seems logical.*❞

— James Clar

Let's compare these three styles: Passive, Assertive, and Aggressive:

	PASSIVE	**ASSERTIVE**	**AGGRESSIVE**
Statements	Hints; Uses indirect messages	Makes clear, concise statements	Speaks for self and others
Social Behavior	Denies own needs and feelings; Lets others choose; Puts self down; Manipulates others into feeling guilty; Absolves self or responsibility for own actions	Respects others; Negotiates conflicts; Chooses for self; Accepts strengths and weaknesses or mistakes; Feels good about one's self	Disregards the rights and needs of others; Chooses for self and others; Blocks communication; May use verbal/physical abuse
Voice	Weak; Quiet; Child-like	Firm; Strong	Loud; Angry
Body Language	Poor eye contact; Moves away and distances self from others; Smiles are forced; Uses few gestures	Uses good eye contact; Relaxed; Uses gestures; Face matches mood; Confident appearance	Moves into others' space; Overreacts
Possible Consequences of Behavior	May feel hurt, angry, anxious; Lack of respect; Others feel guilty or superior; Outcome—needs not met; Others may take advantage	Respect self; Others respect your honesty; Trust; Outcome—needs may or may not get met; Mutual respect	May feel lonely, angry, anxious; Lack of self-respect; Others may feel hurt or defensive; Outcome—may get needs met at the time; Others may avoid you or seek revenge

Which one best describes your communication style? _____

So Why Does the Assertive Communication Approach Result in More Open Communication and Better Interpersonal Relationships?

Because it allows us to express our feelings, needs, opinions, or preferences in a directed and honest manner without threatening, harming, "putting down," or manipulating others. This communication style does NOT guarantee that our needs and wishes will always be met but simply ensures that we have expressed those needs in an appropriate manner. In other words, the rights of both parties in the communication exchange have been acknowledged and protected.

Developing assertive communication behaviors is a learned skill. We are not born being assertive communicators, and we do not generally behave in an assertive manner in all situations. Our ability to practice assertive communication may also change depending on the specific situations. We may feel comfortable expressing positive feelings—giving and receiving compliments, initiating conversations, and expressing affection and love. On the other hand, we may not feel comfortable when we have to request help or make requests of others, when we want to express personal opinions or when we feel annoyance or anger with others. (Aguilar, 188)

To increase our assertiveness levels, we need to consciously practice using assertive communications skills. Easy enough—right?! One way to better our skills is to practice using the "I" message format mentioned earlier under "Strategies for becoming an effective sender" on page 193. "I" messages:

1. Identify your feelings about the conflict/problem.
2. Describe in a nonjudgmental way the specific action or behavior which took place.
3. Focus on the effect or consequence that the action or behavior has on you.

"I" Messages Increase Your Communication and Get Cooperation from the Other Person

When you use "I" messages, you take ownership of your emotions and actions and may also include a statement about what you plan to do about the problem. This approach cannot guarantee a behavior change by the other person, but it lets you control your response to the situation.

"You" Messages Attack the Other Person

They put all the control or ownership of the situation on him or her. They are not likely to make the other person feel sorry about his offenses, which is what you really want.

Instead, that person will probably attack back with insults or complaints about you. An argument will likely happen, and your relationship will suffer.

ASSIGNMENT: Using "I" messages requires practice. Write in your own constructive and appropriate "I" messages as a way of improving each "you" message below.

Instead of this "You" Message: Use this "I" Message:

"Shut up! You always interrupt me."   _____

"You're so lazy! Find someone else to help you." _____

"You never let me know what your plans are!"   _____

"Hey Prof. The grade you gave me on this paper
really sucked!"   _____

"You are always late picking me up from
class—how annoying!"   _____

Here are examples of "I" statements that you can used to express various feelings:

To express anger	To express sadness
I don't like . . .	I feel disappointed . . .
I feel frustrated . . .	I am sad that . . .
I am angry that . . .	I feel hurt . . .
I feel annoyed . . .	I wanted . . .
I want . . .	I want . . .

To express fear	To say you are sorry
I feel worried . . .	I feel embarrassed . . .
I am afraid . . .	I am sorry . . .
I feel scared . . .	I feel ashamed . . .
I do not want . . .	I didn't want . . .
I need . . . , I want . . .	I want . . .

From *College & Career Success,* 3rd edition by Marsha Fralick. Copyright © 2006 by Kendall Hunt Publishing Company. Used with permission.

Assertiveness not only needs practice to become a better communicator, but it comes with a bill of rights and a set of responsibilities. Without respecting and abiding to these rights and responsibilities, you forfeit all of your hard work on the practice of assertive communication. One doesn't come without the other!

ASSERTIVENESS BILL OF RIGHTS	ASSERTIVENESS RESPONSIBILITIES
1. You have the right to request help, assistance, or favors from others without feeling guilty.	1. You have the responsibility to accept "NO" as an answer to your requests for help, assistance, or a favor. Just as you have the right to refuse requests without feeling guilty, you have the responsibility to accept a similar reply from others.
2. You have the right to refuse requests from others without feeling guilty.	2. You have the responsibility to treat others fairly and to make sure that your actions do not hurt or harm others.
3. You have the right to be treated fairly as a person, to make your own decisions, and to have others respect those decisions.	3. You have the responsibility to treat others in a courteous manner just as you expect courteous behavior from others.
4. You have the right to maintain privacy about issues that you feel are private.	4. You have the responsibility to respect the privacy of others.
5. You have the right to express your personal opinions and to expect others to listen to your opinions without being judgmental or making negative comments.	5. You have the responsibility to respect opinions that may differ from your own and to avoid trying to force your opinions on others.
6. You have the right to express justified anger with others as long as you treat them with respect and express your feelings in a non-threatening way.	6. You have the responsibility to take "ownership" of your feelings and to avoid blaming, accusing, or putting down others.
7. You have the right to make mistakes. Becoming more assertive is a learned skill, and your comfort level in using assertive responses will increase with practice.	7. Treat others as though you were one of them.

(Aguilar, 190)

HELPFUL COMMUNICATION IN CRISIS

❝ *When written in Chinese, the word 'crisis' is composed of two characters. One represents danger and the other, opportunity.* ❞

— President John F. Kennedy

Most people have been in a situation where their friends or family are in distress and need immediate help. If you become aware of a dangerous or critical situation, seek professional help. Go to your college counseling center, your doctor, community service organization, or your personal confidant for help and direction. Here are some GENERAL ideas for being a helpful listener to someone in crisis:

- Let the person talk. Talking helps to clarify things.

- Paraphrase or feed back meaning.

- Avoid being critical. Comments such as "You asked for it" or "I told you so" do not help but can make the person angry or make the situation worse.

- Help the person analyze the situation and come up with alternatives for solving the problem.

- Share your experiences but resist giving advice.

- Ask questions to clarify the situation.

- Offer support. Say "I'm here if you need me" or "I care about you."

- Let the person express his or her feelings. It is not helpful to say "Don't feel sad." A person may need to feel sad and deal with the situation. The emotion can motivate change.

- Don't minimize the situation. Saying "It's only a grade" minimizes the situation. It might not be important to the listener, but it is causing pain for the person. Give him or her time to gain perspective on the problem.

- Replace pity with understanding. It is not helpful to say "You poor thing."

From *College & Career Success,* 3rd edition by Marsha Fralick. Copyright © 2006 by Kendall Hunt Publishing Company. Used with permission.

CIVILITY

> *"These small indignities and minor cruelties take a toll. They add to the burden of stress and fatigue that is already present in the workplace, and they have real consequences on the everyday lives of workers."*
>
> — P.M. Forni, Cofounder of the Johns Hopkins Civility Project

Dr. P.M. Forni, cofounder of the Johns Hopkins Civility Project, wrote *Choosing Civility* among other publications. Participants in Dr. Forni's workshops write on a sheet of paper what civility means to them. In no particular order, here are a number of key civility-related notions he has collected over the years from those sheets:

Respect for others	Community service
Care	Tact
Consideration	Equality
Courtesy	Sincerity
Golden rule	Morality
Respect of others' feelings	Honesty
Niceness	Awareness
Politeness	Trustworthiness
Respect of others' opinions	Friendship
Maturity	Table manners
Kindness	Moderation
Manners	Listening
Being accommodating	Compassion
Fairness	Being agreeable
Decency	Going out of one's way
Self-control	Friendliness
Concern	Lending a hand
Justice	Propriety
Tolerance	Abiding by rules
Selflessness	Good citizenship
Etiquette	Peace

This list tells us that

- Civility is complex.

- Civility is good.

- Whatever civility might be, it has to do with courtesy, politeness, and good manners.

- Civility belongs in the realm of ethics.

Courtesy, politeness, manners, and civility are all, in essence, forms of awareness. Being civil means being constantly aware of others and weaving restraint, respect, and consideration on into the very fabric of this awareness. Civility is a form of goodness; it is gracious goodness. But it is not just an attitude of benevolent and thoughtful relation to other individuals; it also entails an active interest in the well-being of our communities and even a concern for the health of the planet on which we live.

Civility, courtesy, politeness, and *manners* are not perfect synonyms, as etymology clearly shows.

Courtesy is connected to *court* and evoked in the past the superior qualities of character and bearing expected in those close to royalty. Etymologically, when we are courteous we are courtierlike. Although today we seldom make this connection, courtesy still suggests excellence and elegance in bestowing respect and attention. It can also suggest deference and formality.

To understand *politeness*, we must think of *polish*. The polite are those who have polished their behavior. They have put some effort into bettering themselves, but they are sometimes looked upon with suspicion. Expressions such as "polite reply," "polite lie," and "polite applause" connect politeness to hypocrisy. It is true that the polite are inclined to veil their own feelings to spare someone else's. Self-serving lying, however, is always beyond the pale of politeness. If politeness is a quality of character (alongside courtesy, good manners, and civility), it cannot become a flaw. A suave manipulator may appear to be polite but is not.

When we think of good *manners* we often think of children taught to say 'please,' 'thank you' and chew with their mouths closed. This may prevent looking at manners with the attention they deserve. *Manner* comes from *mantis*, the Latin word for "hand." *Manner* and *manners* have to do with the use of our hands. A manner is the way something is done, a mode of handling. Thus *manners* came to refer to behavior in social interaction—the way we handle the encounter between Self and Other. We have good manners when we use our hands well—when we handle others with care. When we rediscover the connection of *manner* with *hand*, the hand that, depending on our will and sensitivity, can strike or lift, hurt or soothe, destroy or heal, we understand the importance—for children and adults alike—of having good manners.

Civility's defining characteristic is its ties to *city* and *society*. The word derives from the Latin *civitas*, which means "city," especially in the sense of civic community. *Civitas* is the same word from which *civilization* comes. The age-old assumption behind civility is that life in the city has a civilizing effect. The city is where we enlighten our intellect and refine our social skills. And as we are shaped by the city, we learn to give of ourselves for the sake of the city. Although we can describe the civil as courteous, polite, and well mannered, etymology reminds us that they are also supposed to be good citizens and good neighbors.

Dr. Forni's 25 rules of considerate conduct are as follows:

1. Pay Attention
2. Acknowledge Others
3. Think the Best
4. Listen
5. Be Inclusive

6. Speak Kindly

7. Don't Speak Ill

8. Accept and Give Praise

9. Respect Even a Subtle "No"

10. Respect Others' Opinions

11. Mind Your Body

12. Be Agreeable

13. Keep It Down (and Rediscover Silence)

14. Respect Other People's Time

15. Respect Other People's Space

16. Apologize Earnestly

17. Assert Yourself

18. Avoid Personal Questions

19. Care for Your Guests

20. Be a Considerate Guest

21. Think Twice Before Asking for Favors

22. Refrain from Idle Complaints

23. Accept and Give Constructive Criticism

24. Respect the Environment and Be Gentle to Animals

25. Don't Shift Responsibility and Blame

In 2007, Diane Millett, J.D. formed "CivilSpace," a part of her practice that promotes civility as an antidote to harassment through various programs, activities and writings. Millett discusses five hypothesis for incivility:

Five Hypotheses for Incivility

- Some people treat other people with a profound lack of respect.

- No matter how many laws provide protection, people will find another basis on which to demean others.

- Harassment begins with demeaning, disrespectful behavior.

- If we are more civil to one another there will be less harassment.

- Civility is the antidote to harassment.

CivilSpace is the psychological and physical space created around a person, department, or an organization practicing civility. CivilSpace is a registered trade name for workshops, writings and activities by Diane E. Millett, J.D., in the furtherance of civility to reduce harassment in the workplace. Millett suggests these tips for practicing civility and avoiding harassment:

I. **How We Treat Others**

   A. Our treatment of others suffers when:

   1. We constantly feel that we need to prove ourselves and compete

   2. We are poorly trained in self-restraint

   3. We are used to seeing others as means to the satisfaction of our needs and desires rather than ends in themselves

   4. We are overly concerned about financial gain and professional achievement

   5. We are constantly besieged by stress and fatigue

Behaviors Creating UncivilSpace

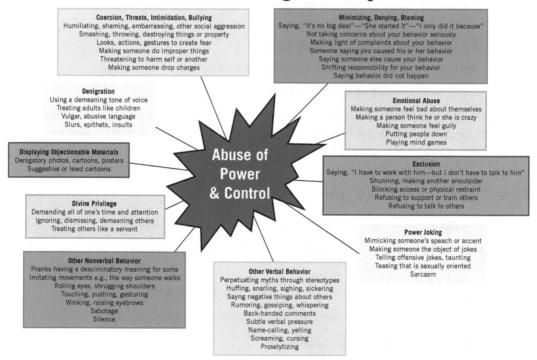

Coercion, Threats, Intimidation, Bullying
Humiliating, shaming, embarrassing, other social aggression
Smashing, throwing, destroying things or property
Looks, actions, gestures to create fear
Making someone do improper things
Threatening to harm self or another
Making someone drop charges

Minimizing, Denying, Blaming
Saying, "It's no big deal"—"She started it"—"I only did it because"
Not taking concerns about your behavior seriously
Making light of complaints about your behavior
Someone saying you caused his or her behavior
Saying someone else cause your behavior
Shifting responsibility for your behavior
Saying behavior did not happen

Denigration
Using a demeaning tone of voice
Treating adults like children
Vulgar, abusive language
Slurs, epithets, insults

Emotional Abuse
Making someone feel bad about themselves
Making a person think he or she is crazy
Making someone feel guily
Putting people down
Playing mind games

Displaying Objectionable Materials
Derogatory photos, cartoons, posters
Suggestive or lewd cartoons

Abuse of Power & Control

Exclusion
Saying, "I have to work with him—but I don't have to talk to him"
Shunning, making another anoutsider
Blocking access or physical restraint
Refusing to support or train others
Refusing to talk to others

Divine Privilege
Demanding all of one's time and attention
Ignoring, dismissing, demeaning others
Treating others like a servant

Power Joking
Mimicking someone's speach or accent
Making someone the object of jokes
Telling offensive jokes, taunting
Teasing that is sexually oriented
Sarcasm

Other Nonverbal Behavior
Pranks having a desciminatory meaning for some
Imitating movements e.g., the way someone walks
Rolling eyes, shrugging shoulders
Touching, pushing, gesturing
Winking, raising eyebrows
Sabotage
Silence

Other Verbal Behavior
Perpetuating myths through stereotypes
Huffing, snarling, sighing, sickering
Sayng negative things about others
Rumoring, gossiping, whispering
Back-handed comments
Subtle verbal pressure
Name-calling, yelling
Screaming, cursing
Proselytizing

6. We are surrounded by strangers who will remain strangers
7. We take everything personally
8. We are insecure about our competence or talent
9. We feel threatened by those around us and are determined to defend our territory from encroachment
10. We are in the grip of jealousy or envy
11. We feel that life is or others are unfair to us

B. To be at your best with others:

1. Think of yourself as a good and accomplished person who does not have to prove his or her worth all the time
2. Exercise restraint and practice empathy
3. See others as ends in themselves
4. Look at financial gain and professional achievement as means rather than ends
5. Defend yourself from toxic stress
6. Get to know the people around you
7. Do not shift the burden of your insecurity onto others in the form of hostility
8. Ask yourself, is this merely self-serving or is it the right thing to do?
9. Consider the consequences the action you are about to take will have on others
10. Wonder whether for others your presence is preferable to your absence
11. In a challenging situation (confronting an angry colleague or customer, for instance) imagine that you are being videotaped and that your video will be used to train others in handling such situation

II. On Being Accountable to Yourself

A. When facing a choice, choose not what makes you feel good now, but what will make you glad with your choice ten minutes from now, tomorrow, and next year. Wisdom is acting in a way that makes you feel good later.

B. Think before acting. Step outside yourself and see yourself in action. Ask yourself:

1. Am I doing this just because it feels good or is it also the right thing to do? Always be aware of the difference between what feels good and what is right.

2. How is what I am about to do going to affect those around me? What are the consequences of my actions?

3. Would I like it if someone did that to me?

4. Am I manipulating this person?

Adapted from the work of P.M. Forni, author of *Choosing Civility, The Civility Solution and The Thinking Life.* Reprinted by permission.

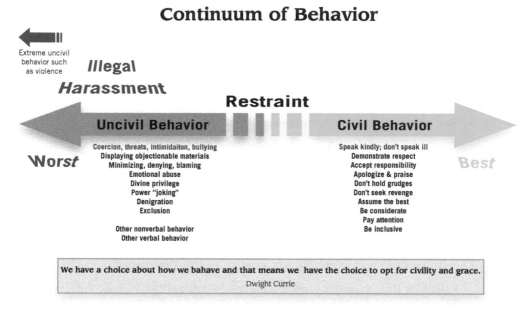

Continuum of Behavior

Extreme uncivil behavior such as violence

Illegal

Harassment

Restraint

Uncivil Behavior   **Civil Behavior**

Worst   **Best**

Coercion, threats, intimidaiton, bullying
Displaying objectionable materials
Minimizing, denying, blaming
Emotional abuse
Divine privilege
Power "joking"
Denigration
Exclusion

Other nonverbal behavior
Other verbal behavior

Speak kindly; don't speak ill
Demonstrate respect
Accept responsibility
Apologize & praise
Don't hold grudges
Don't seek revenge
Assume the best
Be considerate
Pay attention
Be inclusive

We have a choice about how we bahave and that means we have the choice to opt for civility and grace.
Dwight Currie

MULTICULTURALISM/DIVERSITY

> **“**You can't be beautiful and hate.**”**
>
> — Bess Myerson

In a pluralistic society, differences exist among and between various groups of people (e.g., ethnic, racial, religious, gender, sexual orientation, physical, and other groupings). While living in a pluralistic society can create tension as various groups attempt to sustain and develop their traditional cultures or special interests within the confines of a common society, the experience can also create a rich source of energy that can fuel the creative potential of a society and advance it culturally and democratically. To fully develop as a person requires awareness of both the common threads that hold people together as a community, a nation, and a world *AND* the unique threads of various hues and textures that complete the tapestry called humanity.

Multiculturalism is a philosophical belief based on ideals of social justice and equity that recognizes not only that diversity does exist but that it is a valuable resource in a community. Multiculturalism challenges us to recognize multiple perspectives, and, in doing so, we enhance our problem-solving and critical thinking skills. Chapter 6 on Intellectual Wellness will cover critical thinking in more depth. Engaging in unfamiliar or different activities (e.g., talking with people from cultures different from your own and engaging in diverse cultural experiences) helps to create a more complex system of thoughts, perceptions, assumptions, attitudes, feelings, and skills that can lead to a greater learning potential. As a college student, you are in a unique learning situation that offers numerous opportunities to increase your diversity skills. If you have not formed relationships with people who have dissimilar backgrounds from you, now is your chance. People who ignore or resist opportunities may find themselves both vocationally and personally deficient in a global, multicultural society. (Ginter et al., 172–172)

ASSIGNMENT: Who are you? Who are we? Valuing Diversity.

The following questions are intended to help you think and talk about your background and experiences and to learn about the background and experiences of others. This is just one exercise that will enhance your ability to value and respect diversity.

INSTRUCTIONS:

1. Form a random group of three students.
2. Each student should take a few minutes to complete the chart below.
3. When everyone in the group has completed the chart, have each person read his or her responses to the members of the group (members should feel free to ask questions and share experiences).
4. Each student will share with the remainder of the class something interesting learned about another student's background.

My full name:

The name I prefer to be called:

The cultural meaning of my name (if known):

My ethnic background:

Place(s) my parents, grandparents and
great-grandparents were born:

Place were I was born:

The language(s) I speak:

My family's educational achievements:

A person I admire:

An attribute I like about myself:

A characteristic I like about my culture:

A challenge I would like to conquer this semester:

A challenge I would like to achieve in my lifetime:

Belote, G. et al. *The First Year: Making the Most of College.* Fourth Edition. "Developing Relationships." Kendall Hunt Publishing Company (2003):49 (Adapted from materials created by The National Conference's "Actions Speak Louder: A Skills-Based Curriculum for Building Inclusion," 1995.)

Valuing Diversity Through Developing Multicultural Competencies

Valuing diversity begins with understanding yourself. It means taking a closer look at your own experiences, background, and culture. What are the messages from your background that you embrace or that hinder you in some way? How do you view others? How do you view others who are different from you? Once you have faced the first challenge—awareness—you are ready to continue exploring some additional concepts into diversity.

We know that our attitudes and beliefs influence our perceptions. We assimilate attitudes and beliefs throughout our lives, forming assumptions about the way things are and are not, including judgments about people. Unfortunately, we tend to filter out information that does not affirm, or align with, our perception of the world, so we tend to rely on many biased assumptions to guide us through life. There are two concepts that are important if you are to fully understand and begin to value differences. These are prejudices and discrimination.

Prejudice refers to a negative attitude toward members of some distinct group based solely on their membership in that group. Prejudice has behavioral, cognitive, and affective components. In other words, prejudices affect our choices, the way we see the world, the way we interpret information, and the way we feel. All of these components can cause us to take actions that may discriminate against others. We learn prejudice just like we learn everything else: by hearing the views expressed by our parents, teachers, friends, and the media.

Discrimination involves negative actions toward another person. Actions may be mild or severe. Avoidance, for example, is a mild form of discrimination. More severe forms of discrimination include outward aggression and violence. (Belote, 40–42)

Take a moment to become familiar with some of the terms associated with prejudice and discrimination:

abelism	Prejudice or discrimination against people with mental, emotional, and physical disabilities
ageism	Prejudice or discrimination based on age
anti-Semitism	Hostility toward Jewish people
classism	Prejudice or discrimination based on economic background
culture	A group of people bound together by traditions (food, language, religion) and values
ethnocentrism	A belief that one's own culture is more correct or superior
homophobia	An irrational fear of gays, lesbians, or bisexuals
racism	Discrimination based on skin color or ethnicity; a belief that a particular race is superior or inferior
sexism	Prejudice or discrimination based on gender
stereotyping	Overgeneralizing about groups of people based on biased assumptions

To begin combating your own prejudice and that of others, the following steps are useful:

1. Become aware of your own prejudices and their origins.
2. Educate yourself about the customs and beliefs of other cultures and peoples.
3. Challenge others' prejudicial statements, ideas, and beliefs.
4. Increase contacts with individuals and groups you might otherwise avoid or with whom you might not interact on a regular basis.

To begin combating discrimination, the following steps are useful:

1. Be open-minded, ask questions, and be a good listener.
2. Confront your own feelings and attitudes, become better informed about people different from yourself, and challenge others who use stereotypes or discriminate in some way.
3. Become aware of media images and the possible biases presented, both positive and negative. A good way to begin is with your own campus environment.

Valuing Diversity Through Developing a Multicultural View

Developing a multicultural view requires the motivation to develop better diversity skills to interact with a wider range of people. For some people, the motivation to become multiculturally competent arises from a desire to become a social change agent in the community by helping other people develop more tolerant attitudes. Some people view this as a way of supporting their country, since democracy is a system based on mutual respect and equality of rights. There are things you can do to help build a healthier approach to living in a multicultural society.

1. Develop good critical thinking skills. Learn to think through your assumptions about different groups of people. Remember that you base your assumptions on your experiences. The process of critical thinking can help you get beyond preconceived notions formulated over the years and see the truth.

2. Educate others about laws and policies. There are campus policies and laws to deal with acts of bigotry and discrimination. Become familiar with them.

ASSIGNMENT: Evaluate your self-awareness on diversity.

Diversity Spectrum

A. List six different groups that you belong to, which you feel have influenced your personal development.

1.   4.

2.   5.

3.   6.

B. Which one of these groups has had the greatest influence on your personal identity and why?

C. Have you ever felt limited or disadvantaged by being a member of any groups?

D. Have you ever felt that you experienced advantages or privileges because of your membership in any group(s)?

When Have You Felt Different?

A. Describe an experience in your life when you felt that you were different from, or didn't fit in with, the majority of people around you.

B. Why did you feel that way? How do you think members of the majority felt about you?

Questions about Other Groups or Cultures

A. Write down, in a question form, anything that you have wondered about people from a particular group or culture that is different from your own.

B. Would you feel comfortable approaching and posing these questions to someone from this group or culture?

Personal Experience

A. Have you ever been the personal target or prejudice or discrimination?

B. What happened? Who was involved? How did you feel?

Adapted from Cuseo, J. et al. *Thriving in College and Beyond: Research-Based Strategies for Academic Success and Personal Development.* "Diversity." Kendall Hunt Publishing Company Publishing (200?):281–282.

RELATIONSHIPS

> **"**A friend is someone who understands your past, believes in your future and accepts yesterday and you today just the way you are.**"**
>
> — Unknown

Going to college is perhaps the most difficult step that you have ever taken. It is difficult because of the many changes that will occur simultaneously in your life. Relationships will change too. You will change, and others close to you will change. As you begin to explore your new freedoms and choices, you are likely to make some good decisions and poor decisions. Important relationships in your life will begin to change as you learn to handle each situation.

You will meet people who do not view the world the same way you and your family do. Some of these people will be students, and some will be professors. You will make choices about your openness to new experiences and new people. If college is about learning, it includes what we learn from others about ourselves, our values, and our beliefs.

Friendships

College provides the opportunity to make new friendships that can broaden your perspective and make your life richer and more enjoyable. Friendships involve trust and support. Beyond this basic notion, we all have different ideas about what is important in a friendship.

ASSIGNMENT: Evaluate qualities that are important to you in your friendships.

What do you value in a friendship? Here is a list of common qualities of friendships. Place a checkmark next to those qualities that are important to you in establishing your personal friendships.

A friend is a person who:

_____ can keep information confidential.

_____ is loyal.

_____ can be trusted.

_____ is warm and affectionate.

_____ is supportive of who I am.

_____ is honest.

_____ is a creative person.

_____ encourages me to do my best.

_____ spends time with me.

_____ has a sense of humor.

_____ is independent.

_____ has good communication skills.

_____ is an educated person.

_____ is an intelligent person.

_____ knows how to have fun.

_____ cares about me.

What are the top three qualities you would look for in a friend? List them below.

1. _____

2. _____

3. _____

The friends that you choose can have a big influence on your life, so it is important to choose them wisely. Some people make friends easily while others find making new friends more difficult. Ideas for establishing new friendships:

- Be a good listener. Spend equal time listening and talking.

- Talk about yourself. Let others get to know you by sharing your interests, where you come from and what is important to you.

- Be supportive and caring. Help your friends celebrate the good days, and be supportive through life's challenging days.

- Be a friend. Treat your friends the way you would like to be treated.

- Spend time with your friends. Make spending time with friends a high priority.

- Accept your friends for who they are. Accept the idea that you are not going to be able to change people to match your expectations.

- Show appreciation. Say thank you, make honest compliments, and think of something positive to say.

- Be assertive. This means you have the right to your feelings and opinions without being aggressive.

- Be selective. Not everyone makes a good friend. Make friends with people you respect and admire.

(Fralick, 357–359)

A relationship starts as a friendship and then moves a step further. A relationship involves emotional attachment and interdependence. We often get our ideas about good relationships through practice and trial and error. When we make errors, the results are often painful. Although we all have different ideas about what constitutes a good relationship, at minimum it should include: love and caring, honesty, trust, loyalty, mutual support, and acceptance of differences.

Intimate Relationships between Two People

Often people ask the question, "How do you find, maintain, and manage a relationship with a special someone?" Humans ask this question so frequently that our civilization has devoted most of its art, music, and literature to this topic. John Gray, author of *Men Are from Mars, Women Are from Venus,* states that two people can improve their relationship when they demonstrate the following twelve components of love:

1. *Caring.* Show that you are interested in and concerned about each other.

2. *Trust.* Have a positive belief in the intentions and abilities of each other.

3. *Understanding.* Listen without judgment and without presuming that you understand the feelings of the other person. In this way, you can feel free to discuss what is important to him or her.

4. *Acceptance.* It is probably not a good idea to marry a person if you think you can change him or her into the ideal person you have in mind. Love your partner without trying to change him or her. No one is perfect; we are each a work in progress. The key is to trust the people we love to make their own improvements.

5. *Respect.* Have consideration for the thoughts and feelings of each other.

6. *Appreciation.* Acknowledge the behavior and efforts of your partner. Appreciation can be in the form of a simple thank you or sending a card or gift.

7. *Devotion.* Give priority to the relationship so that the other person feels important.

8. *Admiration.* Show approval for the unique gifts and talents of your partner.

9. *Validation.* Do not argue with feelings. Each person has the right to his or her own feelings. We can acknowledge, try to understand, and respect the feelings of another without necessarily agreeing with them.

10. *Approval.* Show approval by acknowledging the goodness and satisfaction you have with each other.

11. *Reassurance.* Show reassurance by repeatedly showing that you care, understand, and respect each other.

12. *Encouragement.* Notice the good characteristics of each other and provide encouragement and support.

How to Survive the Loss of a Relationship

Relationships require work and good communication to keep them going strong. Relationships also change over time as people grow and change. As we search for our soul mates, we may need to end some relationships and start new ones. This process can be very painful. Following the breakup of a relationship, people generally go through three predictable stages:

1. Shock or denial

2. Anger or depression

3. Understanding or acceptance

Dealing with pain is a necessary part of life. Whether the pain is a result of a loss of a relationship or the death of someone important to you, there are some positive steps you can take along the road to acceptance and understanding:

- Recognize that a loss has taken place and give yourself time to adjust to this situation. The greater the loss, the more time it will take to feel better. In the meantime, try to keep up with your daily routines. It is possible to feel sad and to go to work and to school. Daily routines may even take your mind off your troubles for a while.

- It is healthy to feel sad and cry. You will need to experience the pain to get over it. It is not helpful to deny pain, to cover it up, or to run away from it because it will take longer to feel better.

- Talk to a friend or a counselor. Talking about how you feel will help you to understand and accept the loss.

- Don't punish yourself with thoughts that begin with "If only I had . . ."

- Realize that there is a beginning and an end to pain.

- Get plenty of rest and eat well.

- Accept understanding and support from friends and family.

- Ask for help if you need it.

- Don't try to get the old relationship going again. It will just prolong the pain.

- Anticipate a positive outcome. You will feel better in the future.

- Beware of the rebound. It is not a good idea to jump into a new relationship right away.

- Beware of addictive activities such as alcohol, drugs, smoking, or under or overeating.

- Take time to relax and be kind to yourself.

- Use exercise as a way to deal with stress and feel better.

- Keep a journal to help deal with your emotions and to learn from the situation.

- Look at the loss of a relationship as an opportunity for learning.

How can you ever expect anyone else to enjoy your company if you don't enjoy your own company?

Do you treat yourself the way you want other people to treat you?

- When you want to attract a relationship, make sure your thoughts, words, actions, and surroundings don't contradict your desires.

- Your job is you. Unless you fill yourself up first, you have nothing to give anybody.

- Treat yourself with love and respect, and you will attract people who show you love and respect.

- When you feel bad about yourself, you block the love, and instead you attract more people and situations that will continue to make you feel bad about you.

- Focus on the qualities you love about yourself, and the law of attraction will show you more great things about you.

- To make a relationship work, focus on what you appreciate about the other person and not on your complaints. When you focus on the strengths, you will get more of them.

SOURCE: Byrne, R. *The Secret.* "The Secret to Relationships."

ASSIGNMENT: Determine the following regarding relationships in your life.

A. How can you initiate new relationships in your life?

1. _____

2. _____

3. _____

4. _____

5. _____

6. _____

7. _____

B. How do you plan to maintain new or old relationships in your life?

1. _____

2. _____

3. _____

4. _____

5. _____

6. _____

7. _____

C. How would you plan to end a relationship positively if need be?

1. _____

2. _____

3. _____

4. _____

5. _____

6. _____

7. _____

Adapted from Schick, C. et al. *Surviving College: A "Real World" Experience. In Hot Pursuit of Happiness.* Kendall Hunt Publishing Company (2001): 187.

Online Assignment: Influences in Your Life (Timed Test)

Complete this assignment online. Go to:

www.grtep.com

Select >Chapter Content>Chapter 4>Enter your username and password

Tips to becoming socially healthy

> ❝*Take advantage of every opportunity to practice your communication skills so that when important occasions arise, you will have the gift, the style, the sharpness, the clarity, and the emotions to affect other people.*❞
>
> — Jim Rohn

- Begin to understand the details behind your attitude and personality. Doing this will not only help you understand why you may think or react certain ways but it will also help you to begin to understand others' attitudes and personality objectively.

- Develop effective communication skills. This is a "must" for meaningful and successful relationships with others, both personally and professionally. You will need not only to work on how to get your message across to someone else, but you must also learn to be an excellent listener.

- Remember—90% of communication is nonverbal, so be cognizant of your body language as you talk AND listen to others.

- Try to use an assertive communication approach. It allows for respectful expression without "putting down" or manipulating others.

- Knock off any negative self-talk. What you will get for it will be better self-esteem, which will lead to fewer difficulties when communicating with others.

■ Develop awareness of the beautiful multiculturalism around you. Valuing diversity begins with understanding yourself then learning from others.

■ Combat your own prejudices and discriminative thoughts or behaviors as well as those of others.

■ Surround yourself with true friends who will not only love you for you but who can teach or challenge you to be a better person.

■ Follow the twelve components of love stated earlier.

■ Treat yourself as you would want others to treat you.

■ Focus on the positive aspects of other people and always dig deeper and search around potential defenses others might reveal on the surface. There's normally more to what meets the eye.

■ Get involved socially at school or at your job. Get to know the people you're working with to establish a rapport and to learn from others.

■ Find out about community service and volunteer organizations and resources at your school or job.

■ Be the good example in any social situation. It will win you respect and trust.

Helpful Internet Sites

American Association for Marriage and Family Therapy: aamft.org
American Social Health Association: ashastd.org
Amnesty International's Universal Declaration of Human Rights: amnesty.org
CivilSpace: http://www.coactiveconsultants.com/diane_millett_bio.html
Craig's List—Community, Personals, Discussion Forums: craigslist.org
Dr. Phil: drphil.com
Dr. P.M. Forni—Civility: http://krieger.jhu.edu/civility/
Jung Typology Test: humanmetrics.com/cgi-win/JTypes2.asp
Facebook: facebook.com
Good Communication Skills: communication-skills-4confidence.com/good-communication-skills.html
The Personality Page: personalitypage.com
SAMSHA's National Mental Health Information Center: mentalhealth.samhsa.gov/publications/
    allpubs/sma-3716/building.asp
Fight Hate and Promote Tolerance: tolerance.org

References

Aguilar, L. et al. *The Community College: A New Beginning*. Fourth Edition. "Skills to Enhance Communication and Relationships." Kendall Hunt Publishing Company (2005): 182–186; 188–190.

Belote, G. et al. *The First Year: Making the Most of College*. Fourth Edition. "Developing Relationships." Kendall Hunt Publishing Company (2003): 40–42; 49.

Byrne, R. *The Secret*. "The Secret to Relationships." Beyond Words Publishing (2006): 117; 123.

Colgrove, M. et al. *How to Survive the Loss of a Love*. Bantam Books (1988).

Cuseo, J. et al. *Thriving in College and Beyond: Research-Based Strategies for Academic Success and Personal Development*. "Diversity." Kendall Hunt Publishing Company (200?): 281 282.

Cuseo, J. et al. *Thriving in College and Beyond: Research-Based Strategies for Academic Success and Personal Development*. "Interpersonal Relationships." Kendall Hunt Publishing Company Publishing (200?): 357–358.

Forni, P.M. *Choosing Civility*. The Rules. St. Martin's Press, (2002): 35-152.

Forni, P.M. *Choosing Civility*. What is Civility? St. Martin's Press, (2002): 8-12.

Fralick, M. *College & Career Success*. "Learning Style and Intelligence." Kendall Hunt Publishing Company (2005): 240–241; 243–244.

Fralick, M. *College & Career Success*. "Communication and Relationships." Kendall Hunt Publishing Company (2005): 349; 351–354; 358–362.

Ginter, E. et al. *Life Skills for College: A Curriculum for Life*. "Connecting Common Threads across a Diverse World." Kendall Hunt Publishing Company (2005): 171–172; 175; 182.

Gray, J. *Men Are from Mars, Women Are from Venus*. HarperCollins (1992).

Hettler, B. The National Wellness Institute. *The Six Dimensions of Wellness: Social Wellness*. www.nationalwellness.org accessed on 12.7.07.

Maxwell, J. *Attitude 101*. "The Impact of an Attitude" and "The Formation of an Attitude." Thomas Nelson, Inc: 2003: 16; 31–42; 45; 48–49.

Schick, C. et al. *Surviving College: A "Real World" Experience*. In "Hot Pursuit of Happiness." Kendall Hunt Publishing Company (2001): 186–187.

Wellness for Healthy Positive Living. Social Wellness. for.gov.bc.ca/hrb/hw/index.htm accessed on 1.28.08.

CHAPTER 5

Spiritual Wellness

66We are not human beings on a spiritual
journey; we are spiritual beings
on a human journey.99

— Stephen Covey

The objectives in this chapter include the understanding of: —

- The meaning of spiritual wellness and its direct application to you
- Intrinsic motivations
- Positive psychology
- Character and life congruence
- Happiness
- Compassion and concern
- Gratitude
- Respect and tolerance
- Patience
- Forgiveness
- Living in the present

Online Reminders

- Complete the poll question before the next class meeting.
- Complete the interactive activities for this chapter.
- Complete all of the online assignments for this chapter.

Spiritual Wellness—Does this mean that I respect life and nature itself? How religious I am? That I have morals, values, and beliefs that I follow consistently? Yes. Again, the theme continues. You can include these in how you would define spiritual wellness, but there is more . . . Let's explore deeper.

Spiritual wellness is one's search for meaning and purpose in human existence through a deep appreciation for the depth of life, a sense of inner peace, overall satisfaction, and confidence. Your ethics, values, beliefs, and morals contribute to your spiritual wellness through your actions brought to light each and every day. The characteristics of your search will be a peaceful harmony between your personal feelings and emotions and the rough and rugged stretches of your life. You may experience feelings of doubt, despair, fear, disappointment, and dislocation as well as feelings of pleasure, joy, happiness, and discovery. These are all important experiences and components to your search, and the value system you will adapt to bring meaning to your existence will display them. Thus, spiritual wellness enhances the connection between your body, mind, and spirit.

The National Institute of Wellness states that spiritual wellness follows these tenets:

1. It is better to ponder the meaning of life for ourselves and to be tolerant of the beliefs of others than to close our minds and become intolerant.

2. It is better to live each day in a way that is consistent with our values and beliefs than to do otherwise and feel untrue to ourselves.

PRE-CLASS SURVEY: Take your spiritual wellness survey before your next class meeting and identify your level of spiritual wellness. Circle either Yes or No, total up each column, and check your score.

I have a sense of belonging, meaning, and purpose in my life.	YES	NO
I have a belief system (i.e., spiritual, atheist, religious).	YES	NO
I participate in regular spiritual activities with people who share my beliefs, and I am open to hearing about other's beliefs.	YES	NO
I accept my limitations without embarrassment or apology.	YES	NO
I am willing to forgive myself and others.	YES	NO
I keep the purpose of my life clearly in mind and let it guide my decision-making.	YES	NO
I freely give to others.	YES	NO
I am comfortable about knowing things without knowing precisely how I know them (intuition).	YES	NO
I allow others the freedom to believe what they want without pressuring them to accept my beliefs.	YES	NO
I look for and work toward balance in my life.	YES	NO
I continually explore personal beliefs, values, and priorities.	YES	NO
Principles, ethics, and morals provide guides for my life.	YES	NO
TOTAL		

WHAT YOUR TOTAL MEANS:

9 or more Yes answers	Excellent	Your habits are positively enhancing your health.
6–8 Yes answers	Average	You are obviously trying but there is room to improve.
5 or less Yes answers	Not So Good	There is a need for improvement in your daily habits.

SOURCE: "Wellness for Healthy Positive Living." *Spiritual Wellness/Inventory* for.gov.bc.ca/hrb/hw/index.htm

INTRINSIC MOTIVATION

❝*Goodness is the only investment that never fails.*❞
— Henry David Thoreau

Spiritual wellness also includes a level of interaction that occurs in our lives that the processes we observe in the natural world may not always explain. These interactions take place on at least three different levels of our lives. The first and most dramatic is the phenomenal level, which involves miraculous events with no rational explanation that guide or enable our paths. Second is the information level, which is where we receive our thoughts and impressions that clearly do not come from our own minds but that provide us with crucial guidance. Third is the motivational level where the inner forces placed in our lives compel and guide us on how we serve others. Let's call this servanthood.

We can best describe servanthood as love acting in life's relationships. It will express itself in a variety of ways as we serve each other differently based on the differing inner motivations placed within us. We can trace the concept of intrinsic motivation back as far as classical Greek philosophy. However, one of the best classifications of intrinsic motivations can be patterned after seven previously identified by Paul of Tarsus, a leading first-century theologian and keen observer of human nature. Based on historical context, we can define the seven intrinsic motivations as:

Proclaiming	The inward motivation to publicly speak out from internal convictions concerning what is perceived as right and wrong.
Helping	The inward motivation to detect legitimate needs others have and to find practical ways to provide these needs.
Researching	The inward motivation to carefully research truth and to clearly present what we discover to others in such a way that it will be easy to learn.
Exhorting	The inward motivation to encourage others through counsel and to outline practical steps of actions others should take to overcome problems.
Giving	The inward motivation to financially invest in and support other worthwhile projects and to wisely use and invest money to provide for such support.
Managing	The inward motivation to organize and coordinate the activities and efforts of others and to set goals for them to meet in these activities and efforts.
Comforting	The inward motivation to identify with the emotions of others and to provide comfort to those who are in emotional distress.

These motivations will strongly influence the way we respond to people, situations, and problems in the world. The patterns of our inner motivations also help determine the roles we will adopt as a result of these spiritual strengths. As with other strengths, one of the most effective ways to discover our spiritual strengths is to listen to what others who know you say about you.

Our modern society tends to value strengths that we can explain in a rational or natural framework. When we follow this tendency, we end up with a culture where people often ignore the virtue of servanthood. This can lead to misdirection and a self-centered life, and it can cloud the search for the meaning and purpose in our human existence. (Millard, 262–263)

Online Assignment: Intrinsic Motivations

Complete this assignment online. Go to:

www.grtep.com

Select >Chapter Content>Chapter 5>Enter your username and password

POSITIVE PSYCHOLOGY

"Man is what he believes.."

— Anton Chekhov, Russian author

Positive psychology is the scientific study of the strengths and virtues that enable individuals and communities to thrive. This field is founded on the belief that people want to lead meaningful and fulfilling lives, to cultivate what is best within themselves, and to enhance their experiences of love, work, and play.

This information is based largely on Christopher Peterson's book *Primer in Positive Psychology* (2006), Martin Seligman's book *Authentic Happiness* (2002), and an article by *Seligman and Pawelski* (2003).

Is Positive Psychology Just about Making People Happy?

"Happiness" is commonly defined as a state of well being or pleasurable experience, but this notion of happiness is only a small part of positive psychology. Positive psychology is the scientific study of the strengths and virtues that enable individuals and communities to thrive. According to Seligman (2002), positive psychology has three central concerns: positive emotions, positive individual traits, and positive institutions. Understanding positive emotion entails the study of contentment with the past, happiness in the present, and hope for the future. Understanding positive individual traits consists of the study of the strengths and virtues, such as the capacity for love and work, courage, compassion, resilience, creativity, curiosity, integrity, self-knowledge, moderation, self-control, and wisdom. Understanding positive institutions entails the study of meaning and purpose as well as the strengths that foster better communities, such as justice, responsibility, civility, parenting, nurturance, work ethic, leadership, teamwork, purpose, and tolerance.

Each of these three domains is related to a different meaning of the scientifically unwieldy term "happiness," and each has its own road to happiness (Seligman, 2002). Positive emotions lead to the pleasant life, which is similar to the hedonic theories of happiness. Using one's strengths in a challenging task leads to the experience of flow (Csikszentmihalyi, 1990) and the engaged life. Deploying one's strengths in the service of something larger than oneself can lead to the meaningful life (e.g., belonging to and serving institutions such as education, free press, religion, democracy, and family, to name a few).

Is Positive Psychology the Same as Positive Thinking?

Positive psychology is different from positive thinking in three significant ways. First, positive psychology is grounded in empirical and replicable scientific study. Second, positive thinking urges positivity on us for all times and places, but positive psychology does not. Positive psychology recognizes that in spite of the advantages of positive thinking, there are times when negative or realistic thinking is appropriate. Studies find that optimism is associated with better health, performance, longevity, and social success (Seligman, 1991; Lyubomirsky, King & Diener, 2005), but there is evidence that in some situations negative thinking leads to more accuracy and being accurate can have important consequences (Alloy, Abramson, & Chiara, 2000). Optimistic thinking can be associated with an underestimation of risks (Peterson & Vaidya, 2003). For example, we do not necessarily want a pilot or air traffic controller to be an optimist when deciding whether to take off during a storm.

The third distinction between positive thinking and positive psychology is that many scholars of positive psychology have spent decades working on the "negative" side of things – depression, anxiety, trauma, etc. We do not view positive psychology as a replacement for traditional psychology, but merely as a supplement to the hard-won gains of traditional psychology.

Positive psychology research is discovering some things that might not be considered wisdom to all. To name just a few:

1. Wealth is only weakly related to happiness both within and across nations, particularly when income is above the poverty level (Diener & Diener, 1996).

2. Activities that make people happy in small doses—such as shopping, good food and making money—do not lead to fulfillment in the long term, indicating that these have quickly diminishing returns (Myers, 2000; Ryan & Deci, 2000).

3. Engaging in an experience that produces 'flow' is so gratifying that people are willing to do it for its own sake, rather than for what they will get out of it. The activity is its own reward. Flow is experienced when one's skills are sufficient for a challenging activity, in the pursuit of a clear goal, with immediate feedback on progress toward the goal. In such an activity, concentration is fully engaged in the moment, self-awareness disappears, and sense of time is distorted (Csikszentmihalyi, 1990).

4. People who express gratitude on a regular basis have better physical health, optimism, progress toward goals, well-being, and help others more (Emmons & Crumpler, 2000).

5. Trying to maximize happiness can lead to unhappiness (Schwartz et al., 2002).

6. People who witness others perform good deeds experience an emotion called 'elevation' and this motivates them to perform their own good deeds (Haidt, 2000).

7. Optimism can protect people from mental and physical illness (Taylor et al., 2000).

8. People who are optimistic or happy have better performance in work, school and sports, are less depressed, have fewer physical health problems, and have better relationships with other people. Further, optimism can be measured and it can be learned (Seligman, 1991; Lyubomirsky, King & Diener, 2005).

9. People who report more positive emotions in young adulthood live longer and healthier lives (Danner, Snowdon, & Friesen, 2001).

10. Physicians experiencing positive emotion tend to make more accurate diagnoses (Isen, 1993).

11. Healthy human development can take place under conditions of even great adversity due to a process of resilience that is common and completely ordinary (Masten, 2001).

12. There are benefits associated with disclosive writing. Individuals who write about traumatic events are physically healthier than control groups that do not. Individuals who write about the perceived benefits of traumatic events achieve the same physical health benefits as those who write only about the trauma (King & Miner, 2000). Individuals who write about their life goals and their best imagined future achieve similar physical health benefits to those who write only about traumatic events. Further, writing about life goals is significantly less distressing than writing about trauma, and is associated with enhanced well-being (King, 2001).

13. People are unable to predict how long they will be happy or sad following an important event (Gilbert, Pinel, Wilson, Blumberg & Wheatley, 1998; Wilson, Meyers, & Gilbert, 2001). These researchers found that people typically overestimate how long they will be sad following a bad event, such as a romantic breakup, yet fail to learn from repeated experiences that their predictions are wrong.

What Then Is the Connection between Positive Psychology and Character Strengths?

As previously stated, positive psychology is the "scientific study of the strengths and virtues that enable individuals and communities to thrive." According to Peterson, these strengths, termed character strengths, are evolutionary in nature, observable from the age of three and manifest themselves in a range of behaviors, thoughts and emotions and cross-situationally.

Is there a list of personal strengths of character, and are there common virtues, that can be identified across cultures and throughout history? Martin Seligman, past president of the American Psychological Association and founder of the modern positive psychology movement, and especially Christopher Peterson, professor at the University of Michigan since 1986 and member of the Positive Psychology Steering Committee, spent three years researching this.

Peterson and Seligman set out to catalog what's right with people—their psychological strengths, specifically contrasting it with the DSM. The result is what well-known Harvard professor Howard Gardner called "one of the most important initiatives in psychology of the past half century," the 816-page *Character Strengths and Virtues: A Handbook and Classification*.

In *A Primer in Positive Psychology* (2007), Peterson goes on to present a list they used in 2004 summarizing their "possible criteria for signature strengths":

- a sense of ownership and authenticity ("this is the real me") vis-a-vis the strength

- a feeling of excitement while displaying it, particularly at first

- a rapid learning curve as themes are attached to the strength and practiced

- continuous learning of new ways to enact the strength

- a sense of yearning to act in accordance with the strength

- a feeling of inevitability in using the strength, as if one cannot be stopped or dissuaded from its display

- the discovery of the strength as owned in an epiphany

- invigoration rather than exhaustion when using the strength

- the creation and pursuit of fundamental projects that revolve around the strength

- intrinsic motivation to use the strength

The list of personal character strengths is not set in stone. Like other scientific theories it is subject to change as evidence is evaluated over time. Here are the 24 strengths of character at present, grouped in 6 categories of virtues:

The List

Strengths of Wisdom and Knowledge: Cognitive strengths that entail the acquisition and use of knowledge

1. *Creativity*: Thinking of new ways to do things is a crucial part of who you are.

2. *Curiosity*: You like exploration and discovery.

3. *Judgment*: You think things through and examine them from all sides.

4. *Love of learning*: You have a passion for mastering new skills, topics, and bodies of knowledge.

5. *Perspective*: People who know you consider you wise.

   Strengths of courage: Emotional strengths that involve the exercise of will to accomplish goals in the face of opposition, external and internal

6. *Bravery*: You do not shrink from threat, challenge, difficulty, or pain.

7. *Honesty*: You live your life in a genuine and authentic way.

8. *Perserverance*: You work hard to finish what you start.

9. *Zest*: You approach everything you do with excitement and energy.
    Strengths of Humanity: interpersonal strengths that involve tending and befriending others

10. *Kindness*: You are kind and generous to others.

11. *Love*: You value close relations with others.

12. *Social intelligence*: You know how to fit in to different social situations.
    Strengths of Justice: civic strengths that underlie healthy community life

13. *Fairness*: One of your abiding principles is to treat all people fairly.

14. *Leadership*: You excel at encouraging a group to get things done.

15. *Teamwork*: You excel as a member of a group.
    Strengths of Temperance: strengths that protect against excess

16. *Forgiveness*: You forgive those who have done you wrong.

17. *Humility*: You do not seek the spotlight and others recognize and value your modesty.

18. *Prudence*: You are a careful person.

19. *Self regulation:* You are a disciplined person.
    Strengths of Transcendence: strengths that forge connections to the larger universe and provide meaning

20. *Apprec. of beauty*: You notice and appreciate beauty and excellence in all domains of life.

21. *Gratitude*: You are aware of good things that happen and don't take them for granted.

22. *Hope*: You expect the best in the future, and you work to achieve it.

23. *Humor*: Bringing smiles to others people is important to you.

24. *Spirituality*: Your beliefs shape your actions and are a source of comfort to you.

Online Assignment: Character Strengths Survey

Complete this assignment online. Go to:
www.grtep.com
Select >Chapter Content>Chapter 5>Enter your username and password

CHARACTER AND LIFE CONGRUENCE

❝*Character is what you do when no one is looking.***❞**

— Henry Huffman

As we establish foundational values for ourselves, we start by discovering what we hold as true about reality. This becomes the faith on which our lives are built. The question that naturally arises out of this process is how then will we live in response to this faith? The answer to this question becomes the value we hold about ourselves. This value appears far more in our actions than in our statements. This value is character.

Character is what we hold about ourselves that is observable in moral and ethical actions taken in our lives consistent with the faith we have developed. The morals and ethics we have in our lives come from the standards of what is right or just what we have discovered as we have established a foundational faith in our lives. Character-based logic dictates that we should live our lives consistent with these standards, which we can define as life congruence.

If we take this concept of life congruence and apply it to our characters, it implies that the way we live our lives should coincide exactly with the faith we hold for our lives. When we don't live in life congruence, we can end up in a condition that psychologists refer to as cognitive dissonance or "mind disagreement." What it means is that we have a perception or awareness that there is an incompatibility between two patterns of thought in our lives. In the case where we may not be living in life congruence, the incompatibility is between the way we perceive the reality that we live and the way we perceive how to actually live in that reality.

Let's apply your life congruence now. There are three important questions to answer in establishing this value about reality:

1. What do I believe about the design of the universe?
2. What do I believe about the intentionality of the universe?
3. What do I believe about the intentionality of my place in the universe?

Give yourself a moment to think about each of these.

If your answer to #1 leads you to believe that there is some level of design to the overall universe, then in trying to understand your life's purpose, you would want to understand the nature of that design and then live your life congruent with that design. This is the simple principle of *universal harmony*.

If your answer to #2 leads you to believe that there is some level of intentionality to the design of the universe, then in trying to understand your life's purpose, you would want to determine the level of intentionality as best you could with the realization that this intentionality begins to build a sense of reason for your existence. This would encourage you even more to live your life congruent with that design. This is the simple principle of *universal purpose.*

If your answer to #3 leads you to believe that there is a particular intentionality to you personally being a part of the design to the overall universe, then in trying to understand your life's purpose, you would want to understand as best as you could what your particular place in the design is. This would include the realization that this particular intentionality begins to build a sense of meaning for your existence. With a greater sense of both purpose and meaning beginning to emerge in your faith, the need to live your life congruent with the universal design is even greater. This is the simple principal of *universal significance.*

What happens when you do not pursue life congruences in the search for your life's purpose? Almost always you will fall into the "mind disagreement" condition described earlier. When you are in this state, you will try to find ways to lessen the distress caused by this unsettled circumstance. Most commonly, you will try inventing new patterns of thought or revising current ones in such a way that you convince yourself that you are pursuing your life's purpose when in actuality you are NOT. Many people have fallen into this trap; and, at the end of their lives, they often look back with remorse, feeling that they have not achieved what they were placed on this earth to accomplish. The good news: You always have the CHOICE to remedy this situation if it applies to your life. (Millard, 82–84)

Whenever legitimate human needs arise within us, there are three powers (at work in all of us) that go to war. How we respond determines the level of character-based life congruency that will develop in our lives. The three powers are:

1. the self-centered approach (what do I care about and what makes me feel good),
2. the legalistic approach (how do I look to others), and
3. the spiritual approach (what is the principle-centered thing to do).

So . . .

If we respond with a self-centered approach, which is what is congruent with our wants, we will end up doing what is contrary to spiritual values. This is not character-based life congruency.

If we respond with a legalistic approach, our wants are still congruent with the self-centered approach. Although we may end up doing what APPEARS consistent with spiritual values in our outward actions, our inward desires are still consistent with the self-centered approach. This is not character-based life congruency.

If we respond with a spiritual approach that is congruent with the universal principles, we will end up not gratifying the desires of self-centeredness nor will we be under law. Instead we will keep in step with the values and principles of character-based life congruency.

ASSIGNMENT: Evaluate your needs for mentoring and being accountable.

The hectic pace of your social life and the heavy demands of your academic studies can often lead to placing the development of your character on hold during your college experience. Many times in the transition from high school to college, a sense of community is lost. When this happens, there are fewer people around you who can help keep you accountable to live the congruent life you have intended for yourself. One of the best ways to fill this loss is to seek out a relationship with a mentor.

Mentors are individuals who can serve in many different capacities. These include being a spiritual guide, a life coach, a counselor, a teacher, an accountability partner, or a sponsor. A mentor might be a teacher, a staff member, or an older student. Whoever it might be, this mentor has traveled the path before you and can help you make the difficult transitions you face as you start out on your college journey.

Mentoring

STEP 1: **Does my school have a formal mentoring program?**   YES or NO
(If the answer is No, then move on to Step 2.)

What is the location of the mentoring office?

Who is the contact person?

STEP 2: **What kind(s) of mentor do I need?**

☐ Spiritual guide   ☐ Counselor   ☐ Accountability partner

☐ Life coach   ☐ Teacher   ☐ Sponsor

STEP 3: **Who do I know who might fill that desired role?**

STEP 4: **What times do I have available to meet with my mentor?**

STEP 5: **When will I set up time to meet with this person to ask if he or she would mentor me?**

You may also wish to establish a network of peer accountability in addition to a mentoring relationship or as a substitute relationship if mentoring is not available. This approach creates an environment that allows for intentional connections between you and other peers going through the same experience you are. However, it is more than just a way you can connect with other students. It challenges both you and other students to become more accountable to each other for your actions.

Accountability

STEP 1: Who do I know who might want to join me in this type of relationship?
(If you have a formal mentoring office, they can help you find this type of person.)

STEP 2: What times do I have available to meet with my accountability peers?

STEP 3: When will I set up a time to meet with these persons to ask if they would join me?

HAPPINESS

> ❝*The Constitution only gives people the right to pursue happiness.*
> *You have to catch it yourself.*❞
>
> — Benjamin Franklin

In 1996, David Myers and Ed Diener, two investigators of happiness, combined data from 916 surveys of 1.1 million people in 45 nations representing most of the world. They found the average individual's rating of life satisfaction was 6.75. Other more recent studies have shown the same scores involving college students, high school students, and middle school students.

Surprised? It seems that most people think that others are less happy than they really are. Published reports (e.g., Myers 2000) reveal that more than 90% of individuals indicate that they are somewhat or very happy. So what is responsible for all this happiness? What are the characteristics and situations that lead to happy lives?

In Lyobomirsky, King and Diener's *Psychological Bulletin* article "The Benefits of Frequent Positive Affect: Does Happiness Lead to Success?" they discussed their findings as follows:

We have reviewed extensive evidence demonstrating that happy people are successful and flourishing people. Part of the explanation for this phenomenon undoubtedly comes from the fact that success leads to happiness. Our review, however, focuses on the reverse causal direction – that happiness, in turn, leads to success. Happy people show more frequent positive affect, and specific adaptive characteristics. Positive affect has been shown, in experimental, longitudinal, and correlational studies, to lead to these specific adaptive characteristics. Thus, the evidence seems to support our conceptual model that happiness causes many of the successful outcomes with which it correlates. Furthermore, the data suggest that the success of happy people may be mediated by the effects of positive affect and the characteristics that it promotes.

It appears that happiness, rooted in personality and in past successes, leads to approach behaviors that often lead to further success. At the same time, happy people are able to react with negative emotions when it is appropriate to do so.

The desire to be happy is prevalent in Western culture (e.g., Diener, Suh, H. L. Smith, & Shao, 1995; King & Broyles, 1997), and a happy life is very much the preferred life (King & Napa, 1998). If subjective well-being feels good but otherwise leaves people impaired, for example in terms of decision making, social relationships, physical health, or success in life, we might question its net value for society and for the individual. In this article, we reviewed crosssectional, longitudinal, and experimental data showing that happy individuals are more likely than their less happy peers to have fulfilling marriages and relationships, high incomes, superior work performance, community involvement, robust health, and a long life. The three classes of evidence also indicated that positive emotions, as well as chronic happiness, are often associated with resources and characteristics that parallel success and thriving—that is, desirable behaviors and cognitions such as sociability, optimism, energy, originality, and altruism. Although our conclusions run counter to the belief that successful outcomes and desirable characteristics are primarily the causes, rather than the consequences, of happiness, a surprisingly large amount of evidence now appears to challenge this belief.

Psychologist Carol D. Ryff has identified a framework of six core dimensions of happiness (subjective well-being) per her research literature in 1995. These are:

Self-acceptance	■ This means owning all your qualities—good and bad. You are aware of the negative aspects of yourself and don't have to deny them to others. You are okay with being less than perfect, and you are okay with past experiences.
	■ Accepting yourself for who you are is very important. This is easier said than done. As a human being, you realize you are continually in the process of realizing your potential.
Positive relations with other people	■ Happy, healthy people cultivate friendships. Within these interactions, you can experience trust, admiration, respect, affection, and regard.
	■ Scientific research has shown that few variables have proved as powerful in alleviating the effects of stressful events and aiding psychological well-being as having social support from others.
	■ Refer back to the Relationship and Friendship sections in Chapter 5, Social Wellness.
Autonomy	■ Happy people are self-directed and autonomous. Current political correctness and trends do not easily sway them.
	■ Happy people have a good sense of values and are not easily influenced to follow the opinions of the group. Once they have acted, they take ownership for their choice and their behavior.

(continues)

Environmental mastery	▪ Happy people do have some skills in coping with environmental difficulties. However, sometimes it is not so much that they are so accomplished in problem-solving but rather that they structure the situation to ensure success.
	▪ Happy people are much better at choosing realistic goals and actually accomplishing them. This is what makes them happy! One of the best boosters to self-esteem is actually accomplishing something.
	▪ Happy people are able to manipulate their internal voices to turn obstacles into opportunities. They appraise the situation as a challenge rather than as another chance for failure.
Purpose in life	▪ A strong indicator for happiness is whether one has a purpose in life—a sense of meaning about the past, present, and future.
	▪ (From Myers 2000): In 1965 over 80% of college students reported that it was very important/essential to develop a meaningful philosophy of life. Now that number is 40%. Another look: Over 40% of college students in 1965 reported that it was very important/essential to be very "well off" financially. In 1998, that number was 74%, and it is on the rise. For happiness, this is disastrous.
	▪ Our culture's rampant focus on material goods has convinced many young people that this must be the path to well-being. What seems to be sacrificed is the idea of the importance of developing a sense of purpose in one's life. Research suggests that you may pay a high price for these misaligned priorities.
Personal growth	▪ Happy people see themselves as continually growing and expanding.
	▪ Happy people have an orientation toward the future, and they interpret life's experiences as opportunities for learning and personal growth.
	▪ They also take active steps toward ensuring that their lives, values, and relationships are not stagnant.
	▪ You will learn more about continual growth in Chapter 6 on Intellectual Wellness.

(Schick, 181; 186; 188–191)

Online Assignments: General Happiness Scale and Subjective Happiness Scale

Complete this assignment online. Go to:
www.grtep.com
Select >Chapter Content>Chapter 5>Enter your username and password

Compassion and Concern

> ❝*When you want others to be happy, practice compassion.*
> *If you want to be happy, practice compassion.*❞
>
> — The Dali Lama

Dr. Charles Stanley, pastor and author of *When Tragedy Strikes,* talks in his book about the September 11th Terrorist attacks:

"Tragedy can meet you in your home or on the street . . . in your extended family or in your neighborhood schoolyard. Tragedy affects all cultures and societies. It comes in different shapes and sizes. Individuals, families, cities, regions and nations experience tragedies. September 11th has confronted our nation with acts of terrorism never before witnessed on U.S. soil. In these attacks on the World Trade Center, the Pentagon and United Flight 93, these tragic events affect the entire world."

"When we go through adversity it is so reassuring to have someone there to walk with us. One of the things we can do in the midst of tragedy is to reach out to people with compassion and understanding- to walk with those in need, to comfort them. People need someone to reach out to us in troubling times. Reaching out implies doing something, doesn't it? Compassionate people are those who feel the pain of others and act to alleviate the pain.

"A fundamental requisite for those who seek to comfort others is to *forget about self.* It is so easy for us to become enamored of our own affairs and get caught up in our own journey to significance and success. We must work to put others first. We must become successful comforters by *being present* while others weep, by sharing a shoulder for others to lean on and by being a reliable and careful listener. We must be dependable and trustworthy with the thoughts that are shared with us and avoid giving hasty answers or worn-out clichés to others. People need the safety of friends who hold them up rather than hold them accountable for what they express in anger and frustration."

"Has it amazed you that since the terrorist attacks, Americans have united to help one another? We have been responding passionately and positively to the needs of others. It is a beautiful thing to see and a beautiful thing to be a part of, indeed. I am not surprised to see the American flag flying everywhere I look—we are a strong, patriotic nation. Yes I am not surprised but I am thrilled to see compassion in action—people hugging each other, crying on each other's shoulders, lending aid to one another. No one is concerned about skin color, language or heritage. Our primary concern is how people can be helped and how suffering can be alleviated. Clearly a nerve has been touched. A rawness in our national psyche has been uncovered, and we *need each other.*"

(Stanley, 3–17)

Online Assignment: Compassionate Love Scale
Complete this assignment online. Go to:
www.grtep.com
Select >Chapter Content>Chapter 5>Enter your username and password

GRATITUDE

> ❝*When you stop comparing what is right here and now with what you wish were, you can begin to enjoy what is.*❞
>
> — Cheri Huber

Cherie Carter-Scott, Ph.D., is an author, corporate trainer, management consultant, and chairperson of the Motivation Management Service Institute. She has worked with over 200,000 people worldwide leading seminars on self-esteem, communication and leadership skills, and team building. In her book, *If Life is a Game, These Are the Rules,* she discusses gratitude:

To be grateful means you are thankful for and appreciative of what you have and where you are on your path right now. Gratitude fills your heart with the joyful feeling of being blessed with many gifts and allows you to fully appreciate everything that arises on your path. As you strive to keep your focus on the present moment, you can experience the full wonder of "here."

Gratitude is a lesson that needs to be reinforced often. It is too easy to overlook the gifts you have when you focus on those that you hope to obtain, and you diminish the value of where you currently are on your path if you do not pause often to appreciate it.

There are many ways to cultivate gratitude. Here are just a few suggestions you may wish to try:

- Imagine what your life would be like if you lost all that you had. This will most surely remind you of how much you do appreciate it.

- Make a list each day of all that you are grateful for, so that you can stay conscious daily of your blessings. Do this especially when you are feeling as though you have nothing to feel grateful for. Or spend a few minutes before you go to sleep giving thanks for all that you have.

- Spend time offering assistance to those who are less fortunate than you, so that you may gain perspective.

- Look for the gift in each challenging incident.

However you choose to learn gratitude is irrelevant. What really matters is that you create a space in your consciousness for appreciation for all that you have right now, so that you may live more joyously in your present moment.

ASSIGNMENT: Evaluate your gratitude and consciousness for appreciation. Answer accordingly.

What are you grateful for today?

1. _____

2. _____

3. _____

4. _____

5. _____

How can you stay conscious of what you are grateful for?

1. _____

2. _____

3. _____

4. _____

5. _____

Name a recent challenging incident. What gifts can you find in this incident?

_____

Online Assignment: Gratitude Questionnaire

Complete this assignment online. Go to:
www.grtep.com
Select >Chapter Content>Chapter 5>Enter your username and password

TOLERANCE AND RESPECT

❝*Never look down on anybody unless you're helping them up.*❞
— Reverend Jesse Jackson

Continuing on with Dr. Carter-Scott's book, *If Life is a Game, These Are the Rules,* she also discusses tolerance:

Tolerance is the outward extension of acceptance; it is when you learn to embrace all parts of others and allow them to be and express themselves fully as the unique humans that they are. You will need to learn tolerance in order to coexist peacefully with others. Tolerance quiets the inner critic that chatters in your mind so that you can apply the old adage, "live and let live."

When I was sixteen years old, I remember walking down Fifty-seventh Street in New York City and being suddenly aware, for the first time, of a voice in my head talking to me. It sounded like a running commentary on everyone within my field of vision. I heard it broadcasting impressions incessantly, and the majority were far from kind. I realized that I could—and did—find fault with every single person I passed. The next thought that came to me was, "Isn't that amazing, I must be the only perfect person in the universe, since everyone else apparently has something wrong with him."

Once I realized how ridiculous this sounded, it dawned on me that perhaps my judgments of all these people on the street were reflections of myself as opposed to some objective reality. I began to understand that what I was seeing about each of them said more about me than it said about each of them. I also realized that perhaps I was judging everyone else harshly as a way to feel good about myself. By perceiving them as too fat, short, or strangely dressed, I was by comparison thinner, taller, and more stylish. In my mind, my intolerance of them rendered me superior.

Some part of me knew that judging others is a way of covering up feelings of insufficiency and insecurity. I decided to examine each judgment I heard in my head and think of it as a mirror allowing me to glimpse some hidden part of myself. I discovered that there were very few people whom I viewed as "acceptable," and the majority of them were very similar to me. Since I rarely allowed myself to relate to anyone who was nor exactly like me, I had put myself into an isolated box. From that day on, I used every judgment as a gift to learn more about myself.

Making this shift meant that I had to give up judging the world. Giving up my righteous intolerance meant that I could no longer deem myself automatically superior to anyone, and the result was that I needed to take a good look at my own flaws.

I recently had a business lunch with a man who displayed objectionable table manners. My first reaction was to judge him as offensive and his table manners as disgusting. When I noticed that I was judging him, I stopped and asked myself what I was feeling. I discovered that I was embarrassed to be seen with someone who was chewing with his mouth open and loudly blowing his nose into his linen napkin. I was astonished to find how much I cared about how the other people in the restaurant perceived me. I consciously had to shift from perceiving the situation as being about him to it being about me and my embarrassment. This allowed me to use this man's actions as a mirror with which to see my own insecurities about being seen with a person who was less than perfect, and how that reflected on me.

The ultimate goal of making such a shift in perception and learning tolerance is to get to the moment of saying, "So what if this person is . . ." and thereby taking your power back. If I had allowed my lunch partner to continue to disgust me, I would have given all my power to him. I would have allowed his actions to dictate my feelings. By recognizing that my judgment of him had everything to do with me, I neutralized the effect his manners had on me and took back my power.

Whenever you find yourself intolerant of someone, ask yourself, "What is the feeling underneath this judgment that I don't want to feel?" It might be discomfort, embarrassment, insecurity, anxiety, or some other feeling of diminishment that the person is evoking in you. Focus on actually feeling that feeling so that your intolerance can evaporate, and you can embrace both your own emotions and the actions or behavior of the person you are judging.

Remember that your judgment of someone will not serve as a protective shield against you becoming like him. Just because I judged my lunch partner as offensive does not prevent me from ever looking or acting like him, just as extending tolerance to him would not cause me to suddenly begin chewing my food with my mouth open. As tough and rigid as judgment and intolerance may be, it can never protect you from anything but love.

"Patience," "Gratitude," and "Tolerance" from *If Life is a Game, These are the Rules: Ten Rules for Being Human as Introduced in Chicken Soup for the Soul* by Chérie Carter-Scott, copyright © 1998 by Chérie Carter-Scott. Used by permission of Broadway Books, an imprint of the Crown Publishing Group, a division of Penguin Random House LLC. All rights reserved.

PATIENCE

> **"***When you get to the end of your rope, tie a knot and hang on.***"**
> — President Franklin D. Roosevelt

In Cherie Carter-Scott's book, *If Life is a Game, These Are the Rules,* she also discusses patience:

Patience is the display of tolerance while awaiting an outcome. You are presented with the lesson of patience the moment you try to create a change within yourself. You expect immediate results and are often disappointed when your first few attempts to follow through fall short. When people who try to lose weight cheat on their diets, they get very frustrated with themselves for not being able to stay with their new eating regime and berate themselves for not changing their patterns.

As you already know, change is rarely easy, and you need to exercise gentleness and patience with yourself as you work your way through this process. Growth can be a slow, painstaking process and patience will provide you with the stamina you need to become the person you want to be.

If you absolutely hate getting stuck in traffic, chances are you need a little work in the area of patience. And, chances are, you will probably get stuck in more traffic jams than someone who has no issue with patience—and not simply because the universe has a sense of humor. You will just notice the traffic more than someone who has no issues with it.

Remember, a lesson will be repeated until learned. It just takes a little patience.

Angela Brown, International Wellness Spokesperson and Facilitator, said that you can be happy in spite of not having what you want. Often wanting a thing so badly and focusing all of your energy on getting it voids the possibility of enjoying what you do have and what is going on around you right now. Learn to be happy and content right now, with whatever equipment or lack of it you have. And if you can't be happy without the things you want, at least don't make those around you miserable too. If patience is one of your character traits in need of refinement, here are some things to consider:

1. Be open to other options.

2. Patience is letting go of the need to be in control. It is the process of surrendering yourself to the wait.

3. Realize that most things of value take time to create. Be okay with waiting.

4. Use impatience as a reminder to exercise your patience.

5. If you are impatient with another person because he or she is hypersensitive, insecure, whiny, cranky, or immature, realize that the person is growing and developing according to his or her own plan, not yours. Limit your access to these people when possible, and when you do have to be around them, focus on their positive attributes not the negative ones. Remember the behaviors you pay attention to are the ones most often repeated.

6. Don't ask or pray for patience or you might be given more opportunities to exercise patience. Instead ask or pray for strength to endure the waiting period with a good attitude.

FORGIVENESS

Invictus

"Out of the night that covers me,
    Black as the pit from pole to pole,
I thank whatever gods may be
    For my unconquerable soul.

In the fell clutch of circumstance
    I have not winced nor cried aloud.
Under the bludgeonings of chance
    My head is bloody, but unbowed.

Beyond this place of wrath and tears
    Looms but the Horror of the shade,
And yet the menace of the years
    Finds and shall find me unafraid.

It matters not how strait the gate,
    How charged with punishments
    the scroll,
I am the master of my fate,
    I am the captain of my soul. "

— William Ernest Henley

The body of research on forgiveness has grown in the last two decades from nearly nonexistent to hundreds of studies and dozens of books. Researchers are finding a powerful connection between forgiving others and our own well-being.

What Is Forgiveness?

Researchers who study forgiveness and its effects on our well-being and happiness are very specific about how they define forgiveness.

Psychologist Sonja Lyubomirsky calls forgiveness "a shift in thinking" toward someone who has wronged you, "such that your desire to harm that person has decreased and your desire to do him good (or to benefit your relationship) has increased." Forgiveness, at a minimum, is a decision to let go of the desire for revenge and ill-will toward the person who wronged you. It may also include feelings of goodwill toward the other person. Forgiveness is also a natural resolution of the grief process, which is the necessary acknowledgment of pain and loss.

Researchers Are Very Clear about What Forgiveness Is Not

Forgiveness is not the same as reconciliation. Forgiveness is one person's inner response to another's perceived injustice. Reconciliation is two people coming together in mutual respect. Reconciliation requires both parties working together. Forgiveness is something that is entirely up to you. Although reconciliation may follow forgiveness, it is possible to forgive without re-establishing or continuing the relationship. The person you forgive may be deceased or no longer part of your life. You may also choose not to reconcile, perhaps because you have no reason to believe that a relationship with the other person is healthy for you.

Forgiveness is not forgetting. "Forgive and forget" seem to go together. However, the process of forgiving involves acknowledging to yourself the wrong that was done to you, reflecting on it, and deciding how you want to think about it. Focusing on forgetting a wrong might lead to denying or suppressing feelings about it, which is not the same as forgiveness. Forgiveness has taken place when you can remember the wrong that was done without feeling resentment or a desire to pursue revenge. Sometimes, after we get to this point, we may forget about some of the wrongs people have done to us. But we don't have to forget in order to forgive.

Forgiveness is not condoning or excusing. Forgiveness does not minimize, justify, or excuse the wrong that was done. Forgiveness also does not mean denying the harm and the feelings that the injustice produced. And forgiveness does not mean putting yourself in a position to be harmed again. You can forgive someone and still take healthy steps to protect yourself, including choosing not to reconcile.

Forgiveness is not justice. It is certainly easier to forgive someone who sincerely apologizes and makes amends. However, justice—which may include acknowledgment of the wrong, apologies, punishment, restitution, or compensation—is separate from forgiveness. You may pursue your rights for justice with or without forgiving someone. And if justice is denied, you can still choose whether or not to forgive.

Forgiveness is a powerful choice you can make when it's right for you that can lead to greater well-being and better relationships.

We also discussed resiliency in Chapter 3 and its importance in mental wellness. So-the question: Is forgiveness and resiliency linked? A study, conducted on over 490 older adults by Dr. Linda Cox Broyles from the University of Tennessee, psychological resilience and its relationship to forgiveness, descriptive and correlational in nature, was. The results showed a statistically significant correlation between forgiveness and resiliency. Therefore, as forgiveness increased resiliency tended to increase as well which may indicate to all of us that being more open to forgiveness may result in us being more resilient in many circumstances enhancing our mental and spiritual health.

Online Assignment: Transgression-Related Interpersonal Motivations Inventory

Complete this assignment online. Go to:
www.grtep.com
Select >Chapter Content>Chapter 5>Enter your username and password

LIVING IN THE PRESENT

> **❝** *There is no such thing in anyone's life as an unimportant day.* **❞**
> — Alexander Woolcott

The following was forwarded to me in an email I received back when I was in graduate school at Indiana University. The author was unidentified, and there was no reference to its source. However, this profoundly resonated with me then, and it still resonates with me today, so I wanted to pass this message on to you:

Imagine there is a bank that credits your account each morning with $86,400. It carries over no balance from day to day. Every evening it deletes whatever part of the balance you failed to use during the day. What would you do? Draw out every cent, of course!

Each of us has such a bank. Its name is TIME. Every morning, it credits you with 86,400 seconds. Every night it writes off, as lost, whatever of this you have failed to invest to good purpose. It carries over no balance. It allows no overdraft. Each day it opens a new account for you. Each night it burns the remains of the day. If you fail to use the day's deposits, the loss is yours. There is no going back. There is no drawing against the "tomorrow."

You must live in the present on today's deposits. Invest it so as to get from it the utmost in health, happiness, and success. The clock is running. Make the most of today.

- To realize the time value of *one year,* ask a student who failed a grade.

- To realize the time value of *one month,* ask a mother who gave birth to a premature baby.

- To realize the time value of *one week,* ask the editor of a weekly newspaper.

- To realize the time value of *one minute,* ask a person who missed the train.

- To realize the time value of *one second,* ask a person who just avoided an accident.

- To realize the time value of *one millisecond,* ask the person who won a silver medal in the Olympics.

Treasure every moment you have. Treasure it more because you shared it with someone special, special enough to spend your time. Remember, time waits for no one. Yesterday is history. Tomorrow is a mystery. Today is a gift. That's why it's called "the present."

ASSIGNMENT: "If I Had It to Do Over . . ." Complete the sentences accordingly.

Nadine Stair wrote a piece called "If I Had It to Do Over" in which as an older woman she looked back on her life and remarked about the things she would do differently. Some of the things she said were: "I would wear more purple; I would eat fewer beans and more ice cream; I would go barefoot earlier in spring."

And you? Imagine you were 85 years old right now and you were looking back on the life you had lived. What would you do differently?

Complete the following ten sentences.

If I had it to do over again, I would:

1. _____

_____

2. _____

_____

3. _____

_____

4. _____

_____

5. _____

_____

6. _____

_____

7. _____

_____

8. _____

_____

9. _____

_____

10. _____

_____

Of the 10 items you listed, which ones can you begin doing this month?

_____

_____

_____

_____

From *Health & Fitness: A Guide to a Healthy Lifestyle,* 3rd edition by Laura Bounds, Kristin Brekken Shea, Dottiedee Agnor, & Gayden Darnell. Copyright © 2012 by Kendall Hunt Publishing Company. Reprinted with permission.

Online Assignment: Satisfaction with Life Scale

Complete this assignment online. Go to:

www.grtep.com

Select >Chapter Content>Chapter 5>Enter your username and password

TIPS TO BECOMING SPIRITUALLY HEALTHY

> ❝*The human spirit is never finished when it is defeated.*
> *It is finished when it surrenders.*❞
>
> — Ben Stein

- Listen to your inner voice. Pay attention to your feelings, emotions, and thoughts and trust your intuition. Your inner voice will often help you find your direction, but you need to stop and listen.

- A strong mind and body are part of a healthy spiritual life.

- You have the CHOICE about how you can feel about whatever is going on in your life.

- Share your values and count your blessings.

- Be forgiving and grateful.

- Peace is not something you can force on anything or anyone—much less upon one's own mind.

■ Maintain the health and wellness of your soul.

■ Find inner serenity and tranquility. Different people have different ways of centering themselves in a calm place—meditation, prayer, recreation, exercise, or solitude. Find what works for you and then make sure you find the time to pursue it.

■ Reflect on your beliefs: Whether or not you subscribe to any particular religious or spiritual group, think about how you can see and make sense of the world and events that happen.

■ Enhance your spiritual wellness and awareness by using yoga and meditation to tap into the riches of mind-body connection; music and poetry to enhance your self-awareness; soul awareness to find out who you are and your purpose in life; mind calming techniques to obtain inner peace and harmony; philosophy as a way of life, nurturing as your will is always within your power; and/or spiritual journaling as a tool of self-development.

SOURCE: Wellness for Healthy Positive Living: Spiritual Wellness Facts & Tips, Santa Clara University's Wellness Center: Spiritual Wellness Tips for Good Spiritual Health.

Helpful Internet Sites

authentichappiness.com
HeartQuotes: heartquotes.net
Holistic Spirituality: beliefnet.com
meaningandhappiness.com
Prayer & Spirituality in Health: nccam.nih.gov/news/newsletter/2005_winter/prayer.htm
Spirituality & Health: spiritualhealth.com
Spiritual Wellness: skysite.org/wellness.html
viacharacter.org

References

Alloy, L., Abramson, L., & Chiara, A. (2000). On the mechanisms by which optimism promotes positive mental and physical health. In J. Gillham (ed.) The science of optimism and hope: Research essays in honor of Martin E.P. Seligman (pp. 201–212). Philadelphia: Templeton Foundation Press.

Bounds, L. *Health and Fitness: A Guide to a Healthy Lifestyle.* Definition of Spiritual Health. Kendall Hunt Publishing Company (2006): 3.

Bounds, L. *Health and Fitness: A Guide to a Healthy Lifestyle.* If I Had It to Do Over. Kendall Hunt Publishing Company (2006): 19.

Broyles, L.C. Resilience: Its Relationship to Forgiveness in Older Adults. ProQuest Dissertations and Theses (Oct. 2005). gradworks.umi.com/31/77/3177245.html accessed January 11, 2012.

Carter-Scott, C. *If Life Is a Game, These Are the Rules.* Gratitude. Broadway Books, division of Bantam Doubleday Dell Publishing Group, Inc. (1998): 73–75.

Carter-Scott, C. *If Life Is a Game, These Are the Rules*. Patience. Broadway Books, division of Bantam Doubleday Dell Publishing Group, Inc. (1998): 60 61.

Carter-Scott, C. *If Life Is a Game, These Are the Rules*. Tolerance. Broadway Books, division of Bantam Doubleday Dell Publishing Group, Inc. (1998): 86–89.

Danner, D., Snowdon, D, & Friesen, W. (2001). Positive emotion in early life and longevity: findings from the nun study. Journal of Personality and Social Psychology, 80, 804–813.

Diener, E. & Diener, C. (1996). Most people are happy. Psychological Science, 3, 181–85.

Diener, E., Suh, E. M., Smith, H. L., & Shao, L. (1995). National differences in reported well-being: Why do they occur? *Social Indicators Research, 34*, 7–32.

Emmons, R. A. & Crumpler, C.A. (2000). Gratitude as a human strength: Appraising the evidence, Journal of Social & Clinical Psychology, 19, 56–69.

Gilbert, D.T., Pinel, E.C., Wilson, T.D., Blumberg, S.J., & Wheatley, T. (1998). Immune neglect: A source of durability bias in affective forecasting. Journal of Personality and Social Psychology, 75, 617–638.

Haidt, J., The Positive emotion of elevation, Prevention & Treatment, 3.

Hettler, B. The National Wellness Institute. *The Six Dimensions of Wellness: Intellectual Wellness.* nationalwellness.org accessed on 1.3.08.

Isen, A.M. (1993). Positive affect and decision making. In M. Lewis & J.M. Haviland (Eds.), Handbook of emotions (pp. 261–277). New York: Guilford Press.

King, L. A., & Broyles, S. J. (1997). Wishes, gender, personality, and well-being. *Journal of Personality, 65*, 49–76.

King, L. A., & Napa, C. N. (1998). What makes a life good? Journal of Personality and Social Psychology, 75, 156–165.

King, L.A. & Miner, K.N. (2000). Writing about the perceived benefits of traumatic events: Implications for physical health, Personality and Social Psychology Bulletin, 26, 220–230.

King, L.A. (2001). The health benefits of writing about life goals, Personality and Social Psychology Bulletin, 27, 798–807.

Lyubomirsky, S., King, L.A. & Diener, E. (2005). The benefits of frequent positive affect: Does happiness lead to success. Psychological Bulletin, 131, 803–855.

Millard, B. *Explorer's Guide: Starting the College Journey with a Sense of Purpose.* Empowered by Spiritual Strengths. Kendall Hunt Publishing Company (year?): 262–263; 273–274.

Millard, B. *Explorer's Guide: Starting the College Journey with a Sense of Purpose.* Living with Character. Kendall Hunt Publishing Company (year?): 82–84, 93, 97–98.

Myers, D.G. (2000). The funds, friends, and faith of happy people, American Psychologist, 55, 56–67.

Peterson, C. & Vaidya, R.S. (2003). Optimism as virtue and vice. In E.C. Chang & L.J. Sanna (Eds.), Virtue, vice, and personality: The complexity of behavior (pp. 23–37). Washington, D.C.: American Psychological Association.

Peterson, C. (2006). Primer in positive psychology. New York Oxford University Press.

Ryan, R. M. & Deci, E.L. (2000). Self-determination theory and the facilitation of intrinsic motivation, social development, and well-being American Psychologist, 55, 68–78.

Roth, G. *Why Weight? A Guide to Compulsive Eating.* If I Had to Do It Over. Dutton Signet, a division of Penguin Group (USA) Inc. (1989).

Santa Clara University's Wellness Center: Intellectual Wellness Tips for Good Intellectual Health. scu.edu/wellness/Intellectual-Wellness.cfm accessed on 1.3.08.

Schick, C. et al. *Surviving College: A "Real World" Experience*. In Hot Pursuit of Happiness. Kendall Hunt Publishing Company (2001): 181–183; 186; 188–191.

Schwartz, B., Ward, A., Monterosso, J., Lyubomirsky, S., White, K., & Lehman, D.R., Maximizing versus satisfying: Happiness is a matter of choice. Journal of Personality and Social Psychology, 83, Nov 2002, 1178–1197.

Seligman, M.E.P. & Pawelski, J.O. (2003). Positive Psychology: FAQs. Psychological Inquiry. 14, 159–163.

Seligman, M.E.P. (1991). Learned Optimism. New York: Knopf.

Seligman, M.E.P. (2002). Authentic Happiness: Using the New Positive Psychology to Realize Your Potential for Lasting Fulfillment. New York: Free Press/Simon and Schuster.

Seligman, M.E.P., Steen, T.A., Park, N. & Peterson, C. (2005). Positive psychology progress: Empirical validation of interventions. American Psychologist, 60, 410–421.

Stanley, C. *When Tragedy Strikes*. Introduction and Compassion and Care. Thomas Nelson Inc (2001): Introduction (x–xi) and 8–17.

Taylor, S.E., Kemeny, M.E., Reed, G.M., Bower, J.E. & Gruenwald, T.L. (2000). Psychological resources, positive illusions, and health. American Psychologist, 55, 99–109.

Wellness for Healthy Positive Living. Spiritual Wellness. for.gov.bc.ca/hrb/hw/index.htm accessed on 1.3.08.

Wilson, D.T., Meyers, J., & Gilbert, D.T. (2001). Lessons from the past: Do people learn from experience that emotional reactions are short-lived. Journal of Personality and Social Psychology, 78, 821–836.

Words of Wellness with Angela Brown—Patience. wordsofwellness.com accessed on 1.7.08.

CHAPTER 6

Intellectual Wellness

> "The function of education is to teach one to think intensively and to think critically. Intelligence plus character— that is the goal of true education."
>
> — Dr. Martin Luther King, Jr.

This chapter is modified and adapted from "Thinking Critically and Creatively" and "Learning Style and Intelligence" of Fralick, M. *College & Career Success: Thinking Critically and Creatively.* Kendall Hunt Publishing Company (2016).

The objectives in this chapter include the understanding of: ————

- Influences on Behavior
- Critical Thinking
- Creative Thinking
- Bolstering Working Memory
- Learning Style and how it impacts intelligence
- Learning techniques
- Personality and learning preferences
- Making Choices
- Multiple Intelligences
- Practicing Mindfulness and how it affects so much

Online Reminders

- Complete the poll question before the next class meeting.
- Complete the interactive activities for this chapter.
- Complete all of the online assignments for this chapter.

ntellectual Wellness—Intellectual wellness is one's creativity and engagement with stimulating mental activities. Intellectual wellness not only utilizes your own resources but other learning resources to expand knowledge and to improve skills, usually by participating actively in scholastic, cultural, and community activities. Being intellectually healthy also includes the opportunities you take when problem-solving (and how you respond or react); opening your mind to new ideas, thoughts, and cultures; thinking critically; seeking out new challenges; and using your creative skills. As The National Institute of Wellness states, intellectual wellness follows these tenets:

1. It is better to stretch and challenge our minds with intellectual and creative pursuits than to become self-satisfied and unproductive.

2. It is better to identify potential problems and to choose appropriate courses of action based on available information than to wait, worry, and contend with major concerns later.

Why Is This Important? How Does It Apply to You?

People who are intellectually healthy are curious and never stop learning on their own will. You may find yourself reading more newspapers, magazines, credible Websites, fiction or non-fiction books, becoming a part of causes and committees for the mere fact of learning more. You may take time to "smell the roses." You may spend more time on your way to and from class noticing the beauty around you, like the scenery, trees, flowers, the sky, people, and buildings. You may find your sense of humor and your sense of place in this world broadening because you have let your mind become more open and accepting. When you open your mind, you become that resource and inspiration for others.

Assimilating what you learn in the classroom with what you experience outside the classroom positively enhances your potential for living a more fulfilling life. Again, it all relates to a balance in your life. Life isn't just lived inside a classroom. Life is lived dependent of physical space or structure, and it is meant to be lived with a respectful balance of all the dimensions of wellness.

PRE-CLASS SURVEY: Take your intellectual wellness survey before your next class meeting and identify your level of intellectual wellness. Circle either Yes or No, total up each column, and check your score.

I have specific intellectual goals, like learning a new skill.	YES	NO
I pursue mentally stimulating interests.	YES	NO
I am generally satisfied with my education or my career path.	YES	NO
I have positive thoughts daily.	YES	NO
I would describe myself as a lifelong learner.	YES	NO
I commit energy and time to professional and self-development.	YES	NO
I access credible and reliable resources and think critically about issues.	YES	NO
I read more than ten books a year.	YES	NO
I regularly use my leisure time for hobbies.	YES	NO
I adapt well to change.	YES	NO

TOTAL

WHAT YOUR TOTAL MEANS:

8 or more Yes answers	Excellent	Your habits are positively enhancing your health.
5–7 Yes answers	Average	You are obviously trying but there is room to improve.
4 or less Yes answers	Not So Good	There is a need for improvement in your daily habits.

Source: "Wellness for Healthy Positive Living." *Intellectual Wellness Inventory.* www.for.gov.bc.ca/hrb/hw/index.htm

CRITICAL THINKING

❝*Never be afraid to sit awhile and think.***❞**

— Unknown

What does thinking critically mean? Critical thinking involves questioning established ideas, creating new ideas, and using information to solve problems. In critical thinking, reasoning is used in pursuit of the truth. While in college or beyond college, critical thinking is helpful in being a good citizen and a productive member of society.

When thinking critically, your brain cells communicate with each other through fiber-like branches called dendrites. When brain cells are stimulated, dendrites grow, increasing the number of connections between cells. This improves your memory, attention span, and ability to learn.

Language, Media Messages and the Brain: Influences on Behavior

The next book by Drew Westen, expert in neuro-linguistics, is called "The Political Brain: The Role of Emotion in Deciding the Fate of the Nation." In this book, the author relies on research about the brain and advertising to explain political choices made by U.S. citizens. Two main ideas presented are that humans make decisions based more on emotions (80%) than reason and political advertising is designed to arouse emotions, not reason. Furthermore, brain research on advertising has revealed dual systems of emotional processing as shown in Figure 4, the behavioral approach system activated by positive words, images, sounds, music, backdrop, tone of voice, etc. and the behavioral inhibition system activated by negative words, images, sounds, music, backdrop, tone of voice, etc. Different parts of the brain and different neurotransmitters are involved in each system. Dopamine creates a pleasurable emotional state to be welcomed. Norepinephrine arouses anxiety, fear and the inclination to "fight or flee." Whether individuals are aware or unaware, messages can activate one or the other system and create either a positive or negative emotional association with an object.

These dual systems serve important functions. They provide internal checks and balances, leading to the pursuit of enjoyable activities but putting the brakes on when individuals are about to get themselves into trouble. Those individuals who are too high on one system and too low on the other may risk psychological problems, being vulnerable to depression and anxiety on the one hand or to excessive risk taking and antisocial behavior on the other. Given time and repetition, media messages that appeal to emotion can distort reality and create malfunctions of internal regulation and cause individuals to make choices that are against their own best interests.

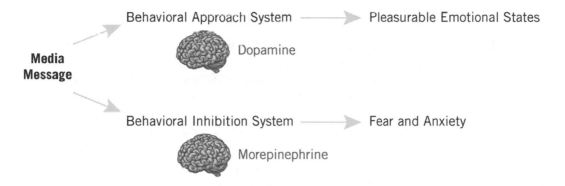

Brain Research and Advertising and the Dual Systems of Emotional Processing Activated in Response to Media Messages

Our next book, "The End of Overeating Taking Control of the Insatiable American Appetite" by former head of the U.S. Food and Drug Administration, David Kessler, reaffirms many of Westen's points. Kessler contends that the business of the food industry is to encourage consumption by creating highly rewarding stimuli based on the layering of the three most satiable ingredients for humans: sugar, fat and salt (SFS), in many food products. The food industry takes advantage of our brain chemistry by using SFS as a reinforcer which humans will consume even when they don't feel hungry, leading to overeating. The food and beverage industry deliberately utilizes consumption reinforcers such as sight, smell, location and anticipation to get us to want and buy their products. Additionally, neurotransmitters that are involved with positive emotions (comfort, stress relief), including dopamine, are imbedded in cues to eat. Neurons in the brain that are activated by appearance, smell, taste and texture of SFS are part of a circuit that produces endorphins and opioids, which can actually relive pain and stress and produce calming—"comfort foods."

Through media literacy you learn to answer five essential questions:

- Who created this message?

- What creative techniques are being used to attract my attention?

- How might different people understand this message differently?

- What lifestyles, values, and points of view are represented in or omitted from this message?

- Why is this message being sent?

Critical Thinking

Critical thinking involves questioning established ideas, creating new ideas, and using information to solve problems. In critical thinking, reasoning is used in the pursuit of truth. Part of obtaining a college education is learning to think critically. Understanding the concepts of critical thinking will help you succeed in college courses in which critical thinking is used.

Beyond college, critical thinking is helpful in being a good citizen and a productive member of society. Throughout history, critical thinkers have helped to advance civilization. Thoughts that were once widely accepted were questioned, and newer and more useful ideas were introduced. For example, it was once assumed that bloodsucking leeches were helpful in curing diseases. Some critical thinkers questioned this practice, and the science of medicine was advanced. It was not so long ago that women were not allowed to vote. Critical thinkers questioned this practice so that women could participate in a democratic society.

A lack of critical thinking can lead to great tragedy. In his memoirs, Adolf Eichmann, who played a central role in the Nazis' killing of six million Jews during World War II, wrote:

> *"From my childhood, obedience was something I could not get out of my system. When I entered the armed services at the age of 27, I found being obedient not a bit more difficult than it had been during my life at that point. It was unthinkable that I would not follow orders. Now that I look back, I realize that a life predicated on being obedient and taking orders is a very comfortable life indeed. Living in such a way reduces to a minimum one's own need to think."[1]*

© art4all/Shutterstock.com

Critical and creative thinking are closely related. If you can think critically, you have the freedom to be creative and generate new ideas. The great American jurist and philosopher Oliver Wendell Holmes noted:

> *"There are one-story intellects, two-story intellects, and three-story intellects with skylights. All fact-collectors who have no aim beyond their facts are one-story men. Twostory men compare, reason, generalize, using the labor of the fact-collectors as their own. Three-story men idealize, imagine, predict—their best illumination comes from above through skylights."*

Use the information in this chapter to become a three-story intellect with skylights. And by the way, even though Oliver Wendell Holmes talked about men, women can be three-story intellects too.

Fallacies in Reasoning

To think critically, you need to be able to recognize fallacies in reasoning.[2] Fallacies are patterns of incorrect reasoning. Recognizing these fallacies can help you to avoid them in your thinking and writing. You can also become aware of when others are using these fallacies to persuade you. They may use these fallacies for their own purpose, such as power or financial gain. As you read through these fallacies in reasoning, think about examples you have experienced in your personal life.

- **Appeal to authority.** It is best to make decisions by reviewing the information and arguments and reaching our own conclusions. Sometimes we are encouraged to rely on experts for a recommendation because they have specialized information. Obviously, we need to have trust in the experts to accept their conclusions. However, when we cite some person as an authority in a certain area when they are not, we make an appeal to a questionable authority. For example, when a company uses famous sports figures to endorse a product, a particular brand of athletic shoes or breakfast cereal, they are appealing to a questionable authority. Just because the athletes are famous does not mean they are experts on the product they are endorsing. They are endorsing the product to earn money. Many commercials you see on TV use appeals to a questionable authority.

- **Jumping to conclusions.** When we jump to conclusions, we make hasty generalizations. For example, if a college student borrows money from a bank and does not pay it back, the manager of the bank might conclude that all college students are poor risks and refuse to give loans to other college students.

- **Making generalizations.** We make generalizations when we say that all members of a group are the same, as in:

  All lawyers are greedy.
  All blondes are airheads.

Of course, your occupation does not determine whether or not you are greedy, and the color of your hair does not determine your intelligence. Such thinking leads to harmful stereotypes and fallacies in reasoning. Instead of generalizing, think of people as unique individuals.

■ **Attacking the person rather than discussing the issues.** To distract attention from the issues, we often attack the person. Political candidates today are routinely asked about personal issues such as extramarital affairs and drug use. Of course personal integrity in politicians is important, but attacking the person can serve as a smokescreen to direct attention away from important political issues. Critical thinkers avoid reacting emotionally to personalities and use logical thinking to analyze the issues.

■ **Appeal to common belief.** Just because something is a common belief does not mean that it is true. At one time people believed that the world was flat and that when you got to the edge of the earth, you would fall off. If you were to survey the people who lived in that period in history, the majority would have agreed that the earth was flat. A survey just tells us what people believe. The survey does not tell us what is true and accurate.

■ **Appeal to common practice.** Appealing to common practice is the "everyone else is doing it" argument. Just because everyone else does it doesn't mean that it is right. Here are some common examples of this fallacy:

> It is okay to cheat in school. Everyone else does it.
> It is okay to speed on the freeway. Everyone else does it.
> It is okay to cheat on your taxes. Everyone else does it.

■ **Appeal to tradition.** Appeal to tradition is a variation of the "everyone else is doing it" argument. The appeal to tradition is "we've always done it that way." Just because that is the way it has always been done doesn't mean it is the best way to do it. With this attitude, it is very difficult to make changes and improve our ways of doing things. While tradition is very important, it is open to question. For example, construction and automotive technology have traditionally been career choices for men, but not for women. When women tried to enter or work in these careers, there was resistance from those who did not want to change traditions. This resistance limited options for women.

■ **Two wrongs.** In this fallacy, it is assumed that it is acceptable to do something because other people are doing something just as bad. For example, if someone cuts you off on the freeway, you may assume that it is acceptable to zoom ahead and cut in front of his or her car. The "two wrongs" fallacy has an element of retribution, or getting back at the other person. The old saying, "Two wrongs do not make a right," applies in this situation.

■ **The slippery slope or domino theory.** The slippery slope or domino theory is best explained with an example. A student might think: If I fail the test, I will fail this class. If I fail this class, I will drop out of college. My parents will disown me and I will lose the respect of my friends. I will not be able to get a good job. I will start drinking and end up homeless. In this fallacy, the negative consequences of our actions are only remotely possible, but are assumed to be certain. These dire consequences influence people's decisions and change behavior. In this situation, it is important to evaluate these consequences. One does not necessarily lead to the other. If you fail the test, you could study and pass the next test. As a child you were probably cautioned about many slippery slopes in life:

> Brush your teeth or your teeth will fall out.
> Do your homework or you will never get into college and get a good job.

■ **Wishful thinking.** In wishful thinking, an extremely positive outcome, however remote, is proposed as a distraction from logical thinking. For example, a new sports stadium may be proposed. Extremely positive outcomes may be presented, such as downtown redevelopment, the attraction of professional sports teams, increased revenue, and the creation of jobs. Opponents, on the other hand, might foresee increased taxes, lack of parking, and neglect of other important social priorities such as education and shelter for the homeless. Neither position is correct if we assume that the outcomes are certain and automatic. Outcomes need to be evaluated realistically.

Wishful thinking is often used in commercials to sell products. Here are a few examples:

> Eat what you want and lose weight.
> Use this cream and look younger.
> Use this cologne and women will be attracted to you.
> Invest your money and get rich quick.

■ **Appeal to fear or scare tactics.** Sometimes people appeal to fear as a way of blocking rational thinking. For example, a political commercial showed wolves chasing a person through the forest. It was clearly designed to evoke fear. The message was to vote against a proposition to limit lawyers' fees. The idea was that if lawyers' fees were limited, the poor client would be a victim of limited legal services.

This commercial used scare tactics to interfere with rational thinking about the issue.

■ **Appeal to pity.** In an appeal to pity, emotion is used to replace logic. It is what is known as a "sob story." Appeals to pity may be legitimate when used to foster charity and empathy. However, the sob story uses emotion in place of reason to persuade and is often exaggerated. College faculties often hear sob stories from students having academic difficulties:

> Please don't disqualify me from college. I failed all my classes because I was emotionally upset when my grandmother died.

> Please don't fail me in this class. If you fail me, my parents will kick me out of the house and I will not be able to get health insurance.

> If you fail me in this class, I won't be eligible to play football and my future as a professional will be ruined.

- **Appeal to loyalty.** Human beings are social creatures who enjoy being attached to a group. We feel loyalty to our friends, families, schools, communities, teams, and favorite musicians. Appeals to loyalty ask you to act according to a group's best interests without considering whether the actions are right or wrong. Critical thinkers, however, do not support an idea just to show support for a group with which they identify.

  Peer pressure is related to the loyalty fallacy. With peer pressure, members of a group may feel obliged to act in a certain way because they think members of the group act that way. Another variation of the loyalty fallacy is called the bandwagon argument. It involves supporting a certain idea just to be part of the group. This tendency is powerful when the group is perceived to be powerful or "cool." In elections, people often vote for the candidate that is perceived to be the most popular. If everyone else is voting for the candidate, they assume the candidate must be the best. This is not necessarily true.

- **Appeal to prejudice.** A prejudice is judging a group of people or things positively or negatively, even if the facts do not agree with the judgment. A prejudice is based on a stereotype in which all members of a group are judged to be the same. Speakers sometimes appeal to prejudice to gain support for their causes. Listen for the appeal to prejudice in hate speeches or literature directed against different ethnicities, genders, or sexual orientations.

- **Appeal to vanity.** The appeal to vanity is also known as "apple polishing." The goal of this strategy is to get agreement by paying compliments. Students who pay compliments to teachers and then ask for special treatment are engaging in apple polishing.

- **Post hoc reasoning, or false causes.** Post hoc reasoning has to do with cause and effect. It explains many superstitions. If I play a good game of golf whenever I wear a certain hat, I might conclude that the hat causes me to play a good golf game. The hat, however, is a false cause of playing a good game of golf. I may feel more comfortable wearing my lucky hat, but it is a secondary reason for playing well. I play well because I practice my golf skills and develop my self-confidence. In scientific research, care is taken to test for false causes. Just because an event regularly follows another event does not mean that the first event caused the second event. For example, when the barometer falls, it rains. The falling barometer does not cause the rain; a drop in atmospheric pressure causes the rain. If falling barometers caused the rain, we could all be rainmakers by adjusting our barometers.

■ **Straw man or woman.** Watch for this fallacy during election time. Using this strategy, a politician creates a misleading image of someone else's statements, ideas, or beliefs to make them easy to attack. For example, politicians might accuse their opponents of raising taxes. That may only be part of the story, however. Maybe their opponents also voted for many tax-saving measures. When politicians or anyone else use the straw man fallacy, they are falsifying or oversimplifying. Use your critical thinking to identify the straw man or woman (political opponent) in the next election. Of course you don't have to be a politician to use this strategy. People use this strategy when they spread gossip or rumors about someone they want to discredit.

■ **Cult behavior.** Cults and doomsday forecasters spread unorthodox and sometimes harmful beliefs with great fervor. These thoughts are perpetuated through mindcontrol techniques. With mind control, members of a group are taught to suppress natural emotions and accept the ideas of the group in exchange for a sense of belonging. These groups do not allow members to think critically or question the belief system. Mind control is the opposite of critical thinking. It is important to use critical thinking when you encounter beliefs for which there is no hard evidence. An example is the Heaven's Gate cult:

> It all seems perfectly ludicrous: 39 people don their new sneakers, pack their flight bags and poison themselves in the solemn belief that a passing UFO will whisk them off to Wonderland.

© elder nurkovic/Shutterstock.com

How to Become a Critical Thinker

The Critical Thinking Process

When thinking about a complex problem, use these steps in the critical thinking process:

1. **State the problem in a clear and simple way.** Sometimes the message is unclear or obscured by appeals to emotion. Stating the problem clearly brings it into focus so that you can identify the issue and begin to work on it.

2. **Identify the alternative views.** In looking at different views, you open your mind to a wider range of options. The diagram entitled "Alternative Views" below gives a perspective on point of view. For every issue, there are many points of view. The larger circle represents these many points of view. The individual point of view is represented by a dot on the larger circle. Experience, values, beliefs, culture, and knowledge influence an individual's point of view.

3. **Watch for fallacies** in reasoning when looking at alternative views.

4. **Find at least three different answers.** In searching for these different answers, you force yourself to look at all the possibilities before you decide on the best answer.

5. **Construct your own reasonable view.** After looking at the alternatives and considering different answers to the problem, construct your own reasonable view. Practice this process using the critical thinking exercises at the end of this chapter.

ISSUE PERSON TOPIC

Individual Point of View Based on:
· Experience
· Values
· Beliefs
· Culture
· Knowledge

Alternative Views

Tips for Critical Thinking

1. **Be aware of your mindset.** A mindset is a pattern of thought that you use out of habit. You develop patterns of thinking based on your personal experiences, culture, and environment. When the situation changes, your old mindset may need to change as well.

2. **Be willing to say, "I don't know."** With this attitude you are open to exploring new ideas. In today's rapidly changing world, it is not possible to know everything. Rather than trying to know everything, it is more important to be able to find the information you need.

3. **Practice tolerance for other people's ideas.** We all have different views of the world based on our own experiences and can benefit from an open exchange of information.

4. **Try to look for several answers and understand many points of view.** The world is not either-or or black-and-white. Looking at all the possibilities is the first step in finding a creative solution.

5. **Understand before criticizing.** Life is not about justifying your point of view. It is important to understand and then offer your suggestions.

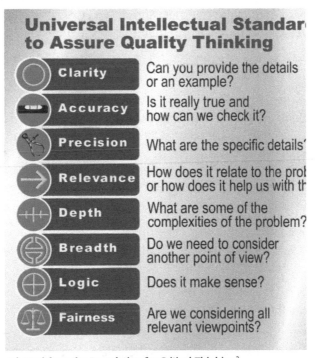

Adapted from the Foundation for Critical Thinking[3]

6. **Realize that your emotions can get in the way of clear thinking.** We all have beliefs that are important to us. It is difficult to listen to a different point of view when someone questions your personal beliefs. Open your mind to see all the alternatives. Then construct your reasonable view.

7. **Notice the source of the information you are analyzing.** Political announcements are required to include information about the person or organization paying for the ad. Knowing who paid for an advertisement can help you understand and evaluate the point of view that is being promoted.

8. **Ask the question,** "What makes the author think so?" In this way, you can discover what premises the author is using to justify his or her position.

9. **Ask the question,** "So what?" Ask this question to determine what is important and how the author reached the conclusion.

Critical Thinking over the Internet

The Internet is revolutionizing the way we access and retrieve information today. Through the use of search engines, websites, electronic periodicals, and online reference materials, it is possible to find just about any information you need. The Internet is also full of scams, rumors, gossip, hoaxes, exaggerations, and illegal activity. Anyone can put anything on the Internet. You will need to apply critical thinking to the information that you find on the Internet. Author Reid Goldsborough offers these suggestions for thinking critically about material on the Internet:

- **Don't be fooled by appearances.** It is easy to create a flashy and professionallooking website. Some products and services are legitimate, but some are scams.

- **Find out about the person or organization providing the information.** There should be links to a home page that lists the author's background and credentials. You need to be skeptical if the author is not identified. If you cannot identify the person who authored the website, find out what organization sponsored the site. Most of the Internet resources cited in this text are provided by educational or government sources. It is the goal of these organizations to provide the public with information.

- **Look for the reason the information was posted.** What is the agenda? Keep this in mind when evaluating the information. Many websites exist to sell a product or influence public opinion.

- **Look for the date that the information was created or revised.** A good website posts the date of creation or revision.

- **Try to verify the information elsewhere,** especially if the information is at odds with common sense or what you believe to be true. Verify the information through other websites or your local library.[4]

© Sam72/Shutterstock.com

How to Recognize a Scam

Use your critical thinking skills to recognize a scam or hoax. How can you recognize a scam? Here are some signs to watch for:

- **Be aware of big promises.** If something sounds too good to be true, it probably is a hoax. If you are promised $5,000 a month for working part time out of your home, be careful. If you are offered a new TV in a box for $50, the box may contain stolen goods or even rocks!

- **The word "free" is often used to catch your attention to make a sale.** Few things in life are free.

- **A similar tactic is to offer money or a prize.** The scam goes like this: "Congratulations! You have just won a . . ." Be especially careful if you have to pay money to claim your prize.

- **Beware of high-pressure tactics.** A common scam is to ask you to pay money now or the price will go up. Take your time to think carefully about your expenditures. If the deal is legitimate, it will be there tomorrow.

- **To avoid identity theft, be careful about disclosing personal information** such as Social Security numbers and credit card numbers. Disclose this information only to people and organizations you know and trust.

- **If you suspect a scam, research the offer on the Internet.** Use a search engine such as yahoo.com or google.com and type in the word "scam." You can find descriptions of many different types of scams. You can also find information on the latest scams or file a complaint at the Federal Trade Commission website at www.ftc.gov.

CREATIVE THINKING

What Is Creativity?

To see creativity in action, all we need to do is to look at young children. Movie producer Steven Spielberg describes their creativity:

> *"The greatest quality that we can possess is curiosity, a genuine interest in the world around us. The most used word—and I have five kids, so I know what I'm talking about—the most used word in a child's vocabulary is 'why.' A child doesn't blindly accept things as they are, doesn't blindly believe in limits, doesn't blindly believe in the words spoken by some authority figure like me."[5]*

Creativity involves both divergent and convergent thinking. **Divergent thinking** is the ability to discover many alternatives. The creative individual looks for problems, asks why, and comes up with many different answers. J. P. Guilford, a researcher on creativity, said that "the person who is capable of producing a large number of ideas per unit of time, other things being equal, has a greater chance of having significant ideas."[6] After many ideas are created, **convergent thinking** is used to combine the ideas to find new and creative solutions. These creative ideas are used to make a new plan of action.

Creative thinking is useful in fields such as the arts, science, and business. Creativity helps in the enjoyment of outside activities, such as hobbies, that help us to lead

© Hermin/Shutterstock.com

satisfying lives. Creativity is important in generating alternatives necessary for effective problem solving and coming up with creative solutions to the challenges we all face in life. Creative individuals are motivated, engaged, and open to new ideas. Guilford defines creative behavior as follows:

> *"The individual who behaves creatively is oriented toward selecting and solving meaningful problems, using an inner drive to recombine his or her storehouse of experiences in new ways. In attacking problems, he or she does not act as a conformist; instead, he or she pioneers often, is not afraid to fail frequently, but is productive in the long run."[7]*

The Three S's of Creativity: Sensitivity, Synergy, and Serendipity

The creative process involves sensitivity, synergy, and serendipity. Creative persons use their **sensitivity** to discover the world and spot problems, deficiencies, and incongruities. A person who is sensitive asks, "Why does this happen?" Sensitive persons are also inventive and ask the question, "How can I do this?" They are problem finders as well as problem solvers.

Synergy occurs when two or more elements are associated in a new way and the result is greater than the sum of the parts. For example, imagine a machine that combines the telephone, the computer, the television, and a music player. The combining of these familiar devices into one machine is changing the way we live. Another example of synergy is the old saying, "Two heads are better than one." When two or more people work together and share ideas, the result is often greater than what one person could produce alone. This is the essence of creativity.

The word **serendipity** is attributed to Horace Walpole, who wrote a story about the Persian princes of Serendip. The princes made unexpected discoveries while they were looking for something else. Serendipity is finding something by a lucky accident. You can only take advantage of a lucky accident if you look around and find new meaning and opportunity in the event. An example of serendipity comes from a story about the famous musician Duke Ellington. He was playing at an outdoor concert when a noisy plane flew over the stage. He changed the tempo of the music to go with the sounds of the airplane and directed the plane along with the orchestra. Another example of serendipity is Alexander Fleming's discovery of penicillin. He was growing bacteria in his lab when a spore of *penicillium notatum* blew in the window, landed on the bacteria, and killed it. Instead of throwing away a ruined experiment, he discovered the antibiotic penicillin, one of the most important medical discoveries ever made. Serendipitous people are flexible and open to possibilities as well as fearless in trying something new. They learn to seize the opportunities that just happen in life.

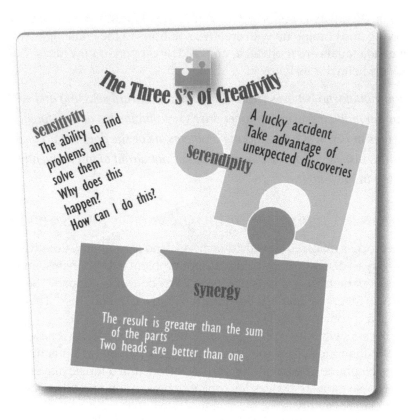

Sensitivity, synergy, and serendipity are the three S's of creativity.

Courtesy of Charlotte Moore. © Kendall Hunt Publishing Company.

Creative Thinking Techniques

- **Brainstorming.** One of the most important components of creativity is the ability to use divergent thinking to generate many ideas or alternatives. Brainstorming is one of the most frequently used techniques to develop divergent thinking. The key to brainstorming is to delay critical judgment to allow for the spontaneous flow of ideas. Critical judgment about the merit of ideas can hinder the creative process if it is applied too early. Here are the rules of brainstorming:

  - Generate a large quantity of ideas without regard to quality. This increases the likelihood that some of the ideas will be good or useful.

  - Set a time limit to encourage quick thinking. The time limit is generally short, from three to five minutes.

© VLADGRIN/Shutterstock.com

- Set a goal or quota for the number of ideas you want to generate. The goal serves as a motivator.

- The wilder and more unusual the ideas, the better. It is easier to tame down crazy ideas than to think up new ideas.

- Use synergy by brainstorming with a group of people. Build on other people's ideas. Sometimes two ideas combined can make one better idea.

- Select the best ideas from the list.

- **Relaxed attention.** Can you imagine being relaxed and paying attention at the same time? Robert McKim describes this as the paradox of the Ho-hum and the Aha![8] To be creative, it is first necessary to relax. The brain works better when it is relaxed. By relaxing, the individual releases full energy and attention to the task at hand. Athletes and entertainers must master the art of relaxation before they can excel in athletics or entertainment. If the muscles are too tense, blood flow is restricted and energy is wasted. However, totally relaxed individuals cannot think at all. They might even be asleep!

    Some tension, but not too much, is needed to think and be creative; hence the term "relaxed attention." In the creative process, the person first thinks about a task, problem, or creation and then relaxes to let the ideas incubate. During this incubation period, the person often gets a flash of insight or feeling of "Aha!" Famous artist Pablo Picasso described this process:

    > "For me creation first starts with contemplation, and I need long, idle hours of meditation. It is then that I work most. I look at flies, at flowers, at leaves and trees around me. I let my mind drift at ease, just like a boat in the current. Sooner or later, it is caught by something. It gets precise. It takes shape . . . my next painting motif is decided."[9]

As a student you can apply the principle of relaxed attention to improve your creativity. If you are thinking about a problem and get stuck, relax and come back to it later. Take a break, do something else, or even sleep on it. You are likely to come up with creative inspiration while you are relaxing. Then get back to solving the problem and pay attention to it.

- **Use idea files.** Keep files of ideas that you find interesting. People in advertising call these "swipe files." No one creates in a vacuum. Some of the best creative ideas involve recombining or building on the ideas of others or looking at them from a different perspective. This is different from copying other people's ideas; it is using them as the fertilizer for creative thinking.

  As a college student, you might keep files of the following:

  - Interesting ideas and their sources for use in writing term papers

  - Information about careers

  - Information for your resume

  - Information that you can use to apply for scholarships

- **Practice using visualization and imagination.** Visualizing and imagining are important in the creative process. Young children are naturally good at these two skills. What happens as we grow older? As we grow older, we learn to follow the rules and color between the lines. We need rules to have an orderly society, yet we need visualization and imagination to move forward and create new ideas.

  Visualization and imagination can be fun and interesting activities to help you relax. We have often been told not to daydream, but daydreams can be a tool for relaxation as well as creativity. It is important to come back to reality once we are finished daydreaming. The last step in the creative process is doing something with the best of our creative ideas.

- **Read.** One of the best ways to trigger your creativity is to read a wide variety of materials, including newspapers, magazines, novels, nonfiction books, and articles on the Internet. The ideas that you discover will provide background information, helping you gain perspective on the world, and give you ideas for making your own contributions. When you read, you expose your mind to the greatest people who have ever lived. Make reading a habit.

- **Keep a journal.** Keep a journal of your creative ideas, thoughts, and problems. Writing often will help you think clearly. When you write about your problems, it is almost like having your own private therapist. In college, your journal can be a source of creative ideas for writing term papers and completing assignments.

■ **Think critically.** Approach learning with a sense of awe, excitement, and skepticism. Here is another paradox! Creative and critical thinkers have much in common. Both ask questions, look at the world from different perspectives, and generate new alternatives.

Acquiring Wisdom and Knowledge

Positive psychologist Christopher Peterson describes wisdom and knowledge as a character strength that includes the acquisition and use of knowledge for the general good. Wisdom and knowledge include these components:[10]

■ **Creativity** which includes new ways of thinking about things.

■ **Curiosity** which includes taking an interest, exploring and discovering throughout life.

■ **Love of learning** which includes the motivation to learn new things over a lifetime.

■ **Open-mindedness** which includes looking at issues from all sides, weighing the evidence and being willing to change one's mind.

■ **Perspective** which involves understanding different points of view.

Use the information about critical thinking and creativity in this chapter to acquire wisdom as well as knowledge.

© iQoncept/Shutterstock.com

Psychology of Learning: Why Bolster Working Memory?

A book called "Why Don't Students Like School?" by Daniel Willingham, a cognitive psychologist who has studied learning for more than 20 years.

Many valuable concepts Willingham are explained and identified in Figure 3. This depiction represents a relatively new concept called "working memory" and its interaction with long-term memory and the environment. The heading of Figure 3 also contains two related concepts. The first, implied, is that humans do not like to think but, rather, when faced with a new situation draw on past memory and rely on that to decide how to act, assuming that applicable knowledge is stored in long-term memory. The second, overt concept is that the acquisition of meaning requires thinking. Fortunately, humans enjoy thinking if the goal is to solve novel problems.

Behavior begins with sensing information in the environment that draws our attention. That information is realized in working memory and, in order to determine whether and how to react, the individual searches for factual information (i.e., what to do) and procedural information (i.e., how to do it) from long-term memory and uses what is found to guide actions. If the information in long-term memory does not adequately address the situation or if no appropriate information exists, the individual works through a new approach to the environmental cue. If that works, s/he will learn something new and store that in long-term memory for future use. As stated, the more information an individual can hold and manipulate in working memory, the better thinker s/he will be. Additionally, for knowledge to "stick" in long term memory it usually must be recalled and applied repeatedly; information in both working and long-term memory can be forgotten if seldom recalled.

Relating to health and wellness, most inexperienced individuals make unhealthy decisions because of: (1) lack of awareness that they are facing a risky situation, (2) time pressure, and/or (3) peer pressure. Health skills (i.e., procedural knowledge) learned in the classroom can mitigate all three reasons if drawn from long-term memory into working memory and applied, because individuals can identify a risky situation and employ procedures for resisting pressure from peers without needing a lot of time to process.

Learning Results from Thinking about Meaning*

Environment

Attention

Information

Working Memory
(site of awareness
and of thinking)

Learning | Remembering

NOTE: The greater
the capacity in
working memory, the
better the thinker

Long-Term Memory
(factual knowledge
and procedural
knowledge)

Interaction between Working Memory, Long-Term Memory and the Environment

*Adapted from *Why Students Like School* by Daniel T. Willingham

ASSIGNMENT: Describe at least two creativity techniques that you use or are willing to try.

1. _____

   _____

   _____

2. _____

   _____

   _____

LEARNING STYLE AND INTELLIGENCE

❝I am always doing that which I cannot do, in order that I may learn how to do it.❞

— Pablo Picasso

Just as each individual has a unique personality, each individual has a unique learning style. There are no good or bad learning styles. Learning style is simply your preferred way of learning. It is how you like to learn and how you learn best. By understanding your learning style, you can maximize your potential and productivity by choosing the learning techniques that work best for you. Gary Price of Price Systems, Inc. developed the Productivity Environmental Preferences Survey (PEPS), which identifies 20 different elements of learning style and environment. These elements include the immediate environment, emotional factors, sociological needs, and physical needs. As you read the description of each of these elements, think about YOUR preferences:

Sound   You may prefer a quiet environment for study or you may find it distracting if it is too quiet.

Light   You may prefer bright light to see what you are studying or you may find bright light uncomfortable or irritating.

Temperature   You may perform better in cool temperatures or prefer warmer temperatures.

Design   You either study best in a more formal environment (desk and chair) or less formal environment (couch, pillows, soft chair).

Motivation   You may be self-motivated to learn or you may lack motivation. If you lack motivation, think about your reasons for attending college and what may help motivate you to learn.

Persistence   You finish what you start or you have many things going on at once and may not finish them.

Responsibility/Conforming   You like to please others by doing what is asked of you or you are less likely to conform. (You prefer to complete things because YOU want to complete them rather than because someone else asked you to.)

Structure   You prefer more (details, clear directions) or less structure (more choices about assignments or tasks, organize material on your own).

Alone/Peer   You prefer to study alone or to study with others.

Authority Figures Present   You are a more independent learner (prefer to have professor available to guide learning) or a less independent learner (prefer to work on your own and report later).

Several Ways   You learn in several ways or you have definite preferences in the way you like to learn.

Auditory   You may or may not prefer to learn through listening and talking.

Visual   You may or may not prefer to learn through reading or seeing things.

Tactile   You may or may not prefer to touch the material as you learn.

Kinesthetic   You may learn best by acting out material to learn or by moving around while learning.

Intake   You may or may not need to chew or drink something while learning.

Evening/Morning   You are most productive in the morning and prefer to go to bed early. If this is your preference, schedule time to study during this period.

Late Morning   You are most productive from 10:00 A.M. until noon. If this is your preference, schedule time to study during this period.

Afternoon   You are most productive in the afternoon. If this is your preference, schedule time to study in during this period.

Mobility   You may or may not like to move around while studying.

ASSIGNMENT: What are your learning styles and preferences? Circle (in the above list) which learning styles apply to you. Write a note to the side on how you plan to accommodate these styles. Doing this will help you better figure out the best learning environment tailored to your needs and preferences.

LEARNING TECHNIQUES

Neuroscience and Practical Learning Strategies

Recent discoveries in neuroscience can be translated into practical and efficient learning strategies for students. Neuroscientists have shown that learning can be increased by **using and integrating all the senses**, not just the preferred ones. This process is called **multi-sensory integration**.

© VLADGRIN/Shutterstock.com

Learning is optimized when more senses are used when trying to remember what we are studying. Researchers note that "it is likely that the human brain has evolved to develop, learn, and operate optimally in multi-sensory environments."[11]

The senses work together as a team to optimize learning by encoding the information into the brain in the form of long-term memories. Sensory inputs include

- **Visual:** learning through reading, observing, or seeing things.

- **Auditory:** learning through listening and talking.

- **Tactile:** learning through touching the material or using a "hands-on approach."

- **Kinesthetic:** learning through movement as in learning to ride a bicycle.

- **Olfactory:** learning by smell.

- **Gustatory:** learning through taste.

Use all of your senses to help you to remember. For example, when studying Spanish, motivate yourself to learn by watching videos of Spanish speaking countries, listen to the words and say them out loud, use flash cards you can touch to practice the vocabulary, imagine the smell of Mexican food, eat some salsa and chips, and if possible, travel to a Spanish speaking country where you can practice the language.

Are there differences between the left brain and right brain that affect how we learn? Educators have often taught students that there is a difference between the right brain and left brain, with one side being more creative and the other more analytical. This idea is not supported by current brain research that shows that **both sides of the brain work together**. New findings show that the right side of the brain tends to remember the main ideas and the left side remembers the details, but every brain is unique.[12] It is suggested that to improve memory, it is important to begin with the main idea (right brain) and then remember the details (left brain).

Visual Learning Strategies

Some scientists have found that vision is the best tool for learning anything. The more visual the input, the more likely it is to be remembered. It was found that 72 hours after learning something, people recalled only 10% of material presented orally versus 65% recollection when a picture was added.[3] When we animate the pictures, learning is further improved. It is important to use visualization as an aid to studying and remembering. Make a visual picture of what you need to remember. If you can make a mental video, recall is further enhanced.

Here are some visual learning strategies. Highlight or place a checkmark in front of the learning strategies that you can use:

_____Make a visual image of what you are learning. For example, while reading history, picture in your mind's eye what it would be like to live in that historical period. Even better, make a video.

_____If you are having difficulties understanding a concept, find an online video that explains it.

_____Use color to highlight the important points in the text while reading. Review the important points by looking at the highlighted passages again.

_____Take notes and use underlining and highlighting in different colors to highlight the important points. Include flow charts, graphs, and pictures in your notes.

_____Make summary sheets or mind maps to summarize and review your notes.

_____Use pictures, diagrams, flow charts, maps, graphs, time lines, videos, and multimedia to aid in learning and preparing for exams.

_____Use flash cards to remember the details.

_____Sit in front of the class so you can carefully observe the professor. Copy what is written on the board or use your cell phone to photograph it.

_____Create visual reminders to keep on track. Make lists on note pads or use sticky notes as reminders.

_____Before answering an essay question, picture the answer in your mind and then make an outline or mind map.

_____Use mind maps and outlines to review for exams.

_____When learning new material, begin with visual learning strategies and then reinforce them with audio, kinesthetic, tactile, or olfactory strategies.

Audio Learning Strategies

Audio learning strategies involve using the sense of hearing to learn new information. Use these techniques to reinforce visual learning. Highlight or place a checkmark next to the strategies you can use.

____As you are reading, ask questions or say out loud what you think will be important to remember.

____Make it a priority to attend lectures and participate in classroom discussions.

____To prepare for exams, rehearse or say the information verbally. For example, while studying math, say the equations out loud.

____Discuss what you are learning with other students or friends. Form a study group.

____Use memory devices, rhymes, poems, rhythms, or music to remember what you are studying. For example, turn facts into a rap song or musical jingle to aid in recall.

____Memorize key concepts by repeating them aloud.

____If you are having problems reading your textbook or understanding the directions, read them out loud.

____Some students can study better with music. However, if your attention shifts to the music, you are multi-tasking and it will take longer to complete your work. On the other hand, some students use music for relaxation, which can be beneficial to studying. Experiment to see if you can be more efficient with the music on or off.

Tactile Learning Techniques

You can increase your learning by using your sense of touch to learn new information. Here are some tactile learning strategies: highlight or place a checkmark next to the ones you can use:

____Writing is one of the best tactile learning strategies. Take notes, write a journal, list key ideas, make an outline, or create a mind map.

____Use real objects to help you learn. For example, in a physics course, if you are studying levers, make a simple lever and observe how it works. If you are studying geography, use a globe or map to aid in studying.

____Use flash cards to review the key ideas as well as the details.

Kinesthetic Learning Strategies

These strategies involve moving around while studying. Highlight or place a checkmark in front of the strategies that you can use.

____Move while studying. For example, review material while on your exercise bike or stair stepper.

____Participate in kinesthetic learning experiences such as drama, building, designing, visiting, interviewing, and going on field trips.

____Take frequent breaks and study in different locations.

____Use a study group to teach the material to someone else.

PERSONALITY AND LEARNING PREFERENCES

"The only real mistake in life is the one from which we learn nothing."

— Unknown

Learning preferences are also connected to personality type. There are learning strategies in the following online assignment that offer some suggestions along with some cautions for each personality type (refer back to Chapter 4's Social Wellness chapter on what you selected as your personality type).

Online Assignment: Personality and Learning Preferences

Complete this assignment online. Go to:

www.grtep.com

Select >Chapter Content>Chapter 6>Enter your username and password

Intrinsic or Extrinsic Motivation

Intrinsic motivation comes from within. It means that you do an activity because you enjoy it or find personal meaning in it. With intrinsic motivation, the nature of the activity itself or the consequences of the activity motivate you. For example, let's say that I am interested in learning to play the piano. I am motivated to practice playing the piano because I like the sound of the piano and feel very satisfied when I can play music that I enjoy. I practice because I like to practice, not because I have to practice. When I get tired or frustrated, I work through it or put it aside and come back to it because I want to learn to play the piano well.

You can be intrinsically motivated to continue in college because you enjoy learning and find the college experience satisfying. Look for ways to enjoy college and to find some personal satisfaction in it. If you enjoy college, it becomes easier to do the work required to be successful. Think about what you say to yourself about college. If you are saying negative things such as "I don't want to be here," it will be difficult to continue.

Extrinsic motivation comes as a result of an external reward from someone else. Examples of extrinsic rewards are certificates, bonuses, money, praise, and recognition. Taking the piano example again, let's say that I want my child to play the piano. The child does not know if he or she would like to play the piano. I give the child a reward for practicing the piano. I could pay the child for practicing or give praise for doing a good job. There are two possible outcomes of the extrinsic reward. After a while, the

© Arson0618/Shutterstock.com

child may gain skills and confidence and come to enjoy playing the piano. The extrinsic reward is no longer necessary because the child is now intrinsically motivated. Or the child may decide that he or she does not like to play the piano. The extrinsic reward is no longer effective in motivating the child to play the piano.

You can use extrinsic rewards to motivate yourself to be successful in college. Remind yourself of the payoff for getting a college degree: earning more money, having a satisfying career, being able to purchase a car and a house. Extrinsic rewards can be a first step in motivating yourself to attend college. With experience and achievement, you may come to like going to college and may become intrinsically motivated to continue your college education.

If you use intrinsic motivation to achieve your goal, you will be happier and more successful. If you do something like playing the piano because you enjoy it, you are more likely to spend the time necessary to practice to achieve your goal. If you view college as something that you enjoy and as valuable to you, it is easier to spend the time to do the required studying. When you get tired or frustrated, tell yourself that you are doing a good job (praise yourself) and think of the positive reasons that you want to get a college education.

Locus of Control

Being aware of the concept of locus of control is another way of understanding motivation. The word **locus** means place. The locus of control is where you place the responsibility for control over your life. In other words, who is in charge? If you place the responsibility on yourself and believe that you have control over your life, you have an internal locus of control. If you place the responsibility on others and think that luck or fate determines your future, you have an external locus of control. Some people use the internal and external locus of control in combination or favor one type in certain situations. If you favor an internal locus of control, you believe that to a great extent your actions determine your future. **Studies have shown that students who use an internal locus of control are likely to have higher achievement in college**.[13] The characteristics of students with internal and external locus of control are listed below.

Students with an internal locus of control:

- Believe that they are in control of their lives.
- Understand that grades are directly related to the amount of study invested.
- Are self-motivated.
- Learn from their mistakes by figuring out what went wrong and how to fix the problem.
- Think positively and try to make the best of each situation.
- Rely on themselves to find something interesting in the class and learn the material.

ACTIVITY: Internal or External Locus of Control

Decide whether the statement represents an internal or external locus of control and put a checkmark in the appropriate column.

INTERNAL   EXTERNAL

_____ _____ 1. Much of what happens to us is due to fate, chance, or luck.

_____ _____ 2. Grades depend on how much work you put into it.

_____ _____ 3. If I do badly on the test, it is usually because the teacher is unfair.

_____ _____ 4. If I do badly on the test, it is because I didn't study or didn't understand the material.

_____ _____ 5. I often get blamed for things that are not my fault.

_____ _____ 6. I try to make the best of the situation.

_____ _____ 7. It is impossible to get a good grade if you have a bad instructor.

_____ _____ 8. I can be successful through hard work.

_____ _____ 9. If the teacher is not there telling me what to do, I have a hard time doing my work.

_____ _____ 10. I can motivate myself to study.

_____ _____ 11. If the teacher is boring, I probably won't do well in class.

_____ _____ 12. I can find something interesting about each class.

_____ _____ 13. When bad things are going to happen, there is not much you can do about it.

_____ _____ 14. I create my own destiny.

_____ _____ 15. Teachers should motivate the students to study.

_____ _____ 16. I have a lot of choice about what happens in my life.

As you probably noticed, the even-numbered statements represent internal locus of control. The odd-numbered statements represent external locus of control. Remember that students with an internal locus of control have a greater chance of success in college. It is important to see yourself as responsible for your own success and achievement and to believe that with effort you can achieve your goals.

Students with an external locus of control:

- Believe that their lives are largely a result of luck, fate, or chance.

- Think that teachers give grades rather than students earning grades.

- Rely on external motivation from teachers or others.

- Look for someone to blame when they make a mistake.

- Think negatively and believe they are victims of circumstance.

- Rely on the teacher to make the class interesting and to teach the material.

MAKING CHOICES

> "*The assumption is that if choice is good, more choice is better.*
> *That's not necessarily true.*"
>
> — Barry Schwartz, PhD, Professor of Social Theory
> and Social Action, Swarthmore College

Choosing well is difficult, and most decisions have several different dimensions. When leasing an apartment, you consider location, spaciousness, condition, safety, and rent. When buying a car, you look at safety, reliability, fuel economy, style, and price. When choosing a job, it is salary, location, opportunity for advancement, potential colleagues, as well as the nature of the work itself, that factor into your deliberations.

Most good decisions will involve these steps:

1. Figure out your goal or goals.

2. Evaluate the importance of each goal.

3. Array the options.

4. Evaluate how likely each of the options is to meet your goals.

5. Pick the winning option.

6. Later use the consequences of your choice to modify your goals, the importance you assign them, and the way you evaluate future possibilities.

The first choice you must make is between the goal of choosing the absolute best and the goal of choosing something that is good enough.

If you seek and accept only the best, you are a *maximizer*.

Maximizers need to be assured that every purchase or decision was the best that could be made. Yet how can anyone truly know that any given option is absolutely the best possible? The only way to know is to check out all the alternatives. As a decision strategy, maximizing creates a daunting task, which becomes all the more daunting as the number of options increases.

The alternative to maximizing is to be a *satisficer*. To satisfice is to settle for something that is good enough and not worry about the possibility that there might be something better. A satisficer has criteria and standards.

Of course no one is an absolute maximizer. They spend a great deal of time and effort on the search, reading labels, checking out consumer magazines, and trying new products. Worse, after making a selection, they are nagged by the options they haven't had time to investigate. In the end, they are likely to get less satisfaction out of the exquisite choices they make than will satisficers. When reality requires maximizers to compromise—to end a search and decide on something—apprehension about what might have been takes over.

To a maximizer, satisficers appear to be willing to settle for mediocrity, but that is not the case. A satisficer may be just as discriminating as a maximizer. The difference between the two types is that the satisficer is content with the merely excellent as opposed to the absolute best.

When Nobel Prize–winning economist and psychologist Herbert Simon initially introduced the idea of "satisficing" in the 1950s, he suggested that when all the costs (in time, money, and anguish) involved in getting information about all the options are factored in, satisficing *is,* in fact, the maximizing strategy. In other words, the best people can do, all things considered, is to satisfice.

Distinguishing Maximizers from Satisficers

ASSIGNMENT: Distinguishing Maximizers from Satisficers—Try it for yourself. Write a number from 1 (completely disagree) to 7 (completely agree) next to each question. Now add up these thirteen numbers. Your score can range from a low of thirteen to a high of 91. If your total is 65 or higher, you are clearly on the maximizing end of the scale. If your score is 40 or lower, you are on the satisficing end of the scale.

MAXIMIZATION SCALE

1. Whenever I'm faced with a choice, I try to imagine what all the other possibilities are, even ones that aren't present at the moment.

2. No matter how satisfied I am with my job, it's only right for me to be on the lookout for better opportunities.

3. When I am in the car listening to the radio, I often check other stations to see if something better is playing, even if I am relatively satisfied with what I'm listening to.

4. When I watch TV, I channel surf, often scanning through the available options even while attempting to watch one program.

5. I treat relationships like clothing: I expect to try a lot on before finding the perfect fit.

6. I often find it difficult to shop for a gift for a friend.

7. Renting videos is really difficult. I'm always struggling to pick the best one.

8. When shopping, I have a hard time finding clothing that I really love.

9. I'm a big fan of lists that attempt to rank things (the best movies, the best singers, the best athletes, the best novels, etc.).

10. I find that writing is very difficult, even if it's just writing a letter to a friend, because it's so hard to word things just right. I often do several drafts of even simple things.

11. No matter what I do, I have the highest standards for myself.

12. I never settle for second best.

13. I often fantasize about living in ways that are quite different from my actual life.

(Courtesy of American Psychological Association)

1. **Whenever I'm faced with a choice, I try to imagine what all the other possibilities are, even ones that aren't present at the moment.**

   The maximizer would agree. How can you tell you have the "best" without considering all the alternatives? What about the sweaters that might be available in other stores?

2. **No matter how satisfied I am with my job, it's only right for me to be on the lookout for better opportunities.**

   A "good" job is probably not the "best" job. A maximizer is always concerned that there is something better out there and acts accordingly.

3. **When I am in the car listening to the radio, I often check other stations to see if something better is playing, even if I am relatively satisfied with what I'm listening to.**

   Yes, the maximizer likes this song, but the idea is to get to listen to the *best* song, not to settle for one that is good enough.

4. When I watch TV, I channel surf, often scanning through the available options even while attempting to watch one program.

   Again, a maximizer seeks not just a good TV show, but the best one. With all these stations available, there might be a better show on somewhere.

5. I treat relationships like clothing: I expect to try a lot on before finding the perfect fit.

   For a maximer, somewhere out there is the perfect lover, the perfect friend. Even though there is nothing wrong with your current relationship, who knows what's possible if you keep your eyes open.

6. I often find it difficult to shop for a gift for a friend.

   Maximizers find it difficult because somewhere out there is the "perfect" gift.

7. Renting videos is really difficult. I'm always struggling to pick the best one.

   There are thousands of possibilities in the video store. There must be one that's just right for my current mood and the people I'll be watching with. I'll just pick out the best of the current releases and then scour the rest of the store to see if there's a classic that would be even better.

8. When shopping, I have a hard time finding clothing that I really love.

   The only way a maximizer can "really love" a clothing item is by knowing that there isn't a better alternative out there somewhere.

9. I'm a big fan of lists that attempt to rank things (the best movies, the best singers, the best athletes, the best novels, etc.).

   People concerned with finding the best will be much more interested in ranking things than people happy with "good enough." (If you read the novel or saw the movie *High Fidelity,* you've seen how this tendency can get wildly out of hand.)

10. I find that writing is very difficult, even if it's just writing a letter to a friend, because it's so hard to word things just right. I often do several drafts of even simple things.

    Maximizers can edit themselves into writer's block.

11. No matter what I do, I have the highest standards for myself.

    Maximizers want *everything* they do to be just right, which can lead to unhealthy self-criticism.

12. I never settle for second best.

    Here, self-editing and selfcriticism can lead to inertia.

13. I often fantasize about living in ways that are quite different from my actual life.

    Maximizers spend more time than satisficers thinking about "roads not traveled." Whole shelves of psychological self-help books testify to the dangers of this "shoulda, woulda, coulda" thinking.

This survey was given to several thousand people. The high score was 75, the low 25, and the average about 50. Perhaps surprisingly, there were no differences between men and women. In another study, respondents were asked several questions that would reveal their maximizing tendencies in action. Not surprisingly, it was found that:

1. Maximizers engage in more product comparisons than satisficers, both before and after they make purchasing decisions.

2. Maximizers take longer than satisficers to decide on a purchase.

3. Maximizers spend more time than satisficers comparing their purchasing decisions to the decisions of others.

4. Maximizers are more likely to experience regret after a purchase.

5. Maximizers are more likely to spend time thinking about hypothetical alternatives to the purchases they've made.

6. Maximizers generally feel less positive about their purchasing decisions.

Example of a Maximizer

1. Maximizers savor positive events less than satisficers and do not cope as well (by their own admission) with negative events.

2. After something bad happens to them, maximizers' sense of well-being takes longer to recover.

3. Maximizers tend to brood or ruminate more than satisficers.

Does it follow that maximizers are less happy than satisficers? We tested this idea by having the same people who filled out the Maximization Scale fill out a variety of other questionnaires that have been shown over the years to be reliable indicators of well-being. One questionnaire measured happiness. A sample item from that questionnaire asked people to rate themselves on a scale that went from "not a very happy person" to "a very happy person." Another questionnaire measured optimism. A sample item asked people how much they agreed that "in uncertain times, I usually expect the best."

Another questionnaire was the Satisfaction with Life Scale. A sample item asked people how much they agreed that "the conditions of my life are excellent." A final questionnaire measured depression, and asked people how sad they felt, how much satisfaction they got out of various activities, how much interest they had in other people, and what they thought of their appearance, among other things.

Our expectation was confirmed: people with high maximization scores experienced less satisfaction with life, were less happy, were less optimistic, and were more depressed than people with low maximization scores. In fact, people with extreme maximization scores—scores of 65 or more out of 91—had depression scores that placed them in the borderline clinical depression range.

What these studies show is that being a maximizer is *correlated* with being unhappy. They do not show that being a maximizer *causes* unhappiness, because correlation does not necessarily indicate cause and effect.

Maximizing and Regret

Maximizers are much more susceptible than satisficers to all forms of regret, especially that known as "buyer's remorse."

What is even worse is that you can actually experience regret in *anticipation* of making a decision. You imagine how you'll feel if you discover that there was a better option available. And that leap of imagination may be all it takes to plunge you into a mire of uncertainty—even misery—over every looming decision.

> **ASSIGNMENT:** Maximizing and Regret—To score yourself on this scale, just put a number from 1 ("Disagree Completely") to 7 ("Agree Completely") next to each question. Then subtract from 8 the number you put next to the first question, and add the result to the other numbers.

REGRET SCALE

1. Once I make a decision, I don't look back.

2. Whenever I make a choice, I'm curious about what would have happened if I had chosen differently.

3. If I make a choice and it turns out well, I still feel like something of a failure if I find out that another choice would have turned out better.

4. Whenever I make a choice, I try to get information about how the other alternatives turned out.

5. When I think about how I'm doing in life, I often assess opportunities I have passed up.

(Courtesy of American Psychological Association)

The higher your score, the more susceptible you are to regret.

Our findings with the Regret Scale have been dramatic. Almost everyone who scores high on the Maximization Scale also scores high on regret. As important as the instrumental value of choice may be, choice reflects another value that might be even more important. Freedom to choose has what might be called *expressive* value. Choice is what enables us to tell the world who we are and what we care about. This is true of something as superficial as the way we dress. The clothes we choose are a deliberate expression of taste, intended to send a message. "I'm a serious person," or "I'm a sensible person," or "I'm rich." Or maybe even "I wear what I want and I don't care what you think about it." To express yourself, you need an adequate range of choices.

The same is true of almost every aspect of our lives as choosers. The food we eat, the cars we drive, the houses we live in, the music we listen to, the books we read, the hobbies we pursue, the charities we contribute to, the demonstrations we attend—each of these choices has an expressive function, regardless of its practical importance. And some choices may have *only* an expressive function.

Every choice we make is a testament to our autonomy, to our sense of self-determination. Almost every social, moral, or political philosopher in the Western tradition since Plato has placed a premium on such autonomy. And each new expansion of choice gives us another opportunity to assert our autonomy, and thus display our character.

But choices have expressive functions only to the extent that we can make them freely.

Autonomy is what gives us the license to hold one another morally (and legally) responsible for our actions. It's the reason we praise individuals for their achievements and also blame them for their failures.

Why Decisions Disappoint: The Problem of Adaptation

While regret and opportunity costs can focus our attention on what we've passed up, there is also plenty of room for dissatisfaction with the options that we actually choose. Because of a ubiquitous feature of human psychology, very little in life turns out quite as good as we expect it will be. You're hit with a double whammy—regret about what you didn't choose, and disappointment with what you did.

This ubiquitous feature of human psychology is a process known as *adaptation*. Simply put, we get used to things, and then we start to take them for granted.

Because of adaptation, enthusiasm about positive experiences doesn't sustain itself. And what's worse, people seem generally unable to anticipate that this process of adaptation will take place. The waning of pleasure or enjoyment over time always seems to come as an unpleasant surprise.

Researchers have known about and studied adaptation for many years, but for the most part they emphasized *perceptual adaptation*—decreased responsiveness to sights, sounds, odors and the like as people continue to experience them. The idea is that human beings, like virtually all other animals, respond less and less to any given environmental event as the event persists.

Even though we don't expect it to happen, such adaptation to pleasure is inevitable, and it may cause more disappointment in a world of many choices than in a world of few.

Hopes, Expectations, Past Experience, and the Experience of Others

When people evaluate an experience, they are performing one or more of the following comparisons:

1. Comparing the experience to what they hoped it would be

2. Comparing the experience to what they expected it to be

3. Comparing the experience to other experiences they have had in the recent past

4. Comparing the experience to experiences that others have had

Each of these comparisons makes the evaluation of an experience relative, and this may diminish the experience or enhance it.

Social scientist Alex Michalos, in his discussion of the perceived quality of experience, argued that people establish standards of satisfaction based on the assessment of three gaps: "the gap between what one has and wants, the gap between what one has and thinks others like oneself have, and the gap between what one has and the best one has had in the past." Michalos found that much of the individual variation in life satisfaction could be explained in terms not of differences in objective experience, but in terms of differences in these three perceived gaps. To these three comparisons I have added a fourth: the gap between what one has and what one expects. As our material and social circumstances improve, our standards of comparison go up. As we have contact with items of high quality, we begin to suffer from "the curse of discernment." The lower quality items that used to be perfectly acceptable are no longer good enough. The hedonic zero point keeps rising, and expectations and aspirations rise with it.

What to Do about Choice

I believe there are steps we can take to mitigate—even eliminate—many of these sources of distress, but they aren't easy. They require practice, discipline, and perhaps a new way of thinking. On the other hand, each of these steps will bring its own rewards.

1. **Choose When to Choose**
   1. Review some recent decisions that you've made, both small and large (a clothing purchase, a new kitchen appliance, a vacation destination, a retirement pension allocation, a medical procedure, a job or relationship change).
   2. Itemize the steps, time, research, and anxiety that went into making those decisions.
   3. Remind yourself how it felt to do that work.
   4. Ask yourself how much your final decision benefited from that work.

2. **Be a Chooser, Not a Picker**
   1. Shorten or eliminate deliberations about decisions that are unimportant to you;
   2. Use some of the time you've freed up to ask yourself what you really want in the areas of your life where decisions matter;
   3. And if you discover that none of the options the world presents in those areas meet your needs, start thinking about creating better options that do.

3. **Satisfice More and Maximize Less**
   1. Think about occasions in life when you settle, comfortably, for "good enough";
   2. Scrutinize how you choose in those areas;
   3. Then apply that strategy more broadly.

4. **Think about the Opportunity Costs of Opportunity Costs**
   1. Unless you're truly dissatisfied, stick with what you always buy.
   2. Don't be tempted by "new and improved."
   3. Don't "scratch" unless there's an "itch."
   4. And don't worry that if you do this, you'll miss out on all the new things the world has to offer.

5. **Make Your Decisions Nonreversible**

What we don't realize is that the very option of being allowed to change our minds seems to increase the chances that we *will* change our minds. When we can change our minds about decisions, we are less satisfied with them. When a decision is final, we engage in a variety of psychological processes that enhance our feelings about the choice we made relative to the alternatives. If a decision is reversible, we don't engage these processes to the same degree.

I think the power of nonreversible decisions comes through most clearly when we think about our most important choices. Knowing that you've made a choice that you will not reverse allows you to pour your energy into improving the relationship that you have rather than constantly second-guessing it.

6. **Practice an "Attitude of Gratitude"**
   1. Keep a notepad at your bedside.
   2. Every morning, when you wake up, or every night, when you go to bed, use the notepad to list five things that happened the day before that you're grateful for. These objects of gratitude occasionally will be big (a job promotion, a great first date), but most of the time, they will be small (sunlight streaming in through the bedroom window, a kind word from a friend, a piece of swordfish cooked just the way you like it, an informative article in a magazine).
   3. You will probably feel a little silly and even self-conscious when you start doing this. But if you keep it up, you will find that it gets easier and easier, more and more natural. You also may find yourself discovering many things to be grateful for on even the most ordinary of days. Finally, you may find yourself feeling better and better about your life as it is, and less and less driven to find the "new and improved" products and activities that will enhance it.

7. **Regret Less**
   1. Adopting the standards of a satisficer rather than a maximizer.
   2. Reducing the number of options we consider before making a decision.
   3. Practicing gratitude for what is good in a decision rather than focusing on our disappointments with what is bad.

8. **Anticipate Adaptation**
   1. As you buy your new car, acknowledge that the thrill won't be quite the same two months after you own it.
   2. Spend less time looking for the perfect thing (maximizing), so that you won't have huge search costs to be "amortized" against the satisfaction you derive from what you actually choose.
   3. Remind yourself of how good things actually are instead of focusing on how they're less good than they were at first.

9. **Control Expectations**
   1. Reduce the number of options you consider.
   2. Be a satisficer rather than a maximizer.
   3. Allow for serendipity.

10. **Curtail Social Comparison**
    1. Remember that "He who dies with the most toys wins" is a bumper sticker, not wisdom.
    2. Focus on what makes *you* happy, and what gives meaning to *your* life.

11. **Learn to Love Constraints**

Routine decisions take so much time and attention that it becomes difficult to get through the day. In circumstances like this, we should learn to view limits on the possibilities we face as liberating not constraining. By deciding to follow a rule, we avoid having to make a deliberate decision again and again. This kind of rule-following frees up time and attention that can be devoted to thinking about choices and decisions to which rules don't apply.

Excerpts from pp. 47, 77–88, 167–8, 182 [3458 words] from *The Paradox of Choice: Why More is Less* by Barry Schwartz. Copyright © 2004 by Barry Schwartz. Reprinted by permission of HarperCollins Publishers.

MULTIPLE INTELLIGENCES

Becoming aware of your multiple intelligences, interests, and values will enhance self-understanding, increase positive thinking about your abilities, and help you to make good decisions about your college major and future career. If you can match your career with your abilities, interests, and values, you will be more intrinsically motivated to excel in it.

Exploring Multiple Intelligences

In 1904, the French psychologist Alfred Binet developed the IQ test, which provided a single score to measure intelligence. This once widely used and accepted test came into question because it measured the intelligence of students in a particular culture. In different cultures, the test was less valid. As an alternative to traditional IQ tests, Harvard professor Howard Gardner developed the theory of multiple intelligences. He looked at intelligence in a broader and more inclusive way than people had done in the past.

© VLADGRIN/Shutterstock.com

Howard Gardner[14] observed famous musicians, artists, athletes, scientists, inventors, naturalists, and philosophers who were recognized contributors to society to formulate a more meaningful definition of intelligence. **He defined intelligence as the human ability to solve problems or design or compose something valued in at least one culture.** His definition broadens the scope of human potential. He identified nine different intelligences: musical, interpersonal, logical–mathematical, spatial, bodily–kinesthetic, linguistic, intrapersonal, naturalist, and existential. He selected these intelligences because they are all represented by an area in the brain and are valued in different cultures. His theory helps us to realize that there are many different kinds of talents and to think more positively about our abilities. To assess your multiple intelligences, take the MI Advantage using the access code on the inside front cover of your textbook.

These intelligences are measured by looking at performance in activities associated with each intelligence. A key idea in this theory is that most people can develop all of their intelligences and become relatively competent in each area. Another key idea is that these intelligences work together in complex ways to make us unique. For example, an athlete uses bodily–kinesthetic intelligence to run, kick, or jump. They use spatial intelligence to keep their eye on the ball and hit it. They also need linguistic and interpersonal skills to be good member of a team.

Developing intelligences is a product of three factors:

1. Biological endowment based on heredity and genetics

2. Personal life history

3. Cultural and historical background[15]

For example, Wolfgang Amadeus Mozart was born with musical talent (biological endowment). Members of his family were musicians who encouraged Mozart in music (personal life history). Mozart lived in Europe during a time when music flourished and wealthy patrons were willing to pay composers (cultural and historical background).

Each individual's life history contains **crystallizers** that promote the development of the intelligences and **paralyzers** that inhibit the development of the intelligences. These crystallizers and paralyzers often take place in early childhood. For example, Einstein was given a magnetic compass when he was four years old. He became so interested in the compass that he started on his journey of exploring the universe. An example of a paralyzer is being embarrassed or feeling humiliated about your math skills in elementary school so that you begin to lose confidence in your ability to do math. Paralyzers involve shame, guilt, fear, and anger and prevent intelligence from being developed.

ACTIVITY: Describing Your Multiple Intelligences

Below are some definitions and examples of the different intelligences. As you read each section, think positively about your intelligence in this area. Highlight or place a checkmark in front of each item that is true for you.

MUSICAL

Musical intelligence involves hearing and remembering musical patterns and manipulating patterns in music. Some occupations connected with this intelligence include musician, performer, composer, and music critic. Place a checkmark next to each skill that you possess in this area.

_____ I enjoy singing, humming, or whistling.

_____ One of my interests is playing recorded music.

_____ I have collections of recorded music.

_____ I play or used to play a musical instrument.

_____ I can play the drums or tap out rhythms.

_____ I appreciate music.

_____ Music affects how I feel.

_____ I enjoy having music on while working or studying.

_____ I can clap my hands and keep time to music.

_____ I can tell when a musical note is off key.

_____ I remember melodies and the words to songs.

_____ I have participated in a band, chorus, or other musical group.

Look at the items you have checked above and summarize your musical intelligence.

_____

_____

_____

INTERPERSONAL

Interpersonal intelligence is defined as understanding people. Occupations connected with this intelligence involve working with people and helping them, as in education or health care. Place a checkmark next to each skill that you possess in this area.

_____ I enjoy being around people.

_____ I am sensitive to other people's feelings.

_____ I am a good listener.

_____ I understand how others feel.

_____ I have many friends.

_____ I enjoy parties and social gatherings.

_____ I enjoy participating in groups.

_____ I can get people to cooperate and work together.

_____ I am involved in clubs or community activities.

_____ People come to me for advice.

_____ I am a peacemaker.

_____ I enjoy helping others.

Look at the Items you have checked above and summarize your interpersonal intelligence.

_____

_____

_____

LOGICAL-MATHEMATICAL

Logical-mathematical intelligence involves understanding abstract principles and manipulating numbers, quantities, and operations. Some examples of occupations associated with logical-mathematical intelligence are mathematician, tax accountant, scientist, and computer programmer. Place a checkmark next to each skill that you possess. Keep an open mind. People usually either love or hate this area.

_____ I can do arithmetic problems quickly.

_____ I enjoy math.

_____ I enjoy doing puzzles.

_____ I enjoy working with computers.

_____ I am interested in computer programming.

_____ I enjoy science classes.

_____ I enjoy doing the experiments in lab science courses.

_____ I can look at information and outline it easily.

_____ I understand charts and diagrams.

_____ I enjoy playing chess or checkers.

_____ I use logic to solve problems.

_____ I can organize things and keep them in order.

Look at the items you have checked above and summarize your logical-mathematical intelligence.

_____

_____

_____

SPATIAL

Spatial intelligence involves the ability to manipulate objects in space. For example, a baseball player uses spatial intelligence to hit a ball. Occupations associated with spatial intelligence include pilot, painter, sculptor, architect, inventor, and surgeon. This intelligence is often used in athletics, the arts, or the sciences. Place a checkmark next to each skill that you possess in this area.

_____ I can appreciate a good photograph or piece of art.

_____ I think in pictures and images.

_____ I can use visualization to remember.

_____ I can easily read maps, charts, and diagrams.

_____ I participate in artistic activities (art, drawing, painting, photography).

_____ I know which way is north, south, east, and west.

_____ I can put things together.

_____ I enjoy jigsaw puzzles or mazes.

_____ I enjoy seeing movies, slides, or photographs.

_____ I can appreciate good design.

_____ I enjoy using telescopes, microscopes, or binoculars.

_____ I understand color, line, shape, and form.

Look at the items you have checked above and summarize your spatial intelligence.

_____

_____

_____

BODILY-KINESTHETIC

Bodily-kinesthetic intelligence is defined as being able to use your body to solve problems. People with bodily-kinesthetic intelligence make or invent objects or perform. They learn by doing, touching, and handling. Occupations connected to this type of intelligence include athlete, performer (dancer, actor), craftsperson, sculptor, mechanic, and surgeon. Place a checkmark next to each skill that you possess in this area.

_____ I am good at using my hands.

_____ I have good coordination and balance.

_____ I learn best by moving around and touching things.

_____ I participate in physical activities or sports.

_____ I learn new sports easily.

_____ I enjoy watching sports events.

_____ I am skilled in a craft such as woodworking, sewing, art, or fixing machines.

_____ I have good manual dexterity.

_____ I find it difficult to sit still for a long time.

_____ I prefer to be up and moving.

_____ I am good at dancing and remember dance steps easily.

_____ It was easy for me to learn to ride a bike or skateboard.

Look at the items you checked above and describe your bodily-kinesthetic intelligence.

_____

_____

_____

LINGUISTIC

People with linguistic intelligence are good with language and words. They have good reading, writing, and speaking skills. Linguistic intelligence is an asset in any occupation. Specific related careers include writing, education, and politics. Place a checkmark next to each skill that you possess in this area.

_____ I am a good writer.

_____ I am a good reader.

_____ I enjoy word games and crossword puzzles.

_____ I can tell jokes and stories.

_____ I am good at explaining.

_____ I can remember names, places, facts, and trivia.

_____ I'm generally good at spelling.

_____ I have a good vocabulary.

_____ I read for fun and relaxation.

_____ I am good at memorizing.

_____ I enjoy group discussions.

_____ I have a journal or diary.

Look at the items you have checked above and summarize your linguistic intelligence.

_____

_____

_____

INTRAPERSONAL

Intrapersonal intelligence is the ability to understand yourself and how to best use your natural talents and abilities. Examples of careers associated with this intelligence include novelist, psychologist, or being self-employed. Place a checkmark next to each skill that you possess in this area.

_____ I understand and accept my strengths and weaknesses.

_____ I am very independent.

_____ I am self-motivated.

_____ I have definite opinions on controversial issues.

_____ I enjoy quiet time alone to pursue a hobby or work on a project.

_____ I am self-confident.

_____ I can work independently.

_____ I can help others with self-understanding.

_____ I appreciate quiet time for concentration.

_____ I am aware of my own feelings and sensitive to others.

_____ I am self-directed.

_____ I enjoy reflecting on ideas and concepts.

Look at the items you have checked above and summarize your intrapersonal intelligence.

_____

_____

_____

NATURALIST

The naturalist is able to recognize, classify, and analyze plants, animals, and cultural artifacts. Occupations associated with this intelligence include botanist, horticulturist, biologist, archeologist, and environmental occupations. Place a checkmark next to each skill you possess in this area.

_____ I know the names of minerals, plants, trees, and animals.

_____ I think it is important to preserve our natural environment.

_____ I enjoy taking classes in the natural sciences such as biology.

_____ I enjoy the outdoors.

_____ I take care of flowers, plants, trees, or animals.

_____ I am interested in archeology or geology.

_____ I would enjoy a career involved in protecting the environment.

_____ I have or used to have a collection of rocks, shells, or insects.

_____ I belong to organizations interested in protecting the environment.

_____ I think it is important to protect endangered species.

_____ I enjoy camping or hiking.

_____ I appreciate natural beauty.

Look at the items you have checked above and describe your naturalist intelligence.

_____

_____

_____

EXISTENTIAL

Existential intelligence is the capacity to ask profound questions about the meaning of life and death. This intelligence is the cornerstone of art, religion, and philosophy. Related occupations include minister, philosopher, psychologist, and artist. Place a checkmark next to each skill that you possess in this area.

_____ I often think about the meaning and purpose of life.

_____ I have strong personal beliefs and convictions.

_____ I enjoy thinking about abstract theories.

_____ I have considered being a philosopher, scientist, theologian, or artist.

_____ I often read books that are philosophical or imaginative.

_____ I enjoy reading science fiction.

_____ I like to work independently.

_____ I like to search for meaning in my studies.

_____ I wonder if there are other intelligent life forms in the universe.

Look at the items you have checked above and describe your existential intelligence.

_____

_____

_____

Online Assignments: Multiple Intelligences and Health Observances

Complete this assignment online. Go to:

www.grtep.com

Select >Chapter Content>Chapter 6>Enter your username and password

PRACTICING MINDFULNESS AND HOW IT AFFECTS SO MUCH

❝The foundation of greatness is honoring the small things at the present moment instead of pursuing the idea of greatness.❞

— Eckhart Tolle

Mindfulness is certainly a term we have been hearing often in varying mediums. What exactly does the word mean and what is its significance to us as people, to our future learning and outcomes?

According to R.A. Baer and E.L.B. Lykins, authors of *Designing Positive Psychology: Taking Stock and Moving Forward*, "mindfulness occurs through practices which include non-judgmental acceptance and being open to experiences, sensations, thoughts and emotions." They also go on to illustrate the some of the benefits we humans derive from practices of mindfulness which include:

- Opens avenues for being more observant and accepting

- Enhances sense of meaning and purpose in life

- Provides consistency when aligning behavior with values and goals

- Improves healing, immune response and stress

- Promotes curiosity

- Promotes healthy, productive relationships

- Enhances clarity and the ability to form more constructive responses to experiences

- Improves the ability to sustain attention and memory

- Helps with improving patterns of thinking and regulate emotions

- Improves critical thinking, creativity, wisdom, authenticity, learning, vitality, emotional intelligence, kindness, compassion, empathy and self-regulation.

In his *Reflections on The Mindful Brain* overview (an adaptation of his earlier work *The Mindful Brain: Reflection and Attunement in the Cultivation of Well-Being*), Daniel Siegel, MD, states "being mindfully aware, attending to the richness of our experiences, creates scientifically recognized enhancements in our physiology, our mental functions, and our interpersonal relationships." He describes the term "mindful brain" as the "notion that our awareness, our mindful 'paying attention or taking care' is intimately related to the dance between our mind and our brain."

Dr. Siegel suggests a triangle of human experience with a tridirectional flow representing the reality of human experience" the mind is how we regulate energy and information flow; the brain embeds the pathways of energy information flow and relationships are the way we share energy and information flow."

He also illustrates that via "the process of attunement (which is the examination of how one person focuses attention on the internal world of another) the brain may grow in ways that promote balanced self-regulation and a process, called neural integration, enables flexibility and understanding." Therefore, he suggests a new approach to understanding mindfulness which is that mindful awareness is a form of intra-personal attunement.

Dr. Siegel's research indicates that prefrontal function is integrative which means "that the long lengths of the prefrontal neurons reach out to distant and differentiated areas of the brain and body which is seen as the underlying common mechanism beneath various pathways leading to well-being."

How might one cultivate such mindfulness? A good example is that of Jon Kabat-Zinn. He is the founder and former Executive Director of the Center for Mindfulness in Medicine, Health Care, and Society at the University of Massachusetts Medical School, founder and former director of its renowned Stress Reduction Clinic and Professor of Medicine Emeritus at the University of Massachusetts Medical School, began teaching mindfulness-based stress reduction in 1979 by using moment-to-moment awareness. He states "an operational working definition of mindfulness is the awareness that emerges through paying attention on purpose, in the present moment, and nonjudgmentally to the unfolding of experience moment by moment." Over 200 medical centers and clinics in the US and elsewhere now use Kabat-Zinn's model. Mindfulness meditation is shown to enhance the same circuitry that Dr. Siegel discussed that involve insight and empathy.

TIPS TO BECOMING INTELLECTUALLY HEALTHY

"I'm afraid of nothing except being bored."
— Greta Garbo

- Develop the curiosity of a child. Children have a knack for being curious about everything around them. Try to regain this curiosity about the world. You may be amazed by what you learn.

- Plan for effective study and time management skills. You'll need them at an even higher intensity when you graduate from college and enter the working world.

- Learn to trust your ability to make good decisions.

- Challenge yourself to see more than one side of an issue.

- Recognize and value learning as a lifelong process.

- Be that creative and resourceful person.

- If your mind is stuck on a problem, ask around for other opinions, then disregard them and form your own.

- When your brain is full, try to digest a little before consuming more.

- Every day, find one thing around you to see for its beauty.

- Avoid idle thoughts and boredom.

- Read for fun. By choosing books just for fun, you not only learn about a subject or a particular interest, you learn about how others express themselves.

- As stated in the Social Wellness chapter, find a community service or volunteer organization or resource on your campus or at work that will enhance your intellectual and social wellness.

- Don't believe all you read or see on TV; instead, think critically about it.

- Learn to laugh at life. According to neurophysicist Richard Hamilton, positive thinking helps the brain produce serotonin, a neurotransmitter linked with feelings of happiness. So smile and be happy as you work on making positive changes in your life.

SOURCE: *Wellness for Healthy Positive Living: Intellectual Wellness Facts & Tips,* Santa Clara University's Wellness Center: Intellectual Wellness Tips for Good Intellectual Health.

Helpful Internet Sites

American Psychological Association: http://www.apa.org/
Blurtit: blurtit.com/q403886.html
Creative Thinking Techniques: virtualsalt.com/crebook2.htm
Dr. Barry Schwartz homepage: http://www.swarthmore.edu/SocSci/bschwar1/
Dr. Howard Gardner: http://www.howardgardner.com/
The Critical Thinking Community: criticalthinking.org/aboutct/define_critical_thinking.cfm
Learning Styles: mindtools.com/mnemlsty.html
Learning Styles Online.com: learning-styles-online.com/overview/
The Myers & Briggs Foundation: myersbriggs.org
National Health Observances: healthfinder.gov/library/nho/nho.asp

References

Anderson, N. B. (with Anderson, P. E.). (2003). *Emotional longevity: What really determines how long you live*. New York: Viking.

Armstrong, T. *Multiple Intelligences in the Classroom.* Association for Curriculum Development (1994).

Brown, R.P. & Gerbarg, P.L. (2005). Sudarshan Kriya Yogic Breathing in the Treatment of Stress, Anxiety, and Depression: Part II—Clinical Applications and Guidelines. *The Journal of Alternative and Complementary Medicine, 11(4)*, 711–717.

Chen, KW (2004): An analytic review of studies on measuring effects of external Qi in China. *Altern Ther Health Med; 10* (4): 38–50.

Davidson, R. J., Kabat-Zinn, J., Schumacher, J., Rosenkranz, M., Muller, D., Santorelli, S. F., Urbanowski, F.,

Fralick, M. College & Career Success. Learning Style and Intelligence. Kendall Hunt Publishing Company: (?): 236–248; 257–259.

Fralick, M. *College & Career Success.* Thinking Critically and Creatively. Kendall Hunt Publishing Company: (?): 383–391; 392–395; 399

Gardner, H. *Intelligence Reframed: Multiple Intelligence for the Twenty-First Century.* Basic Books (1999).

Heller, B. The National Wellness Institute. The Six Dimensions of Wellness: Intellectual Wellness. nationalwellness.org accessed on 12.7.07.

Horne, A. Positive, Negative or Mindful? *Positive Psychology News Daily* (2011): Dec. 6. Institute for Teaching and Learning website Mission Critical. sjsu.edu/depts/itl/index.html.

Irwin, M. (2005). The impact of Tai Chi on elderly subjects. *Presented at the Mindful Awareness Research Center, University of California, Los Angeles.*

Jones, B: (2001): Changes in cytokine production in healthy subjects practicing Guolin Qigong: a pilot study. *BMC Complementary and Alternative Medicine, 1,* 1–8.

Kabat-Zinn, J. (1990). Full Catastrophe Living: Using the Wisdom of Your Body and Mind to Face Stress, Pain, and Illness, New York: Delacorte Press

Kabat-Zinn, J. (2003). Mindfulness-based interventions in context: Past, present, and future. *Clinical Psychology: Science and Practice, 10(2),* 144–156.

Kornfield, J. (1993). *A path with heart.* New York: Bantam Books.

Kornfield, J. (in press). The Wise Heart. New York: Bantam Books.

Lazar, S.W., Kerr, C.E., Wasserman, R.H., Gray, J.R., Greve, D.N., Treadway, M.T., McGarvey, M., Quinn, B.T., Dusek, J.A., Benson, H., Rauch, S.L., Moore, C.I., Fischl, B. (2005). Meditation experience is associated with increased cortical thickness. *Neuroreport, 16(17),* 1893–1897.

Price, G. "Productivity Environmental Preference Survey," Price Systems, Inc. Box 1818 Lawrence, KS, 66044-8818.

Siegel, D. Reflections of a Mindful Brain (A Brief Overview Adapted from *The Mindful Brain: Reflection and Attunement in the Cultivation of Well-Being;* New York: WW Norton 2007). 1–21.

Siegel, D.J. (1999). *The developing mind.* New York: Guilford Press.

Siegel, D.J. (2001). Toward an interpersonal neurobiology of the developing mind: Attachment, "mindsight", and neural integration. *Infant Mental Health Journal, 22,* 67–94.

Siegel, D.J. (2006). An interpersonal neurobiology approach to psychotherapy. *Psychiatric Annals, 36(4),* 248–256.

Wall, R.B. (2005). Tai chi and minfulness-based stress reduction in a Boston public middle school. *Journal of Pediatric Health Care, 194,* 230–237.

Wellness for Healthy Positive Living. for.gov.bc.ca/hrb/hw/index.htm accessed on 12.7.07.

The Wellness Center at Santa Clara University. scu.edu/wellness/Intellectual-Wellness.cfm accessed 12.11.07.

CHAPTER 7

Environmental Wellness

"You must be the change you wish to see in the world."

— Ghandi

The objectives in this chapter include the understanding of:

- The meaning of environmental wellness and its direct application to you
- What is being proposed to solve the climate crisis
- What comprises greenhouse gas emissions
- The meaning behind carbon footprint
- How to apply energy savings everyday with computers, cars, fuel, homes and apartments, appliances, electricity, and insulation
- How to reduce, reuse and recycle materials
- How YOU can make a difference everyday by being conscious and doing your part to help and protect our planet

Online Reminders

- Complete the poll question before the next class meeting.
- Complete the interactive activities for this chapter.
- Complete all of the online assignments for this chapter.

Environmental wellness—Environmental wellness is one's awareness and engagement of the upkeep of environmental quality. Access to clean air, nutritious food, sanitary water and adequate clothing in one's environmental surroundings is one essential component to being environmentally well. An individual's environment should, at the least, be clean and safe. Consideration for self-protection from ultra-violet rays, sunlight, noise, and secondhand smoke is also a must. We will discuss how to take responsibility for yourself and your surroundings later in Chapter 10. However, we must not only consider our environment at home, we must also consider the environment at school, at work, in our city, in our state, in our nation, and in the world. Being environmentally healthy includes the opportunities you take (and how you respond or react) when opening your mind to ways to do your part in helping solving the climate crisis.

Environmental wellness follows these tenets:

1. It is better to challenge ourselves with pursuits of being a part of the solution of protecting our environment than to become apathetic and wait for others to solve the problem for us.

2. It is better to identify how you can be more environmentally friendly on a daily basis and choose appropriate (and possibly new) courses of action than not to try them at all.

PRE-CLASS SURVEY: Take your environmental wellness survey before your next class meeting and identify your level of environmental wellness. Circle either Yes or No, total up each column and check your score.

Are you aware of the world's environmentally sensitive areas?	YES	NO
Are you proactive in practicing environmental management within your community?	YES	NO
Do you respect your local rivers, creeks, and waterways?	YES	NO
Do you protect birds, mammals, and other animals within your environment?	YES	NO
Do you support healthy habitats and ecosystems throughout your community?	YES	NO
Are you aware of what animals are currently listed as endangered species?	YES	NO
Do you participate in reducing, reusing, and recycling materials?	YES	NO
Are you starting to make your personal living space "green friendly" (if you're not already doing so)?	YES	NO
Have you set your computer to hibernate or go into standby when you walk away from it?	YES	NO
Do you advise others against littering and don't litter yourself?	YES	NO
Do you REALLY know what greenhouse gas emissions are?	YES	NO
Do you know what global warming means?	YES	NO
Do you protect yourself from secondhand smoke?	YES	NO
	TOTAL	

WHAT YOUR TOTAL MEANS:

9 or more Yes answers	Excellent	Your habits are positively enhancing your health.
6–8 Yes answers	Average	You are obviously trying but there is room to improve.
5 or less Yes answers	Not So Good	There is a need for improvement in your daily habits.

SOURCE: "Wellness for Healthy Positive Living." *Environmental Wellness/Inventory* for.gov.bc.ca/hrb/hw/Index.htm

SOLVING THE CLIMATE CRISIS

"We must forever realize that the time is always ripe to do right."

— Nelson Mandela

"Our home, Earth, is in danger. [W]e have begun to put so much CO_2 into the thin shell of air surrounding our world that we have literally changed the heat balance between Earth and the Sun . . . This is a moral issue, one that affects the survival of human civilization."

— Al Gore, Vice President of the United States of America from 1993 to 2001, Chairman of the Alliance for Climate Protection and 2007 Nobel Peace Prize Winner

Balancing the needs of today with the prospects for the same—or better—quality of life for tomorrow's generations is referred to as "sustainability." With a growing world population and a rapidly expanding global economy, significant stress will be placed on the earth's resources and our ability to maintain or Improve environmental quality. The challenge is to prevent or mitigate the negative consequences that can come with growth, while ensuring continual Improvement in environmental quality, human health protection, and the global standard of living.

In order to move toward an environment that can support generations to come, new problem-solving approaches are required—approaches that launch us beyond current strategies that have historically focused on pollutant emissions. We now understand that environmental problems are rarely contained within a single resource area or within a single product's life cycle. We know that environmental problems extend across geographic regions and time frames, and need proactive solutions. Sustainability means meeting basic environmental, economic, and social needs now and in the future without undermining the natural systems upon which life depends. This perspective guides the U. S. EPA's Sustainable Environments Research Program.

The program is a natural outgrow of EPA's pollution prevention research effort, which was chiefly concerned with the development and implementation of environmentally better technologies and procedures. But because environmental problems do not respond well to one-dimensional environmental management approaches, the next logical step is to consider the full complexity of the interactions between the socioeconomic, technological, and ecological parts of a system.

Building on environmental stewardship and creating an integrated understanding of our environmental problems leads to measurable sustainable outcomes that prepare us for a healthy environmental future.

Mission: To advance the understanding, development and application of technologies and methods of prevention, removal and control of environmental risks to human health and ecology.

What Is a Carbon Footprint?

A carbon footprint is defined as:

The total amount of greenhouse gases produced to directly and indirectly support human activities, usually expressed in equivalent tons of carbon dioxide (CO_2).

In other words: When you drive a car, the engine burns fuel which creates a certain amount of CO_2, depending on its fuel consumption and the driving distance. When you heat your house with oil, gas or coal, then you also generate CO_2. Even if you heat your house with electricity, the generation of the electrical power may also have emitted a certain amount of CO_2. When you buy food and goods, the production of the food and goods also emitted some quantities of CO_2.

Your carbon footprint is the sum of all emissions of CO_2 (carbon dioxide), which were induced by your activities in a given time frame. Usually a carbon footprint is calculated for the time period of a year.

The best way is to calculate the carbon dioxide emissions based on the fuel consumption. In the next step you can add the CO_2 emission to your carbon footprint. Below is a table for the most common used fuels:

FUEL TYPE	UNIT	CO2 EMITTED PER UNIT
Petrol	1 gallon (UK)	10.4 kg
Petrol	1 liter	2.3 kg
Gasoline	1 gallon (USA)	8.7 kg
Gasoline	1 liter	2.3 kg
Diesel	1 gallon (UK)	12.2 kg
Diesel	1 gallon (USA)	9.95 kg
Diesel	1 liter	2.7 kg
Oil (heating)	1 gallon (UK)	13.6 kg
Oil (heating)	1 gallon (USA)	11.26 kg
Oil (heating)	1 liter	3 kg

Examples:

- For each (UK-) gallon of petrol fuel consumed, 10.4 kg carbon dioxide (CO_2) is emitted.

- For each (US-) gallon of gasoline fuel consumed, 8.7 kg carbon dioxide (CO_2) is emitted.

- If your car consumes 7.5 liter diesel per 100 km, then a drive of 300 km distance consumes $3 \times 7.5 = 22.5$ liter diesel, which adds 22.5×2.7 kg = 60.75 kg CO_2 to your personal carbon footprint.

Each of the following activities add 1 kg of CO_2 to your personal carbon footprint:

- Travel by public transportation (train or bus) a distance of 10 to 12 km (6.5 to 7 miles)

- Drive with your car a distance of 6 km or 3.75 miles (assuming 7.3 litres petrol per 100 km or 39 mpg)

- Fly with a plane a distance of 2.2 km or 1.375 miles.

- Operate your computer for 32 hours (60 Watt consumption assumed)

- Production of 5 plastic bags

- Production of 2 plastic bottles

- Production of 1/3 of an American cheeseburger (yes, the production of each cheeseburger emits 3.1 kg of CO_2!)

To calculate the above contributions to the carbon footprint, the current UK mix for electricity and trains was taken into account.

Carbon dioxide is a so called greenhouse gas causing global warming . Other greenhouse gases which might be emitted as a result of your activities are e.g. methane and ozone. These greenhouse gases are normally also taken into account for the carbon footprint. They are converted into the amount of CO_2 that would cause the same effects on global warming (this is called equivalent CO_2 amount).

The carbon footprint is a very powerful tool to understand the impact of personal behaviour on global warming. Most people are shocked when they see the amount of CO_2 their activities create! If you personally want to contribute to stop global warming, the calculation and constant monitoring of your personal carbon footprint is essential.

In the medium- and long term, the carbon footprint must be reduced to less than 2,000 kg CO_2 per year and per person. This is the maximum allowance for a sustainable living.

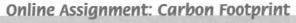

Online Assignment: Carbon Footprint

Complete this assignment online. Go to:
www.grtep.com
Select >Chapter Content>Chapter 3>Enter your username and password

GREENHOUSE GAS EMISSIONS

"Don't blow it — good planets are hard to find."

— Quoted in *Time*

We Count

Every day, all over the world, we participate in activities that produce global warming gases. How much pollution are we generating? The global greenhouse gas emissions counter on the collage started from zero on January 1st, 2007 and increases at a rate of approximately 1,268.51 tonnes CO_2-equivalent per second. We refer to global emissions in metric tonnes (rather than short tons, with which we're more familiar in the US) because metric units are the standard for global reporting and analysis.

Greenhouse gases trap heat and make the planet warmer. Human activities are responsible for almost all of the increase in greenhouse gases in the atmosphere over the last 150 years. The largest source of greenhouse gas emissions from human activities in the United States is from burning fossil fuels for electricity, heat, and transportation.

The primary sources of greenhouse gas emissions in the United States are:

- **Electricity production** (29 percent of 2015 greenhouse gas emissions)— Electricity production generates the largest share of greenhouse gas emissions. Approximately 67 percent of our electricity comes from burning fossil fuels, mostly coal and natural gas.

- **Transportation** (27 percent of 2015 greenhouse gas emissions)—Greenhouse gas emissions from transportation primarily come from burning fossil fuel for our cars, trucks, ships, trains, and planes. Over 90 percent of the fuel used for transportation is petroleum based, which includes gasoline and diesel.

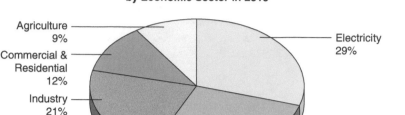

Total U.S. Greenhouse Gas Emissions by Economic Sector in 2015

Agriculture 9%

Commercial & Residential 12%

Industry 21%

Electricity 29%

Transportation 27%

Total Emissions in 2015 = 6,587 Million Metric Tons of CO_2 equivalent

© Kendall Hunt Publishing Company.

■ **Industry** (21 percent of 2015 greenhouse gas emissions)—Greenhouse gas emissions from industry primarily come from burning fossil fuels for energy, as well as greenhouse gas emissions from certain chemical reactions necessary to produce goods from raw materials.

■ **Commercial and Residential** (12 percent of 2015 greenhouse gas emissions)—Greenhouse gas emissions from businesses and homes arise primarily from fossil fuels burned for heat, the use of certain products that contain greenhouse gases, and the handling of waste.

■ **Agriculture** (9 percent of 2015 greenhouse gas emissions)—Greenhouse gas emissions from agriculture come from livestock such as cows, agricultural soils, and rice production.

■ **Land Use and Forestry** (offset of 11.8 percent of 2015 greenhouse gas emissions)—Land areas can act as a sink (absorbing CO_2 from the atmosphere) or a source of greenhouse gas emissions. In the United States, since 1990, managed forests and other lands have absorbed more CO_2 from the atmosphere than they emit.

SOURCE: https://www.epa.gov/ghgemissions/sources-greenhouse-gas-emissions

Emissions and Trends

Since 1990, U.S. greenhouse gas emissions have increased by about 4 percent. From year to year, emissions can rise and fall due to changes in the economy, the price of fuel, and other factors. In 2015, U.S. greenhouse gas emissions decreased compared to 2014 levels. This decrease was largely driven by a decrease in emissions from fossil fuel combustion, which was a result of multiple factors including substitution from coal to natural gas consumption in the electric power sector; warmer winter conditions that

Total U.S. Greenhouse Gas Emissions, 1990–2015

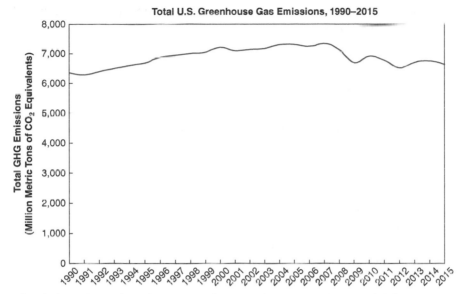

All emission estimates from the *Inventory of U.S. Greenhouse Gas Emissions and Sinks: 1990 2015.*

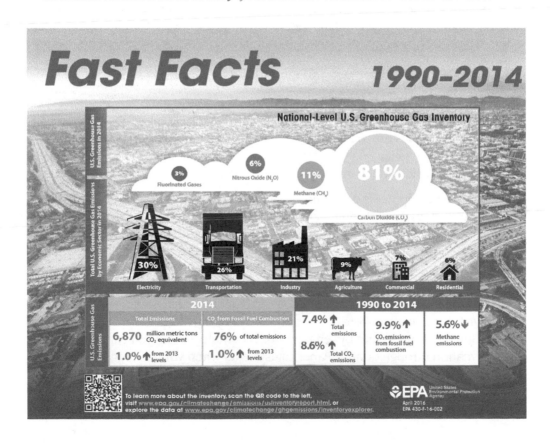

reduced demand for heating fuel in the residential and commercial sectors; and a slight decrease in electricity demand.

ENERGY

> **"**Renewable energy is proven technology, the rest of the world is going that way, that's where our investment should be going as well.**"**
>
> — Bob Brown

Sweet Dreams—Sleeping Computers

Myths abound in the world of office technology: how turning computers on and off shortens their life, how screensavers can save the world, the photographic limits of a copy machine, and how IT department performance is linked to vending machine sales of Jolt.

A final note: Even powered down, a computer draws a small amount of power. For maximum savings shut down and flip the switch on your power strip—new computers can handle 40,000 power cycles. It even makes sense to do this for just an hour at lunch.

Wondering What the Steps Are to Make Your PC More Efficient and Your Company Better Off?

- Two good options are to allow your computer to hibernate or go into standby mode rather than leaving the computer on when you're away and to turn your monitor off when you're away.

- When your computer is on, standby powers down components not in use, but the computer stays on and can reactivate in seconds. Hibernation saves your desktop, including all open files, and then powers down all hardware. When you wake the computer up from hibernation, everything is restored to the state it was when you left it. The start-up time is longer than for standby but shorter than starting your computer when it's been turned off. Hibernate is a lower energy state than standby because all of the hardware is off. You can standby or hibernate from the "Shut Down" menu, which offers buttons for "Stand By," "Turn Off," or "Restart." Press the Shift key, and "Stand By" changes to "Hibernate." In XP you can activate hibernation through Control Panel adjustments when you are logged on as an administrator, or if you're a member of either the Administrators or Power Users group. Some networks may not permit you to do this. Note: Always save open files and try hibernating manually from the "Shut Down" menu before changing

Control Panel options to make hibernation automatic, because some hardware configurations have had problems with hibernation. Also, consider whether you access your computer files remotely when you're away. If so, hibernate is not a good automatic setting for you.

To set your computer to automatically hibernate:

1. Open the Power Options Control Panel. (Click Start, Control Panel, then double-click Power Options.)

2. Click on the Hibernate tab, check the "Enable hibernate support" box, and click Apply. (If this tab is unavailable, your computer can't do it.)

3. Click on the APM tab, choose "Enable Advanced Power Management support" and then click Apply. (On some computers Advanced Power Management is automatic, so this tab is unavailable.)

4. Click on the Power Schemes tab, then set how long before your system hibernates. (Vista's default setting is an hour. You can use this as your setting or change it to match your needs.)

To set your monitor to automatically sleep:

1. Right-click the desktop, then click Properties.

2. In the Display Properties dialog box, click the Screen Saver tab. Click the Power button next to the ENERGY STAR symbol.

3. Now you're looking at the Power Options Properties dialog box. You should be in the first tab, Power Schemes. Click the Turn off monitor list, and the time for monitor sleep to 5 minutes. If this is a laptop, set times for both 'Plugged in' and 'Running on batteries.'

4. Double click 'OK'.

5. To wake your monitor, just move your mouse, or press a key.

What about Apple?

Macs come set to an energy-saving default. To tweak your settings choose "Energy Saver" in "System Preferences" where you can set times for sleeping both the display and the entire system. To schedule automatic shut downs and start ups, click the schedule button on this pane. Click "Options" to explore other power management tweaks.

From www.climateprotect.org by The Alliance for Climate Protection. Copyright © The Alliance for Climate Protection. Reprinted with permission.

Cars, Fuel, and Energy

Increasing concentrations of greenhouse gases are trapping more of the sun's energy in the Earth's atmosphere, causing global climate change.

- Carbon dioxide (CO_2) from burning fossil fuels is the most important of the human-made greenhouse gases.

- Highway vehicles account for 26% of our CO_2 emissions (1.7 billion tons each year).

- 97% of the greenhouse gases emitted from highway vehicles are CO_2.

Transportation Sector Emissions

The Transportation sector includes the movement of people and goods by cars, trucks, trains, ships, airplanes, and other vehicles. The majority of greenhouse gas emissions from transportation are carbon dioxide (CO_2) emissions resulting from the combustion of petroleum-based products, like gasoline, in internal combustion engines. The largest sources of transportation-related greenhouse gas emissions include passenger cars and light-duty trucks, including sport utility vehicles, pickup trucks, and minivans. These sources account for over half of the emissions from the transportation sector. The remaining greenhouse gas emissions from the transportation sector come from other modes of transportation, including freight trucks, commercial aircraft, ships, boats, and trains, as well as pipelines and lubricants.

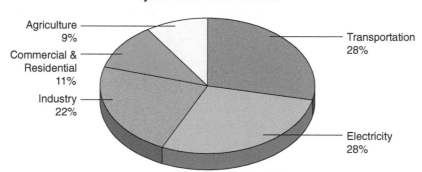

**Total U.S. Greenhouse Gas Emissions
by Economic Sector in 2016**

Agriculture 9%
Commercial & Residential 11%
Industry 22%
Transportation 28%
Electricity 28%

Total Emissions in 2016 = 6,511 Million Metric Tons of CO_2 equivalent

* Land Use, Land-Use Change, and Forestry in the United States is a net sink and offsets approximately 11 percent of these greenhouse gas emissions, not included in total above. All emission estimates from the *Inventory of U.S. Greenhouse Gas Emissions and Sinks: 1990–2016.*

Relatively small amounts of methane (CH_4) and nitrous oxide (N_2O) are emitted during fuel combustion. In addition, a small amount of hydrofluorocarbon (HFC) emissions are included in the Transportation sector. These emissions result from the use of mobile air conditioners and refrigerated transport.

Emissions and Trends

In 2016, greenhouse gas emissions from transportation accounted for about 28.5 percent of total U.S. greenhouse gas emissions, making it the largest contributor of U.S. greenhouse gas emissions. In terms of the overall trend, from 1990 to 2016, total transportation emissions increased due, in large part, to increased demand for travel. The number of vehicle miles traveled (VMT) by light-duty motor vehicles (passenger cars and light-duty trucks) increased by approximately 45 percent from 1990 to 2016, as a result of a confluence of factors including population growth, economic growth, urban sprawl, and periods of low fuel prices. Between 1990 and 2004, average fuel economy among new vehicles sold annually declined, as sales of light-duty trucks increased. Starting in 2005, average new vehicle fuel economy began to increase while light-duty VMT grew only modestly for much of the period. Average new vehicle fuel economy has improved almost every year since 2005, and the truck share is about 43 percent of new vehicles in model year 2015.

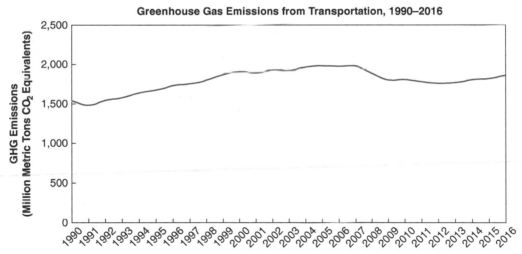

U.S. Environmental Protection Agency (2018). Inventory of U.S. Greenhouse Gas Emission and Sinks: 1990–2016

Emissions involved in the consumption of electricity for transportation activities are included above, but not shown separately (as was done for other sectors). These indirect emissions are negligible, accounting for less than 1 percent of the total emissions shown in the graph.

All emission estimates from the *Inventory of U.S. Greenhouse Gas Emissions and Sinks: 1990–2016.*

Reducing Emissions from Transportation

There are a variety of opportunities to reduce greenhouse gas emissions associated with transportation. The table shown below categorizes these opportunities and provides examples.

EPA's light-duty vehicle greenhouse gas rules are projected to save consumers $1.7 trillion at the pump by 2025, and eliminate 6 billion metric tons of greenhouse gas pollution.

EXAMPLES OF REDUCTION OPPORTUNITIES IN THE TRANSPORTATION SECTOR

TYPE	HOW EMISSIONS ARE REDUCED	EXAMPLES
Fuel Switching	Using fuels that emit less CO_2 than fuels currently being used. Alternative sources can include biofuels; hydrogen; electricity from renewable sources, such as wind and solar; or fossil fuels that are less CO_2-intensive than the fuels that they replace. Learn more about Green Vehicles and Alternative and Renewable Fuels.	Using public buses that are fueled by compressed natural gas rather than gasoline or diesel. Using electric or hybrid automobiles, provided that the energy is generated from lower-carbon or non-fossil fuels. Using renewable fuels such as low-carbon biofuels.
Improving Fuel Efficiency with Advanced Design, Materials, and Technologies	Using advanced technologies, design, and materials to develop more fuel-efficient vehicles. Learn about EPA's vehicle greenhouse gas rules.	Developing advanced vehicle technologies such as hybrid vehicles and electric vehicles, that can store energy from braking and use it for power later. Reducing the weight of materials used to build vehicles. Reducing the aerodynamic resistance of vehicles through better shape design.
Improving Operating Practices	Adopting practices that minimize fuel use. Improving driving practices and vehicle maintenance. Learn about how the freight transportation industry can reduce emissions through EPA's SmartWay Program.	Reducing the average taxi time for aircraft. Driving sensibly (avoiding rapid acceleration and braking, observing the speed limit). Reducing engine-idling. Improved voyage planning for ships, such as through improved weather routing, to increase fuel efficiency.

(continues)

TYPE	HOW EMISSIONS ARE REDUCED	EXAMPLES
Reducing Travel Demand	Employing urban planning to reduce the number of miles that people drive each day. Reducing the need for driving through travel efficiency measures such as commuter, biking, and pedestrian programs. Learn about EPA's Smart Growth Program.	Building public transportation, sidewalks, and bike paths to increase lower-emission transportation choices. Zoning for mixed use areas, so that residences, schools, stores, and businesses are close together, reducing the need for driving.

Energy Star and Energy

The EPA introduced ENERGY STAR in 1992 as a voluntary, market-based partnership to reduce greenhouse gas emissions through energy efficiency. Today you can find the ENERGY STAR label on more than 50 different kinds of products as well as in new homes and buildings. Products that have earned the ENERGY STAR designation prevent greenhouse gas emissions by meeting strict energy-efficiency specifications set by the U.S. government. In 2006 alone, ENERGY STAR helped Americans save about $14 billion on their energy bills while they did their part to protect our environment through reducing greenhouse gas emissions equivalent to those of 25 million vehicles.

From www.climateprotect.org by The Alliance for Climate Protection. Copyright © The Alliance for Climate Protection. Reprinted with permission.

Home Sweet Efficient Home
Commercial and Residential Sector Emissions

The residential and commercial sectors include all homes and commercial businesses (excluding agricultural and industrial activities). Greenhouse gas emissions from this sector come from **direct emissions** including fossil fuel combustion for heating and cooking needs, management of waste and wastewater, and leaks from refrigerants in homes and businesses as well as **indirect emissions** that occur offsite but are associated with use of electricity consumed by homes and businesses.

Direct emissions are produced from residential and commercial activities in a variety of ways:

- Combustion of natural gas and petroleum products for heating and cooking needs emits carbon dioxide (CO_2), methane (CH_4), and nitrous oxide (N_2O). Emissions from natural gas consumption represent about 78 percent of the direct fossil fuel CO_2 emissions from the residential and commercial sectors. Coal consumption is a minor component of energy use in both of these sectors.

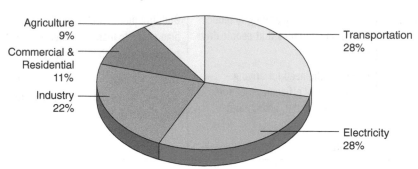

**Total U.S. Greenhouse Gas Emissions
by Economic Sector in 2016**

Agriculture — 9%

Commercial & Residential — 11%

Industry — 22%

Transportation — 28%

Electricity — 28%

Total Emissions in 2016 = 6,511 Million Metric Tons of CO_2 equivalent

* Land Use, Land-Use Change, and Forestry in the United States is a net sink and offsets approximately 11 percent of these greenhouse gas emissions, not included in total above. All emission estimates from the *Inventory of U.S. Greenhouse Gas Emissions and Sinks: 1990–2016.*

- Organic waste sent to landfills emits CH_4.
- Wastewater treatment plants emit CH_4 and N_2O.
- Fluorinated gases (mainly hydrofluorocarbons, or HFCs) used in air conditioning and refrigeration systems can be released during servicing or from leaking equipment.

Indirect emissions are produced by burning fossil fuel at a power plant to make electricity, which is then used in residential and commercial activities such as lighting and for appliances.

More national-level information about emissions from the residential and commercial sectors can be found in the U.S. Inventory's Energy and Trends chapters.

Emissions and Trends

In 2016, direct greenhouse gas emissions from homes and businesses accounted for approximately 11 percent of total U.S. greenhouse gas emissions. Greenhouse gas emissions from homes and businesses vary from year to year based on short-term fluctuations in energy consumption caused primarily by weather conditions. Total residential and commercial greenhouse gas emissions in 2016 have increased by about 7 percent since 1990. Greenhouse gas emissions from on-site direct emissions in homes and businesses have decreased by about 3 percent since 1990. Additionally, indirect emissions from electricity use by homes and businesses have increased by 14 percent since 1990, due to increasing electricity consumption for lighting, heating, air conditioning, and appliances.

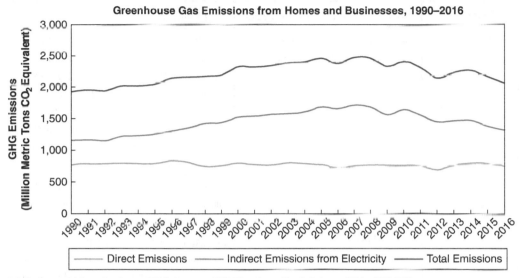

Greenhouse Gas Emissions from Homes and Businesses, 1990–2016

U.S. Environmental Protection Agency (2018). Inventory of U.S. Greenhouse Gas Emission and Sinks: 1990–2016

All emission estimates from the *Inventory of U.S. Greenhouse Gas Emissions and Sinks: 1990–2016.*

Reducing Emissions from Homes and Businesses

The table shown below provides some examples of opportunities to reduce emissions from homes and businesses.

EXAMPLES OF REDUCTION OPPORTUNITIES IN THE RESIDENTIAL AND COMMERCIAL SECTOR

TYPE	HOW EMISSIONS ARE REDUCED	EXAMPLES
Homes and Commercial Buildings	Reducing energy use through energy efficiency.	Homes and commercial buildings use large amounts of energy for heating, cooling, lighting, and other functions. "Green building" techniques and retrofits can allow new and existing buildings to use less energy to accomplish the same functions, leading to fewer greenhouse gas emissions. Techniques to improve building energy efficiency include better insulation; more energy-efficient heating, cooling, ventilation, and refrigeration systems; efficient fluorescent lighting; passive heating and lighting to take advantage of sunlight; and the purchase of energy-efficient appliances and electronics. Learn more about ENERGY STAR®.

(continues)

TYPE	HOW EMISSIONS ARE REDUCED	EXAMPLES
Wastewater Treatment	Making water and wastewater systems more energy-efficient.	Drinking water and wastewater systems account for approximately 3 percent to 4 percent of energy use in the United States. Studies estimate potential savings of 15 percent to 30 percent that are "readily achievable" in water and wastewater plants. Learn more about Energy Efficiency for Water and Wastewater Utilities.
Waste Management	Reducing solid waste sent to landfills. Capturing and using methane produced in current landfills.	Landfill gas is the natural byproduct of the decomposition of solid waste in landfills. It primarily consists of CO_2 and CH_4. Well established, low-cost methods to reduce greenhouse gases from consumer waste exist, including recycling programs, waste reduction programs, and landfill methane capture programs. Learn about EPA's waste reduction and resource conservation efforts. Learn about EPA's Landfill Methane Outreach Program, which promotes the recovery and use of landfill gas.
Refrigeration	Reducing leakage from refrigeration equipment. Using refrigerants with lower global warming potentials.	Commonly used refrigerants include ozone-depleting hydrochlorofluorocarbon (HCFC) refrigerants, often HCFC-22, and blends consisting entirely or primarily of hydrofluorocarbons (HFCs), both of which are potent greenhouse gases. In recent years there have been several advancements in refrigeration technology that can help food retailers reduce both refrigerant charges and refrigerant emissions. Learn more about EPA's GreenChill Program to reduce greenhouse gas emissions from commercial refrigerators.

Nearly one-fifth of America's greenhouse gases come from home energy use. Half of that is used to heat and cool our living spaces, while the other half goes to lighting, appliances, and your electronic entertainment infrastructure. That means a 10% reduction in heating and cooling expenditure would result in a 1% drop in the nation's total greenhouse gases emissions! And that can be achieved so easily with a variety of energy saving options. In fact, according to the EPA ENERGY STAR program, a 20% reduction of heating and cooling costs is in easy reach for most houses. Similar efficiencies are available for electrical appliances in the home.

A climate friendly house begins with just one step that may take one minute and cost nothing. There are quite a few similar options like but, as you get more advanced, they might take a little time and a little money up front. Keep tackling the list and pretty soon you'll start to see significant reductions in your monthly utility bills. And don't forget to check for available tax credits. Uncle Sam will pay 10% of the cost for many home energy improvements.

One thing that may help you to improve your home efficiency and save money is to get a home energy audit. Local energy efficiency programs or your utility may provide this service for free, and they have specialized tools that might uncover surprise savings. They also know the local contracting and energy folks, and should be able to help you prioritize your project list.

The laundry list below provides many options to get started. Some of these are addressed in detail in other parts of climateprotect.org and we'll keep adding more to make it easy for you to take action and make a difference in solving the climate crisis.

Hot Water

- Make sure your water heater temperature isn't set higher than you need it, 120°F for most purposes—extra unused degrees mean extra energy and extra money out of your pocket.

- Make sure the hot water heater tank is insulated so the money you just spent heating the water in the tank doesn't dissipate—water heater 'blankets' are available from most hardware stores.

- Reduce hot water use by installing efficient showerheads—there are now so many models you can choose the pressure and water pattern to suit your fancy.

- Reduce hot water use by fixing leaky faucets.

- When it is time to replace a water heater, buy the highest efficiency model.

- Consider replacing an old water heater with a solar thermal water heater.

- Wash your clothes in cold water.

- Use an ENERGY STAR washing machine.
- Use an ENERGY STAR dishwasher.

Heating and Cooling

- Plant deciduous trees that shade your home during the summer.
- Close the blinds on hot summer days, open them on cool winter days.
- In the winter, set your thermostat to 68°F and lower the temperature when you go to bed or are away from home, or use a programmable thermostat to do it for you.
- Put on a sweater and cover your feet when you feel cool. It's you that wants to be warm, not the furniture.
- Raise the thermostat a few degrees in the summer—your AC should be set to 78°F (check with your doctor if you have health issues). And definitely don't leave the A/C running full throttle when you leave the house.
- Weatherstrip and insulate your house to lower heating and air conditioning costs and energy use.
- Seal leaks around your foundation and electrical, plumbing, and cable gaps.
- Use storm doors and windows in cool environments.
- Install high-performance windows when it's time to replace them.
- Maintain your heating and cooling system on a regular basis.
- Install your air conditioner out of direct sunlight to help it run more efficiently.
- Avoid using the fireplace when the heating system is on and close the damper if it's not being used.
- Install fireplace inserts (doors and circulation blowers) so less warm air goes up the chimney when the fireplace is going.
- Use passive solar design techniques to heat and cool your home naturally.

Electricity

- Request the green power option from your utility.
- Install solar PV panels on your roof, or if you live in an appropriate location, install a wind turbine.
- Get a smart meter: tell your utility company you want to have a meter that can tell you what you're consuming and spending in real time; and one that can turn appliances off and on in response to changing prices.

Lighting

- Turn off lights when leaving a room.

- Use compact fluorescents throughout your home.

- Use solar-powered outdoor lights.

- During the holidays, install miniature holiday lights instead of jumbo ones. The miniatures last longer and reduce energy use.

Appliances—Big and Small

- Use ENERGY STAR appliances (refrigerators and washing machines) and buy the most efficient of everything that plugs in.

- Unplug items or use a kill-switch (power strip) when not using them; standby power wastes your money and energy.

- Don't bother rinsing your dishes. Scrape with a rubber spatula, then load straight into the dishwasher.

- Set your dishwasher to energy saver or no-heat dry modes and just open the door after the wash is done to let the dishes dry naturally.

- Avoid keeping your old refrigerator plugged in year-round in your garage.

- Line dry your clothes.

Recycling

- Recycle as much waste as possible because recycling takes less energy than producing new products from virgin materials.

- Check with your local utility company to find out what you can and can't recycle curbside.

Want to know more about your home energy use? Use these online tools: The ENERGY STAR yardstick will help you compare your home's energy use to averages in your neighborhood. You'll need a year's worth of utility bills to get a really good reading, but once you're done you'll be able to see how you stack up to the Jones'.

The Home Energy Saver run by Lawrence Berkeley National Laboratory helps you determine which things in your home contribute to your energy bill. Throw in your zip code, answer a few questions about your house, and it will break down your energy use from heating, cooling, water heating, major appliances, lighting, and small appliances. The level of detail available in this calculator is amazing: It will work from regional averages, or you can tell it everything from the exterior shading of the house to the wattage of each light fixture and how minutes a day you use your toaster oven. Save your session number and you can come back to it later for further insights.

All these details can be overwhelming unless you recognize that every single one is another opportunity to minimize your energy costs and lessen your climate footprint. The Home Energy Saver will also provide an upgrade report of places to look for improvements. And there is a lot of work to be done: In the average American house the gaps around the windows and doors add up to hole in the wall 3 feet by 3 feet.

Televisions and Energy

The EPA has announced a revised ENERGY STAR specification for televisions. Effective in November 2008, TVs that carry the ENERGY STAR label will be up to 30% more efficient than conventional models and will save energy while they are on and when they are off. After the new specification goes into effect, all TVs sold in the U.S. will meet the Energy Star requirements. The savings in energy costs will grow to about $1 billion annually, reducing greenhouse gas emissions by the equivalent of about one million cars.

TVs first earned the ENERGY STAR label in 1998, and TV manufacturers and the EPA have worked together on efficiency improvements ever since. The U.S. now has more than 275 million TVs in use that consume over 50 billion kilowatts per year.

Are You Kitchen Aware?

If your refrigerator is more than 10 years old, it could be using twice the energy of a new one and costing you twice as much in power bills. If you've been thinking about getting a new refrigerator, energy efficiency is a good excuse to go shopping today.

The fridge used to be one of the major energy hogs in the house, but industry innovation, encouraged by government standards, forced efficiency gains that reduced power consumption almost 75% even as the size of refrigerators went up significantly. That's great news. But even though the average efficiency has greatly improved, you can still end up with a fridge that consumes 50% more than a comparable model of the same size.

You need to look for two things: first is the ENERGY STAR label, which indicates the fridge beats the federal standard by at least 15%. But ENERGY STAR alone is not enough. You also need to look at the EnergyGuide—a card posted on or inside the fridge if you're shopping at the store—because it will tell you the fridge's annual energy consumption as well as how that fridge compares to others of similar size. Ultimately, to save the most money and make the greatest contribution to reducing your fridge's greenhouse footprint you ought to be on the lookout for the model with the lowest energy consumption estimate (measured in kWh/year)—and it may or may not be the smallest refrigerator!

Remember that you pay for your new refrigerator when you buy it and then every month when you pay your utility bill. If you buy an energy efficient model, you will save money every year, up to $50 or more, which adds up over the life of the refrigerator.

If you're shopping for a new fridge, here's how to get the biggest climate bang (and utility bill savings) for your buck:

- Check with your local utility to see if they have a rebate program to help you pay to replace your old refrigerator.

- Design: Freezer-on-top models use about 20% less energy than comparably sized side-by-side models and among available ENERGY STAR models, they're also generally better than freezer-on-bottom. Automatic ice makers, water coolers, and flat panel televisions also increase power consumption.

- Whatever you decide, do go ENERGY STAR and look at the ENERGY GUIDE. A 16 cubic foot Sun Frost uses just 204 kilowatt hours a year compared to 553 for a 20 cubic foot Kenmore side-by-side. But both are much less than the typical 2001 US refrigerator consumption of 1239 kWh per year.

- Remember that one store may not carry the most efficient models so a little comparison shopping can help.

- Don't park your old model in the basement or the garage. If you're going to fire it up once a year as a dedicated beer cooler for your 4th of July bash, fine. But if you keep it plugged in just for backup you'll take a big home efficiency step backwards.

AC/DC Green Power

Consumer choice probably isn't what comes to mind when you think about your electric company. The grid is one-size-fits all: electrons work the same whether they come from organically sourced methane or strip-mined coal, and they don't care if they're pumping tunes from the stereo or milk from a cow.

What does matter is that, unless directed otherwise, regulated utilities often provide energy from the cheapest available option with which they're familiar. That sounds good, except that the formula doesn't account for damage downstream—things like mercury pollution, acid rain, smog, and climate change that arise from reliance on fossil fuels. The deck is stacked against promising clean technologies like solar and wind and in favor of old-school, carbon-belching coal plants. In 2005, non-renewable electricity produced 1.9 billion metric tonnes of CO_2. That's 81% of CO_2 emissions from the US electrical sector and about one-fourth of total US greenhouse emissions.

Electricity markets are changing, though, and if you want to buy power with a lighter carbon footprint there are plenty of utilities who want to sell you electricity produced by wind, biomass, solar, or even landfill gas. Green power can be less, the same, or a little more expensive. But regardless, it plays an important role in today's energy economy: when combined with improving energy efficiency in your home, you can lower your electricity bills and CO_2 impact. Even though it now accounts for less than 1% of the US electricity market, green power grew 37% in 2005. It's proving that there is a growing appetite for clean renewable energy. And as customer demand increases, utilities, from linesmen to CEOs, are becoming renewable energy's strongest advocates.

The simplest scenario for buying green power is to check and see what your local utility offers. Or, if you're in a deregulated state in which you can choose your power company, check and see what the competition is offering as well. Some companies offer to purchase electricity from renewable sources to meet all of your power demands; others provide packages in which some of your power will be sourced from particular kinds of renewable energy like wind or solar. Still, others offer programs in which a portion of your power is met from green sources. The pricing packages vary based on the specific mix of renewables (i.e., how much wind, biomass, solar, landfill gas and geothermal comprise the product), local regulations and the individual utility's overall cost structure. More than 600 utilities in 37 states offer green power products and they try to make it simple to sign up. To find out what your options are, see the US Department of Energy map.

If you can't access green electricity through a utility servicing your area, you can still actively support the renewable energy industry by purchasing Renewable Energy Certificates.

Green power marketing is how to green your juice in the 10 states (plus D.C.) where electricity is deregulated. You choose your provider, and among them are green power options. Depending on your state you can buy some or all of your power from renewables, support new wind investment, or get a mix of power. Some of the products are certified by third parties (Environmental Resources Trust or green-e). You can compare the products in your area here.

Renewable Energy Certificates

If you don't live in state with a deregulated electricity market and your utility isn't offering greenpower, green tags, or renewable energy certificates (RECs) are your best option for getting green power, apart from installing your own. A REC or green tag represents one megawatt hour (MWh) of renewable electricity. Because the grid doesn't care where electricity comes from it can be generated and delivered anywhere. So what you're really buying are the renewable attributes—carbon free, renewable, pollution free—of the electricity that is displacing dirty power. RECs use electricity's unique portability to deliver low carbon power, wherever you need it.

Consumer Voice

If your local utility ISN'T offering green power right now, make sure to write to them, their regulator (e.g. the state utility commission) and your hometown newspaper to say you want your power to come from renewables—so they should get on with it!

From www.climateprotect.org by The Alliance for Climate Protection. Copyright © The Alliance for Climate Protection. Reprinted with permission.

ASSIGNMENT: Energy Savings Assignment.

1. What are you currently doing to save energy at school or at home?

    a. _____

    b. _____

    c. _____

    d. _____

    e. _____

2. What will you do to make a difference with saving energy at school or at home?

    a. _____

    b. _____

    c. _____

    d. _____

    e. _____

3. What is your plan to increase awareness of energy savings for your friends, family, roommates, and others at home or on campus?

a. _____

b. _____

c. _____

d. _____

e. _____

REDUCING, REUSING AND RECYCLING

"America is shifting to a 'green culture' where all 300 million citizens are embracing the fact that environmental responsibility is everyone's responsibility."

— U.S. Environmental Protection Agency

Don't throw those empty water bottles into the trash, recycle them! The same goes for the empty cereal box. New data released by the U.S.'s Environmental Protection Agency (EPA) shows that Americans generated 251 million tons of municipal solid waste and recycled and composted 82 million tons (about 32%) in 2006. Each American generated 4.6 pounds of waste each day, of which they recycled about 1.5 pounds. In addition, approximately 31 million tons of municipal solid waste was composted for energy recovery in 2006.

Recycling offers opportunities for everyone to help reduce climate change, save energy, and conserve natural resources. For example, recycling just one ton of aluminum cans saves the energy equivalent of 36 barrels of oil or 1,655 gallons of gasoline. Furthermore, using recycled materials instead of new materials saves energy and reduces greenhouse gas emissions. Using recycled glass instead of new materials consumes 40% less energy.

When Americans combine their personal recycling with industrial recycling, they significantly contribute to the protection of the global environment. Americans also contribute to recycling by purchasing products with recycled content, less packaging, and fewer harmful materials.

Recycling reduces costs to businesses and creates jobs. The American recycling and reuse industry is a $200 billion dollar enterprise involving more than 50,000 recycling and reuse establishments, employing more than 1 million people, and generating an annual payroll of approximately $37 billion.

Pack Lightly

When the good people at the Environmental Protection Agency get around to counting your trash, the numbers get scary. Containers and packaging are the single largest category in the waste stream, making up 31% (76.7 million tons) of total municipal solid waste (the waste that goes to the city landfill or gets recycled).

Plastic and paper are the two biggest players here, accounting for 65% of the packaging market. On the receiving end, that leads to 3.7 million tons of plastic, only 9% recycled, and 39 million tons of paper and cardboard, 59% of which gets recycled. Aluminum, steel, and glass round out the potpourri.

And what does waste have to do with climate change? Well, two things. First, all of that waste material—the packaging, the paper, the containers—was produced with the assistance of energy as part of its manufacturing process and, in most situations today, that means greenhouse gas emissions. Second, all that packaging means that products take up more space during transport to the store, which can lead to more fossil fuels being consumed by ships, trains, and trucks than are really needed.

The greenhouse gas statistics are about as mixed up as a landfill on a windy day, and smell just about as nice. Here are some of the factors: About 4% of total U.S. energy consumption is used to produce raw plastic materials. Metals are more likely to get recycled than glass, but just replacing the aluminum cans that don't make it back to the smelter uses enough energy to power 2.7 million American households. And these emissions don't even count the transportation emissions associated with carrying the usually over-packaged items by ship, train, and truck to your local store. Savings can be had across the board with a familiar three-step plan: reduce, reuse, recycle.

Reduce

The biggest savings come when we DON'T make something to begin with. At least 28 nations have some kind of legislation to reduce packaging waste.

The biggest packaging offenders are manufacturers and retailers, and they're beginning to get the picture with rising energy prices pushing up the cost of pretty much everything. You can bring things in focus by:

- Where possible, choose products based on economy of packaging. Look for concentrated products like soaps and detergents, products that don't come in their own serving ware (i.e. noodles in a cup), and products that are sold individually without a package (i.e. lip balms sold from a big cookie jar rather than in separate plastic containers or boxes). The Kiss My Face Lip Action sold at Whole Foods (a portion of the proceeds go to the Alliance for Climate Protection) is a good example of minimal packaging.

- Write a quick note to the company that didn't get your business and explain why. Enclose a copy of the receipt showing the competitor's sale to make sure they get the point.

- Buy in bulk. For example, buy produce from a big bin rather than in a plastic container of four items. Some stores sell grains, pasta, and other dry goods in bulk as well.

- Buy larger packages with greater quantities. If you're buying non-perishables and you have the storage space, you can also buy items in larger packages. The larger the package the better the ratio of product to packaging. Plus, you will save a trip to the store and its associated fuel use and emissions.

- Bring your own reusable bags to market.

- Skip the new giftwrap and the gift box, if not needed to protect the contents: Reclaim wrapping paper, and for an informal gift, reuse an outdated road map.

Reuse

We know you hate clutter, but dedicate a corner of your attic or closet to keeping a second-hand collection of boxes and packing materials. It will save time, money, and reduce climate impacts.

Recycle

Recycled materials typically use only a fraction of the energy needed to make the same product from scratch. In 2005, the U.S. recycled approximately 32% of its waste which saved enough in greenhouse gases to equal taking more than 10 million cars off the road. Raising recycling rates just 3% would be like taking another million cars off the road.

Be Mindful during the Busiest Time of Year

Helpful hints from the EPA to reduce, reuse, and recycle holiday waste:

- Thousands of paper and plastic shopping bags end up in landfills every year. Reduce the number of bags thrown out by bringing reusable cloth bags for holiday gift shopping. Tell store clerks you don't need a bag for small or oversized purchases.

- Wrap gifts in recycled or reused wrapping paper or funny papers. Also remember to save or recycle used wrapping paper.

- Give gifts that don't require much packaging, such as concert tickets or gift certificates.

- Send recycled-content greeting cards to reduce the amount of virgin paper used during the holidays. Remember to recycle any paper cards you receive or use the fronts of the cards as gift labels for the next holiday season. You can also try sending electronic greeting cards to reduce paper waste.

- About 40% of all battery sales occur during the holiday season. Buy rechargeable batteries to accompany your electronic gift and consider giving a battery charger as well. Rechargeable batteries reduce the amount of potentially harmful materials thrown away and can save money in the long run.

- During the holidays, install miniature holiday lights instead of jumbo ones. The miniatures last longer and reduce energy use.

- Turn off or unplug holiday lights during the day. Doing so will not only save energy but will also help your lights last longer.

- Approximately 33 million live Christmas trees are sold in North America every year. After the holidays, look for ways to recycle your tree instead of sending it to a landfill. Check with your community solid waste department and find out if they collect and mulch trees. Your town might be able to use chippings from mulched trees for hiking trails and beachfront erosion barriers.

- To help prevent waste from cutting down and disposing of live trees, you can buy a potted tree and plant it after the holidays.

- Have a create-your-own-decorations party! Invite family and friends to create and use holiday decorations such as ornaments made from old greeting cards or cookie dough, garlands made from strung popcorn or cranberries, wreaths made from artificial greens and flowers, and potpourri made from kitchen spices such as cinnamon and cloves.

- Consider the durability of a product before you buy it as a gift. Cheaper, less durable items often wear out quickly, creating waste and costing you money.

- When buying gifts, check product labels to determine if you can recycle an item and whether it is made from recycled materials. Buying recycled encourages manufacturers to make more recycled-content products available.

- Use your own camera instead of a disposable one to reduce waste while capturing holiday memories. Consider buying a digital camera so that you don't have to use film and only print the pictures you want to keep.

Cell Phones and Recycling

Recycling an old cell phone offers an opportunity for everyone to help reduce greenhouse gas emissions, to save energy, and to conserve natural resources. An estimated 100 to 130 million cell phones are no longer in use; many are just in storage. If Americans recycled 100 million cell phones, we could save enough upstream energy to power more than 194,000 U.S. households for a year. If consumers reused those 100 million cell phones, the environmental savings would be even greater, saving enough energy to power more than 370,000 U.S. homes each year. By dropping off your unused cell phone at a store or sending it through the mail, Americans have more recycling options today than ever before. As a part of the EPA's Plug-In to eCycling program, partners supporting this endeavor include AT&T Wireless, Best Buy, LG Electronics, Motorola, Nokia, Office Depot, Samsung, Sony Ericsson, Sprint, Staples, and T-Mobile.

What Is the Plug-In to eCycling All About?

This is a voluntary partnership between EPA and electronics manufacturers, retailers, and service providers to offer consumers more opportunities to donate or recycle their used electronics. In 2007, as part of their commitment to the program, retailers and electronics manufacturers voluntarily recycled more than 47 million pounds of electronics, mostly computers and televisions. Efforts like these have helped the Plug-In program to recycle more than 142 million pounds of electronics since 2003.

Batteries and Recycling

When you need a portable, convenient power source, you can rely on batteries. The different sizes and shapes reflect the versatility of batteries, but all batteries have two common elements that combine to make power: an electrolyte and a heavy metal (such as mercury, lead, cadmium, and nickel, which can contaminate the environment when we improperly dispose of batteries). When incinerated, certain metals might release into the air or concentrate in the ash produced by the combustion process.

One way to reduce the number of batteries in the waste stream is to purchase rechargeable batteries. Americans purchase nearly three billion dry-cell batteries every year to power cell phones, laptops, radios, toys and power tools. But nearly one in five dry-cell batteries purchased in the United States is rechargeable. Over its useful life, each rechargeable battery may substitute for hundreds of single-use batteries.

What Do I Need to Know about Battery Recycling?

1. *Lead-Acid Automobile Batteries:* Nearly 90% of all lead-acid batteries become recycled as required by most state laws. They send the plastic to a reprocessor for manufacture into new plastic products and deliver purified lead to battery manufacturers and other industries. A typical lead-acid battery contains 60 to 80% recycled lead and plastic.

2. *Non-Automotive Lead-Based Batteries:* Gel cells and sealed lead-acid batteries are commonly used to power industrial equipment, emergency lighting, and alarm systems. The same recycling process applies as with automotive batteries. An automotive store or a local waste agency may accept the batteries for recycling.

3. *Dry-Cell Batteries:* These batteries include alkaline and carbon zinc (9-volt, D, C, AA, AAA), mercuric-oxide (button, some cylindrical and rectangular), silver-oxide and zinc-air (button), and lithium (9-volt, C, AA, coin, button, rechargeable). On average, each person in the United States discards eight dry-cell batteries per year.

   - *Alkaline and Zinc-Carbon Batteries:* Alkaline batteries are the everyday household batteries used in flashlights, remote controls, and other appliances. Several reclamation companies now process these batteries

   - *Button-Cell Batteries:* Most small, round "button-cell" type batteries found in items such as watches and hearing aids contain mercury, silver, cadmium, lithium, or other heavy metals as their main component. Recyclers are increasingly targeting button cells for recycling because of the value of recoverable materials, their small size, and their easy handling relative to other battery types.

   - *Rechargeable Batteries:* The Rechargeable Battery Recycling Corporation (RBRC), a nonprofit public service organization, targets four kinds of rechargeable batteries for recycling: nickel-cadmium (Ni-CD), nickel metal hydride, lithium ion, and small-sealed lead.

Where Can I Recycle These Batteries?

You can search for local battery recycling facilities by zip code at earth911.org

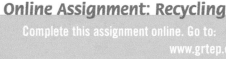

Online Assignment: Recycling

Complete this assignment online. Go to:
www.grtep.com
Select >Chapter Content>Chapter 7>Enter your username and password

I Pledge, You Pledge, We All Win

Talk is cheap, but inaction is expensive, especially when the climate is in crisis. Take this pledge and then post it on your fridge, make it your screensaver, tape it near the back door or put a tiny version inside your wallet. Then explain to others why this is important so that they too will take the pledge. Hang it up in the coffee room at work. Post it on the community bulletin boards downtown or at the local library. This is all about doing something for yourself and your loved ones. For your wife, husband, partner, mom, dad, sister, brother, niece, nephew, cousin; it's for your neighbor, your teacher, your car mechanic, your mailman, your doctor, your best friend, your worst enemy; it's for your children... it's for everybody's children. It's for today, tomorrow, and every tomorrow that follows. Take the pledge for you and for everyone. I pledge:

- To demand that my country join an international treaty within the next 2 years that cuts global warming pollution by 90% in developed countries and by more than half worldwide in time for the next generation to inherit a healthy earth;

- To take personal action to help solve the climate crisis by reducing my own CO_2 pollution as much as I can and offsetting the rest to become "carbon neutral";

- To fight for a moratorium on the construction of any new generating facility that burns coal without the capacity to safely trap and store the CO_2;

- To work for a dramatic increase in the energy efficiency of my home, workplace, school, place of worship, and means of transportation;

- To fight for laws and policies that expand the use of renewable energy sources and reduce dependence on oil and coal;

- To plant new trees and to join with others in preserving and protecting forests; and,

- To buy from businesses and support leaders who share my commitment to solving the climate crisis and building a sustainable, just, and prosperous world for the 21st century.

TIPS TO BECOMING ENVIRONMENTALLY HEALTHY

*"It is not the language of the painters but the language
of Nature to which one has to listen."*

— Vincent Van Gogh

- Ensure that your living space is conducive for studying, sleeping, eating and a healthy lifestyle but also that it provides access to clean air and sanitary water. Safety and cleanliness are also a big part of being environmentally well.

- Be cognizant of ways you can save energy at home, school, or work.

- Be aware of the limits of the earth's natural resources.

- Enjoy and appreciate the outdoors by spending time in the splendor of our natural settings.

- Make sure your personal environment and surroundings are safe, healthy, and conducive to learning, positive thinking, and living.

- Get a grip on what greenhouse gases mean and how they affect our environment.

- Choose products that are environmentally-friendly or recycled.

- Read and stay updated on the latest news and helpful tips on environmental wellness.

- Make a plan to save energy with your vehicle even if it's a matter of just your driving habits.

- Save water: Turn off the water when brushing your teeth, shaving, or washing the dishes. Fill the sink with water as opposed to letting the faucet run.

- Remember to reduce, reuse, and recycle at home, at school, at work, and in your community.

- Preserve aquatic life. Maintain the balance of the food chain by using low-phosphate or phosphate free soaps.

- Become familiar with your community's Earth Day or climate protection initiatives and get involved!

- Educate others about environmental wellness and protecting our planet.

SOURCE: Wellness for Healthy Positive Living: Environmental Wellness Facts.

Helpful Internet Sites

The Alliance for Climate Protection: climateprotect.org
Battery Recycling or Recycling in General: earth911.org/recycling/battery-recycling/
Global Warming: fightglobalwarming.com
The Green Guide: thegreenguide.com
Green Power: eere.energy.gov/greenpower/buying/buyingpower.shtml
Green Power Certificates: eere.energy.gov/greenpower/markets/certificates.shtml
Home Energy Yardstick: energystar.gov/index.cfm?fuseaction=home_energy_yardstick.showStep2
hes.lbl.gov
Insulation and Energy: eere.energy.gov/consumer/tips/insulation.html
Insulation Tips: ornl.gov/sci/roofs+walls/insulation/ins_01.html
Insulation Tips: simplyinsulate.com
Planet Earth: planetearth.com
Tax Credits for Insulation Improvements: energystar.gov/index.cfm?c=Products.pr_tax_credits
U.S. Environmental Protection Agency Go Green Newsroom: epa.gov/newsroom/gogreen
U.S. Environmental Protection Agency Transportation: epa.gov/climatechange/wycd/tools_
transportation.html
U.S. Environmental Protection Agency Green Vehicles: epa.gov/greenvehicles/Index.do;jsessionid=
8230789614d963306f33
U.S. Environmental Protection Agency Cell Phone Recycling: epa.gov/cellphone
U.S. Environmental Protection Agency Plug-In Program: epa.gov/plug-in/
U.S. Environmental Protection Agency Fuel Economy: fueleconomy.gov/feg/climate.shtml
U.S. Environmental Protection Agency Driving Habits: fueleconomy.gov/feg/driveHabits.shtml

References

Bounds, L. *Health and Fitness: A Guide to a Healthy Lifestyle.* Definition of Environmental Health. Kendall Hunt Publishing Company (2006): 4.

EPA (2012). Energy Efficiency for Water and Wastewater Utilities. Accessed 03/13/2012.

IPCC (2007). Summary for Policymakers. In: *Climate Change 2007: The Physical Science Basis.* Exit *Contribution of Working Group I to the Fourth Assessment Report of the Intergovernmental Panel on Climate Change* [Solomon, S., D. Qin, M. Manning, Z. Chen, M. Marquis, K.B. Averyt, M. Tignor and H.L. Miller (eds.)]. Cambridge University Press, Cambridge, United Kingdom and New York, NY, USA.

Kahn Ribeiro, S., S. Kobayashi, M. Beuthe, J. Gasca, D. Greene, D. S. Lee, Y. Muromachi, P. J. Newton, S. Plotkin, D. Sperling, R. Wit, P. J. Zhou (2007). *Transport and its infrastructure. In Climate Change 2007: Mitigation.* Exit *Contribution of Working Group III to the Fourth Assessment Report of the Intergovernmental Panel on Climate Change* [B. Metz, O.R. Davidson, P.R. Bosch, R. Dave, L.A. Meyer (eds.)], Cambridge University Press, Cambridge, United Kingdom.

The Alliance for Climate Protection. AC/DC Green Power. climateprotect.org accessed on 1.5.08.

The Alliance for Climate Protection. Sweet Dreams Sleeping Computers. climateprotect.org accessed on 1.5.08.

The Alliance for Climate Protection. We Count. climateprotect.org accessed on 1.8.08.

The Alliance for Climate Protection. Wrap it Up- Save Energy with R-49. climateprotect.org accessed on 1.8.08.

The Alliance for Climate Protection. Are You Kitchen Aware? climateprotect.org accessed on 1.14.08.

The Alliance for Climate Protection. Home Sweet Efficiency Home. climateprotect.org accessed on 1.14.08.

The Alliance for Climate Protection. Taking Action on the Pledge. climateprotect.org accessed on 1.14.08.

The Alliance for Climate Protection. Solving the Climate Crisis. climateprotect.org accessed on 1.14.08.

U.S. Energy Information Administration (2016). *Electricity Explained - Basics.*

U.S. Environmental Protection Agency (EPA). Cell Phone Recycling is an Easy Call. epa.gov. newsroom accessed on 1.8.08.

U.S. Environmental Protection Agency (EPA). America Recycles Day. epa.gov/newsroom/gogreen accessed on 1.11.08.

U.S. Environmental Protection Agency (EPA). Climate Change- What Can You Do: On The Road. epa.gov/climatechange/wycd/road.html accessed on 1.27.08.

U.S. Environmental Protection Agency (EPA). Fuel Economy Guide: Driving More Efficiently. fueleconomy.gov/feg/driveHabits.shtml accessed on 1.27.08.

U.S. Environmental Protection Agency (EPA). Fuel Economy Guide: Why is Fuel Economy Important? fueleconomy.gov/feg/why.shtml accessed on 1.27.08.

U.S. Environmental Protection Agency (EPA). Fuel Economy Guide: Many Factors Affect MPG. fueleconomy.gov/feg/factors.shtml accessed on 1.27.08.

U.S. Environmental Protection Agency (EPA). Global Climate Change. fueleconomy.gov/feg/climate.shtml accessed on 1.28.08

U.S. Environmental Protection Agency (EPA). Packing Lightly. epa.gov/newsroom/gogreen. accessed on 1.13.08.

U.S. Environmental Protection Agency (EPA). Sustainable Environments Research. epa.gov/nrmrl/std/scb/basic.html accessed on November 7, 2011.

U.S. Environmental Protection Agency (EPA). Televisions Must Meet New Requirements to Earn Energy Star Label. epa.gov.newsroom accessed on 2.5.08

U.S. Environmental Protection Agency (EPA). Batteries. epa.gov/msw/battery.htm accessed on 2.24.08

Wellness for Healthy Positive Living. Environmental Wellness. for.gov.bc.ca/hrb/hw/index.htm accessed on 1.15.08

CHAPTER 8

Occupational Wellness

"The quality of a person's life is in direct proportion to their commitment to excellence, regardless of their chosen field of endeavor."

— Vincent T. Lombardi

The objectives in this chapter include the understanding of:

- ■ **The meaning of occupational wellness and its direct application to you**
- ■ **Keys to choosing a major**
- ■ **Keys to choosing a career**
- ■ **Keys to choosing a vocation**
- ■ **Self-exploration and self-marketing**
- ■ **Work/life balance**
- ■ **Leadership and living**

Online Reminders

- ■ Complete the poll question before the next class meeting.
- ■ Complete the interactive activities for this chapter.
- ■ Complete all of the online assignments for this chapter.

Occupational Wellness—Occupational wellness begins with determining what roles, activities, and commitments take up a majority of an individual's time. These roles, activities, or commitments could include but are not limited to: being a student, volunteering in an organization, parenting, or working part-time or full-time. Occupational wellness occurs when each of these areas are integrated and balanced in a personally or professionally fulfilling way.

Recognizing your personal satisfaction, meaning, and enrichment throughout your student life and eventually your work life is a major part of being occupationally well. The other major part to developing occupational wellness can relate to your attitude about your studies or work because your attitude controls your outlook and mindset.

Ask yourself: Can I see the bigger picture when it comes to doing an assignment or taking a class that isn't within my major? Do I understand that there is a purpose (from the professionals who set my curriculum) for being required to taking that class or doing that assignment? These are important questions to ask yourself—NOW—because your attitude will play a huge role in your work life and productivity as well. Supervisors will ask you to do projects or presentations on items that aren't as much of an interest to you while they will ask your co-worker to do the project or presentation you would like to do. *How will you handle this?*

Remember, you can consider college a "dress rehearsal" for work. Choosing a profession and taking coursework to complete your degree toward doing that profession is the ultimate goal. However, you cannot reach this goal just by coursework alone. As we discussed in earlier chapters, it not only takes having career ambitions but also conveying your strengths through involvement in activities and organizations at school or in your community. Occupational wellness is also the understanding of your own interests, abilities, skills, and values and how these affect the ways you make career choices as well as vocational choices.

According to the National Wellness Institute, occupational wellness follows these tenets:

1. It is better to choose a path of study or career that is consistent with our personal values, interests, and beliefs than to select one that is unrewarding to us.

2. It is better to develop functional, transferable skills through structured involvement opportunities than to remain inactive and uninvolved.

PRE-CLASS SURVEY: Take your occupational wellness survey before your next class meeting and identify your level of occupational wellness. Circle either Yes or No, total up each column, and check your score.

I am involved in several student and/or professional organizations and activities.	YES	NO
I participate in my own personal leisure and recreational activities.	YES	NO
I am happy with the balance between my studies/work time and my leisure time.	YES	NO
I am looking forward to working in my career area.	YES	NO
I am stimulated and personally satisfied with my studies/career choices.	YES	NO
I view the payoffs in my studies/career choices as aligned with my personal values.	YES	NO
I feel that I am respected and viewed as a leader among my peers at school/work.	YES	NO
I feel that my major/career choice contributes to my stability and happiness in life.	YES	NO
I seek out other students or professionals if I feel that I need help with certain assignments or projects.	YES	NO
I feel that my attitude is one that is open-minded and finds purpose in all of my classes/job duties.	YES	NO
I am happy with my major/career path.	YES	NO
I feel my major/career path will allow me, if not already, to make a difference.	YES	NO
I practice the notion of teamwork and "pulling my weight" with team assignments or projects.	YES	NO
	TOTAL	

WHAT YOUR TOTAL MEANS:

9 or more Yes answers	Excellent	Your habits are positively enhancing your health.
6–8 Yes answers	Average	You are obviously trying but there is room to improve.
5 or less Yes answers	Not So Good	There is a need for improvement in your daily habits.

Source: "Wellness for Healthy Positive Living." *Occupational Wellness/Inventory* for.gov.bc.ca/hrb/hw/index.htm

> ❝*I will study and get ready, and perhaps my chance will come.*❞
> — President Abraham Lincoln

Six Factors that Align and Enhance Motivation

The theories and research of social scientists and the comments made by highly motivated students reveal that various elements and characteristics contribute to being highly motivated. It is also apparent that these elements are intertwined. To summarize, highly motivated students

- Are willing to put forth effort to achieve their goals
- Possess a strong sense of belonging on campus
- Possess firm goals that are explicit (clear and not built on fantasy), linked to careful planning, and established by obtaining useful information from various resources
- Possess skills for personal problem-solving and decision-making
- Report having support from others
- Experience a range of motivations, but are mostly driven by intrinsic forms of motivation

Final Suggestions to Help Develop and Maintain One's Motivation

Develop a motivating perspective toward the world

David E. Schmitt, who wrote *The Winning Edge*, writes about a motivating attitude. Based on our experiences and the views of Schmitt, we have concluded that it is important to feed and strengthen (1) an optimistic perspective, (2) a passion for our identified goals, (3) a critical, truthseeking approach to learning, (4) an ability to approach situations with curiosity, (5) a desire to achieve, (6) a belief in ourselves, (7) our creative potential, and (8) our sense of control. While some of these elements will be discussed in greater detail in other chapters, we will expand on a few here.

When you experience anxiety or fear about a college course, you should not allow such feelings to affect your motivation. For example, let's say you are required to enroll in an introductory speech class and you have always found it difficult to speak in front of others. You could dwell on the negative aspects of the situation, or you could take control of the situation by approaching it from a positive, optimistic perspective. For example, a student enrolled in a speech class could take control of his fear. The student could write out the first speech. He could go to the classroom when no one is there and sit in his chair and then imagine being called upon by the professor. The student would then go to the front of the classroom and give the speech. Reciting a speech while picturing one's classmates being present and seeing oneself earning a good grade can significantly reduce one's fear in many cases.

When a student uses this technique, frequently the student is able to do what is required—to take control of a situation rather than letting it control him or her. An optimistic perspective enables a person to focus on what he or she can do rather than what he or she cannot do.

Possessing the various elements of a motivating perspective enables one to recover sooner from the stress and confusion that is sometimes encountered during one's academic journey toward graduation. For example, sometimes a person becomes confused as to why he or she is attending a college. Goals are no longer clear, and the student finds it difficult to concentrate on class work because the student is unsure about what the future holds. There is a sense of lacking direction. If you ever find yourself in a situation where you doubt your original reasons for going to college, you should stop and ask, "Why did I want to attend college in the first place?" Such self-examination may lead you to realize that the motivation that has carried you this far is weak and your motivational energy is missing. The solution is to establish new goals or modify old ones by moving through these steps, keeping in mind that intrinsic motivation is associated with high rates of persistence.

- Examine your priorities (values).
- Examine alternatives.
- Obtain needed information and assistance.
- Find something that will generate passion.
- Finally, reestablish goal(s).

The following examples illustrate the connection between values and motivation:

A student may value and be motivated by a desire to help others.

A student may value and be motivated by an interest in working as a member of a team.

Other values that may motivate someone are competition, power and authority, working alone, acquiring knowledge, or financial security.

The college career of one of the authors provides a case in point: I (Ginter) started college wanting to gain knowledge, but also to guarantee myself financial security after graduating. As a beginning freshman, I decided to major in philosophy. But over time, maintaining my motivation became difficult because I became very concerned about whether I would ever obtain a job teaching philosophy, since such jobs are rare. This meant I did not see myself as having a financially secure future (something I valued). I gathered information and sought assistance. The result of these efforts was that I examined appropriate alternatives and decided to switch to a major in psychology, a major that at the time promised a future career. I had a passion for both philosophy and psychology. Thus, by carefully considering my values and the alternatives, I was able to reestablish a clear goal, and this boosted my motivation level to do well in college.

Everyone has strengths. Students admitted to a college are not selected with the aim of having those students fail. Colleges want students to succeed. This is where having carefully thought-out goals pays off. Keep in mind that your college goals should be tied to your strengths. If you are interested in working with people, you might want to consider going into majors related to social work, nursing, or psychology. If you are the type of person who likes to be in a position of leading others or convincing others, you might want to consider going into law or business. If you enjoy investigating problems and you enjoy science-related activities, you may want to consider biology, math, or computer programming as a career.

Achievement and Motivation are Inseparable.

Image © gulsev, 2010. Used under license from Shutterstock, Inc.

The right major can be a powerful contributor to success. Some students even change colleges (once they figure out the question of what to major in) because the new college offers the major desired. As indicated earlier, students without a clear direction often do not see themselves as a part of the college they attend. They have a difficult time seeing anything positive about the college. These students are more likely to lose whatever motivation they started college with, perform poorly, and even drop out.

When a successful, motivated student begins to feel alienated, the student works to establish a connection in some manner. The main point here is that if you major in an area that fits your personality, the more likely you will be to remain optimistic and curious, develop critical thinking skills, and foster your creative potential: that is, the more likely you will be to stay motivated in college.

Use motivational boosters to maintain your motivational level

In addition to possessing a motivating attitude, there are many simple techniques that you can employ to maintain a high level of motivation. Time-management techniques can be helpful. Keeping a list of what needs to be done in each of your college classes, breaking the tasks down into manageable units of time, and marking off what has been accomplished can reduce stress and help maintain your motivation.

Another motivational aid is to plan for a vacation, but only work on the details of the vacation after reaching a goal—for example, after having completed and turned in a major assignment on time. Such a reward system will help you stay motivated.

Sources

Cokley, K. O., Bernard, N., Cunningham, D., & Motoike, J. (2001). A psychological investigation of the academic motivation scale using a United States sample. *Measurement and Evaluation in Counseling and Development*, 34, 109–119.

Glauser, A., Ginter, E. J., & Larson, K. (2002). *Composing a meaningful life in an ever-increasing diverse world*. Presentation made at the 2002 World Conference of the American Counseling Association, New Orleans, LA.

Maslow, A. H. (1968). Abraham H. Maslow. In W. S. Sahakian (Ed.), *History of psychology: A source book in systematic psychology* (pp. 411–416). Itasca, IL: F. E. Peacock.

Reeves, J. (Producer). (1997). *Getting motivated*. [Videotape]. Athens, GA: GPTV. Earl J. Ginter (Writer of script).

Reeves, J. (Producer). (1997). *Maintaining motivation*. [Videotape] Athens, GA: GPTV. Earl J. Ginter (Writer of script).

Rotter, J. B. (1966). Generalized expectancies for internal versus external control of reinforcement. *Psychological Monographs*, 80 (1, Whole No. 609).

Ryan, M. (2000, October 8). My middle name is persistence. *Parade Magazine*, pp. 24–25.

Schmitt, D. E. (1992). *The winning edge: Maximizing success in college*. New York: HarperCollins.

Exercise 1. End Goals and Getting There

1. During the next ten minutes, list all the things you want to do in the future (after graduation). These can be thought of as **end goals**. At this stage in the exercise, the number of items listed is more important than how well-thought-out each one may be. Just list things as you think about them without being too critical of what has popped into your head.

2. Select two of the **end goals** listed that you find personally meaningful. Rewrite these end goals in a manner that is clear and specific. Provide details.

   End Goal 1

   End Goal 2

3. Devote five minutes to listing **intermediate goals** and **stepping-stone goals**. These are smaller goals that lead to completing your **two end goals**.

   Stepping-stone goals are the smallest goals. They might be accomplished in a day or a week. Their contributions lead to the next category of goals (intermediate goals). Think of *intermediate goals* as goals that might take several weeks or longer to accomplish.

   List **End Goal 1** here: _____

   Stepping-Stone Goals

   Intermediate Goals

List **End Goal 2** here: _____

Stepping-Stone Goals

Intermediate Goals

4. This exercise has allowed you to establish an outline of a motivationally driven plan to accomplish two longterm goals. In 50–100 words, indicate what you have learned about the necessary steps to achieve your two end goals.

Exercise 2. *Academic Motivational Orientation Assessment (AMOA)*

Using the rating scale below, indicate to what extent the following statements correspond to your decision to attend college. Place the appropriate number in the space before each statement.

1	2	3	4	5	6	7
Had no influence on my decision	Influenced me a little		Had a moderate influence on my decision	Influenced me a lot		Is the exact reason for my decision

WHY DO YOU GO TO COLLEGE?

1. _____ My family has always stressed the importance of me getting a college education.
2. _____ I really enjoy engaging in the academic tasks of college.
3. _____ Earning a college education will make my family very proud of me.
4. _____ I'm earning a college education mainly to ensure a good standard of living.
5. _____ The things I will learn while in college will make me a more competent person in many areas of my life.
6. _____ Without a college education, I risk an uncertain financial future.
7. _____ I will feel very guilty if I do not earn a college degree.
8. _____ I do not really have a clear reason for being in college at this time.
9. _____ Because I need a college education if I want to secure an important career in the future.
10. _____ A college education will provide the opportunity to hone many life skills I will need in the future.
11. _____ My primary reason for getting a college education is to maximize my earning potential.
12. _____ Being college-educated symbolizes who I am as a person.
13. _____ For the inherent pleasure I experience doing academic work.
14. _____ Because I believe that my career options would be seriously limited without a college education.
15. _____ A college education will allow me to utilize, throughout my life, the knowledge I gain.
16. _____ A college education is an integral part of my own personal value system.
17. _____ I enjoy the academic work involved in college.
18. _____ A college education is necessary to ensure that I obtain a well-paying job.

SOURCE: Pisarik, C. (2009). *Academic Motivational Orientation Assessment (AMOA)*. Athens, GA: Author.

19. _____ The things I learn in college will enable me to face important life challenges.

20. _____ The academic tasks involved in college are pleasurable.

21. _____ My intentions for pursuing a college education are not yet clear.

22. _____ A college education will make me competitive within the job market.

23. _____ I feel I owe it to my family to get a college education.

24. _____ A college education will make me a more capable individual.

25. _____ I enjoy meeting the academic challenges in college.

26. _____ A college education will define me as a person.

27. _____ There was nothing better to do.

28. _____ It will be difficult to support myself without a college degree.

29. _____ The knowledge I gain in college will be important in many ways.

30. _____ In many ways, I am following the flow.

31. _____ I do not want to disappoint my family.

32. _____ I have come to realize how central a college education is to my own identity.

33. _____ It is very satisfying to accomplish difficult academic tasks.

34. _____ I want to secure a meaningful career in the future.

35. _____ I grew up believing that I should get a college education.

36. _____ I am in college passing time until I know what I want to do.

Instructions

Sum the values you assigned for each group of items listed below to determine your overall score for each category of motivation.

Sum the ratings for items 8, 21, 27, 30, 36

_____+_____+_____+_____+_____ = _____ (Amotivation)

Sum the ratings for items 4, 6, 9, 11, 14, 18, 22, 28, 34

_____+_____+_____+_____+_____+_____+_____+_____+_____ = _____ (External Regulation)

Sum the ratings for items 1, 3, 7, 23, 31, 35

_____+_____+_____+_____+_____+_____ = _____ (Introjected Regulation)

Sum the ratings for items 5, 10, 15, 19, 24, 29

_____+_____+_____+_____+_____+_____ = _____ (Identified Regulation)

Sum the ratings for items 12, 16, 26, 32

____+____+____+____ = ____ **(Integrated Regulation)**

Sum the ratings for items 2, 13, 17, 20, 25, 33

____+____+____+____+____+____ = ____ **(Intrinsic Motivation)**

INTERPRETATION OF RESULTS

The higher the score, the more likely you are to rely upon this form of motivation. The lower the score, the less likely you are to rely upon this form of motivation.

Review

Read over the explanation for each type of motivation.

- **Amotivation** represents the lowest level of autonomy. It is difficult to tie the person's behavior to either an intrinsic or an extrinsic explanation because the person sees his or her actions as beyond his or her control (e.g., "*I am doing poorly in my psychology class and there is nothing I can do because the professor comes up with tests I can't prepare for.*").
- **External regulation** occurs when there is a definite outside consequence that drives an activity (e.g., "*I can get my own apartment if I earn a B average fall semester.*").
- **Introjected regulation** occurs when the external reason for acting in a certain manner has "taken up residence" in the person, and this typically takes the form of an inner voice or monologue that persuades or pressures the person to act in a certain way (e.g., "*When I go out the night before a test I feel guilty, so I stay in and study to reduce the amount of self-scolding that goes on in my head.*").
- **Identified regulation** occurs when the person acts in a certain fashion because the person has adopted a ready-made set of rules or established guidelines from someone else. The person has allowed himself or herself to identify with another person's or group's standards (e.g., "*My parents socialize only with other professionals and I see no reason to socialize differently.*"). In this case, the person is essentially governed by unexamined rules.
- **Integrated regulation** refers to when a person has evaluated those regulations which were assimilated into the self. In addition, an effort is made by the person to maintain congruence between behaviors and goals and needs and values. However, any particular activity carried out by the person is done to obtain a desired outcome, not because of the inherent enjoyment one may find in carrying out the activity itself (e.g., "*I decided to attend college because I value having a college degree, not because I enjoy learning a lot of stuff.*").
- **Intrinsic motivation** comes into play when a person performs a certain activity because the activity itself creates pleasure or satisfaction. Regardless of the specific type of pleasurable pursuit that drives a person to act, intrinsic motivation is believed by the experts to reflect a form of **self-determined behavior** (i.e., "*Since I like to read about history, I decided to enroll in this class.*").

1. Of the various types of motivation listed above, which one most accurately reflects your reason for attending UGA? Explain why this is true.

2. Which of the above types of motivation least accurately reflects your reason for attending UGA? Explain why this is true.

CHOOSING A CAREER

> **"**The golden opportunity you are seeking is in yourself.**"**
> — Margaret Engelbert

Why Should Career Planning Begin in the First Year of College?

It is true that college graduation and career entry are years away, but the process of investigation, planning, and preparing for career success should begin during your first year of college. Also consider the fact that once you begin full-time work, you will spend the majority of your waking hours at work. The fact is, the only other single activity that you will spend more time doing in your lifetime is sleeping. When you consider that such a sizable amount of our lifetime is spent working, plus the fact that work can influence our sense of self-esteem and personal identity, it is never too early to start thinking about your career choices. Remember, when you are doing career planning, you're also doing life planning. You are planning how to spend your future life doing what you want to do.

Reaching an effective decision about a career involves four important steps:

Step 1: Self-Awareness	The more you know about yourself, the better your choices and decision will be. One way to gain greater self-awareness of your interests (what you like to do), abilities (what you do well), and values (what brings you satisfaction and fulfillment in life) is by taking career assessments. Another way is to use learning style to help you select a career path. Lastly, understand your personal needs and when you are doing something that makes your life more satisfying or fulfilling.
Step 2: Awareness of your options	In order to make effective decisions about your career path, you need to have accurate knowledge about the nature of different careers and the realities of the work world. Working with your school's career development center will be key in this step. There are also Websites available through the U.S. Department of Labor's Occupational Outlook Handbook (bls.gov) that lists thousands of jobs, the necessary training and education, earnings, expected job prospects, what workers do on the job and working conditions. Again, working closely with your school's career development center is important in this step too. Other avenues you can take are interviewing people in different career fields, job shadowing, internships, co-op programs, volunteer service, and part-time work.

Step 3: Awareness of what particular options best fit you

What should carry the greatest amount of influence in career decision making is how compatible your choice is with your personal abilities, interests, needs, and values. After you have determined this, then you also need to consider other factors, such as working conditions (physical and social environments, location of the work, work schedule, work-related travel), career entry (easy or competitive/difficult), career advancement (opportunities for promotion), career mobility (easy or difficult to move in or out of this career due to rise or fall of demand or your interests or values change), financial benefits (salary, fringe benefits such as paid vacation time, paid sick time, health insurance, etc.), and impact on personal life (family life, time for friends, time for leisure activities, time for exercise, etc.).

Step 4: Awareness of how to prepare for and gain entry into the career of your choice

You can start building your personal skills and the qualities that you know employers want in a candidate by self-monitoring, which is watching or observing yourself and keeping track of the skills you are using and developing during your college experience. One specific strategy is to track your developing skills by keeping a journal of your completed academic tasks and assignments or extra-curricular activities accompanied by the specific skills you used to complete them. Since skills are actions, it is best to record them as action verbs in your journal. Another strategy is to package and present your personal strengths and achievements by self-marketing. You can market your personal skills, qualities, and achievements to future employers by your college transcript, extra-curricular experiences, personal portfolio, personal resume, letter of application (cover letters), letters of recommendations (letters of reference), networking skills, and personal interviews.

(Cuseo, J et al., 286–304)

CHOOSING A VOCATION

❝*Dance like no one is watching, love like you've never been hurt and work like you don't need the money.*❞

— Unknown

Although people tend to use the words job, career, and vocation interchangeably, the words do not share a common definition. A job has to do with specific tasks and responsibilities that someone is employed to carry out. A career is a line of work such as a teacher, a nurse, a botanist, or an author. But one's career may not be one's vocation. According to Butler and Waldroop, vocation derives from the Latin *vocare* (to call) and describes what one does that brings meaning and purpose to one's life via work. Some callings are to do something while others are to be someone. Vocational planning is a developmental process that involves self-exploration, career exploration, and occupational exploration (the same process discussed earlier), but it does require purposeful planning to discover the kinds of opportunities needed to build life skills for optimal growth. The goal is for you to become more aware, through self-exploration, of your interests, abilities, and values as previously noted but also how your personality relates to career choice. (Ginter et al., 238) Let's look at self-exploration first.

ASSIGNMENT: Identify your personal needs when considering making career choices.

As you read the needs below, make a note after each one in the right column, indicating how strong the need is for you (high, moderate, or low). When exploring career options, keep in mind how different careers may or may not satisfy your level of need for the following items.

Autonomy The need to work independently without close supervision or control.	Individuals high in this need may experience greater satisfaction working in careers that allow them to be their own boss, to make their own decisions, and to control their own work schedule. Individuals low in this need may become more satisfied working in more structured careers that involve a supervisor who provides direction, assistance, and frequent feedback.
Affiliation The need for social interaction, a sense of belongingness, and the opportunity to collaborate with others.	Individuals high in this need may become more satisfied working in careers that involve frequent interpersonal interaction and teamwork with colleagues or co-workers. Individuals low in this need may become more satisfied working alone, or in competition with others, rather than in careers that emphasize interpersonal interaction or collaboration.
Achievement The need to experience challenge and to achieve a sense of personal accomplishment.	Individuals high in this need may become more satisfied working in careers that push them to solve problems, to generate new ideas, and to continually learn new information or master new skills. Individuals low in this need may become more satisfied with careers that do not continually test their abilities and do not repeatedly challenge them to stretch their skills by taking on new tasks or different responsibilities.

Sensory Stimulation The need to experience variety, change, and risk.	Individuals high in this need may become more satisfied working in careers that involve frequent changes of pace and place (e.g. frequent travel), unpredictable events (e.g. work tasks that vary considerably from day to day), and moderate stress (e.g. working under pressure of competition or deadlines). Individuals with a low need for sensory stimulation may feel more comfortable working in careers that involve regular routines, predictable situations, and minimal levels of risk or stress.

Cuseo, J. et al. *Thriving in College and Beyond: Research-Based Strategies for Academic Success and Personal Development.* "Finding a Path to Your Future Profession." Kendall Hunt Publishing Company: (2006): 288.

ASSIGNMENT: Identify your interests.

Most people are more likely to feel motivated to accomplish a task if they are interested in the task. Chances are good that if your interests are congruent with your occupational environment, you will achieve more than job satisfaction. By answering the questions below you will start to highlight activities you enjoy.

1. What subjects do you like?

2. What books or magazines do you read?

3. What do you like to do for fun? What do you do in your spare time?

4. What jobs have you had? What did you like or dislike about them? (Remember to include volunteer work.)

5. Based on your responses, write a short statement about the things you like to do and why. What types of activities did you include or exclude?

Belote, G. et al. *The First Year: Making the Most of College.* Fourth Edition. "Planning for a Career." Kendall Hunt Publishing Company (2003): 143

ASSIGNMENT: Identify your values and work values and complete the following checklists.

A. Look over the list of values and identify 15 values that are significant to you. Rank them from 1 to 15, with 1 being the most important.

_____ Spiritual well-being	_____ Good job	_____ Diversity
_____ Relationships	_____ Success and achievement	_____ Loyalty
_____ Respect	_____ Happiness	_____ Freedom
_____ Empathy/compassion	_____ Courage	_____ Intelligence
_____ Sense of humor	_____ Strength	_____ Health
_____ Autonomy	_____ Acceptance	_____ Endurance
_____ Competition	_____ Appreciation of nature	_____ Intimacy
_____ Security	_____ Adventure	_____ Creativity
_____ Wealth	_____ Learning/education	_____ Love
_____ Challenges	_____ Helping others	_____ Appreciation of beauty
_____ Recognition	_____ Ambition	_____ Pleasure and joy
_____ Other:	_____ Other:	_____ Other:

What are your top three values _____ _____ _____

How does your life reflect these?

B. Work values are qualities about a job that are most significant and meaningful to you. Without them the job would not be satisfying. Identify 10 work values that are important to you and rank them from 1 to 10, with 1 being the most important.

_____ Great salary	_____ Recognition from others	_____ Security
_____ Fun	_____ Autonomy	_____ Variety
_____ Excitement	_____ Lots of leisure time	_____ Leadership role
_____ Helping others	_____ Prestige	_____ Creativity
_____ Improving society	_____ Influencing others	_____ Continuity
_____ Professional position	_____ Flexible work schedule	_____ Working outside
_____ Having an office	_____ Congenial workplace	_____ Competition
_____ Travel	_____ Affiliation	_____ Decision making

_____ Supervising others   _____ Work flexibility   _____ Public contact

_____ Working alone   _____ Other: _____ Other:

What are your top three values _____   _____   _____

Describe why each of these values is important to you.

Will your career choice satisfy these values? Explain.

Ginter, E. et al. *Life Skills for College: A Curriculum for Life.* "Vocation." Kendall Hunt Publishing Company (2005): 251–254

ASSIGNMENT: Identify your skills and abilities.

Write down your top ten skills and abilities—*again, the things you do well.* Refer back to Chapter 6, Intellectual Wellness, when you identified your multiple intelligences for help with this assignment.

1. _____

2. _____

3. _____

4. _____

5. _____

6. _____

7. _____

8. _____

9. _____

10. _____

ASSIGNMENT: Identify your achievements.

A. Think about all the goals you have set for yourself thus far in life and all of your achievements. List five achievements that you consider the most significant.

1. _____

2. _____

3. _____

4. _____

5. _____

B. List five *skills* that you used to reach your achievements.

1. _____

2. _____

3. _____

4. _____

5. _____

C. List five *interests* that your achievements reflect.

1. _____

2. _____

3. _____

4. _____

5. _____

D. List five *values* that your achievements reflect.

1. _____

2. _____

3. _____

4. _____

5. _____

Ginter, E. et al. *Life Skills for College: A Curriculum for Life.* "Vocation." Kendall Hunt Publishing Company (2005): 255

PERSONALITY AND VOCATION

When talking about personality, we are referring to a set of motivations, beliefs, attitudes, traits, and response patterns that are consistent over time and that distinguish one person from another. Each person is a unique composite of physical, biological, mental, emotional, and spiritual traits and potentials. Personality factors do influence vocational exploration. How does personality affect career choice? When your personality types match up with a career, you will tend to find more support for challenges you undertake and greater understanding for failed attempts. While no combination of preferences is inherently better than any other type, knowing your personality type can help you understand not only your behavior in a work environment but also those around you. Let's now explore your personality type and how it is associated with career choice. Look back on page 191 in this chapter to refer to your personality types and keep these in mind when reading the following.

Extroversion and Introversion

Extroverts tend to define themselves by how others recognize and respond to them, whereas introverts tend to be private and may not share what is significant and valuable about themselves with colleagues. In working situations, extroverts prefer to be around people and to seek opportunities to interact with others. Introverts need time and space to think through their thoughts carefully before answering a question or giving an opinion. A person with an extroverted personality generally prefers a job that offers a lot variety and activity and can become impatient with long, tedious tasks.

Intuition and Sensation

Intuitive types in the workplace want appreciation for generating ideas and theories, whereas sensing types want appreciation for all the details and facts they can bring to the work situation. People who rely on sensing prefer to use skills that they have already developed. They prefer work environments that have standardized procedures, and they do well in work that involves precision. Intuitive types are the opposite. They tend to dislike repetitive tasks and prefer careers that offer numerous opportunities to learn a variety of skills.

Thinking and Feeling

Feeling personality types like to work in harmonious environments. They generally enjoy pleasing people and are genuinely interested in the people they work with. Thinking personality types respond more to ideas than people at work and are good at analyzing situations. They tend to be firmer in their decisions and seek careers that encourage the use of logical reasoning.

Judging and Perceiving

In a work situation, judging types are most productive when they have lists and plans to follow as well as the necessary resources (supplies, tools, and people) needed to begin work. Perceiving types are good at adapting to changes that arise at work and prefer to start projects rather than finish them. People who rely mostly on judging seek careers that require organization, whereas people who rely mostly on perceiving prefer work situations in which they can create their own work schedule.

(Ginter, F. et al., 61–65)

Online Assignment: Personality Clusters

Complete this assignment online. Go to:
www.grtep.com
Select >Chapter Content>Chapter 8>Enter your username and password

TIPS FOR CONDUCTING INFORMATION INTERVIEWS

1. Thank the person for taking the time to speak with you. This should be the first thing you do after meeting the person, before you officially begin the interview.

2. Take notes during the interview to help you remember what was said but also to show the person you are interviewing that the input is valuable and helpful to you.

3. Prepare your interview questions in advance. Here are some questions to consider:

   - How did you decide on your career?
   - What qualifications or prior experiences did you have that enabled you to enter your career?
   - How does someone find out about openings in your field?
   - What specific steps did you take to find your current position?
   - What advice would you give to beginning college students about things they could start doing now to help them prepare to enter your career?

- During a typical day's work, what do you spend most of your time doing?
- What do you like most about your career?
- What are the most difficult or frustrating aspects of your career?
- What personal skills or qualities do you see as critical for success in your career?
- How does someone advance in your career?
- Are there any moral issues or ethical challenges that tend to arise in your career?
- Are you likely to find members of diverse racial and ethnic groups in your career field?
- What impact does your career have on your home life or personal life outside of work?
- If you had to do it all over again, would you choose the same career?
- Would you recommend that I speak with anyone else to obtain additional information or a different perspective on this career field?

4. If the interview goes well, consider asking if it is possible to observe or "shadow" the person during a day at work.

(Cuseo et al., 316)

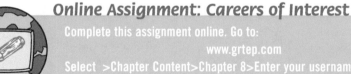

Online Assignment: *Careers of Interest*

Complete this assignment online. Go to:

www.grtep.com

Select >Chapter Content>Chapter 8>Enter your username and password

SELF-MARKETING: PACKAGING AND PRESENTING YOUR PERSONAL STRENGTHS AND ACHIEVEMENTS

You're attending college ultimately to learn more and to get your degree, which then leads to getting a better job, better pay, better incentives, and better benefits. But how will you let employers know what you can bring to the table? Even if you are two or three years away from graduating, it is important to start thinking now of how you will "package" and "present" all that you have to offer to employers. Most of all, you will need to figure out how you will stand apart from other candidates applying for the same job.

To do this most effectively, it might be useful to view yourself as an eventual "product" and employers as future "customers." As a freshman or sophomore, it could be said that you are in the early stages of the product-development process. You want to begin the process of developing yourself into a high-quality product, so that by the time you graduate, employers will choose your "finished product." The primary tools you can use to showcase yourself to employers are:

1. College transcript (a listing of the types of courses you completed and grades you earned in these courses)
2. Extracurricular experiences (involvement in clubs and organizations)
3. Personal portfolio (a collection of your educational and personal development)
4. Personal resumé (a summary of your most important accomplishments, skills, and credentials)
5. Letters of application (cover letters)
6. Letters of recommendation (letters of reference)
7. Networking skills (expanding your circle of people who know your career interests and abilities)
8. Personal interviews (opportunities to make a positive "in-person" impression).

(Cuseo et al., 303–304)

ASSIGNMENT: Describe yourself.

List 10 words that describe you.

1.	5.	8.
2.	6.	9.
3.	7.	10.
4.		

Which words identify work-related strengths or assets?

Which identify work-related weaknesses or liabilities?

Belote, G. et al. *The First Year: Making the Most of College.* Fourth Edition. "Planning for a Career." Kendall Hunt Publishing Company (2003): 149.

Online Assignment: Construct Your Resume
Complete this assignment online. Go to:
www.grtep.com
Select >Chapter Content>Chapter 8>Enter your username and password

Again, you need to start thinking ahead now. Your letters of recommendation (or reference letters) can be one of your most powerful selling points whether for a summer job or for a job after you graduate from college. However, to maximize the power of your recommendations, you need to give careful thought to whom you want to serve as your references, how to approach them, and what to provide them. Below are effective strategies and common courtesies for requesting letters of recommendation:

- Select recommendations from people who know you well. Think about people with whom you've had an ongoing relationship, who know your name, and who know your strengths, like an instructor, an academic advisor, a supervisor, or a family friend.

- Seek a balanced blend of letters from people who have observed you perform in different settings or situations (e.g., the classroom, on campus, off campus).

- Pick the right time and place to make your request. Be sure to make your request well in advance of the letter's deadline date. First, ask the person if he or she is willing to write the letter, then supply forms, envelopes, fact sheets, etc. Do not approach the person with these materials in hand because this may send a message that you have assumed or presumed the person will automatically say "yes." Remember—you are asking for a favor.

- Waive your right to see the letter. By waiving your right to see the letter, you show confidence that the letter about you will be positive, and you assure the person who receives the letter that you didn't inspect or screen it before it was sent off.

- Provide your references with a fact sheet about yourself that includes your specific experiences and achievements—both inside and outside the classroom. It would also be smart to supply your resume. Your fact sheet should be a documentation of your strengths, and this is the time to "toot your own horn."

- Provide your references with a stamped, addressed envelope. This is a simple courtesy that makes their job a little easier and demonstrates your social sensitivity.

■ Follow up with a thank you note to your references about the time they should be sending your letters of recommendation. This shows your appreciation for their time, but it can also serve as a gentle reminder to them to write and send their letters.

■ Let your references know the outcome of your efforts. This is a courteous thing to so, and your references are likely to remember your courtesy, which could strengthen the quality of any future letters they may write for you.

(Cuseo et al., 310–311)

WORK/LIFE BALANCE

> **❝***Nobody, when they were on their deathbed, ever said,
> 'I wish I'd spent more time at the office'.***❞**
>
> — Paul Tsongas

Internationally respected leadership authority, Stephen R. Covey, discusses work and life balance and answers questions on his blog: "With today's technology, multi-taskers are using PDAs, cell phones, text messaging and emails to stay in connected 24 hours a day. While lighthearted nicknames like 'crackberry' have been coined to describe this almost obsessive behavior, what happens when we become addicted to this connectivity? Do we exclude the other important dimensions of our life?"

What Does It Mean to Have Work/Life Balance?

"This is a very personal thing and it is different for everyone. Generally speaking, having a good work/life balance means that your actions and priorities are aligned in a way that is taking care of what is really important to you. Today, the average college student or corporate worker considers him or herself a 'multi-tasker'. It's not unusual to meet people in their twenties who are working, going to school, starting their own company, married, raising kids and enjoying hobbies. They end up with a huge list of things that fracture their attention. This isn't wrong in any way–for the most part it's admirable—but there is an old saying: to a hammer, everything looks like a nail. To a chronic multi-tasker, everything is a task. Soon, the things in life that are really important to them are in the same list as everything else, and the only tasks that get done are the ones that have become urgent, but often aren't very important. Because of this they are driven by an addiction to the urgent and continually respond to the four P's—those things that are Pressing, Proximate, Pleasant and Popular—leaving very little time to do those things that are truly important."

What Can Happen to You When You Allow Yourself to Become Out of Balance?

"One of the main implications of being out of balance, however you define it, is that you neglect other areas of your life; family, health, etc. are often some of the first. When you become so addicted to only dealing with your urgent tasks you don't think there is time for the non-urgent. You think that there will be time to deal with them later. But often, when you ask people what they feel is most important in their life, things they really want to accomplish, they are things that take time and long-term investment. By the time these things become urgent, it's often too late to affect them. For example, take a relationship. If you only invest in your relationships when they become urgent (you are on the brink of divorce or your child has become self-destructive) you can't just 'take care of it.' It becomes a dominant issue that could take decades to 'fix.' These issues can often be avoided if you invest in your relationships when they are important, but not urgent. This might mean turning off the computer and cellphone when you get home and really investing in your loved ones. Another example is your health. If you don't eat well or exercise because you don't think you have the time or because it isn't urgent, you could find yourself in a life-risking situation later. When a health issue becomes urgent, it stops everything else. But if you take the time daily to eat well and exercise in some form, you take care of your body so that you lessen your chances of ill health."

So, I Have to Say "No" to Some Things— What Should I Say No To?

"First, you have to decide what is important. What do you really want to be and do with your life? What is your mission? What do you want people to say about you 30 or 40 years from now? Then, look at what is being asked of you and see if those things are a part of your life's important goals. If not, smile and say 'no.' If you've really decided what is important, you can become an agent in helping the people you work with, your family, friends and boss, know and understand your top priorities. This takes courage. It means you have to stand up for what you feel is important and help others understand why.

"There are no quick-fixes to achieving work/life balance. Your priorities may change as your circumstances change. Thus, I invite you to consider the things that you value most and allow those to serve as the foundation. Then commit to consistently re-evaluate your current priorities, given your current circumstances and based on what you have identified as your core values. It takes courage, but remember not to trade in what you want most, for what you want now."

An unhealthy work/life balance affects not only our health and well-being, but our families and our society as a whole. John de Graaf, president of Take Back Your Time and documentary filmmaker of *Affluenza: The All-Consuming Epidemic,* talks about how Americans are getting fewer and fewer days off work, and his article, *No Vacation Nation,* talks about how it translates into an unhealthy work/life balance. "Americans get the shortest vacations in the world—when they get them at all. A recent Harris poll found that only 14% of Americans were taking the traditional two-week summer vacation in 2007. More and more of us take what vacation days we have one by one, here and there, and use them to catch up on the errands for which our ever-increasing work demands leave little time. Americans may be materially richer than almost anyone else, but we have the poorest health in the industrial world despite spending far more per capita on healthcare than any other country. In 1980, we ranked 11th in the world in longevity; now we're 42nd. We are twice as likely as Europeans to suffer from anxiety and depression. In large part, these deficits are caused by lack of time. Overwork means we spend less time with friends and family and less time exercising and eating healthy."

"Although American workers are promised an average of about two weeks of vacation a year, according to Expedia.com they give back about three days, on average, to their employers, mostly because they feel they'll be seen as slackers if they take all their time (and therefore be singled out in the next round of layoffs) or because they simply don't want to return to an inbox filled with emails. Of those who do take vacations, studies show that at least a third take their work with them, a habit made easier by cell phones, laptops and the Internet."

"In his book, *Work to Live,* Joe Robinson, a life-balance trainer for corporations and government agencies, provides data from several studies indicating that people who take vacations are less likely to experience heart attacks or other illnesses than those who don't. 'But it only starts to work that way when you take at least a two-week block of time,' says Robinson. 'Men reduce their risk of a heart attack by 30% and women by 50%,' he adds, citing data from the ongoing Framingham Heart Study and a State University of New York at Oswego study. 'There seems to be no positive effect when you just take a day off here and there. It may help you de-stress a little mentally, but it doesn't reduce your risk of heart failure. You need a block of time to do that.' Most recently, Robinson and the activist organization I founded, Take Back Your Time, have proposed a bill called The Minimum Leave Protection, Family Bonding and Personal Well-Being Act of 2007. The bill, which Robinson drafted, calls for annual, federally mandated three-week paid vacation for all workers. The struggle for vacation time comes down to a question of values. What is our economy for anyway? What is progress for? If what we're trying to do is improve our quality of life, then it's time we acknowledged that vacations really do matter.'" Let's see what happens.

LEADERSHIP AND LIVING

> ❝*Be who you are and say what you feel, because those who mind*
> *don't matter and those who matter don't mind.*❞
>
> — Dr. Seuss

Responding to the world begins with the decision to take action that effects change by mobilizing others to accomplish a shared vision. That is the true meaning of the word leadership. In order to make a better world, we need more of these kinds of leaders. Citizenship requires leadership. So does professional success. If you can lead no one, your education is incomplete. Leadership doesn't have to be a formal, exalted position. Personal leadership is taking action (in any setting) that brings about change by mobilizing others (they don't have to be a formal group) to accomplish a shared vision. (Millard) The six characteristics that make for successful leadership include:

- Vision (a sense of the future and its possibilities)

- Ethics and integrity (a commitment to think carefully about the public good and our own values when we act)

- Service orientation (the habit of working for others)

- Communication skills (the ability to say and write what we mean, simply and powerfully, as well as the ability and commitment to listen with understanding to the concerns of others)

- Self-awareness (the ongoing realization of personal strengths and weaknesses, of knowledge of interests, values, temperament, aspirations, and abilities)

- Teamwork in diverse groups (skills to accomplish common goals by working with others who bring a variety of experiences to the task). (Osher-Ward)

Learning to lead is imperative for every college student. Yet many students are notoriously indifferent to the leadership opportunities available to them. Leadership requires careful reflection. You will be cheating yourself and jeopardizing your career if you do not resolve to improve as a leader. (Millard)

Online Assignment: Leadership Self-Assessment

Complete this assignment online. Go to:
www.grtep.com
Select >Chapter Content>Chapter 8>Enter your username and password

TIPS TO BECOMING OCCUPATIONALLY HEALTHY

"I know the price of success: dedication, hard work and an unremitting devotion to the things you want to see happen."

— Frank Lloyd Wright

- Remember, you don't know all the answers. Ask for help with assignments or jobs you dislike and find support from others.

- Try out new interests. Use this time to explore all kinds of interests. Volunteer in your community. You may find hidden talents and gain work-related skills.

- Encourage laughter to reduce stress in your environment—school or work.

- Practice grace under pressure.

- Find satisfaction and meaning in your studies and at work—at the very least one thing.

- Study or work in an environment conducive to learning.

- Accurately assess your strengths and weaknesses as well as how you can accommodate others' strengths and weaknesses.

- Find confidence and be comfortable in your place of study or work where stress is at a minimum.

- Have hobbies, interests, and activities that bring you pleasure outside of your coursework or career.

- Be comfortable with the direction of your future plans. If you're not, ask yourself "why"?

- Believe that you have the qualities of a valuable and valued student or employee.

- Feel good about what you want to do with your life.

- Find out how to obtain an internship or volunteer experience and get an insider's view.

SOURCE: Wellness for Healthy Positive Living: Environmental/Occupational Wellness Facts & Tips, Santa Clara University's Wellness Center: Occupational Wellness Tips for Good Occupational Health.

Helpful Internet Sites

Dale Carnegie® Training: dalecarnegie.com

InternDirect Internships: internships.com

Stephen R. Covey—Internationally Respected Leadership Authority: stephencovey.com

Take Back Your Time: timeday.org

U.S. Department of Labor—Bureau of Labor Statistics: bls.gov

U.S. Department of Labor—Bureau of Labor Statistics Occupational Outlook Handbook: bls.gov/oco/home.htm

U.S. Department of Labor—Bureau of Labor Statistics Occupational Employment Statistics: bls.gov/oes/current/oes_stru.htm

Vault Reports Career Information: vaultreports.com

References

Belote, G. et al. *The First Year: Making the Most of College,* Fourth Edition. Planning for a Career. Kendall Hunt Publishing Company (2003): 143; 149.

Bounds, L. *Health and Fitness: A Guide to a Healthy Lifestyle.* Definition of Occupational Health. Kendall Hunt Publishing Company (2006): 3.

Covey, S. *How to Strike a Work and Life Balance.* stephencovey.com/blog/?p=12a accessed on 3.11.08.

Cuseo, J et al. *Thriving in College and Beyond: Research-Based Strategies for Academic Success and Personal Development.* Finding a Path to Your Future Profession. Kendall Hunt Publishing Company: (2007): 286–304; 309–311; 316.

Dale Carnegie Training ®. *Dale Carnegie's Golden Book.* Principles from How to Win Friends and Influence People and Principles from How to Stop Worrying and Start Living. Dale Carnegie and Associates, Inc. (2003): 1–9.

de Graaf, J. *Experience Life Magazine.* No Vacation Nation. Lifetime Fitness (2008): March: 48–53.

Ginter, E. et al. *Life Skills for College: A Curriculum for Life.* Vocation. Kendall Hunt Publishing Company (2005): 238; 242; 251–255.

Hettler, B. The National Wellness Institute. The Six Dimensions of Wellness: Occupational Wellness. *www.nationalwellness.org.*

Holland, J. *The Psychology of Vocational Choice.* Blaisdell: (1966).

Millard, B. *Explorer's Guide: Starting the College Journey with a Sense of Purpose.* Personal Mission. Kendall Hunt Publishing Company (2007): 334; 345–352.

Regents of the University of California. *The University Mind: Essential Skills for Academic Success.* Second Edition. Choosing a Major. Kendall Hunt Publishing Company (2005): 128–130.

Robinson, J. *Work to Live.* Perigree (2003).

Webber, A. *Fast Track.* Is Your Job Calling? (2000): January: pp. 13–16.

CHAPTER 9

Financial Wellness

"Happiness is not in the mere possession of money; it lies in the joy of achievement, in the thrill of creative effort."

— President Franklin D. Roosevelt

The objectives in this chapter include the understanding of:

- The meaning of financial wellness and its direct application to you
- Common mistakes college students make with money and how to avoid them
- Money management: what you need to know about your credit, credit cards, checks and checking accounts and problem gambling
- Identity theft
- Saving for the future
- Money and happiness

Online Reminders

- Complete the poll question before the next class meeting.
- Complete the interactive activities for this chapter.
- Complete all of the online assignments for this chapter.

Financial Wellness—Financial wellness is your stability with a personal budget and financial obligations—meaning that you have planned a budget, are sticking to it, are aware of where your money goes, are paying your bills on time, are using credit cards wisely, and that you also have a long-term financial plan for yourself. Whether or not you have or make a lot of money, financial wellness is a state of living with your means and having a comfortable relationship with money.

College may be the first time that some live away from home and from their parents where they find much independence, like no curfews and no asking for permission. Maybe you are still living with your parents, but now you are in fully in charge of your personal finances and financial decisions. Either way, though it may seem like a "no-brainer," being financially responsible for yourself and managing your money can be an overwhelming task.

According to the InCharge Institute of America (a non-for-profit community service organization specializing in personal finance education and credit counseling), college students owe enormous credit card debt—on average about $2,700 with close to one-quarter of students owing more than $3,000. About 10% owe more than $7,000.

According to Nellie Mae, a leading provider of higher education loans, a study of last year's applicants showed that students held an average of three separate credit cards, 78% have at least one credit card, 32% had four or more credit cards, and 95% of graduate students carried credit cards. This means that there is a rising prevalence of students getting in over their heads with debt, in particular credit card debt, and living outside of their means. Getting hold of their personal finances from the very beginning and practicing some self-control may have helped these students from getting in debt in the first place.

Financial wellness follows these tenets:

1. It is better to prepare and plan your finances and to live within your means than to become complacent about misusing your money and irresponsible about using it.

2. It is better to fix any mistakes you have made financially as soon as possible and to learn money management than not to attempt to fix them at all or not to be proactive about financial issues.

PRE-CLASS SURVEY: Take your financial wellness survey before your next class meeting and identify your level of financial wellness. Circle either Yes or No, total up each column, and check your score.

I know what my weekly and monthly budget is.	YES	NO
I have a credit card, and I pay my bill in full every month.	YES	NO
I pay all my bills on time.	YES	NO
I stay within my budget on a weekly and monthly basis.	YES	NO
I safeguard my financial information and Social Security number.	YES	NO
I use a credit card with a low interest rate.	YES	NO
I use my own financial institution's ATM or the ATMs owned by financial institutions that don't charge fees to non-customers.	YES	NO
I have not bounced a check in over two years.	YES	NO
Each month, I put money into my savings account or retirement savings account for my future.	YES	NO
I often read articles about personal finance so I am up to date with the latest information.	YES	NO
I balance my checkbook every week or two weeks.	YES	NO
I understand that money might buy me some security but not happiness.	YES	NO
TOTAL		

WHAT YOUR TOTAL MEANS:

9 or more Yes answers	Excellent	Your habits are positively enhancing your health.
6–8 Yes answers	Average	You are obviously trying but there is room to improve.
5 or less Yes answers	Not So Good	There is a need for improvement in your daily habits.

SOURCE: "Wellness for Healthy Positive Living." *Financial Wellness/Inventory* for.gov.bc.ca/hrb/hw/index.htm

Financial Stress Affects Academics for College Students, Survey Finds

Findings released today illuminate how financial challenges affect college students. A majority of students surveyed worry about paying for college, and as many as one in three frequently opt not to purchase required academic materials due to cost. Full-time students working more than 20 hours per week face the greatest financial stress: three in five said that their job interfered with their academic performance, yet just as many had considered working more hours.

The survey also shows that social media can be a mixed blessing. Nine out of ten students use social media (Facebook, Twitter, etc.), primarily to connect with friends and family. Many also use social media in educationally purposeful ways, such as to plan study groups or complete class assignments. Frequent interaction with peers, faculty, and campus offices by way of social media corresponded to higher engagement and satisfaction. But those who used social media during class for nonclass activities had lower grades and were less satisfied with college.

These findings, released by the National Survey of Student Engagement (NSSE), demonstrate the need for colleges and universities to monitor how emerging issues and trends facing today's college students affect their ability to thrive and succeed.

The report, ***Promoting Student Learning and Institutional Improvement: Lessons from NSSE at 13—Annual Results 2012***, details results from a 2012 survey of 285,000 firstyear students and seniors attending 546 U.S. colleges and universities. NSSE's annual survey provides diagnostic, comparative information about the prevalence of effective educational practices at participating bachelor's degree-granting colleges and universities.

On the eve of launching an updated survey in 2013, NSSE dedicated a part of this year's report to revisiting key findings from its first 13 years. New analyses reinforce the educational benefits of deep approaches to learning—approaches that favor higher-order thinking over rote memorization, that call on students to integrate knowledge from multiple sources, and that inspire them to rethink and revise their prior beliefs. Students participating in high-impact practices such as service-learning and culminating senior experiences (e.g., capstone courses and senior theses) showed higher levels of deep approaches to learning.

A core purpose of the NSSE project is to provide actionable information to inform the improvement of undergraduate education. An updated analysis of multi-year, institution-level results in student engagement at more than 400 colleges and universities found that more than half showed positive trends for first-year students, as did more than one-third for seniors. Only 7-8% evidenced negative trends. Positive trends were found at public as well as private, and large as well as small institutions.

"These findings offer compelling evidence that positive change is not only possible, it's happening on many campuses. Size and institutional structure are not insurmountable obstacles. Across the range of institutional types, many faculty and college leaders are taking up the challenge to improve undergraduate education," said Alexander C. McCormick, NSSE director and associate professor of educational leadership and policy studies at Indiana University Bloomington.

NSSE seeks to refocus the discourse about college quality on what matters for student learning. "Along with a rich pool of evidence of effective practices, NSSE provides insightful guidelines for interpretation and productive use of the data," according to Daniel J. Bernstein, professor of psychology and director of the Center for Teaching Excellence at The University of Kansas.

Other noteworthy findings from the 2012 survey and its companion surveys, the Beginning College Survey of Student Engagement (BCSSE) and the Faculty Survey of Student Engagement (FSSE), include:

- First-year students spent an average of 15 hours per week preparing for class, and seniors averaged one half-hour more. Those earning grades of A or A- studied about four more hours per week than their first-year peers with grades of C+ or lower.

- In most fields, full-time seniors devoted about one to two hours less to class preparation than faculty expected. Engineering majors studied more than faculty expected. But when asked how much they believe students *actually* study, faculty estimates in all fields fell short of student accounts by five to eight hours per week.

- On average, distance education students spent about one hour more per week preparing for class than their on-campus counterparts.

- Support for learning in college was beneficial regardless of how engaged students had been in high school. Although high school engagement was related to subsequent engagement in college, on average, students who experienced a more supportive campus environment evidenced higher levels of engagement.

- Job opportunities were cited by the majority of seniors among the factors motivating their choice of major, but this varied by racial/ethnic background and field of study. Students of color were generally more concerned than Whites about their ability to find a job. Seniors majoring in science, technology, engineering, and math were more likely than others to cite job opportunities as a motivating factor.

NSSE's *Annual Results 2012* is sponsored by The Carnegie Foundation for the Advancement of Teaching.

Reprinted by permission of National Survey of Student Engagement.

Common Mistakes College Students Make with Money and How to Avoid Them

Everybody makes mistakes with money. The important thing is to keep them to a minimum. And one of the best ways to accomplish that is to learn from the mistakes of others. Here is the U.S. Federal Deposit Insurance Corporation's (FDIC) list of the top mistakes college students (and also people way older than college students) make with their money and what you can do to avoid these mistakes in the first place.

#1

Buying Items You Don't Need and Paying Extra for Them in Interest.

- Every time you use your credit card but you don't pay in full by the due date, you could be paying interest on that purchase for months or years to come. *Example:* If you pay only the minimum payment due on a $1,000 computer, let's say it's about $20 a month, your total cost at an Annual Percentage Rate (APR) of more than 18% can be close to $3,000, which will take you nearly 19 years to pay off.

- Research major purchases and comparison shop before you buy. Ask yourself if you really need the item. Even better, wait a day or two, or just a few hours, to think things over rather than making a quick and costly decision you may come to regret.

- There are good reasons to pay for major purchases with a credit card, such as extra protections if you have problems with the items. But if you charge a purchase with a credit card instead of paying by cash, check, or debit card (that automatically deducts the money from your bank account), be smart about how you repay. For example, take advantage of offers of "zero-percent interest" on credit card purchases for a certain number of months (but understand when and how interest charges could begin).

- And pay the entire balance on your credit card or as much as you can to avoid or minimize interest charges that can add up significantly.

#2

Getting Too Deeply in Debt.

- Being able to borrow allows us to buy clothes or computers, to take a vacation, or to purchase a home or a car. But taking on too much debt can become a problem, and each year millions of adults of all ages find themselves struggling to pay their loans, credit cards, and other bills.

- Learn to be a good money manager and to recognize the warning signs of a serious debt problem. These may include borrowing money to make payments on loans you already have, deliberately paying bills late, and putting off doctor visits or other important activities because you think you don't have enough money.

- If you believe you're experiencing debt overload, take corrective measures. For example, try to pay off your highest interest-rate loans (usually your credit cards) as soon as possible, even if you have higher balances on other loans. For new purchases, instead of using your credit card, try paying with cash, a check, or a debit card.

- Companies called credit bureaus prepare credit reports for use by lenders, employers, insurance companies, landlords, and others who need to know someone's financial reliability, based largely on the person's track record paying bills and debts. Credit bureaus, lenders, and other companies also produce "credit scores" that attempt to summarize and evaluate a person's credit record using a point system.

- While one or two late payments on your loans or other regular commitments (such as rent or phone bills) over a long period may not seriously damage your credit record, making a habit of it will count against you. Over time you could receive a higher interest rate on your credit card or a loan that you really want and need. You could be turned down for a job or an apartment. It could cost you extra when you apply for auto insurance. A bankruptcy filing or a court order to pay money as a result of a lawsuit also can damage your credit record.

- So, pay your monthly bills on time. Also, periodically review your credit reports from the nation's three major credit bureaus—Equifax, Experian, and TransUnion—to make sure their information accurately reflects the accounts you have and your payment history, especially if you intend to apply for credit for something important in the near future.

- Two to four cards (including any from department stores, oil companies and other retailers) are the right number for most adults. Why not more cards?

- The more credit cards you carry, the more inclined you may be to use them for costly impulse buying. In addition, each card you own—even the ones you don't use—represents money that you *could* borrow up to the card's spending limit. If you apply for new credit, you will appear as someone who, in theory, could get much deeper in debt, and you may only qualify for a smaller or costlier loan.

- Also be aware that card companies aggressively market their products on college campuses, at concerts, ball games, or other events often attended by young adults. Their offers may seem tempting and even harmless—perhaps a free T-shirt or a Frisbee, or 10% off your first purchase if you just fill out an application for a new card—but you've got to consider the possible consequences we've just described.

- It's very easy to overspend in some areas and take away from other priorities, including your long-term savings. Our suggestion is to try any system—ranging from a computer-based budget program to handwritten notes—that will help you keep track of your spending each month and enable you to set and stick to limits you consider appropriate.

- Want some specific ideas for ways to cut back on spending? A good place to start is the Website for the "66 Ways to Save" campaign: 66ways.org.

#6

Not Saving for
Your Future.

- It can be tough to scrape together enough money to pay for a place to live, a car, and other expenses each month. But experts say it's also important for young people to save money for their long-term goals, too, including perhaps buying a home, owning a business, or saving for retirement (even though it may be 40 or 50 years away).

- Start by "paying yourself first." That means even before you pay your bills each month you should put money into savings for your future. Often the simplest way is to arrange with your bank or employer to automatically transfer a certain amount each month to a savings account or to purchase a U.S. Savings Bond or an investment, such as a mutual fund that buys stocks and bonds.

- Eventually, you will want to automatically transfer a certain amount each month into your retirement account, like a 401K.

- Even if you start with just $25 or $50 a month you'll be significantly closer to your goal so you can benefit from the effect of compound interest. Compound interest refers to when an investment earns interest, and later that combined amount earns more interest, and on and on until a much larger sum of money is the result after many years.

- Banking institutions pay interest on savings accounts that they offer. However, bank deposits aren't the only way to make your money grow. James Williams, an FDIC Consumer Affairs Specialist, says, "Investments, which include stocks, bonds and mutual funds, can be attractive alternatives to bank deposits because they often provide a higher rate of return over long periods, but remember that there is the potential for a temporary or permanent loss in value. Young people especially should do their research and consider getting professional advice before putting money into investments."

#7

Paying Too Much
in Fees.

- Whenever possible, use your own financial institution's automated teller machines or the ATMs owned by financial institutions that don't charge fees to non-customers. You can pay $1 to $4 in fees if you get cash from an ATM that your financial institution doesn't own or that isn't part of an ATM "network" that your bank belongs to.

- Try not to "bounce" checks—that is, writing checks for more money than you have in your account, which can trigger fees from your financial institution (about $15 to $35 for each check) and from merchants. The best precaution is to keep your checkbook up to date and to closely monitor your balance.

- Remember to record your debit card transactions from ATMs and merchants so that you will be sure to have enough money in your account when your bank processes those withdrawals.

#7

Paying Too Much in Fees. (continued)

- Financial institutions also offer "overdraft protection" services that can help you avoid the embarrassment and inconvenience of having a check returned to a merchant. But be careful before signing up because these programs come with their own costs.

- Again, paying off your credit card balances each month can help you avoid or minimize interest charges. Also send in your payment on time to avoid additional fees. If you don't expect to pay your credit card bill in full most months, consider using a card with a low interest rate and a generous "grace period" (the number of days before the card company starts charging you interest on new purchases).

#8

Not Taking Responsibility for Your Finances.

- Do a little comparison shopping to find accounts that match your needs at the right cost. Be sure to review your bills and bank statements as soon as possible after they arrive or monitor your accounts periodically online or by telephone. You want to make sure there are no errors, unauthorized charges, or indications that a thief is using your identity to commit fraud.

- Keep copies of any contracts or other documents that describe your bank accounts, so you can refer to them in a dispute.

- Also remember that the quickest way to fix a problem usually is to work directly with your bank or other service provider.

- Resolving these issues can be time consuming and exhausting, but doing so can add up to hundreds of dollars.

Even if you are fortunate enough to have parents or other loved ones you can turn to for help or advice as you start handling money on your own, it's really up to you to take charge of your finances. Doing so can intimidate anyone. It's easy to become overwhelmed or frustrated. And everyone makes mistakes. The important thing is to take action. Start small if you need to. Stretch to pay an extra $50 a month on your credit card bill or other debts. Find two or three ways to cut your spending. Put an extra $50 a month into a savings account. Even little changes can add up to big savings over time.

WHAT YOU NEED TO KNOW ABOUT YOUR CREDIT

"If you would know the value of money, go and try to borrow some."
—Benjamin Franklin

What's Credit?

Being out on your own can be fun and exciting, but it also means taking on new financial responsibilities. The decisions you make now about how you manage your finances and borrow money will affect you in the future—for better or for worse. *Did you know that there are companies that keep track of whether you pay your debts and if you make payments on time?* Then these companies make this information available in the form of a credit report and score. A bad credit history can haunt you for a long time—seven years or more. That's why the best thing to do is to learn how to maintain good credit BEFORE there's a problem. While this might seem complicated at first, it gets easier once you understand the basics of credit and how it works.

Credit is more than just a plastic card you use to buy things. It is your financial trustworthiness. Good credit means that your history of payments, employment, and salary makes you a good candidate for a loan, and creditors—those who lend money or services—will be more willing to work with you. Having good credit usually translates into lower payments and more ease in borrowing money. Bad credit, however, can be a big problem. It usually results from making payments late or borrowing too much money, and it means that you might have trouble getting a car loan, a credit card, a place to live, and, sometimes, a job.

Need Credit or Insurance? Your Credit Score Helps Determine What You'll Pay

Ever wonder how a lender decides whether to grant you credit? For years, creditors have been using credit scoring systems to determine if you'd be a good risk for credit cards, auto loans, and mortgages. These days, many more types of businesses—including insurance companies and phone companies—are using credit scores to decide whether to approve you for a loan or service and on what terms. Auto and homeowners insurance companies are among the businesses that are using credit scores to help decide if you'd be a good risk for insurance. A higher credit score means you are likely less of a risk, and in turn, means you will be more likely to get credit or insurance—or pay less for it.

The Federal Trade Commission (FTC), the nation's consumer protection agency, wants you to know how credit scoring works.

What Is Credit Scoring?

Credit scoring is a system creditors use to help determine whether to give you credit. It also may be used to help decide the terms you are offered or the rate you will pay for the loan.

Information about you and your credit experiences, like your bill-paying history, the number and type of accounts you have, whether you pay your bills by the date they're due, collection actions, outstanding debt, and the age of your accounts, is collected from your credit report. Using a statistical program, creditors compare this information to the loan repayment history of consumers with similar profiles. For example, a credit scoring system awards points for each factor that helps predict who is most likely to repay a debt.

A total number of points—a credit score—helps predict how creditworthy you are—how likely it is that you will repay a loan and make the payments when they're due.

Some insurance companies also use credit report information, along with other factors, to help predict your likelihood of filing an insurance claim and the amount of the claim. They may consider these factors when they decide whether to grant you insurance and the amount of the premium they charge. The credit scores insurance companies use sometimes are called "insurance scores" or "credit-based insurance scores."

Credit Scores and Credit Reports

Your credit report is a key part of many credit scoring systems. That's why it is critical to make sure your credit report is accurate. Federal law gives you the right to get a free copy of your credit reports from each of the three national credit reporting companies once every 12 months.

The Fair Credit Reporting Act (FCRA) also gives you the right to get your credit score from the national credit reporting companies. They are allowed to charge a reasonable fee, generally around $8, for the score. When you buy your score, often you get information on how you can improve it.

To order your free annual report from one or all the national credit reporting companies, and to purchase your credit score, visit www.annualcreditreport.com, call toll-free 877-322-8228, or complete the Annual Credit Report Request Form and mail it to: Annual Credit Report Request Service, P. O. Box 105281, Atlanta, GA 30348-5281. For more information, see Your Access to Free Credit Reports.

How Is a Credit Scoring System Developed?

To develop a credit scoring system or model, a creditor or insurance company selects a random sample of its customers, or a sample of similar customers, and analyzes it statistically to identify characteristics that relate to risk. Each of the characteristics then is assigned a weight based on how strong a predictor it is of who would be a good risk. Each company may use its own scoring model, different scoring models for different types of credit or insurance, or a generic model developed by a scoring company.

Under the Equal Credit Opportunity Act (ECOA), a creditor's scoring system may not use certain characteristics—for example, race, sex, marital status, national origin, or religion—as factors. The law allows creditors to use age in properly designed scoring systems. But any credit scoring system that includes age must give equal treatment to elderly applicants.

What Can I Do to Improve My Score?

Credit scoring systems are complex and vary among creditors or insurance companies and for different types of credit or insurance. If one factor changes, your score may change—but improvement generally depends on how that factor relates to others the system considers. Only the business using the scoring knows what might improve your score under the particular model they use to evaluate your application.

Nevertheless, scoring models usually consider the following types of information in your credit report to help compute your credit score:

- Have you paid your bills on time? You can count on payment history to be a significant factor. If your credit report indicates that you have paid bills late, had an account referred to collections, or declared bankruptcy, it is likely to affect your score negatively.

- Are you maxed out? Many scoring systems evaluate the amount of debt you have compared to your credit limits. If the amount you owe is close to your credit limit, it's likely to have a negative effect on your score.

- How long have you had credit? Generally, scoring systems consider the length of your credit track record. An insufficient credit history may affect your score negatively, but factors like timely payments and low balances can offset that.

- Have you applied for new credit lately? Many scoring systems consider whether you have applied for credit recently by looking at "inquiries" on your credit report. If you have applied for too many new accounts recently, it could have a negative effect on your score. Every inquiry isn't counted: for example, inquiries by creditors who are monitoring your account or looking at credit reports to make "prescreened" credit offers are not considered liabilities.

- How many credit accounts do you have and what kinds of accounts are they? Although it is generally considered a plus to have established credit accounts, too many credit card accounts may have a negative effect on your score. In addition, many scoring systems consider the type of credit accounts you have. For example, under some scoring models, loans from finance companies may have a negative effect on your credit score.

Scoring models may be based on more than the information in your credit report. When you are applying for a mortgage loan, for example, the system may consider the amount of your down payment, your total debt, and your income, among other things.

Improving your score significantly is likely to take some time, but it can be done. To improve your credit score under most systems, focus on paying your bills in a timely way, paying down any outstanding balances, and staying away from new debt.

Are Credit Scoring Systems Reliable?

Credit scoring systems enable creditors or insurance companies to evaluate millions of applicants consistently on many different characteristics. To be statistically valid, these systems must be based on a big enough sample. They generally vary among businesses that use them.

Properly designed, credit scoring systems generally enable faster, more accurate, and more impartial decisions than individual people can make. And some creditors design their systems so that some applicants—those with scores not high enough to pass easily or low enough to fail absolutely—are referred to a credit manager who decides whether the company or lender will extend credit. Referrals can result in discussion and negotiation between the credit manager and the would-be borrower.

What If I Am Denied Credit or Insurance, or Don't Get the Terms I Want?

If you are denied credit, the ECOA requires that the creditor give you a notice with the specific reasons your application was rejected or the news that you have the right to learn the reasons if you ask within 60 days. Ask the creditor to be specific: Indefinite and vague reasons for denial are illegal. Acceptable reasons might be "your income was low" or "you haven't been employed long enough." Unacceptable reasons include "you didn't meet our minimum standards" or "you didn't receive enough points on our credit scoring system."

Sometimes you can be denied credit or insurance—or initially be charged a higher premium—because of information in your credit report. In that case, the FCRA requires the creditor or insurance company to give you the name, address, and phone number of the credit reporting company that supplied the information. Contact the company to find out what your report said. This information is free if you ask for it within 60 days of being turned down for credit or insurance. The credit reporting company can tell you what's in your report; only the creditor or insurance company can tell you why your application was denied.

If a creditor or insurance company says you were denied credit or insurance because you are too near your credit limits on your credit cards, you may want to reapply after paying down your balances. Because credit scores are based on credit report information, a score often changes when the information in the credit report changes.

If you've been denied credit or insurance or didn't get the rate or terms you want, ask questions:

- Ask the creditor or insurance company if a credit scoring system was used. If it was, ask what characteristics or factors were used in the system, and how you can improve your application.

- If you get the credit or insurance, ask the creditor or insurance company whether you are getting the best rate and terms available. If you're not, ask why.

- If you are denied credit or not offered the best rate available because of inaccuracies in your credit report, be sure to dispute the inaccurate information with the credit reporting company. To learn more about this right, see How to Dispute Credit Report Errors.

The FTC works to prevent fraudulent, deceptive and unfair business practices in the marketplace and to provide information to help consumers spot, stop and avoid them. To file a complaint or get free information on consumer issues, visit ftc.gov or call toll-free, 1-877-FTC-HELP (1-877-382-4357); TTY: 1-866-653-4261. Watch a video, How to File a Complaint, at ftc.gov/video to learn more. The FTC enters consumer complaints into the Consumer Sentinel Network, a secure online database and investigative tool used by hundreds of civil and criminal law enforcement agencies in the U.S. and abroad.

Online Assignment: Estimate Your Credit Score

Complete this assignment online. Go to:
http://webcom8.grtxle.com/totalpackage
Select >Chapter Content>Chapter 9>Enter your username and password

FACTA

The Fair and Accurate Credit Transactions Act's (FACTA) gives new rights to free credit reports. FACTA also provides new rights to obtain your credit score. FACTA became law in December 2003.

FACTA affects your ability to obtain your credit report and your credit score in the following ways:

- Under FACTA, you will have the right to obtain one free copy of your credit report from each of the three major credit bureaus every 12 months. Rules issued by the Federal Trade Commission (FTC) provide for free credit reports to become available in stages, beginning in western states December 1, 2004, and gradually moving east with completion due by September 1, 2005. FACTA also requires the major credit bureaus to provide a single point of contact so you can request your reports from all three companies with one toll-free phone call, letter or Internet request.

- Prior to FACTA, some providers of credit scores voluntarily made them available to consumers. But starting December 1, 2004, you will have new rights to obtain your score from a credit bureau as well as an explanation of the key factors used in computing the score.

- Title V of the FACTA established the Financial Literacy and Education Commission with the purpose of improving the financial literacy and education of persons in the United States. To reach the widest number of people possible, the Commission established a website (www.mymoney.gov) and a toll-free telephone number (1 (888) mymoney (696-6639)) to coordinate the presentation of educational materials from across the spectrum of federal agencies that deal with financial issues and markets.

Credit Cards

As discussed previously, credit cards are one of the biggest money management issues for college students.

5 THINGS YOU SHOULD KNOW ABOUT CREDIT CARDS

1. **Use them carefully.** Credit cards offer great benefits, especially the ability to buy now and pay later. But you've got to keep the debt levels manageable. If you don't, the costs in terms of fees and interest, or the damage to your credit record, could be significant. 392

2. **Choose them carefully.** Don't choose a credit card just to get freebies like T-shirts or sports items or because there's no annual fee. Look for a card that's best for your borrowing habits.

   Example: If you expect to carry a balance on your card from month to month, which means you'll be charged interest, it's more important to look for a card with a low interest rate or a generous "grace period"—more time before your payments are due.

3. **Pay as much as you can to avoid or minimize interest charges.** If possible, pay your bill in full each month. Remember, paying only the minimum due each month means you'll be paying a lot of interest for many years, and those costs could far exceed the amount of your original purchase.

4. **Pay on time.** You'll avoid a late fee of about $35 or more. But more importantly, continued late payments on your credit card may be reported to the major credit bureaus as a sign that you have problems handling your finances. And if your credit rating gets downgraded, your card company could raise the interest rate on your credit card, reduce your credit limit (the maximum amount you can borrow), or even cancel your card. Late payment on your credit card also can be a mark against you on your credit rating the next time you apply for an apartment or a job.

5. **Protect your credit card numbers from thieves.** Never provide your credit card numbers —both the account numbers and expiration date on the front and the security code on the back—in response to an unsolicited phone call, e-mail, or other communication you didn't originate. When using your credit card online make sure you're dealing with a legitimate Website and that encrypts your information (scrambled for security purposes) during transmission. Major credit card companies also are offering more protection by providing "zero-liability" programs that protect consumers from the unauthorized use of their cards. In general, only give your credit card or card numbers to reputable merchants or other organizations.

ASSIGNMENT: Take the FDIC's Financial Aptitude Test.

Do you think you already have a good understanding of financial wellness and can get a good score? Circle true or false based on what you think is the right answer.

1. It's always smart to send in the minimum payment due on a credit card bill each month and to stretch out the card payments as long as possible instead of paying the bill in full.   **TRUE FALSE**

2. Your credit record (your history of paying debts and other bills) can be a factor when you apply for a loan or a credit card, but it cannot affect non-credit decisions, such as applications for insurance or an apartment.   **TRUE FALSE**

3. While one or two late payments on bills may not damage your credit record, making a habit of it will count against you.   **TRUE FALSE**

4. There's no harm in having many different credit cards, especially when the card companies offer free T-shirts and other special giveaways as incentives. The number of cards you carry won't affect your ability to get a loan; what matters is that you use the cards responsibly.   **TRUE FALSE**

5. A debit card may be a good alternative to a credit card for a young person because the money to pay for purchases is automatically deducted from a bank account, thus avoiding interest charges or debt problems.   **TRUE FALSE**

6. It makes no sense for young adults to put money aside for their retirement many years away. People in their twenties should focus entirely on meeting monthly expenses and saving for short-term goals (such as buying a home or starting a business) and not start saving for retirement until their forties at the earliest.   **TRUE FALSE**

7. If you receive an e-mail from a company you've done business with asking you to update your records by re-entering your Social Security number or bank account numbers, it's safe to provide this information as long as the e-mail explains the reason for the request and shows the company's official logo.   **TRUE FALSE**

8. The best way to avoid a "bounced" check—that is, a check that your financial institution rejects because you've overdrawn your account—is to keep your checkbook up to date and to closely monitor your balance. Institutions do offer "overdraft protection" services, but these programs come with their own costs.   **TRUE FALSE**

9. All checking accounts are pretty much the same in terms of features, fees, interest rates, opening balance requirements, and so on.   **TRUE FALSE**

10. If you or your family has $100,000 or less on deposit at an FDIC-insured bank, and the bank fails, your money is completely safe.   **TRUE FALSE**

Federal Deposit Insurance Corporation. Consumer News: Financial Aptitude Test. Spring 2005—A Special Guide for Young Adults. fdic.gov/consumers/consumer/news/cnspr05/test.html

It is important that YOU understand the features of your credit card and know your rights when using your credit card.

What Is the APR?

The APR (Annual Percentage Rate) is the way of stating the interest rate you will pay if you carry over a balance, take out a cash advance, or transfer a balance from another card. The APR states the interest rate as a yearly rate.

What about Multiple APRs?

A single credit card may have several APRs:

- *One APR for purchases, another for cash advances, and yet another for balance transfers.* The APRs for cash advances and balance transfers often are higher than the APR for purchases (for example, 14% for purchases, 18% for cash advances, and 19% for balance transfers).

- *Tiered APRs:* These apply different rates to different levels of the outstanding balance (for example, 16% on balances of $1–$500 and 17% on balances above $500).

- *A penalty APR:* The APR may increase if you are late in making payments. For example, your card agreement may say, "If your payment arrives more than ten days late two times within a six-month period, the penalty rate will apply."

- *An introductory APR:* A different rate will apply after the introductory rate expires.

- *A delayed APR:* A different rate will apply in the future. For example, a card may advertise that there is "no interest until next March." Look for the APR in effect after March.

If you carry over a part of your balance from month to month, even a small difference in the APR can make a big difference in how much you will pay over a year.

What about Fixed vs. Variable APRs?

Some credit cards are "fixed rate"—the APR doesn't change or at least doesn't change often. Even the APR on a "fixed rate" credit card can change over time. However, the credit card company must tell you before increasing the fixed APR. Other credit cards are "variable rate"—the APR changes from time to time. The rate is usually tied to another interest rate, such as the prime rate or the Treasury bill rate. If the other rate changes, the rate on your card may change, too. Look for information on the credit card application and in the credit card agreement to see how often your card's APR may change (the agreement is like a contract—it lists the terms and conditions for using your credit card).

What Is a Grace Period?

The grace period is the number of days you have to pay your bill in full without triggering a finance charge. For example, the credit card company may say that you have "25 days from the statement date, provided you paid your previous balance in full by the due date." The bill gives the statement date. The grace period usually applies only to new purchases. Most credit cards do not give a grace period for cash advances and balance transfers. Instead, interest charges start right away. If you carried over any part of your balance from the preceding month, you may not have a grace period for new purchases. Instead, you may be charged interest as soon as you make a purchase (in addition to being charged interest on the earlier balance you have not paid off). Look on the credit card application for information about the "method of computing the balance for purchases" to see if it includes or excludes new purchases.

What Are Finance Charges and How Are They Calculated?

The finance charge is the dollar amount you pay to use credit. The amount depends in part on your outstanding balance and the APR. Credit card companies use one of several methods to calculate the outstanding balance. The method can make a big difference in the finance charge you'll pay. Your outstanding balance may be calculated: (1) over one billing cycle or two, (2) using the adjusted balance, the average daily balance, or the previous balance, and (3) including or excluding new purchases in the balance. Depending on the balance you carry and the timing of your purchases and payments, you'll usually have a lower finance charge with one-cycle billing and either: (1) the average daily balance method excluding new purchases, (2) the adjusted balance method, or (3) the previous balance method.

What Is a Minimum Finance Charge?

Some credit cards have a minimum finance charge. You'll be charged that minimum even if the calculated amount of your finance charge is less. For example, the company may calculate your finance charge as 35¢—but if the company's minimum finance charge is $1.00, you'll pay $1.00. A minimum finance charge usually applies only when you must pay a finance charge, that is, when you carry over a balance from one billing cycle to the next.

What Do I Need to Know about Credit Card Fees?

Most credit cards charge fees under certain circumstances:

- *Annual fee* (sometimes billed monthly). Charged for just having the card.

- *Cash advance fee.* Charged when you use the card for a cash advance; may be a flat fee (for example, $3.00) or a percentage of the cash advance (for example, 3%).

- *Balance-transfer fee.* Charged when you transfer a balance from another credit card. (Your credit card company may send you "checks" to pay off the other card. The balance is transferred when you use one of these checks to pay the amount due on the other card.)

- *Late-payment fee.* Charged if your payment is received after the due date.

- *Over-the-credit-limit fee.* Charged if you go over your credit limit.

- *Credit-limit-increase fee.* Charged if you ask for an increase in your credit limit.

- *Set-up fee.* Charged when a new credit card account is opened.

- *Return-item fee.* Charged if you pay your bill by check and the check is returned for non-sufficient funds (that is, your check bounces).

- *Other fees.* Some credit card companies charge a fee if you pay by telephone (that is, if you arrange by phone for payment transfer from your bank to the company) or to cover the costs of reporting to credit bureaus, reviewing your account, or providing other customer services. Read the information in your credit card agreement to see if there are other fees and charges.

How Do I Find Information about Credit Cards?

You can find lists of credit card plans, rates, and terms on the Internet, in personal finance magazines, and in newspapers. The Federal Reserve System surveys credit card companies every six months. You'll need to get the most recent information directly from the credit card company by phoning the company, looking on the company's

Website, or reading a solicitation or application. Under federal law, all solicitations and applications for credit cards must include certain key information in a disclosure box similar to the one shown.

Annual percentage rate (APR) for purchases	2.9% until 11/1/06 after that, 14.9%
Other APRs	Cash-advance APR: 15.9% Balance-Transfer APR: 15.9% Penalty rate: 23.9% See explanation below.*
Variable-rate information	Your APR for purchase transactions may vary. The rate is determined monthly by adding 5.9% to the Prime Rate.**
Grace period for repayment of balances for purchases	25 days on average
Method of computing the balance for purchases	Average daily balance (excluding new purchases)
Annual fees	None
Minimum finance charge	$.50
Transaction fee for cash advances: 3% of the amount advanced Balance-transfer fee: 3% of the amount transferred Late-payment fee: $25 Over-the-credit-limit fee: $25	

* Explanation of penalty. If your payment arrives more than ten days late two times within a six-month period, the penalty rate will apply.

** The Prime Rate used to determine your APR is the rate published in the *Wall Street Journal* on the 10th day of the prior month.

TABLE 9.1 TRUTH IN LENDING

Signed into law during 2009
■ A credit card issuer has to wait until a person is 60 days behind in making a payment before it increases the interest rate.
■ The issuer of a credit card must post on the Internet the full agreement that outlines what to expect when a credit card is issued.
■ Instead of 14 days, the issuer must now allow 21 days to elapse between sending a statement and the due date for payment.
■ Persons younger than 21 years old must provide proof of their ability to pay charges; otherwise parental or guardian assumption of responsibility for nonpayment is required before a credit card can be issued.
■ Issuers of credit cards are no longer permitted to sponsor "giveaway campaigns" on college campuses.
■ A "pay-to-pay fee" can no longer be charged when someone pays a fee over the Internet or by phone.
SOURCE: Starrs, C. (2009, November 8). Credit card changes. *Athens Banner-Herald*, pp. 1, 6.

From *Life Skills for the University and Beyond*, 4th Edition by Earl Ginter and Ann Shanks Glauser. Copyright © 2010 by Earl J. Ginter and Ann Shanks Glauser. Reprinted by permission of Kendall Hunt Publishing Company.

These days, it's hard to imagine life without gadgets and high-tech helpers. We want to make sure you know about some of the attractive electronic banking services beyond ATMs:

- **Internet banking** enables you to transfer money between your accounts at the same bank and view account information, deposits as well as loans, at any time.

- **Internet bill paying** allows you to pay monthly and one-time bills over the Internet. Some banks offer electronic bill payment free of charge, others charge a fee that is usually less than what you would spend on postage.

- **Debit cards** look like credit cards, but they automatically withdraw the money you want from your account. You can use a debit card to get cash from an ATM or to pay for purchases.

- **Direct deposit** enables the automatic transmission of your paycheck and certain other payments into your bank account. "Direct deposit is free and it's fast—there's no waiting for the check to arrive at home and no waiting in the teller lines," said Kathryn Weatherby, an Examination Specialist for the FDIC.

- **Telephone banking** allows you to use your touch-tone phone to confirm that a check or deposit has cleared, to get your latest balance, to transfer money between separate accounts at the same bank, and to obtain details about services.

- **Automatic withdrawals** from your bank account can be arranged free of charge to pay recurring bills (such as phone bills or insurance premiums) or to systematically put a certain amount of money into a savings account, a U.S. Savings Bond, or an investment.

STUDENT LOANS

"Any informed borrower is simply less vulnerable to fraud and abuse."
—Alan Greenspan, Former Chairman of the Federal Reserve

BUDGETING: THE KEY TO MONEY MANAGEMENT

*Money management begins with looking at your attitude toward money. Pay attention to how you spend your money so that you can accomplish your financial goals such as getting a college education, buying a house or car, or saving for the future. One of the most important things that you can do to manage your money and begin saving is to use a budget. A budget helps you become aware of how you spend your money and will help your make a plan for the future. It is important to control your money, rather than letting your money control you. Managing Your Money

- Monitor your spending

- Prepare a budget

- Beware of credit and interest

- Watch spending leaks

Monitor how you spend your money

The first step in establishing a workable budget is to monitor how you are actually spending your money at the present time. For one month, keep a list of purchases with the date and amount of money spent for each. You can do this on a sheet of paper, on your calendar, on index cards, or on a money management application for your phone. If you write checks for items, include the checks written as part of your money monitor. At the end of the month, group your purchases in categories such as food, gas, entertainment, and credit card payments, and add them up. Doing this will yield some surprising results. For example, you may not be aware of just how much it costs to eat at a fast-food restaurant or to buy lunch or coffee every day.

© koya979/Shutterstock.com

Prepare a budget

One of the best tools for managing your money is a budget. At the end of this chapter, you will find a simple budget sheet that you can use as a college student. After you finish college, update your budget and continue to use it. Follow these three steps to make a budget:

1. Write down your income for the month.

2. List your expenses. Include tuition, books, supplies, rent, phone, utilities (gas, electric, water, cable TV, Internet), car payments, car insurance, car maintenance (oil, repairs), parking fees, food, personal grooming, clothes, entertainment, savings, credit card payments, loan payments, and other bills. Use your money monitor to discover how you are spending your money and include categories that are unique to you.

3. Subtract your total expenses from your total income. You cannot spend more than you have. Make adjustments as needed.

Beware of credit and interest

College students are often tempted to use credit cards to pay for college expenses. This type of borrowing is costly and difficult to repay. It is easy to pull out a plastic credit card and buy items that you need and want. Credit card companies earn a great deal of money from credit cards. Jane Bryant Quinn gives an example of the cost of credit cards. She says that if you owe $3,000 at 18 percent interest and pay the minimum payment of $60 per month, it will take you 30 years and 10 months to get out of debt! Borrowing the $3,000 would cost about $22,320 over this time! If you use a credit card, make sure you can pay it off in one to three months. It is good to have a credit card in order to establish credit and to use in an emergency.

Watch those spending leaks

We all have spending problem areas. Often we spend small amounts of money each day that add up to large spending leaks over time. For example, if you spend $3 on coffee each weekday for a year, this adds up to $780 a year! If you eat lunch out each weekday and spend $8 for lunch, this adds up to $2,080 a year. Here are some common areas for spending leaks:

- Fast food and restaurants
- Entertainment and vacations
- Clothing
- Miscellaneous cash
- Gifts

© Andrey Armyagov/Shutterstock.com

Need More Money?

You may be tempted to work more hours to balance your budget. Remember that to be a full-time college student, it is recommended that you work no more than 20 hours per week. If you work more than 20 hours per week, you will probably need to decrease your course load. Before increasing your work hours, see if there is a way you can decrease your monthly expenses. Can you make your lunch instead of eating out? Can you get by without a car? Is the item you are purchasing a necessity, or do you just want to have it? These choices are yours.

"Money is, in some respects, like fire; it is a very excellent servant, but a terrible master."

P. T. Barnum

"Empty pockets never held anyone back. Only empty heads and empty hearts can do that."

Norman Vincent Peale

1. **Check out financial aid.** All students can qualify for some type of financial aid. Visit the Financial Aid Office at your college for assistance. Depending on your income level, you may qualify for one or more of the following forms of aid.

   - **Loans.** A loan must be paid back. The interest rate and terms vary according to your financial need. With some loans, the federal government pays the interest while you are in school.

   - **Grants.** A grant does not need to be repaid. There are both state and federal grants based on need.

   - **Work/study.** You may qualify for a federally subsidized job depending on your financial need. These jobs are often on campus and provide valuable work experience for the future.

   The first step in applying for financial aid is to fill out the Free Application for Federal Student Aid (FAFSA). This form determines your eligibility for financial aid. You can obtain this form from your college's financial aid office or over the Internet at https://fafsa.ed.gov/

   Here are some other financial aid resources that you can obtain from your financial aid office or over the Internet.

   - Federal Student Aid Resources. This site provides resources on preparing for college, applying for aid, online tools, and other resources: https://studentaid.ed.gov/sa/resources.

   - How to apply for financial aid. Learn how to apply for federal financial aid and scholarships at www.finaid.org.

2. **Apply for a scholarship.** Applying for a scholarship is like having a part-time job, only the pay is often better, the hours are flexible, and you can be your own boss. For this part-time job, you will need to research scholarship opportunities and fill out applications. There are multitudes of scholarships available, and sometimes no one even applies for them. Some students do not apply for scholarships because they think that high grades and financial need are required. While many scholarships are based on grades and financial need, many are not. Any person or organization can offer a scholarship for any reason they want. For example,

scholarships can be based on hobbies, parent's occupation, religious background, military service, and personal interests, to name a few.

There are several ways to research a scholarship. As a first step, visit the financial aid office on your college campus. This office is staffed with persons knowledgeable about researching and applying for scholarships. Organizations or persons wishing to fund scholarships often contact this office to advertise opportunities.

You can also research scholarships through your public or college library. Ask the reference librarian for assistance. You can use the Internet to research scholarships as well. Use any search engine such as Google.com and simply type in the keyword scholarships. The following websites index thousands of scholarships:

- The Federal Student Aid Scholarship site is located at https://studentaid.ed.gov/sa/types/grants-scholarships/finding-scholarships

- fastweb.com

- http://www.scholarships.com/

- collegenet.com/mach25

- studentscholarshipsearch.com

- collegeboard.com/paying

To apply for scholarships, start a file of useful material usually included in scholarship applications. You can use this same information to apply for many scholarships.

- Three current letters of recommendation

- A statement of your personal goals

- A statement of your financial need

- Copies of your transcripts

- Copies of any scholarship applications you have filled out

Be aware of scholarship scams. You do not need to pay money to apply for a scholarship. No one can guarantee that you will receive a scholarship. Use your college scholarship office and your own resources to research and apply for scholarships.

© mangostock/Shutterstock.com

The Best Ideas for Becoming Financially Secure

Financial planners provide the following ideas as the best ways to build wealth and independence. If you have financial security as your goal, plan to do the following:

1. **Use a simple budget to track income and expenses.** Do not spend more than you earn.

2. **Have a financial plan.** Include goals such as saving for retirement, purchasing a home, paying for college, or taking vacations.

3. **Save 10 percent of your income.** As a college student, you may not be able to save this much, but plan to do it as soon as you get your first good-paying job. If you cannot save 10 percent, save something to get in the habit of saving. Save to pay for your tuition and books.

4. **Don't take on too much debt.** Be especially careful about credit cards and consumer debt. Credit card companies often visit college campuses and offer high interest credit cards to students. It is important to have a credit card, but pay off the balance each month. Consider student loans instead of paying college fees by credit card.

5. **Don't procrastinate.** The earlier you take these steps toward financial security, the better.

Tips for Managing Your Money

Keeping these guidelines in mind can help you to manage your money.

- Don't let friends pressure you into spending too much money. If you can't afford something, learn to say no.

- Keep your checking account balanced or use online banking so you will know how much money you have.

- Don't lend money to friends. If your friends cannot manage their money, your loan will not help them.

- Use comparison shopping to find the best prices on the products that you buy.

- Get a part-time job while in college. You will earn money and gain valuable job experience.

- Don't use shopping as a recreational activity. When you visit the mall, you will find things you never knew you needed and will wind up spending more money than intended.

- Make a budget and follow it. This is the best way to achieve your financial goals.*

*From *College & Career Success*, 7th Edition by Marsha Fralick. Copyright © 2016 by Kendall Hunt Publishing Company. Reprinted by permission.

Finding your way through the peaks and pitfalls of student loan repayment can be a daunting task and many borrowers head down the repayment trail without having the tools they need. Some situations may cause you to stray from making payments while other obstacles simply leave you bewildered.

You may have several different types of student loans, each being held by a different lender or servicer. For example, if your school participated in the Federal Family Education Loan (FEEL) Program, you borrowed from a commercial lender and your loans are guaranteed by a guaranty agency. If your school participated in the Federal Direct Loan Program (FDLP), your lender is the U.S. Department of Education. If you were a "high need" student, you may have received a Perkins Loan which must be repaid to your school or its servicer. Finally, you may have borrowed an "alternative loan," which is a non-federal loan made by a private lender.

PROBLEM GAMBLING

> **"**If you must play, decide upon three things at the start: the rules of the game, the stakes, and the quitting time.**"**
>
> —Chinese Proverb

What Is Problem Gambling?

Problem gambling includes all gambling behavior patterns that compromise, disrupt, or damage personal, family, or vocational pursuits. The essential features are increasing preoccupation with gambling, a need to bet more money more frequently, restlessness or irritability when attempting to stop, "chasing" losses, and loss of control manifested by continuation of the gambling behavior in spite of mounting, serious, negative consequences. In extreme cases, problem gambling can result in financial ruin, legal problems, loss of career and family, or even suicide.

Isn't Problem Gambling Just a Financial Problem?

No. Problem gambling is an emotional problem that has financial consequences. If you pay all of a problem gambler's debts, the person will still be a problem gambler. The real problem is that he or she has an uncontrollable obsession with gambling.

Isn't problem gambling really the result of irresponsible or weak-willed people?
No. Many people who develop problems have been viewed as responsible and strong by those who care about them. Precipitating factors often lead to a change in behavior, such as retirement or job-related stress.

What Kind of People become Problem Gamblers?

Anyone who gambles can develop problems if he or she is not aware of the risks and does not gamble responsibly. When gambling behavior interferes with finances, relationships, and the workplace, a serious problem already exists.

Do Casinos, Lotteries, and Other Types of Gambling "Cause" Problem Gambling?

The cause of a gambling problem is the individual's inability to control the gambling. This may be due in part to a genetic tendency to develop addiction, ability to cope with normal life stress, and even social upbringing and moral attitudes about gambling. The casino or lottery provides the opportunity for the person to gamble. It does not, in and of itself, create the problem any more than a liquor store would create an alcoholic.

What Types of Gambling Cause the Most Problem Gambling?

Again, the cause of a gambling problem is the individual's inability to control the gambling. Therefore, any type of gambling can become problematic, just as an alcoholic can get drunk on any type of alcohol. But some types of gambling have different characteristics that may exacerbate gambling problems. While these factors are still poorly understood, anecdotal reports indicate that one risk factor may be a fast speed of play. In other words, the faster the wager to response time with a game, the more likely players may develop problems with a particular game.

Can You Be a Problem Gambler if You Don't Gamble Every Day?

The frequency of a person's gambling does not determine whether or not a gambling problem exists. Even though the problem gambler may only go on periodic gambling binges, the emotional and financial consequences will still be evident in the gambler's life, including the effects on the family.

How much money do you have to lose before gambling becomes a problem? The amount of money lost or won does not determine when gambling becomes a problem. Gambling becomes a problem when it causes a negative impact on any area of an individual's life.

How Can a Person Be Addicted to Something That Isn't a Substance?

Although the problem gambler ingests no substance, he or she gets the same effect from gambling as someone else might get from taking a tranquilizer or having a drink. The gambling alters the person's mood, and the gambler keeps repeating the behavior in an attempt to achieve that same effect. But just as tolerance develops to drugs or alcohol, the gambler finds that it takes more and more of the gambling experience to achieve the same emotional effect as before. This creates an increased craving for the activity, and the gambler finds less and less ability to resist as the craving grows in intensity and frequency.

How Widespread Is Problem Gambling in the U.S.?

The estimate is that 2 million (1%) U.S. adults meet criteria for pathological gambling in a given year. Another 4–8 million (2–3%) would be considered problem gamblers; that is, they do not meet the full diagnostic criteria for pathological gambling, but they do meet one or more of the criteria and are experiencing problems due to their gambling behavior. Research also indicates that most adults who choose to gamble are able to do responsibly.

"FAQs—Problem Gambling" from *www.ncpgambling.org* by National Council on Problem Gambling. Copyright © by National Council on Problem Gambling. Reprinted by permission.

IDENTITY THEFT

> **"***Identity theft is a huge problem. This is not a question of six degrees of separation—everybody knows somebody who's been a victim.***"**
>
> — Edward Mierzwinski

In the course of a busy day, you may write a check for your monthly rent, charge tickets to a ball game or clothes from the mall, change service providers for your cell phone, or apply for a credit card. Chances are you don't give these everyday transactions a second thought. But an identity thief does.

Identity theft is a serious crime! According to the Federal Trade Commission (FTC), people with stolen identities can spend months or years and thousands of dollars cleaning up the mess the thieves have made of a good name and credit record. In the meantime, victims of identity theft may lose job opportunities, be refused loans for education, housing, or cars, and even get arrested for crimes they didn't commit. Humiliation, anger, and frustration are among the feelings victims experience as they navigate the process of rescuing their identities.

How Does Identity Theft Occur?

Despite your best efforts to manage the flow of your personal information or to keep it to yourself, skilled identity thieves may use a variety of methods to gain access to your data.

How Identity Thieves GET Your Personal Information

- They get information from businesses or other institutions by stealing records or information while they're on the job, by bribing an employee who has access to these records, by hacking these records, or by conning information out of employees.

- They may steal personal information from you through email or phone by posing as legitimate companies and claiming that you have a problem with your account. This practice is known as "phishing" online or pretexting by phone.

- They may steal your mail, including bank and credit card statements, credit card offers, new checks, and tax information.

- They may steal your wallet or purse or steal personal information they find in your home.

- They may rummage through your trash and the trash of businesses or public trash dumps in a practice known as "dumpster diving."

- They may complete a "change of address form" to divert your mail to another location.

- They may get your credit reports by abusing their employers' authorized access to them, or by posing as a landlord, an employer, or someone else who may have a legal right to access your report.

- They may steal your credit or debit card numbers by capturing the information in a data storage device in a practice known as "skimming." They may swipe your card for an actual purchase, or attach the device to an ATM machine where you may enter or swipe your card.

How Identity Thieves USE Your Personal Information

- They may call your credit card issuer to change the billing address on your credit card account. The imposter then runs up charges on your account. Because your bills are being sent to a different address, it may be some time before you realize there's a problem.

- They may open new credit card accounts in your name. When they use the credit cards and don't pay the bills, your credit report shows the delinquent accounts.

- They may establish a phone or wireless service in your name. They may open a bank account in your name and write bad checks on that account.

- They may buy a car by taking out an auto loan in your name and may get identification in your name, such as a driver's license issued with their picture.

- They may counterfeit checks or credit or debit cards or authorize electronic transfers in your name and drain your bank account.

- They may get a job or file fraudulent tax returns in your name.

- They may file for bankruptcy under your name to avoid paying debts they've incurred under your name or to avoid eviction.

- They may give your name to the police during an arrest. If they don't show up for their court date, the court issues a warrant for arrest in your name.

What Happens If I Become a Victim of Identity Theft?

Take the following four steps as soon as possible, and keep a record with the details of your conversations and copies of all correspondence.

1. Place a fraud alert on your credit reports and review your credit reports. Fraud alerts can help prevent an identity thief from opening any more accounts in your name. Contact the toll-free fraud number of any of the three consumer reporting companies below to place a fraud alert on your credit report. You only need to contact one of the three companies to place an alert. The company you call is required to contact the other two, which will place an alert on their versions of your report, too. Once you place the fraud alert in your file, you're entitled to order free copies of your credit reports, and, if you ask, only the last four digits of your SSN will appear on your credit reports. Once you get your credit reports, review them carefully. Look for inquiries from companies you haven't contacted, accounts you didn't open, and debts on your accounts that you can't explain. Check that information, like your SSN, addresses, name or initials, and employers are correct. If you find fraudulent or inaccurate information, get it removed.

    a. EQUIFAX: 800.525.6285;equifax.com; P.O. Box 740241, Atlanta, GA 30374.0241

    b. EXPERIAN: 888.EXPERIAN (397.3742); experian com; P.O. Box 9532, Allen, TX 75013

    c. TRANSUNION: 800.680.7289; transunion.com; Fraud Victim Assistance Division, P.O. Box 6790, Fullerton, CA 92834.6790

2. Close the accounts that you know, or believe, have been tampered with or opened fraudulently. Call and speak with someone in the security or fraud department of each company. Follow up in writing and include copies (NOT originals) of supporting documents. It's important to notify credit card companies and banks in writing. Send your letters by certified mail, return receipt requested, so you can document what the company received and when. Keep a file of your correspondence and enclosures.

   When you open new accounts, use new Personal Identification Numbers (PINs) and passwords. Avoid using easily available information like your mother's maiden name, your birth date, the last four digits of your SSN, or your phone number, or a series of consecutive numbers. If the identity thief has made charges or debits on your accounts, or on fraudulently opened accounts, ask the company for the forms to dispute those transactions. Once you have resolved your identity theft dispute with the company, ask for a letter stating that the company has closed the disputed accounts and has discharged the fraudulent debts. This letter is your best proof if errors relating to this account reappear on your credit report or you are contacted again about the fraudulent debt.

3. File a report with your local police or the police in the community where the identity theft took place. Then, get a copy of the police report or, at the very least, the number of the report. It can help you deal with creditors who need proof of the crime. If the police are reluctant to take your report, ask to file a "Miscellaneous Incidents" report, or try another jurisdiction, like your state police. You also can check with your state Attorney General's office to find out if state law requires the police to take reports for identity theft.

4. File a complaint with the Federal Trade Commission. By sharing your identity theft complaint with the FTC, you will provide important information that can help law enforcement officials across the nation track down identity thieves and stop them. The FTC can refer victims' complaints to other government agencies and companies for further action, as well as investigate companies for violations of laws the agency enforces. You can file a complaint online at consumer.gov/idtheft. If you don't have Internet access, call the FTC's Identity Theft Hotline, toll-free: 877.IDTHEFT (438.4338); TTY: 866.653-.4261; Identity Theft Clearinghouse, Federal Trade Commission, 600 Pennsylvania Avenue, NW, Washington, DC 20580.

Be sure to call the Hotline to update your complaint if you have any additional information or problems.

MONEY MANAGEMENT

> **"***Money is a good servant but a bad master.***"**
> — French proverb

BUDGETING: THE KEY TO MONEY MANAGEMENT

Money management begins with looking at your attitude toward money. Pay attention to how you spend your money so that you can accomplish your financial goals such as getting a college education, buying a house or car, or saving for the future. One of the most important things that you can do to manage your money and begin saving is to use a budget. A budget helps you become aware of how you spend your money and will help your make a plan for the future. It is important to control your money, rather than letting your money control you.

Managing Your Money

- Monitor your spending

- Prepare a budget

- Beware of credit and interest

- Watch spending leaks

Monitor how you spend your money

The first step in establishing a workable budget is to monitor how you are actually spending your money at the present time. For one month, keep a list of purchases with the date and amount of money spent for each. You can do this on a sheet of paper, on your calendar, on index cards, or on a money management application for your phone. If you write checks for items, include the checks written as part of your money monitor. At the end of the month, group your purchases in categories such as food, gas, entertainment, and credit card payments, and add them up. Doing this will yield some surprising results. For example, you may not be aware of just how much it costs to eat at a fast-food restaurant or to buy lunch or coffee every day.

© koya979/Shutterstock.com

Prepare a budget

One of the best tools for managing your money is a budget. At the end of this chapter, you will find a simple budget sheet that you can use as a college student. After you finish college, update your budget and continue to use it. Follow these three steps to make a budget:

1. Write down your income for the month.

2. List your expenses. Include tuition, books, supplies, rent, phone, utilities (gas, electric, water, cable TV, Internet), car payments, car insurance, car maintenance (oil, repairs), parking fees, food, personal grooming, clothes, entertainment, savings, credit card payments, loan payments, and other bills. Use your money monitor to discover how you are spending your money and include categories that are unique to you.

3. Subtract your total expenses from your total income. You cannot spend more than you have. Make adjustments as needed.

Beware of credit and interest

College students are often tempted to use credit cards to pay for college expenses. This type of borrowing is costly and difficult to repay. It is easy to pull out a plastic credit card and buy items that you need and want. Credit card companies earn a great deal of money from credit cards. Jane Bryant Quinn gives an example of the cost of credit cards. She says that if you owe $3,000 at 18 percent interest and pay the minimum payment of $60 per month, it will take you 30 years and 10 months to get out of debt! Borrowing the $3,000 would cost about $22,320 over this time! If you use a credit card, make sure you can pay it off in one to three months. It is good to have a credit card in order to establish credit and to use in an emergency.

Watch those spending leaks

We all have spending problem areas. Often we spend small amounts of money each day that add up to large spending leaks over time. For example, if you spend $3 on coffee each weekday for a year, this adds up to $780 a year! If you eat lunch out each weekday and spend $8 for lunch, this adds up to $2,080 a year. Here are some common areas for spending leaks:

- Fast food and restaurants
- Entertainment and vacations
- Clothing
- Miscellaneous cash
- Gifts

© Andrey Armyagov/Shutterstock.com

Need More Money?

You may be tempted to work more hours to balance your budget. Remember that to be a full-time college student, it is recommended that you work no more than 20 hours per week. If you work more than 20 hours per week, you will probably need to decrease your course load. Before increasing your work hours, see if there is a way you can decrease your monthly expenses. Can you make your lunch instead of eating out? Can you get by without a car? Is the item you are purchasing a necessity, or do you just want to have it? These choices are yours.

"Money is, in some respects, like fire; it is a very excellent servant, but a terrible master."

P. T. Barnum

"Empty pockets never held anyone back. Only empty heads and empty hearts can do that."

Norman Vincent Peale

1. **Check out financial aid.** All students can qualify for some type of financial aid. Visit the Financial Aid Office at your college for assistance. Depending on your income level, you may qualify for one or more of the following forms of aid.

   - **Loans.** A loan must be paid back. The interest rate and terms vary according to your financial need. With some loans, the federal government pays the interest while you are in school.

   - **Grants.** A grant does not need to be repaid. There are both state and federal grants based on need.

   - **Work/study.** You may qualify for a federally subsidized job depending on your financial need. These jobs are often on campus and provide valuable work experience for the future.

   The first step in applying for financial aid is to fill out the Free Application for Federal Student Aid (FAFSA). This form determines your eligibility for financial aid. You can obtain this form from your college's financial aid office or over the Internet at https://fafsa.ed.gov/

   Here are some other financial aid resources that you can obtain from your financial aid office or over the Internet.

   - Federal Student Aid Resources. This site provides resources on preparing for college, applying for aid, online tools, and other resources: https://studentaid.ed.gov/sa/resources.

   - How to apply for financial aid. Learn how to apply for federal financial aid and scholarships at www.finaid.org.

2. **Apply for a scholarship**. Applying for a scholarship is like having a part-time job, only the pay is often better, the hours are flexible, and you can be your own boss. For this part-time job, you will need to research scholarship opportunities and fill out applications. There are multitudes of scholarships available, and sometimes

no one even applies for them. Some students do not apply for scholarships because they think that high grades and financial need are required. While many scholarships are based on grades and financial need, many are not. Any person or organization can offer a scholarship for any reason they want. For example, scholarships can be based on hobbies, parent's occupation, religious background, military service, and personal interests, to name a few.

There are several ways to research a scholarship. As a first step, visit the financial aid office on your college campus. This office is staffed with persons knowledgeable about researching and applying for scholarships. Organizations or persons wishing to fund scholarships often contact this office to advertise opportunities.

You can also research scholarships through your public or college library. Ask the reference librarian for assistance. You can use the Internet to research scholarships as well. Use any search engine such as Google.com and simply type in the keyword scholarships. The following websites index thousands of scholarships:

- The Federal Student Aid Scholarship site is located at https://studentaid.ed.gov/sa/types/grants-scholarships/finding-scholarships
- fastweb.com
- http://www.scholarships.com/
- collegenet.com/mach25
- studentscholarshipsearch.com
- collegeboard.com/paying

To apply for scholarships, start a file of useful material usually included in scholarship applications. You can use this same information to apply for many scholarships.

- Three current letters of recommendation
- A statement of your personal goals
- A statement of your financial need
- Copies of your transcripts
- Copies of any scholarship applications you have filled out

Be aware of scholarship scams. You do not need to pay money to apply for a scholarship. No one can guarantee that you will receive a scholarship. Use your college scholarship office and your own resources to research and apply for scholarships.

© mangostock/Shutterstock.com

The Best Ideas for Becoming Financially Secure

Financial planners provide the following ideas as the best ways to build wealth and independence. If you have financial security as your goal, plan to do the following:

1. **Use a simple budget to track income and expenses.** Do not spend more than you earn.

2. **Have a financial plan.** Include goals such as saving for retirement, purchasing a home, paying for college, or taking vacations.

3. **Save 10 percent of your income.** As a college student, you may not be able to save this much, but plan to do it as soon as you get your first good-paying job. If you cannot save 10 percent, save something to get in the habit of saving. Save to pay for your tuition and books.

4. **Don't take on too much debt.** Be especially careful about credit cards and consumer debt. Credit card companies often visit college campuses and offer high-interest credit cards to students. It is important to have a credit card, but pay off the balance each month. Consider student loans instead of paying college fees by credit card.

5. **Don't procrastinate.** The earlier you take these steps toward financial security, the better.

Tips for Managing Your Money

Keeping these guidelines in mind can help you to manage your money.

- Don't let friends pressure you into spending too much money. If you can't afford something, learn to say no.

- Keep your checking account balanced or use online banking so you will know how much money you have.

- Don't lend money to friends. If your friends cannot manage their money, your loan will not help them.

- Use comparison shopping to find the best prices on the products that you buy.

- Get a part-time job while in college. You will earn money and gain valuable job experience.

- Don't use shopping as a recreational activity. When you visit the mall, you will find things you never knew you needed and will wind up spending more money than intended.

- Make a budget and follow it. This is the best way to achieve your financial goals.

To successfully reach your financial goals, a lot depends on what you do and when. For many people, the word "budget" sounds negative. Instead, think of it as a means to achieve success. A successful budget will include categories that reflect your needs and the way you eat, exercise, interact with health care providers, and, yes, spend money.

Here are just a few ideas you can consider during college: Realize that as you pay bills and debts on your own you are building a "credit record" that could be important when you apply for a loan or a job in the future. Pay your bills on time and borrow only what you can repay. If you decide to get your own credit card, choose carefully. Take your time, understand the risks as well as the rewards, and do some comparison shopping. Protect your Social Security number (SSN), credit card numbers, and other personal information from thieves who use others' identities to commit fraud. Use your SSN as identification only if absolutely necessary and never provide it to a stranger. Safeguard your personal information when using the Internet or borrowing a computer provided by your school. Consider a paying job or even an unpaid internship at a workplace related to a career you're considering. If possible, set money aside into savings and investments. Try to take a class in personal finance. Read money-related magazine and newspaper articles.

Here are just a few ideas you can consider when you start your career: Keep your credit card and other debts manageable. Maintain a good credit record. Save money for both short-term and long-term goals. Contribute as much as you can to retirement savings, which you often can use for other purposes, including a first time home purchase. Take advantage of matching contributions that your employer will put into your retirement savings. Do your best to stick to a budget and control your spending, especially if you're still paying back student loans or working at an entry-level job. Although insurance sometimes seems like a waste of money, you only need one accident or catastrophe to wipe you out financially. Think about disability insurance (to replace lost income if you become seriously ill) and health insurance (to cover big medical bills). Check into low-cost or free insurance offered through your employer.

Online Assignments: Monthly Budget and How Do You Spend Your Money?

Complete this assignment online. Go to:

http://webcom8.grtxle.com/totalpackage

Select >Chapter Content>Chapter 9>Enter your username and password

ASSIGNMENT: Having completed the previous assignments, answer the following questions about money management.

MONEY MANAGEMENT

1. Based on the material in this chapter, what area of money management do you believe you need to concentrate on the most? Explain.

2. How do you plan to work on this money management area? Be as specific as possible.

3. How does your personality affect your ability to manage money?

4. Describe how you see yourself financially in five years. What obstacles will you have to overcome to achieve your financial goals? What can you do during the next year to move closer toward these goals? How are these goals tied to your *personal values* (e.g., helping others, time, freedom, power, creativity, stability, independence, security, and so forth)?

Adapted from Ginter, E. et al. *Life Skills for College: A Curriculum for Life.* Acquiring Financial Skills. Kendall Hunt Publishing Company: (2005): 951–954.

SAVING FOR THE FUTURE

> **"**The question isn't at what age I want to retire, it's at what income.**"**
>
> — George Foreman

Six Key Principles of Saving for Retirement

by Ben Stein

Miles to Go

The first set of principles come from my old pal and colleague, financial planning whiz Raymond J. Lucia (or Ray Lucia, as I call him). He's written a fine new book called "Ready . . . Set . . . Retire!: Financial Strategies for the Rest of Your Life" in which he lays out the six most fundamental considerations for retiring.

But the main point to bear in mind is that you're probably going to live about 20 years after you retire. That's a long, long time if you don't have enough money saved up.

The Six Principles

The principles that will influence how you live financially after you retire. Specifically, they are:

1. **How much you save.**

   Simply put, if you're a typical American (who happens to save close to zero right now), you have to save more. When you're young, 10 percent of your income will get you there. If you don't start saving until middle age, aim closer to 15 or 20 percent. If you don't start until later than middle age, save every penny you can.

2. **How long you give your savings to compound.**

   The great Milton Friedman famously said that the greatest invention of man was compound interest. Maybe he was joking, maybe not.

   In any event, compound interest is a great gift to young people. If you start early, tiny amounts grow to immense amounts, and pretty soon you're all set for retirement. My pal, the genius investment advisor Phil DeMuth, says that if you're old enough to start thinking about sex, you're old enough to start saving for retirement.

   A thousand dollars socked away when you're 20 and growing at 10 percent per year will be almost $73,000 when you're 65. The same sum saved when you're 50 will grow to $4,200 at age 65. That's a stunning truth that should compel any young person to start saving early —and the rest of us to start right now.

As for timing your retirement, Ray advises that if you can push it back by even five years you'll allow your money to grow and have fewer years to need it.

3. **How you allocate your assets.**

    Typically, for those who start early, stocks are the answer. Over long periods, a diversified basket of common stocks wildly outperforms bonds, cash, and real estate. The differences are breathtaking.

    But, as we've seen lately, there's also a lot of volatility in stocks. As you age, you'll want more of your money in bonds and money market accounts. These have lower returns than stocks, but they also have far lower volatility.

4. **How much your investment returns annually.**

    Now, this is largely unknown from year to year. But over long periods, stocks return close to 6.5 percent after inflation, and about 10 percent before inflation.

    The supernova-genius of investing, the investor's absolutely best pal ever, John Bogle, who founded index investing through Vanguard Funds, says—and his evidence is powerful indeed—that you'll do best as a stock investor with index funds that cover the largest possible universe of stocks in the free world. These tend to be very low-cost in terms of fees and loads (sales charges), and beat almost all actively managed funds in terms of return over long periods.

5. **How low you keep your fees and costs.**

    This principle is largely about using index funds and no-load mutual funds, which makes perfect sense.

6. **How closely you keep an eye on taxes.**

    Finally, Ray advises maxing out your tax-protected accounts like IRAs and 401(k)s; keeping high-dividend stocks in accounts that are tax-deferred; and, when retiring, carefully considering what bracket you'll be in and drawing out your funds to remain in the lowest possible one.

Remember the Basics

These are basic principles to be sure, but they're vital. The three most important to remember are: (1) Start saving for retirement when you're young; (2) Save as much as you can; and (3) Maximize your returns by using index funds with low costs and high diversification. (Diversification and time are probably the investor's best friends.)

It may sound simple, but it isn't easy. If you're diligent, though, you'll be well on your way.

Online Assignment: Longevity

Complete this assignment online. Go to:

http://webcom8.grtxle.com/totalpackage

Select >Chapter Content>Chapter 9>Enter your username and password

MONEY AND HAPPINESS

❝*If you want to feel rich, just count the things you have that money can't buy.*❞

— Proverbs

Does Money Buy Happiness?

Sharon Begley's 2007 *Newsweek* article, "When Money Doesn't Buy Happiness," discusses this topic in great detail. "According to Daniel Gilbert, Harvard University psychologist and author of Stumbling on Happiness, concludes that 'wealth increases human happiness when it lifts people out of abject poverty and into the middle class but that it does little to increase happiness thereafter.' According to standard economics, the most important commodity you can buy with additional wealth is choice. Additional wealth also lets you satisfy additional needs and wants, and the more of those you satisfy the happier you are supposed to be. Satisfying needs brings less emotional well-being than satisfying wants. Curiously, although money doesn't buy happiness, happiness can buy money. Young people who describe themselves as happy typically earn higher incomes, years later, than those who said they were unhappy. It seems that a sense of well-being can make you more productive and more likely to show initiative and other traits that lead to a higher income. Contented people are also more likely to marry and stay married, as well as to be healthy, both of which increase happiness."

Again, I Ask Does Money Buy Happiness?

Matthew Herper's 2004 *Forbes* article, "Money Won't Buy You Happiness," also elaborates on this discussion. "Sure, if a person is handed $10, the pleasure centers of his brain light up as if he were given food, sex or drugs. But that initial rush does not translate into long-term pleasure for most people. Surveys have found virtually the same level of happiness between the very rich individuals on the Forbes 400 and the Maasai herdsman of East Africa. Lottery winners return to their previous level of happiness after five years. Increases in income just don't seem to make people happier—and most negative life experiences likewise have only a small impact on long-term satisfaction.

"Why doesn't wealth bring a constant sense of joy? 'Part of the reason is that people aren't very good at figuring out what to do with the money,' says George Loewenstein, an economist at Carnegie Mellon University. People generally overestimate the amount of long term pleasure they'll get from a given object. Sometimes, Loewenstein notes, the way people spend their money can actually make them less happy. For example, people derive a great deal of pleasure from interacting with others. If the first thing lottery winners do is quit their job and move to a palatial but isolated estate where they don't see any neighbors, they could find themselves isolated and depressed."

"The central problem is that the human brain becomes conditioned to positive experiences. Getting a chunk of unexpected money registers as a good thing, but as time passes, the response wears off. An expected paycheck doesn't bring any buzz at all—and doesn't contribute to overall happiness. You can get used to anything, be it hanging by your toenails or making millions of dollars a day. Mood may be set more by heredity than by anything else: Studies of twins have shown that at least half a person's level of happiness may be determined by some of the genes that play a role in determining personality. But this raises another question. How important is happiness anyway? Some of life's most satisfying experiences don't bring happiness. 'I think it's possible to way overestimate the importance of happiness,' says Loewenstein. 'Part of the meaning of life is to have highs and lows. A life that was constantly happy was not a good life.'

"However, there may be at least one important relationship between money and happiness, according to Ed Diener, the University of Illinois researcher who surveyed the Forbes 400 and the Maasai. Diener has also written that happy people tend to have higher incomes later on in their lives. So, while money may not help make people happy, being happy may help them make money."

So, Can You Find Money and Happiness Living Together in Harmony?

Maybe. Most people will find a sense of happiness and fulfillment as they selflessly give a portion of their hard-earned money charitably. According to the National Center for Charitable Statistics, there are currently more than 850,000 public charities, more than 104,000 private foundations, and more than 463,000 nonprofit organizations registered with the Internal Revenue Service (IRS). You also might possibly be giving of your time—charitably—to an organization or charity, but when you are in a place to "give back" financially, you'll have to figure out how best to choose such a charity. You can begin by doing a little research on what organization is dedicated to your chosen cause. Make sure to also research how much or what percentage of donations actually go toward the cause and how much is spent on administration. According to the Charities Review Council, a charity should spend no more than 30% of its revenues on administration.

ASSIGNMENT: Determine your meaning of money.

1. What does money mean to you?

2. Do you think money means the same thing to your friends as it does to you? Explain.

3. Does every member of your family (parents, siblings, etc.) view money the same way? Explain.

4. Does money make you happy? Explain.

5. Are there other things than money that make you happy?

6. Are there aspects about money that make you unhappy?

7. How can you meet a balance between your different feelings about money?

Ginter, E. et al. *Life Skills for College: A Curriculum for Life.* "Acquiring Financial Skills." Kendall Hunt Publishing Company: (2005): 949.

TIPS TO BECOMING FINANCIALLY HEALTHY

"A penny saved is a penny earned."

— Benjamin Franklin

- Make a plan and develop a budget. Just by tracking your expenses you'll start to curb your expenses, especially the "extra-curricular" expenses.

- It's okay to spend money on "extra-curricular" items, but you have to make room in your budget for them. Live within your means!

- Don't let friends pressure you into spending money.

- Make good choices when it comes to getting and using credit cards. Get cards that come with low, fixed APRs and read the "fine print" before sealing the deal.

- Keep your checkbook balanced.

- Don't rack up unnecessary ATM fees.

- Be cautious when loaning money to anyone.

- Research products before you make a purchase. You might just save yourself money by putting in a little extra time. This can include books, room and board needs, etc.

- It is important to start saving now for your future-event, though it may seem like light years away. Getting started early will pay off in your later years.

- Make sure you have funds saved up for emergencies.

- Take steps to protect your identity and financial information.

- Know how your actions (financially) can affect your credit score.

- Read and stay current with the latest financial information.

- Ask for help when you need it. Do not "sit" on financial issues—be proactive and think how best you can solve the problems at hand.

Helpful Internet Sites

American Institute of Certified Public Accountants (AICPA) Financial Literacy: 360financialliteracy.org
InCharge Institute of America: inchargeinstitute.org
Internal Revenue Service (IRS) Tax Fraud: treas.gov/irs/ci
National Information Center of the Federal Reserve System: ffiec.gov/nic/
The National Council on Problem Gambling: ncpgambling.org
Northwestern Mutual Finance Network Free Interactive Calculators: nmfn.com/tn/listpages—calculator_list_pg
Principal Financial Group Budgeting Calculators: principal.com/PAGA
State Attorney General: naag.org
Social Security Administration (SSA) Number Misuse: ssa.gov
Suze Orman International Acclaimed Personal Finance Expert: suzeorman.com
Urban Institute: National Center for Charitable Statistics: nccs.urban.org
U.S. Department of Education Student Loan Fraud: ed.gov/about/offices/list/oig/hotline.html?src=rt;
U.S. Department of State (USDS) Passport Fraud: travel.state.gov/passport/passport_1738.html
U.S. Federal Communications Commission (FCC) Cell Phone and Long Distance Fraud: fcc.gov
U.S. Federal Trade Commission: ftc.gov
U.S. Federal Trade Commission Identity Theft: consumer.gov/idtheft
U.S. Federal Trade Commission Finding Reputable Credit Counselors: ftc.gov/bcp/conline/edcams/credit/coninfo_debt
U.S. Federal Trade Commission Access to Free Credit Reports: ftc.gov/bcp/conline/pubs/credit/freereports.
U.S. Federal Deposit Insurance Corporation (FDIC): fdic.gov
U.S. Financial Literacy and Education Commission: mymoney.gov
U.S. Financial Literacy and Education Commission (calculators): mymoney.gov/calculators.html
U.S. Postal Inspection Service (USPIS) Mail Theft: usps.gov/websites/depart/inspect

U.S. Securities and Exchange Commission (SEC) Investment Fraud: sec.gov
U.S. Trustee (UST) Bankruptcy Fraud: usdoj gov/ust
Young Money Blog: youngmoney.com
66 Ways to Save Money Campaign: 66ways.org

References

Begley, S. *Newsweek Web Exclusive.* Why Money Doesn't Buy Happiness (2007): Oct. 15. newsweek.com/id/43884/page/2 accessed on 3.2.08.

Federal Deposit Insurance Corporation. Credit Reports and Scores: *FACTA.* fdic.gov/consumers/consumer/alert/facta html accessed on 1.12.12.

Federal Deposit Insurance Corporation. *Consumer News: Financial Aptitude Test. Spring 2005—A Special Guide for Young Adults.* fdic.gov/consumers/consumer/news/cnspr05/test.html accessed on 2.26.08.

Federal Deposit Insurance Corporation. *Consumer News: If At First You Don't Succeed: Common Mistakes Young Adults Make with Money and How to Avoid Them. Spring 2005—A Special Guide for Young Adults.* fdic.gov/consumers/consumer/news/cnspr05/cvrstry.html accessed on 2.26.08.

Federal Deposit Insurance Corporation. *Consumer News: Ages and Stages of Money Management: A To Do List. Spring 2005—A Special Guide for Young Adults.* fdic.gov/consumers/consumer/news/cnspr05/cvrstry.html accessed on 2.26.08.

Federal Deposit Insurance Corporation. *Consumer News: Five Things You Should Know About Credit Cards. Spring 2005—A Special Guide for Young Adults.* fdic.gov/consumers/consumer/news/cnspr05/cvrstry.html accessed on 2.26.08.

Federal Deposit Insurance Corporation. *Consumer News: Five Things You Should Know About Checks and Checking Accounts.. Spring 2005—A Special Guide for Young Adults.* fdic.gov/consumers/consumer/news/cnspr05/cvrstry.html accessed on 2.26.08.

Federal Deposit Insurance Corporation. *Consumer News: High-Tech Banking, 24/7. Spring 2005—A Special Guide for Young Adults.* fdic.gov/consumers/consumer/news/cnspr05/cvrstry.html accessed on 2.26.08.

The Federal Reserve Board. *Choosing a Credit Card.* federalreserve.gov/pubs/shop/default.htm accessed on 3.2.08

Federal Trade Commission. *Your Credit Report.* ftc.gov/bcp/edu/pubs/consumer/credit/cre24.shtm accessed on 5.23.12.

Federal Trade Commission. *Getting Credit: What You Need to Know About Credit.* ftc.gov/bcp/conline/pubs/credit/gettingcredit.shtm accessed on 3.2.08.

Federal Trade Commission. *Take Charge: Fighting Back Against Identity Theft.* ftc.gov/bcp/edu/pubs/consumer/idtheft/idt04.shtm accessed on 2.25.08.

Fralick, M. *College & Career Success.* Managing Time and Money. Kendall Hunt Publishing Company: (2006): 83.

Ginter,E. et al. *Life Skills for College: A Curriculum for Life.* Acquiring Financial Skills. Kendall Hunt Publishing Company: (2005): 949; 133–134.

Herper, M. Forbes.com. *Money Won't Buy You Happiness* (2004): Sept. 21. forbes.com/2004/09/21/cx_mh_0921happiness.html accessed on 3.2.08.

Kirchner, D. Plan Ahead Get Ahead. *Seven Retirement Savings Myths.* Principal Financial Group: (Winter 2008): 14–17.

The National Council on Problem Gambling. *FAQs—Problem Gambling.* ncpgambling.org/i4a/pages/Index.cfm?pageID=3314 accessed on 3.5.08.

Northwestern Mutual Financial Network. *The Longevity Game.* nmfn.com/tn/learnctr—lifeevents—longevity accessed on 3.5.08.

Stein, B. Yahoo Finance. *How Not to Ruin Your Life: Six Key Principles for Saving for Retirement* (2007): March 30. finance.yahoo.com/expert/article/yourlife/27943 accessed on 3.4.08.

Urban Institute-National Center for Charitable Statistics. nccs.urban.org accessed on 3.3.08.

Weston, L. money.msn.com. *Raise Your Credit Score to 740* (2010): Sept. 21. money.msn.com/credit-rating/your-credit-score.aspx accessed on 1.12.12.

CHAPTER 10

Being Responsible for You

> "It is not the strongest of the species that survives, nor the most intelligent, but the ones most responsive to change."
>
> — Charles Darwin

The objectives in this chapter include the understanding of:

- Rising health care costs and the impact it has on you
- Healthy People 2020
- Risk factors for and prevention of heart disease and stroke
- Risk factors for and prevention of metabolic syndrome and diabetes
- Risk factors for smoking and using tobacco products and the importance to quit
- Risk factors for and prevention of cancers
- Sleep health
- Oral health
- Eye health
- Low back health
- Risk factors for and prevention of sexually transmitted diseases
- Risk factors for and prevention of substance abuse
- Risk factors for and prevention of alcohol dependence and abuse
- Safety awareness of motor vehicles, motorcycles, bicycles, watercrafts, and personal safety measures

Online Reminders

- Complete the poll question before the next class meeting.
- Complete the interactive activities for this chapter.
- Complete all of the online assignments for this chapter.
- Complete the Post-Course Assessment: Multi-Dimensional Wellness Inventory.

Taking Responsibility—We are responsible for what happens in our lives. We make decisions and choices that create the future. Our behavior leads to success or failure. Too often we believe we are victims of circumstance. We often look for others to blame for how our lives are going:

- My parents did it to me. My childhood experiences shaped who I am.
- Society did it to me. I have no opportunity.
- My boss did it to me. She gave me a poor evaluation.
- My teacher did it to me. He gave me a poor grade.

Author Stephen Covey suggests that we look at the word responsibility as "response-ability." It is the ability to choose responses and to make decisions about the future. When you are dealing with a problem, it is useful to ask yourself what decisions you made that led to the problem. At times you may ask, "How did I create this?" and find that the answer is that you did not create the situation. But we do create or at least contribute to many of the things that happen to us. Even if you did not create your circumstances, you CAN CREATE YOUR REACTION to the situation.

Stephen Covey believes that we can use our resourcefulness and initiative in dealing with most problems. Use your resourcefulness and initiative to create the future that you want. (Fralick, 249–250) Being responsible for you involves taking responsibility for all the dimensions of wellness in your life and taking "hold" of your overall health.

Healthy People 2020

The following news release announces the nation's new health promotion and disease prevention plans:

The U.S. Department of Health and Human Services unveiled Healthy People 2020, the nation's new 10-year goals and objectives for health promotion and disease prevention, and "myHealthyPeople," a new challenge for technology application developers in December 2010.

For the past 30 years, Healthy People has been committed to improving the quality of our Nation's health by producing a framework for public health prevention priorities and actions.

Chronic diseases, such as heart disease, cancer and diabetes, are responsible for seven out of every 10 deaths among Americans each year and account for 75 percent of the nation's health spending. Many of the risk factors that contribute to the development of these diseases are preventable.

According to Assistant Secretary for Health Howard K. Koh, M.D., M.P.H, too many people are not reaching their full potential for health because of preventable conditions. Healthy People is the nation's roadmap and compass for better health, providing our society a vision for improving both the quantity and quality of life for all Americans.

Healthy People 2020 is the product of an extensive stakeholder feedback process that is unparalleled in government and health. It integrates input from public health and prevention experts, a wide range of federal, state and local government officials, a consortium of more than 2,000 organizations, and perhaps most importantly, the public. Based on this input, a number of new topic areas are included in the new initiative, including:

- Adolescent Health

- Blood Disorders and Blood Safety

- Dementias, including Alzheimer's Disease

- Early and Middle Childhood

- Genomics

- Global Health

- Health-Related Quality of Life and Well-Being

- Healthcare-Associated Infections

- Lesbian, Gay, Bisexual and Transgender Health

- Older Adults

- Preparedness

- Sleep Health

- Social Determinants of Health

The development of Healthy People 2030 includes establishing a framework for the initiative—the vision, mission, foundational principles, plan of action, and overarching goals—and identifying new objectives.

PRE-CLASS SURVEY: Take your "being responsible for you" wellness survey before your next class meeting and identify your level of wellness. Circle either Yes or No, total up each column, and check your score.

I know the risk factors for heart disease and stroke and practice prevention measures.	YES	NO
I know the risk factors for metabolic syndrome and diabetes and practice prevention measures	YES	NO
I avoid smoking and using tobacco products and avoid secondhand smoke.	YES	NO
I know the risk factors for developing cancer and practice prevention measures.	YES	NO
I am aware of my family history as it relates to any disease state (cancer, heart disease, etc.)	YES	NO
I practice consistent and proper oral hygiene and go to my regular dental check-ups.	YES	NO
I get 7–9 hours of sleep per night and/or have talked with my doctor about my sleep problems	YES	NO
I practice prevention of eye and vision problems by getting regular eye exams and being on the lookout for any vision changes.	YES	NO
I practice low back prevention measures by exercising, watching my posture when sitting, or taking other preventive measures.	YES	NO
I practice safe sex and prevention measures against getting a sexually transmitted disease.	YES	NO

I am aware of the dangers that involve using drugs and alcohol, don't use drugs, and drink responsibly.	YES	NO
I practice safety measures when I'm in the car, on a motorcycle, on a bicycle, or on a watercraft.	YES	NO
I practice safety measures at home and on campus	YES	NO
	TOTAL	

WHAT YOUR TOTAL MEANS:

9 or more Yes answers	Excellent	Your habits are positively enhancing your health.
6–8 Yes answers	Average	You are obviously trying but there is room to improve.
5 or less Yes answers	Not So Good	There is a need for improvement in your daily habits.

Source: "Wellness for Healthy Positive Living." *Being Responsible for You/Inventory* for.gov.bc.ca/hrb/hw/index.htm

WHAT YOU NEED TO KNOW ABOUT CARDIOVASCULAR HEALTH

Heart Disease

Cardiovascular disease (CVD) death rates are declining, but CVD is still the No. 1 cause of death in the United States, and risk factor control remains a challenge for many. This is according to the most recent data from the American Heart Association's *Heart Disease and Stroke Statistics—2017 Update*. CVD includes heart disease, stroke, high blood pressure, heart failure, and several other conditions, including arrhythmias, atrial fibrillation, cardiomyopathy, and peripheral arterial disease. CVD has been the LEADING CAUSE OF DEATH in the United States EVERY YEAR SINCE 1900 except during the 1918 flu epidemic.

Risk Factors and Coronary Heart Disease

AHA Scientific Position

Extensive clinical and statistical studies have identified several factors that increase the risk of coronary heart disease and heart attack. Major risk factors are those that research has shown significantly increase the risk of heart and blood vessel (cardiovascular) disease. Other factors are associated with increased risk of cardiovascular disease, but their significance and prevalence haven't yet been precisely determined. They're called contributing risk factors.

The American Heart Association has identified several risk factors. Some of them can be modified, treated or controlled, and some can't. The more risk factors you have, the greater your chance of developing coronary heart disease. Also, the greater the level of each risk factor, the greater the risk.

What Are the Major Risk Factors That Can't Be Changed?

The risk factors on this list are ones you're born with and cannot be changed. The more of these risk factors you have, the greater your chance of developing coronary heart disease. Since you can't do anything about these risk factors, it's even more important for you to manage the risk factors that can be changed.

- **Increasing Age**—The majority of people who die of coronary heart disease are 65 or older. At older ages, women who have heart attacks are more likely than men are to die from them within a few weeks.

- **Male Sex (Gender)**—Men have a greater risk of heart attack than women do, and they have attacks earlier in life. Even after menopause, when women's death rate from heart disease increases, it's not as great as men's.

- **Heredity (Including Race)**—Children of parents with heart disease are more likely to develop it themselves. African Americans have more severe high blood pressure than Caucasians and a higher risk of heart disease. Heart disease risk is also higher among Mexican Americans, American Indians, native Hawaiians and some Asian Americans. This is partly due to higher rates of obesity and diabetes. Most people with a strong family history of heart disease have one or more other risk factors. Just as you can't control your age, sex and race, you can't control your family history. Therefore, it's even more important to treat and control any other risk factors you have.

What Are the Major Risk Factors You Can Modify, Treat or Control by Changing Your Lifestyle or Taking Medicine?

- **Tobacco smoke**—Smokers' risk of developing coronary heart disease is much higher than that of nonsmokers. Cigarette smoking is a powerful independent risk factor for sudden cardiac death in patients with coronary heart disease. Cigarette smoking also acts with other risk factors to greatly increase the risk for coronary heart disease. Exposure to other people's smoke increases the risk of heart disease even for nonsmokers.

- **High blood cholesterol**—As blood cholesterol rises, so does risk of coronary heart disease. When other risk factors (such as high blood pressure and tobacco smoke) are present, this risk increases even more. A person's cholesterol level is also affected by age, sex, heredity and diet. Here's the lowdown on:

    Total Cholesterol: Your total cholesterol score is calculated using the following equation: HDL + LDL + 20 percent of your triglyceride level.

Low-density-lipoprotein (LDL) cholesterol = "bad" cholesterol

A low LDL cholesterol level is considered good for your heart health. However, your LDL number should no longer be the main factor in guiding treatment to prevent heart attack and stroke, according to the latest guidelines from the American Heart Association. For patients taking statins, the guidelines say they no longer need to get LDL cholesterol levels down to a specific target number. Lifestyle factors, such as a diet high in saturated and trans fats can raise LDL cholesterol.

High-density-lipoprotein (HDL) cholesterol = "good" cholesterol

With HDL (good) cholesterol, higher levels are typically better. Low HDL cholesterol puts you at higher risk for heart disease. People with high blood triglycerides usually also have lower HDL cholesterol. Genetic factors, type 2 diabetes, smoking, being overweight and being sedentary can all result in lower HDL cholesterol.

- **Triglycerides**—Triglyceride is the most common type of fat in the body. Normal triglyceride levels vary by age and sex. A high triglyceride level combined with low HDL cholesterol or high LDL cholesterol is associated with atherosclerosis, the buildup of fatty deposits in artery walls that increases the risk for heart attack and stroke.

- **High blood pressure**—High blood pressure increases the heart's workload, causing the heart muscle to thicken and become stiffer. This stiffening of the heart muscle is not normal, and causes the heart not to work properly. It also increases your risk of stroke, heart attack, kidney failure and congestive heart failure. When high blood pressure exists with obesity, smoking, high blood cholesterol levels or diabetes, the risk of heart attack or stroke increases even more.

- **Physical inactivity**—An inactive lifestyle is a risk factor for coronary heart disease. Regular, moderate-to-vigorous physical activity helps reduce the risk of heart and blood vessel disease. Even moderate-intensity activities help if done regularly and long term. Physical activity can help control blood cholesterol, diabetes and obesity, as well as help lower blood pressure in some people.

- **Obesity and overweight**—People who have excess body fat—especially if a lot of it is at the waist—are more likely to develop heart disease and stroke even if they have no other risk factors. Overweight and obese adults with risk factors for cardiovascular disease such as high blood pressure, high cholesterol, or high blood sugar can make lifestyle changes to lose weight and produce clinically meaningful reductions in triglycerides, blood glucose, HbA1c, and risk of developing Type 2 diabetes. Many people may have difficulty losing weight. But a sustained weight loss of 3 to 5% body weight may lead to clinically meaningful reductions in some risk factors, larger weight losses can benefit blood pressure, cholesterol, and blood glucose.

- **Diabetes mellitus**—Diabetes seriously increases your risk of developing cardiovascular disease. Even when glucose levels are under control, diabetes increases the risk of heart disease and stroke, but the risks are even greater if blood sugar is not well controlled. At least 68% of people >65 years of age with diabetes die of some form of heart disease and 16% die of stroke. If you have diabetes, it's extremely important to work with your healthcare provider to manage it and control any other risk factors you can. Persons with diabetes who are obese or overweight should make lifestyle changes (e.g., eat better, get regular physical activity, lose weight) to help manage blood sugar.

What Other Factors Contribute to Heart Disease Risk?

- **Stress**—Individual response to stress may be a contributing factor. Some scientists have noted a relationship between coronary heart disease risk and stress in a person's life, their health behaviors and socioeconomic status. These factors may affect established risk factors. For example, people under stress may overeat, start smoking or smoke more than they otherwise would.

- **Alcohol**—Drinking too much alcohol can raise blood pressure, increase risk of cardiomyopathy and stroke, cancer and other diseases. It can contribute to high triglycerides, and produce irregular heartbeats. Excessive alcohol consumption contributes to obesity, alcoholism, suicide and accidents. However, there is a cardioprotective effect of moderate alcohol consumption. If you drink, limit your alcohol consumption to no more than two drinks per day for men and no more than one drink per day for women. The National Institute on Alcohol Abuse and Alcoholism defines one drink as 1-1/2 fluid ounces (fl oz) of 80-proof spirits (such as bourbon, Scotch, vodka, gin, etc.), 5 fl oz of wine or 12 fl oz of regular beer. It's not recommended that nondrinkers start using alcohol or that drinkers increase the amount they drink.

- **Diet and Nutrition**—A healthy diet is one of the best weapons you have to fight cardiovascular disease. The food you eat (and the amount) can affect other controllable risk factors: cholesterol, blood pressure, diabetes and overweight. Choose nutrient-rich foods—which have vitamins, minerals, fiber and other nutrients but are lower in calories—over nutrient-poor foods. Choose a diet that emphasizes intake of vegetables, fruits, and whole grains; includes low-fat dairy products, poultry, fish, legumes, nontropical vegetable oils, and nuts; and limits intake of sweets, sugar-sweetened beverages, and red meats. And to maintain a healthy weight, coordinate your diet with your physical activity level so you're using up as many calories as you take in.

Goal 1: Know Your Treatment Plan

The goal is to help you learn to reduce the risk factors—such as smoking, high blood pressure, high cholesterol, physical inactivity and being overweight—that increase your chances of future health problems.

The American Heart Association and the American College of Cardiology have developed national guidelines to help you reduce the risk of future problems. These guidelines can help your doctor develop a treatment plan—including medicines and lifestyle changes such as diet and physical activity—for all your risk factors. Make sure you know your goal numbers and work with your healthcare team professionals to achieve them.

RISK FACTOR	GOAL
Smoking	Quit for good
Blood Pressure	Less than 120 mmHg (systolic) and less than 80 mmHg (diastolic)
LDL (Bad) Cholesterol	Less than 100 mg/dL
Triglycerides	Less than 150 mg/dL
HDL (Good) Cholesterol	60mg/dL or higher
Physical Activity	At least 150 minutes of moderate-intensity exercise per week. Exercise recommendations can be met through 30-60 minutes of moderate-intensity exercise (five days per week) or 20-60 minutes of vigorous-intensity exercise (three days per week)
Weight	Ideal body mass index (BMI) Is 18.5–24.9 kg/m^2
	Waist circumference not more than 40 inches for men and not more than 35 inches for women (Recommendations are lower for people of Asian descent: 37–39 inches for men and 31–35 inches for women.)
Blood Sugar (Glucose)	Normal fasting blood glucose of less than 100 mg/dL
Diabetes	If you are diabetic, a HbA1c (glycosylated hemoglobin) of less than 7 percent

ASSIGNMENT: Determine if you are at risk for heart disease.

Are you at risk? Do you know what your numbers are? It might be a good idea to find out especially since heart disease is the #1 killer of men AND women.

On the following page, answer yes or no (per the risk factors you just read about) in the "Are you at risk?" column. If you are unsure, put a "?" in this column and write below what action(s) you will take to find out if you are indeed at risk or not.

RISK FACTORS THAT CAN'T BE CHANGED	ARE YOU AT RISK?	RISK FACTORS THAT CAN BE CHANGED	YOUR NUMBERS	ARE YOU AT RISK?
Age		Smoking		
Gender		High cholesterol*		
Heredity		High blood pressure		
		Physical Inactivity		
		Obesity/Overweight		
		Diabetes		
		Stress		
		Alcohol		

* If any of the 4 items listed under "High Cholesterol" are in an unhealthy range, you are at risk.

For any risk factor I put a "?" above, I will find out if I am at risk by:

1. _____

_____

2. _____

_____

3. _____

_____

4. _____

_____

5. _____

_____

List three prevention measures YOU will take to prevent heart disease:

1. _____

2. _____

3. _____

HEART ATTACK, STROKE AND CARDIAC ARREST WARNING SIGNS

Dial 9-1-1 Fast

Some heart attacks are sudden and intense—the "movie heart attack," where no one doubts what's happening. But most heart attacks start slowly, with mild pain or discomfort. Often people affected aren't sure what's wrong and wait too long before getting help.

Immediately call 9-1-1 or your emergency response number so an ambulance (ideally with advanced life support) can be sent for you. As with men, women's most common heart attack symptom is chest pain or discomfort. But women are somewhat more likely than men to experience some of the other common symptoms, particularly shortness of breath, nausea/vomiting, and back or jaw pain. Learn more about heart attack symptoms in women.

Learn the signs, but remember this: Even if you're not sure it's a heart attack, have it checked out (tell a doctor about your symptoms). Minutes matter! Fast action can save lives—maybe your own. Call 9-1-1 or your emergency response number.

Calling 9-1-1 is almost always the fastest way to get lifesaving treatment. Emergency medical services (EMS) staff can begin treatment when they arrive—up to an hour sooner than if someone gets to the hospital by car. EMS staff are also trained to revive someone whose heart has stopped. Patients with chest pain who arrive by ambulance usually receive faster treatment at the hospital, too. It is best to call EMS for rapid transport to the emergency room.

Heart Attack Symptoms

- **Chest discomfort.** Most heart attacks involve discomfort in the center of the chest that lasts more than a few minutes, or that goes away and comes back. It can feel like uncomfortable pressure, squeezing, fullness or pain.

- **Discomfort in other areas of the upper body.** Symptoms can include pain or discomfort in one or both arms, the back, neck, jaw or stomach.

- **Shortness of breath** with or without chest discomfort.

- **Other signs** may include breaking out in a cold sweat, nausea or lightheadedness.

Stroke Symptoms

Spot a stroke F.A.S.T.

- **Face drooping.** Does one side of the face droop or is it numb? Ask the person to smile.

- **Arm weakness.** Is one arm weak or numb? Ask the person to raise both arms. Does one arm drift downward?

- **Speech difficulty.** Is speech slurred, are they unable to speak, or are they hard to understand? Ask the person to repeat a simple sentence, like "the sky is blue." Is the sentence repeated correctly?

- **Time to call 9-1-1.** If the person shows any of these symptoms, even if the symptoms go away, call 9-1-1 and get them to the hospital immediately.

Cardiac Arrest Symptoms

- **Sudden loss of responsiveness.** No response to tapping on shoulders.

- **No normal breathing.** The victim does not take a normal breath when you tilt the head up and check for at least five seconds.

What Is Stroke?

Stroke is a type of cardiovascular disease. It affects the arteries leading to and within the brain. A stroke occurs when a blood vessel that carries oxygen and nutrients to the brain is either blocked by a clot or bursts. When that happens, part of the brain cannot get the blood (and oxygen) it needs, so it starts to die.

What Are the Types of Stroke?

Stroke can be caused either by a clot obstructing the flow of blood to the brain or by a blood vessel rupturing and preventing blood flow to the brain.

Diagnosis of Stroke

When someone has shown symptoms of a stroke or a TIA (transient ischemic attack), a doctor will gather information and make a diagnosis. A doctor may use many different tests. The ones listed here are just some of the more common options.

Acute and Preventative Treatments of Stroke

Because their mechanisms are different, the treatments for the types of stroke are different.

What Are the Effects of Stroke?

The brain is an extremely complex organ that controls various body functions. If a stroke occurs and blood flow can't reach the region that controls a particular body function, that part of the body won't work as it should.

Stroke Risk Factors

Some stroke risk factors are hereditary. Others are a function of natural processes. Still others result from a person's lifestyle. You can't change factors related to heredity or natural processes, but those resulting from lifestyle or environment can be modified with the help of a healthcare professional.

Stroke Risk Factors that You Can Control, Treat or Improve

Keep your stroke risks low with regular checkups and treatment for these conditions if you have them.

- **High blood pressure—If you have high blood pressure (or hypertension), know your numbers and keep them low.** High blood pressure is the leading cause of stroke and the most significant controllable risk factor for stroke. Many scientists attribute our current decline in stroke-related deaths to the successful treatment of high blood pressure. Manage HBP.

- **Smoking—If you smoke cigarettes, take steps to stop.** Recent studies confirm that cigarette smoking is another crucial risk factor for stroke. The nicotine and carbon monoxide in cigarette smoke damage the cardiovascular system and pave the way for a stroke to occur. Additionally, the use of birth control pills combined with cigarette smoking can greatly increase the risk of stroke. Quit smoking now and lower risks.

- **Diabetes—If you have diabetes (Type 1 or 2), keep blood sugar controlled.** Diabetes Mellitus is an independent risk factor for stroke. Many people with diabetes also have high blood pressure, high blood cholesterol and are overweight. This increases their risk even more. While diabetes is treatable, the presence of the disease still increases your risk of stroke. Learn how to lower risks with diabetes and pre-diabetes. Statistics on diabetes and cardiovascular risks.

- **Diet—If your diet is poor, eat foods that improve your heart and brain health.** Diets high in saturated fat, trans fat and cholesterol can raise blood cholesterol levels. Diets high in sodium (salt) can increase blood pressure. Diets with high calories can lead to obesity. Also, a diet containing five or more servings of fruits and vegetables per day may reduce the risk of stroke. Learn how you can eat better.

- **Physical activity—If you're physically inactive, start moving and being more active.** Physical inactivity can increase your risk of stroke, heart disease, becoming overweight, developing high blood pressure, high blood cholesterol and diabetes, heart disease and stroke. So go on a brisk walk, take the stairs, and do whatever you can to make your life more active. Try to get a total of at least 30 minutes of activity on most or all days. Learn how to move more and get active.

- **Obesity—If you're obese or overweight, take steps to get your body mass into a healthy range.** Excess body weight and obesity are linked with an increased risk of high blood pressure, diabetes, heart disease and stroke. Losing as little as 5 to 10 pounds can make a significant difference in your risks. Even if weight control has been a lifelong challenge, start by taking small steps today to manage your weight and lower risks.

- **High blood cholesterol—If you have high blood cholesterol, get it under control.** People with high blood cholesterol have an increased risk for stroke. Large amounts of cholesterol in the blood can build up and cause blood clots, leading to a stroke. Also, it appears that low HDL ("good") cholesterol is a risk factor for stroke in men, but more data is needed to verify if this is true for women as well. Take control of your cholesterol.

- **Carotid artery disease—If you have carotid artery disease or other artery disease, get treatment to lower your risks.** The carotid arteries in your neck supply blood to your brain. A carotid artery narrowed by fatty deposits from atherosclerosis (plaque buildups in artery walls) may become blocked by a blood clot. Because they're located so close to the brain, carotid arteries may more easily cause a stroke, but any artery disease may contribute to a stroke.

- **Peripheral artery disease—If you have peripheral artery disease or PAD, get treatment to lower your risks.** PAD is the narrowing of blood vessels carrying blood to leg and arm muscles. It's caused by fatty buildups of plaque in artery walls. People with peripheral artery disease have a higher risk of carotid artery disease, which raises their risk of stroke.

- **Atrial fibrillation—If you have atrial fibrillation (AFib), know your AFib-Stroke risks and keep them low.** AFib (a heart rhythm disorder) increases stroke risks fivefold. That's because it causes the heart's upper chambers to beat incorrectly, which can allow the blood pool and clot to travel to the brain and cause a stroke. A resulting clot can travel to the brain and cause a stroke. If you have AFib, know your stroke risks. If you're at risk, get treatment to keep risks low. Also, sleep apnea can be linked to AFib and is associated with increased stroke risks.

- **Other heart disease—If you have other heart disease, manage related conditions and work with your healthcare provider.** People who have coronary heart disease or heart failure are at higher risk of stroke than people who have healthy hearts. Dilated cardiomyopathy (an enlarged heart), heart valve disease and some types of congenital heart defects can also raise the risk of stroke.

- **Sickle cell disease—If you have sickle cell disease (also called sickle cell anemia), seek treatment early.** This treatable genetic disorder mainly affects African-American and Hispanic children. "Sickled" red blood cells are less able to carry oxygen to the body's tissues and organs. These cells also tend to stick to blood vessel walls, which can block arteries to the brain and cause a stroke.

Stroke Risk Factors that Are Not within Your Control

You can't control some risk factors, but knowing that they exist may help motivate you to work harder on the ones you can change.

- **Age matters.** The likelihood of having a stroke nearly doubles every 10 years after age 55. Although stroke is more common among the elderly, a lot of people under 65 also have strokes. Even babies and children can sometimes have a stroke.
- **A family history of stroke can raise your risk.** If your parent, grandparent, sister or brother has had a stroke—especially before reaching age 65—you may be at greater risk. Sometimes strokes are caused by genetic disorders like CADASIL, which can block blood flow in the brain.
- **Race can make a difference.** Statistics show that African-Americans have a much higher risk of death from a stroke than Caucasians do. This is partly because blacks have higher risks of high blood pressure, diabetes and obesity. Visit our Empowered to Serve program to learn more. Hispanics and latinos also have unique risks for stroke.
- **Your sex (gender) can affect your risks.** Each year, women have more strokes than men, and stroke kills more women than men, too. Factors that may increase stroke risks for women include: pregnancy, history of preeclampsia/eclampsia or gestational diabetes, oral contraceptive use (especially when combined with smoking) and post-menopausal hormone therapy. Be sure to discuss your specific risks with your doctor.
- **Prior stroke, TIA or heart attack can raise your risk.** A person who has had a prior stroke has a much higher risk of having another stroke than a person who has never had one. Transient ischemic attacks (TIAs) or are also strong predictors of stroke. TIAs are smaller, temporary blockages in the brain that can produce milder forms of stroke-like symptoms but may not leave lasting damage. A person who's had one or more TIAs is almost 10 times more likely to have a stroke than someone of the same age and sex who hasn't. Recognizing and treating TIAs can reduce your risk of a major stroke. TIA should be considered a medical emergency and followed up immediately with a healthcare professional. If you've had a prior heart attack, you're at higher risk of having a stroke, too. A heart attack is a plaque buildup that causes blockages in the blood vessels to the heart. Similarly, most strokes are caused by buildups of plaque that cause blockages in the brain.

Additional Factors that May Be Linked to Higher Stroke Risks

- **Geographic location can make a difference.** Strokes are more common in the southeastern United States than in other areas. These are the so-called "stroke belt" states. Check out your state and consider how it supports healthy habits.

- **Socioeconomic factors may have an impact.** There's some evidence that strokes are more common among those with lower incomes. One reason may be because smoking and obesity rates are also higher. Another reason may be that access to quality healthcare is often more limited at lower income levels. Support quality healthcare for all.

- **Alcohol abuse can raise risk multiple.** In fact, in can lead to medical complications, including stroke. If you drink alcohol, we recommend no more than two drinks per day for men and no more than one drink per day for non-pregnant women, based on current evidence for lowering stroke risk. See recommendations. As always, pregnant women are advised to abstain from alcohol. Speak with your doctor or a local support group if you need help overcoming addiction to alcohol.

- **Drug abuse is associated with increased risk.** The most commonly abused drugs, including cocaine, amphetamines and heroin, have been associated with an increased risk of stroke. Drug addiction is often a chronic relapsing disorder associated with a number of societal and health-related problems. Strokes caused by drug abuse are often seen in a younger population. Steer clear of potentially addicting substances and see a doctor if you need support for overcoming substance abuse.

- **Sleep habits can affect stroke risk factors.** Recent studies have begun to clarify the reasons that people who get regular, good quality sleep tend to have lower heart disease and stroke risks. Adopt habits that promote healthy sleep patterns.

Whether your risks are related to changeable factors or are primarily outside of your control, you can benefit your heart and your brain with healthy lifestyle choices.

ASSIGNMENT: Determine if you are at risk for stroke.

Are you at risk? Do you know what your numbers are?

Answer yes or no (per the risk factors you just read about) in the "Are you at risk?" column. If you are unsure, put a "?" in this column and write below what action(s) you will take to find out if you are indeed at risk or not.

RISK FACTORS THAT CAN'T BE CHANGED	ARE YOU AT RISK?	RISK FACTORS THAT CAN BE CHANGED	YOUR NUMBERS	ARE YOU AT RISK?
Age		High Blood Pressure		
Gender		Cigarette Smoking		
Heredity		Diabetes		
Prior Stroke, TIA, or Heart Attack		Carotid or Other Artery Disease		
		Atrial Fibrillation		
		Other Heart Disease		
		Sickle Cell Disease		
		High Cholesterol		
		Poor Diet		
		Physical Inactivity/Obesity		
		Geographic Location		
		Socioeconomic Factors		
		Alcohol		
		Drug Abuse		

For any risk factor I put a "?" above, I will find out if I am at risk by:

1. _____

_____

2. _____

_____

3. _____

_____

4. _____

_____

5. _____

_____

List three prevention measures YOU will take to prevent stroke:

1. _____

2. _____

3. _____

Metabolic Syndrome

What Is

Metabolic syndrome is the name for a group of risk factors that raises your risk for heart disease and other health problems, such as diabetes and stroke.

The term "metabolic" refers to the biochemical processes involved in the body's normal functioning. Risk factors are traits, conditions, or habits that increase your chance of developing a disease.

In this article, "heart disease" refers to coronary heart disease (CHD). CHD is a condition in which a waxy substance called plaque builds up inside the coronary (heart) arteries.

Plaque hardens and narrows the arteries, reducing blood flow to your heart muscle. This can lead to chest pain, a heart attack, heart damage, or even death.

Causes

Metabolic syndrome has several causes that act together. You can control some of the causes, such as overweight and obesity, an inactive lifestyle, and insulin resistance.

You can't control other factors that may play a role in causing metabolic syndrome, such as growing older. Your risk for metabolic syndrome increases with age.

You also can't control genetics (ethnicity and family history), which may play a role in causing the condition. For example, genetics can increase your risk for insulin resistance, which can lead to metabolic syndrome.

People who have metabolic syndrome often have two other conditions: excessive blood clotting and constant, low-grade inflammation throughout the body. Researchers don't know whether these conditions cause metabolic syndrome or worsen it.

Researchers continue to study conditions that may play a role in metabolic syndrome, such as:

- A fatty liver (excess triglycerides and other fats in the liver)

- Polycystic ovarian syndrome (a tendency to develop cysts on the ovaries)

- Gallstones

- Breathing problems during sleep (such as sleep apnea)

Risk Factors

People at greatest risk for metabolic syndrome have these underlying causes:

- Abdominal obesity (a large waistline)

- An inactive lifestyle

- Insulin resistance

- Some people are at risk for metabolic syndrome because they take medicines that cause weight gain or changes in blood pressure, blood cholesterol, and blood sugar levels. These medicines most often are used to treat inflammation, allergies, HIV, and depression and other types of mental illness.

Populations Affected

Some racial and ethnic groups in the United States are at higher risk for metabolic syndrome than others. Mexican Americans have the highest rate of metabolic syndrome, followed by whites and blacks.

Other groups at increased risk for metabolic syndrome include:

- People who have a personal history of diabetes

- People who have a sibling or parent who has diabetes

- Women when compared with men

- Women who have a personal history of polycystic ovarian syndrome (a tendency to develop cysts on the ovaries)

- Heart Disease Risk

- Metabolic syndrome increases your risk for coronary heart disease. Other risk factors, besides metabolic syndrome, also increase your risk for heart disease. For example, a high LDL ("bad") cholesterol level and smoking are major risk factors for heart disease. For details about all of the risk factors for heart disease, go to the Coronary Heart Disease Risk Factors Health Topic.

Even if you don't have metabolic syndrome, you should find out your short-term risk for heart disease. The National Cholesterol Education Program (NCEP) divides short-term heart disease risk into four categories. Your risk category depends on which risk factors you have and how many you have.

Your risk factors are used to calculate your 10-year risk of developing heart disease. The NCEP has an online calculator that you can use to estimate your 10-year risk of having a heart attack.

- **High risk:** You're in this category if you already have heart disease or diabetes, or if your 10-year risk score is more than 20 percent.

- **Moderately high risk:** You're in this category if you have two or more risk factors and your 10-year risk score is 10 percent to 20 percent.

- **Moderate risk:** You're in this category if you have two or more risk factors and your 10-year risk score is less than 10 percent.

- **Lower risk:** You're in this category if you have zero or one risk factor.

Even if your 10-year risk score isn't high, metabolic syndrome will increase your risk for coronary heart disease over time.

Screening and Prevention

The best way to prevent metabolic syndrom is to adopt heart-healthy lifestyle changes. Make sure to schedule routine doctor visits to keep track of your cholesterol, blood pressure, and blood sugar levels. Speak with your doctor about a blood test called a lipoprotein panel, which shows your levels of total cholesterol, LDL cholesterol, HDL cholesterol, and triglycerides.

Signs, Symptoms, and Complications

Metabolic syndrome is a group of risk factors that raises your risk for heart disease and other health problems, such as diabetes and stroke. These risk factors can increase your risk for health problems even if they're only moderately raised (borderline-high risk factors).

Most of the metabolic risk factors have no signs or symptoms, although a large waistline is a visible sign.

Some people may have symptoms of high blood sugar if diabetes—especially type 2 diabetes—is present. Symptoms of high blood sugar often include increased thirst; increased urination, especially at night; fatigue (tiredness); and blurred vision.

High blood pressure usually has no signs or symptoms. However, some people in the early stages of high blood pressure may have dull headaches, dizzy spells, or more nosebleeds than usual.

Treatment

Heart-healthy lifestyle changes are the first line of treatment for metabolic syndrome. If heart-healthy lifestyle changes aren't enough, your doctor may prescribe medicines. Medicines are used to treat and control risk factors, such as high blood pressure, high triglycerides, low HDL ("good") cholesterol, and high blood sugar.

Goals of Treatment

The major goal of treating metabolic syndrome is to reduce the risk of coronary heart disease. Treatment is directed first at lowering LDL cholesterol and high blood pressure and managing diabetes (if these conditions are present).

The second goal of treatment is to prevent the onset of type 2 diabetes, if it hasn't already developed. Long term complications of diabetes often include heart and kidney disease, vision loss, and foot or leg amputation. If diabetes is present, the goal of treatment is to reduce your risk for heart disease by controlling all of your risk factors.

Heart-Healthy Lifestyle Changes

Heart-healthy lifestyle changes include heart-healthy eating, aiming for a healthy weight, managing stress, physical activity, and quitting smoking.

Medicines

Sometimes lifestyle changes aren't enough to control your risk factors for metabolic syndrome. For example, you may need statin medications to control or lower your cholesterol. By lowering your blood cholesterol level, you can decrease your chance of having a heart attack or stroke. Doctors usually prescribe statins for people who have:

- Diabetes

- Heart disease or had a prior stroke

- High LDL cholesterol levels

- Doctors may discuss beginning statin treatment with those who have an elevated risk for developing heart disease or having a stroke.

Your doctor also may prescribe other medications to:

- Decrease your chance of having a heart attack or dying suddenly.

- Lower your blood pressure.

- Prevent blood clots, which can lead to heart attack or stroke.

- Reduce your heart's workload and relieve symptoms of coronary heart disease.

- Take all medicines regularly, as your doctor prescribes. Don't change the amount of your medicine or skip a dose unless your doctor tells you to. You should still follow a heart-healthy lifestyle, even if you take medicines to treat your risk factors for metabolic syndrome.

SOURCE: www.nhlbi.nih.gov

ASSIGNMENT: Determine if you are at risk for metabolic syndrome.

Are you at risk? Do you know what your numbers are?

Answer yes or no (per the risk factors you just read about) in the "Are you at risk?" column. If you are unsure, put a "?" in this column and write below what action(s) you will take to find out if you are indeed at risk or not.

RISK FACTORS	YOUR NUMBERS	ARE YOU AT RISK?
Waist measurement (men > 40 inches; women > 35 inches)		
Blood Pressure of 130/85 + or on blood pressure medications		
Triglycerides of 150 +		
Blood Glucose of 100 + or on glucose lowering medications		
HDL (<40 for men; <50 for women)		

For any risk factor I put a "?" above, I will find out if I am at risk by:

1. _____

_____

2. _____

_____

3. _____

_____

4. _____

_____

5. _____

_____

List three prevention measures YOU will take to prevent stroke:

1. _____

2. _____

3. _____

DIABETES MELLITUS

What Is Diabetes Mellitus?

Diabetes is a disease in which the body doesn't produce or properly use insulin. Insulin is a hormone produced in the pancreas, an organ near the stomach. Insulin is needed to turn sugar and other food into energy. When you have diabetes, your body either doesn't make enough insulin or can't use its own insulin as well as it should, or both. This causes sugars to build up too high in your blood.

Diabetes mellitus is defined as a fasting blood glucose of 126 milligrams per deciliter (mg/dL) or more. "Pre-diabetes" is a condition in which blood glucose levels are higher than normal but not yet diabetic. People with pre-diabetes are at increased risk for developing type 2 diabetes, heart disease and stroke, and have one of these conditions:

- **impaired fasting glucose** (100 to 125 mg/dL)

- **impaired glucose tolerance** (fasting glucose less than 126 mg/dL and a glucose level between 140 and 199 mg/dL two hours after taking an oral glucose tolerance test)

What Are Type 1 and Type 2 Diabetes?

Type 2 diabetes is the most common form. It appears most often in middle-aged adults; however, adolescents and young adults are developing type 2 diabetes at an alarming rate. It develops when the body doesn't make enough insulin and doesn't efficiently use the insulin it makes (insulin resistance).

Type 1 diabetes usually occurs in children and young adults. In type 1, the pancreas makes little or no insulin. Without daily injections of insulin, people with type 1 diabetes won't survive.

Both forms of diabetes may be inherited in genes. A family history of diabetes can significantly increase the risk of developing diabetes. Untreated diabetes can lead to many serious medical problems. These include blindness, kidney disease, nerve disease, limb amputations and cardiovascular disease (CVD).

How Are Insulin Resistance, Diabetes and CVD Related?

Diabetes is treatable, but even when glucose levels are under control, it greatly increases the risk of heart disease and stroke. In fact, most people with diabetes die of some form of heart or blood vessel disease.

Pre-diabetes and subsequent type 2 diabetes usually result from insulin resistance. When insulin resistance or diabetes occur with other CVD risk factors (such as obesity, high blood pressure, abnormal cholesterol and high triglycerides), the risk of heart disease and stroke rises even more.

Insulin resistance is associated with atherosclerosis (fatty buildups in arteries) and blood vessel disease, even before diabetes is diagnosed. That's why it's important to prevent and control insulin resistance and diabetes. Obesity and physical inactivity are important risk factors for insulin resistance, diabetes and cardiovascular disease.

How Is Diabetes Treated?

When diabetes is detected, a doctor may prescribe changes in eating habits, weight control and exercise programs, and even drugs to keep it in check. It's critical for people with diabetes to have regular checkups. Work closely with your healthcare provider to manage diabetes and control any other risk factors. For example, blood pressure for people with diabetes and high blood pressure should be **lower than 120/80 mm Hg.**

AHA Recommendation

Diabetes is a major risk factor for stroke and coronary heart disease, which includes heart attack. People with diabetes may avoid or delay heart and blood vessel disease by controlling the other risk factors. It's especially important to control weight and blood cholesterol with a low-saturated-fat, low-cholesterol diet and regular aerobic physical activity. It's also important to lower high blood pressure and not to smoke.

Reprinted with permission. www.americanheart.org © 2012, American Heart Association, Inc.

ASSIGNMENT: Determine if you are at risk for diabetes.

Are you at risk? Do you know what your numbers are?

Take the American Diabetes Association's Diabetes Risk Test (diabetes.org/risk-test.jsp) and find out if you are at risk.

- What was your score?
- Are you at very low risk, low to medium risk, or high risk?
- What does your score mean?
- What is their advice for how to keep your risk low?

Answer yes or no (per the risk factors you just read about) in the "Are you at risk?" column. If you are unsure, put a "?" in this column and write below what action(s) you will take to find out if you are indeed at risk or not.

RISK FACTORS	YOUR NUMBERS	ARE YOU AT RISK?
I have been experiencing one or more of the symptoms indicated on page xx.		
Body Mass Index > 25 or Waist Circumference (men > 40 in; women > 35 in)		
Blood Pressure of 120/80 +		
Triglycerides of 150 +		
Prediabetes: Impaired fasting glucose (100 to 125 mg/dL)		
Prediabetes: Impaired glucose tolerance (fasting glucose less than 126 mg/dL and a glucose level between 140 and 199 mg/dL two hours after taking an oral glucose tolerance test)		
Parent or sibling with type 2 diabetes		
African American, Latino, Native American, and Asian American/Pacific Islander		
HDL (<40 for men; < 50 for women)		
Physical Inactivity		
Women only: Gestational diabetes or delivered a baby weighing more than 9 pounds		
Women only: Diagnosed with polycystic ovary syndrome		

For any risk factor I put a "?" above, I will find out if I am at risk by:

1. _____

_____

2. _____

_____

3. _____

_____

4. _____

_____

5. _____

_____

List three prevention measures YOU will take to prevent stroke:

1. _____

2. _____

3. _____

How Do I Prevent or Delay Diabetes?

Pre-diabetes is a serious medical condition that is treatable. The good news is that the recently completed Diabetes Prevention Program (DPP) study conclusively showed that people with pre-diabetes can prevent the development of type 2 diabetes by making changes in their diet and increasing their level of physical activity. They may even be able to return their blood glucose levels to the normal range.

While the DPP also showed that some medications may delay the development of diabetes, diet and exercise worked better. Just 30 minutes a day of moderate physical activity, coupled with a 5–10% reduction in body weight, produced a 58% reduction in diabetes.

WHAT YOU NEED TO KNOW ABOUT SMOKING AND TOBACCO USE

Health Effects of Smoking

Cigarette smoking is the number one cause of preventable disease and death worldwide. Smoking-related diseases claim more than 480,000 American lives each year. Smoking cost the U.S. at least $289 billion each year, including at least $150 billion in lost productivity and $130 billion in direct healthcare expenditures.[1] This is an average of close to $7,000 per adult smoker.[1]

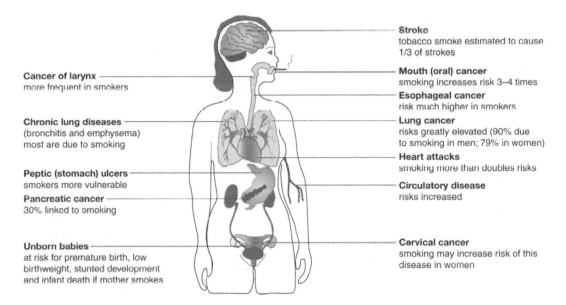

Stroke
tobacco smoke estimated to cause
1/3 of strokes

Mouth (oral) cancer
smoking increases risk 3–4 times

Esophageal cancer
risk much higher in smokers

Lung cancer
risks greatly elevated (90% due
to smoking in men; 79% in women)

Heart attacks
smoking more than doubles risks

Circulatory disease
risks increased

Cervical cancer
smoking may increase risk of this
disease in women

Cancer of larynx
more frequent in smokers

Chronic lung diseases
(bronchitis and emphysema)
most are due to smoking

Peptic (stomach) ulcers
smokers more vulnerable

Pancreatic cancer
30% linked to smoking

Unborn babies
at risk for premature birth, low
birthweight, stunted development
and infant death if mother smokes

The Health Effects of Smoking
Adapted from "The Human Effects of Smoking" *Lifetime Physical Fitness & Wellness* by Hoeger and Hoeger, Wadsworth Publishing.

Key Facts about Smoking

Cigarette smoke contains more than 7,000 chemicals, at least 69 of which are known to cause cancer.[2] Smoking is directly responsible for approximately 90 percent of lung cancer deaths and approximately 80 percent of deaths caused by chronic obstructive pulmonary disease (COPD), including emphysema and chronic bronchitis.[3]

Among adults who have ever smoked daily, 87 percent had tried their first cigarette by the time they were 18 years of age, and 95 percent had by age 21.[1]

Among current smokers, chronic lung disease accounts for 73 percent of smoking-related conditions. Even among smokers who have quit, chronic lung disease still accounts for 50 percent of smoking-related conditions.[4]

Smoking harms nearly every organ in the body, and is a main cause of lung cancer and COPD. It also is a cause of coronary heart disease, stroke and a host of other cancers and diseases.[1]

Smoking Rates among Adults & Youth

In 2015, an estimated 36.5 million, or 15.1 percent of adults 18 years of age and older were current smokers.[5]

Men tend to smoke more than women. In 2015, 16.7 percent of men currently smoked compared to 13.6 percent of women.[5]

Prevalence of current smoking in 2015 was highest among American Indians/ Alaska Natives (21.9 percent), non-Hispanic whites (16.6 percent) and non-Hispanic blacks (16.8 percent), and was lowest among Hispanics (10.1 percent) and Asian-Americans (7.0 percent).[5]

In 2015, 9.3 percent of high school students and 2.3 percent of middle school students were current cigarette users.[6]

Facts about Quitting Smoking

Nicotine is the chemical in cigarettes that causes addiction. Smokers not only become physically addicted to nicotine; they also link smoking with many social activities, making smoking an extremely difficult addiction to break.[7]

In 2015, an estimated 52.8 million adults were former smokers. Of the 36.5 million current adult smokers, 49.2 percent stopped smoking for a day or more in the preceding year because they were trying to quit smoking completely.[5]

Quitting smoking for good often requires multiple attempts. Using counseling or medication alone increases the chance of a quit attempt being successful; the combination of both is even more effective.[8]

There are seven medications approved by the U.S. Food and Drug Administration to aid in quitting smoking. Nicotine patches, nicotine gum and nicotine lozenges are available over the counter, and a nicotine nasal spray and inhaler are currently available by prescription. Buproprion SR (Zyban®) and varenicline (Chantix®) are non-nicotine pills.[8]

Individual, group and telephone counseling are effective. Telephone quitline counseling is available in all 50 states and is effective for many different groups of smokers.[8]

Learn about the American Lung Association's programs to help you or a loved one quit smoking, and join our advocacy efforts to reduce tobacco use and exposure to secondhand smoke. Visit Lung.org or call the Lung HelpLine at 1-800-LUNGUSA (1-800-586-4872).

SOURCES:

1. U.S. Department of Health and Human Services. The Health Consequences of Smoking—50 Years of Progress: A Report of the Surgeon General. 2014.

2. U.S. Department of Health and Human Services. How Tobacco Smoke Causes Disease: The Biology and Behavioral Basis for Smoking-Attributable Disease A Report of the Surgeon General.

3. Centers for Disease Control and Prevention. Health Effects of Cigarette Smoking Fact Sheet. 2014.

4. U.S. Department of Health and Human Services. The Health Consequences of Smoking: A Report of the Surgeon General, 2004.

5. Centers for Disease Control and Prevention. National Center for Health Statistics. National Health Interview Survey, 2015. Analysis performed by the American Lung Association Epidemiology and Statistics Unit using SPSS software.

6. Centers for Disease Control and Prevention. Tobacco Use Among Middle and High School Students—United States, 2011–2014. *Morbidity and Mortality Weekly Report.* April 17, 2015; 64(14):381–5.

7. National Institute on Drug Abuse. Tobacco/Nicotine Research Report: Is Nicotine Addictive? 2012.

8. National Health Interview Survey Raw Data, 2012. Analysis by the American Lung Association Epidemiology and Statistics Unit Using SPSS Software.

9. Fiore M, Jaen C, Baker T, et al. Treating Tobacco Use and Dependence: 2008 Update. Clinical Practice Guideline. Vol 35. Rockville, MD; 2008.

Benefits of Quitting

As soon as you quit, your body begins to repair the damage caused by smoking. See the health benefits you'll experience as soon as 20 minutes to 15 years after quitting.

20 Minutes After Quitting:

- Your heart rate drops to a normal level.

12 Hours After Quitting:

- The carbon monoxide level in your blood drops to normal.

2 Weeks to 3 Months After Quitting:

- Your risk of having a heart attack begins to drop.
- Your lung function begins to improve.

1 to 9 Months After Quitting:

- Your coughing and shortness of breath decrease.

1 Year After Quitting:

- Your added risk of coronary heart disease is half that of a smoker's.

5 to 15 Years After Quitting:

- Your risk of having a stroke is reduced to that of a nonsmoker's.
- Your risk of getting cancer of the mouth, throat, or esophagus is half that of a smoker's.

10 Years After Quitting:

- Your risk of dying from lung cancer is about half that of a smoker's.
- Your risk of getting bladder cancer is half that of a smoker's.
- Your risk of getting cervical cancer or cancer of the larynx, kidney or pancreas decreases.

15 Years After Quitting:

- Your risk of coronary heart disease is the same as that of a nonsmoker.

SOURCE: U.S. Department of Health and Human Services. The Health Consequences of Smoking: A Report of the Surgeon General. Atlanta, GA: U.S. Department of Health and Human Services, Centers for Disease Control and Prevention, National Center for Chronic Disease Prevention and Health Promotion, Office on Smoking and Health, 2004.

What Is Nicotine Withdrawal?

According to the National Institutes of Health, almost all people who try to quit have some form of nicotine withdrawal. Generally, people who smoked longer or a higher number of cigarettes are more likely to have withdrawal symptoms. The severity of the symptoms is also dependent on the duration of smoking and number of cigarettes smoked. People who are regular smokers tend to have particularly strong cravings and worsening of withdrawal symptoms at certain times, places, or situations associated with smoking.

Common feelings of nicotine withdrawal include:

- Feeling depressed

- Not being able to sleep

- Getting cranky, frustrated, or mad

- Feeling anxious, nervous, or restless

- Having trouble thinking clearly

- Feeling hungry or gaining weight

Not everyone has feelings of withdrawal. You may have one or many of these problems. And they may last different amounts of time.

Steps to Take on Your Quit Day

1. Quitting smoking is easier with the support of others. Tell your family, friends, and coworkers that you plan to quit. Tell them how they can help you. Some people like to have friends ask how things are going. Others find it nosy. Tell the people you care about exactly how they can help. Here are some ideas:

   - Ask everyone to understand your change in mood. Remind them that this won't last long. (The worst will be over within two weeks.) Tell them this: "The longer I go without cigarettes, the sooner I'll be my old self."

   - Does someone close to you smoke? Ask them to quit with you, or at least not to smoke around you.

   - Do you take any medicines? Tell your doctor and pharmacist you are quitting. Nicotine changes how some drugs work. You may need to change your prescriptions after you quit.

   - Get support from other people. You can try talking with others one-on-one or in a group. You can also get support on the phone. You can even try an Internet chat room. This kind of support helps smokers quit. The more support you get, the better. But even a little can help.

2. Keep Busy.

   - Go to a movie.

   - Exercise.

   - Take long walks.

- Go bike riding.

- Spend as much free time as you can where smoking isn't allowed. Some good places are malls, libraries, museums, theaters, department stores, and places of worship.

- Do you miss having a cigarette in your hand? Hold something else. Try a pencil, a paper clip, a marble, or a water bottle.

- Do you miss having something in your mouth? Try toothpicks, cinnamon sticks, lollipops, hard candy, sugarfree gum, or carrot sticks.

- Drink a lot of water and fruit juice. Avoid drinks like wine and beer. They can trigger you to smoke.

3. Stay Away from What Tempts You.

   - Instead of smoking after meals, get up from the table. Brush your teeth or go for a walk.

   - If you always smoke while driving, try something new: Listen to a new radio station or your favorite music. Take a different route. Or take the train or bus for a while, if you can.

   - Stay away from things that you connect with smoking. Do it today and for the next few weeks. These may include:

     - Watching your favorite TV show

     - Sitting in your favorite chair

     - Having a drink before dinner

   - Do things and go places where smoking is not allowed. Keep this up until you're sure that you can stay smoke-free.

   - Remember, most people don't smoke. Try to be near nonsmokers if you must be somewhere you'll be tempted to smoke, for example at a party or in a bar.

4. Know Your Smoking Triggers. Certain things trigger, or turn on, your need for a cigarette. They can be moods, feelings, places, or things you do. Knowing your triggers is very important. It can help you stay away from things that tempt you to smoke. It can prepare you to fight the urge when you are tempted.

   - Stay away from places where smoking is allowed. Sit in the non-smoking section at restaurants.

   - Keep your hands busy. Hold a pencil or paper clip. Doodle or write a letter. Carry a water bottle.

   - Stay away from people who smoke. Spend time with non-smoking friends.

- Put something else in your mouth. Chew sugarfree gum. Snack on a carrot or celery stick. Keep your mouth and hands busy with a toothpick, sugarfree lollipop, or straw.

- Drink less or stay away from alcohol. Drinking alcohol often makes people want to smoke. Drink juice, soda, or ice water instead.

- Remember: The urge to smoke will come and go. Cravings usually last only for a very brief period of time. Try to wait it out.

What to Do If You Do Slip

Don't be discouraged if you slip up and smoke one or two cigarettes. It's not a lost cause. One cigarette is better than an entire pack. But that doesn't mean you can safely smoke every now and then, no matter how long ago you quit. One cigarette may seem harmless, but it can quickly lead back to one or two packs a day.

Many ex-smokers had to try stopping many times before they finally succeeded. When people slip up, it's usually within the first three months after quitting. Here's what you can do if this happens:

- Understand that you've had a slip. You've had a small setback. This doesn't make you a smoker again.

- Don't be too hard on yourself. One slip up doesn't make you a failure. It doesn't mean you can't quit for good.

- Don't be too easy on yourself either. If you slip up, don't say, "Well, I've blown it. I might as well smoke the rest of this pack." It's important to get back on the non-smoking track right away. Remember, your goal is no cigarettes—not even one puff.

- Feel good about all the time you went without smoking. Try to learn how to make your coping skills better.

- Find the trigger. Exactly what was it that made you smoke? Be aware of that trigger. Decide now how you will cope with it when it comes up again.

- Learn from your experience. What has helped you the most to keep from smoking? Make sure to do that on your next try.

- Are you using a medicine to help you quit? Don't stop using your medicine after only one or two cigarettes. Stay with it. It will help you get back on track.

- Know and use the tips in this booklet. People with even one coping skill are more likely to stay nonsmokers than those who don't know any. START to stop again!

- See your doctor or another health professional. He or she can help motivate you to quit smoking.

Visit the smokefree.gov or the American Cancer Society's website (cancer.org) for help with quitting. Above all, don't get discouraged if you aren't able to quit smoking the first time. Nicotine addiction is a hard habit to break. Try something different next time.

ASSIGNMENT: Complete the following smoking tests. If you do not smoke, please note this for your instructor below.

"WHY DO YOU SMOKE? TEST

	ALWAYS	FREQUENTLY	OCCASIONALLY	SELDOM	NEVER
A. I smoke cigarettes to keep myself from slowing down.	5	4	3	2	1
B. Handling a cigarette is part of the enjoyment of smoking it.	5	4	3	2	1
C. Smoking cigarettes is pleasant and relaxing.	5	4	3	2	1
D. I light up a cigarette when I feel angry about something.	5	4	3	2	1
E. When I have run out of cigarettes, I find it almost unbearable until I can get them.	5	4	3	2	1
F. I smoke cigarettes automatically without even being aware of it.	5	4	3	2	1
G. I smoke cigarettes for the stimulation, to perk myself up.	5	4	3	2	1
H. Part of the enjoyment of smoking a cigarette comes from the steps I take to light up.	5	4	3	2	1
I. I find cigarettes pleasurable.	5	4	3	2	1
J. When I feel uncomfortable or upset about something, I light up a cigarette.	5	4	3	2	1
K. I am very much aware of the fact when I am not smoking a cigarette.	5	4	3	2	1
L. I light up a cigarette without realizing I still have one burning in the ashtray.	5	4	3	2	1
M. I smoke cigarettes to give me a "lift."	5	4	3	2	1
N. When I smoke a cigarette, part of the enjoyment is watching the smoke as I exhale it.	5	4	3	2	1
O. I want a cigarette most when I am comfortable and relaxed.	5	4	3	2	1

(continues)

	ALWAYS	FREQUENTLY	OCCASIONALLY	SELDOM	NEVER
P. When I feel "blue" or want to take my mind off cares and worries, I smoke cigarettes.	5	4	3	2	1
Q. I get a real gnawing hunger for a cigarette when I haven't smoked for a while.	5	4	3	2	1
R. I've found a cigarette in my mouth and didn't remember putting it there.	5	4	3	2	1

SCORING YOUR TEST:

Enter the numbers you have circled on the test questions in the spaces provided below, putting the number you circled for question A on line A, for question B on line B, etc. Add the three scores on each line to get a total for each factor. For example, the sum of your scores for lines A, G, and M gives you your score on "Stimulation," lines B, H, and N give the score on "Handling," etc. Scores can vary from 3 to 15. Any score 11 and above is high; any score 7 and below is low.

A _____ + G _____ + M _____ = _____ Stimulation

B _____ + H _____ + N _____ = _____ Handling

C _____ + I _____ + O _____ = _____ Pleasure/Relaxation

D _____ + J _____ + P _____ = _____ Crutch: Tension Reduction

E _____ + K _____ + Q _____ = _____ Craving: Psychological Addiction

F _____ + L _____ + R _____ = _____ Habit

U.S. Department of Health and Human Services.

"DO YOU WANT TO QUIT?" TEST

	STRONGLY AGREE	MILDLY AGREE	MILDLY DISAGREE	STRONGLY DISAGREE
A. Cigarette smoking might give me a serious illness.	4	3	2	1
B. My cigarette smoking sets a bad example for others.	4	3	2	1
C. I find cigarette smoking to be a messy kind of habit.	4	3	2	1
D. Controlling my cigarette smoking is a challenge to me.	4	3	2	1
E. Smoking causes shortness of breath.	4	3	2	1
F. If I quit smoking cigarettes, it might influence others to stop.	4	3	2	1
G. Cigarettes damage clothing and other personal property.	4	3	2	1
H. Quitting smoking would show that I have willpower.	4	3	2	1
I. My cigarette smoking will have a harmful effect on my health.	4	3	2	1

J. My cigarette smoking influences others close to me to take up continue smoking.	4	3	2	1
K. If I quit smoking, my sense of taste or smell would improve.	4	3	2	1
L. I do not like the idea of feeling dependent on smoking.	4	3	2	1

SCORING YOUR TEST:

Write the number you have circled after each statement on the test in the corresponding space to the right. Add the scores on each line to get your totals. For example, the sum of your scores A, E, I gives you your score for the Health factor. Scores can vary from 3 to 12. Any score of 9 or over is high, and a score of 6 or under is low.

A _____ + E _____ + I _____ = Health
B _____ + F _____ + J _____ = Example
C _____ + G _____ + K _____ = Aesthetics
D _____ + H _____ + L _____ = Mastery

U.S. Department of Health and Human Services.

WHAT YOU NEED TO KNOW ABOUT CANCER AND CANCER PREVENTION

According to the CDC, cancer is the #2 cause of death among Americans.

What Is Cancer?

Cancer is a term for diseases in which abnormal cells divide without control and can invade other tissues. Cancer cells can spread to other parts of the body through the blood and lymph systems. Cancer is not just one disease but many diseases. There are more than 100 different types of cancer. The main categories of cancer include:

- Carcinoma—cancer that begins in the skin or in tissues that line or cover internal organs.

- Sarcoma—cancer that begins in bone, cartilage, fat, muscle, blood vessels, or other connective or supportive tissue.

- Leukemia—cancer that starts in blood-forming tissue such as the bone marrow and causes the production of large numbers of abnormal blood cells that then enter the blood.

- Lymphoma and myeloma—cancers that begin in the cells of the immune system.

- Central nervous system cancers—cancers that begin in the tissues of the brain and spinal cord.

All cancers begin in cells, the body's basic unit of life. To understand cancer, it's helpful to know what happens when normal cells become cancer cells. The body is made up of many types of cells. These cells grow and divide in a controlled way to produce more cells as needed to keep the body healthy. When cells become old or damaged, they die, and new cells replace them.

But sometimes this orderly process goes wrong. The genetic material (DNA) of a cell can become damaged or changed, producing mutations that affect normal cell growth and division. When this happens, cells do not die when they should, and new cells form when the body does not need them. The extra cells may form a mass of tissue called a tumor. Not all tumors are cancerous; tumors can be benign or malignant.

- Benign tumors aren't cancerous. They can often be removed, and, in most cases, they do not come back. Cells in benign tumors do not spread to other parts of the body.

- Malignant tumors are cancerous. Cells in these tumors can invade nearby tissues and spread to other parts of the body. The spread of cancer from one part of the body to another is called metastasis.

Most cancers are named for the organ or type of cell in which they begin. For example, cancer that begins in the stomach is called stomach cancer. Some cancers do not form tumors. For example, leukemia is a cancer of the bone marrow and blood.

Cancer Signs and Symptoms

Cancer can cause many different symptoms. These are some of them:

- A thickening or lump in the breast or any other part of the body

- A new mole or a change in an existing mole

- A sore that does not heal

- Hoarseness or a cough that does not go away

- Changes in bowel or bladder habits

- Discomfort after eating

- A hard time swallowing

- Weight gain or loss with no known reason

- Unusual bleeding or discharge

- Feeling weak or very tired

Most often, these symptoms are not due to cancer. They may also be caused by benign tumors or other problems. Only a doctor can tell for sure. Anyone with these symptoms or other changes in health should see a doctor to diagnose and treat problems as early as possible. Usually, early cancer does not cause pain. If you have symptoms, do not wait to feel pain before seeing a doctor.

To learn more about specific cancers, you can visit the National Cancer Institute's website (cancer.gov) or the American Cancer Society's website (cancer.org) and click on "Learn about Cancer/Choose a Cancer Topic."

Cancer Risk Factors

Doctors often cannot explain why one person develops cancer and another does not. But research shows that certain *risk factors* increase the chance that a person will develop cancer. These are the most common risk factors for cancer:

- Growing older
- Tobacco
- Sunlight
- Ionizing radiation
- Certain chemicals and other substances
- Some viruses and bacteria
- Certain hormones
- Family history of cancer
- Alcohol
- Poor diet, lack of physical activity, or being overweight

You can avoid many of these risk factors. Others, such as family history, you cannot avoid. People can help protect themselves by staying away from known risk factors whenever possible. Over time, several factors may act together to cause normal cells to become cancerous. When thinking about your risk of getting cancer, these are some things to keep in mind:

- Not everything causes cancer.
- An injury, such as a bump or a bruise, does not cause cancer.
- Cancer is not contagious. Although being infected with certain viruses or bacteria may increase the risk of some types of cancer, no one can "catch" cancer from another person.
- Having one or more risk factors does not mean that you will get cancer. Most people who have risk factors never develop cancer.
- Some people are more sensitive than others to the known risk factors.

Cancer Prevention

A variety of different factors can cause cancer, and they may develop over a number of years. *You can control some risk factors.* Choosing the right health behaviors and preventing exposure to certain environmental risk factors can help prevent the development of cancer. For this reason, we will focus on two major groups of risk factors: Behavioral and Environmental.

BEHAVIORAL FACTORS

Scientists estimate that human behaviors such as smoking, physical inactivity, and poor dietary choices cause as many as 50–75% of cancer deaths in the U.S. The following are all behaviors that can help to prevent cancer.

Tobacco Use

Smoking causes about 30% of all U.S. deaths from cancer. *Avoiding tobacco use is the single most important step Americans can take to reduce the cancer burden in this country.* The younger a person starts smoking, the greater the lifelong risk of developing smoking-related cancers. That is because young smokers are more likely to become addicted, and the more years a person smokes, the greater the risk of cancer.

Diet

Maintaining a healthy weight and eating a moderate-fat diet and enough fruits and vegetables while limiting consumption of red meat and avoiding too much alcohol is also an important step in reducing cancer risk. People whose diets are rich in plant foods such as fruits and vegetables have a lower risk of getting cancers of the mouth, pharynx, larynx, esophagus, stomach, and lung, and there is some suggested evidence for colon, pancreas, and prostate. To help prevent these cancers and other chronic diseases, experts recommend 4 to 13 servings of fruits and vegetables daily, depending on energy needs. This includes 2 to 5 servings of fruits and 2 to 8 servings of vegetables, with special emphasis on dark green and orange vegetables and legumes. There is no evidence that the popular white potato protects against cancer.

Physical Activity

Compelling evidence exists that prevention of obesity reduces the risk for many of the most common cancers, such as colon, postmenopausal breast, uterine, esophageal, and renal cell cancers. Estimates are that 20–30% of these cancers—some of the most common cancers in the United States—may relate to being overweight and/or lack of physical activity. Obesity is estimated to cause 14% of cancer deaths in men and 20% of cancer deaths in women.

Sun Protection

The number of new cases of melanoma skin cancer has increased between 1975 and 2004, with an estimated number of 60,000 new cases in 2007. More than one million people receive diagnoses of basal cell and squamous cell (non-melanoma) skin cancer in the United States every year. Basal and squamous cell cancers are the two most common types of skin cancers in the country. Although 40–50% of Americans who live to age 65 will have these two types of skin cancer at least once, they can prevent most of these cancers and melanoma skin cancers. Studies suggest that reducing unprotected exposure to the sun and to artificial light from tanning beds, tanning booths, and sun lamps can lower the risk of skin cancer. Avoiding sunburns, intermittent high intensity exposure, and other damage from these sources—especially in children and teens—reduces the chances of getting melanoma skin cancer. All of these types of skin cancers are most common in light-skinned people, although they also occur in people with darker skin.

ENVIRONMENTAL FACTORS

Certain chemicals, biological agents, toxins, etc. are associated with cancer development. This section reports national trends data associated with environmental exposures and their relationship to cancer.

Secondhand Smoke

Secondhand smoke (SHS), also known as environmental tobacco smoke, is a mixture of the sidestream smoke released by the smoldering cigarette and the mainstream smoke exhaled by the smoker. Like mainstream smoke, it is a complex mixture containing thousands of chemicals, including formaldehyde, cyanide, carbon monoxide, ammonia, and nicotine. At least 250 chemicals in SHS are known to be toxic and/or cancer causing agents.

Exposure of adults to SHS has immediate adverse effects on the cardiovascular system and causes coronary heart disease and lung cancer. In 2005, the California Environmental Protection Agency estimated that SHS exposure causes approximately 3,400 lung cancer deaths and approximately 46,000 heart disease deaths among nonsmoking adults in the United States annually, as well as causing 430 SIDS deaths annually among U.S. infants. There is no risk-free level of exposure to SHS, and only eliminating smoking in indoor spaces fully protects nonsmokers from exposure to SHS.

Chemical Exposures

Pesticides are chemicals used to eliminate or control unwanted or harmful insects, plants, fungi, animals, or microorganisms in order to protect food crops and other plants. Some pesticides have been classified as carcinogens. Chlordane and dichlorodiphenyltrichloroethane (DDT) are possible human carcinogens. General studies of people with high exposures to pesticides, such as farmers, pesticide applicators, manufacturers, and crop dusters, have found high rates of blood and lymphatic system cancers and cancers of the lip, stomach, lung, brain, and prostate, as well as melanoma and other skin cancers.

Dioxins are chemicals produced through paper and pulp bleaching; burning of municipal, toxic, and hospital wastes; certain electrical fires; and smelters. Dioxins can also exist in some insecticides, herbicides, wood preservatives, and cigarette smoke. There are at least 100 different kinds of dioxins, including Tetrachlorodibenzo-p-dioxin (TCDD). The most common routes of exposure for dioxins occur through the diet, particularly from animal fats. Not all dioxins can cause cancer. TCDD is a particular dioxin that is likely to cause cancer in humans. The general population becomes exposed to low levels of TCDD primarily from eating dairy products, fish, and meat.

LEADING SITES OF NEW CANCER CASES AND DEATHS—2007 ESTIMATES		
CANCER TYPE	ESTIMATED NEW CASES	ESTIMATED DEATHS
Bladder	81,190	17,240
Breast (Female—Male)	266,120–2,550	40,920–480
Colon and Rectal (Combined)	140,250	50,630
Endometrial	63,230	11,350
Kidney (Renal Cell and Renal Pelvis) Cancer	65,340	14,970
Leukemia (All Types)	60,300	24,370
Liver and Intrahepatic Bile Duct	42,220	30,200
Lung (Including Bronchus)	234,030	154,050
Melanoma	91,270	9,320
Non-Hodgkin Lymphoma	74,680	19,910
Pancreatic	55,440	44,330
Prostate	164,690	29,430
Thyroid	53,990	2,060

SOURCE: www.cancer.gov

ASSIGNMENT: Take the Torabi Cancer Prevention Test.

Torabi Cancer Prevention Scale

Please read each behavioral statement carefully. Using the following scale, record your reaction to the statement by writing the letter that best characterizes YOUR BEHAVIOR concerning each numbered item in the space provided.

a = Always   b = Most of the time   c = Sometimes   d = Rarely   e = Never

1. I talk to a cancer patient.   _____
2. I am a volunteer for institutions that deal with cancer education.   _____
3. I read materials on cancer.   _____
4. I talk with my friends about cancer.   _____
5. I drink alcoholic beverages daily.   _____
6. I have been drinking alcoholic beverages for several years.   _____
7. I smoke cigarettes daily.   _____

8. I have been smoking cigarettes for several years. _____

9. I chew tobacco. _____

10. I observe my body carefully for any kind of physical changes. _____

11. I have regular physical checkups. _____

12. I update myself with new discoveries in cancer prevention. _____

13. I stay away from polluted areas. _____

14. I see a doctor as soon as I feel any problems with my lungs. _____

15. I sit in the smoking section of restaurants. _____

16. I look for a lump or deformity in my own/partner's breasts when I do breast examination. _____

17. I read materials on breast self-examination. _____

18. I ask professionals about preventing breast cancer. _____

19. I encourage my friends to have regular pelvic exams. _____

20. I distribute materials on prevention of uterine cancer. _____

21. I read materials on uterine cancer. _____

22. I exclude refined food from my daily diet. _____

23. I have a daily diet high in fiber. _____

24. I stay away from a high-fat diet as much as I can. _____

25. I use sunscreens whenever I am exposed to the sun. _____

26. I sunbathe before 10:00 A.M. or after 3:00 P.M. _____

27. I sunbathe with no protection. _____

28. I encourage my friends to get a prostatic checkup. _____

29. I read some materials on prevention of prostate cancer. _____

30. I distribute materials on prevention of prostate cancer. _____

SCORING:

For items 5 through 9, 38, and 50, "always" equals 1 point; "most of the time," 2 points; "sometimes," 3 points; "rarely," 4 points; and "never," 5 points. For the remaining items, reverse the order of values assigned to alternatives, with "always" equaling 5 points; "most of the time," 4 points; "sometimes," 3 points; "rarely" 2 points; and "never," 1 point. The higher score is interpreted as more healthy behavior in cancer prevention.

SOURCE: Torabi, M.R. (1991). A Cancer Prevention Behavior Scale. *American Journal of Health Behavior,* formerly *Health Values,* 15(3), 21–25. Copyright © 1991 by PNG Publications. Reprinted with permission.

WHAT YOU NEED TO KNOW ABOUT SLEEP AND YOUR HEALTH

Sleep Facts and Stats

For the Sleep Facts & Figures Section

Good health was related to good sleep: Americans were asked to rate their general health, quality of life, physical health and mental health.

- Almost half (48%) rated their general health highly, as very good or excellent, and just over half (54%) also rated their quality of life highly.

- In addition, 44% rated their physical health highly and 60% rated their mental health highly. Likewise, greater stress was associated with less sleep and worse sleep quality.

- Approximately 1 in 10 people (12%) had severe or very severe stress in the previous 7 days and another 31% reported moderate levels of stress.

Pain was also associated with lower sleep quality, more sleep problems, and greater sleep debt: Those experiencing pain in the past 7 days slept less and had worse sleep quality than those without pain.

- On average, those with no pain slept 7.3 hours in the past week, while those with acute pain slept 7.0 hours and those with chronic pain slept 6.7 hours. Those with an average pain severity that was mild got an average of 7.0 hours of sleep, compared to 6.5 hours for those with severe or very severe pain (and 6.9 hours for those with moderate pain).

- Likewise, when asked how often they get a good night's sleep, 68% of Americans with no pain said often or always in the past 7 days, compared to 47% of those with acute pain and only 39% of those with chronic pain.

- Among those with mild pain, 53% report always/often getting a good night's sleep, compared to only 39% of those with moderate pain and 27% of those with severe or very severe pain.

- Those with chronic pain were 3 times more likely to have been diagnosed with a sleep disorder than those with no pain or acute pain. Specifically, 23% of those with chronic pain were diagnosed with sleep disorder compared with 6% of everyone else.

- People in pain felt less in control of their sleep and they reported worrying more about the effects of poor sleep on their health.

Difficulty sleeping interferes with life more among people with either acute or chronic pain: 40% reported sleep problems in the last week according to the NIH.

- They people were asked how the sleeping difficulties interfered with 5 domains of life: their mood, daily activities, enjoyment of life, relationships with other people and ability to do work, chores, child care, or other duties.

- People who have chronic or acute pain are more likely to have sleeping difficulties interfere with their life. For example, 52% of those with chronic pain indicate that sleeping difficulties interfere with their work, compared to 23% of those without pain. Thus, sleep difficulties appear to have a greater impact on the lives of those in pain.

Sleep attitudes associated with better sleep: Sleep attitudes were associated with longer sleep durations and better sleep quality.

- People who said they were very or extremely motivated to get enough sleep reported sleeping 36 more minutes per night across the week compared to those were not that motivated or not motivated at all (7.3 vs. 6.7 hours).

- Those who were more motivated also said they needed more sleep to feel their best.

- Those who were very or extremely motivated said they wanted 7.4 hours of sleep per night compared to 7.0 hours for those who were not motivated.

- Sleep quality was also higher among those more motivated to get enough sleep: 62% reported good or very good sleep quality compared with 41% of those who were not that motivated or not at all motivated.

- People who were very or extremely motivated were less likely to report difficulty sleeping in the past 7 days compared with those not that motivated or not motivated at all (29% vs 39%).

Overall Sleep Patterns

- On average people went to bed at 11:02PM and woke at 7:05AM on workdays and went to bed at 11:24PM and woke at 8:13AM on free days.

- They spent 7.9 hours in bed on work days and 8.6 hours on free days.

- They reported sleeping 6.9 hours on work days and 7.6 hours on free days resulting in an average of 7.1 hours across the week.

- *Sleep efficiency*, a commonly-used marker of sleep quality, was calculated by dividing sleep duration by time spent in bed. The average sleep efficiency was 88% on work days and 89% on free days.

- Americans indicated that they would prefer to sleep 7.3 hours per night on average. Comparing the preferred sleep amount to actual time spent sleeping gives us an estimate of *sleep debt*.

- The average sleep debt on work days was approximately 26 minutes, indicating that on average Americans would prefer to sleep 26 minutes more than they do on work days.

- On free days, however, the average was -17 minutes, indicating that on average on free days Americans were getting 17 minutes more sleep than they felt they needed.

- When asked about sleep quality in the past 7 days, 52% reported very good or good sleep quality, 36% reported fair sleep quality, and 13% reported poor or very poor sleep quality.

- When asked about how often they get a good night's sleep in general, 13% of Americans reported rarely or never, 32% reported sometimes and 54% said often or always.

- When asked how often health problems make it difficult to get a good night's sleep, only 29% said Never. 40% said rarely, 20% said sometimes, and 10% reported Often or Always.

- 9% of Americans report they had been diagnosed with a sleep disorder by a doctor or medical professional. Of them, 71% were diagnosed with apnea and 24% with insomnia.

SOURCE: http://www.sleephealthjournal.org/pb/assets/raw/Health%20Advance/journals/sleh/2015Sleepin AmericaPollSummaryofFindings.pdf

How Much Sleep Do We Really Need?

Ellen Caroll has often asked herself this exact question—especially when it comes to helping her family members get the amount of sleep they need. With a son in preschool and a daughter in high school, a husband who works over 50 hours a week and aging parents, one with Parkinson's disease, Ellen's family runs the gamut when it comes to age and sleep needs. Because all of Ellen's family members have busy schedules, they often forget to put their sleep needs ahead of their other priorities. Not only does Ellen need to convince her family that getting the right amount of sleep is important, but she also needs to figure out how much sleep they really need!

If you're like Ellen and her family, you're probably also confused about how to know when "enough is enough" in regards to your sleep. While news media and health organizations are regularly saying to get more sleep, it might be unclear to you how many hours of sleep you should be getting and how to tell if you are adequately rested. Keep reading and we'll explore how you can make educated decisions about your sleep and that of your family members'.

What the Research Says about Sleep Duration

The first thing experts will tell you about sleep is that there is no "magic number." Not only do different age groups need different amounts of sleep, but sleep needs are also *individual.* Just like any other characteristics you are born with, the amount of sleep you need to function best may be different for you than for someone who is of the same age and gender. While you may be at your absolute best sleeping seven hours a night, someone else may clearly need nine hours to have a happy, productive life. In fact, a 2005 study confirmed the fact that sleep needs vary across populations, and the study calls for further research to identify traits within genes that may provide a "map" to explain how sleep needs differ among individuals.

Another reason there is "no magic number" for your sleep results from two different factors that researchers are learning about: a person's *basal sleep need*—the amount of sleep our bodies need on a regular basis for optimal performance—and *sleep debt,* the accumulated sleep that is lost to poor sleep habits, sickness, awakenings due to environmental factors or other causes. Two studies suggest that healthy adults have a basal sleep need of seven to eight hours every night, but where things get complicated is the interaction between the basal need and sleep debt. For instance, you might meet your basal sleep need on any single night or a few nights in a row, but still have an unresolved sleep debt that may make you feel more sleepy and less alert at times, particularly in conjunction with *circadian dips,* those times in the 24-hour cycle when we are biologically programmed to be more sleepy and less alert, such as overnight hours and mid-afternoon. You may feel overwhelmingly sleepy quite suddenly at these times, shortly before bedtime or feel sleepy upon awakening. The good news is that some research suggests that the accumulated sleep debt can be worked down or "paid off."

Though scientists are still learning about the concept of basal sleep need, one thing sleep research certainly has shown is that sleeping too little can not only inhibit your productivity and ability to remember and consolidate information, but lack of sleep can also lead to serious health consequences and jeopardize your safety and the safety of individuals around you.

For example, short sleep duration is linked with:

- Increased risk of motor vehicle accidents

- Increase in body mass index—a greater likelihood of obesity due to an increased appetite caused by sleep deprivation

- Increased risk of diabetes and heart problems

- Increased risk for psychiatric conditions including depression and substance abuse

- Decreased ability to pay attention, react to signals or remember new information

According to researchers Michael H. Bonnet and Donna L. Arand, "There is strong evidence that sufficient shortening or disturbance of the sleep process compromises mood, performance and alertness and can result in injury or death. In this light, the most common-sense 'do no injury' medical advice would be to avoid sleep deprivation."

On the other hand, some research has found that long sleep durations (nine hours or more) are also associated with increased morbidity (illness, accidents) and mortality (death). Researchers describe this relationship as a "U-shaped" curve where both sleeping too little and sleeping too much may put you at risk. This research found that variables such as low socioeconomic status and depression were significantly associated with long sleep. Some researchers argue that these other variables might be the cause of the longer sleep: the fact that individuals with low socioeconomic status are more likely to have undiagnosed illnesses because of poor medical care explains the relationship between low socioeconomic status, long sleep and morbidity/mortality. Researchers caution that there is not a definitive conclusion that getting more than nine hours of sleep per night is consistently linked with health problems and/or mortality in adults, while short sleep has been linked to both these consequences in numerous studies.

"Currently, there is no strong evidence that sleeping too much has detrimental health consequences, or even evidence that our bodies will allow us to sleep much beyond what is required," says Kristen L. Knutson, PhD, Department of Health Studies, University of Chicago. "There is laboratory evidence that short sleep durations of 4–5 hours have negative physiological and neurobehavioral consequences. We need similar laboratory and intervention studies to determine whether long sleep durations (if they can be obtained) result in physiological changes that could lead to disease before we make any recommendations against sleep extension."

But a key question is how much is too much or too little. Researchers Shawn Youngstedt and Daniel Kripke reviewed two surveys of more than 1 million adults conducted by the American Cancer Society and found that the group of people who slept seven hours had less mortality after six years than those sleeping both more and less. The group of people who slept shorter amounts and those who slept longer than eight hours had an average mortality risk that was greater, but the risk was higher for longer sleepers. Youngstedt and Kripke argue that for those who would normally sleep longer than eight hours, restricting their sleep may actually be healthier for them, just as eating less than one's appetite may be healthier in a more sendentary society.

What Your Body Is Saying about Your Sleep Needs

After looking at the research, the next step in identifying your sleep need is taking a "snapshot" of your sleeping habits. Ellen began this process by looking qualitatively at each family member's sleep habits and their behaviors during the day. Here's what she found:

Her teenage daughter was a lot of fun to be around at night—she was energetic and in high spirits, chatting with her family during dinner, talking on the phone with friends, playing on her computer and squeezing in an hour of TV. Whenever Ellen would try and get her off to bed, she'd complain that she didn't feel tired. Nevertheless, when her alarm would usher in another day of high school at 6:30 AM, Ellen's daughter Terri was NOT fun to be around. Irritable, tired and unhappy, Terri would head off to school with a bad start to the day, not to mention the fact that she had difficulty staying awake in her classes. What Ellen and Terri may not know is that Terri's biology and age play a large role in her sleep habits. As a teenager, her circadian rhythms are geared to stay up later in the evening and to wake later in the morning. As a result, a 10 o'clock bedtime may feel too early to her body, and a 6:30 AM wake time certainly doesn't fit her current sleep/wake schedule. But the biggest problem is that adolescents still need lots of sleep—at least nine hours every night and it is hard to get that much when biology says "stay up late" and school says "start early."

Ellen never thought that her young son could be sleep deprived. After all, she thought, sleep deprivation occurs when you're a "night owl" teenager or over-worked adult, not a four year-old! What Ellen may not know is that children need much more sleep than their adult counterparts to be well-rested. Experts estimate that preschoolers (3 to 5 years-old) need 11–13 hours of sleep, while school-aged children up to age 12 need approximately 10–11 hours of sleep. Ellen's son Josh frequently adapts to his family's late-night schedule and doesn't usually take naps—in fact, when he falls asleep in the car, it is usually past his bedtime or the day after getting too little sleep. As a result of "going along with the family routine," he's often shortchanged on sleep. Unfortunately, it shows up in whiny behavior and even tantrums that he has otherwise outgrown.

As a mother of two in her forties, Ellen is used to sacrificing her own sleep needs for that of her family's. She squeezes in a busy day at work and has lots to do around the house, not to mention spending time with her children and husband. By day's end she feels exhausted, but hasn't had time to herself and doesn't want to sleep. As a woman, Ellen has also had unique sleep experiences from those of her family members. Ellen's sleeping habits have undergone many changes throughout her life. As a pregnant woman her sleep needs changed with each trimester, and she battled common sleep problems during pregnancy such as heartburn, leg cramps and snoring. As Ellen approaches menopause, she will face new sleep challenges like hot flashes and may experience insomnia.

Ellen's husband Roger is a *busy* executive who often spends early mornings and late nights working. When he's not working he's often thinking about working, and this has led to a lot of insomnia and sleeplessness nights. Roger's sleep deprivation is starting to show—he has difficulty enjoying time with his family and has lost his desire to exercise as he used to. This pattern forms a vicious cycle because the less Roger sleeps the more likely he is to eat. Research has found links between appetite increase and sleep deprivation due to hormones that are produced when you're short on sleep. This can not only lead to gaining weight, but his sleep deprivation and weight gain could lead to serious health problems like the onset of sleep apnea, hypertension, heart attack, diabetes and stroke. Roger knows that most adults need 7–9 hours to feel well-rested, but he has trouble "turning off" his mind at the end of the day to get the sleep he needs.

Ellen's aging father has Parkinson's disease and faces a number of unique challenges related to his sleep. Regardless of his illness, as an older adult his sleep is different than when he was younger. For example, elderly people tend to spend very little time in deep sleep and are more easily aroused or awakened. Nevertheless, their average total sleep time increases slightly after age 65, but many older adults divide their sleep between daytime naps and nighttime sleep. Napping, though, may decrease the need to sleep at night and some older people complain of difficulty falling asleep or staying asleep. Lack of exercise may also take a toll on elder sleep and medications may make a person feel drowsy and wanting to sleep during the day. These problems should be discussed with a physician.

As you can see, sleep needs vary across ages and are especially impacted by lifestyle and health. Thus, to determine how much sleep you need, it's important to assess not only where you fall on the "sleep needs spectrum," but also to examine what lifestyle factors are affecting the quality and quantity of your sleep such as work schedules and stress. To get the sleep you need, you must look at the big picture.

Though research cannot pinpoint an exact amount of sleep need by people at different ages, the following table identifies the "rule-of-thumb" amounts most experts have agreed upon. Nevertheless, it's important to pay attention to your own individual needs by assessing how you feel on different amounts of sleep. Are you productive, healthy and happy on seven hours of sleep? Or does it take you nine hours of quality ZZZs to get you into high gear? Do you have health issues such as being overweight? Are you at risk for any disease? Are you experiencing sleep problems? Do you depend on caffeine to get you through the day? Do you feel sleepy when driving? These are questions that must be asked before you can find the number that works for you.

What You Can Do

To begin a new path towards healthier sleep and a healthier lifestyle, begin by assessing your own individual needs and habits. See how you respond to different amounts of sleep. Pay careful attention to your mood, energy and health after a poor night's sleep versus a good one. Ask yourself, "How often do I get a good night's sleep?" If the answer is "not often," then you may need to consider changing your sleep habits or consulting a physician or sleep specialist. When Ellen's family members began this process, they realized that often they weren't getting what they would call a "good night's sleep." This led each of them to reevaluate how much sleep they needed and whether their sleep habits were healthy ones.

To pave the way for better sleep, experts recommend that you and your family members follow these sleep tips:

- Establish consistent sleep and wake schedules, even on weekends

- Create a regular, relaxing bedtime routine such as soaking in a hot bath or listening to soothing music—begin an hour or more before the time you expect to fall asleep

- Create a sleep-conducive environment that is dark, quiet, comfortable and cool

- Sleep on a comfortable mattress and pillows

- Use your bedroom only for sleep and sex (keep "sleep stealers" out of the bedroom—avoid watching TV, using a computer or reading in bed)

- Finish eating at least 2–3 hours before your regular bedtime

- Exercise regularly during the day or at least a few hours before bedtime

- Avoid caffeine and alcohol products close to bedtime and give up smoking

If you or a family member are experiencing symptoms such as sleepiness during the day or when you expect to be awake and alert, snoring, leg cramps or tingling, gasping or difficulty breathing during sleep, prolonged insomnia or another symptom that is preventing you from sleeping well, you should consult your primary care physician or sleep specialist to determine the underlying cause. You may also try keeping a sleep diary to track your sleep habits over a one- or two-week period and bring the results to your physician.

Most importantly, make sleep a priority. You must schedule sleep like any other daily activity, so put it on your "to-do list" and cross it off every night. But don't make it the thing you do only after everything else is done—stop doing other things so you get the sleep you need.

> Take a tip from Ellen Carol. She said that "After our family made a commitment to getting the sleep we need, it seemed that my husband and I were both more productive with the time we had and the kids seemed a little less grumpy and excitable. Overall, making sleep a priority is something we are going to continue to do."

Helping Yourself to a Good Night's Sleep

Difficulty falling or staying asleep is a common problem. About half of Americans report sleep difficulty at least occasionally, according to National Sleep Foundation surveys. These woes—called insomnia by doctors—have far-reaching effects: a negative impact on concentration, productivity and mood.

Fortunately, there are many things you can do to improve your sleep. The first step requires some detective work. You'll need to examine your diet, exercise patterns, sleeping environment, personal habits, lifestyle and current concerns. As you begin to see the connection between, for example, what and/or when you eat and nights of poor sleep, you can develop your own good sleep plan.

Keep in mind that good sleep doesn't always just happen. Like a successful play, a restful night of ZZZs demands a strong director's hand and a stage set appropriately. If you've been sleeping poorly for some time, you may have fallen into some bad sleep habits that reinforce your problem. Read on to learn more about sleep.

Just Say No . . . to Caffeine and Alcohol?

All too often, we eat and drink without thinking about the effects. That afternoon cup of coffee seems like a good idea at the time. The dinnertime wine may appear a fitting celebration of the day's success. But that same drink can prove an enemy of restful sleep.

Coffee contains caffeine, as do many teas, chocolate and cola drinks. Caffeine is a stimulant, which means it has an alerting or wake-up effect. For some people, a small amount of caffeine early in the day can cause problems falling asleep ten to 12 hours later. Others have learned to avoid caffeine-containing drinks and foods within six hours of bedtime.

How you respond to caffeine is individual; it is also related to how much caffeine you have regularly. For example, the more coffee you drink each day, the less powerful its effect as a stimulant.

How to determine caffeine's effect on you? Try eliminating caffeinated food and drink after lunch for a few weeks. Are you sleeping better? If so, you may have identified the culprit.

Alcohol, in contrast, is often thought of as a sedative: a calming drug. However, while alcohol may speed the beginning of sleep, it actually increases the number of times you awaken in the later half of the night. If your sleep isn't restful, alcohol (beer, wine, hard liquor) may be the cause. Skip the nightcap and see if your sleep improves.

Are You What You Eat?

Caffeine and alcohol aren't the only substances that affect your sleep. Everything you eat can affect nighttime slumber. For example, tomato products and spicy foods give many people heartburn (as does eating too fast). What does heartburn have to do with sleep? Lying down makes heartburn worse, and heartburn itself makes falling asleep more difficult. Heartburn also awakens sleepers with middle-of-the-night discomfort.

Drinking too much of any beverage can lead to more awakenings because of the need to urinate during the night. Also, the older we get, the more we experience these nighttime awakenings.

Try to restrict your fluids before bedtime to help promote an uninterrupted night's sleep. If the problem persists, talk to your doctor.

Another cause of sleep problems can be eating too much—of any food—that can make sleep difficult. A heavy meal close to bedtime may make you less comfortable when you settle down for your night's rest. At the same time, going to bed hungry can be just as disruptive to sleep as going to bed too full.

Bedtime Snack Facts

- Do not eat or drink too much close to bedtime.

- Consider a small snack to ease bedtime hunger pains.

Saying Goodbye to Tobacco?

Smokers and nonsmokers alike may not be aware that nicotine, like caffeine, is a stimulant. And when smokers go to sleep, they experience nicotine withdrawal. Research suggests that nicotine is linked to difficulty falling asleep and problems waking up. Smokers may also experience more nightmares. Giving up smoking may cause more sleep problems at first, but the long-term effect on sleep and health is much better. So kick those cigarettes goodbye.

Exercise Has Many Benefits

The next place to look for the cause of a sleep problem is your exercise routine. Exercise can be a boon for good sleep, especially when done regularly in the afternoon and not too close to bedtime. If you don't exercise regularly, add good sleep to a long list of reasons why you should take up the practice.

Why not try an afternoon brisk walk, run or bicycle ride instead of a coffee break? Consider combining aerobic (activity that increases the heart rate) exercise with a weight-bearing or resistance workout. (Be sure to check with your physician before beginning any exercise routine.) Research suggests that exercise at this time can help deepen your sleep, which means that you spend more time in deeper stages of sleep. During the lighter stages of sleep, awakenings are more common. Also, people who exercise may take less time to fall asleep than people who don't.

When you exercise, whether you are physically fit and a regular or occasional exerciser, the type of exercise you select, and your age or sex may all affect sleep. Some studies suggest that exercise 2–3 hours before bedtime can keep sleep at bay.

Traditionally, sleep experts have cautioned people to avoid strenuous exercise right before sleep and even up to three hours before bedtime. That's because exercise has an alerting effect and raises your body temperature. This rise leads to a corresponding fall in temperature five to six hours later, which makes sleep easier then. That's why late afternoon may be the perfect time for your exercise. If you've been exercising close to bedtime and having trouble falling or staying asleep, try to arrange your workout earlier in the day.

Screen Time and Sleep

- Suppresses Melatonin
- Keeps your brain alert
- Wakes you up

https://sleep.org/articles/ways-technology-affects-sleep/

- The bright screen light from devices can cause increased alertness
- Activities on such devices can be stimulating and make us less ready to sleep
- People can become absorbed and continue using technology beyond their usual bedtime

https://www.sleephealthfoundation.org.au/public-information/fact-sheets-a-z/802-technology-sleep.html

Sleep Tips

Want a better night's sleep? Try the following:

- Consume less or no caffeine and avoid alcohol.
- Drink less fluids before going to sleep.
- Avoid heavy meals close to bedtime.
- Avoid nicotine.
- Exercise regularly, but do so in the daytime, preferably after noon.
- Try a relaxing routine, like soaking in hot water (a hot tub or bath) before bedtime.
- Establish a regular bedtime and waketime schedule.
- Keep a sleep diary before and after you try these tips. If the quality of your sleep does not improve, share this diary with your doctor.

Is It Hot . . . or Humid Enough for You?

Finding and maintaining the right temperature for sleep sounds easy . . . but it isn't. Even sleep researchers fail to agree on the ideal temperature. In general, most sleep scientists believe that a slightly cool room contributes to good sleep. That's because it matches what occurs deep inside the body, when the body's internal temperature drops during the night to its lowest level. (For good sleepers, this occurs about four hours after they begin sleeping.)

But how cool should the bedroom be? And what should couples do who share a bed but disagree about the desired sleep temperature? Turning the thermostat down at night in cold weather saves on fuel bills and sets the stage for sleep. Blankets or comforters can lock in heat without feeling too heavy or confining. An electric blanket may help. Or the heat-seeking partner might dress in warmer bedclothes (even socks!), while the warmer partner might shun sleep clothes or bed covering.

In summer, a room that's too hot can also be disruptive. In fact, research suggests that a hot sleeping environment leads to more wake time and light sleep at night, while awakenings multiply. An air conditioner or fan can help.

Remember the common summer complaint: It's not the heat, it's the humidity? If excess humidity is a problem, consider a dehumidifier.

If too dry an environment is your problem, consider a humidifier. Clues like awakening with a sore throat, dryness in your nose, or even a nose bleed are signs of too little humidity. Note: Be sure to change the water daily.

Body Heating and Sleep

Interestingly, body-heating can have a very different effect from a warm room during sleep. Some studies suggest that soaking in hot water (such as a hot tub or bath) before retiring to bed can ease the transition into a deeper sleep.

This may be due to a temperature shift (core body temperature drops after leaving the tub, which may signal the body it's time to sleep). Or the sleep improvement may be related to the water's relaxing properties, which may also have sleep-promoting effects.

A pre-bedtime bath may set the mood for children and adults alike. Why not try soaking in hot water to ease your journey to sleep?

Are You Enlightened about Light . . . and Dark?

People who work at night know all too well the problem of trying to sleep when the world around them is wide awake. When the sun's rays come streaming in, it's even harder. But the sun is more than a sign that it's daytime. Light—strong light, like sunlight—is the most powerful regulator of our biological clock. The biological clock influences when we feel sleepy and when we are alert.

When do you get your sunlight exposure? People who are housebound get little. In fact, the cause of your sleep difficulty may be just that: too little exposure to sunlight.

If you find yourself waking earlier than you'd like, why not try increasing your exposure to bright light in the evening? If sunlight isn't available, consider a lightbox (or light visor) available from a specialty store. Either way, as little as one to two hours of evening bright light exposure appears to help you to sleep longer in the morning. This may be especially helpful for the elderly.

During sleep, bright lights can disturb your sleep. Keep your bedroom dark (consider light-blocking shades, lined drapes, even an eye mask) so light doesn't interfere with your passage to slumber.

A sleep specialist can help determine whether changing your exposure to light might improve your sleep, and when would be the best time for you to experience bright light.

What's All the Noise About?

Do you find your sleep disrupted by noises such as the screech of sirens, the rumble of trains, the rise and fall of conversation, airplanes overhead, a dog's barking, or a partner's snoring? You may be surrounded by a steady stream of noise or it may occur in sudden peaks.

Older people may be particularly bothered by noise. Because their sleep may be frail, it is more likely to be disturbed by lower levels of noise.

Noise Control

If noise is disturbing your sleep, consider:

- ear plugs
- white noise, which comes from a noise-making machine such as a fan or generator
- rugs
- heavy curtains or drapes
- double-pane windows
- relaxing music or tapes

Is Your Bed All That It Can Be?

Many people change where they live or what they drive more often than they change their mattress or pillows. Yet nothing lasts forever.

Although there isn't much published research on mattresses, mattress quality may affect how sleep feels to the sleeper. Discomfort can make falling asleep more difficult and lead to restless slumber.

Does your mattress provide the support you like? Do you wake with your back aching? Is there enough room for you and your sleep partner? Do you sleep better, or worse, when you sleep away from home?

Mattresses may be made of inner springs, foam, fabric, water or air. They may be firmer or more responsive to your body. This, in turn, may affect body temperature and humidity, as well as comfort.

What Does Your Bed Mean to You?

If you can fall asleep easily on your sofa or chair, and it is difficult to fall asleep in your own bed, you may be associating your bed with everything but sleep. Do you use your bed for work? Balance your checkbook while propped against the pillows? Watch television there? These are ways to tell your body to be alert in bed, not to go to sleep.

To teach patients to associate their bed and bedroom with sleep, sleep specialists advise a strategy called stimulus control, performed under the supervision of a specialist. Patients learn to use their bed only for sleep and to follow a regular wake-up schedule.

Another effective approach involves restricting your time in bed, initially, to the number of hours you actually sleep. Then, as you can rely on sleeping these hours regularly, you increase your time in bed by 15–30 minutes per night. A less dramatic approach would be to decrease your time in bed by 30 to 60 minutes.

Reclaiming Your Bed for Sleep

- Use your bed only for sleep and sex.

- Only get into bed when you're tired.

- If you don't fall asleep within 15 minutes, get out of bed. When you're sleepy, go back to bed.

- While in bed, don't dwell on not sleeping or your anxiety will increase.

- Think relaxing thoughts: picture yourself soothed in a tub of hot water, or drifting to sleep, each muscle relaxed.

Are You Trying Too Hard?

Some sleep specialists say that anxiously watching the clock while focusing on how much time you have yet to sleep may actually cause insomnia. Try setting your alarm, then hiding it and your watch before you go to bed.

Are You Playing by the Numbers?

The time you go to sleep and the time you rise may sometimes seem beyond your control. Consistent bedtimes and wake times are advisable for those experiencing insomnia. Sleeping in may make for a more enjoyable weekend, but Monday morning— and Sunday bedtime—may suffer as a result. You choose: sleep late on the weekends . . . or feel refreshed and alert every morning?

Napping Notes

To nap or not to nap, that is the question. If you suffer from insomnia, try not taking a nap. If the goal is to sleep more during the night, napping may steal hours desired later on. However, napping can help promote short-term alertness, for example, to prepare for driving or in the middle of a long car trip.

Napping Tips

- Plan on a nap of just 20–30 minutes.

- If driving, nap in a safe place, such as in your locked car in a well-lit rest stop.

- Don't use a nap to try to substitute for a good night's sleep. If you're a regular napper, and experiencing difficulty falling or staying asleep at night, give up the nap and see what happens.

How Can You Relax?

Relaxing may mean choosing the bedtime ritual that's right for you. Does gentle music lull you to sleep? A calming soak in a warm bath or hot tub? Cozy pajamas? Cuddling with your partner? Meditation or a prayer? Find what works for you . . . and do it! Sweet dreams.

If you find your thoughts turning to worries when bedtime approaches, keep a worry book by your bedside. Jot down a brief note about what's on your mind. Schedule time the next day to focus on the problem and a solution. Problems often seem smaller in the daylight. However, if problems persist, consider talking to your doctor or a psychotherapist.

Getting Help

If your sleep problem persists, there may be an underlying cause that can be successfully treated or controlled once properly diagnosed. Sleep disorders centers are staffed by physicians and other medical professionals who specialize in helping people with persistent sleep problems.

Online Assignment: Sleep Quiz

Complete this assignment online. Go to:

www.grtep.com

Select >Chapter Content>Chapter 10>Enter your username and password

WHAT YOU NEED TO KNOW ABOUT DENTAL HEALTH

Prevent and control oral and craniofacial diseases, conditions, and injuries, and improve access to preventive services and dental care.

The health of the mouth and surrounding craniofacial (skull and face) structures is central to a person's overall health and well-being. Oral and craniofacial diseases and conditions include:

- Dental caries (tooth decay)

- Periodontal (gum) diseases

- Cleft lip and palate

- Oral and facial pain

- Oral and pharyngeal (mouth and throat) cancers

The significant improvement in the oral health of Americans over the past 50 years is a public health success story. Most of the gains are a result of effective prevention and treatment efforts. One major success is community water fluoridation, which now benefits about 7 out of 10 Americans who get water through public water systems.

However, some Americans do not have access to preventive programs. People who have the least access to preventive services and dental treatment have greater rates of oral diseases. A person's ability to access oral health care is associated with factors such as education level, income, race, and ethnicity.

Objectives in this topic area address a number of areas for public health improvement, including the need to:

- Increase awareness of the importance of oral health to overall health and well-being.

- Increase acceptance and adoption of effective preventive interventions.

- Reduce disparities in access to effective preventive and dental treatment services.

Why Is Oral Health Important?

Oral health is essential to overall health. Good oral health improves a person's ability to speak, smile, smell, taste, touch, chew, swallow, and make facial expressions to show feelings and emotions.

However, oral diseases, from cavities to oral cancer, cause pain and disability for many Americans.

Understanding Oral Health

Good self-care, such as brushing with fluoride toothpaste, daily flossing, and professional treatment, is key to good oral health. Health behaviors that can lead to poor oral health include:

Barriers that can limit a person's use of preventive interventions and treatments include:

- Limited access to and availability of dental services

- Lack of awareness of the need for care

- Cost

- Fear of dental procedures

There are also social determinants that affect oral health. In general, people with lower levels of education and income, and people from specific racial/ethnic groups, have higher rates of disease. People with disabilities and other health conditions, like diabetes, are more likely to have poor oral health.

Community water fluoridation and school-based dental sealant programs are 2 leading evidence-based interventions to prevent tooth decay.

- Community water fluoridation is the most effective way to deliver the benefits of fluoride to a community. Studies show that it prevents tooth decay by 18 to 40 percent.

- School-based dental sealant programs, which focus on sealing permanent molar teeth, usually target schools that serve children from low-income families. Dental sealants can prevent up to 60 percent of tooth decay in the treated teeth.

Emerging Issues in Oral Health

Major improvements have occurred in the Nation's oral health, but some challenges remain and new concerns have emerged. One important emerging oral health issue is the increase of tooth decay in preschool children. A recent Centers for Disease Control and Prevention (CDC) publication reported that, over the past decade, dental caries (tooth decay) in children ages 2 to 5 have increased.

Lack of access to dental care for all ages remains a public health challenge. This issue was highlighted in a 2008 Government Accountability Office (GAO) report that described difficulties in accessing dental care for low-income children. In addition, the Institute of Medicine (IOM) has convened an expert panel to evaluate factors that influence access to dental care.

Potential strategies to address these issues include:

Implementing and evaluating activities that have an impact on health behavior.

Promoting interventions to reduce tooth decay, such as dental sealants and fluoride use.

Evaluating and improving methods of monitoring oral diseases and conditions.

Increasing the capacity of State dental health programs to provide preventive oral health services.

Increasing the number of community health centers with an oral health component.

As noted in *Oral Health in America: A Report of the Surgeon General,* community water fluoridation continues to be the most cost-effective, equitable and safe means to provide protection from tooth decay in a community. Scientific studies have found that people living in communities with fluoridated water have fewer cavities than those living where the water is not fluoridated. For more than 50 years, small amounts of fluoride have been added to drinking water supplies in the United States where naturally-occurring fluoride levels are too low to protect teeth from decay. Over 8,000 communities are currently adjusting the fluoride in their community's water to a level that can protect the oral health of their citizens.

Over 170 million people, or 67 percent of the United States population served by public water supplies, drink water with optimal fluoride levels for preventing decay. Of the 50 largest cities in the country, 43 are fluoridated. Although water fluoridation reaches some residents in every state, unfortunately, only 24 states are providing these benefits to 75 percent or more of their residents.

A significant advantage of water fluoridation is that all residents of a community can enjoy its protective benefit—at home, work, school, or play—simply by drinking fluoridated water or beverages and foods prepared with it. A person's income level or ability to receive routine dental care is not a barrier to receiving fluoridation's health benefits. Water fluoridation is a powerful strategy in our efforts to eliminate differences in health among people and is consistent with my emphasis on the importance of prevention.

The U.S. Centers for Disease Control and Prevention has recognized the fluoridation of drinking water as one of ten great public health achievements of the twentieth century. Water fluoridation has helped improve the quality of life in the United States by reducing pain and suffering related to tooth decay, time lost from school and work, and money spent to restore, remove, or replace decayed teeth. An economic analysis has determined that in most communities, every $1 invested in fluoridation saves $38 or more in treatment costs. Fluoridation is the single most effective public health measure to prevent tooth decay and improve oral health over a lifetime, for both children and adults.

While we can be pleased with what has already been accomplished, it is clear that there is much yet to be done. Policymakers, community leaders, private industry, health professionals, the media, and the public should affirm that oral health is essential to general health and well being and *take action* to make ourselves, our families, and our communities healthier. I join previous Surgeons General in acknowledging the continuing public health role for community water fluoridation in enhancing the oral health of all Americans.

Links between Oral Health and Diseases

Diabetes can cause serious problems in your mouth. You can do something about it.

If you have diabetes, make sure you take care of your mouth. People with diabetes are at risk for mouth infections, especially periodontal (gum) disease. Periodontal disease can damage the gum and bone that hold your teeth in place and may lead to painful chewing problems. Some people with serious gum disease lose their teeth. Periodontal disease may also make it hard to control your blood glucose (blood sugar).

Other problems diabetes can cause are dry mouth and a fungal infection called thrush. Dry mouth happens when you do not have enough saliva—the fluid that keeps your mouth wet. Diabetes may also cause the glucose level in your saliva to increase. Together, these problems may lead to thrush, which causes painful white patches in your mouth.

You can keep your teeth and gums healthy. By controlling your blood glucose, brushing and flossing every day, and visiting a dentist regularly, you can help prevent periodontal disease. If your diabetes is not under control, you are more likely to develop problems in your mouth.

Take steps to keep your mouth healthy. Call your dentist when you notice a problem.

If you have diabetes, follow these steps:

- Control your blood glucose.

- Brush and floss every day.

- Visit your dentist regularly. Be sure to tell your dentist that you have diabetes.

- Tell your dentist if your dentures (false teeth) do not fit right, or if your gums are sore.

- Quit smoking. Smoking makes gum disease worse. Your physician or dentist can help you quit.

Take time to check your mouth regularly for any problems. Sometimes people notice that their gums bleed when they brush and floss. Others notice dryness, soreness, white patches, or a bad taste in the mouth. All of these are reasons to visit your dentist.

Remember, good blood glucose control can help prevent mouth problems.

Important Clue in How Certain Oral Bacteria Might Contribute to Heart Condition

Endocarditis is a sometimes life-threatening infection of the inner surface of the heart and/or its valves. Of the approximately 15,000 cases of endocarditis reported each year in the United States, many likely arise when bacteria that naturally attach to our teeth are displaced and pass into the bloodstream during a dental procedure, flossing, or even chewing food. These microbes, while relatively harmless in the mouth, have an affinity for damaged endothelial cells or blood clots in the heart, where they attach, multiply, and form larger bacterial colonies that trigger the endocarditis. Scientists have shown that immune cells called monocytes are prominently found in early inflammatory lesions linked to endocarditis. What's been puzzling is the monocytes tend to disappear from the lesions over time without becoming macrophages, a scavenging immune cell formed from monocytes that removes debris from tissues, such as the damaged, bacteria-laden cells linked to endocarditis. In the August issue of the journal *Infection and Immunity*, NIDCR grantees show that the usual monocyte-macrophage transformation rarely occurs because monocytes infected in studies with the well-known oral bacterium *Streptococcus mutans* instead become dendritic cells, a type of immune cell that initiates an inflammation-producing immune response upon interaction with this bacterium. This finding indicates that oral streptococci mediated changes in a person's normal immune response can contribute to endocarditis. It also suggests that an effective future strategy to treat endocarditis might involve learning to turn off the destructive immune response and/or reprogram the monocytes to produce macrophages to clear away the disease-causing bacterial colonies from the heart.

Smokeless Tobacco

What Is Smokeless Tobacco?

Smokeless tobacco, also known as dip and chew, snuff, or chewing tobacco, comes in two forms. Chewing tobacco comes as loose leaves of tobacco, as plug tobacco (brick form), or in a twist form. Snuff is finely ground (powdered) tobacco that is sold moist, dry, or in tea bag-like pouches called sachets. But no matter what it's called, smokeless tobacco is highly addictive and can harm your health. Here's why:

- Smokeless tobacco is still tobacco. Tobacco contains cancer-causing chemicals called nitrosamines.

- Like cigarettes, smokeless tobacco also contains nicotine—an addictive drug. In fact, holding an average-size dip in the mouth for just 30 minutes can deliver as much nicotine as smoking three cigarettes. Nicotine addiction can make quitting difficult.

- Smokeless tobacco may cause mouth cancer and other health problems.

If You Want to Quit...

Quitting smokeless tobacco is not easy. The most effective way to quit chewing tobacco is to have a quit date and a quitting plan. Successful quitters also include support teams in their plan— friends, family, and co-workers who can help during the difficult times when urges and temptations are strongest.

HIV/AIDS and Oral Health

What Oral Problems Are Caused by HIV/AIDS?

People with human immunodeficiency virus (HIV), the virus that causes acquired immunodeficiency syndrome (AIDS), are at special risk for oral health problems. Many of these problems arise because the person's immune system is weakened and less able to fight off infection.

Some of the most common oral problems for people with HIV/AIDS include:

- oral warts
- fever blisters

- hairy leukoplakia

- oral candidiasis (thrush)

- aphthous ulcers, often called canker sores

People with HIV/AIDS may also experience dry mouth, which increases the risk of tooth decay and can make chewing, eating, swallowing, and even talking difficult.

Treatment

Many of the common oral health problems associated with HIV can often be treated with over-the-counter or prescription medications. There are also self-care steps you can take to help ease dry mouth.

WHAT YOU CAN DO TO MAINTAIN GOOD ORAL HEALTH

You can keep your teeth and gums healthy. Most problems with teeth and gums can be prevented by taking these steps:

- Brush your teeth 2 times a day with fluoride ("FLOOR-ide") toothpaste.

- Floss between your teeth every day.

- Visit a dentist regularly for checkups and cleaning.

- Cut down on sugary foods and drinks.

- Don't smoke or chew tobacco.

- If you drink alcohol, drink only in moderation.

Watch out for plaque. Plaque ("plak") is a sticky substance that forms on your teeth. When plaque stays on your teeth too long, it can lead to tooth decay (cavities) and gum disease. Tooth decay and gum disease are the main causes of tooth loss.

Taking care of your teeth and gums is especially important if you:

- Have diabetes

- Have cancer

- Are an older adult

- Are pregnant

Take Action!
Follow these tips for a healthy, beautiful smile.

Brush your teeth. Brush your teeth 2 times every day. Use fluoride toothpaste and a toothbrush with soft bristles. Fluoride is a mineral that helps protect teeth from decay.

- Brush in circles and use short back-and-forth strokes.

- Take time to brush gently along the gum line.

- Don't forget to brush your tongue.

- Get a new toothbrush every 3 to 4 months. (Replace your toothbrush sooner if it's wearing out.)

WHAT YOU CAN DO TO MAINTAIN GOOD ORAL HEALTH (CONTINUED)

Floss every day. Floss every day to remove plaque and any food between teeth that your toothbrush missed. Rinse your mouth with water after you floss.

If you aren't sure if you are doing it right, ask the dentist or dental assistant to show you how to floss at your next appointment.

Get regular checkups at the dentist. Visit a dentist once or twice a year for checkups and cleaning. Get checkups even if you have no natural teeth and have dentures. If you have problems with your teeth or mouth, see a dentist right away.

If you don't like going to the dentist, make your visit easier. Some people get nervous about going to the dentist. Try these tips to help make your visit to the dentist easier:

- Let your dentist know you are feeling nervous.
- Choose an appointment time when you won't feel rushed.
- Take headphones and a music player to your next appointment.

What about cost? You can still get dental care even if you don't have insurance.

- Find a health center near you to learn more.
- Get tips for finding low-cost dental care.

Cut down on sugary foods and drinks. Choose low-sugar snacks like vegetables, fruits, and low-fat or fat-free cheese. Cut down on sugary soda and drinks that can lead to tooth decay.

Quit smoking. Using tobacco in any form (cigarettes, cigars, pipe, spit tobacco) raises your risk for getting gum disease and oral (mouth) cancer.

Drink alcohol only in moderation. Drinking a lot of alcohol can increase your risk for oral cancer. If you choose to drink, have only a moderate amount. This means no more than 1 drink a day for women or 2 drinks a day for men.

The Dentist Visit and What to Expect

For proper oral health care and prevention of oral disease states, it is recommended that you have regular check-ups with your dentist every six months. First things first, ask a family member or friend for a referral to their dentist if you already don't have one of your own. In order to improve your chances of sticking with your regular check-ups, you will want to find a dentist (and his staff) that you feel most comfortable with visiting.

Regular check-ups can include reporting to your dentist any changes in your health history, a routine and thorough cleaning, a full examination of your teeth, gums and mouth and sometimes X-rays.

Routine and thorough cleaning includes removing built-up plaque and tartar by using a special scraping instrument that can get below the gumline, brushing your teeth, flossing your teeth and possibly giving you a fluoride treatment. These are usually done by the dental hygienist.

Your dentist will then come in to examine your teeth, gums and mouth looking not just for cavities but for signs of disease or other oral health issues. By doing this, your dentist is helping you by preventing any issues from getting more serious and, if a problem is found, treating the issue as quickly as possible.

X-rays may be recommended depending on your age, risk of disease and any symptoms you may have. X-rays are also used as a prevention method as well. X-rays can help the dentist see potentially unnoticed problems like impacted teeth, abscesses, cysts, etc. Most X-ray machines in dental offices are very safe and emit no harmful radiation to you. As a precaution, it is important that you wear a lead apron when having an X-ray and if you are pregnant, it is wise to wait for the X-ray to be taken later after the baby is born unless it is an emergency. There is a special type of X-ray that is now being taken every so often that is called a Panoramic X-ray that provides a complete view of both your upper and lower jaw in a single picture and helps the dentist understand your bite.

During your regular check-up, always make sure to ask your dentist or the dental hygienist any questions you may have. Your oral health is very important to your overall health so keep it a priority.

Periodental (Gum) Disease

Overview

Periodontal (gum) disease is an infection of the tissues that hold your teeth in place. It's typically caused by poor brushing and flossing habits that allow plaque—a sticky film of bacteria—to build up on the teeth and harden. In advanced stages, periodontal disease can lead to sore, bleeding gums; painful chewing problems; and even tooth loss.

Causes

Our mouths are full of bacteria. These bacteria, along with mucus and other particles, constantly form a sticky, colorless "plaque" on teeth. Brushing and flossing help get rid of plaque. Plaque that is not removed can harden and form "tartar" that brushing doesn't clean. Only a professional cleaning by a dentist or dental hygienist can remove tartar.

There are a number of risk factors for gum disease, but smoking is the most significant. Smoking also can make treatment for gum disease less successful. Other risk factors include diabetes; hormonal changes in girls and women; diabetes; medications that lessen the flow of saliva; certain illnesses, such as AIDS, and their medications; and genetic susceptibility.

Symptoms

Symptoms of gum disease include:

- Bad breath that won't go away
- Red or swollen gums
- Tender or bleeding gums
- Painful chewing

- Loose teeth
- Sensitive teeth
- Receding gums or longer appearing teeth

Diagnosis

At a dental visit, a dentist or dental hygienist will:

- Examine your gums and note any signs of inflammation.
- Use a tiny ruler called a "probe" to check for and measure any pockets around the teeth. In a healthy mouth, the depth of these pockets is usually between 1 and 3 millimeters. This test for pocket depth is usually painless.
- Ask about your medical history to identify conditions or risk factors (such as smoking or diabetes) that may contribute to gum disease.

The dental professional may also:

- Take an x-ray to see whether there is any bone loss.
- Refer you to a periodontist. Periodontists are experts in the diagnosis and treatment of gum disease and may provide you with treatment options that are not offered by your dentist.

Treatment

The main goal of treatment is to control the infection. The number and types of treatment will vary, depending on the extent of the gum disease. Any type of treatment requires that the patient keep up good daily care at home. The dentist may also suggest changing certain behaviors, such as quitting smoking, as a way to improve your treatment results.

Oral Cancer

Oral cancer is cancer of the mouth.

Causes, Incidence, and Risk Factors

Oral cancer most commonly involves the lips or the tongue. It may also occur on the:

- Cheek lining
- Floor of the mouth
- Gums (gingiva)
- Roof of the mouth (palate)

Most oral cancers are a type called squamous cell carcinomas. These tend to spread quickly.

Smoking and other tobacco use are linked to most cases of oral cancer. Heavy alcohol use also increases your risk for oral cancer.

Other factors that may increase the risk for oral cancer include:

- Chronic irritation (such as from rough teeth, dentures, or fillings)
- Human papilloma virus (HPV) infection
- Taking medications that weaken the immune system (immunosuppressants)
- Poor dental and oral hygiene

Some oral cancers begin as a white plaque (leukoplakia) or as a mouth ulcer. Men get oral cancer twice as often as women do, particularly men older than 40.

Symptoms

Sore, lump, or ulcer in the mouth:

- May be a deep, hard-edged crack in the tissue
- Most often pale colored, but may be dark or discolored
- On the tongue, lip, or other area of the mouth
- Usually painless at first (may develop a burning sensation or pain when the tumor is advanced)

Other symptoms that may occur with oral cancer include:

- Chewing problems
- Mouth sores
- Pain with swallowing
- Speech difficulties
- Swallowing difficulty
- Swollen lymph nodes in the neck
- Tongue problems
- Weight loss

Signs and Tests

Your doctor or dentist will examine your mouth area. The exam may show:

- A sore on the lip, tongue, or other area of the mouth
- An ulcer or bleeding

Tests used to confirm oral cancer include:

- Gum biopsy
- Tongue biopsy

X-rays and CT scans may be done to determine if the cancer has spread.

Treatment

Surgery to remove the tumor is usually recommended if the tumor is small enough. Surgery may be used together with radiation therapy and chemotherapy for larger tumors. Surgery is not commonly done if the cancer has spread to lymph nodes in the neck.

Other treatments may include speech therapy or other therapy to improve movement, chewing, swallowing, and speech.

Support Groups

You can ease the stress of illness by joining a support group of people who share common experiences and problems. See cancer—support group.

Expectations (Prognosis)

Approximately half of people with oral cancer will live more than 5 years after they are diagnosed and treated. If the cancer is found early, before it has spread to other tissues, the cure rate is nearly 90%. However, more than half of oral cancers have already spread when the cancer is detected. Most have spread to the throat or neck.

About 1 in 4 persons with oral cancer die because of delayed diagnosis and treatment.

Complications

- Complications of radiation therapy, including dry mouth and difficulty swallowing
- Disfigurement of the face, head, and neck after surgery
- Other spread (metastasis) of the cancer

Calling Your Health Care Provider

Oral cancer may be discovered when the dentist performs a routine cleaning and examination.

Call for an appointment with your health care provider if you have a sore in your mouth or lip or a lump in the neck that does not go away within 1 month. Early diagnosis and treatment of oral cancer greatly increases the chances of survival.

Prevention

- Avoid smoking or other tobacco use
- Have dental problems corrected
- Limit or avoid alcohol use
- Practice good oral hygiene

Online Assignment: Dental Health Quiz

Complete this assignment online. Go to:
www.grtep.com
Select >Chapter Content>Chapter 10>Enter your username and password

WHAT YOU NEED TO KNOW ABOUT EYE HEALTH

Most Americans do not know the risks and warning signs of diseases that could blind them if they don't seek timely detection and treatment, according to recent findings of the Survey of Public Knowledge, Attitudes, and Practices Related to Eye Health and Disease. (This survey involved more than 3,000 randomly selected adults. The National Eye Institute, one of the National Institutes of Health, and the Lions Clubs International Foundation sponsored the survey.)

Seventy-one percent of respondents reported that a loss of their eyesight would rate as a 10 on a scale of 1 to 10, meaning that it would have the greatest impact on their day-to-day life. However, only 8% knew that there are no early warning signs of glaucoma, a condition that can damage the eye's optic nerve and result in vision loss and blindness.

Fifty-one percent said that they have heard that people with diabetes are at increased risk of developing eye disease, but only 11% knew that there are usually no early warning signs. Only 16% had ever heard the term "low vision," which affects millions of Americans. Low vision is vision loss that standard eyeglasses, contact lenses, medicine, or surgery cannot correct, making everyday tasks difficult to do. Simple tasks like reading the mail, watching TV, shopping, cooking, and writing become challenging. The survey shows that nearly one-quarter of Americans have not seen or heard anything about eye health or disease, and yet more than 90% have seen a health care provider.

Prevention

Regular eye checkups from an ophthalmologist or optometrist are important. Your doctor will recommend earlier and more frequent exams if you have diabetes or you are already showing early signs of eye problems from diabetes, high blood pressure, or other causes. Some visits will measure the pressure in your eyes to test for glaucoma. Periodically, they will dilate your eyes to examine the retina for any signs of problems from aging, high blood pressure, or diabetes. These important steps can prevent eye and vision problems:

■ Wear sunglasses to protect your eyes.

■ Don't smoke.

- Limit how much alcohol you drink.

- Keep your blood pressure and cholesterol under control.

- Keep your blood sugars under control if you have diabetes.

- Eat foods rich in antioxidants, like green leafy vegetables.

The Eye Doctor Visit and What to Expect

A standard ophthalmic exam, or a routine eye examination, is a series of tests done to check your vision and the health of your eyes. The eye doctor will ask questions about your overall health and your family's medical history. You should tell the doctor if you have noticed any eye problems. The doctor checks your vision (visual acuity) using a chart of random letters of different sizes called the Snellen chart.

To see inside your eye, the doctor looks through a magnifying glass that has a light on the end (an ophthalmoscope). The device allows the doctor to see the retina, fundus (back of the eye), retinal vessels, and optic nerve head (optic disc). Sometimes, the doctor will give you eye drops so that he or she can better view the back of the eye. Another magnifying device called a slit lamp is useful to see the clear surface of the eye (cornea).

Different machines and methods test your eye's reaction to light, eye movement, and peripheral vision. To see if you need glasses, the doctor places several lenses in front of your eye, one at a time, and asks you when the letters on the Snellen chart are easier to see. The doctor may also test for color blindness and glaucoma. The doctor checks for glaucoma using a method called tonometry. Tonometry is a test to measure the pressure inside your eyes. Normal results mean the eye pressure is within the normal range. Abnormal results mean that glaucoma may be detected.

How to Prepare for an Eye Exam

Make an appointment with the eye doctor (some take walk-in patients). Avoid eye strain the day of the test. You will need someone to drive you home if the doctor dilates your eyes. The tests cause no pain or discomfort. If you received drops to dilate your eyes for the ophthalmoscopy, your vision will be blurry and sunlight can damage your eyes. Wear dark glasses or shade your eyes to avoid discomfort until the dilation wears off.

Why Test in the First Place?

The point is—you should have regular eye exams. Such exams allow for early detection of eye problems and help determine the cause of vision changes. A routine eye test can find various eye and medical problems (see abnormal results below). People with diabetes should have their eyes examined AT LEAST once a year.

Normal Results Mean:

- 20/20 vision
- Ability to differentiate colors
- No signs of glaucoma
- Normal optic nerve, retinal vessels, and fundus

Abnormal Results May Mean:

- *Glaucoma* is increased pressure in the eye, causing poor night vision, blind spots and loss of vision to either side.
- *Myopia* (Nearsightedness) is when the eyes focus incorrectly, making distant objects appear blurred.
- *Hyperopia* (Farsightedness) is difficulty seeing objects that are nearby.
- *Damaged optic nerves, vessels, or fundus*
- *Astigmatism* is a condition in which the cornea (has an abnormal curve, causing out-of-focus vision.
- *Presbyopia* is a condition in which the lens of the eye loses its ability to focus, making it difficult to see objects close up.
- *Corneal abrasion* (or dystrophy) describes an injury to the curved, transparent covering on the front of the eye.
- *Color blindness*
- *Strabismus* (crossed eyes) is a disorder that causes misalignment of one eye with the other when focusing.
- *Eye diseases*
- A *cataract* is a cloudy or opaque area (an area you cannot see through) in the lens of the eye.
- *Trauma*
- *Corneal ulcers and infections.* A corneal ulcer is an erosion or open sore in the outer layer of the cornea. It is associated with infection by a bacterium, virus, fungus, or parasite
- *Blocked tear duct* describes a partial or complete blockage in the tear duct system. This duct system carries tears away from the surface of the eye, into the nose.
- *Amblyopia* (Lazy eye) is the loss of an eye's ability to see details. The condition appears in one eye. The cause is lack of using that eye in early childhood.
- *Age-related macular degeneration (ARMD)* is loss of central vision, blurred vision (especially while reading), distorted vision (like seeing wavy lines), and colors appearing faded.
- *Diabetic retinopathy* is a complication of diabetes that can lead to bleeding into the retina.

Vision Changes

Many eye diseases, if detected early, are curable or treatable. There are many types of eye problems and visual disturbances. These include blurred vision, halos, blind spots, floaters, and other symptoms. Blurred vision is the loss of sharpness of vision and the inability to see small details. Blind spots (scotomas) are dark "holes" in the visual field in which nothing can be seen. The most severe form of visual loss is blindness.

A medical professional should always evaluate changes in vision, blurriness, blind spots, halos around lights, or dimness of vision. Whatever the cause, you should NEVER ignore vision changes. They can get worse and significantly impact the quality of your life. As you determine which professional to see, the following descriptions may help:

- Opticians dispense glasses and do not diagnose eye problems.

- Optometrists perform eye exams and may diagnose eye problems. They prescribe glasses and contact lenses. In some states they prescribe eye drops to treat diseases.

- Ophthalmologists are physicians who diagnose and treat diseases that affect the eyes. These doctors may also provide routine vision care services, such as prescribing glasses and contact lenses.

- Sometimes an eye problem is part of a general health problem. In these situations, you should also involve your primary care provider.

Many different conditions can cause vision changes and problems:

- Presbyopia—difficulty focusing on objects that are close. Common in the elderly.

- Cataracts—cloudiness over the eye's lens, causing poor nighttime vision, halos around lights, and sensitivity to glare. Daytime vision eventually becomes affected. Common in the elderly.

- Glaucoma—a major cause of blindness. Glaucoma can happen gradually or suddenly—if sudden, it's a medical emergency.

- Diabetic retinopathy—another common cause of blindness.

- Macular degeneration—the most common cause of blindness in people over age 60.

- Eye infection, inflammation, or injury.

- Floaters—tiny particles drifting across the eye. Although often brief and harmless, they may be a sign of retinal detachment.

- Retinal detachment—symptoms include floaters, flashes of light across your visual field, or a sensation of a shade or curtain hanging on one side of your visual field.

- Optic neuritis—inflammation of the optic nerve from infection or multiple sclerosis. You may have pain when you move your eye or touch it through the eyelid.

- Stroke or TIA.

- Brain tumor.

- Bleeding into the eye.

- Temporal arteritis—inflammation of an artery in the brain that supplies blood to the optic nerve.

- Migraine headaches—spots of light, halos, or zigzag patterns are common symptoms prior to the start of the headache. An ophthalmic migraine is when you have only visual symptoms without a headache.

- Other potential causes of vision problems include fatigue, overexposure to the outdoors (temporary and reversible blurring of vision), and many medications.

- Medications that can affect vision include antihistamines, anticholinergics, digitalis derivatives (temporary), some high blood pressure pills (guanethidine, Reserpine, and thiazide diuretics), indomethacin, phenothiazines (like Compazine for nausea, Thorazine and Stelazine for schizophrenia), medications for malaria, ethambutol (for tuberculosis), and many others.

Safety measures may become necessary if you have any vision problems. For example, if you have trouble seeing at night, you should not drive after dusk. It may be helpful to increase the amount of light in a room or arrange a home to remove hazards. A specialist at a low-vision clinic may be able to help.

When to Contact a Medical Professional

Call 911 if:

- You experience partial or complete blindness in one or both eyes, even if it is only temporary.

- You experience double vision, even if it is temporary.

- You have a sensation of a shade being pulled over your eyes or a curtain being drawn from the side.

- Blind spots, halos around lights, or areas of distorted vision appear suddenly.

- You have eye pain, especially if also red. A red, painful eye is a medical emergency.

Call your provider if you have:

- Trouble seeing objects to either side
- Difficulty seeing at night or when reading
- Gradual loss of the sharpness of your vision
- Difficulty distinguishing colors
- Blurred vision when trying to view objects near or far
- Diabetes or family history of diabetes
- Eye itching or discharge
- Vision changes that seem related to medication (DO NOT stop or change a medication without talking to your doctor)

What to Expect at Your Office Visit When Experiencing Eye Problems

Your provider will check vision, eye movements, pupils, the back of your eye (called the retina), and eye pressure when needed. An overall medical evaluation will take place if necessary. Treatments depend on the cause. Your provider will ask questions about your vision problems, such as:

- When did this begin? Did it occur suddenly or gradually?
- How often does it occur? How long does it last?
- When does it occur? Evening? Morning?
- Is the problem in one eye or both eyes?
- Is your vision blurred or is there double vision?
- Do you have blind spots?
- Are there areas that look black and missing?
- Is side (peripheral) vision missing?
- Do you see halos (circles of light) around shiny objects or lights?
- Do you see flashing lights or zigzag lines?
- Do you have sensitivity to light?
- Do stationary objects seem to be moving?
- Are colors missing? Is it difficult to differentiate colors?
- Is there pain?

- Are your eyes crossed? Does one or both of your eyes "drift"?

- Have you had an injury, infection, allergy symptoms, added stress or anxiety, feelings of depression, fatigue, or headache in the last few weeks to months? Have you been exposed to pollens, wind, sunlight, or chemicals in this time frame? Have you used any new soaps, lotions, or cosmetics?

- Is your vision better after you rest?

- Is it better with corrective lenses?

- Are there other symptoms present like redness, swelling, headache, pain, itching, discharge/drainage, a sense that something is in the eye, increased or decreased tearing, etc.?

- What medications do you take?

- Do you have diabetes or is there a family history of diabetes?

Online Assignment: Eye Health Quiz

Complete this assignment online. Go to:

www.grtep.com

Select >Chapter Content>Chapter 10>Enter your username and password

WHAT YOU NEED TO KNOW ABOUT LOW BACK HEALTH

If you have lower back pain, you are not alone. Nearly everyone at some point has back pain that interferes with work, routine daily activities, or recreation. Americans spend at least $50 billion each year on low back pain, the MOST COMMON CAUSE of job-related disability and a LEADING contributor to missed work. Back pain is the second most common neurological ailment in the United States—only headache is more common. Fortunately, most occurrences of low back pain go away within a few days. Others take much longer to resolve or lead to more serious conditions.

Acute or short-term low back pain generally lasts from a few days to a few weeks. Most acute back pain is mechanical in nature—the result of trauma to the lower back or a disorder such as arthritis. Pain from trauma may result from a sports injury, work around the house or in the garden, or a sudden jolt such as a car accident or other stress on spinal bones and tissues. Symptoms may range from muscle ache to shooting or stabbing pain, limited flexibility or range of motion, or an inability to stand straight. Occasionally, pain felt in one part of the body may "radiate" from a disorder or injury elsewhere in the body. Some acute pain syndromes can become more serious if left untreated.

Chronic back pain is measured by duration—pain that persists for more than three months is considered chronic. It is often progressive, and the cause can be difficult to determine.

What Structures Make Up the Back?

The back is an intricate structure of bones, muscles, and other tissues that form the posterior part of the body's trunk, from the neck to the pelvis. The centerpiece is the spinal column, which not only supports the upper body's weight but houses and protects the spinal cord—the delicate nervous system structure that carries signals that control the body's movements and convey its sensations. Stacked on top of one another are more than 30 bones—the vertebrae—that form the spinal column, also known as the spine. Each of these bones contains a roundish hole that, when stacked in register with all the others, creates a channel that surrounds the spinal cord. The spinal cord descends from the base of the brain and extends in the adult to just below the rib cage. Small nerves ("roots") enter and emerge from the spinal cord through spaces between the vertebrae. Because the bones of the spinal column continue growing long after the spinal cord reaches its full length in early childhood, the nerve roots to the lower back and legs extend many inches down the spinal column before exiting. Early anatomists dubbed this large bundle of nerve roots the cauda equina, or horse's tail. Round, spongy pads of cartilage called intervertebral discs maintain the spaces between the vertebrae. These allow for flexibility in the lower back and act much like shock absorbers throughout the spinal column to cushion the bones as the body moves. Bands of tissue known as ligaments and tendons hold the vertebrae in place and attach the muscles to the spinal column.

Starting at the top, the spine has four regions:

1. the seven cervical or neck vertebrae (labeled C1–C7),

2. the 12 thoracic or upper back vertebrae (labeled T1–T12),

3. the five lumbar vertebrae (labeled L1–L5), which we know as the lower back, and

4. the sacrum and coccyx, a group of bones fused together at the base of the spine.

The lumbar region of the back, where people feel most back pain, supports the weight of the upper body.

What Causes Lower Back Pain?

As people age, bone strength and muscle elasticity and tone tend to decrease. The discs begin to lose fluid and flexibility, which decreases their ability to cushion the vertebrae.

Pain can occur when, for example, someone lifts something too heavy or overstretches, causing a sprain, strain, or spasm in one of the muscles or ligaments in the back. If the spine becomes overly strained or compressed, a disc may rupture or bulge outward. This rupture may put pressure on one of the more than 50 nerves rooted to the spinal cord that control body movements and transmit signals from the body to the brain. When these nerve roots become compressed or irritated, back pain results.

Low back pain may reflect nerve or muscle irritation or bone lesions. Most low back pain follows injury or trauma to the back, but degenerative conditions may also cause pain, such as arthritis or disc disease, osteoporosis or other bone diseases, viral infections, irritation to joints and discs, or congenital abnormalities in the spine. Obesity, smoking, weight gain during pregnancy, stress, poor physical condition, posture inappropriate for the activity performed, and poor sleeping position also may contribute to low back pain. Additionally, scar tissue created when the injured back heals itself does not have the strength or flexibility of normal tissue. Buildup of scar tissue from repeated injuries eventually weakens the back and can lead to more serious injury.

Occasionally, low back pain may indicate a more serious medical problem. Pain accompanied by fever or loss of bowel or bladder control, pain when coughing, and progressive weakness in the legs may indicate a pinched nerve or other serious condition. People with diabetes may have severe back pain or pain radiating down the leg related to neuropathy. People with these symptoms should contact a doctor immediately to help prevent permanent damage.

Who Is Most Likely to Develop Low Back Pain?

Nearly everyone has low back pain sometime. It affects men and women equally. It occurs most often between ages 30 and 50, due in part to the aging process but also as a result of sedentary life styles with too little (sometimes punctuated by too much) exercise. The risk of experiencing low back pain from disc disease or spinal degeneration increases with age.

College students: Backpacks overloaded with schoolbooks and supplies can quickly strain the back and cause muscle fatigue. The U.S. Consumer Product Safety Commission estimates that more than 13,260 injuries related to backpacks were treated at doctors' offices, clinics, and emergency rooms in the year 2000. To avoid back strain, students carrying backpacks should bend both knees when lifting heavy packs, visit their room, car, or apartment between classes to lighten loads or replace books, or purchase a backpack or airline tote on wheels.

What Conditions Are Associated with Low Back Pain?

Conditions that may cause low back pain and require treatment by a physician or other health specialist include:

- *Bulging disc (also called protruding, herniated, or ruptured disc).* The intervertebral discs are under constant pressure. As discs degenerate and weaken, cartilage can bulge or get pushed into the space containing the spinal cord or a nerve root, causing pain. Studies have shown that most herniated discs occur in the lower, lumbar portion of the spinal column.

- A much more serious complication of a ruptured disc is *cauda equina syndrome,* which occurs when disc material gets pushed into the spinal canal and compresses the bundle of lumbar and sacral nerve roots. Permanent neurological damage may result if this syndrome is left untreated.

- *Sciatica* is a condition in which a herniated or ruptured disc presses on the sciatic nerve, the large nerve that extends down the spinal column to its exit point in the pelvis and carries nerve fibers to the leg. This compression causes shock-like or burning low back pain combined with pain through the buttocks and down one leg to below the knee, occasionally reaching the foot. In the most extreme cases, when the pinched nerve is between the disc and an adjacent bone, the symptoms involve not pain but numbness and some loss of motor control over the leg due to interruption of nerve signaling. A tumor, cyst, metastatic disease, or degeneration of the sciatic nerve root may also cause the condition.

- *Spinal degeneration* from disc wear and tear can lead to a narrowing of the spinal canal. A person with spinal degeneration may experience stiffness in the back upon awakening or may feel pain after walking or standing for a long time.

- *Spinal stenosis* related to congenital narrowing of the bony canal predisposes some people to pain related to disc disease.

- *Osteoporosis* is a metabolic bone disease marked by progressive decrease in bone density and strength. Fracture of brittle, porous bones in the spine and hips results when the body fails to produce new bone or absorbs too much existing bone. Women are four times more likely than men to develop osteoporosis. Caucasian women of northern European heritage are at the highest risk of developing the condition.

- *Skeletal irregularities* produce strain on the vertebrae and supporting muscles, tendons, ligaments, and tissues supported by the spinal column. These irregularities include *scoliosis,* a curving of the spine to the side; *kyphosis,* in which the normal curve of the upper back is severely rounded; *lordosis,* an abnormally accentuated arch in the lower back; *back extension,* a bending backward of the spine; and *back flexion,* in which the spine bends forward.

■ *Fibromyalgia* is a chronic disorder characterized by widespread musculoskeletal pain, fatigue, and multiple "tender points," particularly in the neck, spine, shoulders, and hips. Additional symptoms may include sleep disturbances, morning stiffness, and anxiety.

■ *Spondylitis* refers to chronic back pain and stiffness caused by a severe infection to or inflammation of the spinal joints. Other painful inflammations in the lower back include *osteomyelitis* (infection in the bones of the spine) and *sacroiliitis* (inflammation in the sacroiliac joints).

Can Back Pain Be Prevented?

Recurring back pain resulting from improper body mechanics or other nontraumatic causes is often preventable. A combination of exercises that don't jolt or strain the back, maintaining correct posture, and lifting objects properly can help prevent injuries.

Stressors cause or aggravate many work-related injuries. These include heavy lifting, contact stress (repeated or constant contact between soft body tissue and a hard or sharp object, such as resting a wrist against the edge of a hard desk or repeated tasks using a hammering motion), vibration, repetitive motion, and awkward posture. Applying ergonomic principles—designing furniture and tools to protect the body from injury—at home and in the workplace can greatly reduce the risk of back injury and help maintain a healthy back. More companies and homebuilders are promoting ergonomically designed tools, products, workstations, and living space to reduce the risk of musculoskeletal injury and pain.

The use of wide elastic belts that one can tighten to "pull in" lumbar and abdominal muscles to prevent low back pain remains controversial. A landmark study of the use of lumbar support or abdominal support belts worn by persons who lift or move merchandise found no evidence that the belts reduce back injury or back pain. The two-year study, reported by the National Institute for Occupational Safety and Health (NIOSH) in December 2000, found no statistically significant difference in either the incidence of workers' compensation claims for job-related back injuries or the incidence of self-reported pain among workers who reported they wore back belts daily compared to those workers who reported never using back belts or reported using them only once or twice a month. Although there have been anecdotal case reports of injury reduction among workers using back belts, many companies that have back belt programs also have training and ergonomic awareness programs. The reported injury reduction may be related to a combination of these or other factors.

How Is Back Pain Treated?

Most low back pain can be treated without surgery. Treatment involves using analgesics, reducing inflammation, restoring proper function and strength to the back, and preventing recurrence of the injury. Most people with back pain recover without residual functional loss. People should contact a doctor if there is not a noticeable reduction in pain and inflammation after 72 hours of self-care.

- Although science has never proven that ice and heat (the use of cold and hot compresses) quickly resolve low back injury, compresses may help reduce pain and inflammation and allow greater mobility for some individuals. As soon as possible following trauma, you should apply a cold pack or a cold compress (such as a bag of ice or a bag of frozen vegetables wrapped in a towel) to the tender spot several times a day for up to 20 minutes. After two to three days of cold treatment, you should then apply heat (such as a heating lamp or a hot pad) for brief periods to relax muscles and increase blood flow. Warm baths may also help relax muscles. You should avoid sleeping on a heating pad, which can cause burns and lead to additional tissue damage.

- Bed rest—one to two days at most. A 1996 Finnish study found that persons who continued their activities without bed rest following onset of low back pain appeared to have better back flexibility than those who rested in bed for a week. Other studies suggest that bed rest alone may make back pain worse and can lead to secondary complications such as depression, decreased muscle tone, and blood clots in the legs. You should resume activities as soon as possible. At night or during rest, consult your doctor on what sleep position is best for you.

- Exercise may be the most effective way to speed recovery from low back pain and help strengthen back and abdominal muscles (as discussed in Chapter 1). Maintaining and building muscle strength is particularly important for persons with skeletal irregularities. Any mild discomfort felt at the start of these exercises should disappear as muscles become stronger. But if pain is more than mild and lasts more than 15 minutes during exercise, patients should stop exercising and contact a doctor.

- We often use medications to treat acute and chronic low back pain. Effective pain relief may involve a combination of prescription drugs and over-the-counter remedies. You should always check with a doctor before taking drugs for pain relief.

- People often use therapeutic massage for pain relief. According to a survey sponsored by the American Massage Therapy Association® (AMTA®), almost one-quarter of all adult Americans (24%) had a massage at least once in the last

12 months. Almost one-third of adult Americans say they've used massage therapy at least one time for pain relief—just behind those who have turned to chiropractic (38%) and physical therapy (44%). Of people who had at least one massage in the last five years, 30% report that they did so for health conditions such as pain management, injury rehabilitation, migraine control, or overall wellness. People know about the role massage therapy plays in maintaining health and wellness, as 87% agree that massage can effectively reduce pain, 85% agree that massage can be beneficial to health and wellness, and 59% would like to see their insurance plans cover massage therapy.

- People may use acupuncture to remedy low back pain. According to *Acupuncture Today,* researchers believe that based on previously published papers, acupuncture may be most effective for low back pain that is nociceptive (caused by an injury or disease outside the nervous system) in origin. Determining the cause of pain, they feel, is paramount to using a particular therapy for relief. While there is no definitive way to resolve lower back pain, the use of acupuncture to treat back pain has increased dramatically in the past few decades. The basis for this, to a large extent, is due to placebo-controlled studies that have validated it as a reliable method of pain relief. The results of a recent study published in the *Clinical Journal of Pain* provide further proof that acupuncture is a safe and effective procedure for low-back pain, and that it can maintain positive outcomes for periods of six months or longer without producing the negative side-effects that often accompany more traditional pain remedies.

- Other treatments can include: spinal manipulation, acupuncture, biofeedback, interventional therapy, traction, transcutaneous electrical nerve stimulation (TENS), and ultrasound.

Tips to a Healthier Back

Following any period of prolonged inactivity, begin a program of regular low-impact exercises. Speed walking, swimming, or stationary bike riding 30 minutes a day can increase muscle strength and flexibility. Yoga can also help stretch and strengthen muscles and improve posture. Ask your physician or orthopedist for a list of low-impact exercises appropriate for your age and designed to strengthen lower back and abdominal muscles.

- Remember to warm-up and stretch before exercise or other strenuous physical activity. Also be sure to cool-down and always stretch after any activity.

- Following any period of prolonged inactivity, begin a program of regular low-impact exercises and strengthening exercises especially for your core stabilizers (abdominals and low back muscles).

- Yoga, Pilates, and tai chi can also help stretch and strengthen muscles and improve posture.

- Don't slouch when standing or sitting. When standing, keep your weight balanced on your feet. Your back supports weight most easily with reduced curvature.

- At home or work, make sure your work surface is at a comfortable height for you.

- Sit in a chair with good lumbar support and the proper position and height for the task. Keep your shoulders back. Switch sitting positions often and periodically walk around the office or gently stretch muscles to relieve tension. A pillow or rolled-up towel placed behind the small of your back can provide some lumbar support. If you must sit for a long period of time, rest your feet on a low stool or a stack of books.

- Wear comfortable, low-heeled shoes.

- Sleep on your side to reduce any curve in your spine. Always sleep on a firm surface.

- Ask for help when transferring an ill or injured family member from a reclining to a sitting position or when moving the patient from a chair to a bed.

Back Pain and Sitting

Sitting in an office chair for prolonged periods of time can definitely cause low back pain or worsen an existing back problem. The main reason behind this is that sitting, in an office chair or in general, is a static posture that increases stress in the back, shoulders, arms, and legs, and in particular, can add large amounts of pressure to the back muscles and spinal discs.

When sitting in an office chair for a long period, the natural tendency for most people is to slouch over or slouch down in the chair, and this posture can overstretch the spinal ligaments and strain the discs and surrounding structures in the spine. Over time, incorrect sitting posture can damage spinal structures and contribute to or worsen back pain.

Guidelines for Office Chair Setup

An ergonomic office chair is a tool that, when used properly, can help one maximize back support and maintain good posture while sitting. However, simply owning an ergonomic office chair is not enough—it is also necessary to adjust the office chair to the proportions of the individual's body to improve comfort and reduce aggravation to the spine.

The first step in setting up an office chair is to establish the desired height of the individual's desk or workstation. This decision is determined primarily by the type of work to be done and by the height of the person using the office chair. The height of the desk or workstation itself can vary greatly and will require different positioning of the office chair, or a different type of ergonomic chair altogether.

Once the workstation has been situated, then the user can adjust the office chair according to his or her physical proportions. Here are the most important guidelines—distilled into a quick checklist—to help make sure that the office chair and work area are as comfortable as possible and will cause the least amount of stress to the spine:

1. Elbow measure
First, begin by sitting comfortably as close as possible to your desk so that your upper arms are parallel to your spine. Rest your hands on your work surface (e.g. desktop, computer keyboard). If your elbows are not at a 90-degree angle, adjust your office chair height either up or down.

2. Thigh measure
Check that you can easily slide your fingers under your thigh at the leading edge of the office chair. If it is too tight, you need to prop your feet up with an adjustable footrest. If you are unusually tall and there is more than a finger width between your thigh and the chair, you need to raise the desk or work surface so that you can raise the height of your office chair.

3. Calf measure
With your bottom pushed against the chair back, try to pass your clenched fist between the back of your calf and the front of your office chair. If you can't do that easily, then the office chair is too deep. You will need to adjust the backrest forward, insert a low back support (such as a lumbar support cushion, a pillow or rolled up towel), or get a new office chair.

4. Low back support
Your bottom should be pressed against the back of your chair, and there should be a cushion that causes your lower back to arch slightly so that you don't slump forward or slouch down in the chair as you tire over time. This low back support in the office chair is essential to minimize the load (strain) on your back. Never slump or slouch forward in the office chair, as that places extra stress on the structures in the low back, and in particular, on the lumbar discs.

See Office Chair Back Support
5. Resting eye level
Close your eyes while sitting comfortably with your head facing forward. Slowly open your eyes. Your gaze should be aimed at the center of your computer screen. If your computer screen is higher or lower than your gaze, you need to either raise or lower it to reduce strain on the upper spine.

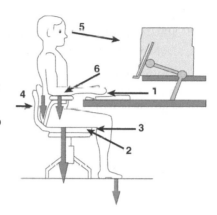

6. Armrest
Adjust the armrest of the office chair so that it just slightly lifts your arms at the shoulders. Use of an armrest on your office chair is important to take some of the strain off your upper spine and shoulders, and it should make you less likely to slouch forward in your chair.

7. Stay Active To Reduce Back Pain in the Office
No matter how comfortable one is in an office chair, prolonged static posture is not good for the back and is a common contributor to back problems and muscle strain.

To avoid keeping the back in one position for a long period, remember to stand, stretch and walk for at least a minute or two every half hour. Even a quick stretch or some minimal movement—such as walking to the water cooler or bathroom—will help.

A twenty minute walk will help even more, promoting healthy blood flow that brings important nutrients to all the spinal structures.

In general, moving about and stretching on a regular basis throughout the day will help keep the joints, ligaments, muscles, and tendons loose, which in turn promotes an overall feeling of comfort, relaxation, and ability to focus productively.

ALTERNATIVES TO TRADITIONAL OFFICE CHAIRS

While this article is about traditional office chairs, some people prefer more active, ergonomic chairs, such as a Swedish kneeling chair or a Swiss exercise ball.

See Exercise Ball Uses

While a traditional office chair is designed to provide complete support, these alternatives help promote good posture without a back support. They also require more active use of one's muscles (e.g. for balance and to sit upright). If you have an injured back or other health problems, it is advisable to first talk with your doctor prior to using one of these types of chairs. For more information, see Alternatives to Traditional Office Chairs.

There is no single type of office chair that is optimal for all patients, and people should determine their individual preference for comfort while following the guidelines explained in this article to promote good posture and back support while sitting in an office chair.

- Don't try to lift objects too heavy for you. Lift with your knees, pull in your stomach muscles, and keep your head down and in line with your straight back. Keep the object close to your body. Do not twist when lifting.

- Maintain proper nutrition and diet to reduce and prevent excessive weight, especially weight around the waistline that taxes lower back muscles. A diet with sufficient daily intake of calcium, phosphorus, and vitamin D helps to promote new bone growth.

- If you smoke, quit. Smoking reduces blood flow to the lower spine and causes the spinal discs to degenerate.

Online Assignment: Low Back Health

Complete this assignment online. Go to:
www.grtep.com
Select >Chapter Content>Chapter 10>Enter your username and password

WHAT YOU NEED TO KNOW ABOUT ADULT IMMUNIZATIONS

The following table illustrates what recommendations your family physician will follow for immunization.

Recommended Adult Immunization Schedule—United States - 2012

Note: These recommendations must be read with the footnotes that follow containing number of doses, intervals between doses, and other important information.

Figure 1. Recommended adult immunization schedule, by vaccine and age group[1]

VACCINE ▼ AGE GROUP ▶	19-21 years	22-26 years	27-49 years	50-59 years	60-64 years	≥ 65 years
Influenza[2]	1 dose annually					
Tetanus, diphtheria, pertussis (Td/Tdap)[3,*]	Substitute 1-time dose of Tdap for Td booster; then boost with Td every 10 yrs					Td/Tdap[3]
Varicella[4,*]	2 Doses					
Human papillomavirus (HPV) Female[5,*]	3 doses					
Human papillomavirus (HPV) Male[5,*]	3 doses					
Zoster[6]					1 dose	
Measles, mumps, rubella (MMR)[7,*]	1 or 2 doses			1 dose		
Pneumococcal (polysaccharide)[8,9]	1 or 2 doses					1 dose
Meningococcal[10,*]	1 or more doses					
Hepatitis A[11,*]	2 doses					
Hepatitis B[12,*]	3 doses					

*Covered by the Vaccine Injury Compensation Program

For all persons in this category who meet the age requirements and who lack documentation of vaccination or have no evidence of previous infection	**Recommended if some other risk factor is present (e.g., on the basis of medical, occupational, lifestyle, or other indications)**	Tdap recommended for ≥65 if contact with <12 month old child. Either Td or Tdap can be used if no infant contact	**No recommendation**

Report all clinically significant postvaccination reactions to the Vaccine Adverse Event Reporting System (VAERS). Reporting forms and instructions on filing a VAERS report are available at www.vaers.hhs.gov or by telephone, 800-822-7967.

Information on how to file a Vaccine Injury Compensation Program claim is available at www.hrsa.gov/vaccinecompensation or by telephone, 800-338-2382. To file a claim for vaccine injury, contact the U.S. Court of Federal Claims, 717 Madison Place, N.W., Washington, D.C. 20005; telephone, 202-357-6400.

Additional information about the vaccines in this schedule, extent of available data, and contraindications for vaccination is also available at www.cdc.gov/vaccines or from the CDC-INFO Contact Center at 800-CDC-INFO (800-232-4636) in English and Spanish. 8:00 a.m. - 8:00 p.m. Eastern Time, Monday - Friday, excluding holidays.

Use of trade names and commercial sources is for identification only and does not imply endorsement by the U.S. Department of Health and Human Services.

Figure 2. Vaccines that might be indicated for adults based on medical and other indications¹

VACCINE ▶ / INDICATION ▲	Pregnancy	Immunocompromising conditions (excluding human immunodeficiency virus [HIV])⁴,⁶,⁷,¹⁴	HIV infection⁴,⁷,¹³,¹⁴ CD4+ T lymphocyte count < 200 cells/μL	HIV infection ≥ 200 cells/μL	Men who have sex with men (MSM)	Heart disease, chronic lung disease, chronic alcoholism	Asplenia¹³ (including elective splenectomy and persistent complement component deficiencies)	Chronic liver disease	Diabetes, kidney failure, end-stage renal disease, receipt of hemodialysis	Health-care personnel
Influenza²	1 dose TIV annually	1 dose TIV annually	1 dose TIV annually	1 dose TIV annually	1 dose TIV or LAIV annually	1 dose TIV annually	1 dose TIV annually	1 dose TIV annually	1 dose TIV annually	1 dose TIV or LAIV annually
Tetanus, diphtheria, pertussis (Td/Tdap)³,*	Substitute 1-time dose of Tdap for Td booster; then boost with Td every 10 yrs									
Varicella⁴,*		Contraindicated	Contraindicated	2 doses	2 doses	2 doses	2 doses	2 doses	2 doses	2 doses
Human papillomavirus (HPV) Female⁵,*		3 doses through age 26 yrs	3 doses through age 26 yrs	3 doses through age 26 yrs	3 doses through age 26 yrs	3 doses through age 26 yrs	3 doses through age 26 yrs	3 doses through age 26 yrs	3 doses through age 26 yrs	
Human papillomavirus (HPV) Male⁵,*		3 doses through age 26 yrs	3 doses through age 26 yrs	3 doses through age 26 yrs	3 doses through age 26 yrs	3 doses through age 21 yrs	3 doses through age 21 yrs	3 doses through age 21 yrs	3 doses through age 21 yrs	
Zoster⁶		Contraindicated	Contraindicated	1 dose	1 dose	1 dose	1 dose	1 dose	1 dose	1 dose
Measles, mumps, rubella (MMR)⁷,*		Contraindicated	Contraindicated	1 or 2 doses	1 or 2 doses	1 or 2 doses	1 or 2 doses	1 or 2 doses	1 or 2 doses	1 or 2 doses
Pneumococcal (polysaccharide)⁸,⁹		1 or 2 doses	1 or 2 doses	1 or 2 doses	1 or 2 doses	1 or 2 doses	1 or 2 doses	1 or 2 doses	1 or 2 doses	
Meningococcal¹⁰,*		1 or more doses	1 or more doses	1 or more doses	1 or more doses	1 or more doses	1 or more doses	1 or more doses	1 or more doses	1 or more doses
Hepatitis A¹¹,*		2 doses	2 doses	2 doses	2 doses	2 doses	2 doses	2 doses	2 doses	2 doses
Hepatitis B¹²,*		3 doses	3 doses	3 doses	3 doses	3 doses	3 doses	3 doses	3 doses	3 doses

Legend:

- For all persons in this category who meet the age requirements and who lack documentation of vaccination or have no evidence of previous infection
- Recommended if some other risk factor is present (e.g., on the basis of medical, occupational, lifestyle, or other indications)
- Contraindicated
- No recommendation

*Covered by the Vaccine Injury Compensation Program

The recommendations in this schedule were approved by the Centers for Disease Control and Prevention's (CDC) Advisory Committee on Immunization Practices (ACIP), the American Academy of Family Physicians (AAFP), the American College of Physicians (ACP), American College of Obstetricians and Gynecologists (ACOG) and American College of Nurse-Midwives (ACNM).

These schedules indicate the recommended age groups and medical indications for which administration of currently licensed vaccines is commonly indicated for adults ages 19 years and older, as of January 1, 2012. For all vaccines being recommended on the Adult Immunization Schedule: a vaccine series does not need to be restarted, regardless of the time that has elapsed between doses. Licensed combination vaccines may be used whenever any components of the combination are indicated and when the vaccine's other components are not contraindicated. For detailed recommendations on all vaccines, including those used primarily for travelers or that are issued during the year, consult the manufacturers' package inserts and the complete statements from the Advisory Committee on Immunization Practices (www.cdc.gov/vaccines/pubs/acip-list.htm). Use of trade names and commercial sources is for identification only and does not imply endorsement by the U.S. Department of Health and Human Services.

U.S. Department of Health and Human Services
Centers for Disease Control and Prevention

WHAT YOU NEED TO KNOW ABOUT ANNUAL PHYSICALS AND PREVENTIVE SCREENINGS/TESTS

Get the Screenings You Need

Screenings are tests that look for diseases before you have symptoms. Blood pressure checks and mammograms are examples of screenings.

You can get some screenings, such as blood pressure readings, in your doctor's office. Others, such as mammograms, need special equipment, so you may need to go to a different office.

After a screening test, ask when you will see the results and who to talk to about them.

Recommended Screenings for Both Men and Women

Colorectal Cancer. Have a screening test for colorectal cancer starting at age 50. If you have a family history of colorectal cancer, you may need to be screened earlier. Several different tests can detect this cancer. Your health care team can help you decide which is best for you.

Depression. Your emotional health is as important as your physical health. Talk to your health care team about being screened for depression, especially if during the last 2 weeks:

- You have felt down, sad, or hopeless.

- You have felt little interest or pleasure in doing things.

Diabetes. Get screened for diabetes if your blood pressure is higher than 135/80 or if you take medication for high blood pressure. Diabetes (high blood sugar) can cause problems with your heart, brain, eyes, feet, kidneys, nerves, and other body parts.

High Blood Pressure. Starting at age 18, have your blood pressure checked at least every 2 years. High blood pressure is determined when it is consistently at 140/90 or higher but new preventative guidelines recommend blood pressure below 120/80. High blood pressure can cause stroke, heart attack, kidney and eye problems, and heart failure.

High Cholesterol. If you are a male and are 35 years or older, have your cholesterol checked. If you are a male or female, starting at age 20, have your cholesterol checked regularly if:

- You use tobacco.

- You are obese.

- You have diabetes or high blood pressure.

- You have a personal history of heart disease or blocked arteries.

- A man in your family had a heart attack before age 50 or a woman, before age 60.

HIV. Talk with your health care team about HIV screening if any of these apply to you:

- You have had unprotected sex with multiple partners.

- You are a male who has sex with men.

- You use or have used injection drugs.

- You exchange sex for money or drugs or have sex partners who do.

- You have or had a sex partner who is HIV-infected, bisexual, or injects drugs.

- You are being treated for a sexually transmitted disease.

- You had a blood transfusion between 1978 and 1985.

- You have any other concerns.

Overweight and Obesity. The best way to learn if you are overweight or obese is to find your body mass index (BMI). You can find your BMI by going to the chart in Appendix A.

A BMI between 18.5 and 25 indicates a normal weight. Persons with a BMI of 30 or higher may be obese. If you are obese, talk to your doctor or nurse about seeking intensive counseling and help with changing your behaviors to lose weight. Overweight and obesity can lead to diabetes and cardiovascular disease.

Recommended Screenings for Women

Breast Cancer. Ask your health care team whether a mammogram is right for you based on your age, family history, overall health, and personal concerns.

Cervical Cancer. Have a Pap smear every 1 to 3 years if you are 21 to 65 years old and have been sexually active. If you are older than 65 and recent Pap smears were normal, you do not need a Pap smear. If you have had a hysterectomy for a reason other than cancer, you do not need a Pap smear.

Chlamydia and Other Sexually Transmitted Diseases. Sexually transmitted diseases can make it hard to get pregnant, may affect your baby, and can cause other health problems.

- Have a screening test for Chlamydia if you are 24 or younger and sexually active. If you are older than 24, talk to your health care team about being screened for Chlamydia.

- Ask your doctor or nurse whether you should be screened for other sexually transmitted diseases.

Osteoporosis (Bone Thinning). Have a screening test at age 65 to make sure your bones are strong. If you are younger than 65, talk to your health care team about whether you should be tested.

Recommended Screenings for Men

Abdominal Aortic Aneurysm. If you are between the ages of 65 and 75 and have ever been a smoker, talk to your doctor or nurse about being screened for abdominal aortic aneurysm (AAA). AAA is a bulging in your abdominal aorta, the largest artery in your body. An AAA may burst, which can cause dangerous bleeding and death.Syphilis. Ask your doctor or nurse whether you should be screened for syphilis.

Note: In May, the U.S. Preventive Services Task Force, a panel of advisors on government medical guidelines, reviewed existing research and reported in its final recommendation that healthy men of all ages should not take a PSA test because the potential harms from a positive test outweigh the benefits from catching the cancer early. It is recommended you work with your physician to determine what is best for you.

Take Preventive Medicines If You Need Them

Immunizations.

- Get a flu shot every year.

- If you are 65 or older, get a pneumonia shot.

- Depending on health problems, you may need a pneumonia shot at a younger age or need shots to prevent diseases like whooping cough or shingles.

- Talk with your health care team about whether you need vaccinations. You can also find which ones you need by going to: www2.cdc.gov/nip/adultimmsched/.

Preventive Medicines for Women

Aspirin. If you are 55 or older, ask your health care team if you should take aspirin to prevent strokes.

Breast Cancer Drugs. If your mother, sister, or daughter has had breast cancer, talk to your doctor about whether you should take medicines to prevent breast cancer.

Estrogen for Menopause (Hormone Replacement Therapy). Do not use estrogen to prevent heart disease or other diseases. If you need relief from symptoms of menopause, talk with your health care team.

Preventive Medicines for Men

Aspirin. If you are 45 or older, ask your health care team if you should take aspirin to prevent strokes.

Take Steps to Good Health

Be physically active and make healthy food choices. Learn how at www.healthfinder .gov/prevention.

Get to a healthy weight and stay there. Balance the calories you take in from food and drink with the calories you burn off by your activities.

Be tobacco free. For tips on how to quit, go to www.smokefree.gov. To talk to someone about how to quit, call the National Quitline: 1-800-QUITNOW (784-8669).

If you drink alcohol, have no more than one drink per day. A standard drink is one 12-ounce bottle of beer or wine cooler, one 5- ounce glass of wine, or 1.5 ounces of 80-proof distilled spirits.

Get More Information on Good Health

Check out these Federal Government Web sites:

Healthfinder.gov. Guides and tools for healthy living, an encyclopedia of health-related topics, health news, and more. Go to: www.healthfinder.gov.

MedlinePlus. Health information from government agencies and health organizations, including a medical encyclopedia and health tools. Go to: www.medlineplus.gov.

Questions Are the Answer. Information on how to get involved in your health care by asking questions, understanding your condition, and learning about your options. Go to: www.ahrq.gov/questionsaretheanswer.

If you don't have access to a computer, talk to your local librarian about health information in the library.

Source: The information provided here is based on research from the U.S. Department of Health and Human Services and the U.S. Preventive Services Task Force (USPSTF). The USPSTF, supported by AHRQ, is a national independent panel of medical experts that makes recommendations based on scientific evidence about which clinical preventive services should be included in primary medical care and for which populations.

For information about the USPSTF and its recommendations, go to: www.uspreventiveservicestaskforce.org.

WHAT YOU NEED TO KNOW ABOUT SEXUALLY TRANSMITTED INFECTIONS

According to the National Institutes of Health, sexually transmitted infections (STIs), also known as sexually transmitted diseases (STDs), are infections that you can get from having sex with someone who has the infection. The causes of STIs are bacteria, parasites, and viruses. STIs caused by viruses include hepatitis B, herpes, HIV, and the human papilloma virus (HPV). STIs caused by bacteria include chlamydia, gonorrhea, and syphilis.

Sexually transmitted diseases (STDs) or STIs are infections that are passed from one person to another through sexual contact. The causes of STDs are bacteria, parasites, yeast, and viruses. There are more than 20 types of STDs, including Chlamydia, Genital herpes, Gonorrhea, HIV/AIDS, HPV, Syphilis and Trichomoniasis.

Most STDs affect both men and women, but in many cases the health problems they cause can be more severe for women. If a pregnant woman has an STD, it can cause serious health problems for the baby.

Antibiotics can treat STDs caused by bacteria, yeast, or parasites. There is no cure for STDs caused by a virus, but medicines can often help with the symptoms and keep the disease under control.

Correct usage of latex condoms greatly reduces, but does not completely eliminate, the risk of catching or spreading STDs. The most reliable way to avoid infection is to not have anal, vaginal, or oral sex.

Sexually Transmitted Diseases (STDs) Prevention

A cornerstone of public health is disease prevention. Tools to prevent STDs, such as vaccines, topical microbicides, and behavioral interventions, are a vital part of protecting the public against infectious diseases. Gardasil, a vaccine against the four most common strains of human papillomavirus (HPV), is an exciting accomplishment in the field of STDs. However, the work to develop safe and effective vaccines against other STDs continues. Most notably are the ongoing clinical trials to evaluate an investigational vaccine to prevent genital herpes.

Barrier methods—such as latex condoms and topical microbicides (a substance applied to the vagina or rectum that kills or disables the microbes that cause STDs)— offer highly effective protection against STDs. NIAID-funded researchers are conducting clinical trials to test new topical microbicides and female-barrier methods to prevent STDs. Used correctly and consistently these products may greatly reduce a person's risk of acquiring or transmitting most STDs, including gonorrhea, chlamydia, trichomonas, syphilis, HPV, and HIV/AIDS.

In addition, NIAID-supported researchers are conducting interventional and behavioral studies to identify social and economic conditions and sexual behaviors that may increase a person's vulnerability to STDs. Results of this work may reduce health disparities, especially among youth, women, and underrepresented minorities.

Sexually Transmitted Diseases (STDs) Diagnosis

Early and rapid diagnosis of STDs increases the chance to limit effects of the disease. Left untreated, STDs, such as gonorrhea, syphilis, chlamydia, genital herpes, and human papillomavirus, can lead to devastating and sometimes long-term complications. These complications include blindness, bone deformities, brain damage, cancer, heart disease, infertility, birth defects, mental retardation, and even death.

Healthcare providers diagnose STDs through physical examination, blood tests, or swabbed cultures. Diagnosis of STDs by self-obtained vaginal swabs was the focus of an NIAID-supported workshop. However, many people infected by an STD have little or no symptoms of the infection. NIAID scientists are conducting immunology studies to address why many STDs in people are asymptomatic. These studies may also uncover how infections mutation contributes to STD drug resistance and the processes associated with repeat infection and coinfection (for example, syphilis and HIV/AIDS).

Sexually Transmitted Diseases (STDs) Treatment

There are many different kinds of STDs, and the types of treatment are as varied as their symptoms. NIAID supports the development and licensure of vaccines, topical microbicides, and drug treatments, such as antibiotics and antifungals, for the microbes that cause STDs. No STD is harmless. Even the curable ones can cause serious consequences if left untreated. HIV is of particular concern as biological evidence demonstrates the increased likelihood of acquiring and transmitting HIV when STDs are present.

Today, scientists at NIAID are testing new vaccines for STDs, such as herpes, and new ways to treat drug-resistant STDs, such as gonorrhea, in animal models and clinical trials. Research findings may lead to faster, safer, and more effective treatments.

SOURCE: www.niaid.nih.gov

STD	TRANSMISSION & SYMPTOMS	PREVENTION & TREATMENT
Chlamydia	Chlamydia is a common sexually transmitted disease caused by bacteria. You get it by having sex or sexual contact with someone who is infected. Both men and women can get it. Chlamydia usually doesn't cause symptoms. If it does, you might notice a burning feeling when you urinate or abnormal discharge from your vagina or penis. In both men and women, chlamydia can infect the urinary tract. In women, infection of the reproductive system can lead to pelvic inflammatory disease, which can cause infertility or serious problems with pregnancy. Babies born to infected mothers can get eye infections and pneumonia from chlamydia. In men, chlamydia can infect the epididymis, the tube that carries sperm. This can cause pain, fever and rarely, infertility.	If you are sexually active, you can decrease your risk of getting it by using condoms. Experts recommend that women 25 and younger get a chlamydia test every year. You can cure chlamydia with antibiotics.
Gonorrhea	Gonorrhea (also called "the clap") is a curable sexually transmitted disease. It is most common in young adults. The bacteria that cause gonorrhea can infect the genital tract, mouth or anus. Gonorrhea does not always cause symptoms, especially in women. In men, gonorrhea can cause pain when urinating and discharge from the penis. If untreated, it can cause epididymitis, which affects the testicles and can lead to infertility. In women, gonorrhea can cause bleeding between periods, pain when urinating and increased discharge from the vagina. If untreated, it can lead to pelvic inflammatory disease, which causes problems with pregnancy and infertility. Gonorrhea can pass from mother to baby during pregnancy.	Correct usage of latex condoms greatly reduces, but does not eliminate, the risk of catching or spreading gonorrhea. You can cure gonorrhea with antibiotics prescribed by your health care provider.

STD	TRANSMISSION & SYMPTOMS	PREVENTION & TREATMENT
Hepatitis B	Hepatitis B is one type of hepatitis—a liver disease—caused by the hepatitis B virus (HBV). Hepatitis B spreads by contact with an infected person's blood, semen or other body fluid. An infected woman can give hepatitis B to her baby at birth. If you get HBV, you may feel as if you have the flu, or you may have no symptoms at all. A blood test can tell if you have it. HBV usually gets better on its own after a few months. If it does not get better, it is called chronic HBV, which lasts a lifetime. Chronic HBV can lead to scarring of the liver, liver failure or liver cancer.	There is a vaccine for HBV. It requires three shots. All babies should get the vaccine, but older children and adults can get it too. If you travel to countries where Hepatitis B is common, you should get the vaccine. There is a vaccine for HBV. It requires three shots. All babies should get the vaccine, but older children and adults can get it too. If you travel to countries where Hepatitis B is common, you should get the vaccine.
Herpes Simplex	Herpes (also called HSV) is an infection that is caused by a herpes simplex virus (HSV). Oral herpes causes cold sores around the mouth or face. Genital herpes affects the genitals, buttocks or anal area. Genital herpes is a sexually transmitted disease (STD). You can get it from having sex, even oral sex. The virus can spread even when sores are not present. Mothers can also infect their babies during childbirth. Some people have no symptoms. Others get sores near the area where the virus has entered the body. They turn into blisters, become itchy and painful, and then heal. The virus can be dangerous in newborn babies or in people with weak immune systems. Most people have outbreaks several times a year. Over time, you get them less often.	Correct usage of latex condoms can reduce, but not eliminate, the risk of catching or spreading herpes. Medicines to help your body fight the virus can help lessen symptoms and decrease outbreaks but there is no cure currently.
HIV/AIDS	AIDS stands for acquired immunodeficiency syndrome. It is the most advanced stages of infection with the human immunodeficiency virus (HIV). HIV is a virus that kills or damages cells of the body's immune system. HIV most often spreads through unprotected sex with an infected person. AIDS may also spread by sharing drug needles or through contact with the blood of an infected person. Women can give it to their babies during pregnancy or childbirth.	There is no cure, but there are many medicines to fight both HIV infection and the infections and cancers that come with it. People can live with the disease for many years.

STD	TRANSMISSION & SYMPTOMS	PREVENTION & TREATMENT
	The first signs of HIV infection may be swollen glands and flu-like symptoms. These may come and go a month or two after infection. Severe symptoms may not appear until months or years later. A blood test can tell if you have HIV infection. Your health care provider can perform the test, or call the National AIDS hotline for a referral at (800) 342-AIDS (1 800 342 2437).	
HPV	Human papillomaviruses (HPV) are common viruses that can cause warts. There are more than 100 types of HPV. Most are harmless, but about 30 types put you at risk for cancer. These types affect the genitals and you get them through sexual contact with an infected partner. They are classified as either low-risk or high-risk. Low-risk HPV can cause genital warts. High-risk HPV can lead to cancers of the cervix, vulva, vagina, and anus in women. In men, it can lead to cancers of the anus and penis. Although some people develop genital warts from HPV infection, others have no symptoms. Your health care provider can treat or remove the warts. In women, Pap smears can detect changes in the cervix that might lead to cancer. Genital warts are a sexually transmitted disease (STD) caused by the human papillomavirus (HPV). The warts are soft, moist, pink or flesh-colored bumps. You can have one or many of these bumps. In women, the warts usually occur in or around the vagina, on the cervix or around the anus. In men, genital warts are less common but might occur on the tip of the penis.	A vaccine can protect against several types of HPV, including some that can cause cancer. Correct usage of latex condoms greatly reduces, but does not eliminate, the risk of catching or spreading HPV. Genital warts might disappear on their own. If not, your health care provider can treat or remove them. The virus stays in your body even after treatment, so warts can come back.
Syphilis	Syphilis is a sexually transmitted disease caused by bacteria. It infects the genital area, lips, mouth, or anus of both men and women. You usually get syphilis from sexual contact with someone who has it. It can also pass from mother to baby during pregnancy. The early stage of syphilis usually causes a single, small, painless sore. Sometimes it causes swelling in nearby lymph nodes. If you do not treat it, syphilis usually causes a non-itchy skin rash, often on your hands	Correct usage of latex condoms greatly reduces, but does not completely eliminate, the risk of catching or spreading syphilis. Syphilis is easy to cure with antibiotics if you catch it early.

STD	TRANSMISSION & SYMPTOMS	PREVENTION & TREATMENT
	and feet. Many people do not notice symptoms for years. Symptoms can go away and come back. The sores caused by syphilis make it easier to get or give someone HIV during sex. If you are pregnant, syphilis can cause birth defects, or you could lose your baby. In rare cases, syphilis causes serious health problems and even death.	
Trichomoniasis	Trichomoniasis is a sexually transmitted disease caused by a parasite. It affects both women and men, but symptoms are more common in women. Symptoms in women include a green or yellow discharge from the vagina, itching in or near the vagina and discomfort with urination. Most men with trichomoniasis don't have any symptoms, but it can cause irritation inside the penis.	Correct usage of latex condoms greatly reduces, but does not eliminate, the risk of catching or spreading trichomoniasis. You can cure trichomoniasis with antibiotics. In men, the infection usually goes away on its own without causing symptoms. But an infected man can continue to infect or reinfect a woman until he gets treated. So it's important that both partners get treated at the same time.

SOURCE: *http://www.nlm.hih.gov/medlineplus/sexually transmitteddisceases.html* accessed on 5.28.08

Online Assignments: Sexual Risk Quiz and STI Knowledge Quiz

Complete this assignment online. Go to:
www.grtep.com
Select >Chapter Content>Chapter 10>Enter your username and password

WHAT YOU NEED TO KNOW ABOUT SUBSTANCE ABUSE

Many people do not understand why individuals become addicted to drugs or how drugs change the brain to foster compulsive drug abuse. They mistakenly view drug abuse and addiction as strictly a social problem and may characterize those who take drugs as morally weak. One very common belief is that drug abusers should be able to just stop taking drugs if they are only willing to change their behavior. What people often underestimate is the complexity of drug addiction—that it is a disease that impacts the brain and, because of that, stopping drug abuse is not simply a matter of willpower. Through scientific advances we now know much more about how exactly drugs work in the brain, and we also know that people can receive successful treatment for drug addiction and help to stop abusing drugs and resume their productive lives.

What Is Drug Addiction?

Addiction is a chronic, often relapsing brain disease that causes compulsive drug seeking and use despite harmful consequences to the addicted individual and to those around them. Drug addiction is a brain disease because the abuse of drugs leads to changes in the structure and function of the brain. Although it is true that for most people the initial decision to take drugs is voluntary, over time the changes in the brain caused by repeated drug abuse can affect a person's self control and ability to make sound decisions, and at the same time send intense impulses to take drugs.

It is because of these changes in the brain that it is so challenging for an addicted person to stop abusing drugs. Fortunately, there are treatments that help people to counteract addiction's powerful disruptive effects and regain control. Research shows that combining addiction treatment medications, if available, with behavioral therapy is the best way to ensure success for most patients. Treatment approaches tailored to each patient's drug abuse patterns and any co-occurring medical, psychiatric, and social problems can lead to sustained recovery and a life without drug abuse.

Similar to other *chronic, relapsing* diseases, such as diabetes, asthma, or heart disease, a person can manage drug addiction successfully. And, as with other chronic diseases, it is not uncommon for a person to relapse and begin abusing drugs again. Relapse, however, does not signal failure—rather, it indicates that the individual should reinstate or adjust treatment, or that alternate treatment is necessary to help regain control and recover.

What Happens to Your Brain When You Take Drugs?

Drugs are chemicals that tap into the brain's communication system and disrupt the way nerve cells normally send, receive, and process information. There are at least two ways that drugs are able to do this: (1) by imitating the brain's natural chemical messengers, and/or (2) by over stimulating the "reward circuit" of the brain.

Some drugs, such as marijuana and heroin, have a similar structure to chemical messengers, called neurotransmitters, which the brain naturally produces. Because of this similarity, these drugs are able to "fool" the brain's receptors and activate nerve cells to send abnormal messages.

Other drugs, such as cocaine or methamphetamine, can cause the nerve cells to release abnormally large amounts of natural neurotransmitters, or prevent the normal recycling of these brain chemicals, which is necessary to shut off the signal between neurons. This disruption produces a greatly amplified message that ultimately disrupts normal communication patterns.

Nearly all drugs directly or indirectly target the brain's reward system by flooding the circuit with dopamine. Dopamine is a neurotransmitter present in regions of the brain that control movement, emotion, motivation, and feelings of pleasure. The overstimulation of this system, which normally responds to natural behaviors linked to survival (eating, spending time with loved ones, etc), produces euphoric effects in response to the drugs. This reaction sets in motion a pattern that "teaches" people to repeat the behavior of abusing drugs.

As a person continues to abuse drugs, the brain adapts to the overwhelming surges in dopamine by producing less dopamine or by reducing the number of dopamine receptors in the reward circuit. As a result, dopamine's impact on the reward circuit lessens, reducing the abuser's ability to enjoy the drugs and the things that previously brought pleasure. This decrease compels those addicted to drugs to keep abusing drugs in order to attempt to bring their dopamine function back to normal. And, they may now require larger amounts of the drug than they first did to achieve the dopamine high—an effect known as *tolerance.*

Long-term abuse causes changes in other brain chemical systems and circuits as well. Glutamate is a neurotransmitter that influences the reward circuit and the ability to learn. When drug abuse alters the optimal concentration of glutamate, the brain attempts to compensate, which can impair cognitive function. Drugs of abuse facilitate non-conscious (conditioned) learning, which leads the user to experience uncontrollable cravings when he or she sees a place or person associated with the drug experience, even when the drug itself is not available. Brain imaging studies of drug-addicted individuals show changes in areas of the brain critical to judgment, decision-making, learning and memory, and behavior control. Together, these changes can drive an abuser to seek out and take drugs compulsively despite adverse consequences—in other words, to become addicted to drugs.

Why Do Some People Become Addicted, While Others Do Not?

No single factor can predict whether or not a person will become addicted to drugs. A person's biology, social environment, and age or stage of development all influence risk for addiction. The more risk factors an individual has, the greater the chance that taking drugs can lead to addiction. For example:

- **Biology.** The genes that people are born with—in combination with environmental influences—account for about half of their addiction vulnerability. Additionally, gender, ethnicity, and the presence of other mental disorders may influence risk for drug abuse and addiction.

- **Environment.** A person's environment includes many different influences—from family and friends to socioeconomic status and quality of life in general. Factors such as peer pressure, physical and sexual abuse, stress, and parental involvement can greatly influence the course of drug abuse and addiction in a person's life.

- **Development.** Genetic and environmental factors interact with critical developmental stages in a person's life to affect addiction vulnerability, and adolescents experience a double challenge. Although taking drugs at any age can lead to addiction, the earlier that drug use begins, the more likely it is to progress to more serious abuse. And because adolescents' brains are still developing in the areas that govern decision-making, judgment, and self-control, they are especially prone to risk-taking behaviors, including trying drugs of abuse.

Prevention Is the Key

Drug addiction is a preventable disease. Results from NIDA-funded research have shown that prevention programs that involve the family, schools, communities, and the media are effective in reducing drug abuse. Although many events and cultural factors affect drug abuse trends, when youths perceive drug abuse as harmful, they reduce their drug taking. It is necessary, therefore, to help youth and the general public to understand the risks of drug abuse and for teachers, parents, and healthcare professionals to keep sending the message that drug addiction can be prevented if a person never abuses drugs.

COMMONLY ABUSED DRUGS

SUBSTANCES: CATEGORY AND NAME	EXAMPLES OF COMMERCIAL AND STREET NAMES	DEA SCHEDULE* AND HOW ADMINISTERED**	INTOXICATION EFFECTS/POTENTIAL HEALTH CONSEQUENCES
Cannabinoids			
hashish	boom, chronic, gangster, hash, hash oil, hemp	I/swallowed, smoked	euphoria, slowed thinking and reaction time, confusion, impaired balance and coordination
marijuana	blunt, dope, ganja, grass, herb, joints, Mary Jane, pot, reefer, sinsemilla, skunk, weed	I/swallowed, smoked	cough, frequent respiratory infections; impaired memory and learning; increased heart rate, anxiety; panic attacks; tolerance, addiction
Depressants			
barbiturates	Amytal, Nembutal, Seconal, Phenobarbital: barbs, reds, red birds, phennies, tooies, yellows, yellow jackets	II, III, V/injected, swallowed	reduced anxiety; feeling of well-being; lowered inhibitions; slowed pulse and breathing; lowered blood pressure; poor concentration/fatigue; confusion; impaired coordination, memory, judgment; addiction; respiratory depression and arrest; death
benzodiazepines (other than flunitrazepam)	Ativan, Halcion, Librium, Valium, Xanax: candy, downers, sleeping pills, tranks	IV/swallowed, injected	Also, for barbiturates—sedation, drowsiness/depression, unusual excitement, fever, irritability, poor judgment, slurred speech, dizziness, life-threatening withdrawal
flunitrazepam***	Rohypnol: forget-me pill, Mexican Valium, R2, Roche, roofies, roofinol, rope, rophies	IV/swallowed, snorted	for benzodiazepines—sedation, drowsiness/dizziness
GHB***	gamma-hydroxybutyrate: G, Georgia home boy, grievous bodily harm, liquid ecstasy	I/swallowed	for flunitrazepam—visual and gastrointestinal disturbances, urinary retention, memory loss for the time under the drug's effects
methaqualone	Quaalude, Sopor, Parest: ludes, mandrex, quad, quay	I/injected, swallowed	for GHB—drowsiness, nausea/vomiting, headache, loss of consciousness, loss of reflexes, seizures, coma, death
			for methaqualone—euphoria/depression, poor reflexes, slurred speech, coma

SUBSTANCES: CATEGORY AND NAME	EXAMPLES OF COMMERCIAL AND STREET NAMES	DEA SCHEDULE* AND HOW ADMINISTERED**	INTOXICATION EFFECTS/POTENTIAL HEALTH CONSEQUENCES
Dissociative Anesthetics			
ketamine	Ketalar SV: cat Valiums, K, Special K, vitamin K	III/Injected, snorted, smoked	increased heart rate and blood pressure, impaired motor function/memory loss; numbness; nausea/vomiting
PCP and analogs	phencyclidine; angel dust, boat, hog, love boat, peace pill	I, II/injected, swallowed, smoked	Also, for ketamine—at high doses, delirium, depression, respiratory depression and arrest
			for PCP and analogs—possible decrease in blood pressure and heart rate, panic, aggression, violence/loss of appetite, depression
Hallucinogens			
LSD	lysergic acid diethylamide: acid, blotter, boomers, cubes, microdot, yellow sunshines	I/swallowed, absorbed through mouth tissues	altered states of perception and feeling; nausea; persisting perception disorder (flashbacks)
mescaline	buttons, cactus, mesc, peyote	I/swallowed, smoked	Also, for LSD and mescaline—increased body temperature, heart rate, blood pressure; loss of appetite, sleeplessness, numbness, weakness, tremors
psilocybin	magic mushroom, purple passion, shrooms	I/swallowed	for LSD—persistent mental disorders
			for psilocybin—nervousness, paranoia
Opioids and Morphine Derivatives			
codeine	Empirin with Codeine, Fiorinal with Codeine, Robitussin A-C, Tylenol with Codeine: Captain Cody, schoolboy; (with glutethimide) doors & fours, loads, pancakes and syrup	II, III, IV, V/injected, swallowed	pain relief, euphoria, drowsiness/nausea, constipation, confusion, sedation, respiratory depression and arrest, tolerance, addiction, unconsciousness, coma, death
			Also, for codeine—less analgesia, sedation, and respiratory depression than for morphine
			for heroin—staggering gait

SUBSTANCES: CATEGORY AND NAME	EXAMPLES OF COMMERCIAL AND STREET NAMES	DEA SCHEDULE*/ HOW ADMINISTERED**	INTOXICATION EFFECTS/POTENTIAL HEALTH CONSEQUENCES
fentanyl and fentanyl analogs	Actiq, Duragesic, Sublimaze: Apache, China girl, China white, dance fever, friend, goodfella, jackpot, murder 8, TNT, Tango and Cash	I, II/injected, smoked, snorted	
heroin	diacetyl-morphine: brown sugar, dope, H, horse, junk, skag, skunk, smack, white horse	I/injected, smoked, snorted	
morphine	Roxanol, Duramorph: M, Miss Emma, monkey, white stuff	II, III/injected, swallowed, smoked	
opium	laudanum, paregoric: big O, black stuff, block, gum, hop	II, III, V/swallowed, smoked	
oxycodone HCL	Oxycontin: Oxy, O.C., killer	II/swallowed, snorted, injected	
hydrocodone bitartrate, acetaminophen	Vicodin: vike, Watson-387	II/swallowed	
Stimulants amphetamine	Biphetamine, Dexedrine: bennies, black beauties, crosses, hearts, LA turnaround, speed, truck drivers, uppers	II/injected, swallowed, smoked, snorted	increased heart rate, blood pressure, metabolism; feelings of exhilaration, energy, increased mental alertness/rapid or irregular heart beat; reduced appetite, weight loss, heart failure, nervousness, insomnia
cocaine	Cocaine hydrochloride: blow, bump, C, candy, Charlie, coke, crack, flake, rock, snow, toot	II/injected, smoked, snorted	Also, for amphetamine—rapid breathing/tremor, loss of coordination; irritability, anxiousness, restlessness, delirium, panic, paranoia, impulsive behavior, aggressiveness, tolerance, addiction, psychosis
MDMA (methylenedioxy-methamphetamine)	Adam, clarity, ecstasy, Eve, lover's speed, peace, STP, X, XTC	I/swallowed	
methamphetamine	Desoxyn: chalk, crank, crystal, fire, glass, go fast, ice, meth, speed	II/injected, swallowed, smoked, snorted	for cocaine—increased temperature/chest pain, respiratory failure, nausea, abdominal pain, strokes, seizures, headaches, malnutrition, panic attacks
methylphenidate (safe and effective for treatment of ADHD)	Ritalin: JIF, MPH, R-ball, Skippy, the smart drug, vitamin R	II/injected, swallowed, snorted	

SUBSTANCES: CATEGORY AND NAME	EXAMPLES OF COMMERCIAL AND STREET NAMES	DEA SCHEDULE*/ HOW ADMINISTERED**	INTOXICATION EFFECTS/POTENTIAL HEALTH CONSEQUENCES
nicotine	cigarettes, cigars, smokeless tobacco, snuff, spit tobacco, bidis, chew	not scheduled/smoked, snorted, taken in snuff and spit tobacco	for MDMA—mild hallucinogenic effects, increased tactile sensitivity, empathic feelings/ impaired memory and earning, hyperthermia, cardiac toxicity, renal failure, liver toxicity
			for methamphetamine—aggression, violence, psychotic behavior/ memory loss, cardiac and neurological damage; impaired memory and learning, tolerance, addiction
			for nicotine—additional effects attributable to tobacco exposure; adverse pregnancy outcomes; chronic lung disease, cardiovascular disease, stroke, cancer, tolerance, addiction
Other Compounds anabolic steroids	Anadrol, Oxandrin, Durabolin, Depo-Testosterone, Equipoise: roids, juice	III/injected, swallowed, applied to skin	no intoxication effects/hypertension, blood clotting and cholesterol changes, liver cysts and cancer, kidney cancer, hostility and aggression, acne; in adolescents,
Dextromethorphan (DXM)	Found in some cough and cold medications; Robotripping, Robo, Triple C	not scheduled/swallowed	premature stoppage of growth; in males, prostate cancer, reduced sperm production, shrunken testicles, breast enlargement; in
inhalants	Solvents (paint thinners, gasoline, glues), gases (butane, propane, aerosol propellants, nitrous oxide), nitrites (isoamyl, isobutyl, cyclohexyl): laughing gas, poppers, snappers, whippets	not scheduled/inhaled through nose or mouth	females, menstrual irregularities, development of beard and other masculine characteristics
			Dissociative effects, distorted visual perceptions to complete dissociative effects/for effects at higher doses see 'dissociative anesthetics'
			stimulation, loss of inhibition; headache; nausea or vomiting; slurred speech, loss of motor coordination; wheezing/ unconsciousness, cramps, weight loss, muscle weakness, depression, memory impairment, damage to cardiovascular and nervous systems, sudden death

* Schedule I and II drugs have a high potential for abuse. They require greater storage security and have a quota on manufacturing, among other restrictions. Schedule I drugs are available for research only and have no approved medical use; Schedule II drugs are available only by prescription (unrefillable) and require a form for ordering. Schedule III and IV drugs are available by prescription, may have five refills in six months, and may be ordered orally. Some Schedule V drugs are available over the counter.

** Taking drugs by injection can increase the risk of infection through needle contamination with staphylococci, HIV, hepatitis, and other organisms.

*** Associated with sexual assaults.

Online Assignment: Drug Abuse Screening Test

Complete this assignment online. Go to:

www.grtep.com

Select >Chapter Content>Chapter 10>Enter your username and password

WHAT YOU NEED TO KNOW ABOUT ALCOHOL DEPENDENCE AND ABUSE

Alcohol Dependence

Alcoholism, also known as alcohol dependence, is a disease that includes the following four symptoms:

1. Craving—A strong need, or urge, to drink.

2. Loss of control—Not being able to stop drinking once drinking has begun.

3. Physical dependence—Withdrawal symptoms, such as nausea, sweating, shakiness, and anxiety after stopping drinking.

4. Tolerance—The need to drink greater amounts of alcohol to get "high."

Researchers have developed formal diagnostic criteria for alcoholism for clinical and research purposes. Such criteria are in the Diagnostic and Statistical Manual of Mental Disorders, Fourth Edition, published by the American Psychiatric Association, as well as in the International Classification Diseases, published by the World Health Organization.

Alcoholism is a disease. The craving that an alcoholic feels for alcohol can be as strong as the need for food or water. An alcoholic will continue to drink despite serious family, health, or legal problems. Like many other diseases, alcoholism is chronic, meaning that it lasts a person's lifetime; it usually follows a predictable course; and it has symptoms. Both a person's genes and his or her lifestyle influence the risk for developing alcoholism.

Alcohol Abuse

Alcohol abuse is a pattern of drinking that results in harm to one's health, interpersonal relationships, or ability to work. Manifestations of alcohol abuse include:

- Failure to fulfill major responsibilities at work, school, or home.

- Drinking in dangerous situations, such as drinking while driving or operating machinery.

- Legal problems related to alcohol, such as being arrested for drinking while driving or for physically hurting someone while drunk.

- Continued drinking despite ongoing relationship problems caused or worsened by drinking.

- Long-term alcohol abuse can turn into alcohol dependence.

What Is a Safe Level of Drinking?

For most adults, moderate alcohol use—up to two drinks per day for men and one drink per day for women and older people—causes few if any problems. (One drink equals one 12-ounce bottle of beer or wine cooler, one 5-ounce glass of wine, or 1.5 ounces of 80-proof distilled spirits.) Certain people should not drink at all, however:

- Women who are pregnant or trying to become pregnant

- People who plan to drive or engage in other activities that require alertness and skill (such as driving a car)

- People taking certain over-the-counter or prescription medications

- People with medical conditions that drinking can worsen

- Recovering alcoholics

- People younger than age 21

Levels and Patterns of Drinking

- *Heavy drinking*

  - For women, more than one drink per day on average

  - For men, more than two drinks per day on average

- *Binge drinking*

  - For women, more than three drinks during a single occasion

  - For men, more than four drinks during a single occasion

Excessive drinking includes heavy drinking, binge drinking, or both

Binge Drinking

Binge drinking is a common pattern of excessive alcohol use in the United States. The National Institute of Alcohol Abuse and Alcoholism defines binge drinking as a pattern of drinking that brings a person's blood alcohol concentration (BAC) to 0.08 grams percent or above. This typically happens when men consume more than four drinks and women consume more than three drinks in about two hours. Most people who binge drink are not alcohol dependent. According to national surveys from the CDC:

- Approximately 92% of U.S. adults who drink excessively report binge drinking in the past 30 days.

- Although college students commonly binge drink, 70% of binge drinking episodes involve adults over age 25.

- The rate of binge drinking among men is three times the rate of women.

- Binge drinkers are 14 times more likely to report alcohol-impaired driving than non-binge drinkers.

- About 90% of the alcohol consumed by youth under the age of 21 in the United States is in the form of binge drinks.

- About 75% of the alcohol consumed by adults in the United States is in the form of binge drinks.

- The proportion of current drinkers that binge is highest in the 18- to 20-year-old groups (52.1%).

There is an association of binge drinking with many health problems, including but not limited to:

- Unintentional injuries (e.g., car crash, falls, burns, drowning)

- Intentional injuries (e.g., firearm injuries, sexual assault, domestic violence)

- Alcohol poisoning

- Sexually transmitted diseases

- Unintended pregnancy

- Children born with Fetal Alcohol Syndrome

- High blood pressure, stroke, and other cardiovascular diseases

- Liver disease

- Neurological damage

BLOOD ALCOHOL CONCENTRATION (BAC): A MEASURE OF DRUNK DRIVING

Within minutes after having a drink, the brain's normal functioning is changed. One measure of how your brain, vision, and decision-making might be impaired is how much alcohol is in your blood. This is called the blood alcohol concentration.

YOUR WEIGHT	NUMBER OF DRINKS (OVER A TWO-HOUR PERIOD) 1.5 OZ. 80 PROOF LIQUOR OR 12 OZ. CAN OF BEER											
100	1	2	3	4	5	6	7	8	9	10	11	12
120	1	2	3	4	5	6	7	8	9	10	11	12
140	1	2	3	4	5	6	7	8	9	10	11	12
160	1	2	3	4	5	6	7	8	9	10	11	12
180	1	2	3	4	5	6	7	8	9	10	11	12
200	1	2	3	4	5	6	7	8	9	10	11	12
220	1	2	3	4	5	6	7	8	9	10	11	12
240	1	2	3	4	5	6	7	8	9	10	11	12

Social Drive with caution BAC to 0.05%	Warning Driving impaired 0.05–0.09%	Intoxicated Do not drive 0.10% and up

This table is only a guide. Information presented is based on averages and may vary according to particular circumstances or from individual to individual.

U.S. Department of Transportation.

- Sexual dysfunction
- Poor control of diabetes

Blood Alcohol Concentration (BAC)

Blood alcohol concentration (BAC) is a measure of the amount of alcohol in a person's bloodstream. Percentages commonly express BAC. For instance, having a BAC of 0.08% means that a person has eight parts alcohol per 10,000 parts blood in the body. State laws generally specify BAC levels in terms of grams of alcohol per 100 milliliters of blood (often abbreviated as grams per deciliter, or g/dL). Breath, blood, or urine tests can detect BAC levels. The laws of each jurisdiction specify the preferred or required types of tests used for measurement.

Does Alcohol Affect Women Differently?

Yes, alcohol affects women differently than men. Women become more impaired than men do after drinking the same amount of alcohol, even when we take differences in body weight into account. This is because women's bodies have less water than men's bodies. Because alcohol mixes with body water, a given amount of alcohol becomes more highly concentrated in a woman's body than in a man's. In other words, it would be like dropping the same amount of alcohol into a much smaller pail of water. That is why the recommended drinking limit for women is lower than for men. In addition, chronic alcohol abuse takes a heavier physical toll on women than on men. Alcohol dependence and related medical problems, such as brain, heart, and liver damage, progress more rapidly in women than in men.

When Taking Medications, Must I Stop Drinking?

Possibly. More than 150 medications interact harmfully with alcohol. These interactions may result in increased risk of illness, injury, and even death. Medicines that depress the central nervous system heighten alcohol's effects. These include sleeping pills, antihistamines, antidepressants, anti-anxiety drugs, and some painkillers. In addition, medicines for certain disorders, including diabetes, high blood pressure, and heart disease, can have harmful interactions with alcohol. If you are taking any over-the-counter or prescription medications, ask your doctor or pharmacist if you can safely drink alcohol.

Are Specific Groups of People More Likely to Have Problems?

Alcohol abuse and alcoholism cut across gender, race, and nationality. In the United States, 17.6 million people—about 1 in every 12 adults—abuse alcohol or are alcohol dependent. In general, more men than women are alcohol dependent or have alcohol problems. **Alcohol problems are highest among young adults ages 18–29.** We also know that people who start drinking at an early age—for example, at age 14 or younger—are at much higher risk of developing alcohol problems at some point in their lives compared to those who start drinking at age 21 or after.

Can a Problem Drinker Simply Cut Down?

It depends. If that person has a diagnosis as an alcoholic, the answer is "no." Alcoholics who try to cut down on drinking rarely succeed. Cutting out alcohol—that is, abstaining—is usually the best course for recovery. People who are not alcohol dependent but who have experienced alcohol-related problems may be able to limit the amount they drink. If they can't stay within those limits, they need to stop drinking altogether.

Is Alcoholism Inherited?

Research shows that the risk for developing alcoholism does indeed run in families. The genes a person inherits partially explain this pattern, but lifestyle is also a factor. Currently, researchers are working to discover the actual genes that put people at risk for alcoholism. Your friends, the amount of stress in your life, and how readily available alcohol is also are factors that may increase your risk for alcoholism. But just because alcoholism tends to run in families doesn't mean that a child of an alcoholic parent will automatically become an alcoholic too. Some people develop alcoholism even though no one in their families has a drinking problem. By the same token, not all children of alcoholic families get into trouble with alcohol. Knowing you are at risk is important, though, because then you can take steps to protect yourself from developing problems with alcohol.

Alcoholism Treatment

Alcoholism treatment programs use both counseling and medications to help a person stop drinking. Treatment has helped many people stop drinking and rebuild their lives. Three oral medications—disulfiram (Antabuse®), naltrexone (Depade®, ReVia®), and acamprosate (Campral®)—currently have approval to treat alcohol dependence. In addition, an injectable, long-acting form of naltrexone (Vivitrol®) is available. These medications have been shown to help people with dependence reduce their drinking, to avoid relapse to heavy drinking, and to achieve and maintain abstinence. Naltrexone acts in the brain to reduce craving for alcohol after someone has stopped drinking. Acamprosate is thought to work by reducing symptoms that follow lengthy abstinence, such as anxiety and insomnia. Disulfiram discourages drinking by making the person taking it feel sick after drinking alcohol.

Other types of drugs are available to help manage symptoms of withdrawal (such as shakiness, nausea, and sweating) if they occur after someone with alcohol dependence stops drinking. Although medications are available to help treat alcoholism, there is no "magic bullet." In other words, no single medication is available that works in every case or in every person. Developing new and more effective medications to treat alcoholism remains a high priority for researchers. Alcoholism treatment works for many people. But like other chronic illnesses, such as diabetes, high blood pressure, and asthma, there are varying levels of success when it comes to treatment. Some people stop drinking and remain sober. Others have long periods of sobriety with bouts of relapse. And still others cannot stop drinking for any length of time. With treatment, one thing is clear, however: the longer a person abstains from alcohol, the more likely he or she will be able to stay sober.

LONG-TERM RISKS ASSOCIATED WITH ALCOHOL ABUSE

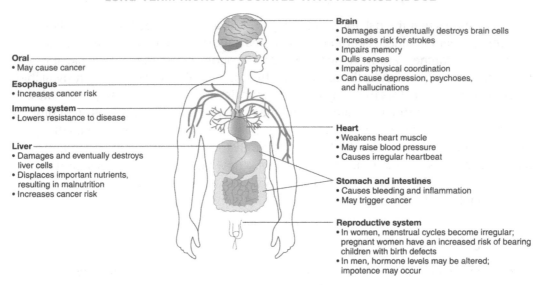

Oral
• May cause cancer

Esophagus
• Increases cancer risk

Immune system
• Lowers resistance to disease

Liver
• Damages and eventually destroys liver cells
• Displaces important nutrients, resulting in malnutrition
• Increases cancer risk

Brain
• Damages and eventually destroys brain cells
• Increases risk for strokes
• Impairs memory
• Dulls senses
• Impairs physical coordination
• Can cause depression, psychoses, and hallucinations

Heart
• Weakens heart muscle
• May raise blood pressure
• Causes irregular heartbeat

Stomach and intestines
• Causes bleeding and inflammation
• May trigger cancer

Reproductive system
• In women, menstrual cycles become irregular; pregnant women have an increased risk of bearing children with birth defects
• In men, hormone levels may be altered; impotence may occur

Adapted from "Long-Term Risk Associated with Alcohol Abuse" *Lifetime Physical Fitness & Wellness* by Hoeger and Hoeger, Wadsworth Publishers.

Online Assignments: Drinking Inventory and Alcohol Screening Test

Complete this assignment online. Go to:

www.grtep.com

Select >Chapter Content>Chapter 10>Enter your username and password

WHAT YOU NEED TO KNOW ABOUT SAFETY AWARENESS: NOT WEARING A SEATBELT, ACCIDENTS, ETC.

According to the ThinkFirst National Injury Prevention Foundation, each year, an estimated 500,000 persons in the United States sustain a brain or spinal cord injury. The most frequent causes of these injuries are motor vehicle crashes, violence, falls, sports, and recreation. The good news is that most injuries are preventable!

The Six Most Common Causes of Automobile Crashes

After the world's first automobile-related fatality, which occurred in London in 1896, the coroner said: "This must never happen again." Little did he know that from then on, some 25 million people would have died in vehicle-related accidents, according to the World Health Organization (WHO).

And even with all the advancements in vehicle safety technology, the number of people killed in auto accidents continues to rise. Nearly 1.3 million people die in road crashes each year, on average 3,287 deaths a day. An additional 20-50 million are injured or disabled. More than half of all road traffic deaths occur among young adults ages 15–44.

SOURCE: http://aslrt.org/initiatives/informing-road-users/road-safety-facts/road-crash-statistics

What's causing all of these accidents, which are, according to the National Highway Traffic Safety Administration (NHTSA), the leading cause of death among people aged 3 to 33, should then be of great interest to all of us drivers out there. Ironically, when you take a look through the top six causes you'll see that the greatest threat to drivers is the drivers themselves.

1. Distracted Drivers

Mark Edwards, Director of Traffic Safety at the American Automobile Association stated, "The research tells us that somewhere between 25–50 percent of all motor vehicle crashes in this country really have driver distraction as their root cause."

The distractions are many, but according to a study conducted by the Virginia Department of Motor Vehicles (DMV) and Virginia Commonwealth University (VCU), rubbernecking—or slowing down to gawk at another accident—caused the most accidents, accounting for 16 percent of all distraction-related crashes.

"I've had as many as three accidents at one scene, at one intersection," says Officer John Carney of the Fairfax County Police. "Rubbernecking is the most dangerous distraction, in my experience."

After rubbernecking, other common driver distractions included:

- Driver fatigue (12 percent, see below)

- Looking at scenery (10 percent)

- Other passengers or children (9 percent)

- Adjusting the radio, cassette or CD player (7 percent)

- Reading the newspaper, books, maps or other documents (less than 2 percent)

Another increasingly serious cause of driver distraction is cell phone use, as more than 85 percent of the estimated 100 million cell-phone users talk on their phone regularly while driving, according to a Prevention magazine survey. At least one study has found that driving and talking on a cell phone at the same time quadruples the risk of crashing, which is why many cities have recently begun banning their use while driving unless a hands-free device is used.

The Dangers of Texting While Driving

There are many different kinds of distracted driving, but texting is one of the most dangerous. Reading or responding to a single text can take a driver's attention off of the road for about five seconds. This may not seem like a lot of time, but in five seconds, a car traveling at 55mph can cover the length of a football field.

Teens are well aware of the dangers of texting while driving. In fact, an AAA poll revealed that 94% of teens acknowledge that texting while driving is dangerous. But unfortunately, this doesn't stop many of them from doing it anyways. Thirty-five percent of teens in this poll admitted to texting while driving even though they know it's not safe.

SOURCE: https://www.teensafe.com/blog/teens-texting-and-driving-facts-and-statistics/

2. Driver Fatigue

Drowsy drivers account for about 100,000 accidents every year in the United States, according to the U.S. National Traffic Safety Administration. The risk is greatest from 11 P.M. to 8 A.M., the time when most people are used to sleeping, however some people also become drowsy from noon to 2 P.M.

Symptoms of driver fatigue include heavy eyelids, frequent yawning, a drifting vehicle that wanders over road lines, varying vehicle speed for no reason, misjudging traffic situations, seeing things "jump out" in the road, feeling fidgety or irritable and daydreaming.

Other than making sure you are well-rested before getting behind the wheel, the Motor Accidents Authority (MAA) offers these tips to help avoid fatigue-related auto accidents:

- Take a break from driving at least every two hours.

- Get a good night's sleep before a long trip.

- Share the driving whenever possible.

- Avoid long drives after work.

- Avoid drinking before driving.

- Pull over and stop when drowsiness, discomfort or loss of concentration occurs.

- Find out whether any medicine you are taking may affect your driving.

3. Drunk Driving

Every day, 28 people in the United States die in motor vehicle crashes that involve an alcohol-impaired driver. This is one death every 51 minutes.[1] The annual cost of alcohol-related crashes totals more than $44 billion.

Source: https://www.cdc.gov/motorvehiclesafety/impaired_driving/impaired-drv_factsheet.html

The only way to prevent this type of accident is to not drink and drive. Whenever alcohol is involved, choose a designated driver in advance. This person should not drink at all before driving.

4. Speeding

Speeding is a multi-tiered threat because not only does it reduce the amount of time necessary to avoid a crash, it also increases the risk of crashing and makes the crash more severe if it does occur. In fact, according to the Insurance Institute for Highway Safety (IIHS), when speed increases from 40 mph to 60 mph, the energy released in a crash more than doubles. Simply slowing down and obeying posted speed limits can go a long way toward making the roads safer.

5. Aggressive Driving

Exactly what is an aggressive driver? According to the New York State Police, it's anyone who: "Operates a motor vehicle in a selfish, bold or pushy manner, without regard for the rights or safety of the other users of the streets and highways." This includes behaviors such as:

- Aggressive tailgating

- Flashing lights at other drivers because you're irritated at them

- Aggressive or rude gestures

- Deliberately preventing another driver from moving their vehicle

- Verbal abuse

- Physical assaults

- Disregarding traffic signals

- Changing lanes frequently or in an unsafe manner

- Failure to yield the right of way

If you come across an aggressive driver, the New York State Police gives these tips to protect yourself:

- Remain calm

- Keep your distance

- Do not pass unless you have to

- Change lanes once it is safe

- If you cannot change lanes and an aggressive driver is behind you, stay where you are, maintain the proper speed and do not respond with hostile gestures

- If the situation is serious, you may call 911 to report an aggressive driver

6. Weather

Inclement weather, including heavy rain, hail, snowstorms, ice, high winds and fog can make driving more difficult. You'll need more time to stop and may have trouble seeing the road clearly, so when the weather gets bad be sure to leave extra room between the car in front of you and slow down. If necessary, pull off the road to a rest stop (or to the side of the road, well out of the traffic lanes) until conditions improve.

Reprinted with Permission from the SixWise.com Security & Wellness e-Newsletter.

Motorcycle Safety

Over 2,800 motorcyclists were killed in the year 2000, and in that same year 53,000 motorcyclists were also injured. Motorcycle deaths had declined since the 1980s, but they began to increase in 1998 and have been on a steady rise ever since. For every mile traveled, a motorcyclist is 18 times more likely than a motor vehicle passenger to be killed and 3 times more likely to be injured.

- About ⅔ of motorcycle deaths are the result of speeding.

- Approximately 60% of motorcycle casualties take place at night.

- In the year 2000, 61% of motorcycle fatalities occurred on the weekend (Friday–Sunday), 49% occurred between 6:00 P.M. and 3:00 A.M., and 75% took place between April and September with June, July, and August having the highest death toll.

- An estimated 70% of collisions between motorcycles and motor vehicles occur at intersections.

In a typical motorcycle incident, the driver has less than two seconds to react. As a result, it is critical for motorcyclists to be constantly aware of their environment. Not only can a crash occur in just seconds, but due to the small size of motorcycles in comparison to cars, drivers easily overlook motorcycles. Motorcycles also lack the protection of enclosure, making injuries much more severe. By taking proper safety precautions and following the rules of the road, everyone involved can enjoy a pleasurable and safe ride:

- Always wear a helmet approved by the U.S. Department of Transportation (look inside the helmet for the DOT label).

- Never wear a helmet someone wore in a crash or dropped or that has obvious defects such as frayed straps, cracks, or loose padding.

- Wear eye and face protection as well as long pants, gloves, boots, and a tough jacket with long sleeves.

- Do not tailgate or speed.

- Ensure parts are properly working before every ride (tires, fluids, lights, clutch, throttle, brakes, mirrors, and horn).

- Always have your headlights on.

- Always drive cautiously and defensively, especially around corners, in bad weather, and at night.

- Only allow a passenger to ride with you once you can skillfully ride in all conditions.

Why helmets are imperative:

- You can reduce the risk of brain injury by 67% by wearing a motorcycle helmet.

- On average, helmet use can save a rider almost 20% in hospital costs.

- An average hospital cost for an un-helmeted rider is $43,053 compared to 23,201 for a helmeted rider.

- From 1984 to 1999, helmet use saved approximately $13.2 billion. If all motorcyclists had worn helmets, it could have saved an additional $11.1 billion.

Bicycle Safety

In the year 2000, crashes with motor vehicles killed 690 bicyclists. In the same year, traffic-related crashes injured 51,000 bicyclists. A bicyclist died every six hours in 2002.

- Bicycle deaths are more likely to occur in the summer between the hours of 3 P.M. and 9 P.M.

- A bicycle crash is likely to occur in a driveway or on a sidewalk.

- Most bicycle crashes occur within 5 blocks of the home.

- Sixty-one percent of bicycle fatalities occur in urban areas.

Before using your bicycle, make sure it is ready to ride. Make sure all parts are working properly, the wheels are inflated, and the brakes work. Bicyclists are considered vehicles, and bicyclists must obey the same rules as motorists. By taking proper safety precautions everyone involved can enjoy a pleasurable and safe ride:

- Always wear a helmet. The helmet should fit snugly and not move from side to side. The front of the helmet should be approximately one inch above the eyebrows, and you should buckle the chinstrap snugly.

- Use helmets that meet or exceed the safety standards developed by SNELL, ANSI and/or the American Society for Testing and Materials (ASTM).

- Always wear bright colors when riding a bicycle and avoid riding at night.

- If you have to ride at night, wear something that reflects light, and make sure you have reflectors on the front and rear of your bike.

- Ride single file and WITH THE FLOW of traffic, never against it.

- Follow all traffic signs, signals, and lane markings.

- Before you enter any street or intersection, check for traffic by looking left-right-left.

- Stay out of drivers' blind spots and use appropriate hand signals.

Why helmets are imperative:

- Wearing helmets is the SINGLE MOST EFFECTIVE WAY to reduce head injuries and fatalities resulting in bicycle crashes.

- In 2000, 90% of bicycle fatalities occurred to riders not wearing helmets.

- Non-helmeted riders are 14 times more likely to be involved in a fatal crash than helmeted riders.

- For every $1 spent on a helmet, $30 is saved in medical expenses.

- Through the use of a bicycle helmet we can avoid 85-88% of critical head and brain injuries.

- By wearing a helmet, a brain injury can be prevented every 4 minutes.

- A helmet worn too far back on the head is 52% less effective.

Water Safety

Just as drowning can cause brain damage or death in minutes, diving can result in spinal cord injuries or death in seconds.

- Alcohol had an association with 25–50% of adolescent and adult water recreation deaths in 2001.

- Approximately 1,000 recreational diving injuries occur each year with 90% of diving injuries resulting in quadriplegia.

- Ninety percent of diving injuries take place in six feet of water or less.

- Natural bodies of water are the site of 75% of diving injuries.

- Personal flotation devices would have prevented approximately 89% of boating-related drownings in the years 2001 and 2002.

- A near drowning victim's medical expenses are around $75,000 initially and $180,000 yearly, while brain damage can cost up to $4.5 million.

Water can provide endless hours of fun and enjoyment for everyone, but in just seconds a day of fun can turn into tragedy. Follow these precautions and enjoy water safely:

- Never drink alcohol when participating in water activities and operating any watercrafts.

- Never dive in water less than nine feet deep.

- Don't dive in above-ground pools.

- Always wear a U.S. Coast Guard-approved life jacket when boating.

- Watch for undercurrents, changing waves, and undertows in a lake or oceans.

- Swim parallel to the shore if caught in a rip tide or current. Once out, swim to the shore.

Personal Safety

Many people cite crime and fear of crime as a determining factor in how they feel about their neighborhood, but in fact criminal victimization in 2004 was at its lowest level since 1973, according to the Justice Department's Bureau of Justice Statistics. PREVENTING CRIME IS EVERYONE'S BUSINESS—children, youth, adults, and seniors must all work together to protect themselves, their families, and their neighborhoods.

- Always keep your doors and windows locked.

- Have adequate lighting around your home or apartment (notify your apartment manager if there are problems).

- Do not open the door to strangers—always ask for credentials from maintenance or repair personnel.

■ Make sure you have sturdy metal or solid wood doors at all entries into your home and properly secured sliding glass and similar doors.

■ Do not give out personal information over the phone, through the mail, or over the Internet unless you have initiated the contact or know with whom you are dealing.

■ If you notice someone following you when you're driving, head for the nearest busy, brightly lighted area. Write down the license number and make and model of the car. Call 911 or your local emergency number.

■ Always lock car doors and take the keys when you leave your car, even if you'll be gone "just for a minute."

■ Don't leave valuables in view in the car. Leave them in the trunk or, better yet, take them home immediately.

■ Always park in well-lit areas.

■ As you walk down the street or through the parking garage, walk alertly and assertively. Don't weigh yourself down with too many parcels. Take several loads to the car if necessary.

■ Always have your keys ready for quick entrance into your home.

■ If you carry a purse, hold it close to your body; if a wallet, keep it in a front pocket.

■ Don't display your cash or any other inviting targets such as pagers, cell phones, hand-held electronic games, or expensive jewelry and clothing.

■ When traveling, carry only the credit and ATM cards you absolutely need. Leave the others at home, safely stored.

■ Make sure your home is secure when you are traveling—all deadbolts locked, lights left on timers, newspapers stopped, and mail held at the post office or collected by a trusted neighbor who has your travel schedule.

■ BE AWARE OF YOUR SURROUNDINGS AT ALL TIMES!

Violent crime—murder, rape, robbery, aggravated assault, and simple assault—was down from a high of 52.3 incidents per 1,000 people in 1981 to just 21.1 incidents per 1,000 in 2004, according to statistics compiled by the Bureau of Justice Statistics at the U.S. Department of Justice. Persons in every demographic category surveyed (gender, race, origin, and household income) experienced the decline in violent victimization.

Young people ages 12 to 24 were still the victims of the most violent crimes (an average of 83.7 victimizations per 1,000 people). Aggravated assault—which involves attack with a weapon or attack without a weapon that results in serious injury—was down even more sharply, from 12.4 incidents per 1,000 people in 1977 to just 4.3 incidents per 1,000 in 2004.

Everyone—and this applies to residents of big cities, small towns, and even rural areas—needs to be careful, but these lower rates of crime are evidence that if people are vigilant and take common-sense precautions, they can prevent crime.

- Don't walk or jog early in the morning or late at night when the streets are deserted.

- When out at night, try to have a friend walk with you.

- Carry only the money you'll need on a particular day.

- If you think someone is following you, switch directions or cross the street. If the person continues to follow you, move quickly toward an open store or restaurant or a lighted house. Don't be afraid to yell for help.

- Try to park in well-lighted areas with good visibility and close to walkways, stores, and people.

- Avoid being alone in isolated areas such as laundry rooms or parking garages.

- Make sure you have your key out as you approach your door.

- Always lock your car, even if it's in your own driveway; never leave your motor running.

- Do everything you can to keep a stranger from getting into your car or to keep a stranger from forcing you into his or her car.

- If a dating partner has abused you, do not meet him or her alone. Do not let him or her in your home or car when you are alone.

- If you are a battered partner, call the police or sheriff immediately. Assault is a crime, whether committed by a stranger or your partner or family member.

- If someone tries to rob you, give up your property—don't give up your life.

- If you are robbed or assaulted, report the crime to the police. Try to describe the attacker accurately. Your actions can help prevent someone else from becoming a victim.

Hate crimes—The U.S. Department of Justice defines hate crime as "the violence of intolerance and bigotry, intended to hurt and intimidate someone because of their race, ethnicity, national origin, religion, sexual orientation, or disability." Forty-one states and the District of Columbia have laws against hate crimes. This means that if bias is involved, a crime such as vandalism, assault, or murder is also a hate crime, and the penalty is more severe than it would be otherwise. People commit hate crimes for many reasons:

- They are ignorant about people who are different from themselves (and terrified of the difference).

- They need to be able to look down on others in order to compensate for their own low self-esteem.

- They have been brutalized themselves (though not by their victims) and therefore see brutalizing others as fair game.

Hate crime is a serious societal problem. The FBI reported 7,722 incidents of hate crimes in 2006, of which the perpetrators directed about 52% at people because of their race; 19% because of the victims' religion; 16% because of their sexual orientation; and 13% because of their ethnicity or national origin. Here are some tips to help reduce the incidence of hate crimes:

- Start an advocacy group for people who come together around an identity that they share (such as shared gender, sexual orientation, or religion).

- Start a peer education program to teach teens or younger children about bias awareness.

- Organize "days of respect" in which all members of the school or community can share strategies about bias awareness and hate crimes.

- Have a teen weekend exchange with a teen of a different culture. Go to each other's home for an afternoon, evening, dinner, or perhaps a weekend.

- Visit an elderly person of a different culture on a regular basis.

- Adopt a Little Brother or a Little Sister of a different culture.

- Actively recruit and include youth from diverse backgrounds in group activities.

- Peer-tutor English as a second language.

- Expose your child to different cultures. Go out to eat at an ethnic restaurant. Visit the local library and check out a book on folk stories from around the world.

- Include your child in a variety of home activities. Have your daughter help with yard work or repairs. Have your son help prepare dinner or care for a sibling. This will help prevent your children from developing gender-based stereotypes.

Adapted and excerpted with permission from *www.ncpc.org* by National Crime Prevention Council. Copyright © 2008 by National Crime Prevention Council. All rights reserved.

College Campus Safety

Many of the crimes on college campuses are crimes of opportunity. Theft is the most frequent crime on campus, yet it is the toughest challenge to convince students that their property can be taken. College students are typically very trusting, leaving their belongings unattended or inside vehicles in open view. Properly identifying your personal property such as backpacks, laptops, CD players, and textbooks becomes extremely important. If you consider the amount of valuables you carry with you in a backpack, including wallet, cell phones, and possibly credit cards, the need for protection against theft becomes crucial. Reducing the opportunity and using common sense is the key to most crime prevention on college campuses.

It is also important to be cautious with the amount of personal information that you make available to the public whether it is on campus or over the Internet. When using the Internet, use a nickname and always keep your Social Security Number, phone number, address, password, or other personal information confidential. The less information given out, the less likely it will be used to harm you.

Stalking is a very common crime on college campuses across the United States, as well as the rest of society. Most stalkers are acquaintances, some with a previous connection to the target. Others can be classmates, neighbors, and co-workers. In a few cases, the stalker may be completely unknown to the target. The victim typically feels powerless, isolated, and confused. Whatever the situation, stalkers can be dangerous. The Department of Justice estimates one out of twelve women and one out of forty-five men are victims of stalking. Victims usually range in age between nineteen–thirty-nine years of age, but that does not mean it does not occur in other age groups. Each year more than 1 million women and 370,000 men are victims of stalking (DOJ, 2002).

If you know you are being stalked:

- Be very direct and tell the individual to leave you alone and never contact you again.

- Tell family, friends, co-workers that you are being stalked.

- Record everything that happens—every phone call, incident, or contact.

- Get an answering machine and keep all messages.

- Break old routines, change your normal patterns.

- Get a cell phone and keep it with you at all times.

The Clery Act was named for Jeanne Clery, a nineteen-year-old freshman who was raped and murdered in her dorm room at Lehigh University in 1986. Her parents were later informed that there had been thirty-eight violent crimes on this campus and the students were unaware of this problem. As a result, her parents, Connie and Howard Clery, along with other campus crime victims, convinced Congress to enact the law known as the "Crime Awareness and Campus Security Act of 1990." The law was amended in 1992 and 1998 to include rights to victims of campus sexual assault and to expand the reporting requirements of the colleges and universities. In 1998, the law was officially named the "Clery Act."

The Clery Act requires all colleges and universities to accurately report the number of campus crimes per category to the campus community and prospective students.

College campuses have often been the site for criminal activity. These offenses include sex offenses, robbery, aggravated assault, burglary, arson, and motor vehicle theft. Hate crimes as well as hazing issues can be included in the reports as well as alcohol and weapons violations. Approximately 80 percent of the crimes that take place on college campuses are student-on-student, with nine out of ten felonies involving alcohol or other drugs.

As of 2002, the Clery Act also requires all states to register sex offenders, under Megan's Law, if they are students or employees of the college or university. This information is available to the campus police as well as students who request such information.

Under this law, colleges and universities can be fined for failure to report campus crimes. Omission of this information is not only illegal but it poses a threat to students' safety. The fines send a strong message for schools to take the obligation of reporting crimes and protecting students seriously.

- Avoid walking alone.

- Do not leave personal possessions unattended.

- Always notice other people—make eye contact.

- Avoid taking shortcuts through campus.

- Do not walk like a victim. Walk like you are on a mission.

- Always be aware of your surroundings.

- Trust your instincts. If someone or something makes you feel uncomfortable, get out of the situation.

- Use well-lighted stops if taking a bus.

- Have key in hand before reaching your room or car.

- Avoid jogging or walking alone.

- Hang up immediately once you realize the nature of a harassing call.

- Call a campus escort when on campus late at night.

Sexual Assault

Sexual assault is a serious, violent, and frightening crime committed against women, men and children. It is an act of violence. Sexual assault is not about sex, it is about power. It is an attempt to control a person using sex as a weapon. Rape can happen to anyone at anytime, and rapists can be anyone. Most rape victims are women, but that does not exclude men as victims. According to the National Crime Victimization Survey, sexual assault is the fastest growing violent crime in the United States. It occurs with increasing frequency but remains the crime least often reported to the police. It is estimated that only about 10 to 15 percent of rape cases are reported and that in one out of seven reported rapes, the male is the victim. Forcible rape is comprised of three elements:

1. the use of force (not necessarily physical),

2. absence of the victim's consent,

3. and oral, penile/vaginal penetration.

Rape can happen to anyone at any age.

On college campuses, 90 percent of sexual assaults occur when the victim or attacker is under the influence of alcohol. The National Institute of Alcohol Abuse and Alcoholism, NIAAA, estimated that drinking by college students contributes to an estimated 70,000 sexual assaults/date rapes each year and also contributes to 500,000 injuries and 1,400 deaths. The probability of a female student being sexually assaulted in the four years of college is approximately 25 percent on a national scale (Clery, 2004).

The Department of Justice estimates that for every sexual assault, there are at least two attempts made on someone. Most rapists plan their attack by familiarizing themselves with the victim's surroundings. In all rape cases, the attacker has the advantage from a surprise standpoint. By being aware and avoiding compromising situations, you can reduce the likelihood of becoming a victim, but this does not mean that all rapes can be prevented. Rapists commit the crime, not victims.

Studies by the Department of Justice have shown that women who used physical resistance at the beginning of the attack were two times more likely to escape rape than those who did not resist. Although choosing to resist increases your chances of injuries, you will have a higher probability of avoiding rape. All studies show that *active resistance* works in most attack situations. One study commissioned by the National Center for the Prevention and Control of Rape showed that women who are the most aggressive and use the most aggressive methods of resistance are the ones most likely to escape rape and serious injury. Are you capable of using physical force? If so, then do it. Learning basic self-defense maneuvers can be extremely helpful in gaining self-confidence. Take advantage of anything that you can use as a weapon: pens, keys, umbrella. Punching, kicking, screaming—whatever it takes, use what you can to survive the situation. If you are inside a building, pull the fire alarm!

How you respond to the situation has a lot to do with where you are, i.e., in a mall parking lot, or in a deserted park. The best defense against an attack is to have a plan, an idea of what you would do if you were ever in a situation that called for a response. This certainly does not mean that in every situation, if you fight back you will survive. It is a good idea to have several plans to choose from. What works in one situation may not work in another—there are no guarantees!

Passive resistance could be effective in some situations. Examples of passive resistance are verbal persuasion, pleading, or submission. This sometimes can be helpful in regaining your stability and possibly giving you a chance to think through the situation and plan a defense. However, research has shown that passive resistance is not as effective as active resistance and does not seem to reduce the chance of victim injury (Bever, 1995). But the bottom line is, if it works it is successful.

Self-defense experts suggest reasons why individuals are easy targets for random violent acts. These reasons include: lack of awareness, body language, and being in the wrong place. Always be aware of your surroundings and walk like you are "on a mission"—making eye contact with everyone you pass. Psychologists have known for years that perpetrators select their victims based on signs and signals given off by the potential victim. Studies have shown that stride length and speed, walking too slow as if you are afraid, and jerky or independent arm swing, as well as slumped posture all play a role in "looking" like a victim (Grayson, 1984).

Avoid being alone in an isolated area. If you feel like you are being followed, cross the street and go to a populated area. If an attacker approaches you, utilize the first rule of self-defense—Run! Most people feel that they cannot escape. Even if the attacker has a gun, if you are not under their control, then run. If you do find yourself in a violent situation, react immediately. Do not allow the attacker to take you to a second location. You have a better chance of surviving by doing whatever it takes at the original site. Do not hesitate to take action. Remember, you are responsible for your own safety, do not rely on someone else to take care of you or protect you from harm!

Acquaintance Rape/Intimate Violence

Acquaintance rape or date rape can be defined as interaction that begins between two people at a social event or on a date and ends with one forcing the other to participate in sexual activity (Sawyer, 1993). This is a particularly volatile issue on college campuses. The prevalence of date rape on campus is difficult to determine because victims are even less likely to report a rape by someone that they know. Studies indicate that as many as one in eight college women will be raped while in college and 84 to 90 percent of the victims knew their attacker, a classmate, friend, previous partner, or acquaintance. Most date rapes occur at either the victim's home or the home of the attacker, with 57 percent occurring on an actual date. Studies also show that alcohol plays a significant role in date rapes involving college students, with almost 75 percent of males and 55 percent of the females being under the influence of alcohol or using other drugs (Koss, 1998).

Women ages sixteen to twenty-four experience the highest per capita rates of *intimate violence* (intimate is defined as current/former spouse or boyfriends/ girlfriends). Alcohol also plays a role in intimate violence. The Bureau of Justice Statistics estimates about three million violent crimes occur each year in which the offenders have been drinking alcohol at the time of the offense. Two-thirds of victims who suffered violence by an intimate reported that alcohol had been a factor. Approximately 31 percent of stranger victimizations were alcohol related.

Safety Tips

- When at a party or club, do not leave beverages unattended or accept a drink from someone you do not know.

- When going to a party or club, go with friends and leave with friends.

- Be aware of your surroundings at all times.

- Do not allow yourself to be isolated with someone you do not know.

- Know the level of intimacy you want in a relationship and state your limits.

- Trust your instincts—if you are uncomfortable, get out of the situation.

- Have your own transportation—if you need to end the date, end it.

- When meeting someone new, meet in a public place.

Steps to Take if Rape Occurs

- Go to a friend's house or call someone you know to come over. You do not need to be alone!

- DO NOT shower or make any attempt to clean yourself; do not change clothes or remove any physical evidence of the attack.

- Call your local Rape Crisis Center for assistance and counseling. A counselor can also accompany you to the hospital.

- Seek immediate medical attention and notify the police.

Domestic Violence

Another form of violence affecting our society is **domestic violence**. This includes partner violence, family violence, spouse abuse, child abuse, and battering. Domestic violence does not always have to be physical. Psychological abuse can be equally as harmful and can progress into physical abuse. A few examples of domestic violence are name calling or put downs, isolation from family and friends, withholding money, threatening or physical harm, sexual assault, disrespect, abusing trust and harassment.

Battering focuses on control of a relationship through violence, intimidation, or psychological abuse in an attempt to create fear in the victim. The violence may not happen often, but the fear of it happening is a terrorizing factor (FBI, 1990).

Approximately 95 percent of the victims are women; however, in a small number of cases the victims are men. According to the Surgeon General, domestic violence is the leading cause of injury to women between the ages of fifteen to forty-four and approximately 70 percent of men, who abuse their female partners, also abuse their children. Every day in America, intimate male partners kill at least four women, and more than 50 percent of all women in the United States are battered at sometime in their lives (FBI, 1991). If you or a friend is the victim of domestic violence, seek help. Call the police or go to a shelter. Realize that the violence could even result in death, so action must be taken immediately.

ASSIGNMENT: Make an action plan of how to keep yourself as safe as possible.

Take a moment and answer each question thoroughly. There are always ways to improve your overall safety.

1. Motor Vehicle Safety: What steps will you start taking to make things safer for you?

2. Motorcycle Safety: What steps will you start taking to make things safer for you?

3. Bicycle Safety: What steps will you start taking to make things safer for you?

4. Water Safety: What steps will you start taking to make things safer for you?

5. Personal Safety: What steps will you start taking to make things safer for you?

6. College Campus Safety: What steps will you start taking to make things safer for you?

ASSIGNMENT: The ReAssessment: Choose one item that you know needs improvement in each dimension of wellness.

Physical Wellness—Exercise: _____

_____

_____

Physical Wellness—Nutrition: _____

_____

_____

Mental Wellness: _____

_____

_____

Social Wellness: _____

_____

_____

Spiritual Wellness: _____

_____

_____

Intellectual Wellness: _____

_____

_____

Environmental Wellness: _____

_____

_____

Occupational Wellness: _____

_____

_____

Financial Wellness: _____

_____

_____

YOUR LAST ASSIGNMENT: Reevaluate your Personal Behavior Change Contract.

A. Write down your three behaviors (long-term goals) relating to wellness that you've identified that you would like to change from page xx.

1. _____ 2. _____ 3. _____

A1. After completing the chapters and assignments in this book, reevaluate your previous three long-term goals (above) and ask yourself if you'd like to change one, two, or all three of them. Realize that if you are going to change one or all of your goals that you are not abandoning these previous goals but instead you are reprioritizing them. You are more than able to work on your previous goals once you have accomplished your new goals. The hope also was to have you realize that there is more to wellness than just one or two dimensions of wellness. Write in your new goals below. If you would like to keep a previous goal, then write "same" in the blank.

1. _____ 2. _____ 3. _____

B. Write down pros for each of these goals.

1. _____ 2. _____ 3. _____

C. Write down cons for each of these goals.

1. _____ 2. _____ 3. _____

D. What will your short-term goals be that will support you reaching your long-term goals? Write down short-term goals for each long-term goal.

1. _____ 2. _____ 3. _____

E. Specific behavior changes that will support my short-term goals are:

1. _____ 2. _____ 3. _____

F. I will achieve my long-term goals by (enter a target date for each goal):

1. _____ 2. _____ 3. _____

G. My rewards for reaching each long-term goal will be:

1. _____ 2. _____ 3. _____

I. _____, agree to what I have written above and will comply with the goals and target dates I have set for myself.

Re-sign your contract with a new date. Have your witness re-sign and date or assign a new witness.

Signature: _____   Date: _____

Witness: _____   Date: _____

A note from the future: After achieving your goals, congratulate yourself and then make new goals. If you did not succeed with your goals, examine what behavior changes you were not able to make in order to support your short-term goals. Learn from your mistakes and try again. Perhaps you made your goals too challenging.

Helpful Internet Sites

Al-Anon/Alateen: al-anon.alateen.org

Alcoholics Anonymous (AA): alcoholics-anonymous.org

American Academy of Family Physicians: aafp.org

American Academy of Family Physicians Family Doctor: familydoctor.org

American Association of Acupuncture and Oriental Medicine Finding a Professional: aaaomonline.org/45000.asp

American Cancer Society Learn about Cancer/Choose a Cancer Topic: cancer.org

American Dental Association Public Oral Health Information: ada.org/public/index.asp

American Diabetes Association: diabetes.org

American Heart Association: americanheart.org

American Lung Association: lungusa.org

American Massage Therapy Association Find a Professional: findmassagetherapist.org

American Stroke Association: strokeassociation.org

Body Health Resource Foundation/The Body—The Complete HIV/AIDS Resource: thebody.com

Cleveland Clinic: clevelandclinic.org

HealthAtoZ: healthatoz.com

Indiana Tobacco Prevention and Cessation: whitelies.tv

National Association for Children of Alcoholics (NACOA): nacoa.org

National Cancer Institute Cancer Stat Fact Sheets: seer.cancer.gov/statfacts/

National Cancer Institute Cancer Treatment: cancer.gov/cancertopics/treatment

National Cancer Institute Tobacco: cancer.gov/cancerinfo/tobacco

National Cancer Institute Smoking Cessation: smokefree.gov

National Crime Prevention Council: ncpc.org

National Coalition on Health Care. *Health Insurance Cost.* nchc.org

National Eye Institute: nei.nih.gov

National Institute on Alcohol Abuse and Alcoholism: niaaa.nih.gov

National Institute on Drug Abuse (NIDA): drugabuse.gov/NIDAHome.html

National Institute of Neurological Disorders and Stroke: ninds.nih.gov

National Sleep Foundation: sleepfoundation.org

RealAge Health Assessments: realage.com

Six Wise—How to Be Safe, Live Longer and Prosper: sixwise.com

Spine Health: spine-health.com

Think First National Injury Prevention Foundation: thinkfirst.org

U.S. Department of Health & Human Services—Centers for Disease Control and Prevention Tobacco: cdc.gov/tobacco

U.S. Department of Health & Human Services—Centers for Disease Control and Prevention Vaccines: cdc.gov/vaccines

U.S. Department of Health & Human Services—Substance Abuse & Mental Health Services Administration Publicly-Funded State Treatment Centers: findtreatment.samhsa.gov

U.S. National Institutes of Health: nih.gov

Vision Council of America—Check Yearly See Clearly: checkyearly.com

WebMD: webmd.com

World Health Organization: who.int/

References

AlcoholScreening.org. *How Much Is Too Much? Alcohol Screening Questions.* alcoholscreening.org/ accessed on 3.26.08

American Academy of Family Physicians. *AAFP Policy Action.* November 1996; Revision 6.1 April 2006: aafp.org accessed on 1.17.08; *STIs: Common Symptoms & Tips on Prevention:* familydoctor.org/online/famdocen/home/common/sexinfections/sti/165.printerview.html

American Cancer Society. *Guide to Quitting Smoking:* cancer.org/docroot/PED/content/PED_10_13X_Guide_for_Quitting_Smoking.asp?sitearea=PED; *Signs and Symptoms of Cancer:* cancer.org/docroot/CRI/content/CRI_2_4_3X_What_are_the_signs_and_symptoms_of_cancer.asp?sitearea=. *Leading Sites of New Cancer Cases and Deaths—2007 Estimates:* cancer.org/downloads/stt/CFF2007LeadingSites.pdf accessed on 3.17.08

American Diabetes Association. *All About Diabetes.* diabetes.org/about-diabetes.jsp; *Type 2 Diabetes.* diabetes.org/type-2-diabetes.jsp; Diabetes Risk Test. diabetes.org/risk-test.jsp; *How to Prevent or Delay Diabetes.* diabetes.org/diabetes-prevention/how-to-prevent-diabetes.jsp accessed 3.16.08

American Heart Association. *Risk Factors and Coronary Heart Disease AHA Scientific Position.* americanheart.org/presenter.jhtml?identifier=4726; *Risk Factors You Can Change.* americanheart.org/presenter.jhtml?identifier=494; Goal 1: *Know Your Treatment Plan.* americanheart.org/presenter.jhtml?identifier=3047847; *Cardiovascular Death Rates Decline,But Risk Factors Still Exact Heavy Toll.* americanheart.org/presenter.jhtml?identifier=3052670; *Heart Attack, Stroke and Cardiac Arrest Warning Signs.* americanheart.org/presenter.jhtml?identifier=3053; *Metabolic Syndrome* americanheart.org/presenter.jhtml?identifier=4756; *Diabetes Mellitus.* americanheart.org/presenter.jhtml?identifier=4546; *Cigarette Smoking and Cardiovascular Disease.* americanheart.org/presenter.jhtml?identifier=4545 accessed on 3.13.08

American Lung Association. *Smoking Cessation Support: Benefits.* lungusa.org accessed on 3.17.08

American Massage Therapy Association. *Wellness Drives Americans' Growing Use of Massage Therapy.* amtamassage.org/media/consumersurvey_factsheet.html accessed on 3.27.08

American Stroke Association. *Learn About Stroke.* strokeassociation.org/presenter.jhtml?identifier=3030387; *Millions of brain cells die each minute a stroke is untreated;* strokeassociation.org/presenter.jhtml?identifier=3036010; *Stroke Risk Factors.* americanheart.org/presenter.jhtml?identifier=4716 accessed on 3.14.08

Bever, D. Safety—A Personal Focus, 3rd edition. Mosby Year Book (1992).

Body Health Resource Foundation. *Assess Your Risk for HIV and Other Similarly Transmitted Diseases.* thebody.com/surveys/sexsurvey.html accessed on 3.19.08

Bounds, L. *Health and Fitness: A Guide to a Healthy Lifestyle.* The Benefits of Quitting Smoking. Kendall Hunt Publishing Company (2006): 200; The Health Effects of Smoking 197; Why Do You Smoke Test. 233–234; Do You Want to Quit Test 235; Reducing Back Pain While Sitting: 96; Long-Term Risks Associated with Alcohol Abuse: 223; Blood Alcohol Concentration (BAC): A Measure of Drunk Driving: 219; What Are the Common Sexually Transmitted Infections: 316–319; Assess Your Risk for HIV and Other STIs: 331; Safety Awareness- College Campuses: 347–351

Cleveland Clinic Center for Consumer Health Information. *Metabolic Syndrome.* clevelandclinic.org/health/health-info/docs/3000/3057.asp?index=10783 accessed on 3.14.08

Colgate-Palmolive Company. *Dental Visits—The Dentist Visit and What to Expect.* colgate.com/app/Colgate/US/OC/Information/OralHealthBasics/CheckupsDentProc/TheDentalVisit/WhatToExpect.cvsp accessed on 3.24.08

Covey, S. *The Seven Habits of Highly Effective People.* Simon and Shuster (1989): 71

Devitt, M. *Acupuncture Today.* Acupuncture Provides Long-Term Relief of Low Back Pain (2002): March, Vol. 3, Issue 3. acupuncturetoday.com/archives2002/mar/03lowbackpain.html accessed on 3.27.08

Fralick, M. *College & Career Success.* Learning Style and Intelligence. Kendall Hunt Publishing Company: (?) 249–250

Health AtoZ. *Test Your Knowledge about Sexually Transmitted Diseases.* healthatoz.com/healthatoz/Atoz/tl/rq/stdquiz.jsp accessed on 3.19.08

Koss, M. "Hidden Rape: Incidence, Prevalence and Description Characteristics of Sexual Aggression and Victimization in a National Sample of College Students." *Sexual Assault,* Vol. II, New York: Garland Publishing Company

National Coalition on Health Care. *Health Insurance Cost.* nchc.org/facts/cost.shtml accessed 3.28.08

National Crime Prevention Council. *Personal Safety:* ncpc.org/topics/personal-safety/; Violence Crime: ncpc.org/topics/violence-/; *Hate/Bias Crime:* .ncpc.org/topics/hate-bias/ accessed on 3.30.08

National Sleep Foundation. *Sleep Facts and Stats:* sleepfoundation.org/site/c.huIXKjM0IxF/b.2419253/k.7989/Sleep_Facts_and_Stats.htm; *How Much Sleep Do We Really Need?* sleepfoundation.org/site/c.huIXKjM0IxF/b.2421183/k.3EA0/How_Much_Sleep_Do_We_Really_Need.htm; *Healthy Sleep Tips:* sleepfoundation.org/site/c.huIXKjM0IxF/b.2417321/k.BAF0/Healthy_Sleep_Tips.htm; *Helping Yourself to a Good Night's Sleep:* sleepfoundation.org/site/c.huIXKjM0IxF/b.2421167/k.238/Helping_Yourself_to_a_Good_Nights_Sleep.htm; *Sleep IQ Quiz:* sleepfoundation.org/site/c.huIXKjM0IxF/b.2466809/ accessed on 3.21.08

Proctor & Gamble™ and Crest. *Dental Hygiene Quiz.* crest.com/dental_hygiene/toothOrFalse.jsp accessed on 3.25.08

RealAge.com. *Worried About Your Back? RealAge back pain care and risk health assessments.* realage.com/health_guides/backpain/introduction.asp accessed on 3.27.08

Six Wise.com. *The Six Most Common Causes of Automobile Crashes.* sixwise.com/newsletters/05/07/20/the_6_most_common_causes_of_automobile_crashes.htm accessed on 3.28.08

Spine-Health.com. *Ergonomic Office Chairs.* spine-health.com/Ergonomic-Office-Chairs.html; Mattresses impact sleep quality: spine-health.com/Mattress-And-Sleep-Advice.html accessed on 3.27.08

Think First National Injury Prevention Foundation. *Fast Facts—Motorcycle Safety:* thinkfirst.org/ Documents/FastFacts/TFmotorcycle227.pdf; *Bicycle Safety:* thinkfirst.org/Documents/FastFacts/ TFbicycle116.pdf; *Water Safety:* thinkfirst.org/Documents/FastFacts/TFwater259.pdf accessed on 3.28.08

Thygerson, A.and Larson, K. *Lab Manual to Accompany Fit to be Well.* Torabi Cancer Prevention Scale. Jones and Bartlett (2006): 107–108

Torabi, M.A Cancer Prevention Behavior Scale. American Journal of Health Behavior (formerly Health Values) PNG Publications (1991): 15 (3), 21–25

U.S. Department of Health and Human Services. *HHS Announces the Nation's New Health Promotion and Disease Prevention Agenda.* HHS News (Dec. 2, 2010). www.hhs.gov/news accessed on January 12, 2012.

U.S. Health & Human Services—Centers for Disease Control and Prevention. *Recommended Adult Immunization Schedule, United States, October 2007–September 2008:* cdc.gov/vaccines accessed on 1.17.08; *Oral Health for Adults:* cdc.gov/oralhealth/publications/factsheets/adult.htm; Links Between Oral and General Health: cdc.gov/oralhealth/publications/factsheets/sgr2000_ fs4.htm; *Oral Cancer: Deadly to Ignore:* cdc.gov/oralhealth/publications/factsheets/oc_facts.htm; *Quick Stats Binge Drinking:* cdc.gov/alcohol/quickstats/binge_drinking.htm accessed on 3.24.08

U.S. National Institutes of Health. National Cancer Institute. Cigarette Smoking and Cancer— Questions and Answers: cancer.gov/cancertopics/factsheet/Tobacco/cancer; Cancer Topics: cancer.gov/cancertopics/what-is-cancer; Prevention: progressreport.cancer.gov/ doc.asp?pid=1&did=2007&mid=vcol&chid=71 accessed on 3.24.08

U.S. National Institutes of Health. National Institute on Alcohol Abuse and Alcoholism. *FAQ for the General Public.* niaaa.nih.gov/FAQs/General-English/default.htm

U.S. National Institutes of Health. National Institute on Drug Abuse. *NIDA InfoFacts: Understanding Drug Abuse and Addiction:* drugabuse.gov/Infofacts/understand.html; *Commonly Abused Drug:* nida.nih.gov/DrugPages/DrugsofAbuse.html accessed on 3.26.08

U.S. National Institutes of Health. National Eye Institute. *Survey Shows Americans Lack Critical Facts about Maintaining Eye Health.* nei.nih.gov/news/pressreleases/031308.asp accessed on 3.25.08

U.S. National Institutes of Health. National Institute of Neurological Disorders and Stroke. *Low Back Pain Fact Sheet:* ninds.nih.gov/disorders/backpain/detail_backpain.htm accessed on 3.27.08

U.S. National Institutes of Health. *Standard Ophthalmic Exam.* nlm.nih.gov/medlineplus/ency/ article/003434.htm; *Vision Problems:* nlm.nih.gov/medlineplus/ency/article/003029.htm accessed on 3.25.08

U.S. National Institutes of Health. *Sexually Transmitted Diseases.* nlm.nih.gov/medlineplus/ sexuallytransmitteddiseases.html accessed on 3.26.08

Vision Council of America. *Check Yearly See Clearly. Sight Saver Quiz.* checkyearly.com/eye-health- 101/sight-saver-prequiz.asp accessed on 3.25.08

Appendices

"Don't cry because it's over, smile because it happened."

— Unknown

Health and Fitness Appraisal Data and Interpretation Information

Fitness Tests

1. **Body composition:**

   A. Body Mass Index (BMI): Height: _____   Weight: _____   BMI: _____

   What's your outcome? (Refer to the top of the next page.) _____

BODY MASS INDEX TABLE

To use the table, find the appropriate height in the left-hand column labeled Height. Move across to a given weight (in pounds). The number at the top of the column is the BMI at that height and weight. Pounds have been rounded off.

BMI	19	20	21	22	23	24	25	26	27	28	29	30	31	32	33	34	35
HEIGHT (INCHES)							BODY WEIGHT (POUNDS)										
58	91	96	100	105	110	115	119	124	129	134	138	143	148	153	158	162	167
59	94	99	104	109	114	119	124	128	133	138	143	148	153	158	163	168	173
60	97	102	107	112	118	123	128	133	138	143	148	153	158	163	168	174	179
61	100	106	111	116	122	127	132	137	143	148	153	158	164	169	174	180	185
62	104	109	115	120	126	131	136	142	147	153	158	164	169	175	180	186	191
63	107	113	118	124	130	135	141	146	152	158	163	169	175	180	186	191	197
64	110	116	122	128	134	140	145	151	157	163	169	174	180	186	192	197	204
65	114	120	126	132	138	144	150	156	162	168	174	180	186	192	198	204	210
66	118	124	130	136	142	148	155	161	167	173	179	186	192	198	204	210	216
67	121	127	134	140	146	153	159	166	172	178	185	191	198	204	211	217	223
68	125	131	138	144	151	158	164	171	177	184	190	197	203	210	216	223	230
69	128	135	142	149	155	162	169	176	182	189	196	203	209	216	223	230	236
70	132	139	146	153	160	167	174	181	188	195	202	209	216	222	229	236	243
71	136	143	150	157	165	172	179	186	193	200	208	215	222	229	236	243	250
72	140	147	154	162	169	177	184	191	199	206	213	221	228	235	242	250	258
73	144	151	159	166	174	182	189	197	204	212	219	227	235	242	250	257	265
74	148	155	163	171	179	186	194	202	210	218	225	233	241	249	256	264	272
75	152	160	168	176	184	192	200	208	216	224	232	240	248	256	264	272	279
76	156	164	172	180	189	197	205	213	221	230	238	246	254	263	271	279	287

www.nhlbi.nih.gov

Department of Health and Human Services • National Institutes of Health

Body mass index (BMI) is measure of body fat based on height and weight that applies to both adult men and women.

BMI Categories:
- Underweight = <18.5
- Normal weight = 18.5–24.9
- Overweight = 25–29.9
- Obesity = BMI of 30 or greater

B. % Body Fat: _____

What's your outcome? Circle one: too little body fat %, healthy range, too much body fat %.

Men	18–39	40–59	60–79
Healthy	8%–19%	11%–24%	13%–24%

Women	18–39	40–59	60–79
Healthy	21–32%	23%–35%	24%–35%

SOURCE: shapeup.org/bodylab/basics/know3.php

C. Waist/Hip Ratio: _____ (waist) /_____ (hip) = _____ (ratio)

What's your outcome? _____

Men	>0.95	Indicating central obesity; Increased risk for cardiovascular disease, diabetes and other disease states. If below this value, you are at less risk.
Women	>0.80	

2. Trunk Flexibility: Attempt 1: _____   Attempt 2: _____   Attempt 3: _____

What's your outcome? _____

Men	18–25	26–35	36–45	46–55	56–65	66+
Well above average	≥22	≥21	≥21	≥19	≥17	≥17
Above average	19–21	18–20	17–20	15–18	14–16	13–16
Average	16–18	15–17	14–16	12–14	11–13	10–12
Below average	14–15	12–14	11–13	9–11	8–10	7–9
Well below average	"12	"11	"10	"8	"7	"6

Women	18–25	26–35	36–45	46–55	56–65	66+
Well above average	≥24	≥23	≥22	≥21	≥20	≥20
Above average	21–23	20–22	19–21	18–20	17–19	17–19
Average	19–20	18–19	17–18	16–17	15–16	14–16
Below average	17–18	16–17	15–16	13–15	12–14	11–13
Well below average	"16	"15	"14	"12	"11	"10

SOURCE: YMCA Fitness Testing and Assessment Manual, 4th ed. 2000

3. **Muscular strength:**   Right Hand: _____   Left Hand: _____   Combined: _____

What's your outcome?_____

Men	20–29	30–39	40–49	50–59	60+
Above average	113–123	113–122	110–118	102–109	98–101
Average	106–112	105–112	102–109	96–101	86–92
Below average	97–105	97–104	94–101	87–95	79–85
Poor	"96	"96	"93	"86	"78

Women	20–29	30–39	40–49	50–59	60+
Above average	65–70	66–72	65–72	59–64	54–59
Average	61–64	61–65	59–64	55–58	51–53
Below average	55–60	56–60	55–58	51–54	48–50
Poor	"54	"55	"54	"50	"47

Results are compared to nationally accepted norms as outlined by the American College of Sports Medicine: acsm.org.

4. **Muscular endurance:**   Curl-Ups: _____   Push-Ups: _____

What's your outcome? _____ (curl-ups)   _____ (push-ups)

RATINGS FOR THE PARTIAL CURL-UP TEST

MEN	NEEDS IMPROVEMENT	NUMBER OF CURL-UPS			
		FAIR	GOOD	VERY GOOD	EXCELLENT
Age: 15–19	Below 16	16–20	21–22	23–24	25
20–29	Below 13	13–20	21–22	23–24	25
30–39	Below 13	13–20	21–22	23–24	25
40–49	Below 11	11–15	16–21	22–24	25
50–59	Below 9	9–13	14–19	20–24	25
60–69	Below 4	4–9	10–15	16–24	25

WOMEN	NEEDS IMPROVEMENT	FAIR	GOOD	VERY GOOD	EXCELLENT
Age: 15–19	Below 16	16–20	21–22	23–24	25
20–29	Below 13	13–18	19–22	23–24	25
30–39	Below 11	11–15	16–21	22–24	25
40–49	Below 6	6–12	13–20	21–24	25
50–59	Below 4	4–8	9–15	16–24	25
60–69	Below 2	2–5	6–10	11–17	18–25

Source: Based on norms from the Cooper Institute for Aerobics Research, Dallas, TX; from *The Physical Fitness Specialist Manual*, revised 2002.

RATINGS FOR THE PUSH-UP AND MODIFIED PUSH-UP TESTS

MEN	NUMBER OF PUSH-UPS					
	VERY POOR	POOR	FAIR	GOOD	EXCELLENT	SUPERIOR
Age: 18–29	Below 22	22–28	29–36	37–46	47–61	Above 61
30–39	Below 17	17–23	24–29	30–38	39–51	Above 51
40–49	Below 11	11–17	18–23	24–29	30–39	Above 39
50–59	Below 9	9–12	13–18	19–24	25–38	Above 38
60+	Below 6	6–9	10–17	18–22	23–27	Above 27

WOMEN	NUMBER OF MODIFIED PUSH-UPS					
	VERY POOR	POOR	FAIR	GOOD	EXCELLENT	SUPERIOR
Age: 18–29	Below 17	17–22	23–29	30–35	36–44	Above 44
30–39	Below 11	11–18	19–23	24–30	31–38	Above 38
40–49	Below 6	6–12	13–17	18–23	24–32	Above 32
50–59	Below 6	6–11	12–16	17–20	21–27	Above 27
60+	Below 2	2–4	5–11	12–14	15–19	Above 19

Source: Based on norms from the Cooper Institute for Aerobics Research, Dallas, TX; from *The Physical Fitness Specialist Manual*, revised 2002.

5. **Cardiovascular Endurance:**

  1.5 Mile Run Test: _____ (time)   OR   1.0 Mile Walk Test _____ (time)

  What's your outcome? _____

FITNESS CATEGORIES FOR COOPER'S 1.5-MILE RUN TEST TO DETERMINE CARDIORESPIRATORY FITNESS

FITNESS CATEGORY	AGE (YEARS)					
	13–19	20–29	30–39	40–49	50–59	60+
Men						
Very poor	>15:30	>16:00	>16:30	>17:30	>19:00	>20:00
Poor	12:11–15:30	14:01–16:00	14:46–16:30	15:36–17:30	17:01–19:00	19:01–20:00
Average	10:49–12:10	12:01–14:00	12:31–14:45	13:01–15:35	14:31–17:00	16:16–19:00
Good	9:41–10:48	10:46–12:00	11:01–12:30	11:31–13:00	12:31–14:30	14:00–16:15
Excellent	8:37–9:40	9:45–10:45	10:00–11:00	10:30–11:30	11:00–12:30	11:15–13:59
Superior	<8:37	<9:45	<10:00	<10:30	<11:00	<11:15
Women						
Very poor	>18:30	>19:00	>19:30	>20:00	>20:30	>21:00
Poor	16:55–18:30	18:31–19:00	19:01–19:30	19:31–20:00	20:01–20:30	20:31–21:31
Average	14:31–16:54	15:55–18:30	16:31–19:00	17:31–19:30	19:01–20:00	19:31–20:30
Good	12:30–14:30	13:31–15:54	14:31–16:30	15:56–17:30	16:31–19:00	17:31–19:30
Excellent	11:50–12:29	12:30–13:30	13:00–14:30	13:45–15:55	14:30–16:30	16:30–18:00
Superior	<11:50	<12:30	<13:00	<13:45	<14:30	<16:30

Times are given in minutes and seconds. (> = greater than; < = less than)

From Cooper, K. *The aerobics program for total well-being.* Bantam Books, New York, 1982.

ROCKPORT 1-MILE WALK TEST

FITNESS CATEGORY	AGE (YEARS)			
	13–19	20–29	30–39	40+
Men				
Very Poor	>17:30	>18:00	>19:00	>21:30
Poor	16:01–17:30	16:31–18:00	17:31–19:00	18:31–21:30
Average	14:01–16:00	14:31–16:30	15:31–17:30	16:01–18:30
Good	12:31–14:00	13:01–14:30	13:31–15:30	14:01–16:00
Excellent	<12:30	<13:00	<13:30	<14:00
Women				
Very Poor	>18:01	>18:31	>19:31	>22:01
Poor	16:31–18:00	17:01–18:30	18:01–19:30	19:01–22:00
Average	14:31–16:30	15:01–17:00	16:01–18:00	16:31–19:00
Good	13:01–14:30	13:31–15:00	14:01–16:00	14:31–16:30
Excellent	<13:00	<13:30	<14:00	<14:30

Because the 1-mile walk test is designed primarily for older or less conditioned individuals, the fitness categories listed here do not include a "superior" category.

Modified from Rockport Fitness Walking Test.

Health Tests

1. Resting Blood Pressure: Reading: _____ /_____ ,   Reading: _____ /_____

What's your outcome? _____

Systolic (mm Hg)	Diastolic (mm Hg)	Category
<120	<80	Normal
120–139	80–89	High Normal
140–159	90–99	Mild (stage 1) Hypertension
160–179	100–109	Moderate (stage 2 Hypertension
180–209	110–119	Severe (stage 3) Hypertension
≥210	≥120	Very Severe (stage 4) Hypertension

Source: U.S. Department of Health and Human Services.

2. Blood Panel: Circle your outcomes for each section.

Your Results	Total Cholesterol	Classification
Total Cholesterol _____	< 200 mg/dl	Desirable level that puts you at lower risk for coronary heart disease. A cholesterol level of 200 mg/dL or higher raises your risk.
	200–239 mg/dl	Borderline high
	> 240 mg/dl	High blood cholesterol. A person with this level has more than twice the risk of coronary heart disease as someone whose cholesterol is below 200 mg/dL.

	LDL Cholesterol	Classification
LDL Cholesterol _____	< 100 mg/dl	Optimal
	100–129 mg/dl	Near or above optimal
	130–159 mg/dl	Borderline high
	160–189 mg/dl	High
	>190 mg/dl	Very high

	HDL Cholesterol	Classification
HDL Cholesterol _____	< 40 mg/dl (for men) and < 50 mg/dl (for women)	Low HDL cholesterol. A major risk factor for heart disease.
	≥ 60 mg/dl	High HDL cholesterol. An HDL of 60 mg/dL and above is considered protective against heart disease.

	Serum Triglycerides	Classification
Triglycerides _____	<150 mg/dl	Normal
	151–199 mg/dl	Borderline High
	200–499 mg/dl	High
	≥ 500 mg/dl	Very High

Reprinted with permission. www.heart.org. © American Heart Association, Inc.

	Risk Ratio	Classification
TC/HDL ratio _____	> 4.0	Desirable
	≥ 5.0	High risk

Your Results	Blood Glucose	Classification
Blood glucose _____	Fasting	
	100 mg/dL	Normal
	100–125 mg/dl	Pre-diabetic
	≥ 126 mg/dl	Diabetic
	Non-fasting	
	≥ 200 mg/dl	Diabetic

Source: Mayo Clinic: mayoclinic.com/health/blood-sugar/SA00102/SI=2279

APPENDIX B

Weekly plans for cardiovascular exercise.

	M	T	W	TH	F	SAT	SUN
Mode							
Frequency							
Duration							
Intensity							

	M	T	W	TH	F	SAT	SUN
Mode							
Frequency							
Duration							
Intensity							

	M	T	W	TH	F	SAT	SUN
Mode							
Frequency							
Duration							
Intensity							

	M	T	W	TH	F	SAT	SUN
Mode							
Frequency							
Duration							
Intensity							

	M	T	W	TH	F	SAT	SUN
Mode							
Frequency							
Duration							
Intensity							

APPENDIX C

Weekly plans for strengthening exercise.

	M	T	W	TH	F	SAT	SUN
Mode							
Frequency							
Duration							
Intensity							

	M	T	W	TH	F	SAT	SUN
Mode							
Frequency							
Duration							
Intensity							

	M	T	W	TH	F	SAT	SUN
Mode							
Frequency							
Duration							
Intensity							

	M	T	W	TH	F	SAT	SUN
Mode							
Frequency							
Duration							
Intensity							

	M	T	W	TH	F	SAT	SUN
Mode							
Frequency							
Duration							
Intensity							

APPENDIX D

Weekly plans for flexibility exercise

	M	T	W	TH	F	SAT	SUN
Mode							
Frequency							
Duration							
Intensity							

	M	T	W	TH	F	SAT	SUN
Mode							
Frequency							
Duration							
Intensity							

	M	T	W	TH	F	SAT	SUN
Mode							
Frequency							
Duration							
Intensity							

	M	T	W	TH	F	SAT	SUN
Mode							
Frequency							
Duration							
Intensity							

	M	T	W	TH	F	SAT	SUN
Mode							
Frequency							
Duration							
Intensity							

Log sheets for pedometer use and keeping track of your steps.

WEEK	DAILY GOAL	MON	TUES	WED	THURS	FRI	SAT	SUN	WEEKLY TOTAL	WEEKLY MILES

NOTE: Your daily goal should be 10,000 steps per day or more and 70,000 steps per week or more. Remember that approximately 2,000 steps equals 1 mile.

APPENDIX F

HR	DATE		DATE		DATE		DATE	COMMENTS
205								
200								
195								
190								
185								
180								
175								
170								
165								
160								
155								
150								
145								
140								
135								
130								
125								
120								
115								
110								
105								
100								
90								
80								
70								
60								
50								
40								
—	TIMES		TIMES		TIMES		TIMES	

SAMPLE: Student's Age = 19, RHR = 72

HR	Zone	1/17 (10)	1/17 (15)	1/17 (20)	1/29 (10)	1/29 (20)	1/29 (30)	2/7 (10)	2/7 (15)	2/7 (25)	3/1 (10)	3/1 (20)	3/1 (30)	COMMENTS
205	201 (Max HR)													**Max HR**
200														
195														1/17 = First time w/ HRMs;
190														Haven't walked/jogged in a while;
185														Need to walk/jog a little faster
180														next time to get to 60% sooner
175														in my workout.
170														
165														
160	80%													1/29 = This time went better;.
155														I worked at 60% and 70% and
150									X					felt good about it; I think
145	70%												X	exercising outside of class
140								X						helped me too.
135												X		
130									X					2/7 = Worked at 60%, 70% and
125						X								into 80%; 80% was tough but
120	60%			X										only for the last 5 minutes
115			X		X			X			X			before cool-down
110														
105														3/1 = Worked at 60–80%
100	50%	X												Again; Feel like I'm making
90														CV progress!!!=)
80														
70	72 (Resting HR)													**Resting HR**
60														
50														
40														
—														
		TIMES			**TIMES**			**TIMES**			**TIMES**			

Index